Communications
in Computer and Information Science   **1420**

More information about this series at http://www.springer.com/series/7899

Constantine Stephanidis ·
Margherita Antona · Stavroula Ntoa (Eds.)

HCI International 2021 - Posters

23rd HCI International Conference, HCII 2021
Virtual Event, July 24–29, 2021
Proceedings, Part II

Editors
Constantine Stephanidis
University of Crete and Foundation
for Research and Technology – Hellas
(FORTH)
Heraklion, Crete, Greece

Margherita Antona
Foundation for Research
and Technology – Hellas (FORTH)
Heraklion, Crete, Greece

Stavroula Ntoa
Foundation for Research
and Technology – Hellas (FORTH)
Heraklion, Crete, Greece

ISSN 1865-0929   ISSN 1865-0937 (electronic)
Communications in Computer and Information Science
ISBN 978-3-030-78641-0   ISBN 978-3-030-78642-7 (eBook)
https://doi.org/10.1007/978-3-030-78642-7

Foreword

Human-Computer Interaction (HCI) is acquiring an ever-increasing scientific and industrial importance, and having more impact on people's everyday life, as an ever-growing number of human activities are progressively moving from the physical to the digital world. This process, which has been ongoing for some time now, has been dramatically accelerated by the COVID-19 pandemic. The HCI International (HCII) conference series, held yearly, aims to respond to the compelling need to advance the exchange of knowledge and research and development efforts on the human aspects of design and use of computing systems.

The 23rd International Conference on Human-Computer Interaction, HCI International 2021 (HCII 2021), was planned to be held at the Washington Hilton Hotel, Washington DC, USA, during July 24–29, 2021. Due to the COVID-19 pandemic and with everyone's health and safety in mind, HCII 2021 was organized and run as a virtual conference. It incorporated the 21 thematic areas and affiliated conferences listed on the following page.

A total of 5222 individuals from academia, research institutes, industry, and governmental agencies from 81 countries submitted contributions, and 1276 papers and 241 posters were included in the proceedings to appear just before the start of the conference. The contributions thoroughly cover the entire field of HCI, addressing major advances in knowledge and effective use of computers in a variety of application areas. These papers provide academics, researchers, engineers, scientists, practitioners, and students with state-of-the-art information on the most recent advances in HCI. The volumes constituting the set of proceedings to appear before the start of the conference are listed in the following pages.

The HCI International (HCII) conference also offers the option of 'Late Breaking Work' which applies both for papers and posters, and the corresponding volume(s) of the proceedings will appear after the conference. Full papers will be included in the 'HCII 2021 - Late Breaking Papers' volumes of the proceedings to be published in the Springer LNCS series, while 'Poster Extended Abstracts' will be included as short research papers in the 'HCII 2021 - Late Breaking Posters' volumes to be published in the Springer CCIS series.

I would also like to thank the Program Board Chairs and the members of the Program Boards of all thematic areas and affiliated conferences for their contribution towards the highest scientific quality and overall success of the HCI International 2021 conference.

This conference would not have been possible without the continuous and unwavering support and advice of Gavriel Salvendy, founder, General Chair Emeritus, and Scientific Advisor. For his outstanding efforts, I would like to express my appreciation to Abbas Moallem, Communications Chair and Editor of HCI International News.

July 2021   Constantine Stephanidis

HCI International 2021 Thematic Areas and Affiliated Conferences

Thematic Areas

- HCI: Human-Computer Interaction
- HIMI: Human Interface and the Management of Information

Affiliated Conferences

- EPCE: 18th International Conference on Engineering Psychology and Cognitive Ergonomics
- UAHCI: 15th International Conference on Universal Access in Human-Computer Interaction
- VAMR: 13th International Conference on Virtual, Augmented and Mixed Reality
- CCD: 13th International Conference on Cross-Cultural Design
- SCSM: 13th International Conference on Social Computing and Social Media
- AC: 15th International Conference on Augmented Cognition
- DHM: 12th International Conference on Digital Human Modeling and Applications in Health, Safety, Ergonomics and Risk Management
- DUXU: 10th International Conference on Design, User Experience, and Usability
- DAPI: 9th International Conference on Distributed, Ambient and Pervasive Interactions
- HCIBGO: 8th International Conference on HCI in Business, Government and Organizations
- LCT: 8th International Conference on Learning and Collaboration Technologies
- ITAP: 7th International Conference on Human Aspects of IT for the Aged Population
- HCI-CPT: 3rd International Conference on HCI for Cybersecurity, Privacy and Trust
- HCI-Games: 3rd International Conference on HCI in Games
- MobiTAS: 3rd International Conference on HCI in Mobility, Transport and Automotive Systems
- AIS: 3rd International Conference on Adaptive Instructional Systems
- C&C: 9th International Conference on Culture and Computing
- MOBILE: 2nd International Conference on Design, Operation and Evaluation of Mobile Communications
- AI-HCI: 2nd International Conference on Artificial Intelligence in HCI

List of Conference Proceedings Volumes Appearing Before the Conference

1. LNCS 12762, Human-Computer Interaction: Theory, Methods and Tools (Part I), edited by Masaaki Kurosu
2. LNCS 12763, Human-Computer Interaction: Interaction Techniques and Novel Applications (Part II), edited by Masaaki Kurosu
3. LNCS 12764, Human-Computer Interaction: Design and User Experience Case Studies (Part III), edited by Masaaki Kurosu
4. LNCS 12765, Human Interface and the Management of Information: Information Presentation and Visualization (Part I), edited by Sakae Yamamoto and Hirohiko Mori
5. LNCS 12766, Human Interface and the Management of Information: Information-rich and Intelligent Environments (Part II), edited by Sakae Yamamoto and Hirohiko Mori
6. LNAI 12767, Engineering Psychology and Cognitive Ergonomics, edited by Don Harris and Wen-Chin Li
7. LNCS 12768, Universal Access in Human-Computer Interaction: Design Methods and User Experience (Part I), edited by Margherita Antona and Constantine Stephanidis
8. LNCS 12769, Universal Access in Human-Computer Interaction: Access to Media, Learning and Assistive Environments (Part II), edited by Margherita Antona and Constantine Stephanidis
9. LNCS 12770, Virtual, Augmented and Mixed Reality, edited by Jessie Y. C. Chen and Gino Fragomeni
10. LNCS 12771, Cross-Cultural Design: Experience and Product Design Across Cultures (Part I), edited by P. L. Patrick Rau
11. LNCS 12772, Cross-Cultural Design: Applications in Arts, Learning, Well-being, and Social Development (Part II), edited by P. L. Patrick Rau
12. LNCS 12773, Cross-Cultural Design: Applications in Cultural Heritage, Tourism, Autonomous Vehicles, and Intelligent Agents (Part III), edited by P. L. Patrick Rau
13. LNCS 12774, Social Computing and Social Media: Experience Design and Social Network Analysis (Part I), edited by Gabriele Meiselwitz
14. LNCS 12775, Social Computing and Social Media: Applications in Marketing, Learning, and Health (Part II), edited by Gabriele Meiselwitz
15. LNAI 12776, Augmented Cognition, edited by Dylan D. Schmorrow and Cali M. Fidopiastis
16. LNCS 12777, Digital Human Modeling and Applications in Health, Safety, Ergonomics and Risk Management: Human Body, Motion and Behavior (Part I), edited by Vincent G. Duffy
17. LNCS 12778, Digital Human Modeling and Applications in Health, Safety, Ergonomics and Risk Management: AI, Product and Service (Part II), edited by Vincent G. Duffy

38. CCIS 1420, HCI International 2021 Posters - Part II, edited by Constantine Stephanidis, Margherita Antona, and Stavroula Ntoa
39. CCIS 1421, HCI International 2021 Posters - Part III, edited by Constantine Stephanidis, Margherita Antona, and Stavroula Ntoa

http://2021.hci.international/proceedings

23rd International Conference on Human-Computer Interaction (HCII 2021)

The full list with the Program Board Chairs and the members of the Program Boards of all thematic areas and affiliated conferences is available online at:

http://www.hci.international/board-members-2021.php

HCI International 2022

The 24th International Conference on Human-Computer Interaction, HCI International 2022, will be held jointly with the affiliated conferences at the Gothia Towers Hotel and Swedish Exhibition & Congress Centre, Gothenburg, Sweden, June 26 – July 1, 2022. It will cover a broad spectrum of themes related to Human-Computer Interaction, including theoretical issues, methods, tools, processes, and case studies in HCI design, as well as novel interaction techniques, interfaces, and applications. The proceedings will be published by Springer. More information will be available on the conference website: http://2022.hci.international/:

General Chair
Prof. Constantine Stephanidis
University of Crete and ICS-FORTH
Heraklion, Crete, Greece
Email: general_chair@hcii2022.org

http://2022.hci.international/

Contents – Part II

Security and Privacy Issues in HCI

AI and Machine Learning in HCI

Interaction Methods and Techniques

Touch: Interactive Exhibition Using the Biometric Information of the Audience

Jooyoung Ha[1] and Yang Kyu Lim[2]([✉])

[1] Chung-Ang University, 84, Heukseok-ro, Dongjak-gu, Seoul, Republic of Korea
[2] Duksung Women's University, 33, Samyang-ro 144-gil, Dobong-gu, Seoul, Republic of Korea
trumpetyk09@duksung.ac.kr

Abstract. This paper shows that the roles of the general audience who were considered as the only customers extend to the parts of producers of the Arts because of Interactive Art. While Interactive Art should be completed by the involvement of speculators, its creatives have to excite their precious visitors and make their works look attractive enough to get interests of the people. In this study, it is the main purpose to compare the previous Interactive Art case in which several interesting devices are used in order to lead speculators with *Touch*. *Touch* as Interactive Art performance uses the biometric information of the audience as its interface. *Touch* sends a message to express that life begins to speculators through light and sound by checking their heartbeat. The heartbeat sensors used in this artwork should be considered as the interactive bride between the Arts and the human minds, not for health care devices. The audience can pay more attention to the Arts via watching the changes of their heartbeat, communicating with the producers of *Touch*. In addition, since it is designed to be used easily, the people can take an active part in the works. In conclusion, the technologies created to make speculators take an active part are introduced; especially *Touch* that is one of Interactive Art. Furthermore, its detail information is provided step by step.

Keywords: Biometric · Heartbeat sensor · Interaction · Interactive art · Media art

1 Introduction

Recently, research into the recognition and communication of human emotions through information technology is increasing. In particular, there is a movement to try to converge with various fields such as medicine and art, technology and social sciences. Art is the field which seeks in a creative way to converge between genres and expresses it in new ways. If you want to fuse with other genres in the process of creation, you must harmoniously combine technical and aesthetic elements. Art works should be able to communicate with viewers through philosophic messages.

Alvin Toffler, a renowned futurist, mentioned, "We are at the end of the information age, and from now on, we are evolving into an era of emotions where dreams and stories dominate." In this way, in the future, with the development of technology, the desire for human sensitivity will rise further. We shall have to deal emotionally with the human senses which have been blunted by the stimulation due to rapid technological

C. Stephanidis et al. (Eds.): HCII 2021, CCIS 1420, pp. 3–7, 2021.
https://doi.org/10.1007/978-3-030-78642-7_1

development. The media art of the modern age, where emotions matter, will transform and express the body in more diverse ways using sensory organs that represent human emotions. In this context, we communicate with the audience by expressing our thoughts through a media artwork known as *Touch*.

Touch is a work which expresses life, the message of the work, by expressing the information of the audience with a virtual eye using a heart rate sensor. The heartbeat is the simplest sign in a person's life. In addition, the heart rate changes continuously as a person's emotions change. Using technology to measure human emotions is called 'emotional interactive art'. In such work, the audience provides its own physiological data and is absorbed into the work.

As well, with machine learning, we've added body tracking technology. The eye becomes a holographic interaction art that makes the illusion of finding and looking at the audience who measured the heartbeat.

2   Theoretical Background

Now we can say that this is a transition period from the information age to the emotional age that Alvin Toffler talked about. The desire to corroborate the human imagination continues to advance in the name of advances in technology. And artificial intelligence starts with the human desire to exceed existing technologies. With the advent of innovative technologies, new media such as social media have arisen. People put their own image, in a virtual space, share it with one another, and enjoy it. Also our work, *Touch*, provides information of my heart rate to a virtual eye. Eventually, viewers can feel the interest and immerse themselves as they see themselves digitally reconstructed by their information.

3   Related Works

Touch doll is an interactive work that expresses a woman's body as an upgraded version of the *Touch* series that was produced in the past [1]. It is a work in the form of illuminating the heart of a doll with information obtained through a heart rate sensor. It also created an erotic atmosphere modeled after a real human body. The audience was surprised and violently reacted to the human-shaped sculpture that measured and responded to the heartbeat. As a series of it, *Touch* has been reborn as an exhibit in the form of an eye, the fourth version.

Pulse of the City, an installation located on the streets of Boston, United States, is a work that makes music by acknowledging the heartbeat in real time. The biological information of the audience is detected by heart rate sensors located on each side of the handle. It is an interesting and enjoyable facility for pedestrians. The heart, which acts as an intermediary between the audience and this work, becomes the part of the human body which expresses emotion. Humans express their emotions at the beat of the heart by accepting stimuli or emotions perceived from the outside by the brain. This work, in which the heartbeat is eventually converted into music and leads to auditory stimulation, is thought to expand the senses and has a very similar direction to *Touch*.

The next piece of art is *Bacchus Self Scanner*, which is installed for promotional purposes. When an audience contacts the palm-shaped sensor, skin temperature, conductivity and heart rate are collected. The work measures the fatigue level of the audience and shows a number called 'discharge rate'. It is a work designed to relieve the fatigue of busy living of modern people and contains the message "Let's check the discharge rate and recharge the life". Interestingly, it uses the complex biometric information of the audience as an interaction in the artwork.

The way of interacting presented in the three works above is not unusual. It is something that everyone can easily measure.

4 Production Process

Modern interactive media art is completed by combining a part of the audience's body with the work. This interactive movement occurs when the audience perceives the work. Firstly, physical, behavioral and sensory elements were applied from the planning stage for the benefit of *Touch* audiences.

Design elements, such as buttons, that affect the actual operation of the work should be made so that the audience can easily manipulate them. The interface of *Touch* is designed to be easy for spectators to use. A device which transmits the hologram of the eye has been installed at a position about the height of the average human size. This is the height at which you can face the artwork even if you inadvertently go through. In addition, the heart rate sensor is set up in the form of a button so that it can be used with simple hand movements.

The second is to induce behavior involvement. The audience's movements are detected by machine learning and manipulated as if the eye was alive and looking at them. When heart rate data is entered into the work, a virtual eye is created to watch the audience. When the audience moves to make changes to the work, which is tracked by machine learning technology connected to a camera. Figure 1 shows the concept of the work *Touch* as a picture.

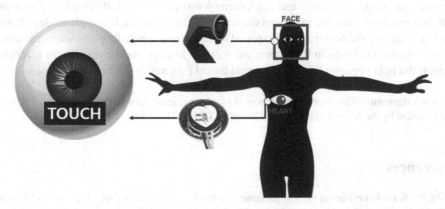

Fig. 1. *Touch* is an interactive media art with face recognition and heart rate measurement.

5 Exhibition

The exhibition was held online due to the COVID-19. The audience's reaction was very regrettable. The reaction of *Touch* can be inferred through the dynamic reaction of the audience that appeared in the past work *Touch* doll (Fig. 2).

Fig. 2. Exhibition of *Touch*

6 Conclusion

Art begins with the human desire to create and evolves by attempting to combine with various technologies to overcome the limitations of expression methods. Through responses to this work, humans can wake up to a dull sense of new technology. This work shows the time of release from sensory palsy mentioned by McLuhan.

The eye is the most sensory part of the human body. Humans accept and store outer stimuli by their eyes. Also, eyes are recognized as normal only when they operate in a perfect pair. This work is also a work in which the eyes and the audience move as one and look at one another in consideration of these features.

Our interactive media art works were constructed by reflecting physical, behavioral and sensory elements. Through this configuration, an environment in which users can approach the work more easily and conveniently was constructed. By observing various audience reactions, we tried to expand the scope of the study, but it is regrettable that we were frustrated by the occurrence of a special situation called non-face-to-face exhibition. If the situation improves in the future, we will try to examine the audience's reaction through the next version of *Touch* produced based on more advanced interactions.

Acknowledgement. This work was supported by the National Research Foundation of Korea Grant funded by the Korean Government (2019S1A5B5A07110229).

References

1. Ha, J.: A study on human body represented by media in interactive art - focused on "Touch Doll". Master thesis. Chung-Ang University, South Korea (2018)
2. McLuhan, M.: Understanding media: human expansion. Translated by Sangho Kim, Communication Books (1994)

3. P5J: https://www.p5js.org. Accessed 25 Mar 2021
4. Pulse of the City – Turning heartbeats into music on Vimeo. https://vimeo.com/74476899. Accessed 26 Mar 2021
5. Ha, J.Y.: [ATF 2020]. https://youtu.be/GyP1YdXp1rw. Accessed 25 Mar 2021
6. Bacchus Self Scanner_Brand Che. https://www.youtube.com/watch?v=HyEErVCmBVM. Accessed 26 Mar 2021

Character Input Using the Motion Sensor on a Smartwatch

Kaito Hino[⊠], Tota Mizuno, Yu Matsumoto, Kazuyuki Mito, and Naoaki Itakura

The University of Electro-Communications, 1-5-1 Chofugaoka, Chofu, Tokyo, Japan

Abstract. The screen of a smartwatch is small, which creates operational issues such as erroneous input and screen occupancy of the keyboard. Therefore, an input method, that does not depend on screen tapping but instead utilizes taps outside the touch screen and a wrist operation, is proposed herein. Five types of tapping movements were used in this study, which were aimed outside the screen and involved wrist movements. With respect to the tapping movements outside the screen, the tapped parts were placed in different locations, and tapping was performed toward the center of the screen. The wrist movement comprised a series of movements ranging from pronation to supination. These movements were assumed to be the character input. As five types of tap movements were used, five vowels of flat kana can be input in a single movement. Ten selections can be made with one input, depending on the tapping movements outside the screen and the presence or absence of wrist movement. By doing this twice, 100 selections can be made, and QWERTY array keyboard input is possible. Accelerometers and angular velocity sensors, built into the smartwatch, were used to determine the movements. In the experiment, the subjects performed each movement and data were acquired. As a result of the analysis, the off-screen tap movement was determined by the acceleration in the x-axis and y-axis. It was suggested that it is possible to discriminate whether the wrist movement is based on the angular velocity of the x-axis. A real-time discrimination experiment based on these revealed that the average discrimination rate was 81.7%. The proposed motions can determine several choices, and the efficacy of the proposed method as a viable input method for smart watches was clearly demonstrated.

Keywords: Interface · Smartwatch · Gesture · Character input

1 Introduction

In recent years, the number of users of wearable devices such as smart watches has increased and continues to do so. Touch and voice are used as the main input methods of smart watches. However, touch input is regarded as a problem from the viewpoint of operability because there are many erroneous inputs due to the small screen of the smart watch and the fact that the screen occupancy rate of the keyboard is large. In addition, voice input is difficult in noisy places, and many people are reluctant to use it in public, thereby limiting the usage environment. Therefore, gesture input is attracting attention

© Springer Nature Switzerland AG 2021
C. Stephanidis et al. (Eds.): HCII 2021, CCIS 1420, pp. 8–13, 2021.
https://doi.org/10.1007/978-3-030-78642-7_2

as a new input method. Gesture input is distinguished by using the sensors built into the smartwatch, so that input is possible regardless of the size of the device screen.

In the previous study [1], gesture input, by the bending and stretching of each finger, was examined. Although the bending and stretching movements of the thumb and index finger sides and of the ring finger and little finger side could be discriminated, it was not possible to discriminate the movements of the entirety of each finger. In the previous study [2], it was examined whether the motion pattern could be determined through the waveform of the vibration, obtained from the keystroke motion of the fingertip. The results revealed that the rotation of the wrist could be discriminated, but not the number of keystrokes.

Previous research [1, 2] shows that it is difficult to distinguish vibrations due to finger movements with a smartwatch. Therefore, in this research we focused on the action of directly tapping the body of smartwatch. Since smart watches are small and lightweight, it is thought that by tapping directly on the body, body movement is caused, and the waveform characteristic of the motion sensor can be obtained. In addition, the waveform obtained differs, depending on the tap position, and multiple operations may be distinguished.

In this research, we examined an input method that does not depend on the size of the touch screen in order to reduce erroneous input, due to the small touch screen. The purpose is to develop character input by tapping outside the touch screen and wrist movement using the acceleration/gyroscope sensor built into the smartwatch.

2 Proposed Method

The movements used in this study were tapping outside the touch screen and wrist movement. The tap positions of the tapping gestures are shown in Fig. 1. The wrist movement involved a series of movements ranging from supination to pronation. We investigated, as part of our research, whether the tapped part of the smartwatch and the wrist movement could be identified from the waveform, obtained from the sensor. Many people who are right-handed wear a watch on their left arm, and thus tap positions are provided on the right and lower sides to make it easier to tap. It is provided on the right side and the lower side. In addition, the tap position is provided on the corner part (LB, RB, RT) and the flat part (B, R) to make it easy to distinguish the operation. Assuming that characters are input using taps outside the touch screen and wrist movements, a total of six movements are prepared, including five types of tap movements and wrist movements. Depending on these five types of tap movements and the presence or absence of wrist movements, ten selections can be made with one input. By doing this twice, 100 selections can be made, and it is possible to input both with the QWERTY array keyboard and Japanese. By utilizing the five types of tapping movements, five vowels of hiragana can be selected; which can be entered in one action.

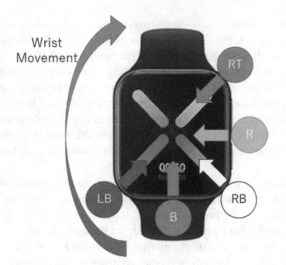

Fig. 1. Proposal actions

3 Waveform Analysis

When the five types of tapping operations, shown in Fig. 1, are performed, a characteristic waveform can be obtained from the x-axis and y-axis acceleration data. When tapping, the acceleration value fluctuates significantly compared to when it is stationary. Figures 2(a) and (b) show the waveform of the acceleration data. The tap operation of the corner part (LB, RB, RT) obtains the waveform on both the x-axis and the y-axis. The tap operation of the flat part (B, R) obtains the waveform on either the x-axis or the y-axis. However, as depicted in Fig. 2(a), there were cases where the waveform appeared on both axes in the operation where the waveform was supposed to appear on only one axis. Therefore, since the speed can be obtained by integrating the acceleration, we decided to use the value obtained by adding the acceleration values. The characteristics of the waveform of the added value became more prominent than the waveform of the raw data. Figures 3(a) and (b) display the data of the added value of acceleration, and Table 1 lists the waveform characteristics of the five movements. The tapping movements could be distinguished using the characteristics listed in Table 1. For the product of the x-axis and the y-axis, the maximum or minimum values that have the larger absolute value were used.

For the wrist movement, the added value of the x-axis of the gyroscope sensor is used. It is considered that the wrist movement can be discriminated because the change in the value is much larger than that of the tap movement.

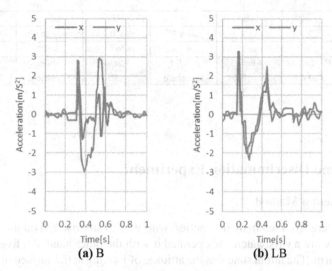

(a) B   **(b)** LB

Fig. 2. Acceleration waveform example

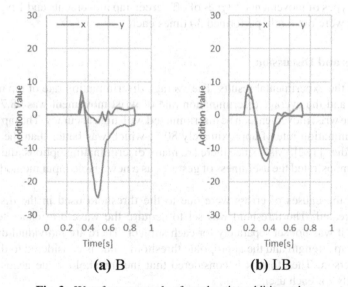

(a) B   **(b)** LB

Fig. 3. Waveform example of acceleration addition value

Table 1. Waveform characteristics of the tap actions

Action		LB	B	RB	R	RT
Waveform Characteristic	X	Plus to Minus		Minus to Plus	Minus to Plus	Minus to Plus
	Y	Plus to Minus	Plus to Minus	Plus to Minus		Minus to Plus
	Product of X and Y	Above Threshold	Under Threshold	Above Threshold	Under Threshold	Above Threshold

4   Real-Time Discrimination Experiment

4.1   Experimental Method

The subjects were five men in their twenties, who wore a smartwatch on the arm where they normally wore a wristwatch and operated it with the other hand. All five men wore it on their left arm. The initial state was the attitude of looking at the surface of the watch. For the experiment, a smart watch (OPPO Watch) equipped with a three-axes acceleration sensor and three-axes gyroscope sensor was used. The motion discrimination rate was calculated by a discrimination algorithm, created based on the characteristics of the waveform obtained by the waveform analysis. The sampling frequency was set to 100 Hz. A total of 6 types of movements, 5 types of off-screen tap movements and 1 type of wrist movements, were randomly performed 30 times each.

4.2   Results and Discussion

Table 2 lists the experimental results. The average discrimination rate of tap movement was 78.3%, and the average discrimination rate of wrist movement was 98.7%. It was found that the wrist movement can be discriminated with high accuracy. The tap operation had a discrimination rate of approximately 80%, which was better than the results of previous studies [1, 2]. Also, since there are many discriminating options, the results of the work demonstrated the usefulness of gestures as a new viable input method for smart watches.

Most of the causes of errors were due to the threshold used in the discriminant algorithm created. The threshold was set to acquire the waveform characteristics in Table 1, but it was not set separately for each subject. There are individual differences in terms of tap strength and the appropriate threshold value is considered to differ from person to person. Therefore, it is considered that the threshold value needs to be set independently for each user.

Consider motions RB and R, which were particularly misjudged. This is probably due to the difficulty of tapping in motion RB. Many subjects stated that motion RB was more difficult to tap than other tap motions. With the exception of movement RB, tapping can be performed by bending the finger. However, to perform movement RB, it is necessary to move the arm in addition to the finger. Furthermore, when performing movement RB, the finger must be tapped with either the thumb or index finger. The movement also

Table 2. Discrimination rate of proposal action

Action \ Subject	LB	B	RB	R	RT	Tap Operation Average	Wrist
A	96.7	76.7	83.3	66.7	90.0	82.7	96.7
B	93.3	83.3	86.7	83.3	63.3	82.0	100.0
C	100.0	90.0	86.7	53.3	70.0	80.0	100.0
D	90.0	93.3	56.7	66.7	83.3	78.0	100.0
E	86.7	70.0	50.0	53.3	83.3	68.7	96.7
Average	93.3	82.7	72.7	64.7	78.0	78.3	98.7

becomes awkward because it is not fixed. It is considered that the direction of the tap motion of RB was similar to other movements and caused misjudgment. In operation R, the waveform should appear only on the y-axis of acceleration, but in many cases the waveform also appeared on the x-axis. This is because the rotation around the belt occurred and the waveform also appeared on the x-axis. It is probable that the threshold value of the product of the axis and the y-axis was exceeded and the error was made.

In order to increase the discrimination rate, it is possible to use the added value, instead of the maximum/minimum of the product of the x-axis and the y-axis. The features appears more prominently, and the discrimination becomes easier by using the added value.

5 Conclusion and Future Issues

In this study, we examined input acquired by a smartwatch from direct tapping and wrist movements. The proposed gestures were effective as a new input method. Wrist movement could be discriminated with high accuracy. However, since the accuracy of discrimination between tap operation RB and R is low, it is necessary to improve the discrimination algorithm.

Some of the tapping movements proposed in this research are difficult to operate. Therefore, we would like to consider other tapping positions and new movements in the future. In addition, we aim to develop an excellent affordance input interface by considering a keyboard design that matches the input operation.

References

1. Sugawara, K., Akehi, K., Farahani, M.A., Mito, K., Mizuno, T., Itakura, N.: Gesture input using forearm movement. IEEE IM Soc. Tokyo/Japan Sect. Jt. Chapter Stud. Meet. IEEE_IM-S18-23 (2018)
2. Inayama, C., Farahani, M.A., Mito, K., Mizuno, T., Itakura, N.: Gesture input for smart watches using finger keystrokes. IEEE IM Soc. Tokyo/Japan Sect. Jt. Chapter Stud. Meet. IEEE_IM-S19-25 (2019)

Phone-Pointing Remote App:
Using Smartphones as Pointers
in Gesture-Based IoT Remote Controls

Ilan Kirsh[1]([⊠])[iD] and Heinrich Ruser[2][iD]

[1] The Academic College of Tel Aviv-Yaffo, Tel Aviv, Israel
kirsh@mta.ac.il
[2] Bundeswehr University Munich, Neubiberg, Germany
Heinrich.Ruser@unibw.de

Abstract. Remote control mobile applications for operating Internet of Things (IoT) devices using smartphones are commonly based on a touch user interface. The effort of using such apps is often disproportionate to the simplicity of carrying out the actions manually. For example, turning a light on or off via menus and forms of a standard remote app might not be very convenient. A voice user interface, while easier to use, gives rise to other issues, including user privacy and distracting others nearby. This paper proposes a new type of universal IoT remote control applications for smartphones: phone-pointing remote apps. Using a phone-pointing remote app, users can physically point their smartphones at IoT devices to select them, and operate them via movement gestures, without needing to turn on the phone screen or talk, and with no need for any additional hardware. This new approach provides a unique combination of advantages. It is simple, intuitive, fast, and voiceless. Instead of using the touchscreen or the microphone as the input source, phone-pointing remote apps will use a combination of standard smartphone sensors, including the GNSS sensor, Wi-Fi scanner, Bluetooth receiver, camera, barometer, magnetometer, g-force meter, accelerometer, and gyroscope. An analysis of the proposed model in light of relevant results from related studies provides positive preliminary indications regarding the feasibility of this novel approach.

Keywords: Universal wireless remote control · Smartphone sensors · Hand-gestures · Internet of Things (IoT) · Smartphone orientation · Azimuth · Pitch · Android · iPhone

1 Introduction

Wireless remote controlling has come a long way from the release of the first TV remote control, the Zenith Space Command [1], in 1956 to modern IoT remote controls [4]. Voice-controlled virtual assistants such as the Amazon Echo Alexa, Google Home Assistant, and Apple HomePod Siri are widely used nowadays to control IoT-enabled devices, such as lights, thermostats, and alarms [3]. Remote

© Springer Nature Switzerland AG 2021
C. Stephanidis et al. (Eds.): HCII 2021, CCIS 1420, pp. 14–21, 2021.
https://doi.org/10.1007/978-3-030-78642-7_3

controls are also available as smartphone apps [2,3]. Voice-controlling is associated with some potential issues regarding security and privacy [3,11] and user acceptance [9]. Therefore, a voiceless operation based on a standard touchscreen user interface may be preferred in certain circumstances. However, touchscreen-based remote apps also have usability issues. For example, controlling the lights using a standard remote control app with a touch user interface often requires turning on the smartphone screen, launching the remote app, navigating through menus, and finally selecting the operation. This process may be considered overly complicated as the required user effort is disproportionate to the simplicity of such a routine operation.

We propose a new type of smartphone IoT remote control: phone-pointing remote apps. Unlike touch-based remote apps, phone-pointing remote apps can be used with the phone's screen turned off. As illustrated in Fig. 1, users select devices by pointing their smartphone at them, and then use movement gestures, while holding the smartphone, to operate the devices. Unlike existing gesture-based pointing remotes that are based on dedicated hardware, such as a hand-held infrared projector and an appropriate receiver at every device [8], which increases costs and restricts their availability, the proposal made in this paper is based on built-in smartphone functionalities, and does not require additional hardware. Phone-pointing remote apps will use standard smartphone sensors for input, including (a) the GNSS (Global Navigation Satellite System, commonly referred to as GPS, based on the most widely used GNSS system) and the Wi-Fi receiver to evaluate the current user location, (b) the magnetometer and the g-force meter (or the accelerometer) to identify 3D pointing directions during device selection, and (c) the accelerometer and the gyroscope to recognize movement gestures while holding the smartphone.

In this paper, we present our vision for phone-pointing remote apps. We define a model based on Machine Learning (ML), which can be used to implement remote control apps of this type. Then we describe relevant technical details and discuss the opportunities as well as the challenges. Results from various related studies provide positive preliminary indications that this novel approach to wireless IoT remote controlling using smartphones is promising, as discussed in this paper.

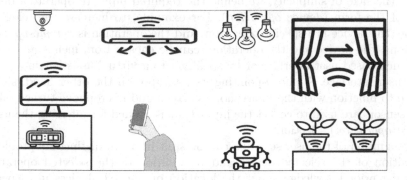

Fig. 1. Controlling an air conditioner using a phone-pointing IoT remote control app

2   Toward Phone-Pointing Remote Apps

Modern remote apps use IoT APIs, such as Google Assistant API, Apple Home-Kit, Amazon Alexa Home Skills API, and others, to communicate with compatible IoT devices, as illustrated in Fig. 2. The arrows in Fig. 2 indicate the main directions of action. To operate IoT devices, users select devices and operations by using either touch or voice user interfaces. Selections are translated by the remote app into instructions that are sent to the devices through the IoT APIs, usually over the local network via Wi-Fi. Information flows also in the opposite direction, where IoT APIs are used to collect information about available devices, which is provided to the user by the app. The main responsibility of an IoT remote app is to provide a user interface that bridges the gap between the users and the relevant IoT APIs and devices.

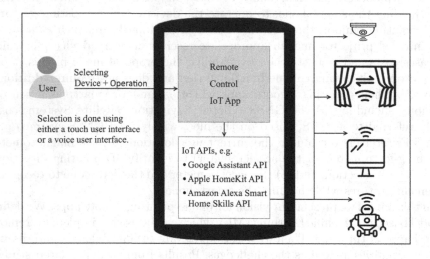

Fig. 2. General structure of IoT remote control apps

For the sake of simplicity, we define the required input to operate a device to be of the form (*device, operation*). For example, to increase the television volume, the device is a specific television, and the operation is *volume-up*. Both selections, the device and the operation, can be chosen from menus and forms in a touch-based user interface or by speaking to a virtual assistant in a voice-based user interface. A phone-pointing remote app, on the other hand, should be able to function with the smartphone's screen and microphone turned off, as other sensors are used to collect the input that is needed for inferring the user's (*device, operation*) selection.

Recognition of the user selection can be split into two distinct subproblems: recognition of the selected device and recognition of the selected operation. Assuming prior knowledge about the location of the IoT devices in a specific environment, an app may be able to identify which device is selected based on the current location of the smartphone (and the user) and its pointing direction. Therefore, the subproblem of recognizing the selected device can be further split into two more fundamental problems (recognition of current location and recognition of pointing direction). The division of our problem into three basic subproblems is illustrated at the top half of Fig. 3 (labeled 'Required Input'). The bottom half of Fig. 3 (labeled 'Phone Sensors') lists standard smartphone sensors that can be used in solving each one of these three basic subproblems.

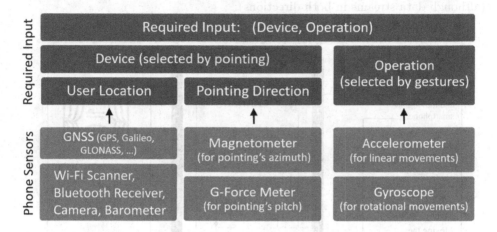

Fig. 3. Using sensors to collect input in phone-pointing remote control apps

GNSS sensors provide the main built-in ability to localize the smartphone. However, to improve accuracy, especially inside buildings, data from other sensors such as the Wi-Fi scanner [10], the Bluetooth receiver [6], and the camera [13] can be used. Barometer values (if available) can help in establishing the 3D location, as barometric pressure values can indicate height (expected to be useful in multi-floor buildings).

The two main sensors for evaluating the 3D pointing direction are the magnetometer and the g-force meter (or the accelerator). Data from the magnetometer can be used to determine the horizontal pointing direction, i.e. the azimuth angle. Data from the g-force meter can be used to determine the vertical pointing direction, i.e. the pitch angle. The g-force (or gravity) meter is often a virtual software sensor, implemented using data from physical hardware sensors, such as the accelerometer. By combining the data from these standard smartphone sensors, the app can establish a 3D pointing direction [7].

After selecting a device by pointing at it with their smartphone, users can specify an operation using arm movement gestures while still holding the smartphone. For example, an upward forearm movement can signal *turn-on*, whereas a downward movement can signal *turn-off*. Similarly, a clockwise rotation can signal *volume-up*, whereas a rotation in the opposite direction, anticlockwise, can signal *volume-down*. The exact gestures can vary from one implementation to another, and even in the same application could be customized by the user. Movement gestures can be identified mainly using data from the linear accelerometer and the gyroscope sensors.

In standard remote apps, the exact physical location of the devices does not play a role (as long as the connection to the network is stable). A phone-pointing remote app, on the other hand, has to be aware of the layout of the devices in a specific environment. We can use Machine Learning (ML) for this purpose, as illustrated in Fig. 4. The arrows in Fig. 4 indicate the main direction of data flow (although data streams in both directions).

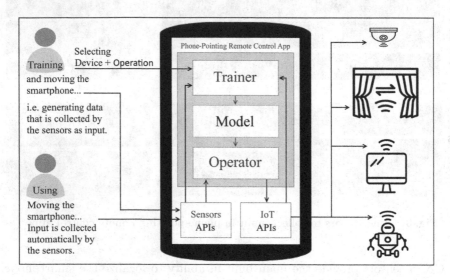

Fig. 4. Structure of phone-pointing IoT remote control apps

During the training phase, the app should learn the environment. This can be achieved by guiding users through on-screen or voice menus and instructions. Users should demonstrate selections of devices by pointing at them from different relevant locations and demonstrate selections of operations by movement gestures. The Trainer component (see Fig. 4) collects data from the relevant sensors and relates the data to devices and operations. An ML-model is built based on this information and when it has trained sufficiently the app is ready for use. Using the trained ML-model, the Operator component can convert sensor data from users (which do not use the touchscreen or voice) into ($device, operation$) values that are then sent to the IoT APIs and processed as commands to the relevant devices.

As shown in Fig. 3, each one of the three basic recognition subproblems (user location, pointing direction, operation by gestures) relates to a different set of sensors, and therefore, can be managed as a separate ML task. Using sub-ML-models for the three subproblems may have some advantages, such as simplicity and the ability to choose the most appropriate ML method for each subproblem separately. On the other hand, one combined ML-model for the complete recognition problem of (*device, operation*) may have some other significant advantages, such as the ability to fill gaps in data for one subproblem by using data available for the other subproblems. For example, if the location information is uncertain, a neural network model for the entire problem can identify a (*device, operation*) pair using only the pointing direction and the movement gestures if they are unique in that environment for a particular (*device, operation*) pair.

3   Discussion

To the best of our knowledge, there are no implementations of phone-pointing remote apps yet, so it is impossible to provide a precise evaluation of the feasibility, usability, and acceptability of this model in this early work.

Regarding usability and acceptability, it is reasonable to expect that phone-pointing remote apps, if they work as expected (i.e. provide a proper level of accuracy) could be usable and acceptable in various situations due to their unique combination of potential advantages as being simple, intuitive, fast, and voiceless (i.e. fewer concerns regarding privacy and distractions compared to voice assistants). Adding phone-pointing capabilities to regular remote apps with conventional user interfaces, rather than providing a separate pointing-only user interface, may improve the overall usability and acceptability, as such hybrid apps could provide the best of both worlds. Definitive answers regarding the usability and the acceptability of phone-pointing remote apps would naturally require implementations of such solutions and field studies.

The key question is whether this model is feasible, i.e. whether a proper level of accuracy can be achieved. Although we cannot provide a definitive answer to this question at this point, we can try to evaluate the possibilities and the challenges of this model in light of relevant results from related studies. It may help, in the context of this discussion, to evaluate each of the three basic recognition subproblems (see Fig. 3) separately.

Out of the three subproblems, the most challenging one might be finding the smartphone location. Although localization is one of the most commonly used capabilities of smartphones nowadays (for navigation and many other uses), pointing remote apps may need higher levels of accuracy and are expected to be used mainly inside buildings, where GNSS sensors are less accurate. Nevertheless, there are several reasons why we can expect this challenge to be manageable. First, there are some successful implementations of indoor localization (including using the camera [13], Wi-Fi signals [10], and Bluetooth signals [6]). Second, remote apps may be used mainly from very specific locations, e.g. while sitting near a desk or on a sofa, lying in bed, etc. In other words, we do not necessarily need a continuous recognition of every point in space, but instead, we mainly want to be able to recognize specific locations, and that may be more tolerant to errors. Third, many circumstantial data, such as the day and time, the way and direction that the user puts the smartphone, and residual movements of the smartphone until it was put to rest, can all help in inferring the location (as well as pointing and gesture operations, i.e. using data related to the two other subproblems as additional hints). Fourth, a pointing remote app with no localization capabilities at all could still be useful, when used from a single location, e.g. from a hospital bed by a patient, or when the current location can be selected by other means.

Regarding the second subproblem (recognizing the pointing direction), recent studies show that the direction of pointing (or the orientation of the smartphone) can be measured with high accuracy using the smartphone's sensors. Although the accuracy varies across different smartphones, the mean inaccuracy per device is up to 2.1 degrees for the pitch orientation [5]. Even when adding up inaccuracies due to deviation of pointing operations by the user, we can expect the total error margin of the orientation measurements to be up to approximately 5 degrees, which should usually be sufficient to select different devices located in a room by pointing at them with the smartphone [7].

The third subproblem, identifying movement gestures based on smartphone sensors, was investigated in recent studies with overall promising results [12,14].

The complete problem of recognizing the (device, operation) input cannot be more difficult than the combination of the three underlying subproblems. As discussed above, it might be even easier, because each of the subproblems contributes data that may assist in solving the other subproblems, by using elimination techniques. For example, a certain pointing direction or a certain gesture could be unique in a particular installation, and therefore sufficient to recognize the (device, operation) selection despite missing data.

4   Conclusions and Further Work

This paper presents a new approach to IoT remote control apps. Using phone-pointing remote apps, users would be able to select devices by pointing at them with the smartphone and operate the devices by movement gestures, detected by the smartphone's built-in sensors. Instead of the usual input sources, such as the touch screen in regular remote apps and the microphone in voice assistants, in the proposed phone-pointing remote apps input is collected from a combination of standard smartphone sensors, including the GNSS sensor, the Wi-Fi scanner, the magnetometer, the g-force (gravity) meter, the accelerometer, and the gyroscope.

The main challenge in implementing phone-pointing remote apps is recognizing (device, operation) inputs that users generate by pointing and gesture operations. Our analysis, based on results from related recent studies, provides preliminary positive indications regarding the feasibility of this novel approach.

Further work should involve the development of phone-pointing remote apps, based on this proposed model, and the evaluation of the feasibility, usability, and acceptability of this approach in field studies.

Acknowledgment. The icons of IoT devices in Figs. 1, 2, and 4 (Air Conditioner, Alarm Clock, Computer, Curtain, Lightbulb, Nature, Robot, and Webcam) are provided by Mavadee from thenounproject.com.

References

1. Acebron, J., Spigler, R.: The remote control and beyond: the legacy of Robert Adler. SIAM News **40**(5), 1–2 (2007)
2. Bai, Y., Su, H., Hsu, W.: Indoor and remote controls and management of home appliances by a smartphone with a four-quadrant user interface. In: IEEE International Conference on Consumer Electronics (ICCE), Las Vegas, USA, pp. 319–320 (2017). https://doi.org/10.1109/ICCE.2017.7889336
3. Hoy, M.B.: Alexa, Siri, Cortana, and more: an introduction to voice assistants. Med. Ref. Serv. Q. **37**(1), 81–88 (2018). https://doi.org/10.1080/02763869.2018.1404391
4. Khan, A., Al-Zahrani, A., Al-Harbi, S., Al-Nashri, S., Khan, I.A.: Design of an IoT smart home system. In: 15th Learning and Technology Conference (L&T), pp. 1–5 (2018). https://doi.org/10.1109/LT.2018.8368484
5. Kuhlmann, T., Garaizar, P., Reips, U.D.: Smartphone sensor accuracy varies from device to device in mobile research: the case of spatial orientation. Behav. Res. Methods **53**(1), 22–33 (2020). https://doi.org/10.3758/s13428-020-01404-5
6. Murata, M., Ahmetovic, D., Sato, D., Takagi, H., Kitani, K.M., Asakawa, C.: Smartphone-based indoor localization for blind navigation across building complexes. In: 2018 IEEE International Conference on Pervasive Computing and Communications (PerCom), pp. 1–10. IEEE (2018)
7. Ruser, H., Kirsh, I.: Point at it with your smartphone: assessing the applicability of orientation sensing of smartphones to operate IoT devices. In: Proceedings of the 23rd HCI International Conference (HCII). Springer, Cham (2021)
8. Ruser, H., Vorwerg, S., Eicher, C.: Making the home accessible - experiments with an infrared handheld gesture-based remote control. In: Stephanidis, C., Antona, M. (eds.) HCII 2020. CCIS, vol. 1226, pp. 89–97. Springer, Cham (2020). https://doi.org/10.1007/978-3-030-50732-9_13
9. Sayago, S., Neves, B.B., Cowan, B.R.: Voice assistants and older people: some open issues. In: Proceedings of the 1st International Conference on Conversational User Interfaces (CUI), pp. 1–3, New York, USA. Association for Computing Machinery (2019). https://doi.org/10.1145/3342775.3342803
10. Shin, B.J., Lee, K.W., Choi, S.H., Kim, J.Y., Lee, W.J., Kim, H.S.: Indoor wifi positioning system for android-based smartphone. In: International Conference on Information and Communication Technology Convergence (ICTC), pp. 319–320 (2010). https://doi.org/10.1109/ICTC.2010.5674691
11. Terzopoulos, G., Satratzemi, M.: Voice assistants and smart speakers in everyday life and in education. Inf. Educ. **19**, 473–490 (2020). https://doi.org/10.15388/infedu.2020.21
12. Wang, X., Tarrío, P., Metola, E., Bernardos, A.M., Casar, J.R.: Gesture recognition using mobile phone's inertial sensors. In: Omatu, S., De Paz Santana, J.F., González, S.R., Molina, J.M., Bernardos, A.M., Rodríguez, J.M.C. (eds.) Distributed Computing and Artificial Intelligence. AISC, vol. 151, pp. 173–184. Springer, Heidelberg (2012). https://doi.org/10.1007/978-3-642-28765-7_21
13. Werner, M., Kessel, M., Marouane, C.: Indoor positioning using smartphone camera. In: International Conference on Indoor Positioning and Indoor Navigation (IPIN), pp. 1–6 (2011). https://doi.org/10.1109/IPIN.2011.6071954
14. Xie, C., Luan, S., Wang, H., Zhang, B.: Gesture recognition benchmark based on mobile phone. In: You, Z. (ed.) CCBR 2016. LNCS, vol. 9967, pp. 432–440. Springer, Cham (2016). https://doi.org/10.1007/978-3-319-46654-5_48

Detection and Localisation of Pointing, Pairing and Grouping Gestures for Brainstorming Meeting Applications

Simon Liechti⬤, Naina Dhingra⁽✉⁾⬤, and Andreas Kunz⬤

Innovation Center Virtual Reality, ETH Zurich,
Leonhardstr. 21, 8092 Zurich, Switzerland
liechtsi@student.ethz.ch, {ndhingra,kunz}@iwf.mavt.ethz.ch
https://www.icvr.ethz.ch

Abstract. The detection of gestures and their interpretation is crucial for blind and visually impaired people (BVIP). In a card-based brainstorming meeting, sighted users use non-verbal communication when referring to cards on a common workspace using pointing, grouping, or pairing gestures. While sighted users could easily interpret such gestures, they remain inaccessible to BVIP. Thus, there is a need for capturing, interpreting and translating gestures for BVIP.

To address this problem, we developed a pointing gesture detection system using Unity with the SteamVR Plugin and HTC Vive. HTC's trackers are attached to a user's hands to measure the hand position in 3D space. With pointing gestures, a user controls a virtual ray that will intersect with a virtual whiteboard. This virtual whiteboard is invisible to the sighted users, but its position and size corresponds to a physical whiteboard. The intersection of the ray with the virtual whiteboard is calculated, resulting in a pointing trajectory on it. The shape of the trajectory is analyzed to determine, which artifacts are selected by the pointing gesture. A pointing gesture is detected when a user is pointing at a card on the screen and then ending the gesture by pointing outside of the screen. A pairing gesture is detected when pointing at one artifact and then on another one before leaving the screen. The grouping gesture is detected when performing an encircling gesture around multiple artifacts before leaving the screen.

Keywords: Blind and visually impaired · Pointing gestures · Virtual reality

1 Introduction

In team meetings, gestures are used together with speech to support arguments during a discussion. These gestures belong to non-verbal communication (NVC), which could make up to 55% of the overall information flow [8]. Since these gestures are inaccessible for the blind and visually impaired (BVIP), they need

C. Stephanidis et al. (Eds.): HCII 2021, CCIS 1420, pp. 22–29, 2021.
https://doi.org/10.1007/978-3-030-78642-7_4

to be detected and interpreted [3], otherwise they would not be able to participate in such meetings to a full extent. Among these NVC elements, pointing gestures are the most important ones, which typically refer to artifacts in the 3D space of a meeting room, e.g. on a common whiteboard. Within this paper, we focus on the so-called "Metaplan" method, which is well established in industry and research as well for idea generation in team meetings. When looking at the NVC elements, most gestures refer to artifacts (cards) on a common whiteboard. These pointing gestures can typically be divided into i) pointing at an artifact, ii) pairing of two artifacts, and iii) grouping. Accordingly, an imaginary "pointing ray" on the whiteboard would be dot-shaped, line-shaped, or encircling.

This paper focuses on the reliable interpretation of pointing gestures. For this, the paper is structured as follows: Sect. 2 will describe the state-of-the-art in this field, followed by Sect. 3 that describes how we track and interpret the gestures. Section 4 will describe the technical setup. Section 6 will show preliminary results, before Sect. 7 will conclude this paper.

2   Related Work

There is only little work in interpreting pointing gestures on artifacts in a common workspace. In [5], an MS Pixelsense table was used together with an MS Kinect depth camera to track pointing gestures above the table. To overcome still existing interference problems between Kinect and Pixelsense, later work used LEAP Motion sensors [6,11]. To interpret the pointing gestures, an information infrastructure was developed in [10] to translate the pointing gestures of sighted users to a BVIP output interface. The application used in this study was a Mindmap tool, and users were supposed to stand around the table [1]. Thus, the users' gestures were close to the artifacts on the Pixelsense table, making their pointing gestures more accurate. However, when users refer to a common whiteboard like in our Metaplan method, their distance to the artifacts is larger and the pointing gestures tend to be less accurate as described in [2]. In their setup, an MS Kinect was placed on the vertical whiteboard, while users performed pointing gestures from a 1.5 m distance. In their study, the pointing accuracy was found to be around 80%, but no other gesture interpretation was involved. If the pointing hand can be captured from a shorter distance like in [7], an accuracy of approximately 90% at a distance of 1m in front of an ideal background for a background segmentation can be achieved. However, no other gesture interpretation was researched. In [9], Hidden Markov Models and Particle Filters were used to improve the detection accuracy of pointing gestures to about 90%. More recently, [12] used convolutional neural networks to detect hand gestures for pointing and also achieved an accuracy of 90%. However, we found no research work that brings hand gestures in relation to artifacts on a common whiteboard for pointing, pairing, and grouping.

While the accuracy of such deep learning approaches is already sufficiently high, these approaches still suffer from the fact that they require a lot of time to train the underlying network properly, and also the detection times are usually in the range of second. Due to this lack of real-time capability, these approaches can yet not be used in lively discussions such as brainstorming session in a team.

3 Method

During a Metaplan session, participants use gestures to support a facilitator in rearranging cards on the whiteboard. The artifacts (cards) are part of the visible whiteboard and it is assumed that all types of gestures are only valid when they are detected inside the whiteboard's area. When gestures are detected to be valid, they mainly differ in their shape. During a brainstorming session, mainly three kinds of gestures will occur: pointing, pairing, grouping (see Fig. 1).

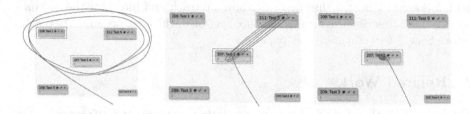

Fig. 1. Trajectories of groupin, pairing, and pointing gestures.

Users typically perform such pointing gestures imprecisely, so that an imaginary pointing ray on the whiteboard would have an elliptic shape even though the user actually wanted i) not to move (pointing), ii) draw a straight line (pairing), or iii) draw a circle (grouping). To differentiate between these gestures, the area of a gesture is approximated as an ellipse and their properties are compared. As a differentiation measure, we use the ratio between the semi-minor and the semi-major axes, as well as the curvature.

In a first step, our algorithm will compute a "G-value" as a basic distinction between circle and ellipse. For this, it connects the sample points (see Sect. 4) by straight lines and calculates the angles between subsequent lines. Summing up all angles and averaging them by the amount of angles will give α_{avg}. Next, each angle α is compared to this average by subtracting it from the average value. If the pointing trajectory has a circular shape, the difference is ideally equal to Zero (or close to it for small "deformations" of the circle. Thus, summing up all differences will result in a G-value close or even equal to zero, or in a high G-value for ellipses, where some angles are significantly different (see Eq. 1).

$$\sum_{i=0}^{n} |\alpha_{\mathrm{avg}} - \alpha_{\mathrm{i}}| = G \tag{1}$$

This G-value is the threshold for distinguishing between circle and ellipse, i.e. between a grouping and a pairing gestures. Based on an empirical study, this G-value was set to be $G = 100$. Once the G-value is determined, a bounding box (blue) is placed around sample points of the ellipse (see Fig. 2).

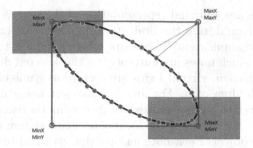

Fig. 2. Determining the orientation of the ellipse and the corner sample points.

Pairing Gesture. If the G-value determines a pairing gesture, the application needs to find the orientation of the ellipse to determine, which two corners of the bounding box will be used for note recognition. For this, the distance of each sample point to each corner of the bounding box is calculated to find the two smallest distances of sample points to the two corners of the bounding box. The two sample points with the smallest distances to the two corners of the bounding box will be further processed (see Fig. 2). For the correct recognition of a note, the distance of the note's center point and the "corner" sample points has to be smaller than a predefined value d. Based on empirical studies, this value was set to be $d = 0.3$ normalized to the size of the whiteboard. To avoid false positives, the pairing gesture's results will only be forwarded to the BVIP if two different cards are detected by the aforementioned method. If the corner sample points refer to the same note, the system will recognize it as a pointing gesture.

Grouping Gesture. If the G-value detects a grouping gesture, the coordinates of all the notes' centerpoints are compared to the bounding box. All notes inside are then checked for their uniqueness. If only one note is inside. The system recognises it as a pointing gesture. If two notes are inside, the system will again recognize it as a pairing gesture of two notes. If more than two notes are inside the bounding box, the system will output a grouping gesture.

4   Implementation

4.1   Modelling

The detection of gestures is done by overlaying an invisible virtual whiteboard on the physical one, having the same form factor and orientation (see Fig. 3). For modeling, the Unity game engine was used. In particular, the following elements or functions were relevant:

– *Screen.* The invisible virtual screen represents the digital whiteboard with the notes attached to it. It is a game object with colliders. The screen's size can be changed by changing its pixel count for the x- and y-axis.

– *Notes.* The notes are a virtual representation of the notes that are displayed on the digital screen during the brainstorming. They are created by a script at the start of the application. This script makes a request to the server to get the information which notes are currently on the selected digital whiteboard. Using this information, virtual twins are created as game objects on the virtual screen as children of it. For any game object being a child of another game object, the child has normalized local coordinates reaching from −0.5 to 0.5 for each axis. The origin of the local coordinate system is in the center of the parent game object. Each note has a script attached to it that holds further information of the note, such as *positionx*, *positiony*, *rotation*, *scale*, *title*, and *body*. This information is updated each frame by a server request. The note also has a unique tag called "note". This tag allows for differentiation of colliders when using the raycasting method.
– *Scripting.* The scripting in Unity is done with C#. To use a script inside Unity, the script needs to be attached to a game object. Variables of that game object like position, scale, and rotation can also be used in the script. In the Unity script, there are two important functions. void Start() and void Update(). The "Start" function is executed when the application is started. The "Update" function is executed for each frame the application is running.
– *Raycasting.* For detecting pointing gestures, Unity's "Raycasting" method is used. It projects a one-dimensional beam from a point of origin in a certain direction. The direction is controlled by the tracker of the HTC Vive. This method returns a "true" value if it hits a collider. Information about the game object with the collider can be accessed with the RaycastHit structure.
– *Rest API.* The visual content on the real whiteboard, i.e. the Metaplan cards, is generated by the sever-based *Rest API* [4]. The script for the communication with the server is attached to a game object. Other scripts can access the function to communicate with the server by referencing that game object. The game objects in Unity will thus communicate their activation to *Rest API*, which in turn will output the card's information (the written text on the card and the cluster it belongs to) to the BVIP interface.
– *Generating Sphere Colliders.* Recognition spheres are primitive sphere game objects with colliders. They are created at the intersection point of the pointing ray with the virtual screen. The spheres are generated with a predefined spawn rate 10 Hz. Each sphere has a specific "Sphere" tag attached to it with a unique ID. This is used to differentiate between sphere collider, screen collider, and note collider. The spheres have also an activation time and a lifetime to avoid any overflow with spheres that might slow down the system's responsiveness. The lifetime determines the duration after which they are deleted. The activation time is the predefined duration of 2 s for a Boolean attached to each sphere to switch from "false" to "true".

As soon as the pointing ray hits a previously generated sphere, the gesture is set as "completed" and the script will perform a gesture recognition as described above by evaluating the position of every sphere (the sampling point).

Fig. 3. Virtual screen overlay.

4.2   Technical Setup

Our application uses the HTC Vive system with two lighthouses and two track-ers. With this, we generated the typical interaction space of 5 × 5 m. The HMD and the controllers are not used. We use the Steam VR plugin for Unity and run it together with our virtual environment on an AMD Ryzen 5 2600 six cores processor at 3.4 GHz and 8 GB RAM. The Rest API runs on an external server and communicated over the Internet.

5   User Study

Each of the three gestures will be tested ten times, together with ten false positive tests by moving randomly in the empty space on the whiteboard. For the study, the user will only see the physical whiteboard together with the artifacts.

– *Pointing gesture test.* The user starts pointing outside of the whiteboard and then moves to an artifact on the whiteboard. He points at the artifact for four seconds. Afterwards he moves outside the whiteboard again.
– *Pairing gesture test.* The user starts pointing outside the whiteboard area. Then he moves to one artifact and instantly continues moving to the second artifact. After pointing at this second artifact the user returns to the first one. This is repeated times before the gesture leaves the whiteboard.
– *Grouping gesture test.* The user starts pointing outside the whiteboard, moves inside, and encircles three artifacts. The circular movement is repeated three times. Finally, the gesture moves outside the whiteboard area.
– *False positive test.* The user starts the pointing outside the whiteboard area. He then moves his pointing direction inside an empty space on the whiteboard. The user moves for four seconds inside this empty space and ends the test by moving outside of the whiteboard area.

6   Results

The results of the user study are summarized in Table 1. The results show that the pointing gesture is detected 100% correctly, which was expected as it can be derived either from the circular or from the elliptic gesture. The recognition of parting was 90% successful, while pairing performed only 80%. The lower performance in detecting the pairing gesture might be due to the fact that the bounding box is only a rough approximation of a circular shape, which might group more cards than actually intended by the users.

Table 1. Detection accuracy for pointing, pairing, grouping and false positives.

Test no.	Pointing	Pairing	Grouping	Random
1	Yes	Yes	No	Yes
2	Yes	Yes	No	Yes
3	Yes	No	Yes	Yes
4	Yes	Yes	Yes	No
5	Yes	Yes	Yes	No
6	Yes	Yes	No	Yes
7	Yes	Yes	Yes	Yes
8	Yes	Yes	Yes	Yes
9	Yes	Yes	Yes	Yes
10	Yes	Yes	Yes	No

7   Summary and Outlook

We presented a system for the recognition of pointing, pairing and grouping gestures. Based on previous work, a new approach using the HTC Vice technology was chosen. The core idea was to create an invisible virtual overlay on the physical digital whiteboard to detect and interpret pointing gestures.

The user study examined three gestures. A comparison of the pointing trajectories on the virtual whiteboard to an ellipse was chosen for differentiating the three gestures. The curvature changes along the ellipse were used to differentiate between the pairing and grouping gesture, while pointing could be detected in both cases. The study with a reduced amount of users due to the COVID disease showed that the recognition performed well with an accuracy of at least 80%, which is comparable to deep learning approaches introduced in Sect. 2.

Future work will focus on increasing the overall performance by taking into account additional information sources. The knowledge of already existing connections between artifacts on the white help increasing the pairing accuracy even though an individual card might not be detected by out algorithm.

References

1. Alavi, A., Kunz, A.: Tracking deictic gestures over large interactive surfaces. Comput. Support. Coop. Work (CSCW) **24**(2), 109–119 (2015). https://doi.org/10.1007/s10606-015-9219-4

2. Dhingra, N., Valli, E., Kunz, A.: Recognition and localisation of pointing gestures using a RGB-D camera. In: Stephanidis, C., Antona, M. (eds.) HCII 2020. CCIS, vol. 1224, pp. 205–212. Springer, Cham (2020). https://doi.org/10.1007/978-3-030-50726-8_27

3. Kane, S.K., Wobbrock, J.O., Ladner, R.E.: Usable gestures for blind people: understanding preference and performance. In: Proceedings of the SIGCHI Conference on Human Factors in Computing Systems, pp. 413–422. ACM, New York (2011). https://doi.org/10.1145/1978942.1979001

4. Koutny, R., Günther, S., Dhingra, N., Kunz, A., Miesenberger, K., Mühlhäuser, M.: Accessible multimodal tool support for brainstorming meetings. In: Miesenberger, K., Manduchi, R., Covarrubias Rodriguez, M., Peňáz, P. (eds.) ICCHP 2020. LNCS, vol. 12377, pp. 11–20. Springer, Cham (2020). https://doi.org/10.1007/978-3-030-58805-2_2

5. Kunz, A., Alavi, A., Sinn, P.: Integrating pointing gesture detection for enhancing brainstorming meetings using kinect and pixelsense. In: 8th International Conference on Digital Enterprise Technology, pp. 205–212 (2014). https://doi.org/10.1016/j.procir.2014.10.031, http://www.det-2014.de/en/home.html

6. Kunz, A., Schnelle-Walka, D., Alavi, A., Poelzer, S., Muehlhaeuser, M., Miesenberger, K.: Making tabletop interaction accessible for blind users. In: Interactive Tabletops and Surfaces, pp. 327–332. ACM, New York (2014). https://doi.org/10.1145/2669485.2669541, http://its2014.org/

7. Le, H.-A., Mac, K.-N.C., Pham, T.-A., Tran, M.-T.: Realtime pointing gesture recognition and applications in multi-user interaction. In: Selamat, A., Nguyen, N.T., Haron, H. (eds.) ACIIDS 2013. LNCS (LNAI), vol. 7802, pp. 355–364. Springer, Heidelberg (2013). https://doi.org/10.1007/978-3-642-36546-1_37

8. Mehrabian, A., Ferris, S.R.: Inference of attitudes from nonverbal communication in two channels. J. Consult. Psychol. **31**(3), 248–252 (1967). https://doi.org/10.1037/h0024648

9. Park, C., Roh, M., Lee, S.: Real-time 3D pointing gesture recognition in mobile space. In: 2008 8th IEEE International Conference on Automatic Face Gesture Recognition, pp. 1–6. IEEE, New York (2008). https://doi.org/10.1109/AFGR.2008.4813448

10. Pölzer, S., Schnelle-Walka, D., Pöll, D., Heumader, P., Miesenberger, K.: Making brainstorming meetings accessible for blind users. In: AAATE Conference (2013)

11. Miesenberger, K., Fels, D., Archambault, D., Peňáz, P., Zagler, W. (eds.): ICCHP 2014. LNCS, vol. 8547. Springer, Cham (2014). https://doi.org/10.1007/978-3-319-08596-8

12. Wang, J., Liu, T., Wang, X.: Human hand gesture recognition with convolutional neural networks for K-12 double-teachers instruction mode classroom. Infrared Phys. Technol. **111**, 103464 (2020). https://doi.org/10.1016/j.infrared.2020.103464

Soft2Soft: Toolkit for the Digital Recognition of Textile Gestures

Maria Jose Melo Betancurt⬛, Yuleisy Rincón-Saavedra⬛, Laura Cortés-Rico$^{(\boxtimes)}$ ⬛, and Alexander Rozo-Torres⬛

Universidad Militar Nueva Granada, Cajicá, Colombia
laura.cortes@unimilitar.edu.co

Abstract. This work in progress presents the toolkit Soft2Soft, for the digital recognition of textile gestures. In this context, the term gesture means a non-verbal way of human-computer interaction (HCI), through the hands, using textile materialities. The first section presents a background of projects that involve HCI with textile elements, which have inspired and informed our work. The second section details the toolkit that provides gesture recognition over wearable textiles (through actions such as button-up, sticking hook and loop pieces, sliding a zipper) and non-wearable textiles (e.g., going through the fabric with a needle, caressing the textile, squeezing, or pinching the fabric). Here, we emphasize calling the interaction through (with) the textile materialities as a gesture, meaning that it intends to express a feeling, an idea, or a thought, not as just a simple, functional action. Finally, we present and discuss some preliminary uses of the toolkit and potential applications that Soft2Soft will allow.

Keywords: Textile gestures · e-textiles · Textile interactions

1 Introduction

Textiles are soft materialities that ancestrally have a strong connection with the body and communities' cultural aspects. Research, technological development, and innovation have recently grown around connections between textiles and digital technologies. For example, how to build human-computer interactions (HCI) through or with textile materials or tools, how to represent, store and even process information through fibers, or how to improve user experiences with digital technologies by taking advantage of the softness of textiles and the emotional ties they represent.

In this field arises Soft2Soft, the proposal toolkit that we present in this paper. With this set of tools, we intend to provide functionalities and examples that facilitate the high-level development of textile interfaces to increase the applications that use textiles to access, represent, store, or manipulate digital information. Due to the phenomenological, embodied, and cultural connotation of textile actions, we conceived the toolkit towards textile gestures. More than just an action, a gesture implies intentionality, a way to express feelings, ideas, thoughts. This gestural quality of textile interfaces presents a possibility to build more inclusive HCI applications, for example, for crafter communities close to textiles but uncomfortable with digital technologies.

© Springer Nature Switzerland AG 2021
C. Stephanidis et al. (Eds.): HCII 2021, CCIS 1420, pp. 30–36, 2021.
https://doi.org/10.1007/978-3-030-78642-7_5

This paper divides into four sections. Background, where we present some of the most significant referents that have guided the conception, design, and development of the toolkit. The toolkit Soft2Soft, which details this work's current state, displaying its components, architecture, functionalities, and potential uses. Preliminary results and discussion, that presents some examples we have crafted while designing and developing the toolkit. Finally, we conclude by indicating the future work and challenges around the sustainability and appropriation of Soft2Soft.

2 Background

Recently, the scientific interest in human-computer interaction has exponentially grown; in this article, we concentrate on presenting some new, much more sophisticated ways of representing and interacting with digital information through textile materialities. The innovation in these interfaces is not limited to software. On the contrary, it focuses and deals with the material parts, both from the electronic and the textile points of view. One of the most cited examples of recent digital-textile technologies is the Jacquard Project of Google, which proposes novel, ubiquitous, soft interactions through textile fibers [1]. In Jacquard Project, the first great challenge was a material one: to develop highly conductive yarns. Next, combining textile and digital techniques, materials, and tools, they provide a proposal to manufacture interactive textiles for wearable computing: clothing such as a jacket, a bag, a suitcase, or even a pair of shoes, through which users can interact with digital data [1].

However, non all the interactions that include textiles are focused on wearables. Referents that have inspired this work are not clothes or even portable, as in accessories or mobile technologies. Some references use the textile as a soft material for non-wearable applications [2–4], and other focus on the technique in itself, for example, because of the time, reflection, and care that require textiles crafting as embroidery, weaving, or knitting [5, 6]. One example is Sara Mlakar and Michael Haller's work at the University of Applied Sciences of Upper Austria. They explore new ways of softening today's interactions through smart non-wearable textiles, taking advantage of their visual and haptic expressiveness power. This exploration includes non-functional prototypes to evaluate user experiences with textiles shapes, textures, colors, and the conception of textile interfaces as a language, with semantics and symbols which may modify the experience according to the materialities (e.g., the yarn or the fabric) [3]. Another non-wearable example corresponds to an application case called "Tangible Textural Interface" by Eunhee Jo. It is a music player with a fabric interface that allows controlling the music through textile gestures: caressing the fabric from side to side to change the track or stretching it to increase the volume [7].

Finally, we present two referents associated with textile crafting as a process. First, the project Spyn, by Daniela Rosner and Kimiko Ryokai, seeks to generate communicative and affective relationships between the weavers and those who receive these weaved pieces as a gift. While weaving, the giver narrates their feelings and thoughts, which Spyn records digitally, along with the geolocation. When the receiver scans the weaved piece, listens to the narrations in the piece's specific positions, and sees where in the world this part was weaved and narrated [8]. Second, a local and localized referent in which the authors propose speculative designs of digital textiles that embody testimonies of reconciliation in the armed conflict in Colombia. One of the designs is, for example, an embroidered speaker that must be embroidered to listen, intimately and carefully, to a testimony recorded previously. The fact of having to embroider the speaker takes time and, according to the authors, allows an emotional connection between survivors, who give testimony, and listeners [9].

3   The Toolkit Soft2Soft

Soft2Soft provides tools that allow the technical recognition of actions performed with e-textiles materials, guides to accompany the design process, and examples of how to craft wearable and non-wearable textile interfaces. For the technical recognition of actions with/over textiles, the toolkit provides an Arduino library, including high-level objects, like a zipper with configurable properties (e.g., its number of teeth), and functions to evaluate object status, e.g., fastenButton(). Table 1. Textile gesture and actions modeled and implemented in the library. summarizes the classification of gestures and textile actions currently available in the library. All the classes are both in Spanish (es) and English (en). The guides, which include the library documentation, and examples are available on the website: http://artesanaltecnologica.org/soft2soft-biblioteca-gestos-tex tiles/. The details of how to craft the interfaces include instructions and examples for

Table 1. Textile gesture and actions modeled and implemented in the library.

Gesture	Textile action	Kind of interface		Kind of interaction	
		Wearable	Non-wearable	Continuous	Discrete
Sheltering	Sliding a zipper	x			x (Discrete levels)
	Sticking hook & loop pieces	x			x(On/Off)
	Fastening a button	x			x(On/Off)
Caressing	Touching a fabric	x	x	x (position of the touch)	x(On/Off)
	Pinching a fabric	x	x	x (pressure levels)	x(On/Off)
Crafting	Going through a fabric with a needle		x	x (position of the needle)	x(On/Off)
	Making a knot	x	x		x(On/Off)
Getting involve	Hugging or squeeze something padded, e.g., a toy		x	x (pressure levels)	
	Stretching/relaxing a fabric	x	x	x (tension levels)	

hardware crafting: embroidering, sewing, connecting soft materials like fabrics, and thread with hard materials as Arduino boards.

As presented in Table 1. Textile gesture and actions modeled and implemented in the library., the library builds around some textile elements present in wearable and non-wearable pieces, like zippers or buttons; tools used in the crafting process of these textiles as needle and thread, and the textile actions related to them. Currently, the library includes six classes to represent textile elements: Button, HookLoop, Zipper, Fabric, Needle, Wool; each of these classes contains methods associated with a textile action (e.g., fastenButton(), riseZipper(), pinchFabric()), and properties such as the pin used or the element's status according to the textile action (Fig. 1).

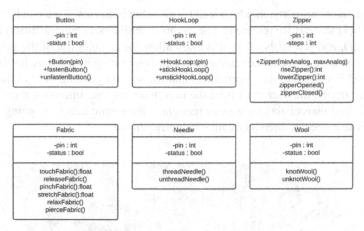

Fig. 1. Classes of the Soft2Soft library

Button class allows the validation and recognition of the gesture of fastening a button through the events fastenButton() and unfastenButton(). This class has two properties: the pin to which the button is connected, and its status, a boolean value where LOW (0) indicates a fastened button, and HIGH (1), an unfastened button. It requires the button connected to a digital pin, and the buttonhole to GND, or vice versa (Fig. 2). The HookLoop class represents the sticking of hook and loop, or *velcro*, pieces. This class has the properties "pin" and "status." In this case, a LOW (0) value indicates two pieces of *velcro* stuck together, and a HIGH (1) value means these pieces are separated. As in the Button, one part must be connected to a digital pin and the other one to GND. The events available to detect textile actions, in this case, are stickHookLoop() and unstickHookLoop() (Fig. 2).

Zipper class has two properties, pin and steps. The steps property represents a subdivision of the zipper to recognize its current, discrete position. These steps are calculated based on the zipper's minimum and maximum analog values, and the user must train them to use a zipper object correctly, as it depends on each particular crafting. The riseZipper() and lowerZipper() methods allow the recognition of the zipper action, whether it goes up or down and in which step it lands. Also, it is possible to detect when if the zipper is fully open or closed with the events zipperOppened() and zipperClosed() (Fig. 3). Fabric

Fig. 2. Left. Hand making the action of unfastening the button. Right. Hand sticking hook and loop pieces.

class has the status property, in which a LOW(0) value indicates if we touch the fabric and a HIGH (1) value if we release it. The events touchFabric(), pinchFabric() (Fig. 3), stretchFabric(), and relaxFabric() of this class allow the recognition of the gestures of touch, pinch, stretch and relax fabric, capturing and estimating its pressure levels. Those levels are highly related to the materialities and the way they are crafted. In this sense, like with the zipper, the user must train the minimum and maximum for their objects. With the method pierceFabric(), we can recognize the textile action of going through the textile with a needle, threading with conductive thread.

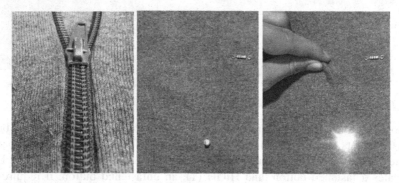

Fig. 3. Left. Zipper interface. Center. Relaxed fabric. Right. Hand pinching the fabric.

With the Needle class, we can validate the status of needle textile actions of threading and unthreading a needle with threadNeedle() and unthreadNeedle(). The status property indicates a LOW (0) value when it is thread and a HIGH (1) value when it is not. In the Wool class, the status property indicates if a wool piece is tied in a knot or not. We can validate it with the methods knotWool() and unknotWool().

4   Preliminary Results and Discussion

For this project, we used a participatory approach, conceiving us both as designers and as potential users. İn this sense, we created some textile interfaces while conceiving, designing, and developing the toolkit (Arduino library and guidelines). This exploration resulted in nine textile actions, in different pieces (Fig. 4), involving the Soft2Soft classes conceived in four gestures: sheltering, caressing, crafting, and getting involved (Table 1).

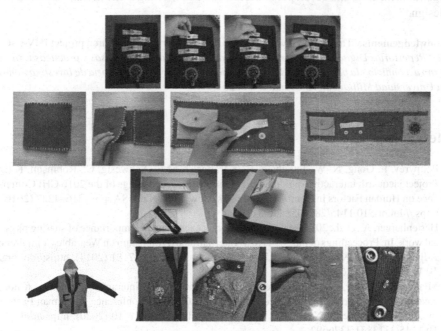

Fig. 4. From the top: i & ii) Textile interface book samplers, iii) Sampler prototype, iv) Jacket with textile interfaces.

While making-designing Soft2Soft, we realized that although this toolkit includes a specific library for Arduino, for being one of the most used electronic prototyping platforms, this does not limit its use to only Arduino boards; the identification and characterization of textile actions gestures allow their implementation in other platforms, such as Raspberry. Likewise, having public documentation, examples, and an open library constitutes an invitation to develop hybrid applications that integrate textile and digital components and materialities.

5 Conclusions

The toolkit Soft2Soft is a textile gesture recognition set of tools that provide a flexible approach to transform and create novel, soft objects with textile and digital properties for different purposes. Ranging from wearable applications to approaches in which textile processes, with their softness, required times, and cares, are the core component (e.g., [10]).

This set of tools is still a work in progress. On the one hand, future work will allow the inclusion of more textile actions and exemplify a greater diversity of textile gestures. These gestures contemplate the soft-hard connections between the body (the hands, for example), the textile, and the electronic and a deep semantic analysis of the relationships between us, the textiles, and the digital information. On the other hand, it will be fundamental to create strategies for the divulgation of Soft2Soft and a rigorous evaluation with users and developers interested in contributing to the library's continuous re-design.

Acknowledgements. This development is a product derived from the research project INV-ING-3192 "*Repertorios Digitales: Representaciones computacionales de procesos y prácticas textiles en torno al conflicto y la paz, caso Sonsón, Antioquia*", funded by "*Vicerrectoría de Investigaciones de la Universidad Militar Nueva Granada*", 2020

References

1. Poupyrev, I., Gong, N.-W., Fukuhara, S., Karagozler, M.E., Schwesig, C., Robinson, K.E.: Project jacquard: interactive digital textiles at scale. In: Proceedings of the 2016 CHI Conference on Human Factors in Computing Systems, New York, NY, USA, pp. 4216–4227 (2016). https://doi.org/10.1145/2858036.2858176
2. Hertenberger, A., et al.: 2013 e-textile swatchbook exchange: the importance of sharing physical work. In: Proceedings of the 2014 ACM International Symposium on Wearable Computers: Adjunct Program, New York, NY, USA, September 2014, pp. 77–81 (2014). https://doi.org/10.1145/2641248.2641276
3. Mlakar, S., Haller, M.: Design investigation of embroidered interactive elements on non-wearable textile interfaces. In: Proceedings of the 2020 CHI Conference on Human Factors in Computing Systems, New York, NY, USA, April 2020, pp. 1–10 (2020). https://doi.org/10.1145/3313831.3376692
4. Posch, I., Kurbak, E.: CRAFTED LOGIC towards hand-crafting a computer. In: Proceedings of the 2016 CHI Conference Extended Abstracts on Human Factors in Computing Systems, New York, NY, USA, pp. 3881–3884 (2016). https://doi.org/10.1145/2851581.2891101
5. Pérez-Bustos, T.: "Let Me Show You": a caring ethnography of embodied knowledge in weaving and engineering. In: Åsberg, C., Braidotti, R. (eds.) A Feminist Companion to the Posthumanities, pp. 175–187. Springer, Cham (2018). https://doi.org/10.1007/978-3-319-62140-1_15
6. Rosner, D.K., Shorey, S., Craft, B.R., Remick, H.: Making core memory: design inquiry into gendered legacies of engineering and craftwork. In: Proceedings of the 2018 CHI Conference on Human Factors in Computing Systems, New York, NY, USA, pp. 531:1–531:13 (2018). https://doi.org/10.1145/3173574.3174105
7. Chalcraft, E.: Tangible textural interface by Eunhee Jo at show RCA 2012. In: Dezeen (2012). https://www.dezeen.com/2012/06/28/tangible-textural-interface-by-eunhee-jo-at-show-rca-2012/. Accessed 26 Feb 2021
8. Rosner, D.K., Ryokai, K.: Spyn: augmenting the creative and communicative potential of craft. In: Proceedings of the SIGCHI Conference on Human Factors in Computing Systems, New York, NY, USA, pp. 2407–2416 (2010). https://doi.org/10.1145/1753326.1753691
9. Cortés Rico, L., Patarroyo, J., Pérez Bustos, T., Sánchez Aldana, E.: How can digital textiles embody testimonies of reconciliation? In: Proceedings of the 16th Participatory Design Conference 2020 - Participation(s) Otherwise - Volume 2, Manizales, Colombia, June 2020, pp. 109–113 (2020). https://doi.org/10.1145/3384772.3385137
10. Patarroyo, J., Cortés-Rico, L., Sánchez-Aldana, E., Pérez-Bustos, T., Rincón, N.: Testimonial digital textiles: material metaphors to think with care about reconciliation with four memory sewing circles in Colombia. In: Presented at the NORDES 2019, Finlandia (2019)

Analysis of Conducting Waves Using Multichannel Surface EMG Based on Arc-Shaped Electrode

Kohei Okura[✉], Yu Matsumoto, Kazuyuki Mito, Tota Mizuno, and Naoaki Itakura

The University of Electro-Communications, 1-5-1 Chofugaoka, Chofu, Tokyo, Japan
o2030024@edu.cc.uec.ac.jp

Abstract. Surface electromyogram (EMG) is recorded as the interference of action potentials, which are produced by some motor units of a muscle. If the composition of the interference wave can be analyzed, the detailed mechanism of muscle contraction may be elucidated. Therefore, we proposed a multichannel method, extracted all the conducting waves existing in the surface EMG, and examined the characteristics of each conducting wave. Consequently, it became possible to consider the detailed mechanism of muscle contraction. In the previous study, biceps brachii and triceps surae were used as test muscles, and it was found that the number of conducting waves obtained by triceps surae was smaller than that of biceps brachii. Therefore, in this study, we proposed and measured an arc-shaped electrode. We aimed to consider whether a conducting wave could be obtained even with electrodes having different electrode widths or influence on the conducting waveform, owing to the difference in shape between the ladder-type and arc-shaped electrodes. Accordingly, first, the maximal voluntary contraction of muscle was measured. Thereafter, the biceps brachii and triceps surae muscles were tested, and myoelectric potential data were acquired under load. The analysis was performed using the multichannel method. Based on the experimental results, it was found that the number of conducting waves increased using the arc-shaped electrode, regardless of the test muscle. Moreover, the conducting waves obtained from the ladder-type electrode were characteristic.

Keywords: Surface electromyogram (EMG) · Interference wave · Multichannel method

1 Introduction

The action potential of the muscle fibers, comprising skeletal muscle, is generated by chemical actions at the neuromuscular junction, and propagates along the muscle fiber from the neuromuscular junction to the tendons at both ends. The conduction velocity of the action potential is known as muscle fiber conduction velocity. This velocity is derived via a surface electromyogram (EMG) using the cross-correlation method. The waveform obtained from the surface EMG is not the action potential of a single motor unit, but the interference potential of multiple motor units. Therefore, if we pay attention to the

© Springer Nature Switzerland AG 2021
C. Stephanidis et al. (Eds.): HCII 2021, CCIS 1420, pp. 37–44, 2021.
https://doi.org/10.1007/978-3-030-78642-7_6

waveform shape that propagates across multiple channels, it differs from the conduction velocity. It is assumed that a new index will be derived.

Therefore, Kosuge et al. [1] have proposed a method that quantitatively determines conduction waves, which obtained using a multichannel surface EMG (hereinafter, referred to as the m-channel method), and a method that analyzes conditions and conduction velocity. Using this method, the conducting waves were extracted from the surface EMG waveforms using an array electrode, and the characteristics of each conducting wave, i.e., conduction velocity, amplitude, wavelength, etc., were examined. As a result, it became possible to consider the muscle contraction mechanism in more detail.

In a study conducted by Takagi et al. [2], the m-channel method was used with the surface EMG; however, the average number of propagated waves obtained from the biceps surae was 16.83 pcs/s, which is the lower leg. The average number of conducting waves obtained from the biceps surae was 2.3 pcs/s, and the number of conducting waves obtained was different. One of the causes is that the biceps muscle is a parallel muscle, in which the contraction direction of the muscle and the motion of the muscle fiber are the same, whereas the gastrocnemius muscle has several short muscle fibers diagonally on both sides along the long tendon. It is a pinnate muscle running along the direction. Therefore, to analyze the conducting wave of the pinnate muscle, we propose new electrodes that spread along the muscle fiber direction (Fig. 1). There are two pairs of ladder-type electrodes, in which five sterling silver wires with a diameter of 1 mm are arranged in parallel, and nine arc-shaped electrodes that allow gradual expansion.

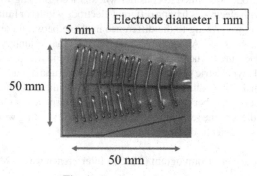

Fig. 1. Proposed electrode.

In this study, using the m-channel method and proposed electrode, a conducting wave can be obtained using arcuate electrodes with different electrode widths. The purpose is to consider the difference in features.

2   Method

2.1   Experimental Method Using Biceps Brachii

First, to examine whether conducting waves can be obtained with different electrode widths, the parallel muscle (biceps brachii) was used as the test muscle. The muscles to be examined were self-reported dominant arms, and the subjects were seven healthy adults. In the measurement of the biceps brachii muscle, the subject maintained the elbow joint angle at 90° in the sitting position, and measured the maximum exerted muscle strength (100% MVC). After that, 20% MVC was used as a load and maintained for 10 s. In addition, the left and right sides of the ladder-type electrode were placed along the muscle fiber direction; as a result of considering the position of the end-plate, they were attached as follows (Fig. 2). The sampling frequency in the experiment was 5 kHz; the amplifier settings were set at high and low cutoff frequencies of 1 and 5 Hz, respectively; and the amplification factor was 80 dB.

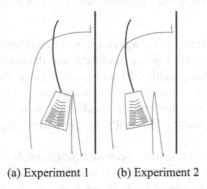

(a) Experiment 1   (b) Experiment 2

Fig. 2. Direction of attaching electrodes to the biceps brachii muscle.

The data, which were obtained from the experiment, were subjected to an FIR filter at a high cutoff frequency of 1 kHz, and the results were used for analysis.

2.2 Experimental Method Using Triceps Surae

During the experiment, the subject maintained the same posture for 10 s, and the heel was lifted from the floor while standing. The proposed electrodes (mentioned in Sect. 1) were used to derive the surface EMG. The test muscles included the lateral head of the gastrocnemius muscle, the medial head of the gastrocnemius muscle, and the central surface of the backside of the lower leg (Fig. 3). The myoelectric potential was derived via adjacent electrodes using the bipolar method. The amplifier settings and sampling frequency were the same as those in Sect. 2.1. The 10-s data that were obtained for each muscle were transferred to a PC for analysis.

2.3 Analysis Method

The m-channel method was used for analysis. In the m-channel method, one of the adjacent electrodes of the same shape is defined as the conduction source, and the other is defined as the conduction destination. The section where zero crossing occurs twice from the source is extracted as one waveform; it is determined whether the signal has propagated over multiple channels. Then, the conduction speed is calculated. When

Experiment 3

Fig. 3. Direction of attaching electrodes to the triceps surae muscle.

performing conduction judgment, one waveform, which is obtained from the conduction source, is used as the conduction wave candidate, and the conduction wave candidate of the conduction destination, existing 10 ms before and after the initiation point of the conduction wave candidate of the conduction source, is extracted. Then, to calculate waveforms with different wavelengths, the conduction wave candidates are resampled based on the sampling theorem; additionally, the similarity, amplitude, and wavelength ratios are calculated.

When analyzing a conduction wave over multiple channels, thresholds are set for the similarity, amplitude, and wavelength ratios, which are based on the assumption that, if the waveform shapes between adjacent channels are similar, the action potential has propagated between the two channels. When the conduction wave candidate is equal to or larger than the threshold, it is a conduction wave. The conduction speed is defined as the time difference Δt between channels and the value that is obtained by dividing the distance between channels (5 mm) by Δt between channels. In addition, the conduction velocity variation coefficient (hereinafter, referred to as CV) is used as the conduction determination condition to consider the velocity variable of the waveform for which conduction is determined. In this study, the conduction judgment conditions were similarity ratio, wavelength ratio (0.9 or more), and amplitude ratio (0.7 or more); and the CV was 30% or less. Furthermore, only conduction waves over three channels were extracted and used for analysis.

3   Results and Discussion on the Biceps Brachii

3.1   Comparison of Relative Frequency Distribution

To compare the relative frequency distribution of amplitude and conduction velocity for each trial, with respect to the propagated waves obtained using the analysis method, the overall percentage of propagated waves in each trial was set to 100%. The amplitude of each conducting wave and the proportion of the conducting velocity were calculated.

First, the relative frequency distributions of Experiments 1 and 2 for subject A are shown for each electrode shape in Fig. 4(a)–(f).

Based on Fig. 4, as a result of attaching the left and right ladder-shaped electrodes along the muscle fiber direction, the conducting waves were extracted from all the

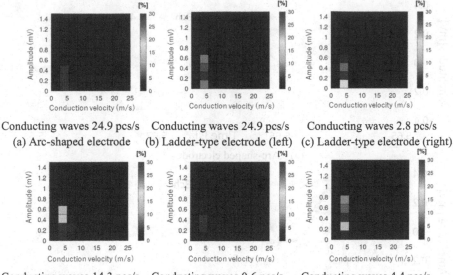

Conducting waves 24.9 pcs/s   Conducting waves 24.9 pcs/s   Conducting waves 2.8 pcs/s
(a) Arc-shaped electrode   (b) Ladder-type electrode (left)   (c) Ladder-type electrode (right)

Conducting waves 14.3 pcs/s   Conducting waves 0.6 pcs/s   Conducting waves 4.4 pcs/s
(d) Arc-shaped electrode   (e) Ladder-type electrode (left)   (f) Ladder-type electrode (right)

Fig. 4. Relative frequency distribution of subject A. (a)–(c) are attached with the left ladder-type electrode along the muscle fiber direction; (d)–(f) are attached with the right ladder-type electrode along the muscle fiber direction.

electrodes. However, based on the experimental results of subjects B–G, the conducting waves often could not be obtained with the ladder-type electrodes. This is because the positions at which the left and right ladder-type electrodes were attached did not follow the muscle fiber direction well. In addition, the number of ladder-type electrodes was as small as five compared with the nine arc-shaped electrodes. Furthermore, based on the experimental results of subjects A, B, C, and E, several conducting waves of 2.5–5.0 m/s were extracted at each electrode; however, as with raw data, the ladder-type electrode was better than the arc-shaped electrode. There was a tendency for the amplitude value to be high.

3.2 EMG Data

The raw data of three channels at the same time, when the left ladder-shaped electrode is attached along the muscle fiber in biceps brachii, are shown in Fig. 5.

As shown in Fig. 5, when the conduction waveforms obtained at the same time with three types of electrodes were compared, the waveforms with the left ladder-type electrode were confirmed with the arc-shaped electrodes. However, when the conduction waveforms of the left ladder-shaped and arc-shaped electrodes were compared, the amplitude value of the arc-shaped electrode was lower than that of the ladder-shaped electrode. It was considered that the amplitude value became smaller because more muscle fibers interfered and averaged in the arcuate electrode. Conversely, in the narrow

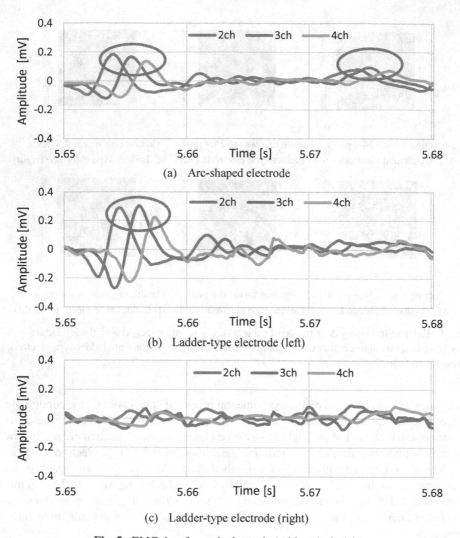

Fig. 5. EMG data for each electrode (subject A, 2–4ch).

ladder-type electrode, the conduction waveform was emphasized more than in the arcuate electrode, and it has been assumed that it is possible to consider muscle activities in detail.

4 Results and Discussion on the Triceps Surae

The average frequency of conduction waves generated at each electrode is listed in Table 1.

Moreover, it is shown in the raw data of three channels when the arcuate electrode was attached along the muscle fiber on the central surface of the triceps surae muscle (Fig. 6).

Table 1. Average frequency of transmission in the triceps surae.

Arc-shaped electrode	Ladder-type electrode (left)	Ladder-type electrode (right)
1.39 pcs/s	0.01 pcs/s	0.01 pcs/s

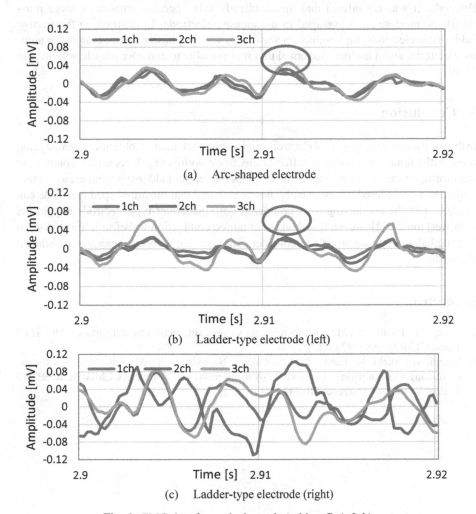

(a)   Arc-shaped electrode

(b)   Ladder-type electrode (left)

(c)   Ladder-type electrode (right)

Fig. 6. EMG data for each electrode (subject G, 1–3ch).

As listed in Table 1, unlike the left and right ladder-type electrodes, the arc-shaped electrodes confirmed the conducting waves; however, there was a significant difference when they were compared in terms of the biceps brachii muscle. Therefore, it is difficult to extract the conducting wave similar to the parallel muscle even if the proposed electrode is used.

As shown in Fig. 6, when the conduction waveforms obtained at the same time with the three types of electrodes were compared, the waveforms with the left ladder-type electrode were confirmed with the arc-shaped electrodes. However, when the conduction waveforms of the left ladder-shaped and arc-shaped electrodes were compared, the amplitude value of the arc-shaped electrode was lower than that of the ladder-shaped electrode. It was considered that the amplitude value became smaller as more muscle fibers interfered and averaged in the arcuate electrode. In contrast, in the narrow ladder-type electrode, the conduction waveform was emphasized more than in the arcuate electrode, and it has been assumed that it is possible to consider muscle activities in detail.

5 Conclusion

In this study, using the proposed electrode and m-channel method, obtaining a propagated wave with arcuate electrodes of different electrode widths or effects on the conduction waveform, owing to the difference in shape between the ladder-type and arcuate electrodes, was considered. Consequently, it was clarified that the arc-shaped electrode can easily extract the conducting wave compared with the ladder-type electrode, regardless of the test muscle. However, based on the obtained conduction waveform, it was evident that the ladder-type electrode can consider more muscle activities than the arc-shaped electrode.

References

1. Kosuge, T., Itakura, N., Mito, K.: Conducting waves using multi-channel surface EMG. IEEJ Trans. **C134**(3), 390–397 (2014)
2. Takagi, M., Akehi, K., Farahani, M.A., Itakura, N., Mizuno, T., Mito, K.: Analyses for the conducting wave of triceps surae muscle by using multi-channel surface EMG. In: IEEE 2nd Student Research Conference 2017 (2017)

Exploration of a Deformation System for Digital 2D Objects Using a Sponge

Natsumi Sagara[1]([✉]), Naomi Itagaki[2], and Yu Suzuki[1]

[1] School of Project Design, Miyagi University, 1-1 Gakuen, Taiwa-cho,
Kurokawa-gun, Miyagi 981-3298, Japan
{p1820084,suzu}@myu.ac.jp
[2] JASTEC Co., Ltd., Tokyo, Japan

Abstract. Deformation of digital two-dimensional objects (2D objects) is one of the most frequent operations in design work using computers. To deform a digital 2D object, it is necessary to manipulate parameters or use a puppet tool, which requires specialized knowledge, skills, and proficiency. The purpose of this research is to make it possible for users without specialized knowledge or skills to easily deform digital 2D objects. In this study, we use a physical object having the same shape as a digital 2D object as an input interface to help users intuitively understand the deformation operation of a digital 2D object. We developed a deformation input system using a sponge. A sponge is an ideal material because it can be easily deformed by a user with a small force and its shape can be easily processed. First, the user deforms a sponge in the same shape as a digital 2D object in front of a camera. Next, the system optically recognizes the deformation of the sponge, and then reflects the shape of the sponge in the digital 2D object. We developed a prototype system and demonstrated the feasibility of a deformation input system using a sponge.

Keywords: Feature point detection · Sponge · Input interface

1 Introduction

Deformation of digital 2D objects is one of the most frequent operations in the design process using graphics editors and CAD software. Typical methods for inputting deformations of digital 2D objects include manipulating parameters and the puppet tool. While manipulating the parameters, it is necessary to predict the output of the deformation and set a numerical value. The method of manipulating the puppet tool is based on the prediction of the output result and mouse operation. Since this act of "prediction" is based on knowledge and experience, it is difficult for users without specialized knowledge or skills in manipulation to handle these existing methods well.

The purpose of this research is to enable users without specialized knowledge or skills to easily deform digital 2D objects.

© Springer Nature Switzerland AG 2021
C. Stephanidis et al. (Eds.): HCII 2021, CCIS 1420, pp. 45–51, 2021.
https://doi.org/10.1007/978-3-030-78642-7_7

2   Related Works

As a study for inputting deformations of digital 2D objects, Su et al. proposed a method for applying motion extracted from a video to a digital 2D object [10]. This method enables users without specialized knowledge or skills to deform a digital 2D object. However, the user cannot necessarily provide arbitrary input because of the use of pre-prepared videos and restrictions on the motion that can be extracted.

Suzuki et al. proposed a method to reflect the posture of each body part of a user in a digital 2D object with head, chest, and limb body parts [11]. In this method, the digital 2D object is deformed into the same pose as the user simply by moving the user's body. Since the input can be obtained by simple manipulation, there is no need for specialized knowledge, skills, or proficiency in operation. However, in this method, the deformation of a digital 2D object is limited to the range of postures possible for the user. In addition, this method only deals with digital 2D objects with body parts.

In this study, we aim to develop an input interface that can deform a digital 2D object of arbitrary shape into any shape in real time.

3   Input Interface Using a Sponge

Existing methods for inputting deformations of digital 2D objects are difficult because the user is hard to "predict" the result of the deformation at the time of input. To solve this issue, we attempted an approach that makes it easier for users to intuitively understand the deformation operations of digital 2D objects.

To realize this approach, we developed an input interface using a sponge. The sponges can be easily shaped and deformed with little force. In the sponge input interface, the user inputs the deformation by grasping the sponge cut out in the same shape as the digital 2D object. The deformed shape of the sponge was reflected in a digital 2D object in real time. Since the user only needs to deform the sponge into an arbitrary shape to complete the operation, the user does not need to "predict." Therefore, users can easily input the deformation of a digital 2D object.

4   Prototype of a Deformation System Using a Sponge Input Interface

4.1   System Overview

We developed a prototype of a deformation input system using a sponge as the input interface (Fig. 1). The system consists of a web camera, PC, and sponge. The only operation by the user is to deform the sponge, which has the same shape as the digital 2D object, in front of the camera.

This system performs two main processes. First, the system uses a camera to optically read the deformation of the sponge performed by the user. Second, the system applies deformation to a digital 2D object. In the following, we describe each of the mechanisms developed in our prototype.

Fig. 1. Deformation system using a sponge input interface

4.2 Technique to Read the Deformation of a Sponge

To read the deformation of the sponge, we used numerous small holes on the surface of the sponge. We investigated a method for detecting and tracking these feature points using image processing.

Comparison of Feature Point Detectors. We compared seven feature point detectors and investigated a detector suitable for detecting feature points from the surface of a sponge. The seven feature point detectors are AKAZE [1], KAZE [2], FAST [8], ORB [9], MSER [7], SIFT [6], and SURF [3].

The feature points detected by each detector are shown in Fig. 2. As a result of comparison, AKAZE, SIFT, and SURF were able to detect feature points from the sponge surface all over. However, the processing speed of SIFT and SURF was slow and unsuitable for real-time input. The processing speed of AKAZE was relatively high; therefore, we adopted AKAZE for feature point detection in this system.

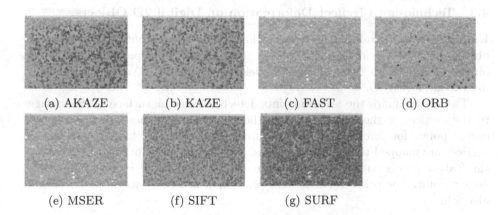

(a) AKAZE   (b) KAZE   (c) FAST   (d) ORB

(e) MSER   (f) SIFT   (g) SURF

Fig. 2. Results of seven feature point detectors

Blackening the Sponge for Stable Detection. When the system has to detect the feature points on the sponge surface using a camera, it is sometimes difficult to detect the feature points depending on the distance between the sponge and the camera. Therefore, we attempted to color the surface of the sponge black to maintain a stable detection.

As shown in Fig. 3, we prepared an uncolored sponge (sponge 1) and three colored sponges of different intensities (sponges 2 to 4), and compared the ease of detection of the feature points. As a result, the darker the sponge, the more feature points the system was able to detect. Because the camera was able to detect a sufficient number of feature points from the surface of sponge 4, we decided to use a sponge with a black surface having the same thickness as sponge 4.

Tracking Method of Feature Points. We examined two methods for tracking the feature points. One is based on feature point matching each frame, and the other is based on optical flow.

In the feature point matching method, the system detects feature points in the image obtained from every frame and matches them with the first feature points detected. In this method, when the system detects many feature points, the process slows down because of the matching of every frame. In addition, the matching of feature points often fails when the sponge is deformed.

In the optical flow method, we used the pyramidal Lucas-Kanade method algorithm [4]. In this method, the first point detected as a feature point is tracked every frame, so the process is faster than the method of feature point matching, and the system allows for real-time input. In addition, it has the advantage that the tracking is less likely to deviate when the sponge is deformed. Therefore, we adopted the tracking method of optical flow.

4.3   Technique to Reflect Deformation on Digital 2D Objects

Using Mesh. To reflect the deformation of the sponge onto the digital 2D object, we used a grid-shaped 2D mesh. First, the system pastes a digital 2D object onto the mesh. Next, the system deforms the digital 2D object by deforming the mesh (Fig. 4).

The system maps the feature points detected from the surface of the sponge to the vertices of the mesh, and uses the corresponding mesh vertices as reference points for deformation. The feature points that are closest to the mesh vertices are mapped to the mesh vertices. The coordinates obtained by tracking the feature points on the sponge surface are reflected in the corresponding reference point. The other vertices were positioned according to the deformation algorithm.

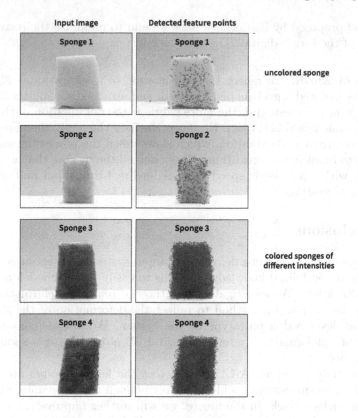

Fig. 3. Result of feature point detection by coloring the sponge

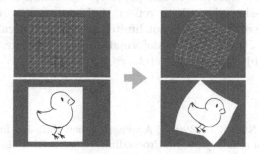

Fig. 4. Deformation of a 2D object using a grid-shaped 2D mesh

Comparison of Mesh Deformation Methods. The free-form deformation (FFD) and the method proposed by Igarashi [5]. Were examined for the deformation algorithm. While FFD requires specifying the positions of the reference points at the four corners, Igarashi's algorithm enables the movement of the entire mesh by specifying two or more arbitrary points. In this research, we use the method proposed by Igarashi because we aim to minimize the restriction of the shape of the target digital 2D object as much as possible.

Fineness of Mesh. To reflect the deformation of a sponge on a digital 2D object, we generated a grid-shaped 2D mesh and attached the digital 2D object to it. The finer the mesh grid, the more subtle is the deformation of the sponge reflected on the digital 2D object. However, the finer the mesh, the more computation is required for deformation, which slows down the processing and makes it difficult to input data in real time. We examined the meshes that were as fine as possible with a processing speed that enabled real-time input and decided to use a 12×12 grid mesh.

5   Conclusions

We developed a prototype of a deformation input system using sponges to enable users without specialized knowledge or skills to easily input any deformation of a digital 2D object. We investigated a method to read the deformation of the sponge by the user and a method to reflect the deformation of the digital 2D object, and developed a prototype of the system. We also demonstrated the feasibility of a deformation system for digital 2D objects using a sponge as an input interface.

In this study, we chose AKAZE to detect the feature points on a sponge surface. Because the system could not detect enough feature points, we colored the sponge surface black. In the future, we will further improve the method to detect feature points on the sponge surface so that the system can detect feature points with uncolored sponges. In the prototype system, a digital 2D object is attached to a grid-shaped mesh to reflect the deformation of the digital 2D object. If the shape of the mesh is not limited to a grid, but can be made more suitable for digital 2D objects, the deformation of the sponge can be reflected on the digital 2D objects more delicately.

References

1. Alcantarilla, P., Nuevo, J., Bartoli, A.: Fast explicit diffusion for accelerated features in nonlinear scale spaces. In: Proceedings of the British Machine Vision Conference, pp. 13.1–13.11 (2013)
2. Alcantarilla, P.F., Bartoli, A., Davison, A.J.: KAZE features. In: Fitzgibbon, A., Lazebnik, S., Perona, P., Sato, Y., Schmid, C. (eds.) ECCV 2012. LNCS, vol. 7577, pp. 214–227. Springer, Heidelberg (2012). https://doi.org/10.1007/978-3-642-33783-3_16
3. Bay, H., Tuytelaars, T., Van Gool, L.: SURF: speeded up robust features. In: Leonardis, A., Bischof, H., Pinz, A. (eds.) ECCV 2006. LNCS, vol. 3951, pp. 404–417. Springer, Heidelberg (2006). https://doi.org/10.1007/11744023_32
4. Bouguet, J.Y.: Pyramidal implementation of the lucas kanade feature tracker description of the algorithm. Intel Corporation, Microprocessor Research Labs, OpenCV Documents (1999)

5. Igarashi, T., Moscovich, T., Hughes, J.F.: As-rigid-as-possible shape manipulation. ACM Trans. Graph. **24**(3), 1134–1141 (2005)
6. Lowe, D.G.: Distinctive image features from scale-invariant keypoints. Int. J. Comput. Vis. **60**(2), 91–110 (2004)
7. Matas, J., Chum, O., Urban, M., Pajdla, T.: Robust wide-baseline stereo from maximally stable extremal regions. Image Vis. Comput. **22**(10), 761–767 (2004)
8. Rosten, E., Drummond, T.: Machine learning for high-speed corner detection. In: Leonardis, A., Bischof, H., Pinz, A. (eds.) ECCV 2006. LNCS, vol. 3951, pp. 430–443. Springer, Heidelberg (2006). https://doi.org/10.1007/11744023_34
9. Rublee, E., Rabaud, V., Konolige, K., Bradski, G.: Orb: an efficient alternative to sift or surf. In: 2011 International Conference on Computer Vision, pp. 2564–2571 (2011) ·
10. Su, Q., Bai, X., Fu, H., Tai, C.L., Wang, J.: Live sketch: video-driven dynamic deformation of static drawings. In: Proceedings of the 2018 CHI Conference on Human Factors in Computing Systems, pp. 662:1–662:12 (2018)
11. Suzuki, Y., Hayashi, R.: Posture control of hand-drawn artworks by generating separate images of body parts and automatically detecting joint points (in Japanese). J. Inform. Process. **60**(11), 1961–1969 (2019)

Improvement of Algorithm in Real-Time Brain–Computer Interface

Shingo Tanaka[✉], Tota Mizuno, Yu Matsumoto, Kazuyuki Mito, and Naoaki Itakura

The University of Electro-Communications, 1-5-1 Chofugaoka, Chofu, Tokyo, Japan
t1610416@edu.cc.uec.ac.jp

Abstract. A brain–computer interface (BCI) using the visual evoked potential (VEP) is being investigated for the use by persons with physical disabilities because it can be input only by looking at the visual stimulus. A transient VEP (TRVEP), which is a type of VEP, is a shape analysis method for synchronous addition during blinking stimuli and was applied only for blinking stimuli below 3.5 Hz. Therefore, in our research, when TRVEP analysis was conducted for high-speed blinking stimuli of ≥ 3.5 Hz, it was possible to discriminate the blinking stimulus gaze in approximately 2 s at 10 Hz. Furthermore, it has been shown that discrimination can be performed using a lighting interval fluctuation stimulus instead of a regular interval blinking stimulus. This approach currently enables the discrimination of a maximum of eight types of gazes.

In this study, we improved the algorithm in the discrimination of eight options by Electroencephalography (EEG) and investigated the discrimination rate using the correlation coefficient with the sample waveform. As a result, the discrimination rate was lower than that reported in previous studies. One of the factors is that the correlation coefficient decreased because the synchronization phenomenon did not occur. Therefore, it is conceivable to discriminate only the synchronized part instead of the correlation coefficient. There is the possibility that the judgment process can be shortened by narrowing the waveform information utilized for the judgment. In a previous study, discrimination was performed using a coefficient of variation that can simultaneously evaluate the waveform amplitude and standard deviation. These methods will also be examined. In addition, since the blinking control has been improved, we will consider using a stimulus that shifts the phase of the 10 Hz blinking stimulus.

Keywords: EEG · BCI

1 Introduction

A brain–computer interface (BCI) using the visual evoked potential (VEP) is being investigated for use by persons with physical disabilities, because it can be input only by looking at the visual stimulus. There are two types of VEP: steady-state VEP (SSVEP) and transient VEP (TRVEP).

The SSVEP is a standing wave that synchronizes with a blinking stimulus of 8 to 13 Hz; a long gaze of approximately 5 to 20 s is required to discriminate the increase in

© Springer Nature Switzerland AG 2021
C. Stephanidis et al. (Eds.): HCII 2021, CCIS 1420, pp. 52–57, 2021.
https://doi.org/10.1007/978-3-030-78642-7_8

its amplitude by frequency analysis [1]. In addition, a long gaze with a blinking stimulus also causes discomfort for the user. On the other hand, the TRVEP is a shape analysis method for synchronous addition during blinking stimuli and was employed only for blinking stimuli below 3.5. Therefore, in our research, when TRVEP analysis was utilized for high-speed flashing stimuli of 3.5 Hz or higher, it was possible to discriminate the flashing stimulus gaze in approximately 2 s at 10 Hz. Furthermore, it has been shown that discrimination can be performed using a lighting interval fluctuation stimulus instead of a regular interval blinking stimulus. This approach currently enables discrimination of a maximum of eight types of gazes [2].

Therefore, we have been researching and developing a brain–computer interface using the TRVEP, which enables real-time gaze discrimination, to achieve miniaturization, wireless communication, and cost reduction of the BCI device. However, there is the possibility that the blinking stimulus is not displayed on the screen at the desired time, or the blinking control and the analysis process are not processed in parallel; thus, a high discrimination rate has not been obtained [3].

Because synchronous addition is performed in TRVEP analysis, it is necessary to precisely control the blinking timing to reliably perform discrimination in a short time. To perform precise control, it is necessary that the blinking timing is not affected even if the judgment process is complicated, that the brain wave acquisition timing and blinking timing are completely synchronized, and that parallel processing is performed while maintaining synchronization. If these conditions are not met, fatal problems such as the inability to obtain characteristic brain waves will occur.

Therefore, the purpose of this study is to complete a real-time algorithm for TRVEP analysis that correctly performs parallel processing and simultaneously satisfies synchronization with blinking.

2 Experiment Outline

In this study, TRVEP analysis was performed in real time in an experiment, in which the subject shown in Fig. 1 gazes at the blinking stimulus displayed on the display.

Figure 1 shows an example of the lighting interval fluctuation stimulus used in the experiment. When the refresh rate was 60 Hz, the number of frames used for turning on and off the lights was 3 for a 10 Hz blinking light. This condition is referred to as 10 Hz blinking. In Fig. 1, the number of frames used for turning off the lights has changed to two, three, and four, so this condition is referred to as 234 blinking. In this study, 432 blinks and 234432 blinks were applied. Four synchronous addition methods were employed. In the case of Fig. 1, 300 ms of data was employed 83 ms after the first lighting was added; 300 ms of data was utilized 100 ms after the second lighting was added; 300 ms of data was applied 117 ms after the third lighting was added, and so on. As previously described, the addition synchronized with the lighting timing of 234 blinking is referred to as 234 addition. In addition, 432 addition, 234432 addition, and a 10 Hz addition that shifts every 100 ms were utilized. In this study, these four types of blinking were divided into two types: high brightness and low brightness. An experiment was conducted using eight types of blinking obtained in this way.

Figure 2 shows the experimental screen. According to the International 10–20 Law, the electrodes were attached at three locations: Pz, Oz, and the earlobe. The subject was seated unrestrained, and a 22-in. display was placed at a viewing distance of approximately 60 cm. A circular stimulus with a fluctuating lighting interval was employed as the blinking stimulus. The standard was 44.6 cd/m^2 for high brightness and 4.6 cd/m^2 for low brightness; adjustments were made so that the subject did not feel discomfort. The screen refresh rate was set to 60 fps. The obtained electroencephalogram was set to 5 Hz for the low-frequency cutoff and 100 Hz for the high-frequency cutoff, amplified at 100 dB, and sampled and stored at 1 kHz. The subject was instructed both in advance of the blinking position and at the onset of blinking to gaze at the blinking, and measurement was performed for 2 s. Measurements were performed to create a sample waveform for each blinking, and then measurements were performed 10 times for each gaze condition.

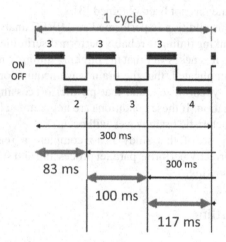

Fig. 1. With lighting interval fluctuation stimulus addition example

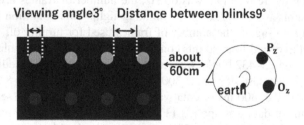

Fig. 2. Experiment screen

3   Results and Discussion

Regarding blinking control, which was problematic in previous research, the blinking timing could be improved by synchronizing the screen redraw command in the program with the refresh rate of the monitor. In addition, by reviewing the implementation of parallel processing, we were able to align the start timing of blinking and the start timing of EEG acquisition.

Table 1 shows the results of the eight choice discrimination. For discrimination, the correlation coefficient with the eight sample waveforms prepared in advance was calculated. Of these, the stimulus with the largest value was employed as the discrimination result. The overall discrimination rate was lower than that reported in previous studies (86%). However, the discrimination rate varied depending on the type of blinking applied. Possible causes for the decrease in the discrimination rate: In the waveform obtained by synchronous addition, synchronization occurs only when the addition is synchronized with the lighting timing, that is, the entire synchronously added waveform does not always exhibit the same tendency. Therefore, the correlation coefficient with the sample waveform does not increase. As another discrimination method, a two-step procedure for discriminating by aligning the peak and the position of the waveform can be considered. As an example, Fig. 3 shows four types of synchronous addition waveforms when high-intensity 432 blinking is observed. The largest negative peak in the range of 220 ms to 250 ms surrounded by a red frame is 432 addition. In this way, the blinking cycle is narrowed, and then it is determined whether the brightness is high or low. In the case of high-brightness 432 blinking, a peak was observed between 100 ms and 150 ms surrounded by a green frame. In the case of low brightness, no peak was observed. It is necessary to consider whether other types of blinking can be discriminated by comparing the absolute values and positions of the peaks.

Another factor is the degree of neck tilting due to the positional relationship between the display and the chair. When we talked to the subjects, some indicated that they would be aware of stimuli that were not the subject of gaze. Therefore, to improve the experimental screen, it is necessary to consider a distance so that the next stimulus cannot be seen and so that the stimulus can be caught in the center of the field of view without tilting the head. In addition, by exchanging the positions of the stimuli, it is necessary to examine whether the high or low discrimination rate is associated with position or blinking.

In addition, synchronous addition is more complicated for the 234432 stimulus than for the other stimuli. Since the time lag of blinking could be eliminated in this study, it is conceivable to use a 10 Hz stimulus with a phase shift instead of the 234432 stimulus. At 10 Hz, synchronous addition is relatively simple; thus, there is the possibility that the judgment process can be performed in a shorter time.

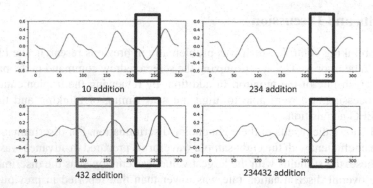

Fig. 3. High-brightness 432 blinking synchronous addition waveform when gazing

Table 1. Discrimination rate for each subject and each blinking

Types of stimuli	sub1	sub2
High brightness 10 Hz	90%	100%
High brightness 234	100%	50%
High brightness 432	100%	50%
High brightness 234432	60%	20%
Low brightness 10 Hz	100%	50%
Low brightness 234	30%	10%
Low brightness 432	60%	20%
Low brightness 234432	30%	50%
Non-gaze	70%	60%
Discrimination rate	71.1%	45.6%

4   Summary

In this study, we improved the algorithm in the discrimination of eight options by EEG and investigated the discrimination rate using the correlation coefficient with the sample waveform. As a result, the discrimination rate was lower than that reported in previous studies. One of the factors for this result is that the correlation coefficient decreased because the synchronization phenomenon did not occur. Therefore, it is conceivable to discriminate only the synchronized part instead of the correlation coefficient. By narrowing the waveform information applied for judgment, it is possible that the judgment process can be shortened. In a previous study, the coefficient of variation, which can simultaneously evaluate the waveform amplitude and standard deviation, was used for discrimination; therefore, these methods were also examined.

In addition, since blinking control has been improved, we will consider using a stimulus that shifts the phase of the 10 Hz blinking stimulus.

References

1. Itai, A., Funase, A.: Trial to build BCI system Brain wave analysis technology. J. Jpn. Soc. Neural Circuits **9**(3), 118–125 (2012)
2. Matsuno Shogo, O., Mumu, S.A., Itakura, N., Mizuno, T., Mito, K.: Examination of multi-choice using changes in index lighting interval and brightness in EEG interface using transient type VEP analysis method. IEEJ Trans. Electr. Eng. C **137**(4), 616–620 (2017)
3. Osano, R., Ikai, M., Matsuno, S., Itakura, N., Mizuno, T.: Development of small device for the brain computer interface with transient VEP analysis. In: Proceedings of IEEE Region 10 Conference, pp. 3786–3789 (2016)

Character Input Method Using Back Tap on Smartphone

Kohei Wajima$^{(\boxtimes)}$, Tota Mizuno, Yu Matsumoto, Kazuyuki Mito, and Naoaki Itakura

The University of Electro-Communications, 1-5-1 Chofugaoka, Chofu, Tokyo, Japan
kohei.wajima0525@uec.ac.jp

Abstract. With the widespread adoption of smartphones, opportunities for character input using the smartphone are increasing. However, character input on a smartphone is challenging. For example, it is erroneous to input owing to the small size button and small size information screen owing to the large size character input screen. To solve these problems, input methods besides touch are being studied. For example, input using sight and gesture. The aim of this study is to develop a gesture input interface that uses a small motion, that is, back tap of the device input. Back tap indicates the motion of tapping the left and right sides of the back of the device once or twice. Furthermore, combinations that can be used for discrimination are considered. The three-axis sensor of acceleration and gyro on a smartphone is used to determine the movement. In addition, the sampling frequency is set to 200 Hz. Using Z-axis of acceleration and Y-axis of gyro, the sensor could determine the analysis acceleration and gyro data of back taps. In the experiment based on the analysis results, four patterns were discriminated. Accordingly, it was possible to determine all patterns with at least 90% accuracy. Because any pattern could be discriminated with high accuracy, we consider character input in consideration of affordances. In addition, the character input speed and accuracy are calculated.

Keywords: Interface · Smartphone · Gesture · Character input

1 Introduction

1.1 Background

In recent years, various devices have been created that make the world more convenient. In particularly, smart devices, such as smartphones and tablets, have become increasingly popular. Despite their small size, these devices can be used for a variety of applications, including personal computers. Smartphone penetration rates, in particular, exceeds the number of fixed-line phones [1], making them indispensable in our daily lives. In addition, there are increasing opportunities to use smartphones for Internet search, e-mail, and social networking service (SNS) [2]. Against the background, opportunities for character input are increasing, however challenges have emerged with regard to this.

For example, the Fat Finger problem in which the button next to the one you tried to enter is selected [3]. This is because each button becomes smaller because of the miniaturization of the device. In addition, the occupancy rate of the screen used for character input is also regarded as a problem. If you make the button larger to solve the problem of incorrect input, the input screen will become larger. In addition, if the input screen is made smaller to solve the problem of screen occupancy, the buttons become smaller and erroneous input increases. These problems are unavoidable as the device becomes smaller. In this manner, in the current character input interface, there is a trade-off relationship between the size of the button and the input screen occupancy rate, therefore a method that achieves both operability and screen occupancy rate is required.

1.2 A Multi-choice Input Method with a Low Degree of Freedom

Matsuno et al. [4] proposed a touch input method with a small degree of freedom of operation and multiple choices using four buttons arranged side by side as an input method that achieves both operability and screen occupancy to solve these problems. The input screen is presented in Fig. 1. The input design used is a port of the qwerty sequence. After tapping the four buttons that lined up side by side, flick it up and down to make eight operations. By repeating this operation twice, 64 choices can be input. 64 choices are enough for character input considering auxiliary keys. A method for achieving both operability and screen occupancy has been developed by inputting characters using only four buttons.

Wajima et al. [5] examined the development of an interface using gestures for the general purpose of touch input interfaces. Similar to touch interface, the input screen used in Fig. 1 is used. Instead of four buttons using touch, four wrist gestures to tilt the device have been used. In addition, the action of tapping the back of the smartphone is used as input. There are eight operations depending on whether this back tap is tilted. Character input is made possible by performing the same operation twice. Although these operations could be discriminated with high accuracy, it is necessary to move the device significantly.

Therefore, this study aimed to develop an interface that allows character input using only small fingertip movements, which is easier than wrist movements, and examined whether it is possible to determine the number of taps and the tap positions at two locations.

Fig. 1. Character input screen

2   Character Input Method by Back Tap

In this study, the basic operation is to tap the back of the smartphone in two places on the left and right as shown in Fig. 2. The three-axis accelerometer and gyro sensor shown in Fig. 2 is used to determine the motion. Assuming that characters are input by tapping on the back, six types of operations including double tap are prepared to increase the types of taps.

The six types of operation are as follows:

Action ①: Tap once on the left side.
Action ②: Tap once on the right side.
Action ③: Two consecutive taps on the left side.
Action ④: Two consecutive taps on the right side.
Action ⑤: Left right alternate tap.
Action ⑥: Right left alternate tap.

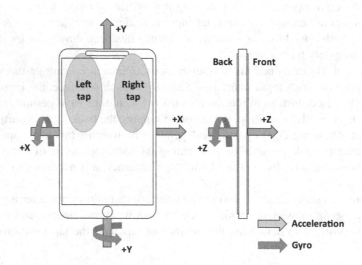

Fig. 2. Basic operation of back tap and three-axis acceleration/gyro

3   Waveform Analysis

As an example, Fig. 3 depicts the waveform when the left side is tapped once. When the back tap is performed, characteristic waveforms are obtained on the acceleration Z-axis and gyro Y-axis.

When the back is tapped, the acceleration Z-axis exhibits positive to negative waveform characteristics. It has very short waveform of about 10 ms from tapping to reaching a negative peak, and then the waveform changes slowly until the device returns to its original state. Therefore, if the acceleration Z-axis exceeds the positive threshold value, then the negative threshold value, and the interval exceeding the threshold value is within a certain period of time, it is considered a tap. For the threshold value, the lowest peak value was set from the data obtained by the preliminary experiment.

For the Y-axis of angular velocity, two peaks are displayed when the back is tapped. When the acceleration Z-axis exceeds the positive and negative thresholds, the left side indicates a positive value and the right side indicates a negative value. It also displays the opposite peak before the device returns to its normal position. Table 1 shows the waveform characteristics of the back tap.

In addition, in the continuous tap, the second tap was input by 450 ms from the data of the preliminary experiment. Therefore, if the acceleration Z-axis exceeds the threshold value again within 450 ms from the first tap, the second tap is considered. The operations are determined by these algorithms.

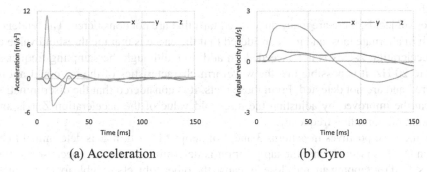

(a) Acceleration   (b) Gyro

Fig. 3. Waveform example (Action ①: Tap once on the left side)

Table 1. Waveform characteristic of back tap.

Action		Left tap	Right tap
Waveform characteristic	**Z-axis acceleration**	Plus→Minus	Plus→Minus
	Y-axis gyro	Plus→Minus	Minus→Plus

4 Discrimination Experiment

4.1 Experiment Method

From the waveform analysis results, the back tap is discriminated using acceleration and gyro sensor in smartphone. A smartphone (HUAWEI P20) is used for the experiment, and the subjects are six in their 20 s. In addition, the hand that normally holds the smartphone is used as the handle. It is for them to perform the movements that randomly ordered 20 times each while sitting on a chair. To input characters, six actions are combined as shown in Table 2 and the discrimination rate for each pattern is calculated.

Table 2. Back tap discrimination pattern.

Pattern 1				Pattern 2			
③ left-left	① left	② right	④ right-right	① left	⑤ left-right	⑥ right-left	② right
Pattern 3				Pattern 4					
③ left-left	⑤ left-right	⑥ right-left	④ right-right	③ left-left	① left	⑤ left-right	⑥ right-left	② right	④ right-right

4.2 Results and Discussion

Tables 3 and 4 show the experimental results. Table 3 shows pattern 1 and 2. Table 4 shows pattern 3 and 4. Except for pattern 2 of subject E and D, the discrimination rate is high.

For subject E, there are many undetected taps that are not considered. The tendency is high in alternate taps, and it is considered that the cause is that the threshold value of the acceleration Z-axis is not exceeded. In addition, although the sampling frequency is set to 20 Hz, it is possible that the waveform characteristics of the tap could not be captured and are not detected. From these facts, it is considered that the discrimination rate can be improved by adjusting the threshold value of the acceleration Z-axis and changing the sampling frequency.

In the false positives in patterns 3 and 4 of subject D, action ⑤ is determined to be motion ③. It is possible that the tap position is determined to be one, because the two fingers used for tapping are too close. Because the other subjects are able to discriminate at almost 100%, it is considered that the discriminant rate will improve as the user learns.

In addition, unintended taps are entered only once throughout. It is considered that the false detection of operations other than tapping is sufficiently suppressed by setting a time constraint on the acceleration Z-axis. It is thought that the accuracy will be further improved by solving these problems.

Table 3. Discrimination result of patterns 1 and 2 [%].

Subject (Handle) \ Action	Pattern 1				Pattern 2			
	③	①	②	④	③	⑤	⑥	④
A(right)	100	100	100	100	100	100	100	100
B(right)	100	100	100	100	100	100	100	100
C(left)	90	95	95	90	100	85	100	100
D(right)	95	100	100	95	100	85	100	95
E(right)	85	85	80	75	100	70	90	95
Average	94	96	95	92	100	88	98	98

Table 4. Discrimination result of pattern 3 and pattern 4 [%].

Action Subject (Handle)	Pattern 3					Pattern 4				
	①	⑤	⑥	②	③	①	⑤	⑥	②	④
A(right)	100	100	100	100	100	100	100	100	100	100
B(right)	100	100	100	100	100	100	100	100	100	100
C(left)	100	95	100	100	100	100	95	95	95	80
D(right)	85	75	95	90	85	100	70	100	100	100
E(right)	90	90	65	95	70	90	80	70	85	95
Average	95	92	92	97	91	98	89	93	96	95

5   Conclusion

In order to solve the problem of character input on smartphones, it focused on gesture input in addition to touch operation. In this research, it focused the two taps on the back of the device that are small and easy for users to input. Using the accelerometer and angular velocity sensor mounted on the smartphone, the movements can be identified with high accuracy. In the future, to support character input, we plan to study operations other than tapping at two locations on the back, and to have the user input characters by making the back tap correspond to the input screen to improve usability. Furthermore, it aims to develop a better interface by combining gesture with touch input.

References

1. Ministry of Finance homepage. Information and communication equipment ownership status. https://www.soumu.go.jp/johotsusintokei/whitepaper/ja/r02/html/nd252110.html. Accessed 11 March 2021
2. Ministry of Finance homepage. Internet usage. https://www.soumu.go.jp/johotsusintokei/whitepaper/ja/r02/html/nd252110.html. Accessed 11 March 2021
3. Siek, K.A., Rogers, Y., Connelly, K.H.: Fat finger worries: how older and younger users physically interact with PDAs. In: Costabile, M.F., Paternò, F. (eds.) INTERACT 2005. LNCS, vol. 3585, pp. 267–280. Springer, Heidelberg (2005). https://doi.org/10.1007/11555261_24
4. Matsuno, S., Chida, S., Itakura, N., Mizuno, T., Mito, K.: A method of character input for the user interface with a low degree of freedom. Artif. Life Robot. **24**(2), 250–256 (2018). https://doi.org/10.1007/s10015-018-0512-4
5. Wajima, K., Farahani, M.A., Itakura, N., Mizuno, T., Mito, K.: Proposal of character input method using hand movement in smart phone. In: IEEE_IM-S19-26 (2019)

Eye-tracking and Facial Expressions Recognition

User State Detection Using Facial Images with Mask Cover

Danushka Bandara(✉) [iD]

Fairfield University, Fairfield, CT 06824, USA
dbandara@fairfield.edu

Abstract. Widespread use of masks was mandated in many countries as a direct result of the covid-19 pandemic. This meant that mask wearing, which was previously restricted to specialized occupations or cities with high levels of pollution became the norm in many places of the world. This has obvious implications for any system that uses facial images to infer user state. This work attempts to gauge the effect of mask wearing on such systems. Arousal classification is used in this study due to its well-studied nature in image processing literature. Using "Affect in the wild" video dataset, the "masks" were synthetically placed on the facial images extracted from videos. A binary classification between high and low arousal shows that there is a drop in accuracy when using masks. However, this drop is larger in across subject classification than within subject classification. The study shows that it is feasible to develop effective user state classification models even with mask cover.

Keywords: Deep learning · Masks · Emotion recognition

1 Introduction

This paper discusses the effect of mask wearing on the image processing-based user state detection methods used today. The goal is to ascertain the possible adverse effect of mask wearing to these systems and quantify the effect using arousal detection which is well studied in literature [1–5].

Many people worldwide work in conditions which require wearing of masks. Some professions like cleaning, maintenance work, mining and firefighting are done in debris or particle filled environments and therefore require specialized masks. Healthcare workers and laboratory workers wear medical grade masks to protect themselves from pathogens and other medical hazards. A lot of these professions are conducted under situations which require intense focus due to safety reasons. And the workers have to be in an optimal mental state in order to perform their tasks correctly and safely. With the increase of particulate matter in the air in large cities, as well as the advent of coronavirus pandemic, wearing of masks have become necessary for health reasons. With the normalization of mask wearing comes a host of challenges for image processing algorithms. In the emotion recognition domain, many of the state-of-the-art algorithms rely on facial image data [1, 2] to do develop emotion classifiers. Features extracted from facial images [6–11] are then fed into a machine learning algorithm to develop a classification model and

© Springer Nature Switzerland AG 2021
C. Stephanidis et al. (Eds.): HCII 2021, CCIS 1420, pp. 67–74, 2021.
https://doi.org/10.1007/978-3-030-78642-7_10

then use that model to classify new images. Facial occlusion is particularly challenging in these approaches due to the sparse nature [14] of the feature matrices obtained. Even though there are suggested methods to deal with this issue such as filling in the gaps of the occluded images [12] or using the causal relations between facial regions [13], the need for hand crafted features has remained a challenge for adaptation of these methods.

Recent advances in deep learning have provided another opportunity to tackle the problem of facial occlusion by using automated feature extraction using CNN techniques [16, 17]. Such approaches have been obtaining state of the art results in the emotion recognition area [18]. This paper therefore leverages this technique in applying it to occluded facial images, specifically images with the lower part of the face occluded as in the case of mask wearing. The affect in the wild video dataset [2] is used as the basis of this work, and the images extracted from the video dataset were augmented to cover the lower part of face. The method is further expanded in the methods section. The results and implications of this work are discussed in the following sections.

2 Methods

There are many facial emotion datasets that are publicly available [19]. The affect in the wild dataset [2] was chosen for this work since, (1) it has a diverse set of faces. (2) The videos were captured in naturalistic settings. (3) In addition to the videos and affect annotations, it also contains 60 facial key points for each frame in each of the videos. This enabled placing an artificial occlusion on the images to simulate facial mask cover.

2.1 The Dataset

The "affect in the wild" dataset consists of 298 videos, with a total length of more than 30 h. The videos were collected using the Youtube video sharing website using the keyword "reaction". The database displays subjects reacting to a variety of stimuli. Subjects display different combinations of emotions. The videos contain subjects from different genders and ethnicities with high variations in head pose and lighting. The videos were annotated using an online annotation procedure in which annotators used joysticks to provide arousal labels continuously (for each frame in the videos) in $[-1, +1]$. All subjects present in each video have been annotated. The total number of subjects is 200, with 130 of them being male and 70 of them female [2].

Dataset Augmentation. All the individual faces were cropped from each frame of the videos for the classification. The bounding box coordinate data from "affect in the wild" dataset was used for this. The annotation for each frame was applied to the individual faces as well. These individual face crops will be referred to as "dataset" from now onwards. Low and high labels were chosen as classification labels for the annotation ranges of $[-1, -5]$ and $[+5, +1]$. The range $[-5, +5]$ was dropped from the dataset due to the ambiguity in assigning high or low labels (Fig. 1).

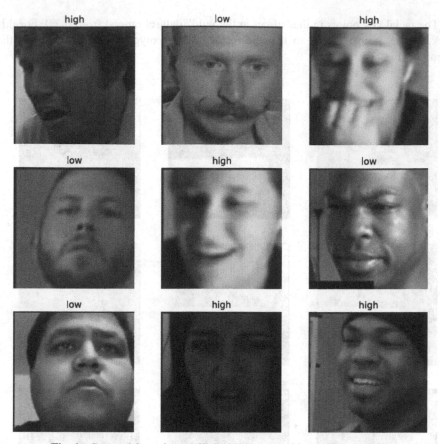

Fig. 1. Cropped faces from Affwild [3] dataset with associated labels.

This dataset was used as the benchmark for classification of faces without masks. Another dataset was created based on these images to represent the faces covered by masks. To achieve this, the facial key point data from "affect in the wild" dataset was used (Fig. 2).

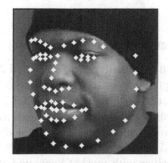

Fig. 2. Facial key points overlayed on a sample face.

The facial key points in the "affect in the wild" dataset ranged from 0–60. For this work, the key points from 2 to 15 were formed into a polygon shape to represent the facemask (Fig. 3).

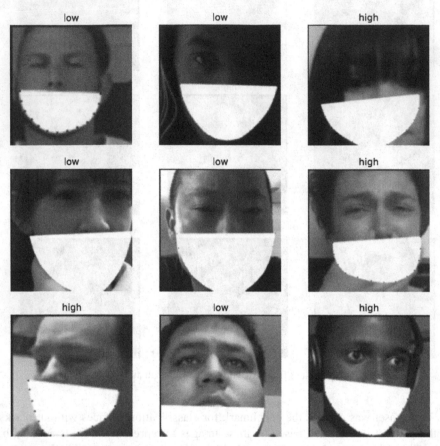

Fig. 3. Cropped faces with mask cover represented by a polygon using the facial key points of the lower half of face.

2.2 Training/Testing Configurations

(Test 1 – Across subject classifier without masks) Separated 20 videos from the without-mask-dataset and used the captured faces from those videos as the test set.

(Test 2 – Across subject classifier with masks) Separated 20 videos from the dataset-with-masks and used the captured faces from those videos as the test set.

(Test 3 – Within subject classifier without masks) Separated 1000 faces of each label at random from the without-mask-dataset as the test set.

(Test 4 – Within subject classifier with masks) Separated 1000 faces of each label at random from the dataset-with-masks as the test set.

For each of the above test methods, the train set, and test set were balanced to get the finalized dataset which contained approximately 40000 training images (20000 in low label and 20000 in high label) and approximately 2000 testing images (1000 in low label and 1000 in high label).

2.3 Preprocessing

The dataset images were rescaled to 180 × 180 before feeding into the classifier. They were converted to grayscale in order to avoid any bias from ambient color or lighting. Finally, they were normalized to the range of 0–1 from the pixel range of 0–255.

2.4 Classification

A RESNET50 [21] Convolutional Neural Network (CNN) classifier was used to train on the dataset and test on the separated test set. RESNET was chosen instead of a vanilla CNN due to the ability of RESNET to support larger number of layers. The batch size used for training was 32. And the validation split was 0.2. The loss was calculated using sparse categorical cross entropy. And the ADAM optimizer [20] was used with learning rate of 0.001, beta1 of 0.9, beta2 of 0.999 and epsilon of 1e−07. Early stopping was used to prevent overfitting the CNN model. The results from the two-label classification are described in the results section.

3   Results

See (Figs. 4 and 5).

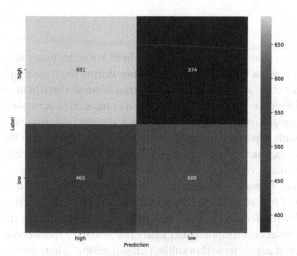

Fig. 4. Confusion matrix for Test 1 without mask overlay. Accuracy 61%

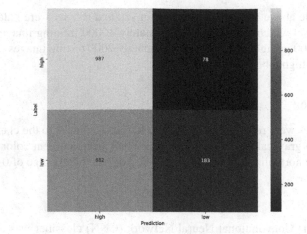

Fig. 5. Confusion matrix for Test 2 with mask overlay. Accuracy 55%

Table 1. Comparison of classification accuracy

Test	Mask cover	Accuracy
1	No	61%
2	Yes	55%
3	No	99%
4	Yes	97%

4 Discussion

The results (Table 1) show that test 1 and 2 obtained lower accuracy levels since the test set videos were not accessed at all by the classifier during the training phase. Test 3 and 4 achieved much better accuracy. This shows that arousal classification performs significantly better in within-subject scenarios when compared to across-subject scenarios. Even though the results indicate that without mask dataset performs better, the accuracy could be higher with hyperparameter optimization. The main goal in this study was not to get the highest accuracy possible, but to offer a fair comparison between the dataset with and without mask cover.

In the test 1 and 2, using masks dropped the accuracy from 61% to 55%. This could be due to the lower half of the face contributing to the arousal detection, this will have to be confirmed by further studies looking at saliency maps from the model.

The accuracy level only dropped marginally (99% to 97%) between masked and non-masked case when it comes to within subject classification. Therefore, we can conclude that across subject classifiers will be more affected from mask cover than within subject classifiers. Arousal was the criteria used in this study. It will be interesting to see if the results translate to other forms of user state as well.

The results show that even with mask cover, it is possible to get acceptable level of accuracy for user state classification.

References

1. Mollahosseini, A., Hasani, B., Mahoor, M.H.: Affectnet: a database for facial expression, valence, and arousal computing in the wild. IEEE Trans. Affect. Comput. **10**(1), 18–31 (2017)
2. Kollias, D., et al.: Deep affect prediction in-the-wild: Aff-wild database and challenge, deep architectures, and beyond. Int. J. Comput. Vis. **127**, 907–929 (2019)
3. Machajdik, J., Hanbury, A.: Affective image classification using features inspired by psychology and art theory. In: Proceedings of the 18th ACM international conference on Multimedia, pp. 83–92, October 2010
4. Nhan, B.R., Chau, T.: Classifying affective states using thermal infrared imaging of the human face. IEEE Trans. Biomed. Eng. **57**(4), 979–987 (2009)
5. Bandara, D., Velipasalar, S., Bratt, S., Hirshfield, L.: Building predictive models of emotion with functional near-infrared spectroscopy. Int. J. Hum Comput Stud. **110**, 75–85 (2018)
6. Buciu, I., Kotsia, I., Pitas, I.: Recognition of facial expressions in presence of partial occlusion. In: Proceedings of the 9th Panhellenic Conference on Informatics (PCI 2003), November 2003sss
7. Kotsia, I., Buciu, I., Pitas, I.: An analysis of facial expression recognition under partial facial image occlusion. Image Vis. Comput. **26**(7), 1052–1067 (2008)
8. Bourel, F., Chibelushi, C.C., Low, A.A.: Recognition of facial expressions in the presence of occlusion. In: BMVC, pp. 1–10 (2001)
9. Zhang, L., Tjondronegoro, D., Chandran, V.: Random gabor based templates for facial expression recognition in images with facial occlusion. Neurocomputing **145**, 451–464 (2014)
10. Towner, H., Slater, M.: Reconstruction and recognition of occluded facial expressions using PCA. In: Paiva, A.C.R., Prada, R., Picard, R.W. (eds.) ACII. LNCS, vol. 4738, pp. 36–47. Springer, Heidelberg (2007). https://doi.org/10.1007/978-3-540-74889-2_4
11. Huang, X., Zhao, G., Zheng, W., Pietikäinen, M.: Towards a dynamic expression recognition system under facial occlusion. Pattern Recogn. Lett. **33**(16), 2181–2191 (2012)
12. Jiang, B., Jia, K.: Research of robust facial expression recognition under facial occlusion condition. In: Zhong, N., Callaghan, V., Ghorbani, A.A., Hu, B. (eds.) AMT. LNCS, vol. 6890, pp. 92–100. Springer, Heidelberg (2011). https://doi.org/10.1007/978-3-642-23620-4_13
13. Miyakoshi, Y., Kato, S.: Facial emotion detection considering partial occlusion of face using Bayesian network. In: 2011 IEEE Symposium on Computers & Informatics, pp. 96–101. IEEE, March 2011
14. Cotter, S.F.: Sparse representation for accurate classification of corrupted and occluded facial expressions. In: 2010 IEEE International Conference on Acoustics, Speech and Signal Processing, pp. 838–841. IEEE, March 2010
15. Hammal, Z., Arguin, M., Gosselin, F.: Comparing a novel model based on the transferable belief model with humans during the recognition of partially occluded facial expressions. J. Vis. **9**(2), 22 (2009)
16. Roy, B., Nandy, S., Ghosh, D., Dutta, D., Biswas, P., Das, T.: MOXA: A deep learning based unmanned approach for real-time monitoring of people wearing medical masks. Trans. Indian Natl. Acad. Eng. **5**(3), 509–518 (2020). https://doi.org/10.1007/s41403-020-00157-z
17. Loey, M., Manogaran, G., Taha, M.H.N., Khalifa, N.E.M.: Fighting against COVID-19: a novel deep learning model based on YOLO-v2 with ResNet-50 for medical face mask detection. Sustain. Cities Soc. **65**, 102600 (2021)

18. Bandara, D., Hirshfield, L., Velipasalar, S.: Classification of affect using deep learning on brain blood flow data. J. Near Infrared Spectrosc. **27**(3), 206–219 (2019)

19. Buciu, I., Kotsia, I., Pitas, I.: Facial expression analysis under partial occlusion. In: Proceedings of the IEEE International Conference on Acoustics, Speech, and Signal Processing ICASSP 2005, vol. 5, pp. v–453. IEEE, March 2005

20. Kingma, D.P., Ba, J.: Adam: a method for stochastic optimization. arXiv preprint arXiv:1412. 6980 (2014)

21. He, K., Zhang, X., Ren, S., Sun, J.: Deep residual learning for image recognition. In: 2016 IEEE Conference on Computer Vision and Pattern Recognition (CVPR), Las Vegas, NV, USA, pp. 770–778 (2016). https://doi.org/10.1109/CVPR.2016.90

A Comparative Analysis of Attention to Facial Recognition Payment Between China and South Korea: A News Analysis Using Latent Dirichlet Allocation

ShaoPeng Che, Dongyan Nan, Pim Kamphuis, and Jang Hyun Kim[✉]

Department of Interaction Science/Department of Human-Artificial Intelligence Interaction, Sungkyunkwan University, Seoul 03063, Korea
cheshao@g.skku.edu, {ndyzxy0926,p.i.m,alohakim}@skku.edu

Abstract. Facial Recognition Payment (FRP) is a new method of digital payment that recently gained popularity in China and South Korea. As of October 2019, although the number of users in China has exceeded 100 million, few studies have focused on this, and media coverage of FRP has not been adequately studied. Therefore, this study examines news articles using Latent Dirichlet Allocation (LDA) topic modeling to compare FRP related news in China and South Korea. The data of China comes from WeChat Public Platform, and the data of South Korea comes from Naver. Chinese search keywords is "人脸识别支付" (facial recognition payment), South Korea's search key word is "안면 인식 결제" (facial recognition payment).Through data cleaning and comparative analysis, each subject is given an description and category, and the differences in 5 aspects of safety concern, application, development, technology and representative products are obtained. The rapid adoption of FRP in China can be explained by a lower public concern of personal information protection and the direct offering of FRP services to independent vendors by market leader Alipay. In South Korea, however, the increased public concern around privacy plays a key role in slower adoption, together with the dominance of franchise stores in the consumer market. It puts forward the suggestion for China and South Korea to learn from each other and for those other countries and enterprises striving to develop and utilize FRP.

Keywords: Facial Recognition Payment · LDA · News analysis · WeChat · Naver

1 Introduction

When WeChat and Alipay both launched their own Facial Recognition Payment (FRP) systems "Frog" and "Dragonfly 2.0" in March and April 2019 respectively, China officially entered the era of facial payments. Attempts in South Korea followed one year later, when Shinhan Card Co. Ltd. installed its first commercial FRP system "Shinhan Face Pay" at Hanyang University in response to the COVID-19 outbreak.

© Springer Nature Switzerland AG 2021
C. Stephanidis et al. (Eds.): HCII 2021, CCIS 1420, pp. 75–82, 2021.
https://doi.org/10.1007/978-3-030-78642-7_11

While the rapid development of innovative payment technologies has served people with a more convenient life, it often comes bundled with novel issues and concerns. As implied in agenda-setting theory [1], news media coverage can be used as an indirect measure of the public's attitude toward a specific technology [2], and analysis can help us to understand the public's concerns and attitude towards FRP. Considering China ranked first in mobile payment usage [3] and South Korea ranked first in terms of Internet usage [4], the authors selected news media outlets from both countries. A web crawler then scraped news articles with the keywords "Facial Recognition Payment" in their respective languages to construct a news article corpus for Latent Dirichlet Allocation (LDA) topic analysis.

The purpose of this research is to understand the public concern regarding FRP through news coverage, to enhance FRP technology and services, to provide insights about the current cases in China and South Korea, and finally to provide valuable information for governments and enterprises.

Therefore, the authors suggest the research questions below:

Q1: What are the key topics in Chinese and Korean news coverage on facial recognition payment?

Q2: What are the differences between the news coverage in China and South Korea and, what are the reasons for the differences?

2   Method

To construct the corpus, Chinese news articles were crawled from "WeChat Public Platform" using a tool called "ScrapeStorm". The software has been used for several studies (e.g., [5]). WeChat is currently the biggest social media platform in China and has, according to the latest data, a number of 1.151 billion monthly active users. To collect South Korean news, the tool "Textom" was used to crawl articles from "Naver News." Naver is the most popular search engine in South Korea with its own news portal, topping the list with a market share of 45% over Google and Daum. "Textom" also has been used by precedent studies (e.g., [6, 7]).

Before crawling the term "Facial Recognition Payment" was translated into the local languages: "人脸识别支付" for Chinese news articles and "안면 인식 결제" for Korean articles. Because the concept of FRP was first introduced in 2013, the data collection was limited to articles published between July 1, 2013 and December 1, 2019. This resulted in a corpus containing 854 Chinese news articles and 741 Korean articles.

After collection of the news articles, the data was preprocessed by dropping duplicates and irrelevant attributes. Stopword correction was applied to delete a large amount of meaningless words and numbers and, finally all news content was tokenized. Then, the LDA-based analysis provided the proper number of topics, titles, and descriptions.

The process of method is shown as Fig. 1.

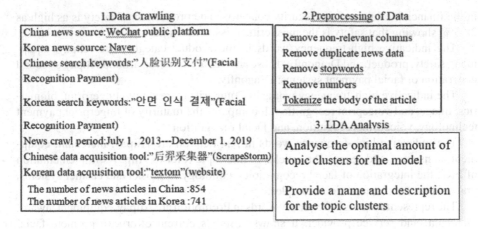

Fig. 1. Flow chart

3 Results

3.1 Chinese Results

Among the 30 highest-frequency words in each topic, 5 representative words were selected to define a title and description for each topic. The results in Table 1 show that Chinese topics can be divided into safety, product, comparison, applications, and promotion. As shown in Table 1.

Table 1. Chinese topics.

Topic	Description	High frequency words
Safety (28.3%)	The risks of facial recognition devices for the financial sector	安全(safety)、生物(biometrics)、金融(finance)、设备(equipment)、风险(risk)
Product (19%)	News of dragonflies (Alipay's FRP product)	支付宝(Alipay)、设备(equipment)、安全(safety)、、产品(product)、蜻蜓(dragonfly)
Comparison (18.8%)	Advantages and disadvantages of fingerprint recognition, voiceprint recognition and facial recognition	安全(safety)、指纹(fingerprint)、生物(biometrics)、图像(image)、声纹识别(Voiceprint Recognition)
Applications (18.1%)	The application of facial recognition in real situations	支付宝(Alipay)、商家(merchant)、设备(equipment)、消费者(consumer)、场景(scene)
Promotion (15.8%)	Merchants are rewarded for completing a specified number of facial recognition transactions	支付宝(Alipay)、设备(equipment)、奖励(award)、商家(merchant)、服务商(service provider)

The indicative high-frequency words in the Safety category are safety, biometrics, finance, equipment, and risk, suggesting that the use of facial recognition technology in the financial industry poses security concerns. The proportion of safety is as high as 28.3%, showing that safety is the most critical issue in China.

The indicative high-frequency words in the Product category are Alipay, equipment, safety, product, and Dragonfly. These articles are centered around Alipay's second generation of facial payment systems: Dragonfly.

The indicative high-frequency words in Comparison are safety, fingerprint, biometrics, image, and voiceprint recognition. It compares the maturity of fingerprint payment technology, voiceprint recognition, and facial recognition.

The indicative high-frequency words in Application are Alipay, merchant, equipment, consumer, and scene. The articles in this topic refer to Alipay's implementation of FRP, the integration of facial recognition technology in kiosks and cashier systems, practical use, and application examples.

The representative high-frequency words in Promotion are Alipay, equipment, award, merchant, and service provider. It shows Alipay's current efforts to promote facial payment products.

3.2 Korean Results

Among the 30 high-frequency words in each topic, 5 representative words were selected to define a title and description for each topic. As shown in Table 2.

Table 2. Korean topics.

Topic	Description	High frequency words
Personal Information (35.2%)	FRPs involve the acquisition of personal information	개인정보 (Personal information), 신한카드 (Shinhan Card), 디지털 (digital), 생체 (biometrics), 편의점 (convenience store)
Application site (24.3%)	FRPs are mainly used in convenience stores	금융 (finance), 편의점 (convenience store), 신한카드 (Shinhan Card), 핀테크 (financial technology), 세븐일레븐 (7-11 convenience stores)
Technical mechanism (23.5%)	FRPs rely on light-sensitive cameras to scan biometric features	신한카드(Shinhan Card), 매읍(store), 카메라(camera), 생체(biometrics), 편의점(convenience store)
Industry impact (17%)	The impact of FRPs on future industry	신한카드(Shinhan Card), 지문(fingerprint), 인공지능(artificial intelligence), 미래(future), 빅데이터(big data)

The results in Table 2 show that Korean topics can be divided into Personal Information, Applications, Technical Principles, and Industry Impact.

The salient high-frequency words in the Personal Information category are personal information, Shinhan Card, digital biometrics, and convenience store. Personal information accounted for the highest proportion, showing that South Koreans are more concerned about the security of personal information.

The high-frequency words in Applications are finance, convenience store, Shinhan Card, finance, and financial technology. Convenience stores, especially 7-Eleven, have the highest correlation with FRP.

The frequent words in Technical Principles are Shinhan Card, store, camera, biometrics, and convenience store; mainly describing the technical principles of FRP.

The outstanding high-frequency words in Industry Impact are Shinhan Card, fingerprint, artificial intelligence, future, and big data. These topics describe the impact of FRP on the future of the industry.

4   Discussion

Through the collection and analysis of news media coverage on FRP in China and South Korea, the research questions can be answered as follows:

Q1: What are the key topics of Chinese and Korean news on facial recognition payment?

LDA analysis of 1595 news articles showed that the topics of articles in both countries could be divided into the following five categories, As shown in Table 3:

Table 3. Comparison of two countries.

Topic	China	Korea
Safety awareness	Finance (e.g., 设备(equipment), 产品(product), 银行(bank))	Personal Information (e.g., 생체(biometrics), 지문(fingerprint))
Product	Alipay's dragonfly (e.g., 支付宝 (Alipay), 蜻蜓(dragonfly), 服务(service))	Shinhan Card (e.g., 신한카드 (Shinhan Card))
Technology	Fingerprint Payment, Voiceprint Recognition, FRP (e.g., 图像 (image), 摄像头(camera))	Technical Principle of FRP (e.g., 인공지능 (Artificial intelligence), 가동(automatic), 계정인증 (Account authentication))
Applications	All kinds of stores (e.g., 场景(application), 商家(shopkeeper))	7-ELVEN (e.g., 편의점 (convenience store chain))
Current situation	Alipay is the market leader and is promoting the market (e.g., 营销(marketing), 奖励(award))	The impact on the future industry is being analyzed and predicted (e.g., 미래(future)、 확웁(expansion)、 분야(field))

4.1 Safety Awareness

Users in both China and South Korea are mostly concerned about security. In China, these concerns seem to rise around financial security, while in South Korea personal information security seemed to be more of a concern. This result can be explained from two perspectives. The first perspective is that the development stage of digital finance between the two countries is not consistent, which is reflected in topic 3 in the analysis below. The second perspective may be caused by the varying degree of personal information protection in the two countries.

4.2 Representative Products

In both countries, most FRP news coverage can be related to one leading service: Alipay's Dragonfly in China and Shinhan Card's "Shinhan Face Pay" in South Korea.

4.3 Technology

Chinese media make more comparisons between fingerprint payments, voiceprint recognition payments and facial recognition payments, while Korean media introduces FRP's technical mechanism. This reflects the speed difference between the two countries in the development of digital payment systems. Due to the strong development of the internet economy, China has accumulated many years of digital payments experiences. Until recently, South Korea has had a strong "credit card culture" before starting to experiment with FRP. The shift from credit cards to biometric payments face psychological barriers in Korea.

4.4 Applications

The applications of FRP in China are more diversified and can be found in any private store, food court, and shopping mall. In South Korea, however, 7-Eleven is the only chain store that adopted FRP services comprehensively.

4.5 Stage of Development

When defining the status quo by examining the high-frequency words among topics, one can conclude that the FRP technology in China has matured into mainstream under the hood of Alibaba, while South Korea is still in a trial phase led and marketed by the Shinhan Card company.

Q2: What are the differences in media coverage between China and South Korea and what are the reasons for the differences?

4.6 Privacy Sensitivity

Because personal information disclosure has become the normalcy in China [6], the low demand for personal information protection may have contributed to the rapid development of FRP. Personal information protection seems to be a prominent issue in South

Korea, which may lead to the slower development and adoption of FRP. Considering this situation, in future progress, China should strengthen relevant laws and policies (strengthen the punishment of personal information misuse), improve the protection of personal information, and popularize the importance of personal information protection among citizens to avoid the side effects of "savage growth" in electronic payments.

4.7 Environmental Regulation

A significant amount of news articles covering FRP in South Korean media refer to the current situation in China, which shows that South Korea's FRP developments are lagging. The industry could use the help from lawmakers to introduce relevant laws and policies to stimulate and promote the development of FRP.

4.8 Historical Difference in Adoption

In transition from cash to electronic payments, China skipped the era of credit cards. This led to a rapid development in biometric payments, while the mass adoption of credit cards in South Korea slowed down the development and adaption of biometric payments.

4.9 Vendor Adoption

While most potential vendors to use FRP in Korea are a part of a chain or franchise, such as 7-Eleven, most vendors in China are independent – often self-employed. Alipay offers their FRP technology directly to these vendors, which led to rapid adoption. In South Korea, however, negotiation and implementation have to take place on an enterprise level, which significantly slow the adoption.

4.10 Learning and Reference

For countries that have not started the development and adoption of FRP it is important to be aware of the current issues and concerns in China and South Korea. Attention should be payed to how both countries handle the legal, social, and technical aspects of this potential technology. Lawmakers should be aware of the personal information security concerns; the payment providers should consider the market types and the public experiences with biometric payments.

5 Conclusion

This research has been conducted to understand the public concerns regarding Facial Recognition Payments through LDA topic analysis of media coverage in China and South Korea.

Although the detailed topics in Chinese media are different from those in South Korea, the news articles from both countries can be globally divided into five categories.

In terms of concerns it seems that financial security is of a higher concern in China; in South Korea, one of key concerns is the protection of personal information.

The differences in current state of development are clearly led by the two key players in the two countries: Alipay in China and Shinhan Card in South Korea. While the FRP service "Shinhan Face Pay" from the latter is still in a trial phase and mass adoption will depend on partnerships with potential chain stores and franchises, the second generation of Alipay's "Dragon fly" is well adopted by independent vendors and consumers all over China.

Based on the comparison, this study put forwards the suggestion that China and South Korea could learn about the public concern through their media coverage to contribute to FRP development at governmental and enterprise levels.

6   Limitations and Suggestions for Future Research

While news media coverage can provide us with clean and well-structured data, it can only serve as an indirect measure of the public attitude and concerns. When the amount of social media content regarding Facial Recognition Payments has grown, future research could use this data to directly measure attitudes and concerns from a variety of users [8]. Additionally, on the basis of the previous studies on payment services (e.g., [5, 9]), future research also can explore the users' perceptions of FRP by analyzing the survey data from China and South Korea. Furthermore, LDA-topic analysis could be applied to the contents distributed over time series, to understand the change in the public attitude and concerns over time.

References

1. Shaw, M.E.M.D.L., Weaver, D.H., Mc Combs, M.: Communication and Democracy: Exploring the Intellectual Frontiers in Agenda-Setting Theory. Psychology Press (1997)
2. Bengston, D.N., Fan, D.P.: Roads on the US national forests: an analysis of public attitudes, beliefs, and values expressed in the news media. Environ. Behav. **31**(4), 514–539 (1999)
3. eMarketer: China Mobile Payment Users 2019-Moving Toward a Cashless Society (2019)
4. The Korea Herald: Korea No. 1 worldwide in smartphone ownership, internet penetration (2018). http://news.koreaherald.com/view.php?ud=20180624000197&md=201806270 03544_BL
5. Krasna, H., et al.: The future of careers at the intersection of climate change and public health: what can job postings and an employer survey tell us? Int. J. Environ. Res. Pub. Health **17**(4), 1310 (2020)
6. Park, S.U., Ahn, H., Kim, D.K., So, W.Y.: Big data analysis of sports and physical activities among korean adolescents. Int. J. Environ. Res. Pub. Health **17**(15), 5577 (2020)
7. Kim, N.R., Hong, S.G.: Text mining for the evaluation of public services: the case of a public bike-sharing system. Serv. Bus. **14**(3), 315–331 (2020)
8. Che, S., Nan, D., Kamphuis, P., Jin, X., Kim, J.H.: a cluster analysis of lotte young plaza using semantic network analysis method. In: 2021 15th International Conference on Ubiquitous Information Management and Communication (IMCOM), pp. 1–6. IEEE (2021)
9. Zhang, W.K., Kang, M.J.: Factors affecting the use of facial-recognition payment: an example of Chinese consumers. IEEE Access **7**, 154360–154374 (2019)

Tile-Related Factors in Modern User Interface and Their Effects on Gaze Pointing Movement Time

Chin-Lung Chen[✉]

Department of Visual Communication Design, Ming Chi University of Technology,
New Taipei City, Taiwan
lung@mail.mcut.edu.tw

Abstract. This study investigated the feasibility of using gaze pointing in modern user interface (UI). Experiments were conducted to assess the impact of the modern UI layout (tile size, dynamic or static target tile, and interference tile) on gaze pointing movement time. A total of 13 participates were recruited, and their gaze pointing operation movement time under 12 experimental settings were measured. The scenarios contained different tile sizes as well as a dynamic or static target tile and an interference tile. When the interference tile was static, the gaze pointing movement time decreased as the tile size increased. However, when the tile size was larger than 96 pixels, the gaze pointing movement time no longer changed as tile size increased. The individual differences of the participants had a substantial impact on the operational performance of the gaze pointing interface, which is a challenge to be overcome when gaze pointing and the modern UI are integrated for future applications.

Keywords: Graphical user interface · Modern UI · Gaze pointing · Movement time

1 Research Background

A gaze-aware computer interface uses gaze to position and select icons. It can effectively reduce the need for bodily movement [1] and has the advantages of no physical contact and distant control [2]. Therefore, it has long been a research topic interesting interface researchers. However, the low precision of a gaze-aware computer interface makes it difficult to be comparable with commonly used skeuomorphic graphical user interfaces (UIs). This represents an obstacle for the popularization of gaze-aware computer interface design. In 2010, Microsoft released a modern UI design with rectangular tiles placed tightly next to one another. Increasing the size of a tile expands the space available for messages. This design substantially increased the feasibility of using gaze for positioning. The current study assessed the feasibility of using (Microsoft's) modern UI to replace conventional skeuomorphic UI icons in a gaze-aware computer interface.

© Springer Nature Switzerland AG 2021
C. Stephanidis et al. (Eds.): HCII 2021, CCIS 1420, pp. 83–89, 2021.
https://doi.org/10.1007/978-3-030-78642-7_12

2 Literature Review

Gaze pointing refers to using an eye tracker to trace the object the eyes gaze at to interact with the computer. Most studies have concluded that using gaze awareness to mediate human–machine interaction is feasible [3–5]. However, studies have also revealed that although users prefer using eye tracking as the assistive interface, the operational performance of eye- tracking gaze-pointing is inferior to that of a conventional mouse.

In normal eye movement, the angle of view can be accurately fixed to 10 points (0.16°). However, spontaneous movements that cannot be controlled make eyes periodically deviate from the target. Therefore, the precision of eye tracking is limited to approximately ±0.5° [6], which is not conducive to the application of existing computer work stations (where the screen viewing distance is approximately 57 cm, and the size of an icon is approximately 0.74° for the angle of view.) Therefore, low precision is a fundamental problem for eye movement. Improvements relying on increasing the precision of eye tracking devices are difficult to make. Human–machine interaction performance can only be effectively increased by improving the fitting of a graphical UI and eye movement.

Conventional graphical UI designs can be divided into two types, namely a skeuomorphic design and a flat design. A skeuomorphic design uses vivid patterns, shadows, visual metaphors, and stimulants to design interface icons [7, 8]. Microsoft's modern UI is representative of flat design. Its characteristics involve using live tiles to dynamically and instantly present graphics, photos, and videos. Its simple style (involving simple shapes, no color gradient, and no ostentatious detail) provides clear structural two-dimensional appearances and impressions [9].

Discussing eye movement and interface design implications, Drewes [2] proposed the design principles that in a spatial arrangement, elements that interact should be placed close together and that interactive elements should be large rather than small. Conventional graphical UIs suggest that icons should be placed with the space of at least one icon between them [10]. By contrast, modern UI's rectangular live tiles are packed tightly so as to make large space available for the display of messages. Therefore, with the same number of elements, the overall size of modern UI's live tiles can be approximately twice that of conventional UI icons, namely a 1.48° angle of view, which substantially increases the feasibility of using gaze for positioning.

3 Research Methods

An experimental method was used to assess the influences of the modern UI's tile size, dynamic versus static target tiles, and interference tiles on gaze pointing movement time. The participants were 13 students (7 male and 6 female) from Ming Chi University of Technology. Their mean age was 20.44 ± 0.34 years. Their vision (or corrected vision) was 1.0 or higher, and none had an eye disease or impairment. The experimental equipment was a 22-inch LCD monitor, a personal computer, and a gaze tracking system (seeingmachines faceLAB^{TM} 5). The experimental material is shown in Fig. 1. The "+"

sign on the left was the starting point. To the right was a set of three tiles adjacent to one another. The yellow tile in the middle was the target tile, and the blue tiles (on either side of the yellow tile) were interference tiles. The distance from the starting point to the target tile was 600 pixels. In the center of the static tile was the lowercase "e"; in the center of the dynamic tile, a lowercase "e" and an uppercase "E" alternated at a 0.1 s interval.

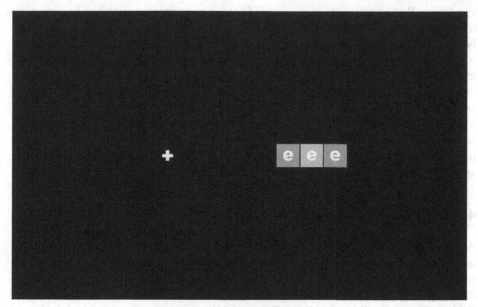

Fig. 1. Gaze pointing experimental material.

Two independent variables were investigated, namely tile type and tile size. Tile type involved dynamic or static target tiles and interference tiles. The possible combinations of target tile–interference tile display were static–static, dynamic–dynamic, static–dynamic, and dynamic–static. Three tile sizes were used, namely small (48 pixels), medium (96 pixels), and large (196 pixels). Thus, 12 (4 × 3) experimental conditions were present. The dependent variable was gaze pointing movement time, which was the time required for gaze pointing from the gaze starting point to the target tile. A within-subjects design was adopted. Each participant completed all experimental conditions. To obtain repeat observations, each participant repeated the test trial twice under each experimental condition. That is, they were asked to complete 24 (12 × 2) trials. To counterbalance the influence of time sequence (practice effect), block randomization was used to assign the experimental conditions to the participants.

Regarding the experimental setting, the screen displaying the experimental stimulus was placed on a table with a height of 75 cm. The center of the screen was 102 cm from the floor. The participants sat in front of the screen. The distance between the screen and the eyes of the participants was 79 cm. When seated, the distance of the participants' eyes from the floor was 116 cm. The parameters for the experimental tasks were fixed for all the participants. Ambient factors such as illumination, temperature, humidity, and noise were set to be comfortable and avoid interference. Before the experiment began, block randomization was used to determine the testing sequence of the experimental conditions. Pretest materials were provided for the participants to conduct five practice trials and familiarize themselves with the experimental procedures. When the experiment began, the participants were asked to gaze at the center of the + sign for 5 s in order to fix the gaze starting point. Subsequently, experimental stimuli were presented according to the sequence of experimental conditions. The participants moved their gaze from the starting point to the target tile as quickly as possible to complete a trial. Again, each experimental condition was repeated. At break of at least 2 min was provided between trials to prevent eye fatigue. During the experiment, the gaze tracking system simultaneously recorded the gaze time and the trajectory of the eye movements of the participants. SPSS (Statistical Product and Service Solutions) was used for statistical analysis.

4 Results and Discussion

Analysis of variance was conducted using single gaze pointing movement time (MT) as the dependent variable and using tile type (T), tile size (W), and participant (S) as independent variables. Single gaze pointing MT was defined as the time required for directing the gaze from the starting point to the target tile. The results are presented in Table 1. The main effect of S ($F(12,153) = 13.83$; $p < .0001$) as well as the interaction terms—T × W ($F(6,153) = 3.46$; $p = .0031$), S × W ($F(24,153) = 2.09$; $p = .0039$), and S × T × W ($F(71,153) = 1.39$; $p = .0475$)—reached the significance level of $\alpha = .05$. The other main effects of independent variables and interaction terms were nonsignificant. In addition to the interaction between T and W significantly affecting MT, then, MT was affected by individual differences among the participants.

Table 2 displays the mean estimation values of gaze pointing MT and 95% confidence interval (CI). Regarding tile type, the dynamic–static combination exhibited the shortest mean MT (590.4 ms), followed by static–dynamic (610.6 ms), dynamic–dynamic (626.2 ms), and then static–static (641.7 ms). However, these differences were not statistically significant. Thus, whether tiles were static or dynamic did not have significant influence on gaze pointing performance. For tile size, the medium tile (96 pixels) had the shortest mean MT (595.9 ms), followed by the small (46 pixels; 626.2 ms) and large (196 pixels; 630.2 ms) tiles. However, these differences too were not statistically significant. In other words, tile size did not have significant influence on gaze pointing performance.

Table 1. Analysis of variance of gaze pointing MT.

Source	SS	df	MS	F	p-value
Participant (S)	7204393.8	12	600366.2	13.83	.0000[**]
Tile type (T)	150407.6	3	50135.9	1.16	.3289
Tile size (W)	55249.0	2	27624.5	.64	.5305
T × W	901151.9	6	150192.0	3.46	.0031[*]
S × T	1972689.4	36	54796.9	1.26	.1679
S × W	2178818.5	24	90784.1	2.09	.0039[*]
S × T×W	4280344.4	71	60286.5	1.39	.0475[*]
Error	6639764.1	153	43397.2		

[*]$p < .05$; [**]$p < .001$

Table 2. Mean estimation value and 95% CI of the gaze pointing MT (ms) for main effects.

Variable	Level	Mean	SE	95% CI
Tile type	Dynamic–static[a]	590.4	24.2	542.5–638.2
	Static–dynamic	610.6	23.9	563.4–657.8
	Dynamic–dynamic	626.2	23.6	579.6–672.8
	Static–static	641.7	23.6	595.1–688.3
Tile size	Medium	595.9	20.6	555.2–636.7
	Small	626.2	20.6	585.5–667.0
	Large	630.2	20.6	589.4–670.9

[a]target tile–interference tile

Table 3 contains the mean estimation values for gaze pointing MT for the T–W interaction and 95% CI. As illustrated by Fig. 2, the static interference tile exhibited the same trend in W when its size was either small or medium (i.e., 46 pixels or 96 pixels), wherein gaze pointing MT decreased as W increased. When W was larger than 96 pixels, gaze pointing MT was constant (no longer increased or decreased as W increased). No other consistent trend was observed for other tile types and their tile size changes.

Table 3. Mean estimation value and 95% CI of gaze pointing MT (ms) for the interaction terms.

Tile type–Tile size	Mean	SE	95% CI
Dynamic–dynamic–Medium[a]	495.6	40.9	414.9–576.3
Static–dynamic–Small	569.7	42.4	485.9–653.4
Dynamic–static–Large	574.2	42.5	490.2–658.2
Dynamic–static–Medium	578.5	42.4	494.8–662.3
Static–dynamic–Large	584.3	40.9	503.6–665.0
Dynamic–static–Small	617.2	40.9	536.4–697.9
Static–static–Medium	631.9	40.9	551.2–712.6
Static–static–Large	637.6	40.9	556.9–718.3
Static–static–Small	655.7	40.9	575.0–736.4
Dynamic–dynamic–Small	662.5	40.9	581.7–743.2
Static–dynamic–Medium	677.8	40.9	597.1–758.5
Dynamic–dynamic–Large	720.4	40.9	639.7–801.1

[a]Target tile–interference tile–Tile size

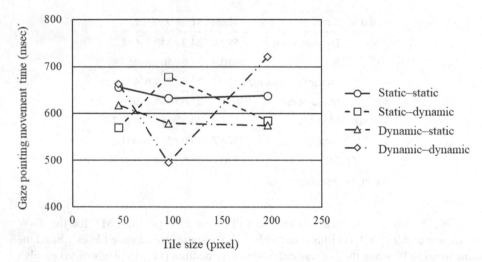

Fig. 2. Mean estimation value distribution of the gaze pointing MT for interaction terms.

5   Conclusions and Suggestions

This study employed an experimental method to explore the feasibility of integrating gaze pointing and the modern UI. The following conclusions and suggestions were discovered and proposed: (1) The participant variable exhibited a significant impact on gaze pointing MT—individual differences between users had a large influence on gaze pointing interface operational performance. Future gaze-aware computer interfaces will have to overcome this. (2) The impact of T and W on single gaze pointing MT was evident in their interaction terms; their main effects were nonsignificant. (3) When interference tiles were static, the gaze pointing mean MT decreased as W increased. However, when W was larger than 96 pixels, the MT was constant (it no longer increased or decreased as W increased).

Acknowledgments. The authors are grateful to the Ministry of Science and Technology for its special topic research project subsidy (project number MOST 106-2410-H-131-003).

References

1. Zhang, X., MacKenzie, I.S.: Evaluating eye tracking with ISO 9241 - part 9. In: Jacko, J.A. (ed.) HCI 2007. LNCS, vol. 4552, pp. 779–788. Springer, Heidelberg (2007). https://doi.org/10.1007/978-3-540-73110-8_85
2. Drewes, H.: Eye Gaze Tracking for Human Computer Interaction. PhD thesis. Media Informatics Group, LMU University of Munich (2010)
3. Murata, A.: Eye-gaze input versus mouse: cursor control as a function of age. Int. J. Hum.-Comput. Interact. **21**(1), 1–14 (2006)
4. Murata, A., Moriwaka, M.: Basic study for development of web browser suitable for eye-gaze input system-identification of optimal click method. In: Fifth International Workshop on Computational Intelligence and Applications, vol. 2009, no. 1, pp. 302–305. IEEE SMC Hiroshima Chapter (2009)
5. Murata, A., Hayashi, K., Moriwaka, M., Hayami, T.: Study on character input methods using eye-gaze input interface. In: 2012 Proceedings of IEEE SICE Annual Conference (SICE), pp. 1402–1407 (2012)
6. Ware, C., Mikaelian, H. H.: An evaluation of an eye tracker as a device for computer input. In: ACM SIGCHI Bulletin, vol. 17, no. SI, pp. 183–188. ACM (1987)
7. Grossman, L.: Flatland: should the virtual world try to look like the real one? Time (2013)
8. Page, T.: Skeuomorphism or flat design: future directions in mobile device user interface (UI) design education. Int. J. Mobile Learn. Organ. **8**(2), 130–142 (2014)
9. Schneidermeier, T., Hertlein, F., Wolff, C.: Changing paradigm – changing experience? In: Marcus, A. (ed.) DUXU 2014. LNCS, vol. 8517, pp. 371–382. Springer, Cham (2014). https://doi.org/10.1007/978-3-319-07668-3_36
10. Lindberg, T., Näsänen, R.: The effect of icon spacing and size on the speed of icon processing in the human visual system. Displays **24**(3), 111–120 (2003)

Touchless Information Provision and Facial Expression Training Using Kinect

Seiji Hayashi[1]([✉]) and Hiroyuki Igarashi[2]

[1] Department of Electronics and Computer Systems, Faculty of Engineering,
Takushoku University, Tokyo, Japan
shayashi@es.takushoku-u.ac.jp
[2] Mechanical and Electronic Systems Course, Graduate School of Engineering,
Takushoku University, Tokyo, Japan

Abstract. In this report, we present a touchless information provision system and facial expression training using Kinect that can be operated intuitively. This system is intended to allow the user to easily acquire various information by hand gestures. Further, the application has a facial expression training application that brings the advantages of a gaming user interface to the field of healthcare. This system was evaluated and its basic design was verified through actual experiments.

Keywords: Kinect · Touchless interface · Information service · Face expression training

1 Introduction

Due to the current coronavirus pandemic, development of an interface system that can be operated without physical contact is regaining attention as a lifestyle tool to prevent infectious disease transmission in the future. As a substitute for the conventional touch screen, recently stationary non-contact devices equipped with a camera and a depth sensor, such as Kinect [1–4], and a wearable artificial intelligence eye-tracking device [5,6] using image analysis technology have been developed. Because the eye-tracking device has drawbacks, such as determining an appropriate installation distance for the device and the wearing of glasses, in this study, we used a touchless interface that allows intuitive operation with the gestures recognized by Kinect. We developed a prototype application that can provide various information and be trained with facial expressions using a gaming interface, and here discuss the results of actual use in experiments. As for the environment to use, we assume that it will be used in welfare facilities and hospitals, and target relatively elderly people who are not familiar with personal computers. We also aim to customize its functions according to the environment.

In previous research, one study focused on the operation of the information presentation interface, and an instruction interface that combines a presentation

C. Stephanidis et al. (Eds.): HCII 2021, CCIS 1420, pp. 90–97, 2021.
https://doi.org/10.1007/978-3-030-78642-7_13

mouse and gesture input by Kinect was proposed [7]. This does not replace all operations with only gesture input, but it enables complex processing by the stepwise operation of the mouse first and gestures second. Our research differs from the main purpose of this previous research because our goal was to develop an application that does not require precise mouse operation.

2 Application Development

We have developed an application that provides various information, such as news, weather, photos, phone and mirror functions, using Kinect. The application implements facial expression training, including some game elements, to judge the state of smiles and blinks in the mirror function.

2.1 Information Provision Using Touchless Interface

Table 1 shows the system development environment in our research.

Table 1. System development environment

Development environment	Visual Studio 2017 WPF C#
Sensor device	Kinect for Windows v2
Software library	Kinect for Windows SDK v2
Application tool	Visual Gesture Builder
API	Face Basics API

In Visual Studio, we developed a touchless interface application using Kinect WPF Controls, and used Kinect Studio to record the capture status of Kinect V2 and Visual Gesture Builder to create a gesture recognition machine by machine learning [8]. The main functions of this application are shown below, and an example of its execution is shown in Fig. 1.

1. With Kinect WPF Controls, the pointer is operated by hand gestures. You can also "click" on the pointer's location by moving your hand forward (equivalent to clicking a mouse button).
2. The following five functions are provided by clicking the relatively large buttons displayed on the home screen: 1) current weather in the specified area, 2) latest news in the specified area, 3) images in the saved folder, 4) call placement using the Skype application, and 5) mirror and facial judgment training functions.
3. The identification machine (bga file) created by Visual Gesture Builder recognizes the specified gesture and is used to terminate the application.

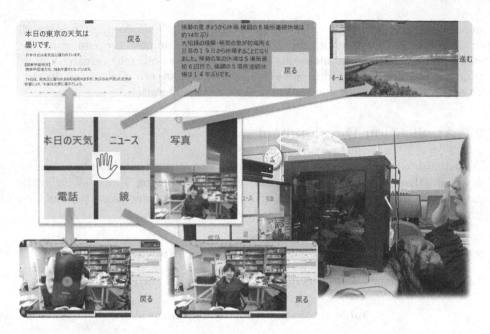

Fig. 1. Execution example of our touchless interface system

2.2 Recognition of Facial Smiling and Blinking

Because the act of moving the facial muscles or making a smirk may have the function of improving immunity [9], we provide the function of such facial conditioning using game-like training with a recognition function. Figures 2 and 3 show examples of when the smile and blink training is started and when it is successful. The training procedure created in our application is as follows [10].

1. The user moves the pointer with his or her hand and clicks the smile and blink training start button.
2. The user makes a smiling expression by following the instructions displayed in the upper right corner of the screen ("Make a smile" in Fig. 2). At this time, the score increases when a smile is recognized, and decreases otherwise.
3. When a certain period of time elapses with a smile (if the score exceeds 200 as shown in Fig. 3), the message "It's a nice smile" is displayed, and the blink training starts.
4. Similarly, blink training is performed in which the eyes are alternately closed. When all training is completed, the program returns to the initial state.

3 Experiments to Confirm Operation of Prototype Application

We asked general subjects who had no experience operating this application to actually use it, consider its difficulty level, and report the problems encountered during the experiment through a questionnaire.

Fig. 2. Screen shot when "smile training" starts

Fig. 3. Screen shot of successful "smile training"

3.1   Experiment Outline

With the cooperation of 10 women in their 50 s to 80 s, we conducted an experiment in a ceremony room as follows.

1. Subjects were asked to display the hand pointer and click on one of the icons in Fig. 1.
2. Then, subjects were asked to perform smile and blink training until smiling and blinking were successfully recorded as shown in Figs. 2 and 3.
3. Finally, subjects filled out a questionnaire after the experiment.

3.2   Experimental Results and Discussion

Figure 4 shows the number of trials until successful icon training and smile and blink training. In the post-experiment questionnaire, the following items were evaluated on a 5-point scale (Fig. 5):

1. Difficulty of making the hand pointer appear (1: difficult to 5: easy)
2. Difficulty in operating the hand pointer (1: difficult to 5: easy)
3. Smile and blink training difficulty (1: difficult to 5: easy)
4. Satisfaction levels other than smile and blink training (1: dissatisfied to 5: satisfied)
5. Would you like to use this application program? (1: No or 5: Yes)

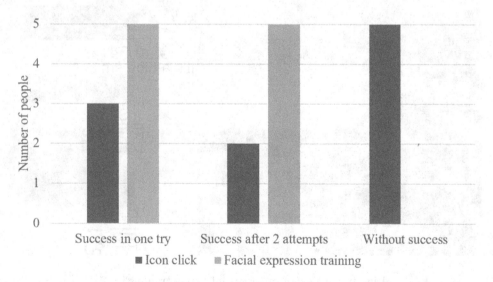

Fig. 4. Number of trials until successful icon training and smile and blink training

In the gesture recognition by icon clicking in Fig. 4, 3 people succeeded in one trial, 2 people performed the operation after more than 2 times, and 5

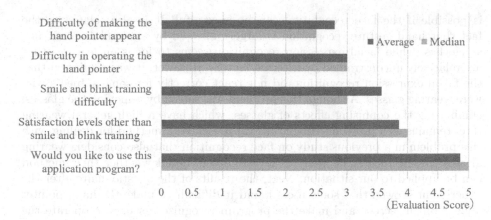

Fig. 5. Questionnaire results after the experiment

subjects could not operate the icon in 5 attempts (the maximum number of trials). This is because elements of "room brightness", "color and material of the subject's clothes", and "subject's age" are related to the recognition performance of Kinect, and it is also due to the difficulty and habituation of operation of Kinect WPF Controls. The specifications for Kinect state that the brightness of the room affects the recognition accuracy. It is considered that the operation of Kinect could not be fully effective, because the brightness of the ceremony room for the experiment was lower than that of a general room. In addition, because the depth sensor of Kinect uses infrared rays, it is considered that the recognition rate will be degraded when the user wears black clothes or clothes made of materials with uneven textures, such as wool, that block light reflection. Most of the subjects wore black clothes and textured clothes to provide warmth due to the season when the experiment was performed. It is considered that such conditions decreased the recognition rate.

Furthermore, a previous study described that the gestures of young people and the elderly have differences [11]. Gesture recognition discriminates the completion of motion using a certain threshold, and it is considered that diminished accuracy of movement due to aging affects the gesture recognition. In the initial gesture operation, it is necessary to place your hand beside your face to make the hand pointer appear, and failure at this point is one of the factors that degraded the success rate. It was found that the application could not recognize this gesture in half of the subjects, even in an environment where the authors could easily make the pointer appear. In the future, it is necessary to confirm the effect of skill level on gesture recognition.

Next, regarding the success rate of smile and blink training shown in Fig. 4, the expressions of 5 people could be recognized in one trial, the expressions of 5 people could be recognized in ≥2 trials, and no-one failed this training in the maximum of 5 trials. The reason why all subjects succeeded in recognition is considered to be deeply related to the fact that training of smiles and blinks is possible if the face recognition can be successful. It is also related to the fact that hand gesture recognition is largely affected by external factors, such as clothes, while facial expression recognition seems to focus on features that are relatively unconstrained by external factors. However, it was confirmed that the facial expression recognition did not react correctly for some subjects who were wearing glasses. Although this problem was solved by removing the glasses, eliminating the confusing effects of glasses, which have a high general wearing rate, remains as a problem. Hua et al. [12] presented a method for dealing with this problem in a previous study on face recognition that also considers wearing glasses. In the future, we want to investigate in detail whether their method can be applied to our situation. Next, the results of the questionnaire after the experiment showed that some users found it difficult to make the hand pointer appear on the screen and make the program recognize gestures to operate the pointer itself after it appears. It was also confirmed that facial expression training is less difficult than training for gesture recognition to manipulate a hand pointer. Moreover, because many subjects wanted to use this application in the future if available, it can be said that our this research is important for the general public by further improving touchless systems.

4   Conclusion

This paper presents an application we developed to provide information using a touchless interface and also provide a smiling and blinking training function. We aimed to create a user interface that is relatively easy for elderly people to use by recognizing gestures and facial expressions using Kinect. We implemented a function to provide basic information, such as news and weather, and implemented a system that stimulates facial activity by eliciting certain facial expressions. Moreover, to evaluate this application, we conducted experiments with general subjects who completed questionnaires to report their experience. As a result, regarding hand gesture recognition, 5 out of 10 people succeeded in using the interface to access information. Various factors, such as the brightness of the room and black clothing color, greatly contributed to failure. In contrast, in the facial expression recognition, it was found that recognition mistakes occurred when the user wore glasses, but all 10 subjects succeeded in the expression recognition task after wearers removed their glasses. In addition, the questionnaire after the experiment confirmed that the application is potentially useful, although some improvements, such as reducing the difficulty of gesture recognition, are needed in the future.

References

1. Kinect for Windows Homepage. https://developer.microsoft.com/en-us/windows/kinect/. Accessed 5 Mar 2021
2. Nakamura, K.: Using Kinect to make gesture-input-compatible home appliances. Nikkei Electronics, Nikkei BP, no. 1065, pp. 121–131 (2011)

3. Chiba, S.: Kinect as a next-gen interface. J. Robot. Soc. Jpn. **32**(3), 231–235 (2014)
4. Nakamura, K., Sugiura, T., Takada, T., Ueda, T.: Kinect for Windows SDK programming Kinect for Windows v2 Sensor handling version. Shuwa System Corporation (2015)
5. Tobii Technology Homepage. https://www.tobii.com/. Accessed 5 Mar 2021
6. Watana, K., Hosoya, K., Gomi, Y.: Analysis of medical care information system UI with eye-tracking and tracing mouse. In: The 78th Information Processing Society of Japan, vol. 2016, no. 1, pp. 373–374 (2016)
7. Hiroyuki, Y., Yusuke, N., Shun, S., Tadachika, O., Toramatsu, S.: On a gesture recognition mechanism for realizing a slide-show presentation. Inform. Process. Soc. Jpn. Inst. Electron. Inform. Commun. Eng. **10**(4), 529–530 (2011)
8. Igarashi, H., Hayashi, S.: A study on information provision by touch-less interface in a hospital room. In: The 2018 IEICE Engineering Sciences Society / NOLTA Society Conference, A-15-10, p. 127 (2018)
9. Social welfare corporation Homepage, Minami Tohoku welfare corporation, General Minami Tohoku welfare center, One point rehabilitation "Effect of laughter". http://www.kaigo-hiwada.com/backnum/2015/07/post-1004.html. Accessed 5 Mar 2021
10. Igarashi, H., Hayashi, S.: Examination of gamification for rehabilitation using face state recognition. In: The 2019 IEICE Engineering Sciences Society / NOLTA Society Conference, A-15-10, p. 108 (2019)
11. Susumu, S.: Development of gymnastics support system for elderly people using Kinect sensor and practical study for social implementation. The Telecommunications Advancement Foundation, Research Investigation Grant Report, no. 32, pp. 1–9 (2017)
12. Chunsheng, H., Haiyuan, W., Tadayoshi, S.: Detecting the existence of glasses and extracting the facial feature points automatically. IEICE Technical report. Pattern recognition and media understanding, vol. 102, no. 554, pp. 91–96 (2003)

A Case Study on the Effect of Movement Expression Activities Using Kinect on the Resilience of the Intellectually Disability

SungHee Hong[(✉)] and TaeWoon Kim

Dongyang University, Yeongju, Gyeongbuk 36040, Republic of Korea
hongsungh22@hanmail.net

Abstract. In this study, the purpose of this study is to find out a case study on the resilience of the intellectually disability by the Kinect sensor-based motion expression activity in a program using ICT. The characteristics of the movement through Laban's LMA include the change of time in which movement occurs through the human body recognizes space and the tension or relaxation of emotional expression. As a result of the experiment, 24 movement expression activities conducted through 10 learning sessions of 5 participants showed a concordance rate of 53.4% or more of the total average. Learning motion games that appear in response to changes in motion had a good effect on positive learning emotions. The purpose of this study is to suggest that the movement expression activity of intellectually disabled people is effective in the learning process of LMA motion recognition based on Kinect sensor.

Keywords: Azure kinect · Laban Motion Analysis (LMA) · Resilience

1 Introduction

With the recent epidemic of the corona19 infectious disease around the world, the government and the Ministry of Education have produced and distributed educational materials to improve youth's resilience. The educational field is also changing a lot as we face the unintended era of un-tact due to Corona 19. In particular, living in group facilities and experiencing unforeseen society has made it more difficult for people with disabilities who are vulnerable to infectious diseases to do outside activities. As they cannot attend school or spend less time with people around them, they are becoming increasingly isolated. It is very important to provide a new learning experience in the educational field for the disabled. People with intellectual disabilities have inadequate changes in their intellectual abilities without training or education, so negative experiences resulting from inexperienced self-expression develop negative self-concepts. As a result, negative self-expression increases, and relationships are also difficult to form. From this point of view, support and efforts to develop self-expression for intellectually disabled people are very important. In particular, in the case of adults with intellectual disabilities who are engaged in shared life and vocational activities, the provision of education and therapeutic support measures that can reduce negative self-expression and

C. Stephanidis et al. (Eds.): HCII 2021, CCIS 1420, pp. 98–104, 2021.
https://doi.org/10.1007/978-3-030-78642-7_14

provide positive interaction experiences is a very important factor for helping adaptive behavior. For people with intellectual disabilities, emotional instability is that negative movements such as lack of confidence and self-expression can be reduced to positive movements of thoughts that appear from the psycho-emotional side. In the game, the movement steps of achieving a set goal, learning, and training are performed. When the goal is to regulate and purify emotions, it induces continuous reproduction of meanings and emission of emotions through repetitive expressions and appreciation. Since the somatosensory elements of the virtual world emphasize interactivity and physical experience, they are closely connected with cognitive, emotional, and sensory stimulation through the physical stimulation of the senses. Also, unlike movies or TV, games are controlled within the game environment because the user is the controller at the point of view. It allows people with intellectual disabilities to construct a flexible ego with multiple perspectives. Resilience decreases the likelihood of having negative consequences in stressful situations caused by psychological and emotional difficulties and anxiety. Positive expectations for the future and positive results for hope can be induced. In the era of on-tect (online + Internet), the educational field is also changing a lot. It is very important to provide new learning experiences in the educational field for disabled people who are becoming increasingly isolated as they cannot attend school or spend time with others around them. Therefore, this study needs a new learning experience while experiencing a motion expression activity program based on the Kinect sensor. It intends to present various content case studies of motion recognition model development by experiencing the motion recognition learning process. In this study, as a convergence and complex study using ICT, motion recognition games were conducted for the disabled, using LMA movement activities as a basis. The quality of movement through Laban's LMA is that movement occurs through the human body that recognizes space. These movements appear differently according to changes in weight, including changes in time and tension or relaxation in emotional expression. In this study, we set the iterative learning process as the basic motion for expressing emotions. Learning effect through repetitive vocational training for intellectually disabled people functional game content proposal for diagnosing and improving cognitive function playing digital textbooks for special education for the disabled Developed as the significance of character education in elementary physical education using games. Therefore, this study aims to present a case study that allows students to have a positive thinking learning process while experiencing a movement activity program based on the Kinect sensor. The research was presented only as an educational game.

2 Methods

2.1 Participants

The subjects of this study were 5 persons with intellectual disabilities and were conducted 2–3 times a week for 10 weeks Table 1.

Table 1. Research subject characteristics

Name (age, gender)	Degree of disability	Disability characteristics
Ma (28, M)	Mild	Communication is possible, lack of expressiveness, and a lot of desire
Kim (25, F)	Mild	Can communicate and tend to do only what they want
Go (19, M)	Mild	Can communicate and have a willingness to actively participate in their favorite programs
Choi (24, M)	Mildly severe	Receiving language is possible, but expressive language is somewhat difficult and sincere, I try hard no matter what I do
Go (24, F)	Mild	Can communicate, somewhat introspective and passive

2.2 Research Design

The progress of the program design was set as the concept of the game. 3 dance doctors (1 Korean dance major, 2 modern dance majors), game program technician, and dance therapist participated in the Laban movement setting. Participants were asked to follow the motion of the silhouette appearing on the game screen. At the same time as the appearance of the motion silhouette, the figure of the participant was also projected on the screen, and if it was adjusted to a certain level of motion (6 equal points in 12 joint values) the score was raised with the sound of 'ding-dong'. This was set to give the game adaptability and motivation, and the skeleton's joint value was assigned to each motion according to motion recognition. At this time, the default value of the joint was set based on the silhouette of the demonstrator's motion (see Fig. 1).

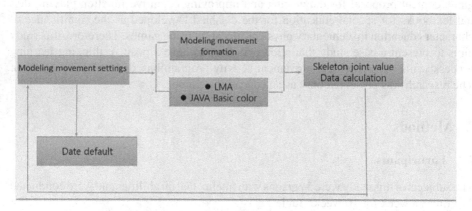

Fig. 1. Research design model

2.3 Azure Kinect

Azure Kinect is a developer with advanced AI sensors that provide visual and audio models with sophisticated computer vision, with more sophisticated sensor functionality than the existing Kinect1 and Kinect360 (see Fig. 2). Azure Kinect includes a depth sensor, an array of spatial microphones with video cameras, and a direction sensor, an all-in-one compact device with multiple modes, options, and SDK (Software Development Kinect).

Fig. 2. Main components of the frame (https://azure.microsoft.com)

2.4 Motion Recognition Program Progress

In the first scene of the motion game, the individual's simple name, gender, and date of birth were recorded to calculate the joint value of each individual skeleton (see Fig. 3).

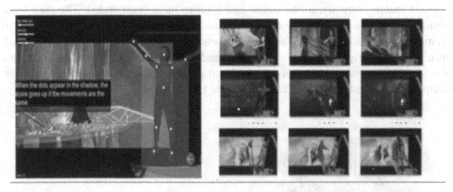

Fig. 3. Program motion recognition progress.

In order to have time to communicate with Kinect, the movement was performed after practicing the three-scene movement at the same time as the start. In this study, in the motion game content setting, four basic emotions of humans (Joy, anger, sadness, reconciliation). The set to move, expressive activity. The rhythm of music and animation images that change according to emotions were set. The motion movement of the movement was connected to the video and the music. All motion movements were produced as videos. Selected music, video, and motion were mapped (see Fig. 4).

※ The animation uses Frozen 1 for educational purposes.

Fig. 4. Emotion in motion.

- As for the emotion of movement, four emotions were selected: anger, sadness, joy, and reconciliation.
- I selected a scene from Frozen 1, an animation that expresses motion and background music that matches the emotions, and this was performed only for educational purposes.
- Repetitively Laban movements that fit the emotion.

3   Results

Motion scores the elements of motion according to the motion performance ability of the game participant. If the picture and movement of the Kinect skeleton provided on the screen match correctly, a bell sound and a score have been added. The data were evaluated for the timing of participation in the movement game and the ability to perform movements after participation. The perfect skeleton value for each movement (head, right-left shoulder, right-left elbow, right-left hand, pelvis, right-left knee, and right- left foot with 12 joint values) was scored. A visual effect on the screen appeared so that participants could recognize the change in score (see Fig. 5).

Fig. 5. Emotion skeleton joint values.

The time given to an action that appears on the screen was set to 20 s, and in this study, eight actions were selected as a case study and the score was measured. The test time required by one participant for the game was set within 2 min 40 s to 3 min. In order to organize the data, it was suggested that the data is collected through the posture of the movements according to the game movement, and the score increases by giving the feedback of the bell sound when the movements matched the movement program. On the other hand, no points were given for the scenes expressing inconsistent motions of the participant's posture, and they rendered their own appearance on the screen and checked their movements through them. Analysis of these data calculated the average of the highest and lowest scores after the performance of movement activity and 10 times participation (see Fig. 6).

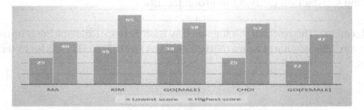

Fig. 6. Emotion skeleton joint values.

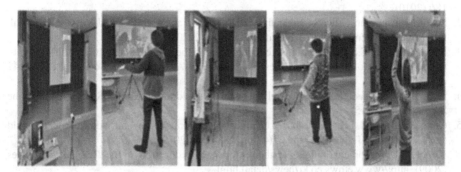

Fig. 7. Participating in a motion recognition game.

4   Conclusion

In this study, Laban's LMA was constructed by using Azure Kinect for the intellectually disabled. The motion recognition program content re cognizes the user's motion information and provides it to the kit sensor. A motion recognition model method generated from each vector was proposed by extracting the feature points of the skeletal model. The design and implementation of the motion recognition model will be described, and the possibility of using the proposed motion recognition model is verified through a simple experiment (see Fig. 7). As a result of the experiment, 24 movement expression activities conducted through 10 learning sessions of 5 participants showed a concordance rate of

53.4% or more of the total average. After the end of the motion work, the score display was set to give the participant the motivation to do better through the recognition of their performance ability and comparison with other participants.

After participating in the Kinect sensor-based LMA movement program, the score continued to increase statistically and significantly.

It was found that it can effectively change the learning time of motion expression activities of intellectually disabled people who participated in the motion recognized model program using ICT. In particular, continuous and systematic development and management of programs provided to intellectually disabled persons residing in facilities can improve the quality of learning about movement activities and contribute to increasing the satisfaction of living in group facilities.

Acknowledgement. This research was supported by Basic Science Research Program through the National Research Foundation of Korea (NRF2020R1I1A1A0107163311) funded by the Ministry of Education.

References

1. Johnson, J., Gooding, P.A., Wood, A.M., Tarrier, N.: Resilience as positive coping appraisals: testing the schematic appraisals model of suicide (SAMS). Behav. Res. Therapy **48**(3), 179–186 (2010)
2. Seoul Metropolitan Office of Education. 2020 Democratic Citizen EDU-Vaccine Proposal. Department of Democratic Citizen Life Education (2020)
3. Kim, M.S., Lee, C.S.: The mediating effect of hope in the relationship between self-elasticity and self-reliance of youth in facilities. J. Korean Ind.-Acad. Technol. Soc. **13**(2), 636–641 (2012)
4. Huh, Y.J.: Analysis of remediation self on game as a medium. J. Korean Soc. Comput. Game **28**(3), 59–64 (2015)
5. Craig, S., Misurell, J.R.: Game-based cognitive-behavioral therapy individual model for child sexual abuse. Int. J. Play Therapy **21**(4), pp. 188–201 (2012)
6. Kim, I.S.: Development of digital textbooks for special education for the disabled with games (2009). http://www.etnws.co.kr/news/detall.html
7. Kwon, J.M., Kim, M.Y.: Job training for the intellectually handicapped using functional games: a study on contents for game use of vocational skills textbook. Korea Comput. Game Soc. **25**(4), 35–46 (2012)
8. Hong, S.H.: A study on the effects of physical activity expression activity on self-expression ability and self-esteem of students with intellectual disabilities. Korean J. Arts Educ. **15**(1), 127–140 (2017)
9. Hong, S.H.: Children with intellectual disabilities movement expression activity: a study on functional game contents using motion graphics and kinect. Korean J. Arts Educ. **7**(3), 121–136 (2019)
10. Ji, S.W., Jung, J.B., Nam, K.C., Choi, M.G.: Design and implementation of cognitive enhancement games for rehabilitation of old mans. J. Korean Comput. Game Soc. **14**, 239–246 (2008)
11. Park, S.J., Lm, H.J.: The significance of elementary physical education class using games as character education. Korean J. Elem. Phys. Educ. **17**(3), 179–190 (2011)

Body-Part Attention Probability for Measuring Gaze During Impression Word Evaluation

Ken Kinoshita$^{(\boxtimes)}$, Michiko Inoue, Masashi Nishiyama⬤, and Yoshio Iwai

Graduate School of Engineering, Tottori University, 101 Minami 4-chome,
Koyama-cho, Tottori 680-8550, Japan
m20j4013x@edu.tottori-u.ac.jp, nishiyama@tottori-u.ac.jp

Abstract. We investigate how to probabilistically describe the distribution of gaze with respect to body parts when an observer evaluates impression words for an individual in an image. In the field of cognitive science, analytical studies have reported how observers view a person in an image and form impressions about him or her. However, a probabilistic representation of their gaze distributions has not yet been discussed. Here, we represent the gaze distribution as a conditional probability according to each body part. To do this, we measured the gaze distribution of observers performing a task that consists of assessing an impression word. We then evaluated whether these distributions change with respect to the impression word and body part specified in the task. Experimental results show that the divergences between the conditional probabilities of gaze distributions are large when the impression words or body parts of the task are changed.

Keywords: Impression words · Body parts · Observers · Gaze distribution · Probability

1 Introduction

A person's impression is important in large, formal occasions, such as weddings and parties. For example, when we attend a wedding ceremony, we take care to make an impression on the attendees that is appropriate for the occasion. In this paper, we analyze the impressions made by individuals in images photographed in formal scenes. We assume that observers are seeing these individuals for the first time.

We consider several words that describe the impressions made by people photographed in formal scenes, such as "beautiful," "cute," "clean," "elegant," and "friendly." When observers are asked about these impression words while looking at an image of a person, many observers are likely to provide the same responses. For example, if we ask observers whether the person shown in Fig. 1(a) is beautiful, we assume that many observers will respond that she is beautiful and some will respond that she is not. Suppose that we ask whether the person in

© Springer Nature Switzerland AG 2021
C. Stephanidis et al. (Eds.): HCII 2021, CCIS 1420, pp. 105–112, 2021.
https://doi.org/10.1007/978-3-030-78642-7_15

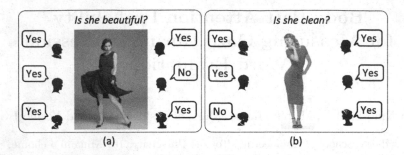

Fig. 1. Examples of observers evaluating whether an impression word describes a person in an image

the image shown in Fig. 1(b) is clean. "Clean," like "beautiful," is an impression word, so we should obtain similar results.

Here, we focus on a technique that automatically predicts the impression words that describe individuals in images. To do this, machine-learning and deep-learning techniques are usually applied. In recent years, methods that incorporate the gaze distribution of image observers into machine- and deep-learning techniques have emerged [4,5,7,9–11]. These existing methods should improve the prediction accuracy in practice even when a large number of training samples cannot be collected. However, these existing methods do not consider how to handle the gaze distribution in terms of impression words in machine- and deep-learning techniques.

In cognitive science, several analytical studies [1,2,6,8] have reported how observers view an image of a person and form impressions of him or her. In these analytical studies, observers were given the task of evaluating their impression words with respect to the image of a person, and their gaze locations were measured. The results showed that the observers spatially located their gaze on various body parts, mainly the face. The results also showed that gaze locations change depending on the impression words given in the task. However, these analytical studies did not discuss how to incorporate the gaze distribution measured from observers into practical applications that perform impression evaluation tasks using machine- and deep-learning techniques. The gaze distribution should be represented probabilistically when applying these techniques.

To achieve this, we propose a method for probabilistically representing the gaze distribution that indicates which body parts are frequently viewed when observers evaluate an impression word for a body part in an image of a person. We also investigate whether there are differences in the probability distributions of impression words by measuring the gaze locations of observers.

2　Measurement of the Gaze Locations of Observers

To investigate whether the probabilistic representation of gaze distribution would be of value if incorporated into machine- and deep-learning techniques, an

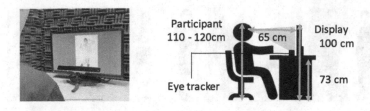

Fig. 2. Settings for measuring the gaze distribution.

impression predictor should be constructed and its prediction accuracy should be evaluated. However, the prediction accuracy will not be improved if the gaze distribution does not change depending on the impression word. In this paper, we first investigate whether the gaze distribution varies by evaluating a probabilistic representation. For our investigation, we hypothesize the following:

- Gaze distribution changes when tasks with different impression words and different body parts are given to the participants.

In our investigation, we assigned observers six tasks ($\mathcal{T} = \{t_1, ..., t_6\}$) in which they evaluated impression words for formal scenes to measure the observers' gaze locations. The tasks are as follows:

- t_1: Do you feel the person's hands are beautiful?
- t_2: Do you feel the person's hands are clean?
- t_3: Do you feel the person's hands are cute?
- t_4: Do you feel the person's feet are beautiful?
- t_5: Do you feel the person's feet are clean?
- t_6: Do you feel the person's feet are cute?

The participants answered yes or no for each stimulus image in each task. Twenty-four participants (12 males and 12 females, average age 22.4 years, Japanese students) participated in the study.

Figure 2 shows the settings for measuring the gaze distribution of the participants. We used a measurement device (Gazepoint GP3 HD) and a 24-inch display for gaze location recording. Figure 3 shows a subset of the 96 stimulus images of people used in our experiments. In all stimulus images, the whole body is contained and the posture of the person is unrestricted. Our method represents the frequency of gaze locations in terms of each body part b of the subject in the stimulus image as a conditional probability of each task t. Figure 4 shows the body parts $b_1, \ldots, b_{12}$ used for computing the conditional probability.

3   Probabilistic Representation of Gaze Distribution

3.1   Pixel-Attention Probability for Each Stimulus Image

We consider a probability that represents how many gaze locations are concentrated on each pixels of a stimulus image when a task t is given to a participant.

Fig. 3. Example stimulus images $\mathcal{X}_x$ of people.

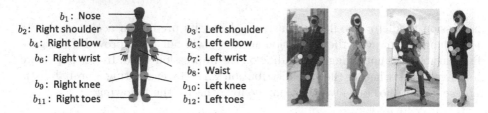

b_1: Nose
b_2: Right shoulder b_3: Left shoulder
b_4: Right elbow b_5: Left elbow
b_6: Right wrist b_7: Left wrist
                        b_8: Waist
b_9: Right knee b_{10}: Left knee
b_{11}: Right toes b_{12}: Left toes

Fig. 4. Body parts $b_1, \ldots, b_{12}$ used for computing the body-part attention probability.

In this study, a stimulus image is represented as a set of pixels $\mathcal{X}_x$. Suppose that a gaze location is measured at location (pixel) $\boldsymbol{x}_f$ from participant i when a certain frame f is shown. We represent the probability as follows:

$$p(\boldsymbol{x}_j|t, i, \mathcal{X}_x, f) = \mathcal{N}(\boldsymbol{x}_j|\boldsymbol{x}_f, \boldsymbol{\Sigma}), \tag{1}$$

where $\mathcal{N}(\boldsymbol{x}_j|\boldsymbol{x}_f, \boldsymbol{\Sigma})$ is a bivariate normal distribution with mean vector $\boldsymbol{x}_f$ and covariance matrix $\boldsymbol{\Sigma}$. Note that this representation satisfies as follows: $\sum_{\boldsymbol{x}_j \in \mathcal{X}_x} p(\boldsymbol{x}_j|t, i, \mathcal{X}_x, f) = 1$.

When gaze is measured, gaze locations will not be observed for some frames because of eye blinks or noise. As a result, the total number of frames varies in each gaze location recording. We use $\mathcal{F}_{ti}$ to denote the set of frames in which gaze locations are measured from a participant i performing task t. Here, we marginalize the probability using all frames $\mathcal{F}_{ti}$ as follows:

$$p(\boldsymbol{x}_j|t, i, \mathcal{X}_x) = \sum_{f \in \mathcal{F}_{ti}} p(\boldsymbol{x}_j|t, i, \mathcal{X}_x, f)p(f). \tag{2}$$

We approximate $p(f)$ using a uniform distribution $1/F_{ti}$ as follows:

$$p(\boldsymbol{x}_j|t, i, \mathcal{X}_x) = \frac{1}{F_{ti}} \sum_{f \in \mathcal{F}_{ti}} p(\boldsymbol{x}_j|t, i, \mathcal{X}_x, f), \tag{3}$$

where F_{ti} is the number of frames of set $\mathcal{F}_{ti}$. Note that this probability satisfies $\sum_{\boldsymbol{x}_j \in \mathcal{X}_x} p(\boldsymbol{x}_j|t, i, \mathcal{X}_x) = 1$.

Next, we marginalize probability $p(\boldsymbol{x}_j|t, i, \mathcal{X}_x)$ according to the set of participants $\mathcal{I}_t$ performing task t as follows:

$$p(\boldsymbol{x}_j|t, \mathcal{X}_x) = \sum_{i \in \mathcal{I}_t} p(\boldsymbol{x}_j|t, i, \mathcal{X}_x) p(i). \tag{4}$$

We approximate $p(i)$ by uniform distribution $1/I_t$ as follows:

$$p(\boldsymbol{x}_j|t, \mathcal{X}_x) = \frac{1}{I_t} \sum_{i \in \mathcal{I}_t} p(\boldsymbol{x}_j|t, i, \mathcal{X}_x), \tag{5}$$

where I_t is the number of participants in set $\mathcal{I}_t$. Note that this equation satisfies $\sum_{\boldsymbol{x}_j \in \mathcal{X}_x} p(\boldsymbol{x}_j|t, \mathcal{X}_x) = 1$. We call $p(\boldsymbol{x}_j|t, \mathcal{X}_x)$ the pixel-attention probability.

Note that the people in the stimulus images have different postures, which means that their body regions are not aligned. Thus, pixel-attention probability can only handle a single stimulus image $\mathcal{X}_x$. In the next section, we describe a probabilistic representation that focuses on body parts to compare the probabilities among various stimulus images.

3.2 Body-Part Attention Probability

We define a probability that represents how many gaze locations are concentrated on body part b when participants observe stimulus image $\mathcal{X}_x$ in task t as follows:

$$p(b|t, \mathcal{X}_x) = \sum_{\boldsymbol{x}_j \in \mathcal{X}_x} p(b|\boldsymbol{x}_j, t, \mathcal{X}_x) p(\boldsymbol{x}_j|t, \mathcal{X}_x). \tag{6}$$

However, it is difficult to obtain this probability directly from the outputs of gaze measurements. We assume that a smaller distance between the measured gaze location and the body-part location means the probability that the gaze is located on that body part is higher. We assume $p(b|\boldsymbol{x}_j, t, \mathcal{X}_x) \propto \mathcal{N}(\boldsymbol{x}_j|\boldsymbol{x}_b, \boldsymbol{\Sigma})$ with the following:

$$p(b|t, \mathcal{X}_x) = \sum_{\boldsymbol{x}_j \in \mathcal{X}_x} \mathcal{N}(\boldsymbol{x}_j|\boldsymbol{x}_b, \boldsymbol{\Sigma}) p(\boldsymbol{x}_j|t, \mathcal{X}_x), \tag{7}$$

where $\boldsymbol{x}_b$ is the location for body part b, $\mathcal{N}(\boldsymbol{x}_j|\boldsymbol{x}_b, and\boldsymbol{\Sigma})$ is a bivariate normal distribution with mean vector $\boldsymbol{x}_b$ and covariance matrix $\boldsymbol{\Sigma}$. Note that this equation satisfies $\sum_{b \in \mathcal{B}} p(b|t, \mathcal{X}_x) = 1$, where $\mathcal{B} = \{b_1, \ldots, b_{12}\}$ is the set of body parts.

Next, we calculate the probability $p(b|t)$ that gaze is located on body part b for a given task t. We marginalize the probability using a set of stimulus images $\mathcal{X}$ as follows:

$$p(b|t) = \sum_{\mathcal{X}_x \in \mathcal{X}} p(b|t, \mathcal{X}_x) p(\mathcal{X}_x). \tag{8}$$

We approximate $p(\mathcal{X}_x)$ using uniform distribution $1/X$ as follows:

$$p(b|t) = \frac{1}{X} \sum_{\mathcal{X}_x \in \mathcal{X}} p(b|t, \mathcal{X}_x), \tag{9}$$

where X is the number of stimulus images. We call $p(b|t)$ the body-part attention probability.

Table 1. Body-part attention probabilities of body parts in the tasks for hands or feet.

Body part	Body-part attention probability (%)	
	Hands $p_{t_{1,2,3}}$	Feet $p_{t_{4,5,6}}$
Nose	16.73	12.73
Right shoulder	9.42	3.06
Left shoulder	10.42	3.16
Right elbow	8.35	2.55
Left elbow	9.46	2.24
Right wrist	17.00	3.98
Left wrist	16.61	4.66
Waist	7.93	13.54
Right knee	1.60	16.04
Left knee	1.48	18.90
Right toes	0.49	8.95
Left toes	0.51	10.19

4   Experimental Results

We first computed the body-part attention probability for the hands with $p_{t_{1,2,3}} = (p(b|t_1) + p(b|t_2) + p(b|t_3))/3$ using tasks t_1, t_2, and t_3. We also computed it for the feet with $p_{t_{4,5,6}} = (p(b|t_4) + p(b|t_5) + p(b|t_6))/3$ using tasks t_4, t_5, and t_6. Table 1 shows the body-part attention probabilities of the body parts under these two conditions (hands or feet). For $p_{t_{1,2,3}}$, the right and left wrists, which are adjacent to the hands, have higher probabilities than all other parts of the body except for the nose. For $p_{t_{4,5,6}}$, the lower body parts (waist, knees, and toes) have higher probabilities than the upper body parts (shoulders, elbows, and wrists). We believe that when a body part is included in the task, it is more likely that the participant's gaze is drawn to the body part itself in the task. We also believe that even if the face (nose) is not explicitly included in the task, the participants frequently look at the face.

Next, we computed the body-part attention probability for "beautiful" with $p_{t_{1,4}} = (p(b|t_1) + p(b|t_4))/2$ using tasks t_1 and t_4. We computed it for "clean" with $p_{t_{2,5}} = (p(b|t_2) + p(b|t_5))/2$ using tasks t_2 and t_5. We also computed it for "cute" with $p_{t_{3,6}} = (p(b|t_3) + p(b|t_6))/2$ using tasks t_3 and t_6. Table 2 shows the probabilities with respect to the impression words in the tasks ("beautiful," "clean," or "cute"). In $p_{t_{1,4}}$, the gaze is likely to be drawn to the wrists, waist, and knees when "beautiful" is evaluated. In $p_{t_{2,5}}$, the gaze is strongly drawn to the nose when "clean" is evaluated. Additionally, in $p_{t_{3,6}}$, the gaze is drawn

Table 2. Body-part attention probabilities for the impression words "beautiful," "clean," and "cute."

Body part	Body-part attention probability (%)		
	Beautiful $p_{t_{1,4}}$	Clean $p_{t_{2,5}}$	Cute $p_{t_{3,6}}$
Nose	9.46	21.55	13.18
Right shoulder	4.99	7.74	5.98
Left shoulder	5.42	8.39	6.56
Right elbow	4.77	6.00	5.58
Left elbow	5.86	5.84	5.85
Right wrist	11.44	9.10	10.93
Left wrist	11.20	9.07	11.65
Waist	12.77	10.43	9.00
Right knee	11.60	5.96	8.90
Left knee	12.85	8.04	9.69
Right toes	4.45	3.86	5.85
Left toes	5.19	4.02	6.83

to the nose and wrists when "cute" is evaluated. We confirmed that there is a tendency for the frequencies of the body parts viewed by the participants to change if the impression word in the task is changed.

Next, we compared how similar the gaze distributions for different impression words were in $p_{t_{1,4}}$, $p_{t_{2,5}}$, and $p_{t_{3,6}}$. To achieve this, we computed the distances between the conditional probability distributions of the tasks using the Jensen–Shannon (JS) divergence [3]. The JS divergence between "beautiful" $p_{t_{1,4}}$ and "clean" $p_{t_{2,5}}$ was $D_{JS}(p_{t_{1,4}}\|p_{t_{2,5}}) = 2.52$. The JS divergence between "clean" $p_{t_{2,5}}$ and "cute" $p_{t_{3,6}}$ was $D_{JS}(p_{t_{2,5}}\|p_{t_{3,6}}) = 1.25$. The JS divergence between "cute" $p_{t_{3,6}}$ and "beautiful" $p_{t_{1,4}}$ was $D_{JS}(p_{t_{3,6}}\|p_{t_{1,4}}) = 0.69$. To understand the meaning of these divergence values, we calculated the differences in the gaze distributions of male and female participants. We obtained $D_{JS}(p_{men}\|p_{women}) = 0.43$. We found that the differences in the body-part attention probabilities with respect to impression words were larger than the differences caused by the gender of the participants. We believe that there is a tendency for the conditional probabilities of gaze on body parts to differ with respect to impression words in formal scenes. Although we have not yet reached the level of incorporating gaze distribution into practical applications, our main contribution is the development of a probabilistic representation of the gaze distribution, which is a fundamental technique that is essential for these applications.

5   Conclusions

We proposed a method for representing a probability that indicates which body parts are frequently viewed when observers evaluate impression words in stimulus images. The experimental results show that the combinations of impression words and body parts contained in the tasks change the values of the JS divergence between conditional probabilities, which means the observers focus their gaze on different body parts of an individual in an image for each task. In future work, we intend to develop a method for predicting impression words using machine- and deep-learning techniques using our probabilistic gaze representation.

Acknowledgment. This work was partially supported by JSPS KAKENHI Grant No. JP20K11864.

References

1. Bareket, O., Shnabel, N., Abeles, D., Gervais, S., Yuval-Greenberg, S.: Evidence for an association between men's spontaneous objectifying gazing behavior and their endorsement of objectifying attitudes toward women. Sex Roles **81**(3), 245–256 (2018)
2. Dixson, B., Grimshaw, G., Linklater, W., Dixson, A.: Eye-tracking of men's preferences for waist-to-hip ratio and breast size of women. Arch. Sex. Behav. **40**, 43–50 (2009)
3. Fuglede, B., Topsoe, F.: Jensen-shannon divergence and hilbert space embedding. In: Proceedings of the IEEE International Symposium onInformation Theory, p. 31 (2004)
4. Murrugarra-Llerena, N., Kovashka, A.: Learning attributes from human gaze. In: Proceedings of IEEE Winter Conference on Applications of Computer Vision, pp. 510–519 (2017)
5. Nishiyama, M., Matsumoto, R., Yoshimura, H., Iwai, Y.: Extracting discriminative features using task-oriented gaze maps measured from observers for personal attribute classification. Pattern Recogn. Lett. **112**, 241–248 (2018)
6. Philippe, B., Gervais, S.J., Holland, A.M., Dodd, M.D.: When do people "check out" male bodies? appearance-focus increases the objectifying gaze toward men. Psychol. Men Masculinity **19**(3), 484–489 (2018)
7. Qiao, T., Dong, J., Xu, D.: Exploring human-like attention supervision in visual question answering. In: Proceedings of the 32nd AAAI Conference on Artificial Intelligence, pp. 7300–7307 (2018)
8. Riemer, A.R., Haikalis, M., Franz, M.R., Dodd, M.D., Dilillo, D., Gervais, S.J.: Beauty is in the eye of the beer holder: an initial investigation of the effects of alcohol, attractiveness, warmth, and competence on the objectifying gaze in men. Sex Roles **79**, 449–463 (2018)
9. Sattar, H., Bulling, A., Fritz, M.: Predicting the category and attributes of visual search targets using deep gaze pooling. In: Proceedings of IEEE International Conference on Computer Vision Workshops, pp. 2740–2748 (2017)
10. Sugano, Y., Ozaki, Y., Kasai, H., Ogaki, K., Sato, Y.: Image preference estimation with a data-driven approach: a comparative study between gaze and image features. Journal of Eye Movement Research, vol. 7, no. 3 (2014)
11. Wu, J., Zhong, S., Ma, Z., Heinen, S.J., Jiang, J.: Gaze aware deep learning model for video summarization. In: Proceedings of the Pacific Rim Conference on Multimedia, pp. 285–295 (2018)

Comparing the Accuracy and Precision of Eye Tracking Devices in Different Monitoring Environments

Roland Nazareth[✉] and Jung Hyup Kim

Department of Industrial and Manufacturing Systems Engineering,
University of Missouri-Columbia, Columbia, USA
Rnbh6@umsystem.edu, Kijung@missouri.edu

Abstract. The eye tracking technology is already being used in various research fields. However, only a few industrial eye tracking applications are available in the market due to the uncontrollable outcomes of the devices. For example, when the devices are used in a multi-monitoring environment, their outcomes are less consistent than a single monitoring environment. In addition, there are variances in accuracy and precision between eye tracking devices. Hence, it is necessary to compare the differences between various eye tracking devices in terms of accuracy and precision in different monitoring environments. In this study, we tested seven eye tracking devices in three different monitoring environments. The current study aims to compare the accuracy and precision of multiple eye tracking devices and identify the pros and cons of each system. The outcomes of this study might help researchers develop a better framework for the next generation of eye tracking devices.

Keywords: Eye tracking · Accuracy · Precision

1 Introduction

Eye tracking (ET) is an approach to measure person's eye movements. By using the eye tracking data, researchers can understand when the person's eyes are moving from one location to another relative to the head and where the person is looking at any given moment (Poole and Ball 2006). ET has become a popular tool in various fields of study (Du and Kim 2016; Kim and Yang 2020; Shotton and Kim 2021; Yang and Kim 2019), and yet it is not very common to have applications in industry (Punde et al. 2017).

Accuracy and precision are the ways to measure the quality of the eye movement data from various ET devices. In this study, the compensation between the recorded gaze point (data collected) and the actual gaze point (the true value) is denoted as accuracy. Besides, the scattering of the recorded gaze points (standard deviation between the gaze points) is called precision (Feit et al. 2017).

This study aims to compare the accuracy and precision of various ET devices and identify the pros and cons of each system in various monitoring tasks. The dependent variables of this experiment are the accuracy and precision of ET devices, whereas the independent variables are the ET devices and the environment.

© Springer Nature Switzerland AG 2021
C. Stephanidis et al. (Eds.): HCII 2021, CCIS 1420, pp. 113–120, 2021.
https://doi.org/10.1007/978-3-030-78642-7_16

2 Methods

2.1 Apparatus

In this study, multiple ET devices were used to collect eye gaze points and fixations from participants. Two types of ET devices were used, mainly classified as screen-based or table-mounted (also known as remote or desktop) and head-mounted (also known as glass type or mobile). This research tested seven different ET devices for three different tasks. We used all the seven ET devices (three table-mounted (A = Cheap, B = Intermediate, C = Expensive) and four head-mounted (D = Cheap, E = Intermediate, F = Intermediate, G = Expensive)) for the first task. However, for the second and third tasks, only three table-mounted and four head-mounted devices were used, respectively.

2.2 Participants

Five participants having an age range from 20–30 years, all of which are students at the University of Missouri, were made to go through the three different tasks in a fixed order. Gender was an irrelevant factor in the experiment and was not taken into consideration when selecting participants. None of the five participants wore glasses.

2.3 Experimental Setup

Task 1

In task 1, every participant was seated at 80 cms from the screen throughout the entire experiment. The height of the seating structure and monitor was adjusted, and the participant's eye was aligned with the center of the screen as indicated by the red line in Fig. 1. The table-mounted ET devices were fixed at a suitable position to capture the eye movement irrespective of the participant's physique (i.e., height, seating posture, and others). The seating position was always constant by keeping a chair in one location. Firstly, the ET devices were calibrated using the 9-point technique. This technique is used as it covers the entire screen, and the accuracy of each device should not only be good around the center of the screen but towards the corners as well. After the calibration is done to capture the participant's eye gaze, a randomized set of targets, was shown up on the screen and the participants were instructed to look at the center of each target. Each target was 2.1" × 2.1" by PowerPoint specifications and was not subjected to change for all ET devices.

Task 2

To compare the capabilities of three table-mounted devices, a multidirectional tapping task, called Fitts's law task, was used as task 2. Since it is commonly used to exam the relationship between the human perceptual processor and the motor processor, it is the most appropriate task to compare the capabilities of the table-mounted ET devices in two dimensions. Figure 2 shows the experiment setup for Fitts's law task in a single monitor environment.

Fig. 1. Experimental setup for Task 1 (Color figure online)

Fig. 2. Experimental setup for Task 2 (Color figure online)

Fig. 3. Experimental setup for Task 3 (Color figure online)

Task 3

Four head-mounted ET devices were tested to investigate their capabilities in a multi-monitor environment (task 3). Fitts's law task was also used in this experiment. The major difference compared to the single monitoring environment was that the participant must perform two Fitts's law tasks simultaneously. Both tasks appeared on dual screens. The experiment setup for task 3 is shown in Fig. 3.

2.4 Procedure

Task 1

Participants were instructed to see nine red calibration dots as accurately as possible until each red dot disappeared. The eye movement data, such as fixation and eye gaze points, were collected from each ET device.

To analyze the data for the table-mounted devices, the nine target points as seen in Fig. 1. were labeled as Top Left (TL), Center Middle (CM), Bottom Right (BR), and so on. Coordinates of the center of each target points were calculated with the help of using a mouse pointer. The mouse pointer was placed at the center of each target, and the coordinates were noted accordingly. In this test, accuracy is defined as how close a measured value is to the actual value. To calculate the accuracy of each device, the distance between the center of the targets and fixation points were calculated using Eq. (1)

$$d = \sqrt{(\Delta x)^2 + (\Delta y)^2} = \sqrt{(x_2 - x_1)^2 + (y_2 - y_1)^2} \tag{1}$$

The calculated distance was then used to convert into degrees, which was the device accuracy at each target.

For precision, it is defined as how close the measured values are to each other. Precision is a measure of how well the eye tracker can reliably reproduce a measurement. In this study, the precision was calculated in a similar way to measure the accuracy, which is using the consecutive fixation points and calculate the distance between them. The average distance at each target gives us the precision of the ET device. The steps for calculating the accuracy and precision of both head-mounted and table-mounted systems are also similar. One difference is that the coordinates of the target center were used as the reference point to calculate the accuracy and precision of the head-mounted tracking systems only.

The experiment was conducted as a two-factor experiment with repeated measures (within-subject). The first factor is the ET device. We compared seven ET devices as we described in Sect. 3.1. The second factor is the target. Based on the location of each target, there were nine levels Top Left (TL), Top Middle (TM), Top Right (TR), Center Left (CL), Center Middle (CM), Center Right (CR), Bottom Left (BL), Bottom Middle (BM), and Bottom Right (BR).

Task 2

Thirteen circles appeared on a monitor screen, and one of the circles was colored red as the initial eye fixation point before the participant start the task (see Fig. 4). When the participant started task 2 by clicking the red circle, the red circle color changed to white. The red color was moved to one of the other twelve circles, which had white color before the clicking. After that, the participant was required to click the red circle continuously.

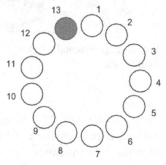

Fig. 4. Targets for task (Color figure online)

The participants must follow the red dots as seen in Fig. 2 and click on it using a mouse. Each set consists of 13 dots, and four sets were tested in each ET device. Each set was designed to test different complexity levels of Fitts's law task. The complexity level was based on the distance between two targets (D) and with (W) are analogous to Shannon's signal and noise theorem. By using the Fitts's index of difficulty ($ID = \log_2 \frac{2D}{W}$, *in bits*), the complexity level of each set was calculated (Set 1: 4 bits, Set 2: 5 bits, Set 3: 2.6 bits, and Set 4: 3.5 bits).

The different sets were designed to cover the entire screen area towards the corners and the center and various sizes to measure how precise the accuracy could be. The seating position, calibration techniques, positioning of screen, metrics, etc. were same as task 1. To analyze the data from the table-mounted devices in a single monitoring environment, the target points as seen in Fig. 4 were labeled 1–13 in a clockwise pattern. The accuracy and precision of each dot were calculated using the center of each dot as the reference point. The coordinates of the center of each target points were calculated with the help of using a mouse pointer on the monitor screen. The mouse pointer was placed at the center of each target, and the coordinates were noted accordingly. As the participant unknowingly had his gaze distributed to both the red dot and the cursor while performing the Fitts's law task, it is observed ET devices provided the corrected values of fixation. The other procedures of measuring both accuracy and precision were similar to task 1.

Task 3

For Task 3, the participants needed to follow and click the red dots similar to the single monitoring environment, i.e., Task 2. There was a total of 13 dots in each set and a total of 26 dots on both screens. The major difference while performing the task in a multi-monitoring environment was that the participants should move their head frequently to glance over the screens from time to time, called task switching. Hence, the participant will be required to carry out a lateral head movement to switch from one monitor to another with the eye and hand motions. The seating position, calibration techniques, positioning of the screen, metrics, etc., were the same as that of task 1. The procedure to analyze the data from the head-mounted ET devices in task 3 was similar to task 2.

3   Results

The eye gaze fixations obtained from the three tasks were compared using ANOVA. As shown in Table 1, the results showed that the overall accuracy of the first task was better than the second task, and the precision showed no significant difference between the task 1 and 2 (P-value = 0.870, F-value = 0.03).

Table 1. Mean and standard deviation for overall Accuracy and Precision of Task 1 and Task 2

	Task 1		Task 2		F-value	P-value
	Mean	SD	Mean	SD		
Accuracy	1.785	1.0212	2.0116	1.0034	17.29	**0.000**
Precision	0.9824	0.9213	0.9901	0.7069	0.03	0.870

Table 2 summarizes the comparisons between the ET devices, the results showed no significant difference between the accuracy of first and second tasks for devices B (P-value = 0.07, F-value = 3.13) and C (P-value = 0.341, F-value = 0.91). However, device A showed a better accuracy during the first task compared to the second task. Similarly, for precision, there was no significant difference between the accuracy of the first and second tasks for device C (P-value = 0.323, F-value = 0.98). For device A, the first task was better than the second task, and the second task was better than the first task for device B.

Table 2. Mean and standard deviation for Accuracy and Precision of Task 1 and Task 2

	Device	Task 1		Task 2		F-value	P-value
		Mean	SD	Mean	SD		
Accuracy	A	**0.9063**	0.4029	1.9329	0.9356	214.34	**0.000**
	B	2.4771	0.9132	2.3052	1.1194	3.13	0.077
	C	1.9145	0.9284	1.8344	0.9047	0.91	0.341
Precision	A	**0.4253**	0.268	1.0082	0.5663	155.54	**0.000**
	B	1.6863	1.111	**1.2874**	0.7228	17.93	**0.000**
	C	0.7983	0.6293	0.7372	0.6906	0.98	0.323

As shown in Table 3, The overall accuracy of the third task was better than the first task. For precision, the first task was better than the third task.

Table 4 outlines the comparisons between the devices, the results showed that the third task had better accuracy than the first task when they used devices E, F, and G. For precision, there was no significant difference on the accuracy between the first and third tasks for device E (P-value = 0.466, F-value = 0.53). The first task was better than the

Table 3. Mean and standard deviation for overall Accuracy and Precision of Task 1 and Task 3

	Task 1		Task 3		F-value	P-value
	Mean	SD	Mean	SD		
Accuracy	1.5786	0.953	1.3123	0.6523	46.91	**0.000**
Precision	0.6199	0.7171	0.8947	2.1848	12.89	**0.000**

Table 4. Mean and standard deviation for Accuracy and Precision of Task 1 and Task 3

	Device	Task 1		Task 3		F-value	P-value
		Mean	SD	Mean	SD		
Accuracy	D	**1.8245**	1.0163	2.1832	0.5474	10.61	**0.001**
	E	1.8375	1.0881	**1.5342**	0.4923	16.32	**0.000**
	F	1.5549	0.9286	**1.3998**	0.5081	5.39	**0.021**
	G	1.1019	0.4612	**0.6814**	0.2987	145.61	**0.000**
Precision	D	**0.6830**	1.1949	2.206	4.064	28.27	**0.000**
	E	0.7291	0.5730	0.7877	1.0803	0.53	0.466
	F	0.6197	0.4871	**0.4257**	0.3151	27.81	**0.000**
	G	0.4500	0.2415	**0.2599**	0.2075	87.00	**0.000**

third task for device D, and the third task was better than the first task for devices F and G.

During the first task, a participant was required only to use the perceptual processor to observe visual information. However, the participants used perceptual, cognitive, and motor responses to see the red dot, process the visual information, and click a mouse during the second task. The third task again uses the perceptual, cognitive, and motor responses. However, since there is an additional switching activity from one monitor to another, the motor response time was increased. Therefore, even as the number of interacting processors (perceptual and motor) increased with each task, the ET devices' accuracy and precision did not have a comprehensive increase or decrease. Overall, we can conclude that the accuracy and precision of the ET devices were decreased when the number of the interacting processor was increased.

4   Discussion and Conclusion

Each ET device has its pros and cons. It is necessary to understand which ET device would be suitable to fulfill the different purposes of various research studies.

Although device A has the best accuracy and precision compared to all table-mounted ET devices, this device showed the highest percentage of unused raw eye movement data (24.94%). It means that device A did not use about 25% of the raw data to generate the outcome results. The inclusion of those unused data points could affect the accuracy negatively. Therefore, if we compare table-mounted ET devices, device C is the most accurate ET device with a low percentage of unused data (5.44%).

Comparing the four head-mounted ET devices, the results clearly showed that device G is the best in terms of accuracy and precision. Also, the percentage of unused data was low (2.15%). The performance of other head-mounted devices (i.e., devices D, E and F) were similar, but device D showed a massive amount of data loss (22.18%) and might misinterpret the outcomes while analyzing data and drawing conclusions. Overall, after considering all tested devices (table-mounted and head-mounted), device G showed the best accuracy when the participants performed task 1.

The current study results also show that the accuracy and precision of device A are better when the participants performed task 1 compared to task 2 (see Table 2). The main difference between task 2 and task 1 is that the participants must respond to a visual stimulus during task 2. They need to click a red circle by using a mouse after they found the visual stimulus. It means that the cognitive process related to this physical response might decrease the performance of device A. For that reason, this ET device can be beneficial to use in settings that do not require a highly sensitive physical response with a fast decision, such as a usability study related to webpage design. For device B, its precision was better when it was used in task 2. However, there was no significant accuracy difference between device B and devices A and C. According to the results, both devices B and C had better stability of generating eye fixation points compared to device A. It means that device B would be good to use in research related to human-computer interactions. Moreover, device C has a better range of headbox compared to device B. Therefore, device C can be employed in similar environments as device B, and where the distance between a user and ET device is longer than 100 cms.

The main difference between task 2 and task 3 is that the participants need to perform continuous task switching activity to execute Fitts's law task in both monitors. With reference to Table 4, the performance of device D was bad, and the device did not successfully record the data from the right side of the second screen during task 3. Hence, the results suggest that device D is not appropriate to use in a multi-monitor environment. For device E, its accuracy was good while performing task 3. However, its precision of task 3 was not good.

In terms of usability perspective, device E has been selected as the most user-friendly ET device among the tested devices, because most participants felt comfortable without any significant interferences. Hence, this ET device would be the best equipment for studies, such as a natural driving experiment where ET device's interference should be small. Devices F and G performed well during task 3. Hence, these devices are recommended in a setting where the margin of error should be low, such as a large-scale manufacturing process requiring a minimum number of human errors.

Overall, the current study shows no single ET device satisfies all three tasks in terms of accuracy and precision. Therefore, selecting the right ET device is crucial based on study needs and the design of the experiment.

References

Du, W., Kim, J.H.: Performance-Based Eye-Tracking Analysis in a Dynamic Monitoring Task. Cham (2016)

Feit, A.M., et al.: Toward everyday gaze input: accuracy and precision of eye tracking and impli-cations for design. Paper presented at the proceedings of the 2017 Chi conference on human factors in computing systems (2017)

Kim, J.H., Yang, X.: measuring driver's perceived workload using fractal dimension of pupil dilation. Proc. Hum. Fact. Ergon. Soc. Ann. Meet. **64**(1), 1620–1624 (2020). https://doi.org/10.1177/1071181320641392

Poole, A., Ball, L.J.: Eye Tracking in HCI and Usability Research Encyclopedia of Human Computer Interaction, pp. 211–219. IGI Global (2006)

Punde, P.A., Jadhav, M.E., Manza, R.R.: A study of eye tracking technology and its applications. Paper presented at the 2017 1st international conference on intelligent systems and information management (ICISIM) (2017)

Shotton, T., Kim, J.H.: Assessing Differences on Eye Fixations by Attention Levels in an Assembly Environment. Cham (2021)

Yang, X., Kim, J.H.: Measuring workload in a multitasking environment using fractal dimension of pupil dilation. Int. J. Hum.-Comput. Interact. **35**(15), 1352–1361 (2019). https://doi.org/10.1080/10447318.2018.1525022

Human-Robot Interaction

Personal Space Norms Aware Robotic Navigation Model and Its Evaluation in a Virtual Reality Environment

Yotaro Fuse[1]([⊠]) [iD] and Masataka Tokumaru[2]

[1] Kansai University Graduate School, 3-3-35 Yamate-cho, Suita-shi, Osaka, Japan
k359679@kansai-u.ac.jp
[2] Kansai University, 3-3-35 Yamate-cho, Suita-shi, Osaka, Japan
toku@kansai-u.ac.jp

Abstract. In this study, we propose a robotic model that determines a robot's ideal positioning when confronted with changes in personal space within a dynamic human-robot group. Recently, there have been several efforts to develop communication robots suitable for human communities. Determining a robot's position is essential to avoid collisions with humans and allow the robot to maintain a socially acceptable distance from people. However, the interpersonal space maintained by people in a community may depend on the contexts and situation of the community. Thus, in a human–robot group, robots need to dynamically evaluate the changes made in their personal space and subsequently update their location while considering the positions of other group members. Here, we propose a robotic navigation model and evaluate its effectiveness in a virtual reality setting where a robot embedding the proposed model had to keep an appropriate distance from the other moving robots based on an experimental scenario. We examined whether experimental participants could distinguish the model-enabled robot's trajectory from the other robot's trajectory. The results showed that the robot embedding the proposed model could move in a humanlike way (convey an impression of group membership) by constantly finding a suitable position in the group, even when changes of personal space occurred. This suggests the meaningfulness of the proposed model toward enabling robots to behave as group members by selecting their pathway without violating the distance norms maintained by other human group members.

Keywords: Navigation model · Human-robot interaction · Sociable robots · Personal space · Group norms

1 Introduction

The past years have seen increased optimistic views on the possibility that people will interact closely or even live with robots in the future. Such views might be associated with the recent spurt of research on developing communication robots

© Springer Nature Switzerland AG 2021
C. Stephanidis et al. (Eds.): HCII 2021, CCIS 1420, pp. 123–130, 2021.
https://doi.org/10.1007/978-3-030-78642-7_17

that can communicate naturally with people. For instance, many studies have demonstrated that robots can communicate with people using social behaviors, such as expressing emotions and gestures [1]. Some researchers have pointed out that navigation robots tend to position themselves too close to humans, which can create discomfort [2,3]. Thus, robots in human communities must conform to human social norms just like humans.

In social groups, people conform to expectations and common group behaviors. Although individuals have different personalities and decision-making criteria, these criteria converge into one common criterion when a group is formed. To exhibit sociality in a human society, robots need to adapt to group norms that are formed by group members. Group norms are informal rules that groups adopt to regulate the behavior of group members [4]. In our previous work, we proposed a robotic model that enabled a robot to adjust its behavior to group norms by observing other group members, and subsequently behave as a member of that group [5].

An example of a group norm in human communities is the physical distancing people maintain while standing with one another. In human communities, people usually have a region surrounding themselves called the personal space, which is psychologically their own space; if another person intrudes into this space, they may experience discomfort [6]. Although [7] reported that personal space is dynamic and situation-dependent, people in a group usually maintain some appropriate distance from one another while standing together.

Besides, autonomous mobile robots in a human-robot group need to move based on changes in humans' personal spaces. However, most previous studies have only aimed at developing models to prevent robots from colliding with humans and encroaching humans' personal space while the robot moves from an initial to a target point [8,9]. It means that previous robotic navigation models did not consider situations where a robot moves in a human-robot group as a group member and adapts to changes in personal space. Thus, a robot using previous methods might not be able to maintain an appropriate distance with other group members when changes occur. To behave as a full-fledged group member, a robot needs to continuously find an appropriate position as a group member, even when a situation or context induces changes in members' personal space.

In a prior contribution, we proposed a robotic navigation model that considered changes of group members' personal space and evaluated its effectiveness through a simulation [10]. The experimental participants evaluated the robots' movements from a third-person or outside perspective, meaning that they could not assess the robot movements from the standpoint of a group member. To further evaluate the appropriateness of the robot's movement controlled by the proposed model, we thought it would be interesting to get insights from an experimental scenario where participants could evaluate the proposed robot's movement from a group member's perspective.

In this study, we present the evaluation of the proposed robotic navigation model in a virtual reality environment. We prepared a scenario where group robots moved while keeping an appropriate distance from one another. One of the robots' movements was controlled using the proposed model, while others moved based on the experimental scenario. Then, we conducted a survey to assess the participants' impressions of the robots' trajectories and their ability to behave as full-fledged group members.

2   Experiment

In this study, we examined whether a robot using the proposed model can move while keeping an appropriate distance from other robots belonging to the same group. The robot continuously identified its suitable position as a group member in an experimental scenario where the physical distance between the group members gradually shrank.

Figure 1 is a representation of the experiment settings showing a group of four robots. In an experimental scenario, three robots approached the black robot while keeping the physical distance. In our experiment, we prepared two samples of participants. Participants observed robots in the scenario as a group member based on the black robot (Fig. 1). In the experimental scenario, three robots, including the proposed model enabled one, approached the static black robot while keeping a certain distance from one another. Participants in the first condition observed the robot movements from the standpoint of the black robot.

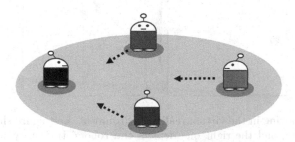

Fig. 1. Experimental scenario showing three robots moving toward the black robot.

2.1   Experimental Flow

In the experimental scenario, each robot was represented with a red, green, blue, or black icon (Fig. 2). During the experiment, the red, green and blue robots moved from their initial respective locations to gather around the black robot, which was static. Participants in the first condition observed robots' trajectories from the black robot's perspective. These participants were equipped with a virtual reality headset tp immerse them in the experimental environment and increase their feeling of group membership. We used HTC Vive headset to this end. Following this approach, they could observe the moving robots gathering around themselves, given that they were observing other robots from the black robot's perspective. However, participants in the second condition, observed the robots from a third-person perspective similar to the viewing perspective of Fig. 1.

After observing robots moving from their initial to the goal position, participants answered a questionnaire asking them to indicate which one of the robots was controlled by a navigation model. Note that we changed the color and the initial position of the robot embedding the proposed model before each new experiment. Then, we compared the results of the questionnaire administrated to participants in both conditions to examine the differences depending on participants' viewpoints.

Fig. 2. Robots in the virtual reality space. (Color figure online)

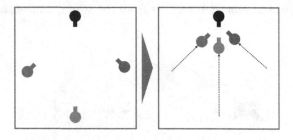

Fig. 3. Robots moving in the virtual reality environment. Left figure shows the initial state of the group, and the right one depicts the robots' trajectory when gathering around the black robot.

2.2   Simulation Environment

The four robots were positioned on a square which was 20 m × 20 m. In the initial state, the robots were kept far away from one another (Fig. 3), to avoid personal space intrusion before they start moving. Besides, 20 initial state patterns, each with different robots' positioning layout were prepared.

To dynamically change distances between robots as they move, we prepared two robots that kept moving toward the static robot until they reach their final goal state. The robot using the proposed model continuously attempted to maintain an appropriate distance with these two robots until the first two stopped moving as they reached the goal location. To sum up, each robot group consists of the robot embedding the proposed model, the static robot, and the two robots that moved toward the static robot (i.e., the black robot).

To express the shrinking of the distance kept by the group members, we defined the parameter *Closeness*. Each robot intends to move shared the *Closeness* parameter, i.e., the robots added the random number $[0.0, 1.0]$ at each step. The range of *Closeness* was $[0, 100]$. By increasing the value of *Closeness*, the physical distance to be maintained by each robot gradually decreased from 7.5 m to 1.0 m. The physical interpersonal distance that robots were to maintain decreased using the following equation:

$$d = 7.5 + ((1.0 - 7.5) * Closeness) / 10 \qquad (1)$$

Considering the closeness and their personal spaces, each robot did not intrude into each other's personal space and kept moving to the grid in its neighborhood, which was the closest to the destination. The robot using the proposed model moved to adjust accordingly its position, while the other two robots attempted to gradually shrink their interpersonal distance.

In this experiment, two groups of participants observed 20 records of the four robots' trajectories in the robot group. The participants in one group observed them from the black robot's location in Fig. 1 while wearing HTC Vive.

2.3   Questionnaire

We conducted a questionnaire to investigate whether the participants can differentiate the robot using the proposed model from the other robots. Before answering the questions, participants were briefed on how robots moved based on the concept of *Closeness* introduced in Sect. 2.2. We explained to them that two of the three moving robots were designed to get closer to the static (black) robot. The other moving robot was controlled by a navigation model and was not assigned the specific goal to move toward the static robot.

They were specifically informed about the following:

- Two robots had the goal of moving toward the black robot;
- These two robots approached the black robot while keeping a certain physical distance from each other;
- The third robot moved while adjusting its location to the maintained distance in the group by learning from the other robots' locations.

2.4   Results

First, we present the robots obtained from the questionnaire that investigated whether the experimental participants could identify the robot that used the proposed model.

Figure 4 shows the correct answers rate among participants and across patterns. The correct answer rate was identical in both conditions and was approximately 34%, which is similar to the correct answer rate in case participants answered the questionnaire randomly (i.e., 1/3).

Figure 5 shows the degree of intrusion of the robots embedding the proposed model in other robots' personal spaces; the distance of these intrusions was less than 20 cm. As the physical distance that each robot wanted to maintain shrank, the robot using the proposed model moved by considering the average maintained distance. The rate of personal spaces encroaching on other robots suggests that the robot using the proposed model did sometimes intrude into other robots' personal space. As the degree of intrusions became low, we deduced that even when a robot encroaches upon the other group members' personal space, it reacted promptly; thus, avoiding further intrusion.

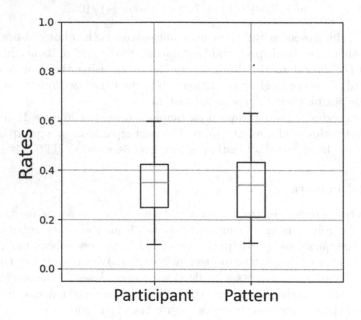

Fig. 4. Average correct answer rate among participants and across patterns. "Participant" of the horizontal axis means the average of the extent to which participants answered the questionnaire correctly. "Pattern" means the average of the extent to which correct answers were provided to patterns.

2.5   Discussion

From the above results, we conclude that the robot using the proposed model moved in a human-like way as other robots get closer to one another, and the physical distances among the robots decrease. This is corroborated at the relatively low rate of correct answers to the questionnaire, which was roughly equal to the correct answer percentage in the case that participants answered the questionnaire randomly. This result indicates that regardless of the initial positioning of the robot, most participants could not distinguish the proposed model enabled robot from other robots. Besides, the trajectories generated by the proposed

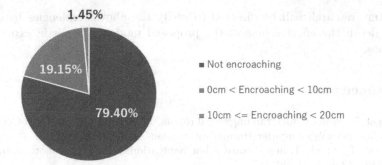

Fig. 5. Degrees of invading personal spaces of the two robots, which moved based on *Closeness*.

model were similar to other robots' trajectories, which moved in the environment considering their personal spaces. It follows that the robot embedding the proposed model could behave as a group member and select its pathway without encroaching upon the personal spaces of the other robots.

Besides, it was not easy for participants to distinguish the trajectories generated by the proposed model from others in the virtual reality space. Although participants knew that the robot using the proposed model did not intend to approach the black robot, most of them could not discover their trajectories. This can be regarded as additional evidence on the fact that the model-controlled robot could determine appropriate positions in the dynamic group environment. This enabled it to convey to the participants the illusion that the robot using the proposed model attempted to move toward the static robot like the other robots. Thus, the proposed model enabled the robot to move suitably as a member of the robot group.

3   Conclusions

In this study, we proposed a navigation model to enable a robot to move in a human or robot group without encroaching upon dynamically changing interpersonal spaces of other group members. Humans in a group tend to maintain physical distancing from one another in accordance with their shared personal space norms or contexts. Thus, to determine an appropriate position at a given time in a group, personal robots that behave as group members in human communities need to learn the physical distancing that humans maintain in groups. We conducted a simulation to evaluate the proposed model, which was used by a robot to move in a robot group without encroaching upon the other members' personal spaces. Besides, we obtained that the proposed model enabled the robot's trajectories to resemble the trajectories of other robots belonging to the same group. These results suggested the meaningfulness of the proposed model and opened new perspectives toward developing mobile robots that are more aware of social norms, which shape human interactions.

Future research will be directed to verify the above tendencies by evaluating in depth the effectiveness of the proposed model in realistic experimental scenarios.

References

1. Hegel, F., et al.: Understanding social robots. In: Second International Conferences on Advances in Computer-Human Interactions, pp. 169–174 (2009)
2. Kruse, T., et al.: Human-aware robot navigation: a survey. Robot. Auton. Syst. **61**(12), 1726–1743 (2013)
3. Rios-Martinez, J., et al.: From proxemics theory to socially-aware navigation: a survey. Int. J. Soc. Robot. **7**(2), 137–153 (2015)
4. Feldman, D.C.: The development and enforcement of group norms. Acad. Manag. Rev. **9**(1), 47–53 (1984)
5. Fuse, Y., et al.: Social influence of group norms developed by human-robot groups. IEEE Access **8**, 56081–56091 (2020)
6. Sundstrom, E., et al.: Interpersonal relationships and personal space: research review and theoretical model. Hum. Ecol. **4**(1), 47–67 (1976)
7. Hayduk, L.A.: Personal space: understanding the simplex model. J. Nonverbal Behav. **18**(3), 245–260 (1994)
8. Chatterjee, I., et al.: Performance of a low-cost, human-inspired perception approach for dense moving crowd navigation. In: 25th IEEE International Symposium on Robot and Human Interactive Communication (RO-MAN), pp. 578–585 (2016)
9. Chen, Y.F., et al.: Socially aware motion planning with deep reinforcement learning. In: 2017 IEEE/RSJ International Conference on Intelligent Robots and Systems (IROS) (2017)
10. Fuse, Y., et al.: Navigation model for a robot as a human group member to adapt to changing conditions of personal space. J. Adv. Comput. Intell. Intell. Inform. **24**(5), 621–629 (2020)

Compilation and Analysis of Requirements for the Design of an Explosive Ordnance Disposal Robot Prototype Applied in UDEX-Arequipa

Joseph Guevara Mamani(✉) ⓘ, Pablo Pari Pinto(✉) ⓘ,
Denilson Vilcapaza Goyzueta(✉) ⓘ, Elvis Supo Colquehuanca(✉) ⓘ,
Erasmo Sulla Espinoza(✉) ⓘ, and Yuri Silva Vidal(✉) ⓘ

Universidad Nacional de San Agustín de Arequipa, Arequipa, Peru
{jguevaram,pparip,dvilcapazag,esupo,esullae,ysilvav}@unsa.edu.pe

Abstract. Advances in the field of robotics will help in the work of the Explosive Ordnance Disposal Unit of Arequipa (UDEX-AQP) allowing to safeguard the lives of the Explosive Ordnance Disposal Technicians (TEDAX). This generates the need to understand the different UDEX procedures in detail in each intervention they perform in order to extract the minimum requirements for the design of the EOD robot that will be accepted by UDEX-AQP.

In the paper we will analyze the different data collected for the development of the EOD robot prototype to be used in UDEX interventions. The information is obtained from the report of reported cases from the period 2013 to 2020 and the support of UDEX-AQP, to extract features and design an intuitive control as well as an optimal user experience. The study revealed the most important aspects for the design of the robot according to the needs of TEDAX such as shape and weight of explosives, frequency of explosives encountered; as well as the most challenging environments in the interventions.

We conducted tests with the Allen Vanguard MK2 robot to innovate the human-robot experience, through surveys we collected aptitudes and skills with this technology by the TEDAX, with this data we can design an interface that generates a friendly user experience.

Keywords: Human-robot experience · Explosive Ordnance Disposal (EOD) · Teleoperation

1 Introduction

In the1980 s, Peru suffered a period of terrorism where there were attacks by terrorist groups such as the Sendero Luminoso and the Tupac Amaru Revolutionary Movement (MRTA); the first 5 years of the decade, the violent attacks were focused on the southern departments [1]. Arequipa suffered those events,

C. Stephanidis et al. (Eds.): HCII 2021, CCIS 1420, pp. 131–138, 2021.
https://doi.org/10.1007/978-3-030-78642-7_18

the use of explosive artifacts on a larger scale to impart fear to the population began. As a result of these events, the Arequipa Explosives Deactivation Unit (UDEX-AQP) was created. There are numerous risks involved in explosive ordnance disposal, and the health and safety of the officers is always a primary concern. Because robots are expendable, they can be easily repaired or replaced, so we sought to design a prototype EOD robot.

The goal of the research is to innovate in human-robot interactions; designing human-robot interfaces to facilitate interaction, operator understanding and situational awareness; translating the qualities of good human teammates into robot characteristics; and fostering human trust in robots. [3,4]. Human operators may have perceptual difficulties in trying to understand a cluttered 3D environment through remote visual feedback, they may become disoriented and lose situational awareness, therefore, explosive ordnance disposal (EOD) robots will not perform optimally [2]. In order to safeguard the lives of the TEDAX, all the information provided by them and also the information obtained from our team will be analyzed in order to obtain the minimum requirements that this bomb disposal robot prototype must have. The remaining sections of this document are as follows. Section 2 is a description of the methodology we will use for data collection and Sect. 3 is a description of the intervention procedure performed by UDEX-AQP. The analysis of the operations report is introduced in Sect. 4. Section 5 describes the tests performed with the MK2 robot to obtain data.

2   Methodology

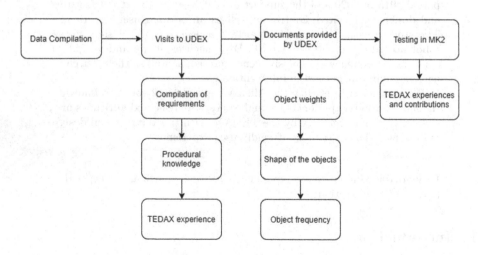

Fig. 1. Methodology used for data collection

Data collection began with visits to UDEX-AQP in search of the needs of the TEDAX, to know their routine (intervention procedures) in detail, in addition to collecting different experiences of the TEDAX, we conducted an analysis to obtain characteristics on explosives. In addition to obtaining additional data from the tests performed on the MK2 robot, we seek to see the handling of the robotic interface by the agents. (see Fig. 1).

3 Procedure Details

In order to understand UDEX-AQP procedures, we visited the unit where an exhibition of the explosives they encounter in their various operations, such as dynamite, grenades, bombs, among others, was shown. The UDEX agents conducted an induction of the procedures (See Fig. 2.) that they carry out in their interventions.

Fig. 2. Procedure UDEX.

1-Observation: First, a TEDAX agent is sent with bomb protection equipment to make a visual analysis of the site where the suspected explosive device was found.
2-Handling: Priority is given to moving the suspected explosive device to an area where its possible explosion will not cause harm to human lives.
3-Deactivation: The suspected explosive device is deactivated, mainly using a disruptor cannon (see Fig. 3).

(a)   **(b)**   **(c)**

Fig. 3. Demonstration of UDEX-AQP intervention (a) observation (b) handling (c) deactivation.

Upon learning the UDEX procedures, we noticed the great involvement of the EOD robot in the marking stage to safeguard human life by avoiding the contact of the TEDAX with the suspect package.

4   Operations Report Analysis

UDEX-AQP provided us with the report for the period 2013 to 2020 of the interventions they carried out among which we found relevant data on the requirements for the design and development of the prototype of the pump deactivating robot equipped with a teleoperated precision actuator. We classified the various data provided by UDEX as shown in Table 1, we considered the data of Grenades, Projectiles, Bombs, Tank which are 88 cases and the false alarms recorded which are 60 cases. These two make 66% of the total cases, hereafter we will call them suspicious packages.

Table 1. Total cases of interventions in the period 2013–2020 by UDEX.

Total cases 2013–2020	223	100%
Grenades, Projectiles, Bombs	**88**	39%
Suspicious artifacts	**60**	27%
Pyrotechnics (Seizure)	**38**	17%
Destruction	**19**	9%
Other (deflagration, blasting work, spills)	**18**	8%

4.1   Efficient Participation

We took the 148 cases obtained above as our new total, being this number of interventions in which our bomb disposal robot prototype would take part (See Table 2). In Table 2 we analyzed the participation of the robot prototype; obtaining 91% of efficient participation, the rest of the cases were not considered efficient participation due to the weight over 20 kg. The factor called "evaluate" included suspicious packages in complicated environments for the robot prototype. The 9 suspicious cases analyzed are discriminated due to weights above 200 kg which requires another procedure for the intervention.

Table 2. Efficient robot participation.

Total cases	148	100%
Yes	**135**	91%
No	**9**	6%
Evaluate	**4**	3%

4.2   Explosive Devices Frequency

We analyzed these 135 cases and obtained data on the objects seized (see Table 3). Grenades, dynamites and suitcases were the most recurrent, accounting for 64% of the cases analyzed. We also obtained the redundancy in the spherical and cylindrical shape of the explosives that will allow us to design the robotic gripper. Another factor we evaluated was the nature of the suspicious packages, whether the explosive was found inside a package (bag, box, suitcase, etc.) or only the explosive was found. It was labeled "Missing Data" because the report provided by UDEX lacked information. From the Table 3, 71 cases were found with only explosives, relevant data for the handling of the explosives. There were also 56 suspicious cases where the explosive was found inside a package. Finally, 9 cases could not be categorized due to lack of data.

Table 3. Total cases of interventions in the period 2013–2020 by UDEX.

Total objects	135	100%
Grenades	37	28%
Dynamite	26	19%
Suitcase	23	17%
Missing data	11	8%
Box	11	8%
Other	11	8%
Bags	10	7%
Pumps	6	5%

4.3   Suspicious Package Weights

At this stage, the average weight of 115 suspicious packages was obtained (discriminating "missing data" from Table 3), but only 33 cases were actually averaged; the rest of the cases we did not have information on the intervened weights. The average of these 33 cases was 3.581 kg, of which the minimum weight was 0.15 kg and the maximum weight was 15 kg. Another factor that was evaluated in the weight of the objects was the frequency of the weight interval (see Table 4), with greater redundancy in objects weighing 0 to 4 kg.

5   Tests on Robot MK2

UDEX-AQP has the opportunity to test the Allen Vanguard MK2 robot on loan from UDEX-Lima (see Fig. 4). The Canadian MK2 robot has a non-actuated keyboard control with visual camera support which we will use as a base reference to design the prototype. In the tests performed, the execution time per requested

Table 4. Weights of analyzed objects.

Kilograms	Frequency	100%
0 a 2	17	51%
2 a 4	8	24%
4 a 6	3	10%
6 a 8	2	6%
8 a 10	2	6%
10 a 12	0	0%
12 a 14	0	0%
14 a 16	1	3%

task was considered, using all the MK2 robot interface, i.e. the key control and the use of the cameras for the observation of the panorama. The task consisted of moving a dynamite from the floor to a box located on top of a table, we considered the total time of the task and the time it took to hold the explosive. At the end of the task, a multidimensional assessment procedure was applied to the agents to give an overall workload score called NASA TLX [5]. This procedure was used to measure the user experience and the workload performed in the test to determine the reliability of the TEDAX agents with the MK2 robot. In Fig. 5 the variables of mental demand and effort were more relevant in the development of the test due to the limited visual assistance of the MK2. This visual assistance by outdated cameras does not provide sufficient information for the manipulation of the explosive. The stress results were due to the time spent in the test while standing still.

Fig. 4. Tests with the MK2 robot.

Test results:

- The total workload of the agents gave us a high value indicating an unintuitive interaction with the interface.

- The cameras of the MK2 robot, being out of phase, do not present a good image quality which is necessary in these procedures. In addition, the control station is delayed in time.
- In the tests, failed attempts were obtained, meaning that in the middle of the manipulation the dynamite fell out of the robotic gripper, if it were a real situation it would cause damage, observing a deficiency in the explosive grip.
- The control of the MK2 robot was not very intuitive among the agents, and after the test they were frustrated when they did not complete the task or did not complete it in a short time.
- The agents in the tests were not aware of the robot's limits due to the limited visual support they had through the robot's cameras, thus damaging the robot's gripper.

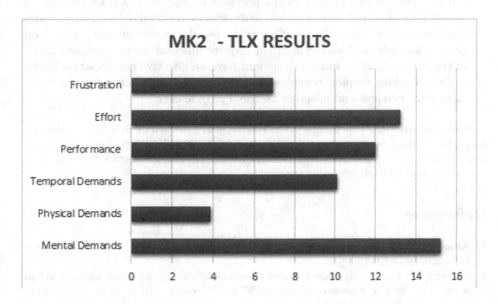

Fig. 5. Variable average-NASA TLX.

6   Conclusions

- The explosive ordnance disposal (EOD) robot prototype would have had an efficient participation in 91% of the suspected cases in the period 2013 to 2020, this result indicates the great help in the work of the Explosive Ordnance Disposal Unit (UDEX) that the project would provide in addition to safeguarding the safety and lives of the agents.

- Grenade, dynamite and suitcase were the objects that were found the most in the period from 2013 to 2020, obtaining that the objects to be manipulated are spherical and cylindrical; this will help us in the design of the robotic gripper.
- The average of the analyzed objects was 3,581 kg, an important data to consider for the design of the robotic arm, with this we can choose the balance of force and speed of the motors of the prototype.
- In the tests the outdated and unintuitive interface for the manipulation of the MK2 robot was observed. Because of this, the TEDAX required more concentration for the completion of the task, the degree of mental effort, concentration, choice and decision is relevant to the tests. These results are reflected in the execution times obtained and also in the data of the applied surveys.
- With all the data collected and the previous literature review we propose to innovate the manipulation of explosive devices through an optimal control and handling experience of the interface with specular imitation using a focused gripper for spherical and cylindrical objects; also an automated assistance system to manipulate small objects and have an effective participation in the stage of marking suspicious explosive devices, achieving a better human-robot experience efficient and effective for the TEDAX user.

Acknowledgments. Our thanks to the Universidad Nacional de San Agustín de Arequipa for funding under contract number IBA-IB-27-2020-UNSA and the Unidad de Desactivacion de Explosivos Arequipa for providing us with the required information, facilities and time to develop this project.

References

1. Alfaro, F.M.: Migraciones Internas en el Perú. Instituto Nacional De Estadítica e Informática(INEI) (2006)
2. Murphy, R., Casper, J.: Human-robot interactions during the robot-assisted urban search and rescue response at the world trade center. IEEE Trans. Syst. Man Cybern. **33**, 367–385 (2003)
3. Billings, D.R., Hancock, P.A., Schaefer, K.E.: A meta-analysis of factors affecting trust in human-robot interaction. Hum. Factors J. Hum. Factors Ergon. Soc. **53**, 517–527 (2011)
4. de Visser, E., Weltman, G., Coeyman Freedy, A.: Measurement of trust in human-robot collaboration. In: Proceedings of the 2007 International Conference on Collaborative Technologies and Systems, pp. 106–114 (2007)
5. Hart, S.G., Staveland, L.E.: Development of NASA-TLX (Task Load Index): results of empirical and theoretical research. In: Human Mental Workload, pp. 139–183 (1988)

Teleoperation of Mobile Robot by Walking Motion Using Saddle Type Device

Shunsuke Kume[✉] (ID) and Masamichi Sakaguchi[✉] (ID)

Nagoya Institute of Technology, Nagoya, Aichi 466-8555, Japan
clf13061@nitech.jp, sakaguchi.masamichi@nitech.ac.jp
http://vrmech.web.nitech.ac.jp

Abstract. Recently, Virtual Reality (VR) which is one of the new Information Technology (IT) constantly keeps making progress. In the VR, there is a concept called "telexistence" [1]. Telexistence is the concept having a meaning of human existence extension that the operator practically exists at the place which is different from the place they are [1]. In the case of telexistence, when the operator handles robot as an avatar robot, we can say that operability is an important viewpoint. In this study, we focused on walking motion as a way of teleoperating robot intuitively. It is clear that walking motion is so fundamental that we experience regularly and it is inherent movement. Besides, we used saddle type device as a locomotion interface which offered safe and stable walking. To propose a method for walking by using saddle type device, we measured the moving loci of the robot and the operator's foot. The result showed that we could get the robot to move forward continuously by using saddle type device.

Keywords: Locomotion interface · Wheeled mobile robot · Teleoperation

1 Introduction

In the last few years, VR technology catches the world's attention. Among the VR technology, there is a concept called telexistence [1]. Telexistence means human existence extension that the operator practically exists at remote place [1]. According to the concept, it releases the operator from temporal and spatial constraints in the conventional real space.

In addition to VR, a wide range of researchers explore usability in the fields of human-robot interaction (HRI). Usability in this field comprehends several aspects, such as various kinds of command control, information feedback, communicability and its applicability on robotic systems [2,3]. In the HRI field, a robot is usually controlled via classic interaction devices like keyboards, mice and joystick [4]. These devices may not be the most suitable options for some applications because they work with complex software systems that commonly require

© Springer Nature Switzerland AG 2021
C. Stephanidis et al. (Eds.): HCII 2021, CCIS 1420, pp. 139–147, 2021.
https://doi.org/10.1007/978-3-030-78642-7_19

training in advance. We can simplify these systems by using a natural interface that requires less learning time. As relative studies, there are some studies about the teleoperation of mobile robot through a natural interface which worked with a body tracking device. Among them, we found the way of controlling the robot by poses defined by different arm positions [5].

In our study, in contrast, we focus on walking among simple physical motion for teleoperating mobile robot intuitively. There are two reasons. First, it is clear that walking motion is so fundamental that we experience regularly. We think that the most fundamental motion is directly linked to the intuition and ease of teleoperation. Secondary, there are not so many studies which focus on controlling the robot by moving the operator's feet as far as we can find. Hence, we approach this unique aspect. Besides, we use saddle type device as a novel locomotion interface which offers safe and stable walking. By using this interface, we can move our entire body and exercise like an actual walking motion. Therefore, we attempt to teleoperate the robot by walking motion intuitively, easily and safely.

The aim of our study is proposing that the use of saddle type device offering telexistence is viable for teleoperating robot. We consider a viable interface for teleoperating robot as a technically feasible interface that enables the operator to control intuitively and easily. Moreover, we judge an ideal gesture-based natural interface should depend on commands that are both easy to learn and execute.

On the next section, divided in three subsections, encloses the methodology followed to make the systems we made, the algorithm and measurement of moving locus. The following section encloses the achieved results of the measurement. Finally, the last section encloses the conclusion we made from this study.

2 Methodology

This section, Methodology, is divided in three subsections. The first contains an explanation of the configuration of the system. Then, the next contains an algorithm of moving forward and stop when to teleoperate robot. The final contains a detailed explanation of the measurement conducted.

2.1 System

The entire system consists of two subunits responsible for complementary parts of the system architecture. The first one is called Control sub-system. It runs a software that detects the operator's physical motions as the commands and send them to the second sub-system, called Robot sub-system. As its name suggests, the Robot contains a robot that works in response to actions which are correspond to the operator's commands by physical motion from the Control. The robot in the Robot also sends visual information about its surroundings to the operator in the Control. In brief, the commands move from the Control to the Robot and visual information moves oppositely.

The Control sub-system contains a personal computer (PC) connected to SteamVR. We choose it due to its ease of use with PC and its possibility of gesture tracking. As for gesture tracking, we can realize it by using VIVE Tracker. This device detects its position coordinates, attitude angle and velocity. Also, it is small and easy to equip anywhere. Regarding reception of visual information, we use HTC VIVE as a Head Mounted Display (HMD). By wearing this device on the head, the operator can see images from the camera on the robot.

In addition to SteamVR, there is another representative component in the Control. As the title of our study implies, we use saddle type device as a locomotion interface (Fig. 1). There are advantages of this interface. One of these is that the interface offers safe and stable walking without risk of falling, for example, when the operator wears HMD. This is because the operator can reduce weight bearing on their legs by straddling the saddle and supporting their upper body. Besides, saddle type device enables the operator to exercise by movement which is similar to actual walking or running because they can move their both hands, arms and feet freely. In this study, we handle commands such as moving forward and stop to control the mobile robot with the use of this interface. About moving forward and stop, we make it possible for the operator to control the robot by VIVE Tracker put on their right feet. This means the operator can control the robot by their own walking motion. Hence, when the operator starts walking, the robot moves forward, and when the operator stops walking, the robot also stops. We will explain the algorithm in the next subsection.

The Robot sub-system contains a robot that works according to the commands sent from the Control. To build a manageable robot, there are two modules needed to deal with. These are an action module and a perception module. They play an important role in controlling the robot and grasping how its surroundings are. Considering these modules, we have judged the Raspberry Pi is suitable for the platform. We use the Raspberry Pi 2 Model B in this study. In addition, we adopt SunFounder PiCar-V Kit V2.0 for Raspberry Pi (Fig. 2) as a wheeled mobile robot. This is a programmable robot and especially Python language is available.

2.2   Algorithm

As mentioned above, we adopt SunFounder PiCar-V Kit V2.0 for Raspberry Pi as a wheeled mobile robot. Conventionally, we teleoperate this robot with keyboard. For example, when we push "w" key, the robot moves forward. Similarly, when we push "s" key, the robot stops. In any case, the robot receives keyboard inputs as commands which are corresponded to some movements. Then, we teleoperate the robot by using VIVE Tracker while riding saddle type device.

First, when we make the robot move forward, we walk while riding saddle type device. Similarly, when we make the robot stop, we stop walking. These physical operations are based on the position coordinates and speed detected by VIVE Tracker put on the operator's right foot. In addition, these numerical data can be sent to the robot as commands which are equivalent to keyboard inputs by Python. Moreover, commands keep being sent constantly while these

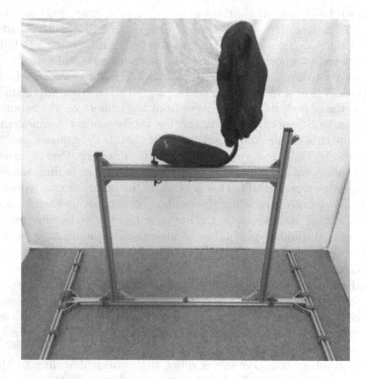

Fig. 1. Saddle type device

Fig. 2. Robot

data meet following requirements, and Raspberry Pi on the robot processes these commands at high speed.

We set the speed boundary of VIVE Tracker between moving forward and stop to 0.3 m/s. This means that the robot moves forward if the speed of VIVE Tracker exceeds 0.3 m/s, otherwise it stops. However, in case of the detection of speed only once, the operator's continuous walking makes the robot move forward intermittently. This is because number sign of velocity of VIVE Tracker changes periodically when the operator walks. This implies there is an inevitable phase that foot stops moving temporarily. Hence, even if the operator intends to make the robot move forward continuously by periodical walking, the robot stops each time when the speed of VIVE Tracker becomes less than 0.3 m/s. Then, we introduced an additional detection of speed of VIVE Tracker into the requirement so that the robot can move forward continuously.

Figure 3 contains an algorithm which enables the robot to move forward continuously. In the Fig. 3, entire structure of the algorithm shows a series of process from receiving an input until working according to the operator's command. However, in contrast to VIVE Tracker detecting velocity at a frequency 100 Hz, it takes from 200 to 300 milliseconds delay for Raspberry Pi on the robot to process command inputs on performance. Therefore, Raspberry Pi receives and processes command inputs 3 to 5 times per second.

Based on these, as can be seen from Fig. 3, the robot moves forward if the speed detected by VIVE Tracker exceeds 0.3 m/s. Additionally, the robot keeps moving forward because the forward command is constantly sent while the speed detected by VIVE Tracker exceeds 0.3 m/s.

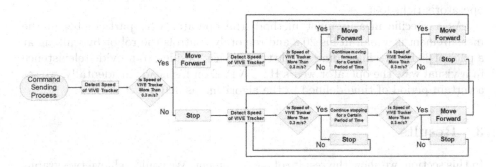

Fig. 3. Algorithm

However, there is phase that foot movement turns in the opposite direction. This gets speed of VIVE Tracker being less than 0.3 m/s inevitably. Then, we implement measures that we intentionally re-detect speed of VIVE Tracker after a certain period of time instead of sending stop command as soon as the speed becomes less than 0.3 m/s. In addition, we send the command corresponded to re-detected speed to the robot as a definitive command. Incidentally, we set the time between the re-detection of the speed and the transmission of a command input to the robot to be the state in which the command corresponding to the first detected speed is sent to the robot.

By taking such measures, even if the speed detected once during walking is less than 0.3 m/s, if the re-detected speed after a certain period of time exceeds 0.3 m/s, the robot judges that the operator is still in the middle of periodical walking process, and the robot continues to move forward. On the contrary, if the re-detected speed is less than 0.3 m/s while the robot is moving forward, the robot judges that the operator has completely stopped walking, and the robot also stops.

Similarly to when the robot stops from the state of moving forward, the robot distinguishes between moving forward and stop by performing such double detection of the speed when the robot moves forward from the state of stop.

2.3   Measurement

In this subsection, we explain the measurement of the moving locus of the robot. As a purpose of the measurement, we perform that to verify an availability of the algorithm we have proposed in the previous subsection.

To verify the availability of the algorithm, we visualize the difference in the moving locus of the robot when measured under the same conditions in each case with or without application of the algorithm.

When measuring the moving locus of the robot, we mount another VIVE Tracker on the robot, and it detects the position coordinates of the robot. In addition, to correspond with the movement of the robot, we also measure the position coordinates and the velocity detected by VIVE Tracker put on the operator's right foot.

As a specific measurement method, the operator who participates in the measurement is a man in his 20 s and remotely controls the robot by walking at a pace of 60 BPM while riding saddle type device. Besides, to provide telexistence in a visual way, the operator wears HTC VIVE on his head. Incidentally, we set a certain period of time defined in the algorithm as 300 ms.

3   Results

In this section, we show the results of measurement. We could achieve two graphs as a result. When explaining the graphs, the horizontal axis shows elapsed time, and the main vertical axis is the coordinate axis provided in the longitudinal direction of saddle type device and shows the displacement of the operator's right foot and the robot. In addition, the second vertical axis is the speed axis of VIVE Tracker put on the operator's right foot. Aside to that, we set the direction in which the foot moves from back to front as the positive direction of the coordinate axis, and the origin is set at the center of saddle type device.

First, Fig. 4 shows the graph without the algorithm applied. In the case of speed detection only once, the robot stops each time because a stop command is sent as soon as a speed close to 0 is detected at the phase where the foot movement turns in the opposite direction in the process of periodical walking. Therefore, we can see from Fig. 4 that the robot moves forward intermittently if the algorithm is not applied.

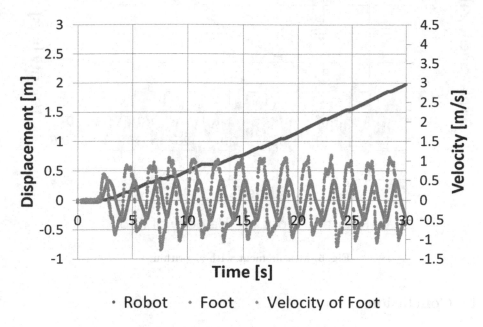

Fig. 4. Measurement without algorithm

Next, Fig. 5 shows the graph with the algorithm applied. In contrast to Fig. 4, the robot can judge whether to move forward or to stop with the algorithm even if the foot movement turns in the opposite direction in the process of periodical walking. In Fig. 5, we can confirm this from the section (range from 3 s to 33 s) in which the forward command is continuously sent by periodical walking and the section (range from 30 s to 35 s) in which the robot also stops when the operator stops walking.

Consequently, we can see that it is possible to teleoperate the robot as the operator intended by applying the algorithm. However, from Fig. 5, there is a slight delay time of about 0.5 s between the time when the speed of VIVE Tracker exceeds 0.3 m/s and the time when the robot starts moving forward, and the time when the speed of VIVE Tracker becomes less than 0.3 m/s and the time when the robot stops. Hence, it is necessary to devise ways to shorten the delay time while maintaining continuous forward movement as a future goal.

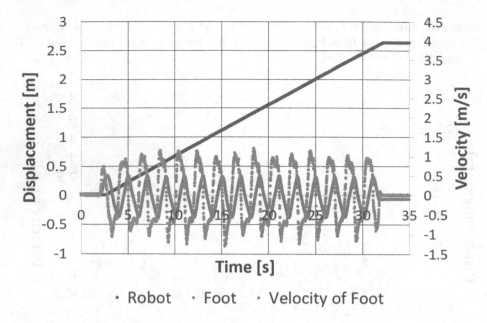

Fig. 5. Measurement with algorithm

4   Conclusion

In this study, we focused on HRI through saddle type device which worked with VIVE Tracker. To test HRI, we proposed an algorithm and measured the moving loci of the robot and the operator's right foot. The results showed that the robot could be teleoperated as the operator intended by applying the algorithm and clarifying the distinction between moving forward and stop commands sent to the robot. Accordingly, we have realized the most basic and intuitive teleoperation by physical movement using saddle type device. Therefore, we will focus on shortening the delay time occurred in the algorithm and realizing a system with more advanced telexistence as a future prospect.

References

1. Tachi, S.: Telexistence 2nd Edition, World Scientific (2015). ISBN 978-981-4618-06-9
2. Inoue, H., Tachi, S., et al.: HRP: humanoid robotics project of MITI. In: Proceedings of the First IEEE-RAS International Conference on Humanoid (Humanoid 2000), Boston, USA, 7 Sep 2000
3. Hasunuma, H., et al.: Development of teleoperation master system with a kinesthetic sensation of presence. In: Proceedings of the 9th International Conference on Artificial Reality and Tele-existence, vol. 99, pp. 53–59. Tokyo, Japan, 16 Dec 1999

4. De Souza, C.S., Leite, J.C., Prates, R.O., Barbosa, S.D.J.: Interacao humanocom-
putador: perspectivas e semioticas. In: Fuks, H. (Org.) Anais das Jornadas de Atu-
alizacao em Informatica. Rio de Janeiro: Edicoes EntreLugar, 1999, pp. 420–470
(1999)
5. Bandeira, G.M., Carmo, M., Ximenes, B., Kelner, J.: Using gesture-based interfaces
to control robots. In: M. Kurosu (Ed.) Human-Computer Interaction, Part II, HCII
2015, LNCS, vol. 9170, pp. 3–12 (2015)

Using a Socially Assistive Robot in a Nursing Home: Caregivers' Expectations and Concerns

Stephanie Lehmann⬤, Esther Ruf(✉)⬤, and Sabina Misoch⬤

Eastern Switzerland University of Applied Sciences, Institute for Ageing Research,
Rosenbergstrasse 59, 9001 St.Gallen, Switzerland
{stephanie.lehmann,esther.ruf}@ost.ch

Abstract. Demographic development and the resulting increase in the proportion of older adults are leading to an increase in the number of people requiring care. At the same time, the shortage of professional caregivers is worsening. Socially assistive robots (SAR) are increasingly being used to assist in the care of older adults. There is evidence of positive effects, but negative effects and ethical concerns are also reported. Therefore, at the beginning of an exploratory study in a nursing home investigating the use of the robotic cushion «Qoobo», caregivers (N = 5) were asked about their expectations and concerns. Positive expectations of the caregivers were that the robotic cushion would be more practical than the already used SAR, that it could improve mood, would be a pastime and boredom would be reduced. Negative expectations were that the robotic cushion could be boring and that it could be rejected because of its shape. Ethical concerns were mainly related to possible deception of older adults and caregivers further expected that older adults might be frightened. For the successful deployment of SAR in a nursing home and to guarantee socially acceptable use, it is important to elicit the expectations and concerns of caregivers in advance, as the fit of a SAR to nursing home residents is always individual.

Keywords: Socially assistive robot · Nursing home · Expectations · Ethical concerns

1 Background

Due to higher life expectancy and low birth rates, the proportion of people over 65 years is increasing in Europe [1, 2]. The increase in the older population group due to the demographic change means that the number of people who need to be cared for in a nursing home is also increasing, as age increases the likelihood that activities of daily living can no longer be performed independently [3]. At the same time, the nursing shortage of professional caregivers is intensifying [4, 5]. This leads to the challenge of ensuring optimal care and support for older adults in institutions in the future. Robotic solutions are increasingly being used to support older adults and caregivers to continue to provide adequate care and support.

Types of robots that can be used are classified differently depending on the authors [6]. This paper focuses on the use of socially assistive robots (SAR) and companion

© Springer Nature Switzerland AG 2021
C. Stephanidis et al. (Eds.): HCII 2021, CCIS 1420, pp. 148–155, 2021.
https://doi.org/10.1007/978-3-030-78642-7_20

robots for older adults. Although these terms are used interchangeably and not always consistently in the literature, the term SAR is used throughout this paper. SAR are a subcategory of robots designed to provide social support and companionship [7] and, as the intersection of assistive robots and socially interactive robots, aim to assist human users through social interaction [8]. SAR are said to support older adults [8, 9], and benefits, as well as a contribution towards the quality of life of older adults, are described [10].

Many studies show various positive effects of SAR. In their review, Pu et al. [11] found that SAR have the potential to reduce agitation and anxiety and improve quality of life of older adults. Similarly, a review showed reduced stress, a sense of safety, and acceptance of SAR among older adults with and without cognitive impairment [12].

Most studies in the aging setting use SAR with an animal-like appearance. For people with dementia who were treated with a pet robot intervention, a meta-analysis showed a statistically significant decrease of behavioral and psychological symptoms of dementia [13]. A meta-analysis of qualitative, mixed-methods, and randomized studies described that interactions with robotic animals positively affect aspects of well-being such as loneliness, depression, and quality of life of residents and staff of long-term care facilities [14]. Examples of animal-like robots which are used are AIBO, a dog-like robot [15], and PARO (Personal Assistant Robot) [16] which has a seal-like appearance and has been used for several years, especially with people with dementia [17]. PARO can significantly improve facial expression and social interaction in people with dementia [18] and reduce loneliness [19]. Petersen et al. [17] showed reduced stress, anxiety, use of psychoactive medications, and pain medication in people with dementia. In summary, positive effects of animal-like robots have been shown in different studies, especially for people with cognitive impairments, by reducing stress and improving their mood, which can relieve caregivers.

However, reported positive effects could only be shown for a short time [20] and undesirable effects as well as obstacles in the application of SAR are supposed. Negative reactions of care recipients, such as fear and aggression, rejection, and skepticism have been reported, although much less frequently [20]. Further barriers to deployment are the high financial costs of a SAR [21, 22]. Besides, physical characteristics of the SAR, such as size and weight are often a barrier for its use with fragile older adults. Further, users require some technical knowledge and experience and interest in technology to use SAR.

Unlike other assistive technologies for older adults, the use of SAR seems to be associated with greater concerns. In their study on care robots, Johansson-Pajala and Gustafsson [23] found that the challenges relate to beliefs in technology, attitudes, ethics, collaboration, and the need for knowledge and skills related to care robots.

It is known that the acceptance of robots depends on the user group [24]. In the care context, a SAR may serve different purposes depending on whether the user is a vulnerable person with cognitive impairments or a formal or informal caregiver [24]. In addition, different user groups may have differing expectations when using a SAR. Regarding the general population, attitudes towards technical and digital applications in care showed that many respondents are in favor of having a robot assist with care and are open to digital helpers in care [25, 26]. But data from the Eurobarometer 2014 showed concerns of the population about robot use in terms of potential negative effects on older adults, with older respondents more dismissive than younger respondents [27]. Zöllick et al. [28] showed that caregivers value the use of technology as a facilitator and to physically support their activities but have strong reservations about using technology for social and emotional care.

In summary, the acceptance of robots by different stakeholders can vary widely. The acceptance can be influenced by end user concerns which are barriers for use. In a Swiss survey, the general population was concerned mainly because they feared reduced human contact for residents and problems with sensitive data [29]. This shows the importance of examining the expectations and concerns of relevant groups regarding a specific robot to be used before it is deployed. Therefore, the Institute for Aging Research (IAF) of the OST – Eastern Switzerland University of Applied Sciences, tested the use of the SAR «Qoobo» in a ward of a retirement home and examined the expectations and concerns of the caregivers. The project was submitted in advance to the Ethics Committee of Eastern Switzerland (EKOS) for clarification of responsibility. The EKOS judged that the project does not fall under the definition of art. 2 of the Federal Act in Research on Human Beings (BASEC No. Req_2020-00928, EKOS 20/138).

2 Method

2.1 Design and Material

As part of an explorative user study which is embedded in the project «Successful use of service robotics in elderly care» [30] on the use of a robot in the ward of a nursing home in Eastern Switzerland, caregivers who already had experience with other SAR were asked about their expectations and concerns prior to the use of «Qoobo». «Qoobo», an animal-like SAR from Yukai Engineering [31], was selected for use as a low-threshold, easily and inexpensively deployable SAR that requires little technical expertise. There is evidence that this SAR can be used with similar effects as PARO [32, 33]. In nursing homes in Japan, «Qoobo» was found to have positive effects on psychological well-being, such as patient satisfaction, happiness, and mood changes [34]. «Qoobo» is a cushion that looks and sounds like a cat and reacts with movements of its tail. Its peculiarity is that it lacks a head.

«Qoobo» was offered to the residents by the caregivers during two months (July to August 2020). After a formal introduction to «Qoobo» but prior to the testing semi-structured telephone interviews were conducted, and a self-compiled questionnaire was completed by the caregivers. The instruments included questions about their previous experience with robots or other assistive devices, their first impression of «Qoobo», what effect on the residents they expect, whether they think the SAR will be accepted, and what difficulties they anticipate in using it. To survey (ethical) concerns regarding the use of the SAR the caregivers indicated their agreement on a four-point rating scale to eleven items that cover the most frequently mentioned ethical topics in literature regarding robot use and older adults [35–38]. Nine items included concerns about what impact the deployment might have on the residents (deception; violation of dignity; restriction of self-determination; reduced human contact; violation of privacy; problems with sensitive data; feeling of being monitored; fear of the robot; injured by the robot) and two items on the caregivers themselves (job loss; feeling of being monitored). To report agreement to concerns response options «yes» and «somewhat yes» were taken together and reported as agreement. Due to the small sample size, the data collected via telephone interview and questionnaire data are presented descriptively, in summary.

2.2 Participants

Five caregivers (including the ward manager and the safety officer) between 16 and 52 years old and with at least one year to several decades of experience in elder care participated. They rated themselves as «somewhat uninterested» to «very intereste» in technology. Their experience with technology ranged from «little» to «a lot» as well as interest in learning how to use and use new or improved equipment. The involved caregivers all had previous experience with the use of PARO.

3   Results

3.1   Expectations Regarding the Effect of « Qoobo»

The first impression of «Qoobo» was rated as not so good on a four-point scale (with the options «very good», «good», «not so good», «not good at all») by all caregivers. The reasons they gave was the headless shape and that they found it difficult to imagine how the residents would react to this. Nevertheless, all participants were curious about the actual effects and were ready to use the SAR.

Positive expectations of the caregivers regarding manageability and practical aspects were that the robotic cushion would be more practical than the already used PARO, as «Qoobo» is smaller and less heavy, and that it is more pleasant due to the less loud sounds emitted, which were perceived to be quite annoying with PARO.

Regarding the effects on the residents, the caregivers expected that the use of «Qoobo» would improve mood, be a pastime, give some joy, reduce boredom, and reduce feelings of loneliness. In general, a more beneficial effect of «Qoobo» compared to the known PARO was not mentioned.

Negative expectations were that «Qoobo» could bore the residents and that it could be rejected because of its shape as it has no features that could enhance interaction like a head. Two caregivers expected that residents would not accept «Qoobo» because of its shape. Difficulties were also seen in the hygiene. In addition, caregivers mentioned that residents who would engage with «Qoobo» might not be taken seriously by other residents or might be excluded, as engaging with robotic pet aids could be perceived as ridiculous.

3.2   (Ethical) Concerns Regarding the Use of «Qoobo»

The main concern that caregivers agreed with was that residents might be afraid of the SAR. Regarding ethical concerns, three of four caregivers agreed with the concern that residents might be deceived. One caregiver agreed that the residents may have less human contact and one that the dignity of residents may be violated as a result of the deployment. Other ethical and general concerns in the questionnaire were not agreed with (Table 1).

Table 1. (Ethical) concerns of the caregivers from interviews and questionnaires.

Ethical concern	Number of caregivers that agreed
(I) Deception of residents	3
(II) Violation of dignity of residents	1
(III) Restriction of self-determination of residents	0
(IV) Reduced human contact of residents	1
(V) Violation of privacy of residents	0
(VI) Problems with sensitive data of residents	0
(VII) Resident's feeling of being monitored	0
(VIII) Resident's fear of the robot	4
(IX) Injury to the residents by the robot	0
(X) Job loss for caregivers	0
(XI) Caregivers' feeling of being monitored	0

4 Discussion

Prior to the use of a SAR in a Swiss nursing home, the expectations and concerns of caregivers experienced in the use of SAR were raised. Caregivers had positive expectations (to improve mood and joy, have fun, pass the time, reduce boredom and loneliness) and negative (boredom, lack of acceptance, hygiene, and making a fool of yourself by using it). Concerns cited were fear and deception of the residents.

Most of the eleven items offered to raise ethical concerns concerned the impact on the residents themselves. Only two items (fear of job loss and feeling of being monitored) related directly to the caregivers. It is notable that the caregivers did not agree with concerns that directly affect themselves. This is surprising since in a Swiss survey on ethical concerns almost half of the respondents agreed with the concern about job loss [29]. In a descriptive qualitative study that explored perceptions and experiences of the use of a SAR in the UK, Italy, and Ireland, it was shown that most participants were positive about the SAR, but some formal caregivers expressed concern that robots might replace care staff [39]. This fear was not expressed by the caregivers in this study. Maybe this could be explained by the good introduction and support at the beginning of the study, so caregivers knew they did not have to fear job loss. This explanation is supported as caregivers agreed to few concerns. The fact that the caregivers disagreed that the robot could injure the residents, is therefore explainable with the study situation. Caregivers were not asked globally if they feared this with robots in general, but specifically with the robot they were using. The lack of concerns can maybe be an expression of strong trust in the study team. But it does not mean that these concerns can be neglected. In a more global setting, these concerns may play a role.

In a study that surveyed the ethical concerns of the general Swiss population concerning the use of robots for older adults reported concerns were mainly related to reduced human contact or problems with sensitive data [29]. Half of the respondents also had concerns about workers losing their jobs or violation of privacy. This may give an indication that there are differences between the concerns of the general population, mostly with no or poor experience with robots, and professional caregivers experienced in the use of SAR, as the caregivers had no concerns of job loss or violation of dignity. But as mentioned, the specific test situation and the very small sample must be considered.

In the future, attitudes, expectations, and concerns should be examined as part of a larger study that includes more participants. It would also be interesting to compare different robots to see if expectations and concerns differ depending on the type of robot. Different stakeholders should be considered. As in a multi-perspective study with older adults, informal and professional caregivers Bedaf, Marti and de Witte [40] showed that some of the robot features mentioned were relevant to only one user group, and some were overarching across all user groups. To guarantee socially acceptable use, the expectations, and concerns of all relevant stakeholders should be considered before the use of a SAR globally and in a specific context.

References

1. Bundeszentrale für politische Bildung. https://www.bpb.de/nachschlagen/zahlen-und-fak ten/europa/70503/altersstruktur#:~:text=Bezogen%20auf%20die%2028%20Staaten,auf% 2028%2C5%20Pro-zent%20erh%C3%B6hen. Accessed on 18 Oct 2021
2. Eatock, D.: https://www.europarl.europa.eu/RegData/etudes/IDAN/2019/637955/EPRS_I DA(2019)637955_DE.pdf. Accessed on 10 March 2021
3. Eurostat. https://ec.europa.eu/eurostat/statistics-explained/index.php/Functional_and_act ivity_limitations_statistics#Functional_and_activity_limitations. Accessed on 10 March 2021
4. Mercay, C., Burla, L., Widmer, M.: Obsan Bericht 71. Gesundheitspersonal in der Schweiz. Bestandesaufnahme und Prognosen bis 2030. Schweizerisches Gesundheitsobservatorium (Obsan), Neuchâtel (2016)
5. Statista. https://de.statista.com/statistik/daten/studie/172651/umfrage/bedarf-an-pflegekra eften-2025/. Accessed on 10 March 2021
6. Ruf, E., Lehmann, S., Pauli, C., Misoch, S.: Roboter zur Unterstützung im Alter. HMD Praxis der Wirtschaftsinformatik **57**, 1251–1270 (2020)
7. Koutentakis, D., Pilozzi, A., Huang, X.: Designing socially assistive robots for alzheimer's disease and related dementia patients and their caregivers: where we are and where we are headed. Healthcare **8**(2), 73 (2020)
8. Feil-Seifer, D., Mataric, M.J.: Defining socially assistive robotics. In: 9th International Conference on Rehabilitation Robotics, ICORR, pp. 465–468. IEEE, Chicago (2005)
9. Broekens, J., Heerink, M., Rosendal, H.: Assistive social robots in elderly care: a review. Gerontechnology **8**(2), 94–103 (2009)
10. Barata, A.N.: Social robots as a complementary therapy in chronic, progressive diseases. In: Sequeira, J.S. (ed.) Robotics in Healthcare. AEMB, vol. 1170, pp. 95–102. Springer, Cham (2019). https://doi.org/10.1007/978-3-030-24230-5_5
11. Pu, L., Moyle, W., Jones, C., Todorovic, M.: The effectiveness of social robots for older adults: a systematic review and meta-analysis of randomized controlled studies. Gerontologist **59**(1), e37–e51 (2019)
12. Góngora Alonso, S., Hamrioui, S., de la Torre Díez, I., Motta Cruz, E., López-Coronado, M., Franco, M.: Social robots for people with aging and dementia: a systematic review of literature. Telemed. J. E-health: Off. J. Am. Telemed. Assoc. **25**(7), 533–540 (2019)

13. Leng, M., et al.: Pet robot intervention for people with dementia: a systematic review and meta-analysis of randomized controlled trials. Psychiatry Res. **271**, 516–525 (2019)
14. Abbott, R., et al.: How do "robopets" impact the health and well-being of residents in care homes? A systematic review of qualitative and quantitative evidence. Int. J. Older People Nurs. **14**(3), e12239 (2019)
15. Veloso, M.M., Rybski, P.E., Lenser, S., Chernova, S., Vail, D.: CMRoboBits: creating an intelligent AIBO robot. AI Mag. **27**(1), 67–82 (2006)
16. Wada, K., Shibata, T., Saito, T., Tanie, K.: Effects of robot assisted activity to elderly people who stay at a health service facility for the aged. In: IEEE/RSJ International Conference on Intelligent Robots and Systems, IROS, vol. 92, pp. 2847–2852. IEEE, Las Vegas (2003)
17. Petersen, S., Houston, S., Qin, H., Tague, C., Studley, J.: The utilization of robotic pets in dementia care. J. Alzheimer's Dis.: JAD **55**(2), 569–574 (2017)
18. Liang, A., et al.: A pilot randomized trial of a companion robot for people with dementia living in the community. J. Am. Med. Dir. Assoc. **18**(10), 871–878 (2017)
19. Robinson, H., MacDonald, B., Kerse, N., Broadbent, E.: The psychosocial effects of a companion robot: a randomized controlled trial. J. Am. Med. Dir. Assoc. **14**(9), 661–667 (2013)
20. Baisch, S., et al.: Emotionale Roboter im Pflegekontext: Empirische Analyse des bisherigen Einsatzes und der Wirkungen von Paro und Pleo. Z. Gerontol. Geriatr. **51**(1), 16–24 (2017)
21. Hung, L., et al.: The benefits of and barriers to using a social robot PARO in care settings: a scoping review. BMC Geriatr. **19**(1), 232 (2019)
22. Moyle, W., Bramble, M., Jones, C.J., Murfield, J.E.: She had a smile on her face as wide as the Great Australian Bite: a qualitative examination of family perceptions of a therapeutic robot and a plush toy. Gerontologist **59**(1), 177–185 (2019)
23. Johansson-Pajala, R.-M., Gustafsson, C.: Significant challenges when introducing care robots in Swedish elder care. Disabil. Rehabil.: Assist. Technol. 1–11 (2020). https://doi.org/10.1080/17483107.2020.1773549
24. Pino, M., Boulay, M., Jouen, F., Rigaud, A.-S.: Are we ready for robots that care for us? Attitudes and opinions of older adults toward socially assistive robots. Front. Aging Neurosci. **7**, 141 (2015)
25. Bitkom. https://www.bitkom.org/Presse/Presseinformation/Grosse-Offenheit-fuer-digitale-Helfer-in-der-Pflege.html. Accessed on 23 March 2021
26. Zentrum für Qualität in der Pflege: ZQP-Report. Pflege und digitale Technik. Berlin, Zentrum für Qualität in der Pflege (2019)
27. Hudson, J., Orviska, M., Hunady, J.: People's attitudes to robots in caring for the elderly. Int. J. Soc. Robot. **9**, 199–210 (2017)
28. Zöllick, J.C., Kuhlmey, A., Suhr, R., Eggert, S., Nordheim, J., Blüher, S.: Akzeptanz von Technikeinsatz in der Pflege. In: Jacobs, K., Kuhlmey, A., Greß, S., Klauber, J., Schwinger, A. (eds.) Pflege-Report 2019, pp. 211–218. Springer, Heidelberg (2020). https://doi.org/10.1007/978-3-662-58935-9_17
29. Ruf, E., Lehmann, S., Misoch, S.: Ethical concerns of the general public regarding the use of robots for older adults. In: Proceedings of the 7th International Conference on Information and Communication Technologies for Ageing Well and e-Health (ICT4AWE 2021) (in press)
30. Fachhochschule Graubünden. https://www.fhgr.ch/fhgr/unternehmerisches-handeln/schweizerisches-institut-fuer-entrepreneurship-sife/projekte/einsatz-von-servicerobotik-in-der-altenbetreuung/. Accessed on 11 March 2021
31. Yukai Engineering. https://qoobo.info/index-en/. Accessed on 15 March 2021
32. Bradwell, H.L., Edwards, K.J., Winnington, R., Thill, S., Jones, R.B.: Companion robots for older people: importance of user-centred design demonstrated through observations and focus groups comparing preferences of older people and roboticists in South West England. BMJ Open **9**(9), (2019)

33. Koh, W.Q., Ang, F.X.H., Casey, D.: Impacts of low-cost robotic pets for older adults and people with dementia: scoping review. JMIR Rehabil. Assist. Technol. **8**(1), (2021)
34. Kolstad, M., Yamaguchi, N., Babic, A., Nishihara, Y.: Integrating socially assistive robots into Japanese nursing care. Stud. Health Technol. Inf. **270**, 1323–1324 (2020)
35. Körtner, T.: Ethical challenges in the use of social service robots for elderly people. Ethische Herausforderungen zum Einsatz sozial-assisitver Roboter bei älteren Menschen. Zeitschrift für Gerontologie und Geriatrie **49**(4), 303–307 (2016)
36. Sharkey, A., Sharkey, N.: Granny and the robots: ethical issues in robot care for the elderly. Ethics Inf. Technol. **14**, 27–40 (2012)
37. Sorell, T., Draper, H.: Robot carers, ethics and older people. Ethics Inf. Technol. **16**, 183–195 (2014)
38. Vandemeulebroucke, T., Dierckx de Casterlé, B., Gastmans, C.: The use of care robots in aged care: a systematic review of argument-based ethics literature. Arch. Gerontol. Geriatr. **74**, 15–25 (2018)
39. Casey, D., et al.: The perceptions of people with dementia and key stakeholders regarding the use and impact of the social robot MARIO. Int. J. Environ. Res. Public Health **17**(22), 8621 (2020)
40. Bedaf, S., Marti, P., De Witte, L.: What are the preferred characteristics of a service robot for the elderly? A multi-country focus group study with older adults and caregivers. Assistive Technology. Off. J. RESNA **31**(3), 147–157 (2019)

Development and Evaluation of a Robot with an Airport Guidance System

Ayako Masuda[1(✉)], Yoshihisa Ohara[2], and Junya Onishi[1]

[1] Honda R&D Co., Ltd., Wako, Saitama, Japan
{ayako_masuda,junya_onishi}@jp.honda
[2] The Japan Research Institute Limited, Shinagawa, Tokyo, Japan
ohara.yoshihisa@jri.co.jp

Abstract. A guide service consisting of a reception robot system and a guide robot system was developed to increase convenience in international airports that are used by a variety of people. This paper describes the functions and evaluation of the reception robot system. Service users perform voice or touch screen operations to search for shops or facilities in the airport and set a destination. This paper evaluated the developed system from two perspectives in order to further enhance the service. The first was evaluation of each function (touch screen usability, impressions of the robot's behavior), and the second was evaluation of the service as a whole (willingness to use when actually encountering the service). The evaluation method used behavioral observation, questionnaires, and interviews . As a result of the evaluation, issues with regards to touch screen usability were extracted. Impressions of the robot's behavior were rated highly overall, with English speakers giving more positive ratings than Japanese speakers. 80% of the survey participants responded that they would like to actually use the service in an airport if the touch screen usability is enhanced, which confirmed the usefulness as a service.

Keywords: Reception robot system · Touch screen usability · Impression of robot's behavior

1 Introduction

Due to labor shortages, the potential for substitution with robots is being increasingly explored in service and distribution industries such as guidance, delivery, and sanitation. Multilingual capability and the ability to support various needs are especially needed in guide operations at international airports, however securing appropriate human resources presents issues. A guide robot service was therefore developed to perform guide operations in place of humans [1].

The service consists of a reception robot system that sets a destination (Fig. 1(a)) and a guide robot system that actually guides the service user to that destination (Fig. 1(b)). The service user can arrive at the destination by communicating the destination to the reception robot system and then following the guide robot system (Fig. 1(c)).This paper discusses the functions and evaluation of the reception robot system.

© Springer Nature Switzerland AG 2021
C. Stephanidis et al. (Eds.): HCII 2021, CCIS 1420, pp. 156–163, 2021.
https://doi.org/10.1007/978-3-030-78642-7_21

(a) Reception   (b) Guide
robot system   robot system   (c) Scenario

Fig. 1. Guide service overview

2 Functions of Reception Robot System

The reception robot system consists of a robot and a touch screen. The service user uses voice and touch screen operations to search for shops or facilities and then set a destination. The reception robot system utilizes the following two features to provide smooth, natural, and approachable service in airports, which are used by a variety of people. The first feature is usability, which is realized by a multilingual support function, a voice dialogue function, and a touch screen function. The second feature is approachability, which is realized by a robot height adjustment function and the robot's behavior [2]. In order to confirm user impressions when using the service, user evaluation was performed with particular focus on touch screen usability and the robot's behavior. This chapter details the functions covered by this evaluation.

First is the touch screen function. The service user can select the language to be used (Fig. 2(a)) and search for destinations on the touch screen. After the language is selected on the tutorial screen, a voice chat screen is displayed (Fig. 2(b)). The service user can select whether to use voice input or button input. When the service user voices the destination to the robot, the search results are listed on the screen (Fig. 2(c)). By selecting the destination from the list, a results screen noting detailed information is displayed (Fig. 2(d)). Lastly, the service user selects whether to proceed to the destination together with the robot or to go alone, ending the reception service.

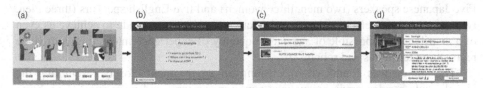

(a)   (b)   (c)   (d)

Fig. 2. User Interface flow

Next is the robot's behavior. The robot performs behaviors according to the system usage scenario and operation contents. For example, the robot behaves as if nodding when it detects utterances by the service user (Fig. 3(a)), and as if thinking by swaying its body from side to side when searching for the destination (Fig. 3(b)).

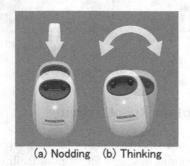

(a) Nodding   (b) Thinking

Fig. 3. Robot motion examples

3   User Evaluation Survey

3.1   Purpose

Evaluation was performed from two perspectives in order to extract functional issues for service enhancement from the evaluation results, as well as to understand users' opinions of the service. The first perspective was evaluation of each function, and the two items of touch screen usability and impressions of the robot's behavior were evaluated. The second perspective was evaluation of the service as a whole, and the willingness to use it when actually encountering the service was evaluated.

3.2   Evaluation Method

Five Japanese speakers (two men, three women) and five English speakers (three men, two women) were selected as survey participants, with effort made to achieve as even of a distribution as possible of age and frequency of experience interacting with voice recognition terminals and robots.

The survey was conducted by creating an environment closely resembling the actual guide service environment in a conference room, and performing a usability test, behavioral observation, and interview. The participants used the reception service and attempted to perform six tasks such as, for example, "Communicate that you wish to go to a lounge, and then go with the robot to that location." At the start of the survey, we explained the nature of the survey to the participants and obtained their informed consent.

In evaluation of touch screen usability, prior research by Nishimoto et al. on Remote Usability Testing [3] was consulted, and a questionnaire suited to evaluation of items such as the text characters, operability, and amount of information was prepared. After completing all of the tasks, the participants evaluated the question items using a 5-point rating scale. The reasons for their ratings were noted in an interview following the evaluation.

In evaluation of the impressions made by the robot's behavior, the GODSPEED [4] questionnaire encompassing the five main concepts (anthropomorphism, animacy, likeability, perceived intelligence, and perceived safety) in the field of Human-Robot Interaction was used. In the case of anthropomorphism, for example, the words "fake – natural" are paired together, and participants rated anthropomorphism on the 5-point scale of 1 point if the robot seemed fake, 2 points for somewhat fake, 3 points for don't know, 4 points for somewhat natural, and 5 points if the robot seemed natural. In this survey, the four items of "Apathetic - Sympathetic," "Fear - Secure," "Unpleasant - Pleasant," and "Inaccurate – Accurate" were added to evaluate the "usability" and "approachability" of the guide service. The participants filled out the questionnaire after completing all the tasks, and were then interviewed to confirm the reasons for their ratings.

In evaluation of the service as a whole, interviews were conducted to confirm the willingness to use it should they actually encounter this service in an airport.

3.3 Results and Discussion

In evaluation of each function, which was the first perspective, touch screen usability is discussed as follows. Figure 4 shows the survey results for all participants. The blue line shows the average ratings by Japanese speakers, and the red line shows the average ratings by English speakers. The average rating was 3.57 for Japanese speakers and 4.06 for English speakers. Except for three items, English speakers tended to rate touch screen usability more positively on average than Japanese speakers. Points rated as easy to use included "Characters were easy to read," "I didn't feel uncomfortable with the written expressions," and "The amount of information displayed on the screen was appropriate," etc. Points rated as not easy to use included "The reaction speed of the voice recognition and button operations was appropriate" and "When using the voice recognition or the interactive buttons, it was easy to know whether I succeeded or did not succeeded," etc.

The survey results, including the interviews, suggested five issues (Table 1). The delay in recognition during voice input was mentioned by all participants, so the priority as a service design was increased, prior research by Shiwa et al. [5] on allowable time was consulted, and the response time was set to 3 s. or less. In addition, the touch screen layout was also modified, such as by increasing map size.

Fig. 4. Results of evaluation of the usability of the touch screen. (Color figure online)

Next, the impressions of the robot's behavior are discussed. Figure 5 shows the survey results for all participants. The blue line shows the average ratings by Japanese speakers, and the red line shows the average ratings by English speakers. English speakers tended to rate anthropomorphism and animacy more positively on average than Japanese speakers. Both Japanese and English speakers tended to rate likeability and perceived intelligence highly, and assigned similar average ratings to perceived safety. Both Japanese and English speakers rated the four added original items positively, but ratings by English speakers tended to be higher on average.

Table 1. Issues extracted in touch screen evaluation

Primary item	Secondary item	Examples of remarks made during interviews
Response during voice input	Delay in recognition	The processing time after speaking is quite long.
	Not easy to know if recognition is successful	I felt uneasy because I wasn't sure if it was not responding or if I needed to speak the phrase again.
	Response when recognition is unsuccessful	It felt like a computer error message, which clearly did not match the system's impression.
Microphone button	Challenging button operation	It is difficult to know if the microphone is on.
	Not easy to understand where to speak to	It is difficult to know how close my face should be when speaking.
List display	Disorganized items	Items should be grouped roughly by genre and listed in order of distance from the present location.
	Inconvenient button behavior	Each item has to be opened one by one in order to know the shop details.
Map screen	Small map size	The displayed map is small and marks and other information are difficult to understand.
	Not easy to notice the Enlarge button	I did not notice the Enlarge button.
Keyboard entry	Challenging text entry	Simple *Hiragana* and alphabet characters are enough.

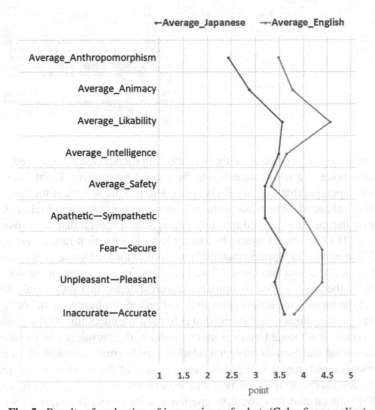

Fig. 5. Results of evaluation of impressions of robot. (Color figure online)

The interview results revealed five viewpoints (Table 2). The robot's appearance, movements, and sound were rated positively, which was found to carry over to anthropomorphism and animacy. In contrast, difficulty using the touch screen and the lack of spontaneous speaking and assistance were found to negatively impact ratings of likeability, perceived intelligence, and the original items "Sympathetic" and "Accurate". Therefore, enhancement of touch screen usability as mentioned above is a potential means for enhancing the service. In addition, responding according to the situation, such as providing advice when voice recognition is repeatedly unsuccessful, is thought to be effective for engendering a sense that the robot is speaking spontaneously and providing assistance.

Table 2. Opinions concerning impressions of the robot's behavior

Item	Positive opinions	Negative opinions
Robot appearance and movement	• The movement is smoother and more like a living creature than robots I have seen so far. • The shape and size look just right.	• It (the movement) makes no sense.
Robot sound	• The sounds that play when the robot is responding are cute. • The sound that the robot emits when the service ends feels like it is saying "Thank you."	• I don't like the whistling sound (that the robot makes when nodding after voice recognition) very much.
Unable to have a conversation using language	• Having the robot express emotions by sounds instead of words is effective in an airport where people of various cultures and languages come and go.	• Due to the lack of verbal conversation, I didn't really feel the robot was necessary.
Relationship between touch screen and robot		• The negative evaluation of the touch screen interfered with the evaluation of the robot, and hindered rating as "pleasant," "competent," "knowledgeable," "intelligent," "sensible," and "responsible". • The lack of notification and explanation of the reason when voice input is unsuccessful was also a factor for negative ratings of "incompetent" and "inaccurate".
Lack of spontaneous speaking and assistance		• The robot moved and emitted sounds but did not help me when I was having trouble during operations, which made a negative impression. • If there was interaction it would feel a bit more intelligent.

Willingness to use it when actually encountering the service is discussed as evaluation of the service as a whole, which was the second perspective. Eight out of the 10 participants responded that they would be willing to use the service if the touch screen usability was enhanced. When asked the reasons, opinions obtained included, "I was fascinated by the fact that I could input by voice, search from a displayed list, and be guided," and "If I had time, I would like to try it as an attraction rather than for guide purposes." In contrast, the opinion that, "When I look at the bird's-eye view of me facing that robot alone, it feels a bit comical," was also obtained as a reason for not actively making use of the service. The participants who responded that they would not make active use of the service due to self-conscious feelings of "embarrassment" or "comicality" were Japanese speakers, suggesting that cultural differences impact the potential for using the service. It is thought that in Oriental culture, the prevalence of an interdependent self-construal that focuses on social relationships [6] may be involved. In addition, participants who said they would not make active use of the service were found from the preliminary survey to have no previous experience conversing with robots. Prior research [7] showed that less contact experience with robots corresponds with more negative attitudes towards dialogue with robots, and willingness to use is also thought to be related to individual characteristics.

4 Conclusion

A reception robot system for setting a destination was developed in order to perform guide service at an international airport. Among the developed functions, the touch screen usability and the impression of the robot's behavior were evaluated. The results of user evaluation showed that enhancement of touch screen usability is needed. The usability of touch screen also impacted ratings of the robot's intelligence. In contrast, the impression of the robot's behavior generally received favorable ratings.

The user evaluation also suggested that, in order to further enhance guide service, spontaneous speaking and assistance from the robot strengthens the impression that the robot is sympathetic to the service user. 80% of the survey participants responded that they would be willing to actually use the service in an airport if the touch screen operations are enhanced, which confirmed the usefulness of the service. In addition, it was suggested that individual characteristics such as cultural sphere and robot contact experience might change the willingness to use the service.

References

1. Saito, Y., Koshiishi, T.: Development and styling design of airport guide robot system. Honda R&D Tech. Rev. **33**(1), 1–9 (2021)
2. Onishi, J., Masuda, A., Obayashi, C., Kawasaki, Y., Takebe, Y.: Development of reception robot for airport guide. Honda R&D Tech. Rev. **33**(1), 10–18 (2021)
3. Nishimoto, K., Nambu, M., Ito, K.: Evaluation an experimental for effectiveness and implementation ease of remote usability testing. In: Proceedings of the 31st JSSST Conference, Ippan 6-4 (2014)
4. Bartneck, C., Kulic, D., Croft, E., Zoghbi, S.: Measurement instruments for the anthropomorphism, animacy, likeability, perceived intelligence, and perceived safety of robots. Int. J. Soc. Rob. **1**, 71–81 (2009). https://doi.org/10.1007/s12369-008-0001-3
5. Shiwa, T., Kanda, T., Imai, M., Ishiguro, H., Hagita, N., Anzai, Y.: How quickly should communication robots respond? J. Rob. Soc. Jpn **27**(1), 87–95 (2009)
6. Markus, H.R., Kitayama, S.: Culture and the self: implications for cognition, emotion, and motivation. Psychol. Rev. **98**, 224–253 (1991)
7. Nomura, R., Kanda, T., Suzuki, T., Yamada, S., Kato, K.: Human attitudes, anxiety, and behaviors in human-robot interaction (HRI). In: Proceedings of the 26th Fuzzy System Symposium, pp. 554–559 (2010)

Social Robotics to Address Isolation and Depression Among the Aging During and After COVID-19

Jordan Miller[1]([⊠]) and Troy McDaniel[2]

[1] Center for Cognitive Ubiquitous Computing (CUbiC), School of Computing,
Informatics, and Decision Systems Engineering (CIDSE),
Ira A. Fulton Schools of Engineering, Arizona State University, Tempe, AZ, USA
jlmill41@asu.edu
[2] The Polytechnic School (TPS), Ira A. Fulton Schools of Engineering,
Arizona State University, Mesa, AZ, USA

Abstract. COVID-19 is exacerbating isolation issues faced by older adults, which may lead to increased risk for depression and other mental health issues. Social robots are being explored for their potential to alleviate these challenges through conversational therapy, companionship, and connectedness regardless of where older adults chose to age in place—from home to long-term care facilities. This is a discussion piece with the objective of raising awareness to the topic of social isolation within older adults and current limitations in the field of social robotics. We discuss the state of the art in social robotics for aging in place and bring attention to remaining challenges for addressing isolation and mental health especially during and after COVID-19. This paper provides a discussion on critical differences between environments where older individuals age, and how designs should account for these variations. Lastly, this paper highlights the physical and mental health issues of caregivers and provides a discussion of challenges that remain toward using social robotics to assist those who take care of the aging population.

Keywords: COVID-19 · Depression · Isolation · Social robotics ·
Elderly · Long-term care · Independent living · Aging in place ·
Pandemics

1 Introduction

Aging in place is defined as a situation where a person can age in the place of his or her choosing for the remainder of his or her life [29]. Many older adults are not able to spend their remaining days living inside their own home due to requiring care not possible in their house. This has led technologist to develop solutions to

Supported by Arizona State University, the National Science Foundation, and the Zimin Institute at Arizona State University.

C. Stephanidis et al. (Eds.): HCII 2021, CCIS 1420, pp. 164–171, 2021.
https://doi.org/10.1007/978-3-030-78642-7_22

allow people to age inside their home longer. Examples include smart homes that monitor a person inside the home [12,13]; and wearables and interactive video games that encourage fitness [14,27]. Robots are being developed to aid people living with dementia and range in their functionality from storytelling and playing music, to engaging users in mathematical problem solving or other cognitive tasks [10,15,21]. An example of a low-cost, commercially-available solution is Joy for All's robotic pets, targeted toward people living with dementia, allowing users to feel as if they are caring for an animal, without the physical burden of a pet [6].

Depression and isolation are often felt as people age due to a myriad of circumstances including the environment in which a person ages; less frequent social interactions; and losing or being separated from friends. The impact depression can have on mental health is detrimental and has been compared to smoking [9]. Isolation is commonly experienced irrespective of where a person chooses to age. Social robots are being explored to assist older adults through companionship, conversation therapy, and connectedness to those around them. Yet much work remains before these technologies, such as conversational therapy products, are brought to the market to address feelings of isolation and depression.

Pandemics, such as COVID-19, necessitate social distancing and quarantining, potentially exacerbating the aforementioned emotions of depression and isolation. For many healthy older adults, COVID-19 interrupted regular visits with family and friends due to quarantining, yet some comfort was found in drive-by visits with their family; using plastic barriers for hugging; waving from windows or front doors; and using video services to connect [17]. Seniors in long-term care facilities were unable to participate in the aforementioned limited yet critical social visits and were completely cut-off from visitors outside the medical staff [1].

COVID-19 has called urgency to social robotics to provide comfort to older adults now and in the future. In this paper, we discuss current trends in social robotics, highlight remaining challenges, and provide insight on how to address these barriers in different environments to assist caregivers of older adults.

2   Aging in Place: How Place Affects Aging

A person can age in place inside their home, a family member's home, a nursing home, or an assisted living facility. When examining these locations separately, a common challenge connected all settings: isolation is irrespective of environment.

Older adults who age inside their home can still feel the effects of isolation and depression. These feelings can be stimulated through limited public and private interaction or living alone [9]. Decreased motor skills that prohibit seniors from leaving the house as often as they would prefer can be another contributing factor to isolation. Infrequent visits by family living far away can contribute to isolation. Seniors, in general, are less tech savvy than younger generations, which can create barriers with staying connected among their social circle.

Health problems can leave an individual feeling isolated if he or she does not have anyone to confide in or cannot receive assistance getting to and from doctor appointments. Disability can also lead to an individual feeling alone. Disability resulting from falls such as hip fractures is a common injury leading to immobility. Difficulties with ambulation and transportation can lead to social isolation depending on how long individuals require to recover; how much time they must spend at home alone; and the extent of surgery.

When a person moves from assisted living to a nursing home, there are social consequences. Older adults often lose friends they made at the assisted living facility as well as the relationship with staff members who are familiar with their medical condition and needs [8].

When an older adult moves in with younger family members, this can cause the informal caregiver to feel isolated and depressed. Usually, informal caregivers have additional people inside the house they provide care to. Caregivers often neglect their own health to assist other people inside the residence which can cause their mental and physical health to decline [16]. For example, they often stop socializing with friends and feel they have no time for themselves.

3   COVID-19, Isolation, and Depression

While isolation and depression are present outside of pandemics, these feelings are heightened during events that require quarantining and social distancing, such as COVID-19. Seniors are more at risk for developing severe illness from COVID-19 than other demographics, which could lead to hospitalization, intensive care, or even death [1]. Therefore, older adults were encouraged to isolate more than the general population. On June 25th, 2020, the Center for Disease Control and Prevention (CDC) reported 8 out of 10 deaths related to COVID-19 were adults 65 and older [1]. In response, many stores created special "Senior Hours" early in the morning for the elderly to shop without the general population [24]. Older adults were encouraged to switch medication from 30- to 90-day supplies as well as store enough food for extended quarantining to help minimize exposure [22]. Grandparents were isolated from their grandchildren who they previously saw regularly, leading to increases in separation anxiety [17]. Grandparents were afraid they would miss watching their grandchildren grow up; their grandchildren would forget them; or their grandchildren would not want to spend as much time with them after the pandemic [17].

For seniors who have underlying health issues, many communities came together to complete shopping and deliver the necessary supplies for community members [19], allowing more at risk demographics to stay safely inside their homes. Concerns for contracting COVID-19 are higher inside care facilities. Many facilities restricted or banned visitors to reduce the risk of infection [1]. In addition, facilities practiced social distancing from other patients [1].

One in three people in the United States serve as an informal caregiver and frequently experience physical and mental stress [26], which can lead to fatigue, anxiety, and/or depression [2]. Informal caregivers are usually the spouse or the adult, female child. During COVID-19, caregivers had to take extreme caution in caring for their loved ones, which included limiting time spent outside their homes; disinfecting groceries and items after shopping; disinfecting mail; and creating a secondary caregiver alternative in case they fell ill [7]. Once caregivers were done sanitizing the outside provisions, they had to sanitize themselves by changing from "outside clothes" to "inside clothes", and taking a shower and washing their hair [7]. Caregivers were advised to not wear jewelry outside the home and wear hair back to reduce the risk of it carrying COVID-19 particles [7]. Finally, caregivers were encouraged to frequently wash their hands up to their elbow [7]. Resources for dealing with the extreme stress and isolation felt from sheltering at home while caring for an older adult include taking short breaks, and contacting loved ones and/or support groups [2, 3, 25, 28].

4   Social Robotics to Assist with Isolation and Depression

Currently, many social robotic applications have only been tested as pilot studies and there are no commercially available conversational robots on the market. Joy for All created a robotic puppy, kitten, and cat intended to sooth older adults living with dementia [6]. These robotic pets interact with the user by barking when conversation is detected. Here, we report only the research in social robotics related to conversational strategies.

In 2019, Magyar et al. [20] developed an autonomous dialogue system to learn conversations from humans to assist older adults living with dementia. The team used a small robot, resembling a baby, which allowed patients to hold onto it for extended periods of time, promoting longer conversations. Magyar et al. reported this work as the first study to demonstrate robots being used to reduce dementia related symptoms such as depression. The had five participants.

Cruz-Sandoval et al. [11] developed a robot named Eva to interact with persons living with dementia by using conversational strategies recommended to caregivers. Eva is semi-autonomous and can handle simple conversations but requires a human operator for more complex interactions. Through her remote app, a human operator can send commands to Eva to play songs, prompt predefined activities (e.g., greetings), change the emotion on her face, and convey personalized phrases. Cruz-Sandoval et al. reported that conversational strategies increased interaction with the robot. The study took place in 2019 in Mexico and included twelve patients who participated in twenty-three group sessions.

Khosla et al. [18] studied how older adults living with dementia in at-home care interacted with a robot named Betty in 2019 over three months. Betty was capable of playing users' favorite songs while dancing, providing the news, telling stories, sharing daily reminders, engaging users in cognitive games, and serving as a medium for SMS messages, phone calls, and video messaging to family members. Results showed users engaged with the robot at least three to six times a day. Videos of the sessions were recorded and showed caregivers preforming other tasks in the background while loved ones engaged with Betty. Four out of the five participants reported feeling that Betty was a friend, showing the potential of social robotics for assisting older adults and their caregivers.

In 2019, Iwabuchi et al. [15] introduced a conversational robot named Sota to help people living with dementia. The robot could greet individuals, ask the user's name, offer topics to discuss, and offer emotion evoking conversations, and play Japanese word games. Participants interacted with Sota for fifteen minutes. Sota was reported as offering positive conversational support; however, the number of participants is unknown.

Abdollahi et al. [5] conducted a pilot study in 2017 with a robot named Ryan. The robot was capable of engaging users through simple question-directed conversation, displaying a photo album along with the story behind each picture, changing facial expressions, or reminding them of their daily schedule. Six participants were selected to have 24/7 access to Ryan inside their home for four to six weeks. The paper reported that participants spent on average two hours interacting with the robot per day. Moreover, users enjoyed having Ryan as a companion, and the interest in interacting with Ryan did not decrease with time.

5 Limitations in the Field

There is a limited amount of research being done around conversational robotics and virtually none for healthy older adults. State-of-the-art technology is still in pilot testing mode, and very few participants are involved during testing.

Much of the technology mentioned above is for older adults living with dementia as opposed to healthy older adults. This could deter healthy older adults from using one of these robotic applications due to a misalignment of needs. The robot in [18] which could have potential given the findings of doll therapy, which has shown to help people living with dementia by providing health benefits associated with caring for another person [23]. The form of a baby could deter healthy older adults given that the robot may feel too childlike instead of filling the role of a companion. Khosla et al. [18] showed that users were engaged with their social robots for extended periods of time, demonstrating the potential for this technology to reduce feelings of isolation and depression.

While hardware, software, and artificial intelligence are advancing at a rapid pace, social robotics is still in its infancy. As of today, no robotic platforms for conversational therapy have made it to market. While apps exist, such as PyxHealth [4], social robots are still nascent. One barrier to their exploration and use is their high cost. Low cost robotic platforms are needed to increase the likelihood of people purchasing and adopting these devices in their homes.

Social robots need to be capable of handling complex and interactive dialogue. Currently, robotic conversation is simple and nonreciprocal. For applications to become widely accepted, communications should be veridical, adaptive, reciprocal, and multimodal. Dyadic interactions between humans include social non-verbal cues such as facial expressions, body language, and hand gestures;

reciprocal engagements; and contextual information from past. None of the current applications are capable of mimicking these behaviors. To reach a wider market, such features will be essential to social companion robots.

The aforementioned challenges leave gaps in the literature including the following questions: Will healthy older adults be willing to accept a social robot for companionship? What physical features of a social robot are important to healthy and burdened adults? What additional tasks or functions, if any, should a social robot be able to perform?

6 Discussion

Isolation and depression were felt by older adults and caregivers before the COVID-19 pandemic. Being forced to shelter at home, sanitizing their provisions, leaving their residence, and being isolated from family and friends has only exacerbated these feelings and taken a toll on their mental health. The recommendation for caregivers is to reach out to a friend or family member for support. Moreover, feelings of isolation and depression among seniors before the pandemic have likely increased due to further restrictions on social interaction. Social robotics have the potential to augment and enhance social interactions during times of isolation, both for older adults and caregivers; yet, as of today, no commercial products exist.

Isolation is felt by caregivers and older adults in all locations they choose to age in place. Most research to address isolation is happening inside care facilities, but other locations, such as the home, are in need of attention. Researchers are urged to shift their area of focus from assisted living to in-home settings to accommodate the majority of seniors aging in home, and work to include healthy older adults in their experiments to enhance the applicability of the devices they develop. By diversify the participant pool, we will gain a better understanding of social robot features valued by healthy older adults as well those requiring assistance. These differences will provide insight into how to generalize social robots to assist as many people suffering from isolation and depression as possible.

COVID-19 has called attention to the urgency and importance of conversational social robotics. These technologies have the potential to assist seniors who are isolated during the time of the pandemic and long after. Caregivers could benefit from the use of a social robot in the home by allowing them to focus on other activities inside the home, take time for themselves, and converse with the robot to release stress. Social robotics capable of engaging the user in veridical, reciprocal, and engaging conversation could alleviate isolation and depression felt by older adults in any location they choose to age.

Acknowledgements. The authors thank Arizona State University, the National Science Foundation (Grant No. 1828010), and the Zimin Institute at Arizona State University for their funding support. Views expressed are those of the authors and do not necessarily reflect those of the NSF.

References

1. Older adults and covid-19. https://www.cdc.gov/coronavirus/2019-ncov/need-extra-precautions/older-adults.html
2. Care for caregivers during covid-19, April 2020. https://ch.kendal.org/2020/04/16/care-for-caregivers-during-covid-19/
3. Caregiver burnout during covid-19: what you should know, May 2020. https://shine365.marshfieldclinic.org/wellness/caregiver-burnout-covid-19/
4. Home, January 2021. https://www.pyxhealth.com/
5. Abdollahi, H., Mollahosseini, A., Lane, J.T., Mahoor, M.H.: A pilot study on using an intelligent life-like robot as a companion for elderly individuals with dementia and depression. In: 2017 IEEE-RAS 17th International Conference on Humanoid Robotics (Humanoids), pp. 541–546. IEEE (2017)
6. Joy for All (2018). https://joyforall.com/
7. Brown, A., Bradford, M., Bresolin, P.: 8 shelter-in-place coronavirus tips for senior care in your home, June 2020. https://dailycaring.com/8-shelter-in-place-tips-for-coronavirus-senior-care-in-your-home/
8. Chapin, R., Dobbs-Kepper, D.: Aging in place in assisted living: philosophy versus policy. Gerontologist **41**(1), 43–50 (2001)
9. Cornwell, E.Y., Waite, L.J.: Social disconnectedness, perceived isolation, and health among older adults. J. Health Soc. Behav. **50**(1), 31–48 (2009)
10. Cruz-Sandoval, D., Favela, J.: A conversational robot to conduct therapeutic interventions for dementia. IEEE Pervasive Comput. **18**(2), 10–19 (2019)
11. Cruz-Sandoval, D., Favela, J.: Incorporating conversational strategies in a social robot to interact with people with dementia. Dement. Geriatr. Cogn. Disord. **47**(3), 140–148 (2019)
12. Demira, E., Köseoğlub, E., Sokulluc, R., Şekerd, B.: Smart home assistant for ambient assisted living of elderly people with dementia. Procedia Comput. Sci. **113**, 609–614 (2017)
13. Enshaeifar, S., et al.: Health management and pattern analysis of daily living activities of people with dementia using in-home sensors and machine learning techniques. PloS One **13**(5), e0195605 (2018)
14. Gerling, K., Livingston, I., Nacke, L., Mandryk, R.: Full-body motion-based game interaction for older adults. In: Proceedings of the SIGCHI Conference on Human Factors in Computing Systems, pp. 1873–1882 (2012)
15. Iwabuchi, Y., Sato, I., Fujino, Y., Yagi, N.: The communication supporting robot based on "humanitude" concept for dementia patients. In: 2019 IEEE 1st Global Conference on Life Sciences and Technologies (LifeTech), pp. 219–223. IEEE (2019)
16. Johnson, R.W., Wang, C.X.: The financial burden of paid home care on older adults: oldest and sickest are least likely to have enough income. Health Aff. **38**(6), 994–1002 (2019)
17. Kaysen, R.: Grandparents face separation anxiety during pandemic, June 2020. https://www.aarp.org/home-family/friends-family/info-2020/grandparents-anxiety-coronavirus.html
18. Khosla, R., Chu, M.T., Khaksar, S.M.S., Nguyen, K., Nishida, T.: Engagement and experience of older people with socially assistive robots in home care. Assistive Technol., 1–15 (2019)
19. Lee, L.: This student created a network of 'shopping angels' to help the elderly get groceries during the coronavirus pandemic, March 2020. https://www.cnn.com/2020/03/17/us/coronavirus-student-volunteers-grocery-shop-elderly-iyw-trnd/index.html

20. Magyar, J., Kobayashi, M., Nishio, S., Sinčák, P., Ishiguro, H.: Autonomous robotic dialogue system with reinforcement learning for elderlies with dementia. In: 2019 IEEE International Conference on Systems, Man and Cybernetics (SMC), pp. 3416–3421. IEEE (2019)
21. Martín, F., et al.: Robots in therapy for dementia patients. J. Phys. Agents **7**(1), 48–55 (2013)
22. Nania, R., Crouch, M.: What you need to know about the coronavirus outbreak. https://www.aarp.org/health/conditions-treatments/info-2020/coronavirus-facts.html
23. Pezzati, R., et al.: Can doll therapy preserve or promote attachment in people with cognitive, behavioral, and emotional problems? A pilot study in institutionalized patients with dementia. Front. Psychol. **5**, 342 (2014)
24. Repko, M.: Stop & shop, other grocers have special shopping hours for seniors. here's how they work, March 2020. https://www.cnbc.com/2020/03/19/coronavirus-how-senior-shopping-hours-work-at-stop-shop-other-grocers.html
25. Schall, J.: Family caregiver mental health and covid-19. https://mhanational.org/family-caregiver-mental-health-and-covid-19
26. Staff, M.C.: Practical solutions for caregiver stress, December 2020. https://www.mayoclinic.org/healthy-lifestyle/stress-management/in-depth/caregiver-stress/art-20044784
27. Steinert, A., Haesner, M., Steinhagen-Thiessen, E.: Activity-tracking devices for older adults: comparison and preferences. Universal Access Inf. Soc. **17**(2), 411–419 (2018)
28. DailyCaring Editorial Team: 8 mental health tips for caregivers during coronavirus. https://dailycaring.com/coronavirus-and-caregiver-mental-health-8-coping-tips/
29. Witt, S., Hoyt, J., Expert, R.B.S.W.E.H.C., Chief, W.B.J.H.E.: Aging in place: What is aging in place and what does it mean? March 2020. https://www.seniorliving.org/aging-in-place/

Development of a Telepresence System Using a Robot Controlled by Mobile Devices

Tatsuya Minagawa$^{(\boxtimes)}$, Ippei Suzuki, and Yoichi Ochiai

University of Tsukuba, Tsukuba, Japan
{mina.tatsu,1heisuzuki}@digitalnature.slis.tsukuba.ac.jp
wizard@slis.tsukuba.ac.jp

Abstract. This study proposes a telepresence system controlled by mobile devices consisting of a conference side and a remote side. The conference side of this system consists of a puppet-type robot that enhances the co-telepresence. The remote side includes a web application that can be accessed by a mobile device that can operate the robot by using a motion sensor. The effectiveness of the robot-based telepresence techniques in the teleconference applications is analyzed by conducting user surveys of the participants in remote and real-world situations. It is observed from the experimental results that the proposed telepresence system enhances the coexistence of remote participants and allows them to attend the conference enjoyably.

Keywords: Design · Operation and evaluation of mobile communications

1 Introduction

Commonly used video conferencing systems (e.g., Skype and Google Meets) face certain limitations when compared to face-to-face meetings. Andres et al. reported that the face-to-face setting is superior to the videoconferencing setting for team productivity [1]. The technologies used for videoconferencing limit the sense of co-presence and the ease of interaction with a person because they have no physical representation of a participant and no support for the use of nonverbal communication. Communication technologies that support remote collaboration in distributed workplaces have also demanded greatly. Previous research in telepresence systems has been proposed to aim to offer solutions to some of these limitations of videoconferencing. This study aims to analyze the effectiveness of a telepresence method using a robot in the interactions between the participants in conference situations by comparing it with a videoconferencing system. Two types of telepresence systems are implemented in this study for teleconferencing. A telepresence robot is used to enhance the presence of a remote person, and the person can control the robot using two methods: a tablet-based interface

© Springer Nature Switzerland AG 2021
C. Stephanidis et al. (Eds.): HCII 2021, CCIS 1420, pp. 172–180, 2021.
https://doi.org/10.1007/978-3-030-78642-7_23

and a motion-based interface with a head mounted display (HMD) system. The results of the user study are presented for both the remote participants and for real-world locations to show how the physical presence of a remote person represented as a robot affects the communication in teleconferencing when compared to a general videoconference. This study also analyzes the advantages and disadvantages of videoconferencing and telepresence conferencing.

2   Related Work

Previous studies have proposed teleconferencing systems combined with robotics to enhance the experience of the remote participants in a conference situation. The PRoPs [6] allow for the remote participants to show their presence in a remote location rather than a virtual environment, using a robot instead of an avatar. Similar telepresence robots are analyzed and used to participate in a conference [2,7,9,11]. However, these proposed robots are equipped with displays to show the participants' faces and do not have a human-like or a bipedal-shaped body; furthermore, the nonverbal gestures are hidden in a display. Therefore, the sense of the presence of a remote person is limited for feeling of the person "being here" together. A few teleoperation robots equipped with actuators have also been proposed in previous studies, which allow for the users to control the robots from remote locations to maintain physical presence instead of using avatars on 2D displays [3,10]. Additionally, human-like remote-controlled android robots have also been developed [5]. Several telepresence systems have been developed for communication and education [4] and for puppetry [8], using robots. These telepresence robots can also be utilized in a conference situation. This study uses a telepresence robot like a puppet, to investigate how it can enhance the presence of a remote person and effectively improve the productivity and the ease of interaction for people in both remote and real-world settings.

3   Implementation

This section presents the details of the telepresence methods used in the analysis. The proposed system consists of two parts: (1) the remote participant side and (2) the conference room side.

3.1   Remote Participant Side

Two types of telepresence systems are implemented for teleconferencing: a tablet-based system and an HMD-based system.

Tablet-Based System. The general mobile terminals (e.g., smartphones and tablets) are used as control and feedback devices, as shown in Fig. 1(a). A web-based application using HTML5 and JavaScript is developed as the client software. The information of the sensor can be acquired by using JavaScript. The

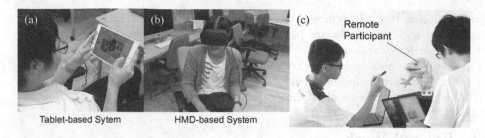

Fig. 1. Remote participants using (a) a tablet-based system and (b) an HMD-based system. (c) The application example of both system used in meeting room.

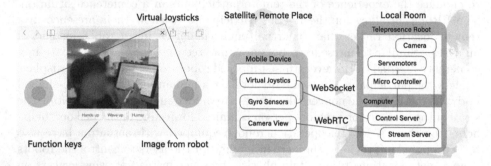

Fig. 2. Left: User interface on mobile device. Right: Configurations of the tablet-based telepresence system.

application uses a virtual joystick to manipulate the arms of the robot on the screen and streams a real-time video from a web camera equipped on the eye of the robot, as shown in Fig. 2 (left). WebSocket is used for data communication between the remote side and a local conference side and WebRTC is used to stream the videos, as shown in Fig. 2 (right). In the experiment, we use Safari 11 which works on an iPad installed with iOS 11 public beta version.

HMD-Based System. A simplified system based on a system used in a previous study [8], is employed as an HMD-based system, as shown in Fig. 1 (b). This system captures the facial movements of a participant from an HMD. The body movements are captured by the Kinect depth camera. The stream of the real-time video of the camera located in the puppet's eyes is shown to be the same as that of the tablet-based system on the screen of the HMD.

3.2   Conference Room Side

The conference room side consists of a telepresence robot and a computer, as shown in Fig. 1 (c). The robot implemented here is based on that of a previous study [8]. It is equipped with a web camera in the eye; each joint is controlled by servo motors and the robot can be operated by a computer using an Arduino microcontroller. A Java-based application and the Node.js (8.5.0) software is used for control. The computer is the core of the system used in this study as it runs the server used for the web-based application for the remote participants, and is also used for the operation of the robot.

4   User Study

User studies have been conducted on both remote and real-world participants to analyze the effectiveness of the proposed system in a conference situation, using three methods: tablet-based telepresence interface, HMD-based telepresence interface, and Skype (typical videoconferencing interface). This section presents the results from the user studies, which include the productivity, the ease of interaction, and the sense of co-presence.

Fig. 3. Left: Interaction between participants and a telepresence robot. Right: Desk space we prepared for the user study.

4.1   Procedure

A simple desk and telepresence system are prepared, as shown in Fig. 3. A three-person group is formed, where one is a remote participant, and the other two are physically present. A remote person participates in a conference using one of three methods: Skype, Tablet/Robot, HMD/Robot. The participants experience each of the methods in a conference for both, the remote person and the physical setting. The participants were asked to answer questionnaires after experiencing each of the methods. They were asked to rate each question on a five-point Likert scale, from extremely productive, easy, clear, enjoyable, or co-present, to not at all, for each of the used methods. Additionally, they were also asked for details on the free-form questions.

4.2   Task

In conference situations, there are two types of tasks, i.e., a decision-making task and a production task, which are the main factors in determining the impact of communication technology on distributed groups or work groups [1]. We set one task that consists of a decision-making and production task at the same time for a distributed group. A card name named Toddles-Bobbles is used. The task is explained as follows:

1. Three cards are provided with an illustration of a character to two physical participants.
2. The group chooses one of the three cards. (Decision-task)
3. The group names the card through discussion. (Production task)

The group does all of the steps above in three minutes. This task is used to determine how each method affects the efficiency of remote collaboration in a conference situation.

4.3   Participants

Twelve participants (3 females, 9 males) aged between 19 and 44 years (M = 23.2, SD = 6.7), participated in this user study. The general participants were recruited by advertising on a few social network services.

4.4   Result

Comparison of Methods from the Perspective of a Remote Side. This section presents the results of the answers to the questionnaires given by the participants who joined a conference as a remote person, as shown in Fig. 4. In the questionnaire, the participants were asked several questions for each of the three systems.

   The first question was to determine how the system motivated the person to participate in a conference. The average for Skype was slightly higher at 3.5 points, but is nearly equal to that of the HMD-based and the tablet-based systems. The second question was to determine the ease of the operation of the system. It shows the differences between Skype, which is commonly used for teleconference, and the telepresence systems implemented in this study. Consequently, the average for Skype was high (4.3 points), which was 0.8 points higher than that of the HMD-based system and the tablet-based system. The third question was to determine the sense of co-presence. In conversation, sharing the atmosphere of a specific place with all the participants in a conference is essential, as in face-to-face meetings. The largest average was for the HMD-based system, followed in order by the tablet-based system and Skype. This implies that the results are affected by immersion, which is one of the advantages. The fourth question was to determine the ease of interaction between the participants when using a system. The average of the HMD-based system was 4.0 points, and the others were 3.5 points. The fifth question determines the ease of the transmission of intention, where all the averages are greater than 3.0 points. The histogram of the answers shows that the point of the HMD-based system is low. The eighth question pertains to the productivity in a conference. The averages of the scores for the HMD-based and the tablet-based methods were 2.8 points, and for that of Skype was 3.2 points. According to the free descriptions of the participants, there were negative opinions about the disadvantages of the HMD-based system. P3: *"I couldn't see around my hands, so it was not easy to drink tea or take notes during a conference."* This description implies that there are some tasks which need to remove HMD during a conference.

Fig. 4. The comparison among three methods (Skype, Tablet/Robot, and HMD/Robot) for remote side.

Comparison of Methods from the Perspective of a Local Side. This section presents the results of the answers to the questionnaires on the participants who are physically present in a local conference room, interacting with a display of a remote participant or a robot, as shown in Fig. 5. In the questionnaire, the participants were asked several questions for each of the three systems. The second question pertains to sharing physical material with the

Fig. 5. The comparison among three methods (Skype, Tablet/Robot, and HMD/Robot) for conference room side.

other participants in a conference. A remote person can only share whatever is visible through the camera in this experiment. Each of the average points was below 3.0 points. P4 mentioned the difficulty of sharing material with a remote person in a tablet-based system. P4: *"It was not easy to see the others' reactions. I did not know if I could share the material."* P1: *"Cards were small, and I needed to take them closer to the camera. As a result, I thought it could not make use of the advantage of the HMD.*" The third question pertains to co-presence. P4 mentioned an HMD-based system. P4: "*Because I couldn't sympathize with other's appearance, like the timing of someone starting to talk, I felt difficult in the interaction with each other.*" The seventh question pertains to the ease of talking. P6 mentioned the ease of talking positively for the HMD-based system in the free descriptions of the participants, and P9 described the opinions about Skype positively. P6: "*I felt easy to talk to a robot looked like a cute puppet.*" P9: "*I feel easy to talk and intimate if I can see others. I felt relieved the best (in Skype) because I could see expressions of others much more than in other methods.*" The eighth question pertains to the productivity of a conference. All the averages were around 3.0 points.

Comparison of Methods as a Whole. In this section, the participants were asked to answer several questions after they experienced the remote and the conference room sides, as shown in Fig. 6.

The first question pertains to the co-presence. P11 describes a tablet-based system. P11: "*The function that I can move my hands lets me feel that I am participating.*" The second question pertains to the enjoyability of the interaction. P8 describes the tablet-telepresence system. P8: "*I came to love the robot gradually, so I felt so enjoyable.*" The third question pertains to ease of interaction. P10 mentions the HMD-based system positively. P10: "*I could understand where I was looking at, so it was easy to interact with each other.*" P12 describes the ease of interaction with others. P12: "*I felt that I could convey my intention only by audio and the movements of my gazing without using a hand.*"

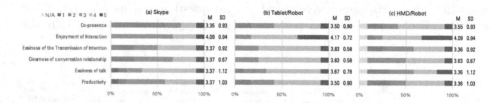

Fig. 6. The comparison among three methods (Skype, Tablet/Robot, and HMD/Robot) as a whole.

5   Conclusion

In this study, the effects of telepresence methods were examined by using a robot in the teleconferencing and by conducting user studies on remote and real-world participants. A telepresence robot is used to enhance the presence of a remote person, and the robot is operated by two methods: tablet-based interface and motion-based interface with an HMD. The results show how the physical presence of a remote person represented as a robot, affects the communication in teleconferencing when compared to general videoconferencing methods. This study suggests that videoconferencing offers certain advantages, such as the ease of talking, though it faces the limitations of non-physical representation. Conversely, the telepresence system enhances the co-presence of a remote participant and allows for the participants to attend a conference enjoyably. The results of this study contribute to the exploration of future applications of conferencing systems.

Acknowledgements. We would like to thank FUJITSU SOCIAL SCIENCE LABORATORY LIMITED for their unfailing support and assistance. We also wish to thank Mose Sakashita for his inputs and great discussion.

References

1. Andres, H.P.: A comparison of face-to-face and virtual software development teams. Team Perform. Manag. Int. J. **8**(1/2), 39–48 (2002). https://doi.org/10.1108/13527590210425077
2. Choi, M., Kornfield, R., Takayama, L., Mutlu, B.: Movement matters: effects of motion and mimicry on perception of similarity and closeness in robot-mediated communication. In: Proceedings of the 2017 CHI Conference on Human Factors in Computing Systems, CHI 2017, pp. 325–335. ACM, New York (2017). https://doi.org/10.1145/3025453.3025734
3. Fritsche, L., Unverzagt, F., Peters, J., Calandra, R.: First-person tele-operation of a humanoid robot. In: 15th IEEE-RAS International Conference on Humanoid Robots, pp. 997–1002, November 2015
4. Lee, J.K., Toscano, R.L., Stiehl, W.D., Breazeal, C.: The design of a semi-autonomous robot avatar for family communication and education. In: RO-MAN 2008 - The 17th IEEE International Symposium on Robot and Human Interactive Communication, pp. 166–173, August 2008. https://doi.org/10.1109/ROMAN.2008.4600661
5. Nishio, S., Ishiguro, H., Hagita, N.: Geminoid: teleoperated android of an existing person. In: Humanoid Robots: New Developments (2012)
6. Paulos, E., Canny, J.: PRoP: personal roving presence (1998)
7. Rae, I., Takayama, L., Mutlu, B.: In-body experiences: embodiment, control, and trust in robot-mediated communication. In: Proceedings of the SIGCHI Conference on Human Factors in Computing Systems, CHI 2013, pp. 1921–1930. ACM, New York (2013). https://doi.org/10.1145/2470654.2466253
8. Sakashita, M., Minagawa, T., Koike, A., Suzuki, I., Kawahara, K., Ochiai, Y.: You as a puppet: evaluation of telepresence user interface for puppetry. In: Proceedings of the 30th Annual ACM Symposium on User Interface Software and Technology, UIST 2017, pp. 217–228. Association for Computing Machinery, New York (2017). https://doi.org/10.1145/3126594.3126608
9. Sirkin, D., Ju, W.: Consistency in physical and on-screen action improves perceptions of telepresence robots. In: Proceedings of the Seventh Annual ACM/IEEE International Conference on Human-Robot Interaction, HRI 2012, pp. 57–64. ACM, New York (2012). https://doi.org/10.1145/2157689.2157699

10. Whitney, J.P., Chen, T., Mars, J., Hodgins, J.K.: A hybrid hydrostatic transmission and human-safe haptic telepresence robot. In: 2016 IEEE International Conference on Robotics and Automation (ICRA), pp. 690–695, May 2016. https://doi.org/10.1109/ICRA.2016.7487195
11. Yankelovich, N., Simpson, N., Kaplan, J., Provino, J.: Porta-person: telepresence for the connected conference room. In: CHI 2007 Extended Abstracts on Human Factors in Computing Systems, CHI EA 2007, pp. 2789–2794. Association for Computing Machinery, New York (2007). https://doi.org/10.1145/1240866.1241080

Effect of Emotion Synchronization in Robot Facial Expressions

Kiruthika Raja(✉), Tipporn Laohakangvalvit, Peeraya Sripian, and Midori Sugaya

College of Engineering, Shibaura Institute of Technology, 3-7-5, Toyosu, Koto,
Tokyo 135-8548, Japan
{am20007,tipporn,peeraya,doly}@shibaura-it.ac.jp

Abstract. With the recent developments in fields like Artificial Intelligence and
Robotics, the rise of social robots is not far away. For social robots to establish
better human interaction, they must be able to interact with people casually. In
this research, we introduce the idea of empathy in robots by syncing our emotions
with the robot's facial expression. The emotions are estimated and synchronized
in real-time using biological signals (i.e., brainwave and heartrate). In this paper,
we (1) investigate the effect that emotion synchronization has in human-robot
interactions by comparing the impressions of a robot that generates synchronized
facial expressions with non-synchronized ones, and (2) clarify the effectiveness
of selecting stimulus according to the individual's interest. The results suggest
that emotion synchronization of facial expressions is an effective way to improve
human-robot interactions.

Keywords: Human-Robot interactions · Affective interactions · Social robots ·
Biological signals

1 Introduction

The use of social robots has been increasing in recent days with the advancements in
fields of robotics and artificial intelligence. Robots have now started to become a part
of our daily lives, resulting in an increase in research related to improving human-robot
interaction (HRI). HRI research focuses on how robots can react to humans in a social
and engaging manner. Robots are now made to look more like humans in an attempt
to improve HRI. Ben Robins et al. [1] studies the effect that robot's appearance has in
facilitating and encouraging interaction. While there has been tremendous improvement
in appearance recent years, it is found that users are disappointed by the lack of empathy
from these robots [2]. In order to interact with humans in a natural manner, robots must
also be able to recognize and respond to our affects naturally. This is closely related with
the idea of empathy.

Empathy can be described in two parts: Cognitive empathy – to understand another
person's emotion and Affective empathy – the capacity to respond with the appropriate
emotions [3]. In order to express empathy to humans, robots must be able to both
understand and respond with appropriate emotions.

© Springer Nature Switzerland AG 2021
C. Stephanidis et al. (Eds.): HCII 2021, CCIS 1420, pp. 181–188, 2021.
https://doi.org/10.1007/978-3-030-78642-7_24

To depict emotions in robots, robots are placed in an affective loop to improve social interactions. Hook [4] defines the affective loop as an interactive process in which "the user (of the system) first expresses her emotions" to which "the system then responds by generating affective expressions… this in turn affects users making them respond and, step-by-step, feel more and more involved with the system". Studies show that this system of affective loops allow for an increase in the user's engagement while interacting with social robots, especially in long term interactions [5].

Therefore, our research focuses on evaluating an affective loop between the user and robot established by an affect recognition system that recognizes the user's affective states through biological signals and the robot that mimics the obtained affective states using various facial expressions. The goal of our research is to study the effect that emotion synchronization has on users through robot facial expressions.

2 Background

Affect recognition or emotion recognition is the process of identifying the user's affective state. This can be done through various observable expressions such as speech annotations (or tone of voice) [6], facial expressions, pupil movement, mouth and head movements [7], etc. A limitation of these approaches is that the emotion obtained can be controlled and are merely observable factors. Ikeda et al. [8] proposed a method of estimating emotions using involuntary biological information aiming to understand true emotions and emotions that are sometimes not expressed.

In this research, we used the same approach of using biological information to recognize the participant's emotions [8]. As shown in Fig. 1, the proposed method classified emotions into two dimensions based on Russell's Circumplex Model of Affect [9] using biological indexes obtained from brainwave and pulse data. Heart rate variability (HRV), pNN50, was proposed as an index for valence or pleasure (x-axis): the point of origin (resting condition) was set to 0.3, values greater than 0.3 indicated pleasure and vice versa. The higher pNN50 value indicated the higher valence. The difference of Attention and Meditation values (Attention-Meditation) obtained from NeuroSky original algorithm of the brainwave sensor was proposed as an index for arousal or awakening (y-axis). The higher the Attention-Meditation value indicated the higher arousal level.

Previous research by Kajihara et al. [10] tested various emotion synchronization methods. They found the method based on periodical emotion value (i.e., when emotion expressed is based on the maximum cumulative value in a defined period) was the best method. A problem with this research was that the employed emotional stimuli, LIRIS-ACCEDCE video database with annotated emotions [11], did not evoke pleasant emotions (e.g., happy) possibly due to the cultural or individual difference. Therefore, we proposed to use emotional stimulus selected based on each individual's interest aiming at evoking pleasant emotions more effectively.

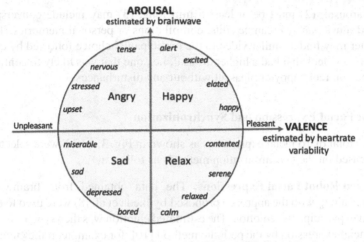

Fig. 1. A method to classify emotions estimated by biological indexes (brainwave and heart rate variability) using Russell's circumplex model.

3 Experiment

The goal of the experiment was to evaluate the impressions of each participants towards the robot with non-synchronized and synchronized facial expressions as they watched a video as emotional stimulus. Figure 2 shows an overview of the experiment. The details of the experiment are described in the following subsections.

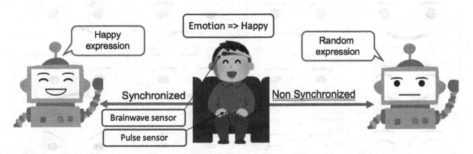

Fig. 2. Overview of synchronized and non-synchronized robot facial expressions.

3.1 Emotional Stimulus

During the experiment, participants were asked to simultaneously observe the robot's facial expression change as they watched an emotional video stimulus that made them feel happy. Rather than using a pre-existing video database for the emotional stimulus, we proposed an improved method that took into account the cultural and individual differences by asking each participant to select one video as emotional stimulus from any online or offline sources following a given criteria: (1) make participant feel happy with high arousal, (2) must be at least 5 min long, (3) may include conversation or background music, and (4) can be edits, compilations or personal memories. Then the experimenter may find a similar video to the participants' choice followed by choosing one of the two videos that had a higher arousal, i.e., one that was likely to continuously make the person feel happy or pleasant without any disturbances.

3.2 Robot Facial Expression and Synchronization

There was a total of 16 facial expressions as shown in Fig. 3, which were selected to be displayed based on the synchronization methods as follows:

Synchronized Robot Facial Expressions. The data obtained from brainwave and pulse sensors along with the approach proposed by Ikeda et al. [8] were used to estimate and recognize participants' emotion. The estimated emotion was then synchronized with the robot facial expression by the periodic method [10], for example, if the emotion was estimated as happy, the robot also showed smiling face as "happy" emotion. This method of synchronization placed the robot in an affective loop and was hypothesized to act in a more empathetic manner.

Non-Synchronized Robot Facial Expressions. The robot's facial expressions were generated to change randomly every 5 s in regardless of participants' emotions.

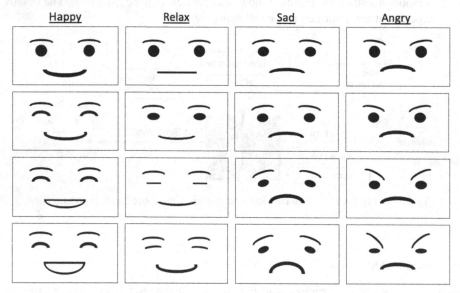

Fig. 3. Images of the 16 robot facial expressions used in our experiment.

3.3 Subjective Evaluation

We used Osgood's Semantic Differential (SD) Method [12] to evaluate the participants impression of the robot's facial expressions. A total of 12 adjective pairs were selected for the evaluation based on the Japanese property-based adjective measurement [13, 14]. Note that the list of adjective pairs is presented along with results in Sect. 4.

In addition, we used Self-Assessment Manikins (SAM) to evaluate the degrees of pleasure and arousal of the video stimulus. The SAM is described as "a non-verbal pictorial assessment technique that directly measures the pleasure, arousal and dominance associated with a person's affective reaction to a wide variety of stimuli" [15].

3.4 Experiment Procedure

The experiment was performed with three participants between ages 13 and 18 years old, two females and one male. The participants were required to wear brainwave sensor (Mindwave Mobile 2; NeuroSky, Inc.) and pulse sensor (World Famous Electronics llc.) throughout the experiment.

There were two conditions in the experiment: (1) Non-Synchronized Facial Expressions, and (2) Synchronized Facial Expressions. The conditions were counterbalanced. For each condition, the experiment procedure is as follows:

1. Baseline measurement: Participants were asked to sit still and close their eyes for 120 s.
2. Stimulus presentation: The robot's expression is changed simultaneously as participants watched video for 120 s.
3. Subjective Evaluation: Participants were asked to evaluate their impression toward the robot's facial expressions using SD method and the stimulus using SAM scale.
4. Repeat the steps (1) to (3) with the other condition.

4 Results

4.1 Biological Information

We calculated the average values of two biological indexes obtained from the three participants. Figure 4(a) shows the average Attention-Meditation values from the brainwave data. The average Attention-Meditation value increased from -27.2 to -5.7 (difference $= 21.5$) between baseline and non-synchronized facial expressions, and from -29.1 to 7.7 (difference $= 36.8$) during synchronized one. The increase in Attention-Meditation value indicates an increase in arousal when stimulus is presented.

Similarly, Fig. 4(b) presents the average pNN50 values from the pulse sensor. The average pNN50 value increased from 0.5 to 0.9 (difference $= 0.4$) during the non-synchronized condition and increases from 0.6 to 1.0 (difference $= 0.4$) during the synchronized one. The increase in pNN50 values indicates an increase in valence when stimulus is presented.

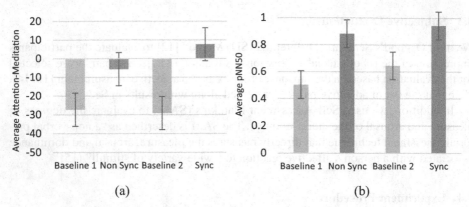

(a)   (b)

Fig. 4. Average values of biological indexes divided into baseline and (synchronized and non-synchronized) stimulus conditions, in which (a) Attention-Meditation average values from brainwave data and (b) pNN50 average values from pulse data.

4.2 Subjective Evaluation

For the degree of pleasure and arousal of video stimulus, the evaluated result from SAM shows that an average of 8.5 for pleasure, and 7 for arousal were obtained.

For the evaluation of the robot's impressions from the three participants, the SD ratings were obtained as shown in Figure. The synchronized facial expressions had overall higher ratings. Only for the adjective "serious" of both conditions had the same ratings (score = 4). Synchronized facial expressions, in particular, had higher sociable (score = 7), friendly (score = 6.3), positive (score = 6.3) and upbeat (score = 6.3) ratings.

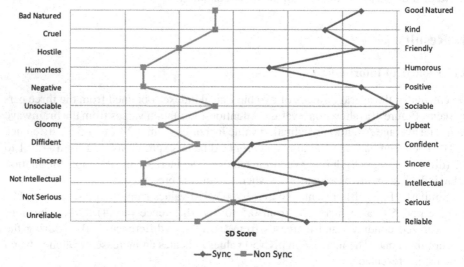

Fig. 5. Average SD ratings of 12 adjective pairs from the three participants.

5 Discussion

By comparing the biological data and subjective evaluation ratings in both conditions, we obtained the following findings:

- There is an increase in the Attention-Mediation value (Fig. 4(a)) and pNN50 value (Fig. 4(b)) every time stimulus is presented. This indicates that the stimulus successfully evokes high arousal and valence among the users.
- The result from SAM scale shows high pleasure and arousal for the video stimulus. Therefore, we confirmed that the video stimulus and method of selecting stimulus according to individual's interests successfully evokes pleasant emotion among the participants.
- Participants found the experience with synchronized robot facial expressions to be much more enjoyable (Fig. 5). This factor of enjoyability can account for the high increase in arousal in the synchronized condition as observed in the result of the biological information (Fig. 4(a)).

Thus, we confirmed that emotion synchronization is an effective way to improve human-robot interactions. From the results, we can thereby state that using biological signals for real-time emotion synchronization along with stimulus selected based on individual interest is an effective method to synchronize emotion.

6 Conclusion and Future Work

Emotion synchronization in robots impacts its social presence and relation with humans in the long-term. The goal of this research was to investigate the effect of emotion synchronization in human-robot interactions. Experiments were conducted to compare the results of non-synchronized and synchronized robot facial expressions. The results show that emotion synchronization based on biological signal measurement and individualized emotion stimulus created a better impression for the users as they found the robot more sociable, friendly and positive.

The current research targeted only one emotion, happiness. Employing negative emotions or emotions associated with lower arousal and lower pleasure, may change the impressions. Future work will also target other emotions with different arousal and valence (e.g., relaxed, sad). In addition, we will investigate other modalities for affect recognition (e.g., facial expressions, voice tones) and create a system combining the various affects modalities in an attempt to further improve human-robot interactions.

References

1. Robins, B., Dautenhahn, K., Te Boekhorst, R.: Robots as assistive technology - does appearance matter? In: Proceedings of the 2004 IEEE Int Workshop on Robot & Human Interactive Communication, pp. 277–282. IEEE, Kurashiki, Okayama, Japan (2004)
2. Fung, P., et al.: Towards empathetic human-robot interactions. In: Gelbukh, A. (ed.) CICLing 2016. LNCS, vol. 9624, pp. 173–193. Springer, Cham (2016). https://doi.org/10.1007/978-3-319-75487-1_14

3. Cuff, B.M.P., Brown, S.J., Taylor, L., Howat, D.J.: Empathy: a review of the concept. Emot. Rev. **8**(2), 144–153 (2016)
4. Höök, K.: Affective loop experiences: designing for interactional embodiment. Philos. Trans. R. Soc. Lond. Biol. Sci. **364**(1535), 3585–3595 (2009)
5. Leite, I., Castellano, G., Pereira, A., Martinho, C., Paiva, A.: Long-term interactions with empathic robots: evaluating perceived support in children. In: Ge, S.S., Khatib, O., Cabibihan, J.J., Simmons, R., Williams, M.A. (eds.) ICSR 2012. LNCS, vol. 7621, pp. 298–307. Springer, Berlin, Heidelberg (2012). https://doi.org/10.1007/978-3-642-34103-8_30
6. Hegel, F., Spexard, T., Vogt, T., Horstmann, G., Wrede, B.: Playing a different imitation game: interaction with an empathic Android robot. In: Proceedings of the 2006 IEEE-RAS International conference on humanoid robots, Genova, Italy, pp. 56–61 (2006)
7. Riek, L.D., Paul, P.C., Robinson, P.: When my robot smiles at me: enabling human-robot rapport via real-time head gesture mimicry. J. Multimodal User Interfaces **3**(1–2), 99–108 (2010)
8. Ikeda, Y., Horie, R., Sugaya, M.: Estimate emotion with biological information for robot interaction. Proc. Comput. Sci. **112**, 1589–1600 (2017)
9. Russell, J.A.: A circumplex model of affect. J. Pers. Soc. Psychol. **39**(6), 1161–1178 (1980)
10. Kajihara, Y., Sripian, P., Feng, C., Sugaya, M.: Emotion synchronization method for robot facial expression. In: Kurosu, M. (ed.) HCII 2020. LNCS, vol. 12182, pp. 644–653. Springer, Cham (2020). https://doi.org/10.1007/978-3-030-49062-1_44
11. Baveye, Y., Dellandrea, E., Chamaret, C., Chen, L.: LIRIS-ACCEDE: a video database for affective content analysis. IEEE Trans. Affect. Comput. **6**(1), 43–55 (2015)
12. Osgood, C.E.: The nature and measurement of meaning. Psychol. Bull. **49**(3), 197 (1952)
13. Hayashi, F.: The fundamental dimensions of interpersonal cognitive structure. Bull. Fac. Educ. Nagoya Univ. **25**, 233–247 (1978)
14. Hayashi, R., Kato, S.: Psychological effects of physical embodiment in artificial pet therapy. Artificial Life and Robotics **22**(1), 58–63 (2017)
15. Bradley, M.M., Lang, P.J.: Measuring emotion: the self-assessment manikin and the semantic differential. J. Behav. Ther. Exp. Psychiatry **25**(1), 49–59 (1994)

Effectiveness of Manga Technique in Expressing Facial Expressions of Welfare Robot

Junpei Sanda and Masayoshi Kanoh(✉)

School of Engineering, Chukyo University, 101-2 Yagoto Honmachi, Showa-ku, Nagoya 466-8666, Japan
mkanoh@sist.chukyo-u.ac.jp

Abstract. We have been developing a communication robot "advice robot" that encourages and suggests actions to an elderly person, such as having a meal, taking a bath, taking medicine, etc. If the robot's affective expressions are weak, an elderly user may not be able to understand or follow the robot's suggestions. We focused on the vertical line and shadow techniques used in *manga*, or Japanese comics, to strengthen the affective expressions of disgust and fear, which can be difficult for the robot to express. The results of our experiment showed that the impression of disgust was strengthened by adding vertical lines. On the other hand, the impression of fear could not be strengthened by using the manga techniques. However, when the vertical lines were added to a happy face, the impression of fear was greater than when the lines were added to a fearful face.

Keywords: Manga technique · Human robot interaction · Welfare robot

1 Introduction

To solve the shortage of elderly caregivers in Japan, the priority areas to which robot technology is to be introduced in nursing care place have been determined by METI[1] and MHLW[2] [1]. One such development is a life aid device using robot technology for communicating with the elderly. In this study, we have been developing a communication robot "advice robot" that encourages and suggests actions to elderly users, such as having a meal, taking a bath, or taking medicine.

If the affective expressions of the robot are weak or lacking, an elderly user may not be able to understand or follow the robot's suggestions. Thus, the robot needs to be able to produce various facial expressions. Robots can express emotions in various ways such as gestures, speech, and facial expressions. In this

---

[1] Ministry of Economy, Trade and Industry.
[2] Ministry of Health, Labour and Welfare.

The research was supported by KAKENHI 19K12192.

C. Stephanidis et al. (Eds.): HCII 2021, CCIS 1420, pp. 189–194, 2021.
https://doi.org/10.1007/978-3-030-78642-7_25

Fig. 1. Appearance of advice robot.

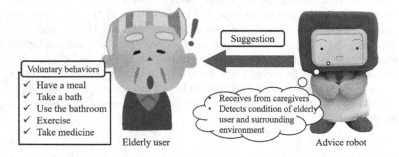

Fig. 2. Robot suggesting actions to elderly user.

study, we focus on visual information, which is said to have the greatest effect on emotion recognition, and aim to improve the affective expression of the robot.

Toward this end, we focused on drawing techniques of *manga* (Japanese comics), which can express various emotions easily. We used these techniques in an effort to strengthen the affective expressions of disgust and fear, which are difficult for the robot to express.

2   Advice Robot

Figure 1 shows the appearance of the advice robot. The neck is rotated by a motor, and the facial expressions are displayed on a smartphone. The robot can respond to commands given by a caregiver. It can also detect the condition of the elderly user and encourage or suggest actions accordingly, as shown in Fig. 2.

3   Manga Techniques

Manga artists use various techniques to convey emotions, including iconography such as sweat drops, anger marks, vertical lines, speed lines, and concentrated linework; solid color expression to express shadow; words such as onomatopoeia and mimetic words; and panel arranging, speech bubbles, and thought bubbles [2]. Out of these techniques, iconography and solid color can be used to depict the facial expressions of the robot. In this study, in addition to the sweat, anger, and tear marks, we use vertical lines and shadows on the face, which are often used to express fear and disgust in manga, to create affective expressions.

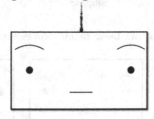

Fig. 3. Neutral facial expression.

Table 1. Facial expressions with highest average scores.

	Anger	Sadness	Joy	Fear	Surprise	Disgust
Average	5.65	5.55	3.65	3.15	4.75	3.05

4   Experiment

4.1   Basic Facial Expressions

We created a total of 88 videos of facial expressions by combining changes in the eyes and eyebrows (11 patterns), changes in the mouth (4 patterns), and the speed of change from the neutral expression (2 patterns) in Fig. 3. Note that the changes in the eyes and eyebrows include patterns that use anger, tear, and sweat marks. We investigated the faces that most strongly conveyed the following six basic emotions; anger, sadness, joy, fear, surprise, and disgust [3,4].

   The investigation was conducted by a questionnaire using a 7-point scale with each item ranging from 0 (no impression) to 6 (strong impression). Twenty university students participated in this study. They rated their impression of the six basic emotions: anger, sadness, joy, fear, surprise, and disgust. The highest rated facial expressions are shown in Fig. 4 and the average scores for each expression are shown in Table 1. The perception of anger increased by 1.91 points with the addition of the anger mark ($p = 0.0001$), and that of sadness increased by 2.51 points with the addition of the tear mark ($p = 0.0001$). The impression of fear also increased by 1.22 points with the addition of the sweat mark ($p = 0.0012$),

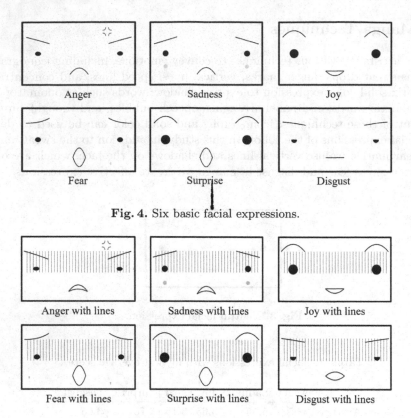

Fig. 4. Six basic facial expressions.

Fig. 5. Facial expressions with vertical lines.

but the sweat mark had nearly no effect on fear impression. As seen in Table 1, the fear impression value is 3.15 points, which is close to the average value of the 7-point scale, i.e., neutral. The marks had no effect on other impressions. These results indicate that fear and disgust are difficult to convey through facial expression marks used in manga.

4.2   Facial Expressions with Vertical Lines or Shadows

Six facial expressions were created by adding vertical lines to each basic facial expression, as shown in Fig. 5, and likewise six facial expressions by adding a shadow, as shown in Fig. 6. Here, as for the presentation timing and the presentation position of the vertical lines and shadow, the least strange one was selected by the preliminary experiment.

4.3   Evaluation

We evaluated a total of 18 facial expressions: the six basic expressions, six expressions with vertical lines, and six with shadows. The participants were asked to

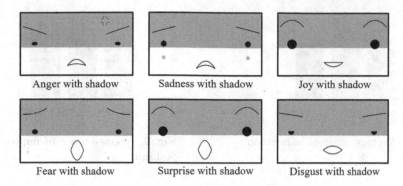

Fig. 6. Facial expressions with shadows.

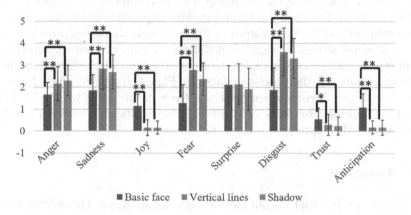

Fig. 7. Average score of each emotion.

watch the 18 facial expressions in random order and rate their impressions in a questionnaire containing eight items (the six basic emotions plus trust and anticipation). For each item, a score from zero (not feel at all) to six (feel strongly) was given. The participants were 20 university students who did not participate the evaluation in Sect. 4.1.

4.4 Results

First, we describe the effects of the vertical lines and shadows. Figure 7 shows the effects of vertical lines and shadows on the participants' affective impressions. The vertical lines and shadow enhanced the impressions of anger, sadness, fear, and disgust but decreased that of joy and anticipation. This indicates that the vertical lines and shadows enhance the impression of negative emotions and decrease that of positive emotions.

Next, we describe the effects of the vertical lines and shadows on the participants' impressions of fear and disgust. Figure 8 shows the result of the effect on

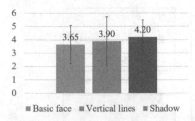

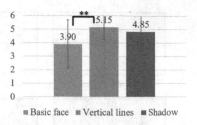

Fig. 8. Average score of impression of fear.

Fig. 9. Average score of impression of disgust.

fear. From left to right, the bars in this graph represent the average scores of the fearful face in Fig. 4, the joyful face in Fig. Figure 5, and the fearful face in Fig. 6. The joyful face with vertical lines had a greater impression of fear than the fearful face with vertical lines. As shown in Fig. 8, the Friedman test for these three facial expressions showed no significant difference. Figure 9 shows the results for the impression of disgust. From left to right, the bars in this graph represent the average scores of the disgusted faces in Figs. 4, 5 and 6. Since there was significance in the Friedman test for these three expressions, we used Scheffe's method for multiple comparisons, verifying the significance between the basic expression and the expression with vertical lines.

5   Conclusion

We designed a robot that encourages or suggests actions of the elderly, and we investigated the use of manga drawing techniques (vertical lines and shadows) to strengthen the impression of fear and disgust, which are difficult emotions to convey. The results of the questionnaire indicated that the impression of disgust could be strengthened by adding vertical lines to the face. On the other hand, the impression of fear could not be strengthened by using either of the manga techniques. However, adding the vertical lines to the joyful face resulted in a stronger impression of fear than when the lines were added to the fearful face. In future work, we intend to investigate new techniques for strengthening the impression of fear.

References

1. Robotic Care Devices Portal - Robotic Devices for Nursing Care Project. http://robotcare.jp/en/home/index.php. Accessed 6 Mar 2021
2. Takeuchi, O.: Manga HyougenGaku Nyumon (An Introduction to Manga Studies). Chikumashobo (2005)
3. Ekman, P.: Darwin and Facial Expressions. Academic Press, Cambridge (1973)
4. Ekman, P.: Emotion in the Human Face. Cambridge University Press, Cambridge (1982)

Effects of Naming Robots on Relationship Between Attachment and Support Acceptability

Kota Tanaka[1], Masayoshi Kanoh[1(✉)], Felix Jimenez[2], Mitsuhiro Hayase[3],
Tomohiro Yoshikawa[4], Takahiro Tanaka[5], and Hitoshi Kanamori[5]

[1] Chukyo University, Nagoya, Japan
mkanoh@sist.chukyo-u.ac.jp
[2] Aichi Prefectural University, Nagakute, Japan
[3] Toyohashi Sozo University, Toyohashi, Japan
[4] Suzuka University of Medical Science, Suzuka, Japan
[5] Nagoya University, Nagoya, Japan

Abstract. To reduce traffic accidents caused by elderly drivers, in recent years we have been developing a robot that reviews their driving with them after they return home. By reviewing their driving together with a robot, they may be more receptive to the robot's advice after developing an attachment to the robot. We conducted an experiment focused on the aspect of naming the robot as a way of increasing the user's attachment to the robot. The results indicated that the correlation between the attachment to the robots and support acceptability was lower when the robot was given a name. Thus, it is possible that increased attachment to robots may not lead directly to improved support acceptability.

Keywords: Robot · Attachment · Support acceptability · Naming

1 Introduction

The percentage of traffic accidents caused by elderly drivers in total traffic accidents has been increasing. One possible way to improve their driving behavior is to reflect on and review their driving. Taking lessons at driving schools to repeatedly review their driving is not always feasible due to time and space limitations. A system is needed that enables elderly drivers to review their driving without being restricted by time or place. In this study, we are developing a driver assistance robot for a system that enables users to review their driving at home.

In developing the driver assistance robot, we focused on increasing the acceptability of assistance (advice) from robots and the continuity of robot use. In a prior study, Tanaka et al. [1] suggested that increased attachment and trust comes from using the driver assistance robot regularly. It is highly likely that the greater the driver's attachment and affinity to the appearance of the robot, the longer the driver will use the robot. These results suggest a relationship between attachment

© Springer Nature Switzerland AG 2021
C. Stephanidis et al. (Eds.): HCII 2021, CCIS 1420, pp. 195–201, 2021.
https://doi.org/10.1007/978-3-030-78642-7_26

to the robot and acceptability and continuous use of the robot, though the effects
of this relationship have not been clarified. In this paper, we focus on attachment
and support acceptability and investigate the effects of naming the driver assistance robot on attachment and support acceptability. We also investigate the relationship between attachment and support acceptability. If naming the driver assistance robot improves the impression of the robot, we expect the driving review to
be effective by asking the users to name the robot or by having them name the robot
voluntarily.

2   Driver Assistance Robot

The driver assistance robot is meant to be integrated into the daily life of the elderly
user. The user brings the robot with them when they drive a car. While driving,
the robot advises the user while recording the driving data. After returning home,
the user reviews his or her driving with the robot using the recorded data.

3   Experiment

3.1   Method

In this experiment, participants were divided into three groups. The first group did
not name the robot (not-naming group), the second group only named the robot
(naming-only group), and the third group named the robot, and the robot use its
name (appealing-name group). We compared the results of the effects of naming
the robot.

In the naming-only group, the research participant names the robot and the
robot never uses the named participant gave it. In the appealing-name group, the
robot used the name given by the participant to refer to itself when speaking. For
example, if the given name of the robot is 'Taro,' then the robot talks like 'Taro
likes your driving.' These two groups were compared to determine whether the act
of naming itself is meaningful (naming-only group) and whether the participant's
strong awareness of the name is meaningful (appealing-name group).

A total of 60 university students with driver's licenses, 30 male and 30 female,
participated in the study. We used stratified sampling to separate them by their
driving frequency.

3.2   Environment

We used RoBoHoN as the driver assistance robot. Also, we used a driving simulator instead of a real car so that the occurrences while driving did not vary
greatly from participant to participant. We used Unity to develop the driving
simulator and Japanese Otaku City from the ZENRIN City Asset Series as the
map. Figure 1 shows the experimental setup with the simulator running.

The course used in the experiment took about six to seven minutes. We created
a total of eight potentially dangerous situations on the course, using the Driver's

Fig. 1. Experimental setup with driving simulator in operation

Fig. 2. Overview of course and danger scenes potentially dangerous situations (numbered)

License Textbook [2, 3] as a reference so that they would not be unnatural. Figure 2 shows the course, in which ① to ⑧ indicate the locations of the following situations: (1) The vehicle in front of the participant coming to a sudden stop, (2) A motorcycle passing the participant from behind on the left when he or she makes a left turn, (3) A pedestrian standing at a crosswalk, (4) An intersection with a stop sign, (5) A stopped vehicle in front of the participant, (6) A vehicle ignoring a stop sign and entering an intersection without a traffic light, (7) A vehicle coming from behind on the right when the participant enters the right-turn-only lane, (8) Turning right at an intersection with multiple points of interest.

3.3 Experimental Procedure

Figure 3 shows the flow of the experiment. First, we administered a pre-questionnaire, modeled after that of prior studies [4–8], containing a total of nine items. The first three items ("Do you find it adorable?" "Do you find it friendly?" "Do you find it attachment?") asked about the participant's impression of the robot. The next three asked about their opinion of the robot's support ("Do you find it uncomfortable?" "Do you find it offensive?" "Do you find the advice easy to accept?"). The last three questions ("Do you want to be taught by a robot?" "Do you want to be taught by a person ?" and "Do you prefer to review alone?") asked about the impression of the robot while reviewing the driving. We asked

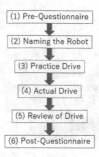

Fig. 3. Experimental procedure

the participants to rate their first impressions of the robot using a 7-point scale ranging from 1 (No impression at all) to 7 (Very strong impression) for all items.

First, the driver assistance robot is given a name by the participants in the naming-only group and appealing-name group.

The participants are instructed by the experimenter to name it. We call it "instructed naming" in this paper. Second, the participant begins with a practice drive. In the practice drive, the experimenter guides the vehicle on the same course as the actual drive, without other vehicles or pedestrians, for the driver to become accustomed to the driving simulator and to roughly learn the route.

After the practice drive, the actual drive is conducted. In the actual drive, the driver assistance robot guided the participant on the road. In the appealing-name group, the name given to the participant was used as the first person when the driver assistance robot provided guidance. The robot was controlled by the Wizard of Oz method. A five-minute break was given after the drive was completed. During this time, we created a video reviewing the drive from the images recorded on the central monitor of the driving simulator. The eight dangerous scenes were reviewed in the footage.

After the break, the participant reviews the drive with the driver assistance robot. We prepared the robot with speech patterns indicating success and failure and responds with an appropriate utterance while reviewing each scene. In the appealing-name group, the name given by the participant was used as the first person when reviewing their driving. The robot was controlled by the Wizard of Oz method.

After reviewing their driving, a post-questionnaire similar to the pre-questionnaire was conducted.

4   Results

The sum of the three items asking about the attachment to the robot (hereafter attachment) and the sum of the three items asking about the impression of

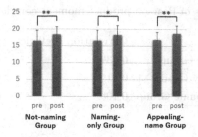

Fig. 4. Changes in attachment

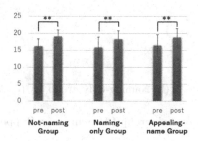

Fig. 5. Changes in support acceptability

the support from the robot (hereinafter support acceptability) were calculated.[1] Figures 4 and 5 show the results of the pre- and post-questionnaires. A t-test between the questionnaires after adjusting the significance level with the Bonferroni correction showed significant differences in all groups. A one-way analysis of variance was conducted on the post-questionnaires of the three groups, and no significant differences were found. Therefore, the results did not show any difference in the degree of improvement between attachment and support acceptability in the three groups.

The correlation between attachment and support acceptability was then calculated using Pearson's product rate correlation coefficient. The results are shown in Table 1 and the scatter plots for the three groups are shown in Fig. 6. The not-naming group showed a positive correlation, the naming-only group showed a positive correlation trend, but the appealing-name group showed no correlation.

5   Discussion

No improvements to attachment and support acceptability were observed in any of the three groups. However, the correlation between attachment and support

---

[1] "Uncomfortable" and "Feel offended" were calculated by reversing the scores.

Table 1. Results of Pearson product-moment correlation coefficient

	Correlation coefficient	p-value
Not-naming Group	0.637	0.0025 **
Naming-only Group	0.419	0.0658 +
Appealing-name Group	0.108	0.6496 n.s

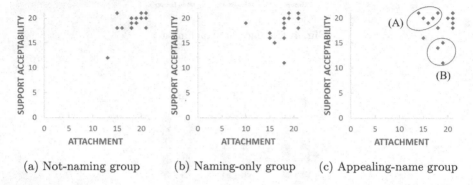

(a) Not-naming group   (b) Naming-only group   (c) Appealing-name group

Fig. 6. Scatter plots of each group (Attachment × Support Acceptability)

acceptability declined in the order of the not-naming group, naming-only group, and appealing-name group. This is likely because the participants were able to perceive the individuality of the robot by naming it personally. In the previous study [1], many people were more likely to accept support from driving instructors, and fewer were more likely to accept support from familiar figures such as husbands, wives, children, grandchildren, and friends. In this experiment, the participants may have perceived the robot as a driving instructor or a familiar person rather than a robot because they gave it a name, though it was instructed. In the appealing-name group (Fig. 6 (c)), the encircled area (A) indicates those who perceived the robot as a driving instructor, their attachment to the robot was not strong, but they were receptive to its support. On the other hand, (B) indicates those who perceived the robot as a familiar person, whose attachment to the robot was strong but were less likely to accept its guidance.

This suggests the possibility that the act of naming the driver assistance robot may reduce support acceptability, or that there may be a way to improve the acceptability of the robot even among people who have a hard time forming a favorable impression of the robot. It is also inferred that this is more pronounced when people are aware of the robot's name.

6   Conclusion

We investigated the change in the relationship between attachment and support acceptability. In the experiment, participants were instructed to give a name to a driver assistance robot. The results suggest that the act of naming the robot may have led some of the participants to perceive the robot as a familiar person. Though the participants' attachment to the robot improved, their support acceptability declined. Other participants perceived the robot as a driving instructor; their support acceptability improved but their attachment to the robot declined. Users of a driver assistance robot are likely to name the robot, and it is possible that naming will naturally lead to increased attachment and decreased support acceptability. In the future, we will conduct medium- to long-term experiments to verify the effects of naming. We also plan to compare instructed naming with spontaneous naming.

Acknowledgements. This research is supported in part by the Center of Innovation Program (Nagoya University COI; Mobility Innovation Center) from Japan Science and Technology Agency.

References

1. Tanaka, T., et al.: Effect of difference in form of driving support agent to driver's acceptability –driver agent for encouraging safe driving behavior (2). J. Transp. Technol. **8**(3), 194–208 (2018)
2. Toyota Nagoya Education Center: Driving Textbook (2017)
3. Japan Automobile Federation: Rules of the Road (2019)
4. Kato, Y., et al.: A robot system using mixed reality to encourage driving review. In: Stephanidis, C. (ed.) HCII 2019. CCIS, vol. 1033, pp. 112–117. Springer, Cham (2019). https://doi.org/10.1007/978-3-030-23528-4_16
5. Watanabe, Y., Onishi, Y., Tanaka, K., Nakanishi, H.: Trainability leads to animacy: a case of a toy drone. In: Human-Agent Interaction (2019)
6. Inoue, M., Kobayashi, T.: The research domain and scale construction of adjective-pairs in a semantic differential method in Japan. Jpn. J. Educ. Psychol. **33**(3), 253–260 (1985). (in Japanese)
7. Takagi, K.: The influence of motivation and experience factors and personality traits on the reduction of negative interpersonal affects. Bull. Graduate School Educ. Hum. Dev. **50**, 49–59 (2003). (in Japanese)
8. Takagi, K.: The influence of interpersonal motivation and social interaction experiences on the reduction of negative interpersonal affect. Jpn. J. Soc. Psychol. **20**(2), 124–133 (2004). (in Japanese)

Robot-Human Partnership is Unique: Partner-Advantage in a Shape-Matching Task

Chia-huei Tseng[1]([✉]), Ti-fan Hung[2], and Su-Ling Yeh[2]

[1] Tohoku University, Sendai, Japan
tseng@riec.tohoku.ac.jp
[2] National Taiwan University, Taipei, Taiwan

Abstract. Human-human interaction studies have shown that we prioritize psychological resources (attention, memory, etc.) to significant others (e.g., family member, friends) and to a stranger assigned to co-work with us. We examine whether the human-robot interaction shares a similar nature.

We adopted a "shape-identity matching task" in which participants first learned to associate 3 shapes with 3 names, and then judged whether the shape-name association in each trial was matched or mismatched. One of the 3 names belong to a social robot with a humanoid face (ASUS Zenbo), who was introduced as a partner to co-work with our participants. The other two names belong to the participant's best friend and to a stranger. In half of the trials, the trials were printed in green, and in the other half of the trials, the names were printed in red. Each participant was instructed to respond to the trials in their assigned color (red or green), and the other half would be completed by their robot partner (co-work on the same task).

We found that a robot partner was endowed with a "partner-advantage" similar to a human partner: the trials associated with the robot's name were responded faster and more accurately than the trials associated with a stranger's name. This advantage toward a robot is developed quickly and requires minimum interaction between human and robot. Interestingly, the effect is further boosted when the robot's expected role (i.e., social companion or functional robot) matches the robot's presence during the behavioral task (i.e., presence or absence). This was never observed among human partners. This unique feature in human-robot interaction implies that we may evaluate a robot partner heavily on the alignment between the expectation and its delivered service.

Keywords: Human-Robot interaction · Social robot · Functionality · Identify-advantage

1 Introduction

One of the significant yet unanswered questions in human-robot design is whether it is possible to create a similar human-human bonding with our robotic partners. This is not a trivial question as our dependency on robotic assistance in recent years has gradually extended from service robots (i.e. labor service provider) to companion robots

C. Stephanidis et al. (Eds.): HCII 2021, CCIS 1420, pp. 202–206, 2021.
https://doi.org/10.1007/978-3-030-78642-7_27

(i.e. emotional support provider). It is of great importance to further understand how the social interaction between human and robots establishes and sustains. Recent studies have suggested sociopsychological benefits from companion robots (e.g. [1, 2]) similar to those from human partners. However, there are also unique features observed in human-robot interaction only (e.g. uncanny valley effect). It is therefore of both theoretical and application values to further elucidate the constraints and opportunities in programming and design of future robots.

In this study, we adopt an experimental paradigm previously applied to investigate the establishment the affiliation with a human partner [3]. When a first-met stranger is introduced to us as a future co-worker, an immediate "partner-advantage" is endowed toward this identity. This effect can be quantified by the speed and accuracy gain attached to a shape associated with the partner's name. We use this paradigm to answer the following questions: (1) Can a robot partner elicit a similar facilitation effect similar to a human partner? (2) Does the functionality of a robot impose an additional limit in this identity-related inference?

2 Methods

2.1 The Perceptual Matching Task

Three geometric shapes (circle, square, and triangle) were associated with three names, including participants' best friends, the robot's name (襌寶), and the neutral stranger's name. The display is illustrated in Fig. 1. Participants' task is to memorize the name-shape matching rules (e.g. friend's name – circle, robot's name – square, stranger's name – triangle) first. During the experiment, they see a name and a shape on the screen and use a key to indicate whether it is a correct or incorrect match. Their response time and accuracy are recordings. During the experiment, they are told that the robot (ASUS, zenbo) will be their partner to share half of the trials (e.g. red trials).

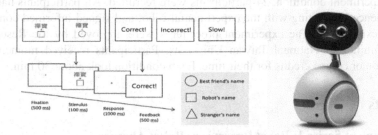

Fig. 1. Experimental Procedure. In the actual experiment, stimuli with an open font represent words colored in red; those with a solid font represent words colored in green. A robot (ASUS, Zenbo) was introduced as a partner to the participants (Color figure online).

2.2 Experiment Design

We designed two series of experiment. In Series 1, we investigated whether the physical presence of the robot is important. In human-human interaction, it was shown that the physical presence is not critical (Cheng and Tseng 2019). We designed a robot absence condition, in which our participants were introduced to a robot partner that never showed up.

In Series 2, we investigated whether the match of robot's design functionality matters. We allowed our participants to briefly interact with the Robot as a tool (i.e. human participants gave instructions to the robot) or as a companion (i.e. robot asks human participants for favors). During the shape matching experiment, the robot either stayed and sat by the participants (i.e. match the expectation of a social companion) or not (i.e. match the fictional robot expectation). Figure 2 summarize the design of Series 2.

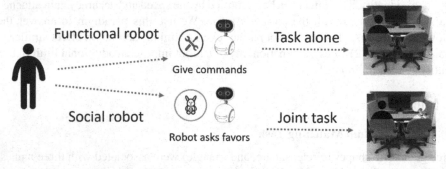

Fig. 2. Experiment Series 2 Design. To match the expectation, huma participants instructed the functional robot and conducted the shape matching experiment alone. Social robots kept human participants companied and had social interaction with the participants prior to the task.

2.3 Participants

For each experiment condition, 24 participants were recruited. All participants had no prior experience interacting with the experimental robot and signed informed consent before the experiment. The experiment procedures were approved by the Research Ethics Committee at National Taiwan University. Participants received momentary compensation or course credits for their time. Each condition took about 30 min.

3   Results

3.1   Experiment Series 1: Robot Presence vs Robot Absence

Results obtained from all 24 participants were included in the data analysis. Responses faster than 200 ms were excluded, eliminating a total of 2.0% of the trials. Only accurate trials were included in the RT analysis, and 10.4% of trials, which had erroneous responses, were not included.

To investigate identity related advantage, we compared the d' (the difference between the Z scores of the hit rate and false alarm rate) and RT in trials relating to different identities with ANOVA tests. We considered there to be an advantage effect if it was observed in either d' or response time.

The results for the robot presence condition are summarized in Fig. 3. A two-way ANOVA test with within-subject factors of shape category and matching judgement (matched and mismatched) revealed a significant interaction effect between shape category and matching judgement. Therefore, follow-up ANOVA tests were conducted separately on matched and mismatched trials. In the matched trials, a significant main effect of shape category was observed, $F(2, 46) = 19.887, p < .001, \eta^2 = .464$. Post hoc tests showed friend-related trials (543 ms) and partner-related trials (583 ms) exhibited a significantly quicker response than stranger-related trials (617 ms, $t(23) = 6.303, p = .08$ and $t(23) = 2.919 p = .023$, respectively). In mismatched trials, friend-advantage was observed, but not partner-advantage.

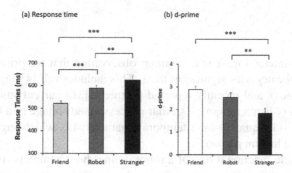

Fig. 3. Experiment Series 1 (Presence Condition) RT and D-prime results for different shape categories. (* p<0.5; ** p < 0.01, *** p < 0.001)

We observed a very similar result pattern in the absence condition (Table 1), which led us to conclude that physical presence is not a pre-requisite to create a partner advantage for robot partners. This is similar to the discovery for human partners.

Table 1. Experiment Series 1: Presence v.s. Absence

Condition	Reaction time	d-prime
Robot Presence	Friend > Robot > Stranger	Friend = Robot > Stranger
Robot Absence	Friend > Robot > Stranger	Friend > Robot = Stranger

3.2 Experiment Series 2: Functionality Match

We use identical analysis methods for the Experiment Series two. The result is summarized in Table 2. The most notable discovery is that when the robot's behavior matches its functional expectation, the partner advantage is enhanced to be as dominant as the "friends." This effect was not observed in human partners.

Table 2. Experiment Series 2: Functionality Match

Condition	Reaction time	d-prime
Match		
Tool	Friend = Robot > Stranger	Friend > Robot = Stranger
Companion	Friend = Robot > Stranger	Friend > Robot = Stranger
Mismatch		
Tool	Friend > Robot > Stranger	Friend > Robot = Stranger
Companion	Friend > Robot > Stranger	Friend = Robot = Stranger

4 Discussion

In human-human interaction, it is a common observation that we prioritize cognitive resources to social categories significant to us. This includes self [4], significant others (e.g. mother, friends), and recently reported partner [3]. In current study, we showed that a co-work robot partner enjoys a similar processing advantage as a human partner. It also shares a similar quickly-built temporal characteristic, which suggests a similar process to that of a human partner.

Interestingly, the functional role of a robot defines how human participants expect from the social interaction. When a functional robot receives instructions to operate, and it leaves the human participants to work during an experiment, it matches the expectation. When the same robot is designed to be social (e.g. it initiates social requests, asks to be picked up) and it stays with human participants during a computer task, it also fulfills the expected social role. Under these circumstances, the bias toward the robot is further enhanced to be similar to a significant other (friend), which usually requires a longer time to acquire. This special mode is never reported in human-human interaction, possibly highlights a unique feature underlying human-robot interaction.

In conclusion, we validated an objective behavioral paradigm which enables us to quantify the information priority toward a robot partner. It also has the potential to distinguish the characteristics unique for human-robot interaction.

References

1. Holzinger, A., Maurer, H.: Incidental learning, motivation, and the Tamagotchi Effect: VR-friends, chances for new ways of learning with computers. In: Computer Assisted Learning, CAL 99 (1999)
2. Wada, K., Shibata, T.: Living with seal robots – its sociopsychological and physiological influences on the elderly at a care house. IEEE Trans. Rob. **23**(5), 972–980 (2007)
3. Cheng, M., Tseng, C.H.: Saliency at first sight: instant identity referential advantage toward a newly met partner. CRPI **4**(1), 1–18 (2019)
4. Sui, J., He, X., Humphreys, G.W.: Perceptual effects of social salience: evidence from self-prioritizeation effects on perceptual matching, JEP:HPP **38**(5), 1105 (2012)

A Study on an Ultrasonic Sensor-Based Following System in Mobile Robots for Worker Assistance

Seung-Ho Yum⬤, Su-Hong Eom⬤, Chol-U Lee, and Eung-Hyuk Lee(✉)

Department of Electronic Engineering, Korea Polytechnic University, Siheung, Gyeonggi-do, Korea
{2020811084,sheom,marinlee2k,ehlee}@kpu.ac.kr

Abstract. The current system where robots follow people is representative of a vision system and a method of using lidar sensors. Systems based on these methods have the advantage of excellent following precision, but cannot guarantee the following precision if there are no distinct features or sufficient calibrations in following targets and surrounding environments. Therefore, this study proposes a following system using ultrasonic sensors that was consist of one receiver and two transmitters. Also, this study proposes an instrumental design and algorithm for fast following restart in the event of a non-following state beyond the sensing cross-region of the two ultrasonic sensors. In addition, this study implements a haptic function to enable the robot to recognize hazardous situations and non-following states for following a target. For quantitative verification of the proposed system, path following experiments with different paths, 'S', 'L', and '8', were conducted in a space of $4m^2$ and the stable following was confirmed through 10 repetitive experiments. Through this study, it is expected that an immediate following system can be implemented in any environment.

Keywords: Following System · Mobile Robot · Interaction

1 Introduction

Collaborative robots enable increased work efficiency through physical interactions in the same space with humans [1, 2]. Therefore, the use of collaborative robots at industrial sites has dramatically improved the inefficiency of traditional field works [3]. Collaborative robots are largely divided into Arm and Mobile platforms [4]. The Mobile platform aims to closely follow workers and allow them to use heavy objects and equipments, providing freedom in the hands of workers, reducing frequent movement, and reducing physical exhaustion. In recent years, for this reason, the Mobile platform-based collaborative robots have been gradually used in different fields as well as industrial sites [5, 6].

The representative sensors currently used by the Mobile platform-based collaborative robots to follow workers are Vision and LiDAR [7, 8]. It cannot guarantee the following precision unless there are distinct characteristics of the following target and surrounding environment, or if sufficient calibration is performed even though this method has the

© Springer Nature Switzerland AG 2021
C. Stephanidis et al. (Eds.): HCII 2021, CCIS 1420, pp. 207–214, 2021.
https://doi.org/10.1007/978-3-030-78642-7_28

advantage of excellent following precision [9, 10]. For this reason, the use of robots to assist medical personnel wearing protective equipments under the Coronavirus disease (COVID-19) pandemic did not meet expectations [11].

Therefore, this study proposes a sensor system that makes the Mobile-based collaborative robots available anytime, anywhere quickly. In this study, the ultrasonic sensor uses two ultrasonic transmitters and one receiver as a single set. This is to estimate the position of a person in terms of distance and direction based on the robot [12].

There are two types of the following failure in following system. The first is when the worker deviates from the horizontal area of transmitting/receiving ultrasonic signals, and the second is when an obstacle appears in the transmission/reception area, or the signal is not detected. This study proposes two ways to solve these problems. The first method is to enlarge the ultrasonic transmission horizontal area by attaching an actuator to the transmitter of the ultrasonic sensor, and the second method is the application of a Haptic interface, which informs the worker as vibrations while the ultrasonic transmission/reception is not possible.

A similar study has been conducted to expand the horizontal area of ultrasonic sensors among the proposed methods. The study can overcome the specification limitations of ultrasonic sensors, but it follows the inconvenience of searching by varying the angle of rotation to the normal ultrasonic transmission/reception process, which causes time delay. This time delay can lead to an out-of-control state of the following in a real-time following system, and a single following failure can lead to a serious accident in the following system without prior interaction.

In this study, therefore, a method that applies a differential rotation method for the ultrasonic sensor transmitter is used to solve this problem. The differential rotation is designed based on link structures and actuators in order to create a wider cross-area through configuring the rotation angle of the outer ultrasonic sensor larger than the inner ultrasonic sensor centered at the rotation radius of the robot.

The ultrasonic sensor configuration proposed in this study consists of two ultrasonic transmitters and receivers as a pair. Although this method shows no significant problem when ultrasonic signals are transmitted/received smoothly, it causes following failures and accidents when the worker deviates from the horizontal area of transmitting/receiving ultrasonic signals, and an obstacle appears in the area, or signals are not detected due to the absence of prior interaction.

Therefore, this paper proposes a solution for each of these two problems where the worker deviates from the horizontal area of transmitting/receiving ultrasonic signals, and the appearance of obstacles and signals are not detected.

2   Method

2.1   Principles for Expanding the Transmission/Reception Horizontal Area

In an ultrasonic sensor system that consists of two ultrasonic transmitters and receivers as a pair, the system positioning is only possible if the receiver exists in the estimated cross-area. Thus, if the target is outside of the estimation area, it is placed in an inestimable, and to address this state, it searches the estimable area.

Currently, a prior study to solve these problems searches the areas where ultrasonic signals can be received by rotating the ultrasonic transmitter as shown in Fig. 1, [A]. Because the estimable area is the intersection of two or more areas of transmitting ultrasonic signals, the search process takes a long time if the receiver of ultrasonic signals is significantly out of the area.

In a target following process, the delay in the estimation process may cause estimation failure. Thus, the estimation delay should be resolved in the shortest possible time.

Therefore, in this paper, the search time is reduced in the same way as presented in Fig. 1, [B]. The proposed method is to rotate the outer ultrasonic sensor module larger than the inner ultrasonic module as rotating the ultrasonic sensor module in order to expand the ultrasonic transmission/reception cross area.

In this study, however, a method that can be implemented as a single link is proposed because individual configurations of actuators for this differential rotation cause an increase in system costs.

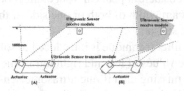

Fig. 1. Search area based on the rotation angle of the distance measurement sensor

2.2 Single Link-Based Asynchronous Rotation Structure for Expanding the Horizontal Area of Ultrasonic Sensors

In this study, a rotating module with a single link structure is designed based on the Ackermann steering mechanism for expanding the horizontal area of ultrasonic sensors. The rotational trajectory of the inside drive of the Ackermann steering mechanism is located inside the rotational trajectory of the center of the rear axle when turning, and the rotational trajectory of the outer drive is located outside the rotation trajectory of the center of the rear axle.

However, the rotation module proposed in this study is the opposite of the Ackermann steering mechanism because the module away from the direction of rotation rotates at a larger angle. This is intended to expand the ultrasonic transmission/reception area in the direction of rotation.

The asynchronous structure of the single link proposed in this study is presented in Fig. 2. The position of the target is assumed to be the sensor maximum incident angle $\angle r$ of both ultrasonic transmission beam widths and the general following distance c. Here, d is the distance from the ultrasonic sensor. In addition, as c is assumed as the inclined plane of a triangle, the center and target of the two ultrasonic sensors can be analyzed as a right triangle, and l, which is the height of the triangle, can be calculated using Eq. (1).

Based on this information, the rotation angles of the ultrasonic sensor module, $\angle a$, $\angle \beta$ can be calculated using Eq. (2) and Eq. (3), respectively.

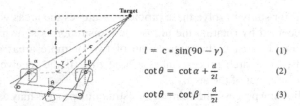

$$l = c * \sin(90 - \gamma) \qquad (1)$$

$$\cot\theta = \cot\alpha + \frac{d}{2l} \qquad (2)$$

$$\cot\theta = \cot\beta - \frac{d}{2l} \qquad (3)$$

Fig. 2. Proposed rotation module

2.3 Single Link-Based Asynchronous Rotation Structure for Expanding the Horizontal Area of Ultrasonic Sensors

The configuration of the ultrasonic sensors proposed in this study causes problems that lead to failure of the following process if both ultrasound transmission signals are not received smoothly at the receiver section of the ultrasonic sensors. One of the causes of this problem is that when an obstacle appears in front of the robot in the following process and then the transmission beam width of both or one side of the ultrasonic sensors does not reach the receiver of the sensors.

In this paper, a software filter technique is introduced to solve these problems, which receive and sum the distance values of left and right ultrasonic sensors respectively, and send the previous values of missing data if one ultrasonic sensor is missing data within a predetermined time. This method allows predictive movements in a state of appearing an obstacle or signal receiving disorder because the robot that acquired the previous data can recognize the approximate worker location without receiving the data value of one side of the sensors.

In this study, therefore, a Haptic interface technique is proposed to inform the robot condition to workers using a vibrator at the same time as predictive movements through the software technique. This technique can be used to prevent accidents using a vibrator attached to the worker, and the worker can recognize the situation in the back through prior interactions.

2.4 Expanding the Transmission/Reception Horizontal Area and an Alternative Algorithm for an Unstable State of Transmission

In this study proposed to implement the expansion of the transmission/reception horizontal area and the notification algorithm shown in Fig. 3. At the beginning of the following process, it will determine whether the transmission/reception horizontal area is expanded or transmission disorder situations according to the values of both distances received.

The expansion of the transmission/reception horizontal area is presented in (a) and (b) shows the rotation of the ultrasonic sensor module to the right as the previous object position is the right side for expanding the reception horizontal area and operates the haptic sensor attached to the worker's waistband (c). Assuming that the following process has been carried out, if the angle between the target and the robot is within $\alpha°$ as shown in (d), it will stop the operation of the haptic sensor and returns the ultrasonic sensor to its original position as shown in (e). The transmission disorder state is presented in (e), and it performs the previous data-based following process because one side of the sensors does not receive transmission data smoothly due to obstacles. Then, the haptic sensor is operated at the same time as shown in (c).

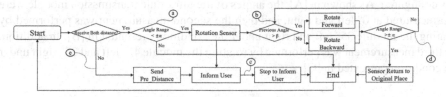

Fig. 3. Operation algorithm based on types of following failures

Figure 4 represents the motion sequence in two different types depending on the received data of the ultrasonic sensors. Figure 4 [A] shows the deviation of the worker from the transmission/reception horizontal area of the ultrasonic signals, where the robot performs the following process by creating a wider cross-area centered at the radius of the rotation, with the rotation angle of the outer ultrasonic sensor larger than the inner ultrasonic sensor. Then, it implements interactions using the haptic device.

Figure 4 [B] represents inharmonic receiving of ultrasonic signals from one side of the sensors due to obstacles, and in this case, the previous ultrasonic distance value is stored for presenting predictive movements, which can also be communicated to the worker for the present condition through the haptic device.

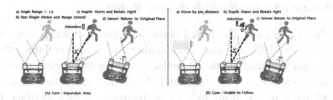

Fig. 4. Operation method based on types of following failures

3 Experiment and Results

3.1 Experiment for Expanding the Transmission/reception Horizontal Area of the Rotation Module Using Ultrasonic Sensors

The rotation module applied in this study cannot recognize the reception module at a point leaning toward the right of 50°. Thus, the reception module was positioned approximately 0.8 m away, taking into account the maximum incident angle of both ultrasonic transmission beam widths of 50°. Here, the rotational angles of the actuators and ultrasonic sensors are derived based on the angle calculation equation of the rotation module proposed in the main subject. Then, the value of α is set to 45° considering the incidence and maximum rotation angles of the ultrasonic sensors, and then the values of β and r are calculated as $25°$ and $35°$ respectively.

For verifying the reliable sensing of the target for the calculated rotation angles of the ultrasonic sensors, the experiment for expanding the following area presented in Fig. 5 was configured. As shown in [A], the angles of the ultrasonic transmission module were first measured at $0°$ left and right, and then the second measurement was performed by rotating the module $35°$ left and right under the condition presented in [B]. In addition, the third measurement was performed by rotating the module $45°$ left and $25°$ right under the condition presented in [C].

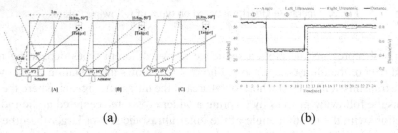

(a)   (b)

Fig. 5. (a) Results of the following area expansion experiment. (b) Experiment scenario of the expansion of following areas

3.2   Experiment for Solving the Following Disorder Through the Driving of an Ultrasonic Sensor-Based Following Robot

In this study, the 'L', 'S', and '8' shaped paths with frequent steep turn sections were marked in advance, and the accuracy was evaluated by accumulating the following trajectories after the walking along the paths based on the ultrasonic reception and notification modules attached to the waistband. Also, data on whether the following area is expanded and haptic notifications are present during steep turn sections. The left side coordinates presented in Fig. 6 (a), (b), (c) represent the path of the robot according to the movement of the user, and the right side shows the angle between the moving robot and the user, the rotation angle of the actuator, and the haptic notification while driving. The following experiment is based on the characteristics of the robot that follows at a certain distance from the user in terms of safety, so the position of the previous user shows a curve and has a delay time because it is after a considerable amount of walking. Thus, in the movement paths of the 'S' and '8' shaped paths within a small space, the robot rotates in place due to the large curvature of the travel distance and indicates the movement paths as shown in Fig. 6 (a), (b).

As the result, when driving 'L', 'S', and '8' and steep turn occurs, the actuator is rotated by $35°$ to expand the following area, which measures more than a limited angle by rotating the outer ultrasonic sensor of the rotation center $45°$ and the inner ultrasonic sensor $25°$. At the same time, the haptic sensor informs the dangerous situation through vibration if the angle between the robot and the user is greater than $35°$. In the repetitive movement trajectory experiments, similar trajectories were identified for the steep turning paths of the robot, and the reliable driving and following with a smooth curve were confirmed without and deviations.

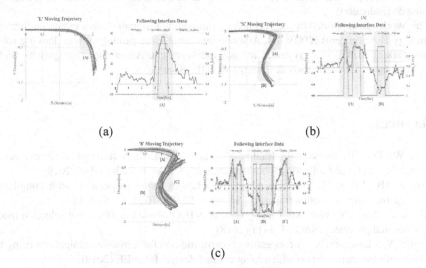

(a)   (b)

(c)

Fig. 6. (a) Results and the robot movement coordinate of the path 'L', (b) Results and the robot movement coordinate of the path 'S', (c) Results and the robot movement coordinate of the path '8'

4 Conclusion

In this study, a sensor system that solves the problem of a disorder in receiving ultrasonic signals during the following process for the worker using ultrasonic sensors in a limited environment without feature points is proposed. In addition, the solution is proposed as two types: the user deviating from the transmission/reception horizontal area of the ultrasonic sensors, and the obstacle appearing and transmission disorder conditions. In the case of the deviation from the ultrasonic transmission/reception horizontal area, a rotation module with a single link structure was designed, see more area than synchronous rotation module and implements haptic system.

For verifying the expansion of the worker following area, the synchronous rotation of ultrasonic sensors and the asynchronous rotation presented in this study were compared, and it showed a wide following range of approximately 70%. In addition, the reliable worker following by repeating the steep turns was verified.

Based on the results of the experiment, it is confirmed that the method proposed in this study can be seen as an improvement in the following technology using conventional ultrasonic sensors and can be used as an interface for various applications of Mobile-based collaborative robots.

Acknowledgement. This research was supported by the MSIT (Ministry of Science and ICT), Korea, under the ITRC (Information Technology Research Center) support program (IITP-2021–2018-0–01426) supervised by the IITP (Institute for Information & Communications Technology Planning & Evaluation).

This work was supported by the Technology Innovation Program (Robot Industrial Strategic Technology Development) (20008764, Autonomous robot valet parking system, Parking robot, Robotic parking management system, Car body measurement, Autonomous navigation) funded by the Ministry of Trade, Industry & Energy (MOTIE, Korea).

References

1. Tai, W., Ilias, B., Shukor, A., Rahim, N., Markom, M.A.: A study of ultrasonic sensor capability in shuman following robot system. IOPSCIENCE. **705**(5), 1–8 (2019)
2. Nemec, B., Likar, N., Gams, A., Ude, A.: Human robot cooperation with compliance adaptation along the motion trajectory. Springer **42**(07), 1023–1035 (2018)
3. Zhou, F., Wang, X., Goh, M.: Fuzzy extended VIKOR-based mobile robot selection model for hospital pharmacy. SAGE J. 1–11 (2018)
4. Naito, Y., Matsuhira, N.: A cooperative control method for a mobile manipulator using the difference the manipulation with a robot control device. In: IEEE (2019)
5. Gao, K., Xin, J., Cheng, H., Liu, D., Li, J.: Multi-mobile robot autonomous navigation system for intelligent logistics. IEEE (2018)
6. Yan, P., Fan, Y., Liu, R., Wang, M.: Distributed optimal deployment on a circle for cooperative encirclement of autonomous mobile multi-agents. IEEE Acces. **8**, 1–7 (2020). https://doi.org/10.1109/ACCESS.2020.2982581
7. Chen, J., Kim, W.J.: A human-following mobile robot providing natural and universal interfaces for control with wireless electronic devices. IEEE ASME Trans. Mech. **24**, 1–8 (2019). https://doi.org/10.1109/TMECH.2019.2936395
8. Wang, M., Liu, Y., Su, D.: Accurate and real-time 3-d tracking for the following robots by fusing vision and ultrasonar information. IEEE ASME Trans. Mech. **23**, 1–9 (2018). https://doi.org/10.1109/TMECH.2018.2820172
9. Pinrath, N., Matsuhira, N.: Simulation of a human following robot with object avoidance function. In: IEEE (2018)
10. Lee, C., Park, G., Ryu, J., Jeong, S., Park, S., Park, J.: Indoor positioning system based on incident angles of infrared emitters. In: IEEE (2004)
11. Dam, A., Verma, A., Pangi, C., Raviteja, R., Prasad, C.: Person following mobile robot using pedestrian dead-reckoning with inertial data of smartphones. In: IEEE (2020)
12. Pandharipande, A., Caicedo, D.: User localization using ultrasonic presence sensing systems. In: IEEE (2012)

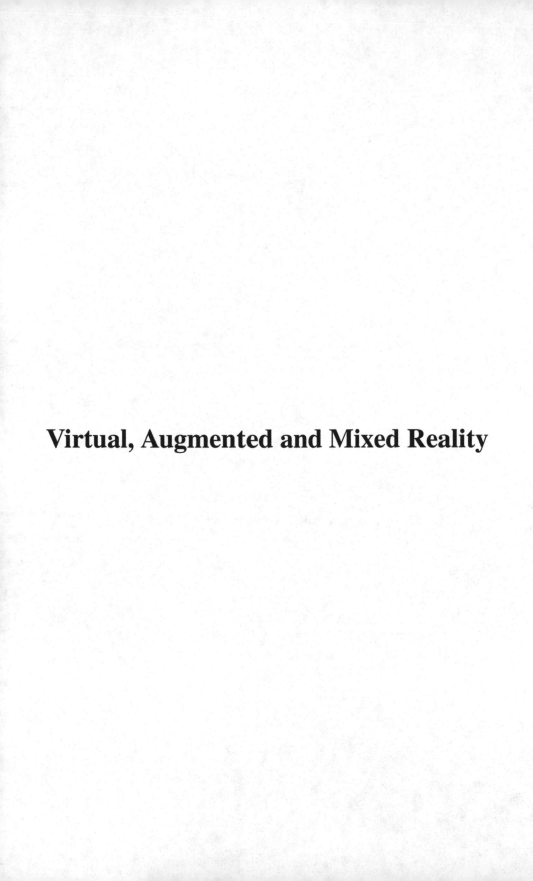

Virtual, Augmented and Mixed Reality

Co-immersive-Creation: A Hybrid Approach for Using Virtual Reality and Telepresence Systems in Co-design Research

M. F. Yang Chen[✉]

The Ohio State University, Columbus, OH 43210, USA
chenyang.1@osu.edu

Abstract. The Covid-19 pandemic is changing the way design researchers conduct research activities with safety regulations restricting much of in-person methods of research. Co-design (or participatory design) utilizes creative toolkits that enable stakeholders from non-design backgrounds to contribute and collaborate in the design process, from front-end to tail-end. The pandemic has forced co-design researchers to reconceptualize and adapt their research methods and toolkits into remote digital formats. This presents new challenges in conducting co-design research such as the varying levels of technological literacy of parties involved and being able to facilitate the same level of engagement and hands-on involvement as in-person co-design activities. This paper examines the exploration of a novel hybrid approach, named Co-Immersive-Creation (CIC), that combines virtual reality (VR) and telepresence systems such as video conferencing applications for remote co-design research. It presents a use case of the co-design of the interior spaces in intensive care unit (ICU) hospital rooms to reduce sleep deprivation and delirium among the patients. An outline of the technical setup and the considerations surrounding this hybrid approach is presented to encourage its continued exploration. The outcome of the exploration highlights the growing potential of CIC and the possibilities offered by integrating technology such as VR for conducting remote co-design research between designers and non-design stakeholders.

Keywords: Co-design · Generative Design Research · Remote · Virtual Reality · Telepresence

1 Introduction

Co-design on a high level can be embraced as a mindset which is the belief that every individual has valuable insights to contribute [5]. It can also be applied as a group of research methods that focus on user participation in the design process. Toolkits for co-design activities are designed to empower creativity in participants, enabling them to better share their insights. Activities such as generative prototyping can be very resource-heavy in preparation and execution depending on the intricacy of toolkits [8]. At the same time, design researchers have to take on the roles of leading and facilitating

© Springer Nature Switzerland AG 2021
C. Stephanidis et al. (Eds.): HCII 2021, CCIS 1420, pp. 217–224, 2021.
https://doi.org/10.1007/978-3-030-78642-7_29

such hands-on activities which are usually conducted in-person [13]. In this case study, a team of co-design researchers identified intensive care unit (ICU) hospital rooms as an area of focus and how the re-design it interior spaces could help to reduce sleep deprivation and delirium in patients. The Covid-19 pandemic, which happened halfway through the study, restricted conducting in-person research due to health-safety regulations. Shifting towards a remote study had introduced new problems; conducting a generative prototyping activity for an interior space in the absence of physical space, creating a workflow that facilitates full remote collaboration between the co-design participants and the researchers, and the varying technological literacy of the researchers and the stakeholders.

2 Definitions

It should be noted that there are varying definitions and uses of certain terms depending on the field that uses them. In this paper, co-design is defined as collective creativity in the design process [13]. Co-design participants or participants refer to the stakeholders involved in the co-design research activities. Co-design researchers or facilitators are used interchangeably to represent the members of the research team. Virtual Reality (VR) refers to the medium of virtual immersion with six degrees of freedom experienced through head-mounted displays (HMD) [10]. Telepresence refers to video conferencing applications that allow for real-time audio and video communication, e.g. Skype, Zoom, Cisco Webex [17].

3 Literature Review

Several studies have investigated remote collaboration for design. Early works explored web-based computer-aided design (CAD) tools for real-time collaborative prototyping between engineers, architects, and designers [14]. Virtual 3D worlds experienced through a computer monitor have been studied as shared spaces for design, creation, and learning [2, 7]. Martelaro and Ju explored remote testing of user interfaces that were real-time prototypes transmitted to participants via screen tablets [11]. These four studies highlight the importance of involved parties being familiar with the prototyping tools with participants either receiving prior training or participating only in the evaluation of prototypes. Madathil and Greenstein measured a higher level of user involvement in VR and telepresence system compared to traditional in-person setups but acknowledged technical challenges of virtual spaces such as interaction delays [1]. Co-design researchers aware of the strengths of virtual tools have explored its integration in studies using virtual environments through CAVE VR, HMD VR, and AR devices [4, 6, 12, 15]. The studies revealed similar key essentials for VR co-design activities such as being able to co-visualize in real-time and real-scale, evaluate, and make decisions in the shared spaces.

The literature reveals the challenges of co-design activities being high in demand for in-person facilitation and resource-heavy in development and execution. In the prototyping of a real-scale hospital room using Velcro toolkits, co-design researchers had to document and reset the space in between sessions [15]. While another co-design study of hospital rooms used real-scale virtual environments for immersive evaluations of only pre-built prototypes because of the limited skills and tools the co-design researchers had in building 3D environments [8]. The design of CIC explores the opportunity for a simpler setup for real-time and real-scale generative prototyping by stakeholders.

4 Background

The co-design study was conducted throughout several months with earlier sessions focused on identifying elements of ICU rooms that contributed to sleep deprivation and delirium in patients; a risk for patients that can be fatal. The interior space of the ICU room was identified as a primary area of focus that could be improved on to address this risk. The co-design team was made up of five researchers and twenty-four stakeholders that included physicians, nurses, hospital volunteers, ex-ICU patients and/or their family members. The later co-design sessions were centered around the creation and implementation of a generative prototyping activity for the interior space of an ICU room. The team explored several prototyping options including miniature models, full-scale makeshift parts of an interior space, sketching, and virtual environments. This task became a bigger challenge when the Covid-19 pandemic happened. The stakeholders involved such as ex-ICU patients and medical personnel made them high-risk individuals for contact and the co-design spaces situated in the hospital became restricted. The researchers also faced the challenge of preparing the rest of the study sessions and toolkits remotely as a team.

5 Co-immersive-Creation

The author who was part of the team had already explored conducting co-design research using VR and developed the collaborative VR design sandbox (VRDS) based on a multi-user cloud base Unity platform [3]. The team decided to integrate VRDS and design a hybrid remote setup combining it with Zoom, a telepresence video conferencing system, for the generative prototyping co-design activity. They named the approach Co-Immersive-Creation (CIC).

5.1 Setup and Preparation

The VRDS was however initially designed to be used in-person because of the technical challenges such as network connectivity and an onboarding training required for participants. Another challenge was the accessibility of VR hardware available to the research team. Only two members, including the author, had access to VR equipment, HTC Vives. The author provided help with the VR setup and trained the other member on the usage of the VRDS remotely. Due to the stress on the bandwidth connecting to a telepresence video call and a networked VR environment, the VR team members had to use wired ethernet connections to ensure a stable connection during the CIC sessions.

The preparation first began with creating a default ICU room environment in VR and the preparation of toolkits for prototyping which included images, 3D models, spatialized audio clips, and basic 3D shapes (see Fig. 1).

Fig. 1. A screen capture of a room in VR with the toolkits prepared, (from left to right) pictures, audio clips, 3D models and basic 3D shapes.

The choices of the toolkits were based on findings and analysis from earlier co-design sessions such as calming images and sounds, with the latter being a unique addition made possible by being in VR. The CIC generative prototyping toolkit and setup went through multiple iterations and tests within the research team with improvements being added to the final setup.

5.2   CIC Process

During each CIC session, the co-design facilitators were connected to participants via a Zoom live video conference call. In the team of five, three facilitators in Zoom led, took notes and coordinated the co-design activity. The other two team members, a VR lead and a VR assistant, were connected to the call from within the VR environment through their HMD (see Fig. 2). Both the facilitators in VR could view the video feed of the call as an overlay within their HMD and communicated via its microphone.

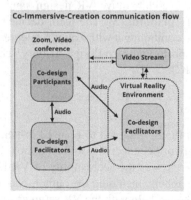

Fig. 2. The visual (video) and audio flow between co-design facilitators and participants in CIC.

The VR lead streamed the video feed from the HMD to Zoom, via share screen, and assumed the role of an embodied representative of the participant in the VR space. Participants were given the freedom to cycle through one out of five different camera views of the ICU room throughout the session (see Fig. 3). They would prototype by instructing the facilitators in VR with their request, utilizing anything available from the toolkits to add or modify in the VR environment. This took away the need to train participants for VR and minimized any risk or concern of motion sickness.

Fig. 3. Five options of camera views, Fullview1 (top-left), Fullview2 (top-right), Patient view (bottom-left), Visitor view (bottom-right) and First-person view; VR lead (center).

6   Data and Analysis

Data for the CIC sessions were captured in the form of screen video and still captures, audio recordings, notes from non-VR facilitators and the actual VR prototyped environments that were saved to the cloud (see Fig. 4).

Fig. 4. Screen captures of two VR prototyped environments co-designed by participants and accessible via the cloud.

After the sessions, the digital nature of the data captured and syncing within the cloud facilitated ease for remote analysis for the co-design researchers. Members of the research team went through the video recordings of the CIC sessions and made notes based on their observations that may have been missed during the live session. This was especially important for the two team members that were within the VR environment and had a different perspective during the sessions. The team also had a post-session walkthrough of the VR environments via the same VR to Zoom setup of CIC. During the walkthrough discussions, key areas of interest within the VR environment were identified and documented as photographs using screen capture. A 360 image capture of each environment was also taken and uploaded to a 360 image viewer [16] for the team to analyze outside of VR. This was a very useful reference for remote analysis.

The analysis in this paper focuses on the approach of CIC and reserves in-depth analysis of the prototyped ICU spaces for reducing sleep deprivation and delirium for a future paper. There were three major patterns identified from the CIC sessions.

1. Each of the CIC sessions ended early with participants satisfied with exploring all their ideas. The research team was also able to conduct consecutive sessions with virtual copies of the default ICU setup. This saved time compared to the physical setup that required time to document and reset between sessions [8].
2. Participants started with simple ideas in the first few minutes, utilizing what was available from the toolkits. The ideas became bolder as the session progressed with participants requesting to play with scale, modifying the structure of the ICU room, changing the colors of the environment and objects, changing the lighting setup and creating new or modifying objects. These options were not planned or included as part of the toolkits.
3. The audio coding revealed that participants talked about a sense of presence in the VR ICU room without being prompted especially with the first person, patient, and visitor camera view with comments such as "I feel like I am walking in the room with you". There were clear indications that participants had a sense of spatial awareness of the VR space with words such as "behind you, by your side, by that wall, on the ceiling".

7 Discussion

CIC enabled the team of co-design researchers to overcome the major problems that emerged when shifting to a remote format. The lack of a physical representation or an actual ICU room was solved by the digital immersive VR environment. The interfacing and interconnectivity of being able to communicate and share the audio and visual environment between VR and the telepresence system made it easier to collaborate remotely. This was essential for the CIC session and in the planning stage where the co-design facilitators were able to collectively make decisions and design the prototyping space together. This approach of mutually sharing gaze has been studied and proven to be beneficial in collaborative setups [9]. CIC reduced the team's concerns with participant's technology literacy which was a major design consideration. All the available options of remote collaborative design platforms considered required a certain level of prior training and handholding.

There were some advantages presented by CIC there were unexpected. From the empirical findings, it seemed that the flexibility of a digital environment combined with the ease of verbalizing their prototyping ideas encouraged participants to demand more than what was offered in the toolkits. Both the VR co-design facilitators ended up using tools or features that were not planned in the toolkits such as altering the dimensions of the VR space, changing of colors, creating new objects either with basic shapes or 3D sketching and altering the lighting within the environment. It is interesting to note that none of these options were promoted or offered but were repeated requests by participants in separate sessions. It was important that both the VR facilitators were well trained with the affordances within the VRDS which allowed such requests to be met in real-time.

Other important considerations identified pertain to the phenomenon of presence which was not part of the design consideration of CIC. However, the feedback from participants and the coding of the audio revealed some level of presence being experienced. This could be due to the ability of being able to view the five different camera views within the environment in real-time. There was also spatial ambient audio of the VR ICU room which included sounds of breathing machines and beeping from medical equipment which may have contributed to the feeling of presence.

8 Conclusion and Future Direction

CIC as an approach has presented preliminary evidence of its effective use for remote co-design activities with the potential of integrating other methods beyond just generative prototyping. Its presentation is an important contribution to the co-design community and provides a foundation on how to carry out co-design activities that extend beyond in-person setups. The approach focuses on the process considerations and is application-agnostic meaning it can be adapted with other similar VR and telepresence systems. CIC facilitates an opportunity to gain valuable insights and engage in co-design research with vulnerable individuals and medical personnel during and beyond the Covid-19 pandemic without additional risk. The approach lessens the demand for technical literacy from participants. Both the VRDS and CIC is continuously being iterated and implemented in other co-design research. The next goal is to publish quantitative data from CIC studies and present an in-depth critical analysis of the approach. Moving forward, the author plans to expand CIC into a higher level of interactivity allowing for participants to have enhanced controls of the VR environment remotely and being able to view a 360 video feed during the live sessions.

Acknowledgments. CIC is a group effort with the author focused on the technical aspects of setup and execution. The author would like to acknowledge the collaborative work by the other co-design researchers from The Ohio State University, Yiting Wang, Noor Murteza, Susan Booher, and Monyk Wecker.

References

1. Chalil Madathil, K., Greenstein, J.S.: An investigation of the efficacy of collaborative virtual reality systems for moderated remote usability testing. Appl. Ergon. **65**, 501–514 (2017). https://doi.org/10.1016/j.apergo.2017.02.011
2. Chau, M., Wong, A., Wang, M., et al.: Using 3D virtual environments to facilitate students sin constructivist learning. Decis. Support Syst. **56**, 115–121 (2013). https://doi.org/10.1016/j.dss.2013.05.009

3. Chen M.F.Y., Manchester, M.F., Yang, C.: Virtual reality in design, a new studio environment. In: YouTube (2020). https://youtu.be/XtRAtxDarRw. Accessed 10 Dec 2020

4. Chowdhury, S., Schnabel, M.A.: Virtual environments as medium for laypeople to communicate and collaborate in urban design. Architect. Sci. Rev. **63**, 451–464 (2020). https://doi.org/10.1080/00038628.2020.1806031

5. Sanders, E.B.-N.: From user-centered to participatory design approaches. In: Design and the Social Sciences, pp. 18–25. CRC Press (2002)

6. Kopeć, W., Wichrowski, M., Kalinowski, K., et al.: VR with older adults: participatory design of a virtual ATM training simulation. IFAC-PapersOnLine **52**, 277–281 (2019). https://doi.org/10.1016/j.ifacol.2019.12.110

7. Koutsabasis, P., Vosinakis, S., Malisova, K., Paparounas, N.: On the value of virtual worlds for collaborative design. Des. Stud. **33**, 357–390 (2012). https://doi.org/10.1016/j.destud.2011.11.004

8. Lavender, S.A., Sommerich, C.M., Sanders, E.B.-N., et al.: Developing evidence-based design guidelines for medical/surgical hospital patient rooms that meet the needs of staff, patients, and visitors. HERD Heal. Environ. Res. Des. J. **13**, 145–178 (2019). https://doi.org/10.1177/1937586719856009

9. Lee, G., et al.: Mutually shared gaze in augmented video conference. In: 2017 IEEE International Symposium on Mixed and Augmented Reality (ISMAR-Adjunct), pp. 79–80. IEEE Nantes, France (2017)

10. Linda, S.E.: Virtual Reality - Virtually Here. PC Magazine (1995)

11. Martelaro, N., Ju, W.: WoZ Way: enabling real-time remote interaction prototyping & observation in on-road vehicles. In: Proceedings of the 2017 ACM Conference on Computer Supported Cooperative Work and Social Computing, pp. 169–182. ACM, Portland Oregon USA (2017)

12. O'Hare, J., Dekoninck, E., Mombeshora, M., et al.: Defining requirements for an augmented reality system to overcome the challenges of creating and using design representations in co-design sessions. CoDesign **16**, 111–134 (2020). https://doi.org/10.1080/15710882.2018.1546319

13. Sanders, E.B.-N., Stappers, P.J.: Co-creation and the new landscapes of design. CoDesign **4**, 5–18 (2008). https://doi.org/10.1080/15710880701875068

14. Smparounis K, et al.: A web-based platform for collaborative product design and evaluation. In: 2009 IEEE International Technology Management Conference (ICE), pp. 1–9. IEEE, Leiden (2009)

15. Tiainen, T., Jouppila, T.: Use of virtual environment and virtual prototypes in co-design: The case of hospital design. Computers **8**, 44 (2019). https://doi.org/10.3390/computers8020044

16. Virtual 360 Tours made easy. Create. Edit. Share Kuula. In: Kuula. https://kuula.co/. Accessed 2 Apr 2020

17. What is Telepresence? - Definition from Techopedia. In: Techopedia.com. http://www.techopedia.com/definition/14600/telepresence. Accessed 20 Mar 2021

A Decision Matrix for Implementing AR, 360° and VR Experiences into Mining Engineering Education

Lea M. Daling[1]([✉]), Samira Khodaei[1], Stefan Thurner[2], Anas Abdelrazeq[1], and Ingrid Isenhardt[1]

[1] Chair of Information Management in Mechanical Engineering (IMA),
RWTH Aachen University, Aachen, Germany
lea.daling@ima.rwth-aachen.de
[2] Educational Technology, Graz University of Technology, Graz, Austria

Abstract. The use of Mixed Reality (MR) technologies is expected to address the current challenges in mining engineering education. Including hands-on experience often conflicts with limited resources for field trips and excursions. Various studies report that MR can support students in fostering knowledge transfer and enhancing the development of professional skills. However, the success of MR technologies in teaching depends significantly on the teachers, who are rarely supported in the introduction and selection of MR technologies. In order to support teachers in the selection of suitable media and technologies, we present a multidimensional matrix to support the decision towards the usage of three different MR experiences in mining engineering education: Augmented Reality (AR), 360°, and Virtual Reality (VR) experiences. This matrix was built based on the result of several conducted interviews with the technology developers and users. The decision matrix differentiates between methodological aspects of teaching, infrastructural factors, individual prerequisites and knowledge of the teacher, all of which play a role in the selection of the right MR technology. In addition, examples of the use of the respective technology in teaching are discussed.

Keywords: Mixed reality · Augmented reality · Virtual reality · Decision matrix · Mining engineering education

1 Introduction

1.1 Mixed Reality Technologies in Mining Engineering Education

Many academic courses at universities aim for including practical experiences, which are often not feasible, or come only at high cost. Furthermore, there is an increasing need for engineering education to enable new and broader perspectives by incorporating the complexity of environmental, economic, and social realities along with systems engineering, enabling technologies, and physical constraints [1, 2]. At the same time, however, the focus of public investment is shifting to growing and economically promising courses of study. Especially in mining engineering education, student numbers continue to decline. Although the mining sector continues to offer attractive job prospects, mining education departments are suffering from severe financial cutbacks [3]. In a situation where real experiences in mines are hardly feasible and field trips are very expensive and time-consuming, teaching institutions have to find new methods to facilitate the transfer of knowledge.

The use of Mixed Reality (MR) technologies is expected to address current challenges in this context. Especially in mining engineering education, using MR can offer experiences in otherwise hardly accessible settings [4], enhance motivation and learning and thus making mining more attractive for students [4, 5]. Various studies report that MR can support students in fostering knowledge transfer and enhancing the development of professional skills [5, 6], allowing them to control their learning processes more actively [7]. Moreover, game-based formats and the possibility of immediate feedback for actions may enable a lasting learning-effect [8]. However, especially with regard to the didactic planning and organizational preparation of MR based teaching, there are still some obstacles preventing their successful implementation.

1.2   Challenges of Implementing MR Experiences into Teaching

Even though numerous studies indicate positive effects and motivation-enhancing aspects of digital technologies in academic teaching [4, 5, 8], there are still severe challenges in the implementation of new digital formats into teaching. Despite the fact that the demands on teachers 4.0 are constantly increasing, there are still very few teachers who are trained in the use of developed technologies [9]. Thus, there is still a large gap between new technical solutions and their actual use by teachers. To date, there are almost no solutions that enable teachers themselves to make an informed decision on the selection of suitable media for teaching.

In order to support teachers in the selection of suitable media and technologies, this paper presents a multidimensional matrix to support the decision towards the usage of three different MR experiences in mining engineering education: Augmented Reality (AR), 360°, and Virtual Reality (VR) experiences. The decision matrix is based on the evaluation of interview results of the project Mixed Reality Books (MiReBooks), funded by the EIT Raw Materials, with over 39 participants from all over Europe [6, 10]. The project addresses the current problems in the field of mining education and develops measures to increase the quality of the studies. The transfer of theoretical knowledge into practice is of particular importance. The project aims to change the way students are taught. Teachers are to be enabled to engage their students more effectively through the use of MR technologies and to provide them with a larger repertoire of content and a better understanding.

In the following, the development of the decision matrix is presented on the basis of an interview study with teachers. Finally, possible fields of application and examples for the use of the matrix are discussed and future research fields in this area are reviewed.

2 Development of a Decision Matrix for Implementing MR Experiences

2.1 Definition and Classification of MR Experiences

According to Milgram and colleagues, MR describes a continuum between reality and virtuality. This makes it possible to merge physical and digital worlds [11]. In the following, we distinguish between three different forms of MR in order to make them distinguishable for teaching: Augmented Reality (AR), 360° experiences, and Virtual Reality (VR). In the context of teaching, AR augments the real world by placing virtual content (e.g., 3D models) in the field of view or by providing a real environment with further digitally represented information (e.g., through annotations) [12]. 360° experiences create an overview of realistic scenarios and environments as images or videos [13]. VR allows the user to experience the sensation of being present in a fully modeled virtual environment [14].

As part of the MiReBooks project, all of the three MR experiences were evaluated in test lectures. Four teachers with many years of teaching experience conducted 12 MR-based teaching units with a total of 120 students. Following the test lectures, participating students and teachers were asked to evaluate the lectures. In the following, only the experiences of the teachers are discussed; a detailed evaluation can be found in previous work [6]. In total, six teachers took part in our interview study. Experienced teachers were asked about their experiences and needs in connection with MR Experiences. In order to evaluate challenges and obstacles of using MR in teaching, interviews were conducted with another three teachers who had no prior experience with MR. Results of these interviews are summarized in the next section.

2.2 Evaluation Results of the Interview Study

The interviews had a duration of 15–30 min, including questions on the effective communication of learning content through MR, areas of application and opinions on challenges. The interviews with experienced teachers focused primarily on reflection on the test lecture, with particular attention to the necessary preparation and optimal teaching conditions. Inexperienced teachers were asked which media they currently use, whether they would be interested in using MR, and what would be necessary to be able to conduct their own lectures with such technologies.

Due to the small sample, the results are summarized in terms of relevant factors for preparing MR-based teaching units. All teachers reported to use traditional teaching material, such as text and manuals, pictures and graphs, videos and films, haptic objects like equipment, as well as excursions and visits to mines. Only few of them used 3D animations. All experienced teachers reported that using MR met their expectations regarding a more practical experience and better transfer from theory to practice.

In particular, 360° Videos were experienced as a feeling of actually being present in a situation, which led to a better understanding of the presented processes. A frequent remark was referring to the use of VR, which was experienced as a barrier between the teacher and students. Teachers reported that especially in large classrooms, they found it difficult to ensure that all students follow and understand the instructions while wearing VR goggles. In addition, they indicated that technical guidance and support was definitely needed so that students could also focus on the content rather than just on the technology. When using AR, students were either asked to use their own smartphones or to use already prepared smartphones, which was perceived as easy to use also with a higher number of students.

All teachers agreed that technical assistance is required to prepare the devices, internet connection and room setup before, during and after the lecture. Moreover, teachers emphasized not to underestimate the importance of technical prerequisites such as s stable Wi-Fi connection or enough space to move in the room. Overall, all teachers agreed that the use of technologies only makes sense if they are used purposefully and integrated into the didactic concept. Thus, the main result of the interviews is that the didactic integration into the teaching concept as well as the consideration of infrastructural and individual prerequisites play a crucial role for the overall success of implementing MR experiences in teaching.

2.3 Derivation of the Decision Matrix Structure

The above-mentioned findings from literature and interviews indicate the need for targeted support for teachers in the selection and preparation of MR technologies. This support should take into account different prerequisites and prior knowledge of the teachers. Since not all teachers in the university context have the opportunity to attend seminars or trainings in didactics, it seems particularly relevant to emphasize the importance of a didactic concept when using new media.

The decision matrix presented in Fig. 1 addresses this problem. It differentiates between methodological aspects of teaching, infrastructural factors, individual prerequisites and knowledge of the teacher, all of which play a role in the selection of the right MR technology. A first version of the matrix has already been presented in 2020 [10]. Since then, the further development of the matrix structure involved teachers, didactical experts and technical developers. Rather than being exhaustive, the matrix presents relevant basics that should be considered when selecting between three different MR technologies: AR, 360° and VR experiences. The horizontal columns of the matrix should be interpreted as a continuum between the different poles. The structure and composition of the matrix are explained in the following:

Teaching Method. The teaching method is condensed to two relevant factors concerning why and how the teaching content is conveyed. *Learning objectives* describe the desired outcome for a student after a learning unit [15]. In the matrix, the formulation of learning objectives is intentionally placed at the beginning, as they should precede any planning of instructional content. Within the matrix, we have divided the taxonomy into meta-levels of lower and higher skills. To formulate a learning objective, three criteria should be met - the desired outcome, the scale, and the conditions.

The *interaction level* describes a spectrum between more teacher-centered or student-centered learning processes. Student-centered approaches allow for consideration of students' individual prerequisites and learning pace and promote self-learning processes [16]. In contrast, we define teacher-centered approaches as frontal teaching. Within the

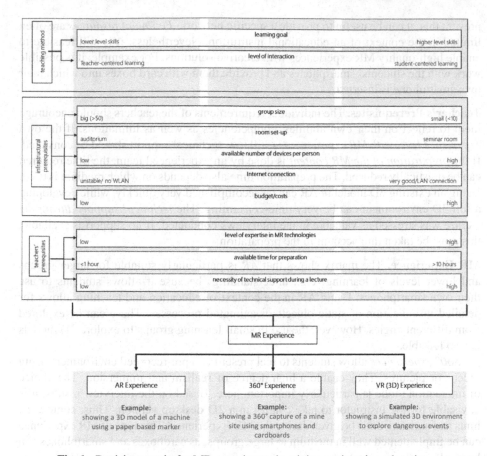

Fig. 1. Decision matrix for MR experiences in mining engineering education.

matrix, it can be seen that higher-level skills are ranked directly above more student-centered learning, indicating that active and self-learning is more likely to contribute to the acquisition of higher-level skills.

Infrastructural Prerequisites. The infrastructural prerequisites refer to *group size, room set-up, devices per person, internet connection* and available *budget or costs*. These prerequisites demonstrate to teachers what options are available to them in order to achieve their defined learning objectives. The *group size* is directly related to the interaction level. For example, events with more than 50 people are usually held as lectures, while smaller groups of about 10 people are more likely to be found in exercises or seminars. The *room set-up*, for example, refers to the possible freedom of movement needed in an MR environment. In a room with fixed rows of tables, the use of VR could be more difficult. The number of *available devices* is strongly related to the teaching method. With a large group and a small number of devices, possibilities such as group work or screen mirroring could be considered. In addition to that, wasting class time with technical issues like establishing an *internet connection* should be avoided. In order to prevent this, it can be useful to provide a specific network. *Financial resources* are often limited in the context of an educational institution. Nevertheless, it is still feasible to enable high-quality MR experiences with creative solutions. For example, it is possible work with the students' smartphones and provide them with card boxes into which their own smartphone is inserted.

Teacher's Prerequisites. The individual requirements of the teachers should encourage them to reflect on their own abilities, competencies as well as limitations. If the own *experience level with MR* experiences is still low, technical support should be consulted. If the *preparation of the MR content* is done by an experienced team, the time required can be drastically reduced. The preparation time also depends on which medium is used. Using an existing 3D model in AR can be accomplished very quickly, while developing a full 3D environment can be very time-consuming. The *technical support during the lecture* was stressed as valuable in the interviews conducted. If no support is available, this must be taken into account in the preparation.

MR Experience. The matrix shows that *AR* is particularly suitable for larger groups and lower levels of learning (e.g., understanding) because it allows students to use their own smartphones. Using AR in the context of education and teaching allows for detailed visualization of static objects or animated processes. These can be explored from different angles. However, the use in small learning groups to explore 3D models is also feasible.

360° experiences allow students to feel present in a pre-recorded environment using videos or pictures. They enable a high degree of realism and immersion. The choice of interaction mode is particularly important here. Based on the interview results, it is advisable for the instructor to take control in a 2D desktop version. Thus, comments, hints and assistance can be given during the MR Experience. This type of MR experience can be implemented well in medium to large groups, as cardboxes and smartphones can be used.

VR or 3D modeled environments can fully simulate reality and thus also dangerous situations. To date, the development of 3D environments is still very time consuming. It requires prior knowledge and programming skills as well as high-quality technical devices and powerful PCs. In the future, more powerful end devices could presumably facilitate the use of VR. In the following section, the use of the matrix is discussed using the three different lecture types as examples.

3   Discussion of Application Areas and Outlook

The presented decision matrix for MR experiences provides a basis for selecting different MR technologies in teaching. In the following, application scenarios of the respective technologies are presented, in which the specifications of the matrix are reflected. Although the three examples presented are related to the mining engineering education, they can be applied to other engineering fields as well.

Based on the matrix, the use of AR is particularly suitable for large lectures. An example would be an introductory lecture on mining equipment. Here it is particularly important for teachers to provide an impression of the functionality, kinematics, size and weight of individual machines. The learning objectives include the ability to understand and reproduce the mentioned features of the presented machines. Students should be given the opportunity to repeat the content even after the lecture is over. At the same time, teachers in mining faculties often have little time and financial resources to learn about new technologies. Using AR offers the possibility to project 3D models and animated processes onto the students' own worksheets. Since the students' own devices are used, they can still access the information after the lecture. It is also not necessary to bring any physical mining equipment to class.

As another example, 360° experiences are particularly suited for seminars that are held in a combination of teacher-centered and student-centered phases. One use case is getting to know a real surface mining area. Here, previously acquired knowledge has to be applied and conditions of the environment have to be analyzed. Teachers can navigate the students, who are all equipped with VR goggles or card-boxes and smartphones, using a 2D desktop version. Since everyone is connected to the same network, the teacher can control which area is to be explored. Live annotations are used to mark danger zones and analyze them with the students.

Finally, an example of VR 3D environments is discussed. In higher semesters and master courses, the focus is often on the independent assessment of situations and scenarios (e.g., compliance with occupational safety measures). In this context, students should be prepared for real situations in mines. Since the course is taken by a small number of students, students can be equipped with the devices of the participating institute. The room is spacious and has a stable internet connection. Students move through the virtual world, have to complete tasks and solve quizzes. If they need information, they can ask the teacher for help or independently use the help buttons provided.

The decision matrix can be a first step to support a conscious choice of technology. Any further development and evaluation of the matrix should be ensured by user studies with teachers. Moreover, future research should focus on enabling teachers to create their own MR experiences [17], adjust them and implement these MR solutions into teaching.

Acknowledgment. This work is part of the project "Mixed Reality Books (MiReBooks)" and was funded by the EIT RAW Materials. The author is responsible for the contents of this publication.

References

1. Shields, D., Verga, F., Blengini, G.A.: Incorporating sustainability in engineering education. Int. J. Sustainabil. Higher Educ. **15**(4), 390–403 (2014)
2. LaSar, R., Chen, K.C., Apelian, D.: Teaching sustainable development in materials science and engineering. Mater. Res. Soc. Bull. **37**(4), 449–454 (2012)
3. Wagner, H.: How to address the crisis of mining engineering education in the western world? Mineral Res. Eng. **8**(4), 471–481 (1999)
4. Abdelrazeq, A., Daling, L., Suppes, R., Feldmann, Y.: A virtual reality educational tool in the context of mining engineering - the virtual reality mine. In: Gómez Chova, L., López Martínez A., Candel Torres I. (eds.) 13th International Technology, Education and Development Conference, INTED2019, pp. 8067–8073. IATED Academy (2019)

5. Dede, C.J., Jacobson, J., Richards, J.: Introduction: virtual, augmented, and mixed realities in education. In: Liu, D., Dede, C., Huang, R., Richards, J. (eds.) Virtual, Augmented, and Mixed Realities in Education, pp. 1–16. Springer Singapore, Singapore (2017)
6. Daling, L., Eck, C., Abdelrazeq, A., Hees, F.: Potentials and challenges of using mixed reality in mining education: a Europe-wide interview study. In: Lloret Mauri J., Saplacan D., Çarçani K., Ardiansyah Prima, O.D., Vasilache, S. (eds.) Thirteenth International Conference on Advances in Computer-Human Interactions, ACHI 2020, pp. 229–235. IARIA (2020)
7. Guo, Q.: Learning in a mixed reality system in the context of Industrie 40. J. Techn. Educ. **3**, 91–115 (2015)
8. Hochschulforum Digitalisierung: The Digital Turn – Hochschulbildung im digitalen Zeitalter, (The Digital Turn – Higher Education in the digital age). Working paper 28. Hochschulforum Digitalisierung, Berlin (2016).
9. Abdelrazeq A., Janßen D., Tummel C., Richert, A., Jeschke, S.: Teacher 4.0: requirements of the teacher of the future in context of the fourth industrial revolution. In: Gómez Chova L., López Martínez A., Candel Torres I. (eds.) 9th International Conference of Education, Research and Innovation, ICERI2016, pp. 8221–8226, IATED Academy (2016)
10. Daling, L., Kommetter, C., Abdelrazeq, A., Ebner, M., Ebner, M.: Mixed reality books: applying augmented and virtual reality in mining engineering education. In: Geroimenko, V. (ed.) Augmented reality in education, pp. 185–195. Springer, Cham (2020)
11. Milgram P., Colquhoun, H.: A taxonomy of real and virtual world display integration. In: Ohta, Y., Tamura, H. (Eds.) Mixed reality: Merging real and virtual worlds, pp. 5–30. Springer, Berlin (1999)
12. Azuma, R., et al.: Recent Advances in Augmented Reality. IEEE Computer Graphics and Applications 21(6), 34–47 (2001).
13. Kalkofen, D., Mori, S., Ladinig, T., Daling, L., Ab-delrazeq, A., et al.: Tools for teaching mining students in virtual reality based on 360° video experiences. In: 2020 IEEE Conference on Virtual Reality and 3D User Interfaces Abstracts and Workshops, VRW, pp. 455-459. IEEE, USA (2020)
14. Milgram P., Kishino F.: A Taxonomy of mixed reality Visual Displays. IEICE Trans. Inf. Syst. 77(12), 1321–1329 (1994)
15. Bloom, B.S., Engelhart, M.D., Furst, E.J., Hill, W.H., Krathwohl, D.R.: Taxonomy of educational objectives: the classification of educational goals, Handbook I: Cognitive domain. David McKay, New York (1956)
16. Wright, G.B.: Student-centered learning in higher education. Int. J. Teach. Learn. Higher Educ. 23(1), 92-97 (2011)
17. Khodaei, S., Sieger, J., Abdelrazeq, A., Isenhardt, I.: Learning goals in 360° virtual excursion-media crea-tion guideline for mixed-reality-based classes. In: Gómez Chova, L., López Martínez, L., Candel Torres, I. (eds.) Proceedings of the 13th International Conference of Education, Research and Innovation, INTED 2019, pp. 2552–2561. IATED Academy (2020)

Smooth Operator

A Virtual Environment to Prototype and Analyse Operator Support in CCTV Surveillance Rooms

Jonas De Bruyne[1], Jamil Joundi[2], Jessica Morton[1], Niels Van Kets[3], Glenn Van Wallendael[3], Durk Talsma[4], Jelle Saldien[2], Lieven De Marez[1], Wouter Durnez[1], and Klaas Bombeke[1]

[1] imec-mict-UGent, Department of Communication Sciences, Ghent University, Miriam Makebaplein 1, 9000 Gent, Belgium
klaas.bombeke@ugent.be

[2] imec-mict-UGent, Department of Industrial Systems Engineering and Product Design, Ghent University, Technologiepark 46, 9052 Zwijnaarde, Belgium

[3] imec-IDLab-UGent, Department of Electronics and Information Systems, Ghent University, Technologiepark-Zwijnaarde 126, 9052 Zwijnaarde, Belgium

[4] Department of Experimental Psychology, Ghent University, Henri Dunantlaan 2, 9000 Gent, Belgium

Abstract. Operators in closed-circuit television (CCTV) control rooms have to monitor large sets of video feeds coming from an ever increasing number of cameras. To assist these operators in their demanding day-to-day tasks, AI-driven support systems accompanied by user-centric interfaces are being developed. However, prototyping these support systems and testing them in operative control rooms can be a challenge. Therefore, in this paper, we present a virtual reality (VR) control room which can be used to investigate the effects of existing and future support systems on operators' performance and behaviour in a fully controlled environment. Important assets of this VR control room include the possibility to subject operators to different levels of cognitive load and to monitor their cognitive-affective states using not only subjective but also behavioural and physiological techniques.

Keywords: Virtual reality · User testing · Design review · Virtual training · WoZ testing · Cognitive load

1 Introduction

To assist human operators in modern closed-circuit television (CCTV) control rooms, AI-driven support systems are increasingly deployed to facilitate or automate certain aspects of the operator's task. In parallel with the continuously increasing number of security cameras in modern cities [9,11], control room operators are charged with monitoring an ever growing amount of video feeds. As a result, new control room interfaces – leveraging the power of computer vision algorithms – are designed to display video feeds in such a way that they

© Springer Nature Switzerland AG 2021
C. Stephanidis et al. (Eds.): HCII 2021, CCIS 1420, pp. 233–240, 2021.
https://doi.org/10.1007/978-3-030-78642-7_31

facilitate the operator's work [12]. However, in order to effectively design such intuitive, AI-driven interfaces, as well as validate the impact they offer towards operator performance and cognitive load, extensive user testing is required.

The construct of cognitive load plays a profound role in cognitive ergonomics. The level of cognitive load in human actors is defined by multiple antecedents [16]. These antecedents are elements of either cognitive work demands or human cognitive architecture. As an example, increased task complexity can increase operators' cognitive load as it places higher demands on their limited working memory capacity. However, the effects of these antecedents on cognitive load can be moderated by numerous factors both related to the individual (e.g., task experience) and to the task (e.g., involving the use of assistive technology). Especially in work contexts, (sub-)optimal cognitive load can impact the actor's work behaviour (e.g., speed and accuracy) and thus overall work performance.

Cognitive load as a multi-dimensional construct [20] is assessed through a wide range of procedures. In literature, adapted versions of the NASA-TLX questionnaire [8] are regularly used as a method to obtain a measure of perceived cognitive workload (e.g., [5,6]). However, other than obtaining a subjective measure through questionnaires, researchers have studied physiological correlates of cognitive load ranging from electrical brain activity [1] to electrodermal activity [13] to pupil dilation (see, [19]). As a study of Vanneste et al. [17] demonstrates, the accuracy of cognitive load assessment increases by using a multimodal approach that includes multiple measures.

To effectuate a multimodal approach to assess cognitive load during CCTV monitoring, immersive virtual reality (VR) appears an advantageous testing environment. By means of a head-mounted display (HMD), people can watch and interact with an immersive virtual environment. Building VR simulators offers multiple advantages over traditional approaches. First, with regards to the present project, it is less time-consuming to prototype and evaluate simulated operator support systems in VR than it is to build fully operational supportive systems in a physical environment. Moreover, virtual environments allow the implementation of the Wizard of Oz prototyping approach [3] to test initial ideas without the need of developing automated systems. This means that researchers can simulate automated systems by manually steering in-scene events so that the participant believes these events to occur automatically. Second, by using VR, the experimental environment is fully controlled. Researchers can control for lightning conditions, background noise, the presence of colleagues, etc. This allows investigating the effects of experimental manipulations (e.g., the addition of supportive systems in surveillance rooms) during numerous different circumstances. In addition, it is possible to log all the participant's actions and interactions. Third, state-of-the-art HMDs with built-in eye-trackers continuously log eye-related indices. As an example, insights on participants' gaze as well as indirect indicators of cognitive load (pupil dilation and blink rate) can be derived from this data. Finally, results of a study by Tauscher et al. [14] demonstrate that, with some optional minor modifications, it is possible to combine EEG and

VR. Furthermore, researchers have already been able to discriminate between different levels of cognitive load using a classical n-back task in an interactive VR environment regardless of the increase in muscle tension and activity as a result of the interactive environment [15].

In the present paper, we present a VR environment to test existing and next-generation AI-based supportive systems or new interfaces in CCTV control rooms. To this extent, we developed a virtual CCTV control room in which an operator's job is simulated using immersive VR technologies. In a pilot experiment, we tested whether we can influence participants' cognitive load in order to create different working conditions. To do so, we introduced a dual task paradigm that is commonly used by experimental psychologists to gain insight into multitasking processes. Participants – who wore an HMD in order to watch the virtual control room and interact with it – had to perform a simplified monitoring task (primary task) while from time to time they were interrupted by auditory requests which they had to respond to (secondary task). This secondary task either consisted of low demanding task rules and long response-stimulus intervals (RSIs; i.e., the time between a participant's response to a trial and the presentation of the stimuli of the next trial) or high demanding task rules and short RSIs. We will refer to these conditions as the low and high demand condition respectively. Manipulating these two features (task difficulty and RSIs) has previously been shown to increase cognitive load [7,18]. Therefore, we hypothesised higher cognitive load in the high demand condition compared to the low demand condition. To investigate this with a multimodal approach, task performance, pupil size, blink rate and subjective reports on perceived cognitive load (using an adapted version of NASA-TLX) were selected as measures for cognitive load, as they are frequently used to measure cognitive load and represent behavioural, physiological and subjective techniques.

2 Virtual Reality CCTV Control Room

The test environment was developed in Unity (version 2019.4.3f1) using a pre-existing police control room asset, which was modified according to the experiment's design needs. The VRTK framework (vrtoolkit.readme.io) was used for in scene interactions. The resulting virtual control room is equipped with a videowall consisting of 8 large screens and two desks with 3 monitors each (Fig. 1). One of the monitors of the operator's (i.e., the participant) personal workspace is used as a response screen with buttons that can be pressed using a pointer and the trigger button of the controller. On the remaining screens, a wide range of various types of content can be rendered such as (interactive) city maps, surveillance camera footage and visualisations of data streams. Moreover, the screen set-up can easily be modified according to assistive technology requirements and the study's needs. Also, other than prerecorded camera footage, real-time video streams can be integrated in the scene through embedded web browsers and virtual desktop screens in Unity.

To manipulate cognitive load in order to test supportive systems during different circumstances, a secondary task with varying difficulty and response-stimulus intervals (RSI) is introduced. In the scene, a walkie talkie radio is present, which is the audio source for the presentation of the auditory stimuli of the secondary task. This secondary task consists of the auditory presentation of digit sequences (max. 6 digits) which require a different response according to the condition participants are in. In the low demand condition, they are asked to click on the on-screen response button corresponding to the last heard digit. In contrast, in the high demand condition, the response depends on the number of digits in the sequence. When the sequence consists of an odd number of digits, participants have to click the last two heard digits. When the number of digits in the sequence is even, participants have to click the first two digits they heard. In addition, the RSI of the secondary task varies over both conditions. In the low demand condition, the RSI varies ad random between 25 and 30 s whereas in the high demand condition the RSI varies between 2 and 7 s. During testing, performance on this task is instantly calculated. Furthermore, all operator actions and UI interactions are automatically logged. Additionally, eye gaze, pupil dilation and blink rate are measured continuously.

Fig. 1. Overview of the virtual control room.

3   Pilot Experiment: Cognitive Load Manipulation

3.1   Method

Participants. Thirteen participants with normal or corrected to normal vision participated to the experiment (3 female, $M_{age} = 21.92$, $SD_{age} = 0.95$). All participants signed informed consent and participated voluntarily to the study. Therefore, they were not credited nor paid.

Materials and Equipment. The VR setup consisted of a computer running SteamVR (v.1.14.16) and an HTC VIVE Pro Eye. The HMD and the controllers were tracked by two Vive SteamVR Base Stations 2.0. The HMD's built-in eye-tracker and the Vive Eye-tracking Software Development Kit (SDK) SRanipal was used to obtain eye-tracking measures (incl. pupil sizes). This built-in eye-tracker had a sampling rate 120 Hz. However, in this experiment, we recorded the eye-tracking data 50 Hz. Perceived workload was assessed at the end of every block using an adapted version of the NASA-TLX [8]. The NASA-TLX is a well-known assessment instrument which results in an indication of perceived workload on six domains of task requirements (e.g., mental demand, physical demand etc.).

The Primary Task. A simplified video monitoring task was used as the primary task. Participants watched surveillance videos that were presented on the eight screens of the videowall and on the left and centre monitor on the personal desk. These videos merely served to create a realistic operator setting and, thus, were irrelevant to the task. However, one of these screens turned green after a variable interval (5–10 s). The task was to press the 'detected' button on the response screen whenever this happened before the response deadline of 4 s was exceeded. Both accuracy and reaction times were measured.

Procedure. Participants signed informed consent upon arrival and were then given a short instruction on the experiment. After the brief introduction, they were helped to put on the headset. Throughout the whole experiment, participants were seated and wore one controller in their hand of preference. Next, all instructions were presented on the centre monitor of the personal workspace in the virtual control room. After reading these on-screen instructions in VR, each participant performed a practice block on the primary task. Next, half of the participants were instructed on the low demand task rules and the other half on the high demand task rules, followed by a practice block on the secondary task. Subsequently, a practice block for the dual task was provided. This was followed by three experimental blocks of approximately 5 min each, separated by self-paced breaks. After these blocks, the task rules of the secondary task changed. Participants who first performed the low demand secondary task were now instructed on the high demand secondary task and vice versa. Next, a practice block to get familiar with these new task rules was performed. Finally, participants were presented with another set of three dual task experimental blocks, now using the new task rules. At the start of every block, participants performed an eye-tracker calibration procedure. At the end of each block, participants were asked to unmount the HMD and fill in the questionnaire on perceived cognitive load.

3.2 Results

The data was analysed with one within-subject factor (i.e., task demands – high or low). All data pre-processing was performed in Python 3 and models were constructed in R using the lme4 package [2] specifying a random intercept for each participant. Reported p-values for the linear mixed effects models are corrected values using the Kenward-Rogers correction [10].

Performance. In the analysis of accuracy on the primary task, we found that people performed better in the low demand condition (M = 93%, SD = 2%) compared to the high demand condition (M = 99%, SD = 6%), $F(1, 12) = 22.02$, $p < 0.001$. Moreover, participants were slower to detect the highlighted screen in the high demand (M = 1194.53 ms, SD = 709.88 ms) compared to the low demand condition (M = 905.93 ms, SD = 514.64 ms), $F(1, 12) = 8.32$, $p = 0.014$. The same trend was found for accuracy on the secondary task where participants performed worse in the high demand (M = 67%, SD = 13%) compared to the low demand condition (M = 95%, SD = 7%), $F(1, 12) = 165.00$, $p < 0.001$.

Cognitive Load. Subjective cognitive load as measured by the adapted version of NASA-TLX was higher in the high demand condition (M = 52.26, SD = 13.74) than in the low demand condition (M = 19.70, SD = 11.86), $F(1, 12) = 81.24$, $p < 0.001$. This effect was found for pupil size as well. Participants had larger mean pupil sizes during the high demand condition (M = 3.17 mm, SD = 0.42 mm) compared to the low demand condition (M = 2.99 mm, SD = 0.28 mm), $F(1, 12) = 11.79$, $p = 0.004$. This effect reflects higher cognitive load when the task rules of the secondary task were more difficult. Blink rate also differed significantly between conditions. Blink rate was higher when the task rules were difficult (M = 18.10 blinks/min., SD = 12.65 blinks/min) relative to the low demand condition (M = 10.50 blinks/min., SD = 4.82 blinks/min.), $F(1, 12) = 7.74$, $p = 0.017$.

4 Discussion

In this project, we developed a VR CCTV control room in order to test the influence of supportive systems and interfaces on operators' performance, behaviour and cognitive load while they are subject to different levels of cognitive load. This allows researchers to gain insight into the effects of assistive technology during different cognitive states of the operator. To validate the cognitive load manipulation, we conducted a pilot experiment in which we investigated whether we can manipulate cognitive load by manipulating difficulty and temporal features of a secondary task. In line with previous research, the results of this experiment highly suggest an increase in cognitive load when the task rules for the secondary task became more difficult and the frequency of secondary task trials was higher. In particular, we found a significant main effect of task demands on reported cognitive load. Moreover, the same effect was found in the behavioural results. Specifically, performance (i.e., accuracy and reaction time) on the primary task decreased with increasing task demands for the secondary task. Since the primary task was identical across conditions, these results indirectly reflect an increase in cognitive load as a result of the demand manipulation in the secondary task. Next, the same effect was found in the analysis of pupil size. As larger pupil sizes reflect higher cognitive load, this result also suggests an increase in cognitive load driven by the secondary task manipulation. For blink rate, which we included as an exploratory measure, a main effect of task demands was found. Specifically, blink rate was higher in the high demand condition compared to the low demand condition. However, since multiple drivers can underlie this effect, we cannot surely attribute this effect to either an increase in mental activity needed to perform the dual task or an increase in using mental rehearsal [4] as a strategy to accomplish the secondary task goals.

Future experiments within the current project will investigate the effects of a specific support system on operators' behaviour, performance and cognitive load. Furthermore, we will explore the gain of adding EEG as a measure of cognitive load. In particular, we will look into parietal alpha suppression, increases in frontal theta power and the cognitive load index [19]. Additionally, using the built-in eye-tracker, we will explore how we can gain insights in visual search and active exploration of monitored video footage using eye gaze data. An example of such a measure would be the proportion of time spent looking at suggested video footage pushed by a camera selection algorithm compared to the proportion of time spent looking at the other videos that are presented on, for example, the videowall. Additionally, from a user testing perspective, it remains important to take into account the perceived usability of professional control room operators when testing new assistive technology. Therefore, this VR tool can also be used to set up qualitative experiments tapping into the subjective experience of users. In sum, these experiments will yield a demonstration of how the VR control room can be used and investigate possible additional dependent measures that might offer insights in how control room operators are affected by introducing AI-based supportive systems.

References

1. Antonenko, P., Paas, F., Grabner, R., Van Gog, T.: Using electroencephalography to measure cognitive load. Educ. Psychol. Rev. **22**(4), 425–438 (2010)
2. Bates, D., Mächler, M., Bolker, B., Walker, S.: Fitting linear mixed-effects models using lme4. arXiv preprint arXiv:1406.5823 (2014)
3. Dahlbäck, N., Jönsson, A., Ahrenberg, L.: Wizard of Oz studies-why and how. Knowl.-Based Syst. **6**(4), 258–266 (1993)
4. De Jong, P.J., Merckelbach, H.: Eyeblink frequency, rehearsal activity, and sympathetic arousal. Int. J. Neurosci. **51**(1–2), 89–94 (1990)
5. Di Nocera, F., Camilli, M., Terenzi, M.: A random glance at the flight deck: pilots' scanning strategies and the real-time assessment of mental workload. J. Cogn. Eng. Decis. Mak. **1**(3), 271–285 (2007)
6. DiDomenico, A., Nussbaum, M.A.: Interactive effects of physical and mental workload on subjective workload assessment. Int. J. Ind. Ergon. **38**(11–12), 977–983 (2008)
7. Haga, S., Shinoda, H., Kokubun, M.: Effects of task difficulty and time-on-task on mental workload. Jpn. Psychol. Res. **44**(3), 134–143 (2002)

8. Hart, S.G., Staveland, L.E.: Development of NASA-TLX (task load index): results of empirical and theoretical research. In: Advances in Psychology, vol. 52, pp. 139–183. Elsevier (1988)
9. Hollis, M.E.: Security or surveillance? Examination of CCTV camera usage in the 21st century (2019)
10. Kenward, M.G., Roger, J.H.: Small sample inference for fixed effects from restricted maximum likelihood. Biometrics 983–997 (1997)
11. Norris, C., McCahill, M., Wood, D.: The growth of CCTV: a global perspective on the international diffusion of video surveillance in publicly accessible space. Surveill. Soc. **2**(2/3) (2004)
12. Pelletier, S., Suss, J., Vachon, F., Tremblay, S.: Atypical visual display for monitoring multiple CCTV feeds. In: Proceedings of the 33rd Annual ACM Conference Extended Abstracts on Human Factors in Computing Systems, pp. 1145–1150 (2015)
13. Setz, C., Arnrich, B., Schumm, J., La Marca, R., Tröster, G., Ehlert, U.: Discriminating stress from cognitive load using a wearable EDA device. IEEE Trans. Inf Technol. Biomed. **14**(2), 410–417 (2009)
14. Tauscher, J.P., Schottky, F.W., Grogorick, S., Bittner, P.M., Mustafa, M., Magnor, M.: Immersive EEG: evaluating electroencephalography in virtual reality. In: 2019 IEEE Conference on Virtual Reality and 3D User Interfaces (VR), pp. 1794–1800. IEEE (2019)
15. Tremmel, C., Herff, C., Sato, T., Rechowicz, K., Yamani, Y., Krusienski, D.J.: Estimating cognitive workload in an interactive virtual reality environment using EEG. Front. Hum. Neurosci. **13**, 401 (2019)
16. Van Acker, B.B., Parmentier, D.D., Vlerick, P., Saldien, J.: Understanding mental workload: from a clarifying concept analysis toward an implementable framework. Cogn. Technol. Work **20**(3), 351–365 (2018). https://doi.org/10.1007/s10111-018-0481-3
17. Vanneste, P., et al.: Towards measuring cognitive load through multimodal physiological data. Cogn. Technol. Work 1–19 (2020)
18. Veltman, J., Gaillard, A.: Physiological workload reactions to increasing levels of task difficulty. Ergonomics **41**(5), 656–669 (1998)
19. van der Wel, P., van Steenbergen, H.: Pupil dilation as an index of effort in cognitive control tasks: a review. Psychon. Bull. Rev. **25**(6), 2005–2015 (2018). https://doi.org/10.3758/s13423-018-1432-y
20. Young, M.S., Brookhuis, K.A., Wickens, C.D., Hancock, P.A.: State of science: mental workload in ergonomics. Ergonomics **58**(1), 1–17 (2015)

Kansei Perception Support System to Promote Daily Life Awareness

Ikuya Edama[1](✉), Emmanuel Ayedoun[2], Hiroshi Takenouchi[3],
and Masataka Tokumaru[2]

[1] Graduate School of Kansai University, 3-3-35 Yamate-cho, Suita-shi, Osaka 564-8680, Japan
k187195@kansai-u.ac.jp
[2] Kansai University, 3-3-35 Yamate-cho, Suita-shi, Osaka 564-8680, Japan
toku@kansai-u.ac.jp
[3] Fukuoka Institute of Technology, 3-30-1 Wajiro-higashi,
Higashi-ku, Fukuoka 811-0295, Japan

Abstract. Kansei is a Japanese word that refers to feeling, sensitivity, intuition, among others. In this paper, we propose a system that facilitates the perception of other people's Kansei to promote daily life awareness. To this end, our approach consists of providing users with the opportunity to visualize other people's Kansei through observation of emoticons attached to various objects in daily scenery. To achieve an immersive experience, we designed a virtual reality environment displaying scenery that subjects are already familiar with. The proposed system is equipped with two modes: Mode 1, where users just add their Kansei to the displayed scenery, and Mode 2, where they are prompted to infer another user's Kansei by finding objects on which emoticons may have been added. We conducted an experiment to evaluate the effectiveness of the proposed system. During the experiment, subjects interacted with the system in Mode 1, Mode 2, and then Mode 1 again, so that we could measure the influence of inferring other's Kansei on their own. The results showed that users could gain new insights by adopting others' Kansei. Besides, we obtained that they were keener to explore the scenery more proactively to gain new awareness.

Keywords: Kansei · Support system · Daily life awareness

1 Introduction

Kansei is a Japanese word, which cannot be smoothly translated into English. It is a broadly encompassing concept, which may refer to people's sensibility, sensitivity, feeling, creativity, imagination, inspiration, intuitive thinking (the list is not exhaustive). In this study, Kansei can be understood as the impression people get when they encounter a certain artifact, environment, or situation, using their senses of touch, sight, hearing, smell, taste, and cognition. Subsequently, a complex mind pattern is developed and stored in the brain, containing all the impressions experienced; thereby, building the foundation for human behavior [1]. We consider that emotions are sensations triggered by a person's Kansei. Thus, it can be seen as a component of Kansei.

© Springer Nature Switzerland AG 2021
C. Stephanidis et al. (Eds.): HCII 2021, CCIS 1420, pp. 241–248, 2021.
https://doi.org/10.1007/978-3-030-78642-7_32

Recently, there has been increasing interest in the Kansei engineering research field. However, while the focus has mostly been on applying Kansei to product design, there has been less study on how to use it to influence people's recognition, behavior, interaction with their environment. Nowadays, people pay less attention to the real world and daily scenery around them, especially when commuting to work or school, due to routinization or accustomization. Accustomization is a phenomenon in which repeated exposure to a particular stimulus may diminish our response to that stimulus. Without a conscious awareness of how we spend our daily lives, our Kansei might get dulled by excessive accustomization.

To enhance people's consciousness of events happening in their daily life, a navigation system that instead of the shortest route to a destination, presents users with routes that may make them happier [2]. The system is beneficial for users as it fostered their ability to look at their surroundings and gain new awareness. The book "The Book of Awesome" summarizes the small joys of daily life that we do not often discuss with others [3]. The author stated that things that we do not usually pay much attention to can be useful when we are conscious of them. Thus, gaining new awareness in our daily lives leads to enriching our Kansei.

To gain new awareness in daily life, it is necessary to encounter unknown perspectives in familiar landscapes. The book "On Looking" features different people with different ways of looking at things [4]. The book shows that when experts in various fields walk along the same road, they pay attention to different places. Kansei is formed by knowledge and experience. Differences in Kansei may produce differences in gazing behavior. Besides, a study uses gaze information to obtain human Kansei information [5]. Gazing behavior may also reflect a person's latent preferences so that it might be possible to use it for accessing other people's Kansei with reduced cognitive load. For this reason, we assume that it might be possible to help people gain new daily life insights by accessing others' Kansei through their gazing behavior.

In this study, we propose a virtual reality (VR)-based system to support the perception of others' Kansei to promote new awareness in daily life scenes. In the proposed system, people's Kansei is visualizable through their gazing behavior and emoticons attached to scenery objects. Emoticons tend to intuitively grasp the reason (i.e., intention) why a given user is interested, is sensible to a place, or a particular object of the scenery. After going through an overview of its features, we present the results of an experimental evaluation of the proposed system before discussing the implications of our findings.

2 Proposed System

2.1 System Overview

The proposed system displays in a VR space, daily life scenery that users are relatively familiar with. Users can select various objects in the displayed scenery and leave their feelings or emotions to these objects using emoticons. The proposed system has two modes: Mode 1, where users attach their Kansei to the scenery using emoticons, and Mode 2, where users can explore the same environment from other people's perspective by visualizing Kansei footprints (i.e., gazing behaviors and emoticons) left by them in the scenery.

2.2 System Interface

In Mode 1, users are presented with a daily scenery displayed in the VR space. According to their interests, they can select some scenery objects to which emoticons reflecting their feelings or emotions can be attached. To visually represent emotions, we use emoticons placed on a graphical representation of Russell's circumplex model of affect. Russell's circumplex model of affect arranges 16 human emoticons in order of proximity [6]. Thus, the resulting emoticon selection user interface (UI) (Fig. 1) consists of 16 emoticons that were carefully selected through a preliminary survey. Figure 2 shows each of the 16 selected emoticons. We use emoticons as a means of accessing a user's Kansei since they informed us what a given user focused on, enabling us to intuitively recognize emotions left on the focused object. Figure 3 shows the UI for attaching emoticons to objects.

Table 1. Questionnaire contents in Mode 2

1	"Were you surprised by others paying attention to this object?"
2	"Can you imagine why others attached this emoticon to this object?"
3	"Can you understand (i.e. sympathize with) the sensitivity associated with this object?"

In Mode 2, users can explore others' Kansei by revisiting the scenery from others' viewpoint. Once users have found an object that others have focused on, the system shows them an emoticon attached to it. Then, users move to the questionnaire UI (cf. Fig. 4). To apprehend someone's Kansei, it is necessary to be able to perceive and interpret it. Thus, it is essential to make users think of inquiries, such as "why did other persons pay attention to this particular object?" or "why did other persons have such feelings toward this object?" For this purpose, Mode 2 is equipped with a questionnaire UI through which users are prompted to answer a set of 5-point Likert style questions. The contents of the questionnaire are shown in Table 1.

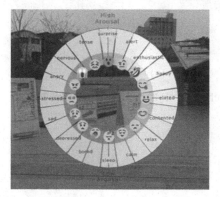

Fig. 1. Emoticon selection UI

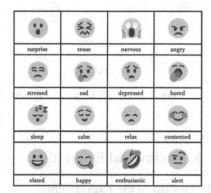

Fig. 2. List of emoticons

Fig. 3. Emoticon attaching UI   **Fig. 4.** Questionnaire UI

2.3 Similarity with Others' Kansei

In Mode 2, the user is presented with the scenery as visited (i.e., objects focused on, emoticons attached) by another user whose Kansei is evaluated to be the least similar. As an example, suppose that the vector of emoticon attached to the object named "obj1" by User A and B is as shown in Fig. 5. Using this vector, we can calculate the Euclidean distance between emoticons and measure the degree of similarity in user Kansei. If the number of objects in scenery is N, the similarity between User A and User B, dis_{AB}, can be calculated using the following Eq. (1).

$$dis_{AB} = \sum_{n=1}^{N} \sqrt{(A_n - B_n)^2} \tag{1}$$

This calculation is performed for all users based on results of Mode 1 so that users with the lowest Kansei similarity are identified and their log data are used as explained above.

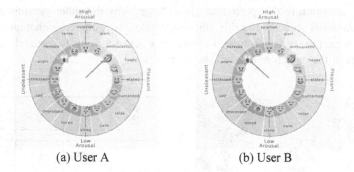

(a) User A   (b) User B

Fig. 5. Example vector of emoticon attached to "obj1" by User A and User B

3 Experimental Evaluation

3.1 Outline of the Experiments

This experiment investigates the following three preoccupations: Can the proposed system be used to live visualize Kansei in daily scenery?, Can the process of inferring others' Kansei affect users' Kansei?, and Can the proposed system promote new daily life scenery awareness among users?

The subjects were ten students from Kansai University. In this experiment, we used three-dimensional (3D) photos taken around and inside the university to reproduce daily scenery that subjects are already reasonably familiar with.

The flow of the experiment is described below. First, the user interacts with the system in Mode 1, consisting of exploring and leaving emoticons on objects in the scenery. This is referred to as Experiment 1. Next, the user moves to Mode 2, where the user is prompted to infer another user's Kansei. This is called Experiment 2. In this experiment, the user explores the scenery from another person's perspective determined using the data of the seven people obtained in advance. Finally, the user moves back to Mode 1. This is called Experiment 3. In Experiment 3, we examine whether and how the user was influenced by accessing others' Kansei.

In Experiment 1, the user can move to the next scenery after discovering five objects in one scene, and the same operation is repeated until going through eight scenery. In Experiment 2, the user can move to the next scenery after successfully guessing five objects that others have focused on. This is repeated for four scenery. To evaluate the system's effectiveness, we administered a survey after subjects completed their three rounds of experiments. Table 2 presents the content of the survey.

3.2 Experimental Results

Figure 6 shows the results of the survey. In Table 3, Kansei similarity is expressed in percentage, and the users are listed in the order of the largest change in the similarity of Kansei. We use Neo4j, a graph database visualization toolkit, to visualize the objects that users focused on and the emotions they left. Results of Experiments 1 and 3 for User A and B, who had the largest change in similarity, and User J, who had the smallest change in similarity.

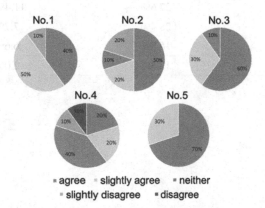

Fig. 6. Survey result for each question

Figure 7 shows the objects that user A and K (who had the lowest Kansei similarity with user A) focused on in scene 8 and the emotions they attached to the scenery in

Table 2. Survey contents

No	Questionnaire contents
1	Did you feel that you were able to visualize your own Kansei?
2	Were you interested in places other than the object?
3	Did the emoticon help you to infer others' intentions?
4	Did you feel the need of using other emoticons?
5	Were you able to gain new awareness in the familiar scenery?

Experiments 1 and 3. Similarly, Fig. 8 shows the objects that user B and K focused on in scene 7 and the emotions they used in Experiments 1 and 3. Figure 9 shows the objects that user J and L focused on in scene 3 and the emotions they attached to objects during Experiments 1 and 3. Figure 10 shows the objects that user J focused on in scene 3 and the emotions he used in Experiments 1 and 3.

Table 3. Changes in Kansei similarity between Experiments 1 and 3

	Similarity (Experiment 1)	Similarity (Experiment 3)	Similarity Difference
UserA	20.5%	46.9%	26.4%
UserB	11.5%	36.1%	24.6%
UserC	22.1%	39.9%	17.8%
UserD	13.7%	30.2%	16.5%
UserE	16.7%	30.5%	13.8%
UserF	15.7%	27.9%	12.2%
UserG	16.2%	27.6%	11.4%
UserH	20.7%	28.4%	7.7%
UserI	10.2%	16.8%	6.6%
UserJ	15.3%	17.3%	2.0%

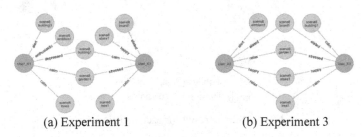

(a) Experiment 1   (b) Experiment 3

Fig. 7. Results of user A and K in scene 8

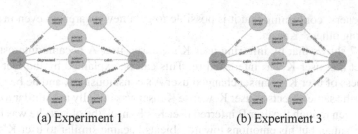

(a) Experiment 1   (b) Experiment 3

Fig. 8. Results of user B and K in scene 7

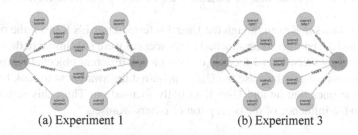

(a) Experiment 1   (b) Experiment 3

Fig. 9. Results of user J and L in scene 3

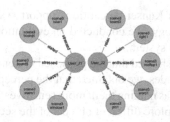

Fig. 10. Results of user J in scene 3 after Experiments 1 and 3

4 Discussion

From the results of the questionnaire shown in Fig. 6, 90% of users answered that they were able to visualize their Kansei, confirming the effectiveness of the proposed system for visualizing Kansei. Besides, 70% of the users answered that they were interested in places other than objects. In the proposed system, given that objects that can be selected are defined in advance, it would be necessary to increase the number of selectable objects to allow users to output their Kansei more accurately.

Furthermore, 90% of users said that emoticons helped them infer others' intentions, indicating that emoticons can be used to assist in inferring others' intentions. However, 40% of users indicated that they want to use different emoticons, suggesting that emoticons alone are not sufficient to express all of a user's intentions. Thus, it might be necessary to consider alternatives to emoticons that can more accurately express user's Kansei. Besides, all users responded that they were able to gain new awareness even in familiar scenery, confirming that it is possible to gain new awareness even in daily life by perceiving others' Kansei.

Figure 7 shows that by inferring user K's Kansei, user A became interested in the same object that user K was interested in. This can be explained by the fact that user A's awareness of user K's Kansei changed user A's consciousness, and he began paying attention to the same objects as user K, whose Kansei was initially not similar to. Figure 8 shows that even though the user B inferred user K's Kansei, the objects he was interested in did not change, but his emotions toward objects became similar to user K's. We can deduct from such a result that the recognition of User K's Kansei changed the way User B felt about the object so that he ended up expressing a different feeling toward the object.

Figure 9 shows that even though the User J inferred User L's Kansei, the objects he focused on and the emoticons he attached to the scenery were not similar to those of User L. Figure 10 shows that User J focused on completely different objects in Experiments 1 and 3. This is probably because the User J acquired the awareness to look for objects other than the ones that he and User K initially focused on. Thus, this result may be attributed to the influence of the perception of others' Kansei.

5   Conclusion

In this study, we proposed a Kansei perception support system to promote daily life awareness using VR technology. We conducted an evaluation experiment to verify the effectiveness of the proposed system.

The experimental results showed that the proposed system enabled users to visualize and infer others' Kansei. Besides, we obtained that the perception of others' Kansei had various effects on users, such as making them more sensitive to the same objects as others or making them keener to explore different objects of the scenery. In future studies, we will investigate on devising methods that could allow us to get a better picture of users' Kansei. Besides, we are looking forward to implementing an interface that could allow users to select objects of interest with more precision.

References

1. Schütte, S.T.W., Eklund, J., Axelsson, J.R.C., Nagamachi, M.: Concepts, methods and tools in Kansei engineering. Theor. Issues Ergon. Sci. **5**, 214–231 (2004)
2. Quercia, D., Schifanella, R., Maria Aiello, L.: The shortest path to happiness: recommending beautiful, quiet, and happy routes in the city. In: HT 2014: Proceedings of the 25th ACM Conference on Hypertext and Social Media, pp.116–125 (2014)
3. Pasricha, N.: The Book of Awesome. Berkley Trade (2011)
4. Horowitz, A.: On Looking. Scribner (2013)
5. Takenouchi, H., Tokumaru, M.: Interactive evolutionary computation system with user gaze information. Int. J. Affect. Eng. **18**(3), 109–116 (2019)
6. Russell, J.A.: A circumplex model of affect. J. Pers. Soc. Psychol. **39**(6), 1161–1178 (1980)

A Robot-in-a-CAVE Setup for Assessing the Tracking Accuracy of AR/VR Devices

Daniel Eger Passos$^{(\boxtimes)}$, Nico Heinrich, and Bernhard Jung

Institute of Computer Science, Technical University Bergakademie Freiberg,
Freiberg, Germany
{egerpas,jung}@informatik.tu-freiberg.de,
nico.heinrich@student.tu-freiberg.de

Abstract. Many XR devices such as AR-headsets, smartphones, as well as a growing number of VR-HMDs rely on visual-inertial tracking for motion estimation and environment mapping. Tracking accuracy is thus strongly affected by properties of the environment, such as number of visual features. In order to systematically assess such environmental influences on the tracking accuracy of XR devices, we have designed a setup where the XR device is attached to a moving robotic arm which itself is situated in a Virtual Reality CAVE. In our experiments, the high-precision robot arm repeatedly moved along the same trajectories in synthetically generated virtual scenes where the number of visual features was systematically increased. As expected, the measured tracking accuracy varied for different XR devices and virtual scenes. At one end of the spectrum, tracking completely failed in very feature-poor scenes. At the other end, sub-millimeter tracking accuracy was achieved for a synthetic scene with a very high number of features in case of a high-end XR device, outperforming the tracking accuracy achieved in a real-world environment with the same robotic setup. We conclude from these results that the proposed Robot-in-a-CAVE setup is in principle well-suited for assessing the tracking accuracy of XR devices.

Keywords: Inside-out tracking · Augmented Reality · Virtual Reality

1 Introduction

Many AR/VR devices such as AR-headsets, smartphones, as well as a growing number of VR-HMDs rely on visual-inertial tracking for motion estimation and environment mapping. It is well known, that their tracking accuracy is strongly affected by properties of the environment. E.g., if the environment has not enough structure, such as a completely white room, computer vision processing will not find enough features and tracking will degrade or fail altogether. On the other hand, if the environment provides too many similar features, such as a room with wall-paper showing a repetitive pattern, tracking performance may also degrade. Similarly, visual feature detection, and thus visual-inertial tracking, generally benefits from well-lit, high-contrast environments.

© Springer Nature Switzerland AG 2021
C. Stephanidis et al. (Eds.): HCII 2021, CCIS 1420, pp. 249–255, 2021.
https://doi.org/10.1007/978-3-030-78642-7_33

Although there are already several methods for measuring the accuracy of tracking algorithms and hardware that are applicable to certain kinds of AR/VR devices (collectively "XR devices"; in the following "D_{XR}" refers to an XR device) and applications [2, 4, 7, 8], none of these methods can easily be adapted for arbitrary XR devices and environments. In order to systematically assess environmental influences on the tracking accuracy of these technologies we have designed a novel setup where the XR device is attached to a moving robotic arm which itself is situated inside of a Virtual Reality CAVE.

Several works exploiting robotic arms to evaluate the precision of particular XR-devices are found: a motorized arm is used in [1] to evaluate latency; [3] mentions that a robotic arm was used in one of their test cases; in [6] a visual tracking system is also mounted on a robot arm. But to the best of our knowledge our previous work [9] is the first research that utilizes a UR5 robotic arm for reproducibly measuring the tracking accuracy of different AR and VR-Devices. We now expand this previous setup by moving it to the inside of a CAVE. There we conducted several experiments in order to evaluate if such high-resolution immersive virtual environments can be used for gaining knowledge about the accuracy of inside-out tracking solutions.

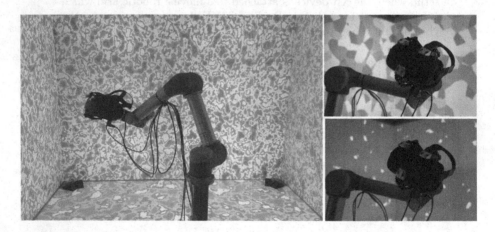

Fig. 1. An AR/VR device is attached to a high-precision UR5 robotic arm inside of a CAVE. Pre-programmed trajectories are executed with repeatability of 0.1 mm while different synthetic virtual scenes are projected, facilitating a systematic analysis of how visual features in the environment affect the positional accuracy of inside-out tracking systems. An attached Oculus Quest achieved e.g. a tracking accuracy of 2.6 mm (left picture), 0.3 mm (top right) and 1.5 mm (bottom right) for the same trajectory under different virtual environments.

2 Methodology

A CAVE is a spatially immersive display room that is usually used for single- and multi-user VR experiences. Our setup uses a high-resolution CAVE (50 mega-pixel) where individual pixels cannot be distinguished by the human eye (and neither by moving cameras of XR devices), i.e. there is no screen-door effect that is present in several of today's VR-HMDs. During our experiments, procedurally generated images were displayed in the CAVE and systematically modified according to visual parameters like feature richness.

In order to systematically investigate if and how visual changes in the virtual environment affect the inside-out tracking quality of the D_{XR} moving along known trajectories inside of the CAVE we used two different functions for rendering patterns that compose diverse synthetic scenes: Perlin [10] and Voronoi noise [12]. We have rendered 10 different scenes for each mentioned function with help of the coherent noise-generating *libnoise* C++ library. These scenes are labeled $V01, V02, ...V10$ for the images created with Voronoi noise, and $P01, P02...P10$ for the images created with Perlin noise (Fig. 2).

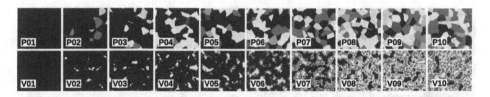

Fig. 2. With the help of Perlin and Voronoi functions we rendered 20 different synthetic scenes that were projected on 3 walls and on the floor of the CAVE. The pictures above show a small section of each scene ("P01...P10" are scenes created with Perlin, "V01...V10" with Voronoi). $V01$ and $P01$ consist of a blue screen only without any noise, where no virtual feature can be located by inside-out tracking systems. The other scenes differ from each other by their noise quality, resulting in varying feature quantity and color contrast. (Color figure online)

The CAVE we use in our experiments is located at the Technical University Bergakademie Freiberg, in Germany, and it is assembled with four seamless projection walls (front, left, right, floor). The side walls are approximately dimensioned at 3×3 m. Because of lacking projection walls (top and back) and also because of its dimensions, the field of regard of the CAVE is less than 100%. We shot 360° photos with an *Insta360 Pro* of some of our scenes in the CAVE and with help of Harris and Shi-Tomasi corner detection [5,11] we concluded that relatively small quantities of visual features can be found outside of the projection screens (Fig. 3).

We call F_R all features that originate from real objects inside of the CAVE: they are actually undesirable for our experiments and need to be avoided or removed. Possible sources of F_R detected by Harris or Shi-Tomasi are structural elements of the CAVE, ceiling light, door, a cabinet, operator table and other small objects inside of the room. We have opted for limiting the movements of the robotic arm so that the field of view of the D_{XR} crosses over as few sources of F_R as possible. Projected images contain only "virtual" features (F_V) that, in contrast to F_R, are desirable and whose quantities are controlled within our synthetic scenes. The number of F_V in the scenes $P01$ and $V01$ is zero.

Although our first analysis with corner detection algorithms gives us an idea of the amount and location of features that the physical environment could contain, they do not necessarily predict the final tracking accuracy of a specific D_{XR}. For example, we have observed some XR devices performing poorly for scenes where Harris and Shi-Tomasi detected a very high number of F_V. Therefore we still need to assess the accuracy for each D_{XR} empirically. For this, based on our previous work [9], we have used a high-precision, industrial robot arm of type UR5 placed in the center of the CAVE (Fig. 1). Pre-programmed movements are executed by the arm with repeatability of 0.1mm, providing very precise ground-truth pose information of its tool center point (TCP). The XR device is attached to the robot with help of a 3-finger adaptive gripper.

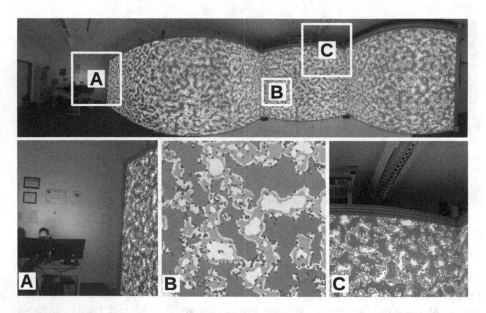

Fig. 3. A 360° photo of the synthetic environment reveals that not only virtual features and objects are found inside of the CAVE. Using algorithms like Harris or Shi-Tomasi corner detection over this and other 360° shots we located several feature sources that might influence the positional accuracy of an XR device. The red dots in pictures A-C represent corners identified by the Harris corner detection. Real objects that spark features like e.g. the operator's desk or wall decoration in A as well as ceiling light in C needs to be manually removed, hidden or avoided when the robot is executing the pre-programmed trajectories. (Color figure online)

3   Experiments

We programmed two different 3DoF and one 6DoF trajectories for the UR5. The first trajectory is used only for initializing the tracking of D_{XR} (about 5 s). The robot executes the second and third trajectory three times each (total time around 1 min), resulting in 6 rounds for each D_{XR}. The TCP starts and finishes a round exactly at the same pose, and between two rounds the robot always waits for 3 s. During this time, while the UR5 is motionless, we collect the tracked pose of the D_{XR} (via wireless UDP connection). After that, we calculate the mean Euclidean error between the start and end pose for all 6 rounds made in one scene.

We carried out first experiments with a Samsung Galaxy S9 (D_{S9}) and a Oculus Quest (D_{Quest}). Although both devices serve completely different purposes in the XR spectrum, this choice is deliberate in order to demonstrate the flexibility of our setup. The XR devices are attached to the robot that runs the pre-programmed trajectories while the synthetic scenes $P01...P10$ and $V01...V10$ are projected, one at a time. For comparison purposes the same trajectories were also conducted outside of the CAVE, in a typical scientist's office at our university. The average tracking accuracy in the office was 14 mm for D_{S9} and 2 mm for D_{Quest}.

The best accuracy values for both D_{S9} and D_{Quest} are achieved in $V10$ (3.5 mm and 0.3 mm accuracy, respectively). For $P01$ and $V01$ the performance of the tracking system dropped to several centimeters or even complete tracking failure. Starting at $P02$ and $V02$ the performance increases significantly for D_{Quest}, while D_{S9} starts a more reliable tracking only after $P04$ and $V03$. Figure 4 summarizes these results.

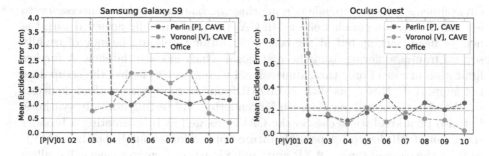

Fig. 4. Tracking accuracy averaged over 6 rounds for each scene of our Robot-in-a-CAVE setup with a Samsung Galaxy S9 (left) and Oculus Quest (right). Scene $V10$ (synthesized with the Voronoi noise function) is best suited for accurate inside-out tracking among the 20 synthetic scenes, achieving a mean Euclidean error in sub-millimeter range for the Oculus Quest (0.3 mm accuracy).

It is also to notice that although the Perlin function generates very interesting and at first sight feature-rich synthetic scenes, the tracking performance of

XR devices does not necessarily improve with the complexity of the image: for instance the accuracy of D_{Quest} is best for scene $V05$ but degraded somewhat for scenes with a higher number of features. A possible explanation is that a high number of similar features could be problematic for the feature matching step of tracking algorithms.

4   Conclusion and Future Work

Our first experiments confirm that the proposed Robot-in-a-CAVE setup is in principle well-suited for assessing inside-out tracking performance. The different XR devices evaluated in this work with the help of a robotic arm reached a very high positional accuracy when operated inside of synthetic, feature-rich scenes. For example, a Samsung Galaxy S9 showed an tracking accuracy of as little as 3.4 mm, and an Oculus Quest as little as 0.3 mm – an excellent tracking performance if compared with measurements while operating outside of the CAVE in environments with only real features.

We also demonstrated that although undesirable visual features (F_R) from real objects are present inside of the CAVE, their number is relatively small if compared to the virtual features (F_V) from the synthetic scenes projected in the CAVE. Furthermore most F_R can be hidden or avoided by the camera path. The tracking accuracy degraded to several centimeters or even failed completely for experiments where $F_V = 0$ (synthetic scenes containing only a blue screen), demonstrating that the CAVE is also well suited for simulating feature-poor environments.

Our Robot-in-a-CAVE approach has so far only been tested with "flat" two-dimensional virtual scenes that are aligned with the projection screens of the CAVE. In order to extend the experiment to fully three-dimensional virtual environments, viewer-dependent rendering mechanisms could be necessary to account for motion parallax effects. In CAVEs, this is usually achieved with the help of head-tracking but at the cost of a motion-to-photon latency of usually several frames, differing from the real world which has zero latency. A further limitation in case of fully three-dimensional virtual worlds is that the setup does not support depth-sensors such as LiDAR found in some current iPad devices.

We plan to expand our research by rendering and testing not only synthetic but also photo-realistic scenes in the CAVE, as well as by evaluating a broader spectrum of XR devices. A possible future application of our Robot-in-a-CAVE setup is the co-prototyping of XR apps and XR-friendly environments that allow for accurate visual-inertial tracking, e.g. for museums, showrooms, libraries and stores.

References

1. Adelstein, B.D., Johnston, E.R., Ellis, S.R.: Dynamic response of electromagnetic spatial displacement trackers. Presence Teleoperators Virtual Environ. **5**(3), 302–318 (1996). https://doi.org/10.1162/pres.1996.5.3.302

2. Agnus, V., Nicolau, S., Soler, L.: Illumination independent marker tracking using cross-ratio invariance. In: Proceedings of the 20th ACM Symposium on Virtual Reality Software and Technology - VRST 2014. ACM Press (2014). https://doi.org/10.1145/2671015.2671119

3. Bleser, G., Stricker, D.: Advanced tracking through efficient image processing and visual-inertial sensor fusion. Comput. Graph. **33**(1), 59–72 (2009). https://doi.org/10.1016/j.cag.2008.11.004

4. Chang, C.M., Hsu, C.H., Hsu, C.F., Chen, K.T.: Performance measurements of virtual reality systems. In: Proceedings of the 2016 ACM on Multimedia Conference - MM 2016. ACM Press (2016). https://doi.org/10.1145/2964284.2967303

5. Harris, C.G., Stephens, M., et al.: A combined corner and edge detector. In: Alvey Vision Conference, vol. 15, pp. 10–5244. Citeseer (1988)

6. Krier, A.: Laser projection tracking. Ph.D. thesis, Wien (2020)

7. Moser, K.R., Axholt, M., Swan, J.E.: Baseline SPAAM calibration accuracy and precision in the absence of human postural sway error. In: 2014 IEEE Virtual Reality (VR). IEEE, March 2014. https://doi.org/10.1109/vr.2014.6802070

8. Niehorster, D.C., Li, L., Lappe, M.: The accuracy and precision of position and orientation tracking in the HTC vive virtual reality system for scientific research. i-Perception **8**(3), 204166951770820 (2017). https://doi.org/10.1177/2041669517708205

9. Passos, D.E., Jung, B.: Measuring the accuracy of inside-out tracking in XR devices using a high-precision robotic arm. In: Stephanidis, C., Antona, M. (eds.) HCII 2020. CCIS, vol. 1224, pp. 19–26. Springer, Cham (2020). https://doi.org/10.1007/978-3-030-50726-8_3

10. Perlin, K.: An image synthesizer. ACM SIGGRAPH Comput. Graph. **19**(3), 287–296 (1985)

11. Shi, J., et al.: Good features to track. In: 1994 Proceedings of IEEE Conference on Computer Vision and Pattern Recognition, pp. 593–600. IEEE (1994)

12. Worley, S.: A cellular texture basis function. In: Proceedings of the 23rd Annual Conference on Computer Graphics and Interactive Techniques, pp. 291–294 (1996)

A Typing Training System for Beginners Using a Mixed Reality Device

Kouki Kakuta, Hidetoshi Miyao$^{(\boxtimes)}$, and Minoru Maruyama

Faculty of Engineering, Shinshu University, Nagano, Japan
{miyao,maruyama}@cs.shinshu-u.ac.jp

Abstract. In order to learn keyboard typing skills effectively, we propose a system which can realize the following functions: (1) It indicates the key position to enter a next key so that a user can memorize key arrangement, (2) it suggests the appropriate finger to be used so that a user can learn correct fingering, and (3) it performs various productions such as sound and visual effects to keep users motivated. To realize the functions, we used a mixed reality device (HoloLens2) where a virtual object can be superimposed and displayed on objects in real world space. For our training system, a yellow plane object is displayed on the key to be entered. HoloLens2 can acquire 3D positions of user's fingers in real-time, so that our system displays the red sphere object at the appropriate finger to be used. Keystroke information is transmitted from a keyboard to HoloLens2 via Bluetooth. Using this information, our system can display a visual effect when a user makes a typo. Moreover, it makes effective sounds when a user makes a typo or when he/she completes a single word entry, respectively. A comparative experiment was performed between our system and a typing practice application on the Web by 12 test users. As a result, it was shown that our system has a higher improvement rate in typing speed.

Keywords: Typing training · HoloLens · Mixed reality

1 Introduction

With the spread of ICT, there is a need for skills that can be typing at high speed to use a computer. However, according to the survey of information utilization ability by MEXT in Japan [1], the average typing speed of high school students is 24.7 characters/minute. This speed is not fast enough since it is said that a speed of 60 characters/minute is required at the practical level [2].

Sono et al. [3] points out that the following three points are important for improving the typing ability of beginners:

1. Remembering key arrangement,
2. Entering keys with an appropriate finger,
3. Doing the above two things without looking at the keyboard.

© Springer Nature Switzerland AG 2021
C. Stephanidis et al. (Eds.): HCII 2021, CCIS 1420, pp. 256–263, 2021.
https://doi.org/10.1007/978-3-030-78642-7_34

To train the item 1, they have proposed a method using a projection mapping [3]. In the system, a projector is set in front of a keyboard, it projects a rectangle object on the key to be entered next so that a user can input quickly even if he/she does not remember the key position. As a result, this system has the effect of encouraging the user to remember the key arrangement. However, when user's fingers are on the home position, it does not project objects precisely on the keys hidden by the fingers.

On the other hand, a mixed reality (MR) device is used in various education field [4, 5], because it can superimpose and display a computer-generated object (virtual object) on objects in real world space. For example, a piano learning support system can support performance by displaying the piano key to be input next [6]. To solve the projection mapping problem, we use a mixed reality head-mounted display (Microsoft HoloLens2) which can accurately display an object on the next key you should enter, even if the key is hidden by your finger.

The system proposed by Sono [3] cannot present fingering. In order to realize the function for the above item 2, HoloLens2 equipped with a hand tracking function is used to present the appropriate fingering. Sono's system has sound and visual effects to keep users motivated, so our system also implements similar effects.

2 Typing Training System Using HoloLens2

In order to effectively acquire keyboard typing skills, we propose a typing practice system with the following functions:

1. It indicates the key position to enter a next key so that a user can memorize key arrangement.
2. It suggests the appropriate finger to be used so that a user can learn correct fingering.
3. It performs various productions such as sound and visual effects to keep users motivated.

2.1 System Configuration

To realize the three functions mentioned above, we use Microsoft HoloLens2 in which a virtual object can be superimposed and displayed on objects in real world space. In our system, to align virtual and real coordinate spaces, we use Vuforia SDK [7] in Unity game engine [8] and an AR marker which is affixed a real-world keyboard (Logicool K480BK). Virtual objects are also generated using Unity. Keystroke information of the keyboard is transmitted to HoloLens2 via Bluetooth. A sound is played by HoloLens2.

2.2 Typing Practice Application

We implement an application to practice keyboard typing. The application starts when a user presses the space key. An application window appears above the keyboard. As shown in Fig. 1, a word to be typed is displayed in the center, and the elapsed time and the number of mistypes up to now are displayed in the lower right. Correctly entered characters are displayed in blue. Here, 10 words randomly selected from pre-prepared

23 words are displayed in turn and each word is composed of four Japanese Hiragana characters. When all the 10 words are entered, the application ends and returns to the initial state.

Fig. 1. Typing practice application

2.3   Realization of the Function 1 (Displaying the Key to be Entered)

The target keys in our system are 48 keys used for Japanese Hiragana input. We exclude characters to be entered while pressing two or more keys at the same time. Virtual objects corresponding to the 48 keys are generated by Unity. Each object is represented by a yellow rectangular plane with the corresponding character on it. In our typing application, only the object corresponding to the key to be entered next is displayed (see Fig. 1).

2.4   Realization of the Function 2 (Displaying Fingering Information)

HoloLens2 can acquire 3D positions of user's fingers in real-time, so that our system always displays sphere objects at all fingertips where the red sphere object indicates the appropriate finger to be used and the cyan sphere objects indicate the other fingers (see Fig. 1).

2.5   Realization of the Function 3 (Sound and Visual Effects)

Keystroke information is transmitted from the keyboard. Using this information, our system can display the red points in a radial pattern at the correct key position when a user mistypes as shown in Fig. 2. Moreover, it makes effective sounds when a user makes a typo or when he/she completes a single word entry, respectively.

Fig. 2. Visual effect when a user makes a typo

3 Experimental Results and Discussion

To verify the effectiveness of our system, we conducted an experiment on 12 test users. They are accustomed to *romaji input* which is a method of inputting Japanese Hiragana using alphabetic characters but have rarely used *kana input* which is a method of directly inputting Hiragana characters. Since our system is intended for beginners, we want to experiment in situations where users do not remember the key arrangement. Therefore, we adopted kana input in our experiment.

As a comparative experiment with our system, we used a web application that is commonly used in typing practice [9]. As with our system, randomly selected 10 words are displayed in turn and each word is composed of four Hiragana characters. The elapsed time and the number of mistypes up to now are displayed while a user is entering a character. It also has the following functions:

(a) The next key to enter is displayed in orange.
(b) Fingering information is displayed at the bottom of the application window.
(c) A buzzer sounds when a user enters a wrong key.

Test users were divided into two groups, half each. The 6 users used our system and the remaining 6 users used the Web application. The flow of the experiment is as follows:

(1) In the situation without the functions, the input time of 10 words is measured and the number of typos is counted.
(2) In the situation with the functions, during the three days, 10 min of training are conducted each day.
(3) The same measurement as in (1) are performed.
(4) Users answer the questionnaire.

Here, "functions" means the functions 1–3 in Sect. 2 in the case of the experiment using our system and the above (a)–(c) in the case of the experiment using the Web application, respectively. Next, we will describe the experimental results.

3.1 Evaluation of the Input Time and the Number of Typos

Table 1 shows the experimental results of the input time and the number of typos. Here, "First time" columns represent the results for the above (1) and "Last time" columns for the above (3), respectively. Since "Rate" means "Last time/First time" for the input time, the smaller the value, the higher the improvement rate after the training. Comparing the two systems with respect to the value, most of the values in our system are far below 50%, while the values in the Web application system are around 50%. From this result, it is considered that the input time is further improved by training with our system rather than the Web application. Regarding the number of typos, typing practice tends to reduce the number of mistakes. However, there was no significant difference in the results for both systems. As some users became accustomed to typing, they tried to input without looking at the keyboard, which tends to increase the number of typos. In the future works, we have to evaluate the followings:

- Will users be able to touch-type after a long period of practice?
- How many mistakes are there if users type in touch typing?

Table 1. Experimental results of the input time and the number of types.

	Test user	Input time			Number of typos	
		(a) First time [s]	(b)Last time [s]	Rate (b/a)	First time	Last time
Our system	A	476	112	24%	2	0
	B	497	182	37%	2	0
	C	285	115	40%	2	2
	D	636	477	75%	5	0
	E	413	111	27%	0	1
	F	351	169	48%	5	0
Web App	G	246	120	49%	0	0
	H	255	135	53%	7	1
	I	362	179	49%	5	0
	J	311	139	45%	4	0
	K	224	106	47%	0	7
	L	147	73	50%	4	4

3.2 User Evaluation

After the experiment, we asked the users to answer the following points:

- Q1: Did you enjoy using the system?
- Q2: Do you want to continue using the system?

- Q3: Were you easy to type with the system?
- Q4: Were you easy to understand proper fingering using the system?
- Q5: Did you feel annoyed by various functions of the system?
- Q6: Did you feel uncomfortable with the virtual object being displayed on an actual finger when the target key was hidden by the finger?
- Q7: Did you feel uncomfortable wearing HoloLens2?

Of these seven questions, all the test users answered Q1–Q5, and only the users who used our system answered Q6 and Q7. As a choice of answers, we used a Five-grade evaluation of Rickert standards: 1: Disagree, 2: Moderately disagree, 3: Neutral, 4: Moderately agree, and 5: Agree. Therefore, for Q1 to Q4, the larger the value, the better the result, while for Q5 to Q7, the smaller the value, the better the result. Table 2 shows the answers to the questionnaire where the better the result, the closer the cell color is to red.

Regarding Q1, Q2, Q3, and Q5, the user group trained using our system tends to have more good evaluations than the Web application system. Therefore, it is shown that our system is easier to use, and that the users can maintain their motivation while training. Regarding Q4, there was no significant difference in the results for both systems. It is considered that the cause is that all the test users have typing experience in alphabet input and have almost mastered proper fingering, so that they can input without looking at the fingering instruction display (Some users commented that the display was annoying). It is necessary to experiment again with users who have no typing experience. For Q6 and Q7, the values were divided into two extremes depending on the users.

Here are some of the comments received from the test users during the experiment using our system:

- It was very easy to type because the key to be entered is indicated and can be seen at a glance.
- When I put my fingers in the home position and the key object in the lower row of the keyboard was displayed, the object was displayed on the finger instead of on the key and it was difficult to know the actual key position.
- It seems that learning efficiency will be improved if the system operates as follows: the input key is not indicated at first, but it is done only when the key is not entered after a certain period of time.
- Wearing HoloLens2 for a long time makes my eyes tired.
- When training, I thought that it would not be effective because I was typing without thinking about anything, but after the training, I was surprised that there was a learning effect.

Table 2. Answers to the questionnaire.

	Test user	Q1	Q2	Q3	Q4	Q5	Q6	Q7
Our system	A	5	5	5	3	2	4	2
	B	5	3	4	2	1	1	1
	C	5	5	5	4	1	1	1
	D	5	5	5	5	1	1	1
	E	3	2	5	5	2	3	5
	F	4	4	4	3	2	4	4
Web App	G	2	4	5	4	3		
	H	3	3	4	4	2		
	I	3	4	5	3	4		
	J	3	4	1	5	1		
	K	4	4	2	4	2		
	L	4	3	4	4	2		

4 Conclusion

To effectively acquire keyboard typing skill, we have proposed the typing practice system using HoloLens2 as follows: (1) It indicates the key position to enter a next key, (2) it suggests the appropriate finger to be used, and (3) it performs various productions by sound and visual effects. The comparative experiment was performed between our system and the typing practice application on the Web, it was shown that our system has higher improvement rate in typing speed. Moreover, from the answers to the questionnaire, it was shown that our system is easier to use, and that the users can maintain their motivation while training.

The future works are as follows:

- Experiments and evaluations for subjects who have no typing experience
- Evaluation with longer training time
- Dynamic change of the functions according to learner's skill
- Re-examination of the display position and design of the virtual object to make it easier to see
- Recognizing whether a user is touch-typing and evaluation of typing speed and number of typos under the condition that the user is touch-typing

Acknowledgments. This work was supported by JSPS KAKENHI Grant Number JP18K11564.

References

1. MEXT: Survey of information utilization ability, pp. 54–56. (2017). https://www.mext.go.jp/a_menu/shotou/zyouhou/detail/__icsFiles/afieldfile/2017/01/18/1381046_02_1.pdf . Accessed 19 Mar 2021
2. MaiPaso: Typing necessity, https://maipaso.net/skill_up/necessity/. Accessed 19 Mar 2021

3. Sono, C., Hasegawa, T.: Interaction to support the learning of typing for beginners on physical keyboard by projection mapping. In: ICIT 2019, pp. 565–569 (2019)
4. Tang, Y.M., Au, K.M., Lau, H.C.W., Ho, G.T.S., Wu, C.H.: Evaluating the effectiveness of learning design with mixed reality (MR) in higher education. Virtual Real. **24**, 797–807 (2020)
5. Kucera, E., Haffner, O., Leskovsky, R.: Interactive and virtual/mixed reality applications for mechatronics education developed in unity engine. In: 29th International Conference on Cybernetics & Informatics (2018)
6. Molero, D., Schez-Sobrino, S., Vallejo, D., Glez-Morcillo, C., Albusac, J.: A novel approach to learning music and piano based on mixed reality and gamification. Multimed. Tools Appl. **80**, 165–186 (2021)
7. Vuforia Developer Portal. https://developer.vuforia.com/. Accessed 19 Mar 2021
8. Unity. https://unity.com/. Accessed 19 Mar 2021
9. FUJITSU: Practice Touch Typing. https://azby.fmworld.net/usage/lesson/keyboard/typing/improve/kana.html?supfrom=menu. Accessed 19 Mar 2021

Developing a Virtual Agent that Exhibits Behavioral Conformity as a Social Interaction in the Atypical Architectural Space

Hong Jung Kim, Ho Min Jo, Hyun Seo Jang, Su Jin Kim, and Yun Gil Lee[✉]

Hoseo University, 20, Hoseo-ro, 79beon-gil, Baebang-eup, Asan-si 31499, Chungcheongnam-do, Korea
{kyong5666,1998kevin}@naver.com, tnwls1797@hanmail.net, yglee@hoseo.edu

Abstract. In atypical buildings, social interaction can appear in various forms, one of which, behavioral conformity, is an atypical space social interaction classified in prior research. Behavioral conformity can be explained as imitating the actions of other people. Many cases of unexpected behaviors occur in atypical buildings because these spaces do not have a standard physical form. As a result, there are also many cases of social behaviors that follow the unexpected behavior of another party, which is classified as behavioral conformity. This study aimed to develop a behavioral conformity function for advanced human behavior simulations. Behavioral conformity involves the observation of another person's behavior. Computationally, when another agent's behavior comes into an agent's field of view, the probability of similar behavior increases and is likely to develop into behavioral conformity. As the simulation progresses, a phenomenon may occur in which there is an increase in the number of agents exhibiting a similar behavior as other users who were found through the observation of field surveys. The behavioral conformity function of virtual users was developed based on ActoViz, a user behavior simulation system in previously developed atypical buildings. Through the behavioral conformity function, which is one of the social interactions of virtual users, it is possible to ensure that the simulation is more like a real-world situation in the designed atypical space.

Keywords: Atypical architecture · Human behavior simulation · Social interaction · Behavioral conformity

1 Introduction

Atypical buildings provide vitality to a uniform city and present new experiences to users, and so the demand for them is gradually increasing. Accordingly, the ability to design atypical buildings has become essential for architects. In the atypical architectural design process, more effort is put into the unusual form of a building, which results in architects easily overlooking the human factor, one of the most important values of an architectural space. To compensate for this problem, a human behavior simulation using

© Springer Nature Switzerland AG 2021
C. Stephanidis et al. (Eds.): HCII 2021, CCIS 1420, pp. 264–268, 2021.
https://doi.org/10.1007/978-3-030-78642-7_35

intelligent virtual users has been proposed, and related technologies are being developed. The proposed method places virtual users in the virtual space during the design process by using an unstructured space design tool and then evaluating the designed plan through the free reaction of the agents to the atypical space. The intelligent behavior of virtual users is central to successful human behavior simulation. Both physical and social interactions must be possible. In terms of physical interaction, virtual users should be able to respond appropriately to the form of the atypical space. In addition, in terms of social interaction, natural circumstances can be produced only when the virtual users exhibit appropriate responses to other virtual users. In atypical buildings, social interaction can appear in various forms, one of which, behavioral conformity, is an atypical space social interaction classified in prior research. Behavioral conformity can be explained as imitating the actions of other people. Many cases of unexpected behaviors occur in atypical buildings because these spaces do not have a standard physical form. As a result, there are also many cases of social behaviors that follow the unexpected behavior of another party, which is classified as behavioral conformity.

This study aimed to develop a behavioral conformity function for advanced human behavior simulations. Behavioral conformity involves the observation of another person's behavior. Computationally, when another agent's behavior comes into an agent's field of view, the probability of similar behavior increases and is likely to develop into behavioral conformity. As the simulation progresses, a phenomenon may occur in which there is an increase in the number of agents exhibiting a similar behavior as other users who were found through the observation of field surveys. The behavioral conformity function of virtual users was developed based on ActoViz, a user behavior simulation system in previously developed atypical buildings. Through the behavioral conformity function, which is one of the social interactions of virtual users, it is possible to ensure that the simulation is more like a real-world situation in the designed atypical space. Figure 3 shows virtual agents who exhibit behavioral conformity as social interaction in ActoViz.

2   Social Behavior in the Atypical Buildings

In the previous study, the social interactions of users in unstructured buildings were studied and classified into four categories as follows: Self-Perception, Behavioral Conformity, In-Group Bias, and Behavior Setting [6]. The present study aims to computerize Behavioral Conformity, one of the most representative social interactions in the atypical space.

Behavioral conformity is easily characterized as witnessing and imitating the actions of others. Since humans live in society, they are affected by the lives of others. Conformity is one of the consequences. We are affected by the behavior of others, whether we are superficially following or simply resonating. The majority of people leaning down against the wall, resting, or sitting on a chair can be interpreted as exhibiting behavior in accordance with the actions of people other than one's self or group. These actions can likewise be interpreted as compliance without deliberate intention. Figure 1 illustrates instances of human social practices linked to interpersonal compliance in peculiar systems [6–8].

Fig. 1. Examples of human social behaviors related to behavioral conformity in atypical buildings [6]

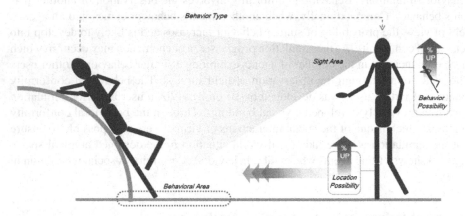

Fig. 2. Strategy to computerize "Behavioral conformity" in human behavior simulation [9]

The technique for computerizing Behavioral Conformity is depicted in Fig. 2. Social activity that conforms to the actions of another group is referred to as behavioral conformity. In other words, it entails observing another person's actions and modeling it in a particular situation. When another agent's behavior crosses an agent's field of view, the possibility of similar behavior increases and is likely to evolve into behavioral conformity. As the simulation continues, a pattern may arise in which the number of agents enacting identical behavior increase, similar to the actions of users discovered through field survey observation [9].

3   Virtual Agent that Exhibits Behavioral Conformity as a Social Interaction in the Atypical Architectural Space

Figure 3 is a representation of the behavioral conformity in ActoViz, which was developed and used as a human behavior simulation platform in this study. Similar to the behavioral conformity development strategy discussed earlier, ActoViz was developed to mimic the behavior of other agents entering an agent's view. As shown in Fig. 3, a much more natural human behavior simulation was produced compared to the agent performing a reaction behavior to each physical space situation. In particular, there is an advantage of being able to visually check affordance of the designed atypical space by imitating the actions of other agents in a space where unpredictable motions are likely to occur, such as an atypical space.

Fig. 3. Virtual agents that exhibits behavioral conformity as a social interaction in ActoViz

4   Conclusion and Discussion

This study aimed to develop a behavioral conformity function for advanced human behavior simulations. This technology development confirmed the possibility of realizing a more natural human behavior simulation. However, the technology developed in this study reproduces preset motions and is limited in reproducing user motions that are difficult to predict in various types of atypical buildings. Therefore, an agent technology capable of performing various actions and social interaction based on these behaviors should be developed in future research.

Acknowledgement. This work was supported by the National Research Foundation of Korea (NRF) grant funded by the Korean government (MSIT) (NRF-2018R1A2B6005827).

References

1. Hong, S., Lee, Y.: The effects of human behavior simulation on architectural major students' fire egress planning. J. Asian Architect. Build. Eng. **17**(1), 125–132 (2018)
2. Lee, Y.: A study on the effect of human factor for atypical design in the architectural design studio. Adv. Intell. Syst. Comput. **876**(1), 130–134 (2018)
3. Hong, S., Schaumann, D., Kalay, Y.E.: Human behavior simulation in architectural design projects: an observational study in an academic course. Comput. Environ. Urban Syst. **60**, 1–11 (2016)
4. Simeone, D., Kalay, Y.E., Schaumann, D., Hong, S.: Modeling and simulating use processes in buildings. In: Proceedings of Education and Research in Computer Aided Architectural Design in Europe, pp. 59–66 (2013)
5. Lee, Y.G.: ActoViz: a human behavior simulator for the evaluation of the dwelling performance of an atypical architectural space. In: Stephanidis, C. (ed.) HCII 2019. CCIS, vol. 1034, pp. 361–365. Springer, Cham (2019). https://doi.org/10.1007/978-3-030-23525-3_48
6. Lee, Y.L., Lee, Y.G.: Psychological interpretation of human social behaviors in the atypical architectural shape. In: Karwowski, W., Ahram, T., Etinger, D., Tanković, N., Taiar, R. (eds.) IHSED 2020. AISC, vol. 1269, pp. 33–38. Springer, Cham (2020). https://doi.org/10.1007/978-3-030-58282-1_6
7. Philbeck, J., Loomis, J.: Comparison of two indicators of perceived egocentric distance under full-cue and reduced-cue conditions. J. Exp. Psychol. Hum. Percept. Perform. **23**(1), 72–85 (1997)
8. Todd, J., Norman, J.: The visual perception of 3-D shape from multiple cues: are observers capable of perceiving metric shape? Percept. Psychophys. **65**(1), 31–47 (2003)
9. Lee, Y., Lee, Y.: A Study on the strategies of developing the autonomous human social behavior of virtual users based on psychological interpretation in an atypical architectural shape. Asia-pacific J. Conver. Res. Interchange (APJCRI) FuCoS **6**(11), 193–202 (2020). ISSN: 2508–9080 (Print); 2671–5325 (Online)

Influence of Visualisation Design of Data Streams on User Experience in Virtual Reality

Tanja Kojić[1(✉)], Maurizio Vergari[1], Rahul Thangaraj[1], Marco Braune[1], and Jan-Niklas Voigt-Antons[1,2]

[1] Quality and Usability Lab, Technische Universität Berlin, Berlin, Germany
tanja.kojic@tu-berlin.de
[2] German Research Center for Artificial Intelligence (DFKI), Berlin, Germany

Abstract. The continuous growth in technology has brought some revolutionary changes in various domains, resulting in considerable data accumulation. Although traditional segregation and displaying data might still be possible, it may be difficult for users to extract the quintessence from them. Data is one of the most practical terms, irrespective of its origin or time, and it does have an interesting story to convey. There is a need for the data to be presented more innovatively, so that obscure and complex data can be comprehended easily. Still, it all may come down to good storytelling in many cases and enabling people to connect with the data. With this research study, we leverage virtual reality concepts to compare two techniques to visualise data - traditionally numerical and creative. The aim is to bring data into virtual reality to help one interact and visualise data in a three-dimensional environment, thereby adding more fun and compelling ways to analyse and evaluate. With this research, we would like to devise various design paradigms that could be used to display or represent data in a virtual environment. Having two different virtual environments representing the office and nature, users (N = 19) of the user study had to evaluate if they could recognise the connection between numerical and creative visualisation. Interestingly, users have reported a higher arousal intensity (measure by SAM questionnaire) when the environment and the expected visualisation are not matching. Further on, results suggest that the different kind of visualisation can be more effective and can be used for future VR applications.

Keywords: User experience · Virtual reality · Data visualisation

1 Introduction

Visualisation is something that has an ever-expanding application in numerous fields and a phenomenon that has been around for ages. It is about creating a more presentable structure of a subject matter. It has to be considered a starting point for understanding, analysing, reasoning, and interpreting a subject matter and its supplementing evidence. With advancements in computer graphics

© Springer Nature Switzerland AG 2021
C. Stephanidis et al. (Eds.): HCII 2021, CCIS 1420, pp. 269–277, 2021.
https://doi.org/10.1007/978-3-030-78642-7_36

and visualisation principles, we have constantly devised new innovative ways to present a subject matter to the consumers.

These visualisation techniques [6] did present us with various opportunities to transform a massive collection of raw data to a more consumable form by an everyday user with a minimal technical background. It should enable one to better comprehend and understand the all nuances before making a well-educated guess. With the current surge and persistent innovation in virtual reality (VR) devices, we seem to have unlocked a new interactive methodology to visualise large chunks of data in a three-dimensional view. This has undoubtedly piqued everyone's interest in studying and understanding how suitable a medium is for virtual reality for data visualisation. The potential of virtual reality [7] in data visualisation is not limited to just the visual display but also provides a broad scope of communicating with these data in real-time. The user can navigate the environment and manipulate or interact with the presented information in a detailed manner. The visual elements might also be an extension of two-dimensional visualisation techniques from a third dimension.

1.1 Related Work

In recent years, the popularity of 3D user interfaces has increased in different areas where 2D solution have been lacking immersive interactions [8], compared to the 3D visualisations [9]. However, perception of 3D data visualisation has been influenced by possibilities to recreate physical worlds, by advancement in VR technologies in virtual environments (VE) [1]. An especially interesting field for research is big data visualisation [5], having focus mainly on digital visualisation. However, when it comes to different media, different forms of data representation have been researched, from traditional data visualisation to the more purely aesthetic forms of visualization art [4].

1.2 Objectives

This research aims to create some visualisation techniques that could be employed to represent data in multiple forms in virtual reality and employ techniques that establish a connection between these different visualisation forms. By establishing a connection, there is a possibility to unlock the opportunity of visualising the same piece of information in multiple forms. Also, we understand how easy or difficult it was for the users to comprehend this connection and what sort of impact the level of comprehension had on the immersion. Therefore, the primary goal of our research project is to address the following questions:

- Do users comprehend the connection between similar data when expressed in different forms (numeral vs creative) of visualisation?
- How do different virtual environments and different visualisation (numerical vs creative) of data influence users' emotional state and user experience?

2   Method

2.1   Scene Design Set-Up

A storyline was created and then implemented in VR using the *Unity* engine [10] to develop a connection between the user and the virtual environment. The user takes the role of a businessman running a tourism agency. The data set contains income information. Besides working in his office, the businessman also loves nature and always finds time to engage in activities that connects him with it. This way, two different environments are brought inside the story, which provides the possibility to represent data in at least two different ways: A numerical data representation in the office environment and a creative data representation in the natural environment. By mixing the data visualisation methods and the environment, four different scenes were created: each of the two environments with the two ways of data representations. But just changing the environment is not enough to give the player an understanding of the data. Each data visualisation was connected to a task to achieve that result. The user was able to interact with every data that was presented to him inside the virtual environment (Fig. 1).

Fig. 1. Visualisation of both scenes, on left is Office, and on right is Nature.

The numerical data representation is more of a typical way of data visualisation. This was done by explicitly showing the numbers on top of objects inside the virtual environment. The user is probably familiar with this kind of data representation, which helps him understand the data easily. The interactions were the following:

– Monitor: The data for one day is shown on a monitor, and by touching another monitor, the user can see the data of another day.
– Sign: The user can discover this sign and notice the change of the presented data after a virtual day passes.
– Money: The amount of money depends on the amount of income. The money can be picked up and put in a money counting machine to see its amount on display (Fig. 2).

Fig. 2. Different graphical representation of data in VR scenes. In upper row from left to right data represented: on Monitor, on Sign, as Money. In lower row from left to right: as Fruits, in Weather, as Fish.

In contrast to that, the creative data representation is done by changing parts of the environment and letting the user interact with them:

– Fruits: Can be picked up and eaten. The kind of food depends on income.
– Weather: It changes accordingly to the income that is presented by the data. Low income equals rainy weather, and high income equals sunny weather. In the office, the player can open the window to inspect the weather. There are different objects to interact with within the natural environment, such as an umbrella for the rainy weather and a fountain to drink from while it is sunny.
– Fish: In the office, the user can open an aquarium to inspect the fish. In the natural environment, the user can go fishing. The colour of the fish corresponds to the income of the virtual day - gold for high income, bronze for low income (Fig. 3).

 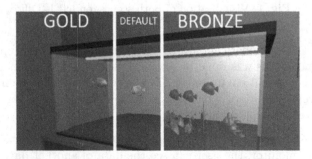

Fig. 3. Examples of different visualisation depending on the change of income data on left as Weather, and on right as Fish.

2.2 Test Set-Up

In order to evaluate the data visualisation in VR, user tests were conducted. The tests were designed as within-subject tests, which means each user has performed each condition (the four different scenes). The participants were invited into a controlled testing environment to conduct the test as a laboratory experiment, where they were instructed with the tasks and controls of the VR application. After each condition the participant was asked to fill out the *Self Assessment Manikin (SAM)* [2]. After the participant went through all four conditions, the *System Usability Scale (SUS)* [3] and ten final questions were asked to be answered. The final questions required to be answered by yes or no (for example: Did you understand the goal of the game?; Did the introduction help you make sense of the game?) or rated on a five-level Likert scale (e.g. the controller was easy to use; it was easy to navigate in the environment; it was easy to locate the necessary objects in the environment; it was easy to recognise the objects in the environment.)

2.3 Participants

In the study had participated 19 persons (12 men and 7 women), from age between 17 and 34 years old (M = 25.58, SD = 3.977). All participants provided written informed consent before participating in the experiment, and the experiment was done before the outbreak of the pandemic, and the experimental procedure did not represent any risk for human health.

3 Results

A repeated measure Analysis of Variance (ANOVA) was performed to determine statistically significant differences. An overview of all significant effects that will be explained in the following sections is given with Table 1. Additionally, results from the final questionnaires and System Usability Scale are as well reported.

Table 1. Two-way repeated-measures ANOVA statistically significant results show effects of Environment and Visualisation on SAM dimensions of valence and arousal (SAM_V, SAM_A).

Parameter	Effect	df_n	df_d	F	p	η_G^2
Environment	SAM_V	1	18	6.552	.020	.267
Environment	SAM_A	1	18	10.059	.005	.358
Environment & Visualisation	SAM_A	1	18	6.429	.021	.263

3.1   Environment

The independent variable Environment has a statistically significant effect on the dependent variables of SAM. Results have shown a main effect of Environment on SAM Valence value, which results in valence being less pleasant for the Office environment (M = 3.658, SE = 0.248) compared to the Nature one (M = 4.105, SE = 0.169). The main effect of Environment found on SAM Arousal has been reported to be less intense for the Office environment (M = 3.211, SE = 0.217) compared to the Nature one (M = 3.711, SE = 0.207) (Fig. 4).

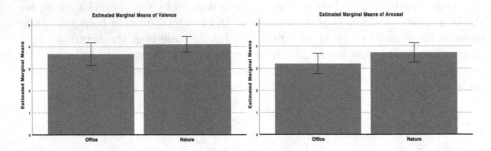

Fig. 4. Average values for the two presented scenes (Office vs. Nature) for valence (on left) and arousal (on right) ratings over all participants.

3.2   Interaction of Environment and Visualisation

Results have shown a significant combined interaction between the independent variables Environment and Visualisation on the dependent variable SAM Arousal. Opposite profile trends (increasing-decreasing) resulted between the

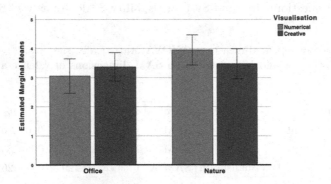

Fig. 5. Average values for arousal ratings for the two presented scenes (Office vs. Nature) and the two visualisation methods (numerical vs. creative) over all participants. Whiskers denote the 95% confidence interval.

Office and Nature environment conditions. In the Office condition, arousal intensity is lower in Numerical than Creative visualisation. On the contrary, in the Nature condition, the arousal intensity is higher for the Numerical visualisation (Fig. 5).

3.3   System Usability Scale

From the analysis of the SUS [3] results, the developed VR experience was rated with a score of 72.79 (SD = 16.82). The score indicates that the application usability is above average (>68), indicating a good usability level.

3.4   Final Questionnaire

From the final questionnaire results, it emerged that 61% of the participants understood the goal of the game. The introduction to the game was helpful instead for 83% of them. When it comes to the ease of following a specific task, it was reported a mean value of 4.17 (SD = 0.786). The visibility of the consequences of each task was rated with a mean value of 3.94 (SD = 0.998). Moreover, 94.4% of the users noticed changes in the environment after fulfilling a task. 66.6% of participants revealed that they thought there was a connection between the Office and Nature environments. In terms of system components, the controller ease of use was rated with a mean value of 4.28 (SD = 0.826). Simultaneously, a mean value of 4.17 (SD = 0.924) resulted in the ease of navigating the virtual environment. Furthermore, ease of locating and recognising objects in the environment got a mean value of 3.94 (SD = 0.938) and 4.39 (SD = 0.608), respectively.

4   Discussion

With the aim to find out about the role of the environment, in which the data are display, on emotional states of users, two different environments Office and Nature, were included. The office environment induces lower emotional responses in terms of valence and arousal, indicating that the Nature environment is more effective in generating a good mood and stronger emotions in intensity. This result confirms the beneficial nature effect of increasing valence already revealed in other studies [11]. At the same time, an increase in arousal was in contrast with previous results for natural environments. This could be related to the fact that what has been used was not a regular natural environment. It was filled with different tasks, changing weather conditions and different type of artificial information (e.g. sign in the numerical condition) that could have created an increase in arousal.

From the results, a statistically significant interaction between Environment and Visualisation on arousal has been found. It is interesting to notice a higher arousal intensity when the environment and the expected visualisation are not matching. In fact, in the office environment where a numerical representation would typically be more appropriate, we had higher arousal with the creative one. Vice versa, in the natural environment, the numerical representation generated a higher intensity in arousal. This is probably to be attributed to the fact that the users were amazed by having such diverse visualisations.

From the final questionnaire results, more than half of the participant can understand the similarities and connection between data in numerical or creative form across the environments. Giving a clear introduction to the user before using the system is crucial to make a successful experience. It has to be also said that the gamification aspect might have pushed some users more to accomplish a task more than understanding its meaning.

5   Conclusion

With the aim to explore different visualisations of environment and data representation, a user study has been done comparing different ways of data representation. The users reported that they could recognise the connection between numerical and creative visualisation, and results have shown that the different kind of visualisation can result as more effective. Knowing that data visualisation in natural environments could provide higher pleasure and intensity of emotions could lead to a better-designed user experience for virtual environments. Therefore in future, the performance of such data visualisation application in different industries could be researched with real-time live data streams.

References

1. Bowman, D.A., Kruijff, E., LaViola, J.J., Jr. Poupyrev, I.: 3D user interfaces: theory and practice (2005)
2. Bradley, M.M., Lang, P.J.: Measuring emotion: the self-assessment manikin and the semantic differential. J. Behav. Ther. Exp. Psychiatry **25**(1), 49–59 (1994). https://doi.org/10.1016/0005-7916(94)90063-9. https://www.sciencedirect.com/science/article/pii/0005791694900639
3. Brooke, J.: SUS: A 'quick and dirty' usability scale. In: Jordan, P.W., Thomas, B., McClelland, I.L., Weerdmeester, B. (eds.) Usability Evaluation in Industry, 1st edn., pp. 189–194. CRC Press (1996)
4. Moere, A.V.: Aesthetic data visualization as a resource for educating creative design. In: Dong, A., Moere, A.V., Gero, J.S. (eds.) Computer-Aided Architectural Design Futures (CAADFutures) 2007, pp. 71–84. Springer, Dordrecht (2007). https://doi.org/10.1007/978-1-4020-6528-6_6
5. Moran, A., Gadepally, V., Hubbell, M., Kepner, J.: Improving big data visual analytics with interactive virtual reality. In: 2015 IEEE High Performance Extreme Computing Conference (HPEC), pp. 1–6. IEEE (2015)
6. Millais, P., Jones, S.L., Kelly, R.: Exploring data in virtual reality: comparisons with 2D data visualizations (2018). https://purehost.bath.ac.uk/ws/portalfiles/portal/168354128/paper1278.pdf
7. Loftin, R.B., Chen, J.X.: Visualization using virtual reality. In: Johnson/Hansen: The Visualization Handbook, pp. 465–476 (2004). http://www.uvm.edu/pdodds/files/papers/others/2004/loftin2004a.pdf

8. Steinicke, F., Bruder, G., Hinrichs, K., Ropinski, T., Lopes, M.: 3D user interfaces for collaborative work. In: Human Computer Interaction. IntechOpen (2008)
9. Stellmach, S., Dachselt, R.: Looking at 3D user interfaces. In: CHI 2012 Workshop on the 3rd Dimension of CHI (3DCHI): Touching and Designing 3D User Interfaces, pp. 95–98 (2012)
10. Unity Technologies: Unity. https://unity.com/
11. Valtchanov, D., Barton, K.R., Ellard, C.: Restorative effects of virtual nature settings. Cyberpsychol. Behav. Soc. Netw. **13**(5), 503–512 (2010)

Developing a Technology of Tracing a Trigger Spot for Human Behavior through Voxelization of Atypical Architectural Shapes

Yun Gil Lee[(⊠)], Hyun Seo Jang, Su Jin Kim, Hong Jung Kim, and Ho Min Jo

Hoseo University, 20, Hoseo-ro, 79beon-gil, Baebang-eup, Asan-si 31499,
Chungcheongnam-do, Korea
yglee@hoseo.edu

Abstract. Human behavior simulation is one of the advancements that have been introduced in atypical building design because this technology makes it possible to overcome various limitations, such as when architects overlook human factors during the design process. To attain a detailed human behavior simulation, the appropriate actions of the virtual user in the right position are crucial. The action possibility of a particular shape of object is called affordance. The affordance of general objects is standardized, so computerization is easy. However, it is difficult to predict where and what behavior will be induced in atypical geometry. This is why it is difficult to realize advanced human behavior simulation technology in atypical designs. This study aimed to develop a technology that automatically calculates action points for the advanced human behavior simulation of atypical buildings. In this study, we developed an algorithm to extract the action trigger points by voxelizing a three-dimensional unstructured shape. By analyzing the positional relationship of voxels through the algorithm developed in this study, it is possible to calculate the point where the action can be triggered. Moreover, appropriate user actions can be placed at calculated points. The results of this study would facilitate complex human behaviors in atypical buildings and constitute a type of core technology that can be used for developing a more meaningful human behavior simulation technology.

Keywords: Voxelization · Human behavior simulation · Atypical architecture · Trigger spot

1 Introduction

The ability to design atypical structures has become an essential skillset for architects. To design an atypical structure, it is necessary to cultivate the ability to freely reproduce curved three-dimensional (3D) sculptures using tools such as Rhino. Architects should also consider whether the modeled unstructured structure is suitable for use by people. Through the architectural design process, architects repeatedly reproduce design alternatives and review them countless times to derive optimal architectural results. There are a multitude of criteria for the review of the designed alternatives, such as law, experience, and the client's request, among others. The most important factor in evaluating the value of a building is the human factor. This is because improvement in user safety and convenience is the ultimate goal of architectural design. In recent years, human behavior simulation has been increasingly used to examine human factors in designs. This is a method that involves placing an intelligent virtual user in a designed building and evaluating the latter through the user's actions. In such a simulation, the architect observes the automatic reaction of the virtual user in relation to the designed architectural shapes in a 3D virtual space. The quality of the simulation is determined by the virtual user's proper actions at the right place. Human behavior simulation has also been introduced in atypical building design because this technology makes it possible to overcome various limitations, such as when architects overlook human factors during the design process. As discussed previously, to attain a detailed human behavior simulation, the appropriate actions of the virtual user in the right position are crucial. The action possibility of a particular shape of object is called affordance. The affordance of general objects is standardized, so computerization is easy. However, it is difficult to predict where and what behavior will be induced in atypical geometry. This is why it is difficult to realize advanced human behavior simulation technology in atypical design.

This study aimed to develop a technology that automatically calculates action points for advanced human behavior simulations in atypical buildings. In this study, we developed an algorithm to extract the action trigger point by voxelizing a 3D unstructured shape. By analyzing the positional relationship of voxels through the algorithm developed in this study, it is possible to calculate the point where the action can be triggered. Moreover, appropriate user actions can be placed at calculated points. The results of this study will facilitate complex human behaviors in atypical buildings and constitute a type of core technology that can be used for developing a more meaningful human behavior simulation technology. Figure 1 shows the method used to trace trigger spots through voxelization.

2 Assigning Trigger Spots for the Agent's Behavior in Human Behavior Simulation

2.1 Human Behavior Simulation and Affordance

Gibson described this feature using the term "affordance," which means that an object triggers a specific possible action [6]. In other words, a chair can induce a user to sit on it through the meaning "thing that can be used to sit on." When a semantic characteristic of an object is given to each virtual space and object, the character's behavior can be automatically determined based on the characteristic. Figure 1 depicts the behavior of furniture and doors. Depending on the shape and function of an object, it can be seen that there is a high probability of occurrence of a specific action around the object. If the concept of affordance is applied in human behavior simulation, the user's behavior that involves furniture and architectural objects can be replicated. However, it is hard to apply this method in atypical architectural objects because it is difficult to predict what kind of motion can occur for an atypical architectural shape.

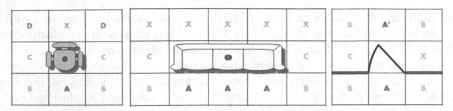

Fig. 1. [7] Expression of affordance in relation to chairs and doors. (a) Action execution point. (b) Access point for performing actions. (c) Evasion or waiting point. (d) Hesitating point. (e) X is a point that has nothing to do with the object [7]

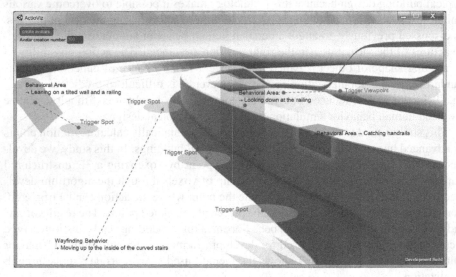

Fig. 2. Methods of specifying the trigger spot, trigger viewpoint and behavioral area using ActoViz (Lee and Lee 2019).

2.2 Trigger Spots in the Atypical Architectural Geometry

Based on prior research, we devised a method to designate the point that induces the action of virtual users in an atypical architectural space. Figure 2 describes how to designate information related to the virtual user's behavior. It observes user behavior in an actual atypical space and systematizes information related to the user's behavior (trigger spot, trigger viewpoint, and behavioral area) based on the result. However, it has not been able to propose a specific method for automatically calculating appropriate action points in various forms of unstructured architectural spaces.

3 Method of Tracing a Trigger Spot for Human Behavior Through Voxelization of Atypical Architectural Shapes

3.1 Background Idea of Voxelization

Voxelization is a method of simplifying complex and difficult-to-interpret forms into units and condensing them into forms that can be interpreted. In computer graphics, voxelization is used to systematize disordered forms into unit forms. Since atypical architectural shapes are also difficult to systematically manage, a method of extracting the affordance of space was devised using voxelization.

If the atypical architectural surface is transformed into units of voxels, there is a possibility that the voxel's affordance can be ascertained through the position and relationship of the voxels. Positional types of voxels can be classified based on the geometrical and topological information of voxels. That is, if neighboring voxels maintain the same height, they are likely to form a flat surface. In addition, if the positions of the neighboring voxels are continuously increased, it is highly likely that they are voxels forming a vertical wall. If the height of the neighboring voxel changes rapidly, it is possible that the surface is bent. Using this strategy, the type of voxel can be determined and the affordance for it can be set.

Fig. 3. Voxel classification through voxelization of atypical architectural surfaces. (a) Red voxel: vertical surface. (b) Green voxel: horizontal surface. (c) Yellow voxel: curved floor. (d) Blue voxel: junction between vertical and horizontal surfaces. (Color figure online)

3.2 Implementation of Tracing Trigger Spots Through Voxelization

Figure 3 shows that the positional type of voxels is determined through the voxelization of an atypical architectural surface. Through prior research, we analyzed the psychological causes of user behavior in an atypical architectural space. It was found that there is a high possibility that user behavior occurs in the folded part of the architectural surface [9]. In addition, through field investigation, it was confirmed that behaviors similar to the content of the theoretical analysis appeared in the atypical architectural space. In this study, after subdividing an atypical architectural surface into mesh, the mesh was converted into voxels by comparing the mesh size with a certain unit size. Figure 4 shows the atypical architectural surfaces that were voxelized using such algorithm. Voxelized atypical architectural surfaces were automatically classified into positional types, as shown in Fig. 5. At the yellow spot, where the possibility of inducing action was high, the action was performed in accordance to the surrounding situation.

Fig. 4. Voxelization of atypical architectural shapes. (a) Left: before voxelization. (b) Right: after voxelization.

Fig. 5. Tracing trigger spots through voxelization (Color figure online)

4   Discussion and Conclusion

This study aimed to develop a technology that automatically calculates action points for the advanced human behavior simulation of atypical buildings. In this study, we developed an algorithm to extract the action trigger point by voxelizing a 3D atypical shape.

Through this study, a basic method was devised to automatically find the point of action on a wide and complex atypical architectural surface. However, this merely constitutes a base study, so additional research is required. Overall, it is necessary to classify the relationship with voxels and analyze their meanings more closely to be able to formulate a more sophisticated human behavior simulation.

Acknowledgement. This work was supported by the National Research Foundation of Korea (NRF) grant funded by the Korean government (MSIT) (NRF-2018R1A2B6005827).

References

1. Hong, S., Lee, Y.: The effects of human behavior simulation on architectural major students' fire egress planning. J. Asian Archit. Building Eng. **17**(1), 125–132 (2018)
2. Lee, Y.: A study on the effect of human factor for atypical design in the architectural design studio. Adv. Intell. Syst. Comput. **876**(1), 130–134 (2018)
3. Hong, S., Schaumann, D., Kalay, Y.E.: Human behavior simulation in architectural design projects: an observational study in an academic course. Comput. Environ. Urban Syst. **60**, 1–11 (2016)
4. Simeone, D., Kalay, Y.E., Schaumann, D., Hong, S.: Modeling and simulating use processes in buildings. In: Proceedings of Education and Research in Computer Aided Architectural Design in Europ, pp. 59–66 (2013)
5. Lee, Y.G.: ActoViz: a human behavior simulator for the evaluation of the dwelling performance of an atypical architectural space. In: Stephanidis, C. (ed.) HCII 2019. CCIS, vol. 1034, pp. 361–365. Springer, Cham (2019). https://doi.org/10.1007/978-3-030-23525-3_48
6. Gibson, J.J.: The theory of affordances. In: Shaw, R., Bransford, J. (eds.) Perceiving, Acting, and Knowing: Toward an Ecological Psychology. Lawrence Erlbaum Associates, Hillsdale (1977)
7. Choi, J., Kim, S., Lee, Y.: Developing a building performance simulation environment based on self-animated virtual characters. J. Architectural Institude of Korea **26**(4), 83–90 (2010)
8. Lee, Y., Lee, Y.: Developing an autonomous behavior of virtual users based on psychological interpretation of human behavior to an atypical architectural shape. Int. J. ICT Aided Archit. Civil Eng. **6**(1), 1–6 (2019)
9. Lee, Y., Lee, Y.: Psychological interpretation of human behavior to atypical architectural shape. In: Ahram, T., Karwowski, W., Pickl, S., Taiar, R. (eds.) IHSED 2019. AISC, vol. 1026, pp. 109–114. Springer, Cham (2020). https://doi.org/10.1007/978-3-030-27928-8_18

Research on Visual Cognitive of Museum Guide System Based on Augmented Reality Technology

Qiang Li[✉], Tian Luo, and Jingjing Wang

Shenyang Aerospace University, Shenyang, China
qiangli@sau.edu.cn

Abstract. In order to meet the cognitive needs of visitors to the large and complex space environment in museums and improve the visiting efficiency, a museum guide system based on augmented reality technology is designed. And user's wayfinding time obtained through experiments in three kinds of guide systems, including traditional graphic, static AR and interactive AR guide systems, are compared and analyzed. Finally, through the method of user questionnaire, the clarity, readability and aesthetics of different guide systems are evaluated. The results show that the interactive AR guide system can effectively improve the efficiency of user wayfinding, and provide users with a good visiting experience.

Keywords: Augmented reality · Guide · Museum · Wayfinding · Experience

1 Introduction

As a place for collecting, protecting, researching, disseminating and displaying human and human environmental witnesses for the purpose of research, education and appreciation, museums often have a very large and complex spatial structure [1, 2]. In complex environment, it is considered a difficult task to search specific location, building or environmental facilities [3]. Therefore, as the direction, instruction and guidance of museum space, the guide system can play a vital role in improving the visitors' experience and efficiency of wayfinding. Many scholars believe that users' needs are changing from two-dimensional static experience to more dynamic experience. For example, HU San (2019) proposed that the performance of dynamic visual interactive guidance is significantly better than that of static visual sign guidance [4]. Xinxiang Liu (2012) proposed that the design method of visual guidance should be based on three-dimensional space, supplemented by graphic design, and combine two-dimensional plane information with three-dimensional space display [5]. Changxue Pan (2019) proposed to interact directly with the media through gesture habits to facilitate the expression of users' emotional demands and meet users' needs for guidance services [6]. Therefore, augmented reality technology is considered to be an ideal guidance system solution [7]. Zeya He (2018) proposed that augmented reality technology can effectively improve visitor experience and willingness to pay [8]. Jessie Pallud (2016) found through surveys and interviews that the use of interactive technology can effectively attract visitors and improve their learning experience in museums [9].

© Springer Nature Switzerland AG 2021
C. Stephanidis et al. (Eds.): HCII 2021, CCIS 1420, pp. 284–289, 2021.
https://doi.org/10.1007/978-3-030-78642-7_38

Based on the above analysis, this research proposes two hypotheses: (1) In a museum environment, the efficiency of users using AR guide system is better than that of traditional plane guide system. (2) By AR guide system, the wayfinding efficiency and user experience of interactive guidance are better than static guidance.

2 Research Method and Process

In order to compare the guide efficiency of the AR and the traditional image guidance system, this research adopts the method of experimental measurement and the method of questionnaires and interviews.

2.1 Experiment

Wayfinding time is affected by many factors such as spatial cognition [4]. Therefore, in order to eliminate the influence of environmental space and individual physical conditions, the settings of this experiment are based on flat images. Participants use the traditional graphic, static AR and interactive AR guide system provided by the researcher to make the optimal route decision to the destination specified by the researcher. And draw the optimal route on the same scale map of the place provided by the researcher (see Fig. 1). The time from when the participant receives the guide image to when the participant completes the route drawing is defined as the decision time (t1). The walking speed of all subjects is assumed to be 1.3 m/s, and the researcher calculates the wayfinding time (t2) required by the subjects through the route drawn by the subjects. The participant's decision time and wayfinding time were calculated in seconds.

请绘制出由坐标位置到达 古代辽宁展 (4) 的最佳路线

Fig. 1. Route questionnaire

Experiment Materials. Three kinds of guide system (traditional graphic, static AR and interactive AR) are selected for testing (see Fig. 2). The traditional graphic guide system is the existing guide system of Liaoning Provincial Museum (LPM). The static AR guide system is developed according to the existing guide system of LPM. And it includes the design elements of graphics, font and color, which is consistent with the

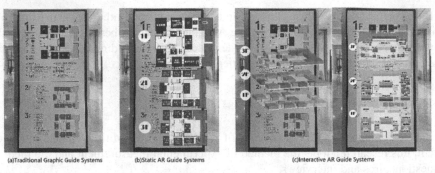

(a)Traditional Graphic Guide Systems   (b)Static AR Guide Systems   (c)Interactive AR Guide Systems

Fig. 2. Three categories of guide system

traditional graphics guide system, and the location and line of sight level of AR logo. The dynamic AR guide system interacts by dragging, rotating, clicking to expand and clicking to recommend the best route.

Participant Selection and Experiment Design. 150 undergraduates were selected as the test subjects. In order to ensure the reliability and validity, all participants were not familiar with the museum space. The participants were divided into three groups, using the graphic guidance, static AR and interactive AR guide system to search the target location. In this experiment, all participants were tested under the same conditions.

Fig. 3. Wayfinding experiment

The experiment was conducted in digital media department of A university. The experimental steps are as follows: (1) The researcher explained the purpose and method of the experiment to the participants. (2) The researcher distributed route questionnaires to three groups of participants. (3) Each participant in different groups were provided with images of traditional guide, static AR guide and interactive AR guide system, and the timing was started. (4) The participants completed the drawing of the best route on the route questionnaires according to their guidance judgment and timing, which was recorded as the decision-making time. (5) According to the route drawn by the subjects, the researchers calculated the distance and the time. (6) Add the decision-making time and wayfinding time to record the completion time of the searching task. The average time of the experiment process was 8 min (see Fig. 3).

2.2 Questionnaire and Interview

After the experiment, 100 participants who used AR guide system were investigated with questionnaires on their satisfaction, and 10 participants were selected from each group as the interview targets. The questionnaire was conducted from 1 (very dissatisfied) to 5 (very satisfied) scales according to the subjective feeling of the subjects. The scale investigated the participants who used AR guide system from four aspects: perceived usefulness, interaction, entertainment and viscosity of key elements of human-computer interaction design.

3 Results and Analysis

3.1 Discussion on Experimental Results

An independent samples T test was conducted for the comparison between the graphic guide system and static AR guide system. As shown in Table 1, the results show that the average task completion time of graphic guide system (M = 156.80) is higher than that of static AR guide system (M = 148.48), and there is a significant difference in task completion time under the guidance of two kinds of guide system (t = 2.282, P = 0.025 < 0.05). As shown in Table 2, the results show that the task completion time of static guide system and interactive guide system in the AR environment is different at the 0.05 significance level (t = 2.618, p = 0.011 < 0.05). Further comparison of the mean values show that the average value of task completion time (M = 148.48) in static AR guide system is higher than in interactive AR guide system (M = 140.40). It can be concluded that interactive AR guide system can effectively improve participants' wayfinding efficiency.

Table 1. Task completion time for graphic guide system and static AR guide system

	Mean (SD)		df	t	p
	Graphic group (N = 50)	Static AR group (N = 50)			
Task completion time	156.80 (17.89)	148.48 (18.56)	98	2.282	0.25

3.2 Discussion of Survey Results

Table 3 shows the evaluation results of static AR and interactive AR group. The average score of four aspects was higher than the average 2.5. Participants considered that the

Table 2. Task completion time of two kinds of guide system in AR environment

	Mean (SD)		df	t	p
	Static AR group (N = 50)	Interactive AR group (N = 50)			
Task completion time	148.48 (18.56)	140.40 (11.47)	81.65	2.618	0.11

interaction of interactive AR guide system was the strongest (4.5), the perceived usefulness of static AR guide system was the weakest (3.0), and the scores of interactive AR guide system were higher than static AR guide system. During the interview, each participant described the sensory experience and expectation of museum guide design in the future. According to the value of key word frequency, the specific results are summarized as follows: (1) 70% of the participants who use graphic guide system believe that they need to judge their position and direction and match the map direction, which will affect the decision time. (2) 90% of the participants who used interactive AR guide system thought they can rotate and adjust the direction and match their own position, and it was unnecessary to judge the position and direction of the destination, which saved a lot of decision time. In the interaction process, the interaction between the hand and the screen focused their attention. (3) More than half of the participants indicated that good interaction effectively improved experience and wayfinding performance. Most of the participants believe that digital technology can serve museums better in future.

Table 3. Satisfaction evaluation

Types	Ratings (Mean)			
	Interactivity	Entertainment	Perceived usefulness	Viscosity
Static AR group	3.6	3.4	3.0	3.2
Interactive AR group	4.5	4.3	3.5	3.8

4 Conclusion

The experience of wayfinding in museum tour plays a key role in the visitor experience. The feasibility of using AR technology in museum guide system and the difference between static guide and AR guide system by using quantitative statistics and qualitative interview methods were discussed. The results show that the efficiency of AR guide system is significantly higher than traditional graphic guide system. And the efficiency and satisfaction of interactive AR guide system are higher than static AR guide system. There are three limitations of this study: (1) The subjects mainly choose the undergraduate students who know about AR technology. (2) Different members of each group have different spatial cognitive ability and visual ability. (3) In the experiment, the route drawing method is chosen to replace the real route finding method. Although it solves the influence of each person's physical condition difference on the experimental results, it also ignores the complexity of the real environment. In the follow-up research, we will improve the experimental environment by expanding the range of subjects and adjusting the inter group test to intra group test, and testing in real museum environment.

Acknowledgement. The work was supported by Liaoning Province Education Department (JYT2020098), Social science development project of Shenyang Federation of Social Sciences (SYSK2020-13-05) and PhD startup fund of Shenyang Aerospace University (20YB15).

References

1. The Statutes of the International Council of Museums Statutes
2. Rui, Z.: The design of museum guidance system based on the concept of space management. Arts Criticism **08**, 90–93 (2015)
3. Iftikhar, H., Shah, P., Luximon, Y.: Human wayfinding behaviour and metrics in complex environments: a systematic literature review. Architectural Science Review, pp. 1–12 (2020)
4. Shan, H., Ming-Yu, Z., Huan, X.: Difference of visual cognition in guiding design. Packag. Eng. **40**(10), 12–17 (2019)
5. Liu, X.: Rigorous analysis of indoor shopping space and visual guidance in hong kong pacific place. Art Des. **07**, 82–83 (2012)
6. Changxue, P., Zhang Weiru, X.: Constructing cruise guidance service system based on visitors' behaviors: taking quantum of the seas as an example. Art Des. **01**, 61–65 + 210 (2019)
7. Han, Y., Lee, H.: Augmented reality signage in mixed-use shopping mall focusing on visual types of directional signage. In: Stephanidis, C., Antona, M., Ntoa, S. (eds.) HCII 2020. CCIS, vol. 1294, pp. 150–155. Springer, Cham (2020). https://doi.org/10.1007/978-3-030-60703-6_19
8. He, Z., Wu, L., Li, X.: When art meets tech: the role of augmented reality in enhancing museum experiences and purchase intentions. Tourism Manag. **68**, 127–139 (2018)
9. Pallud, J.: Impact of interactive technologies on stimulating learning experiences in a museum. Inform. Manag. **54**(4), 465–478 (2016)

The Perception of Avatars in Virtual Reality During Professional Meetings

Britta Nordin Forsberg[1]([envelope]) [iD] and Kathrin Kirchner[2] [iD]

[1] KTH Royal Institute of Technology, Lindstedtsvägen 30, 111 28 Stockholm, Sweden
britta.forsberg@indek.kth.se
[2] Technical University of Denmark, Akademivej, 2800 Kgs. Lyngby, Denmark
kakir@dtu.dk

Abstract. Social Virtual Reality (VR) offers virtual social spaces, where people can meet, collaborate and socialize via head-mounted displays. In VR applications, users can create their own avatars that can control to walk around and interact directly with other users. Recently, social VR gained importance for professional meetings, in order to allow socializing and collaborating during times of travel restrictions. Unlike VR in gaming for the purpose of amusement, where avatars can be fantasy figures, avatars in professional meetings usually look more serious and more like the person behind the avatar. Based on semi-structured interviews in two different scenarios – a conference and a company business meeting – we report about the role and perception of avatars in professional meetings. Our interview results reveal that avatars were perceived differently in both cases. In the conference scenario, avatars were seen as both enablers and obstacles for interaction with other users during the social event. In the company scenario, interviewees did not express any feelings of being restricted in their collaboration with others by the visual appearance of the avatar that represents them.

Keywords: Virtual reality · Avatar · Professional meeting · Socializing · Virtual collaboration

1 Introduction

The usage of virtual solutions for professional meetings have peaked in organizations during the pandemic [1]. Although virtual reality (VR) is not a totally new, but a maturing technology, it is growing in the last years as organizations adopt it for design, data visualization and brainstorming [2].

As a concurrence to video conferences, VR, where users enter 3D-worlds via head mounted devices (HMD), has evolved from being used for on-line gaming to also enabling applications named "social VR". Users do not follow specific rules and story-lines like in games, but instead move and communicate with each other freely. Social VR has the potential to be a substitute to video conferences, since a 3D-space can create a more realistic arena for collaboration [3]. In VR, a character or "avatar" represents a participant. Users can, from a limited set of pre-defined choices, construct an avatar

C. Stephanidis et al. (Eds.): HCII 2021, CCIS 1420, pp. 290–294, 2021.
https://doi.org/10.1007/978-3-030-78642-7_39

that visually represents the user, like a proxy, during participation in the virtual social arena. Being represented by an avatar can give new experiences to the user compared with participating real life or on video conference systems – which might lead to both opportunities and challenges [4]. In gaming scenarios, even fantasy figures can be used as avatars, which is not the case in most professional settings like business meetings and conferences. In this study, we inquire how the usage of avatars as proxy of participants are perceived in professional contexts.

In gaming, the importance of how the avatar is perceived is driven by the logic of the game and the culture of the gamer community. The culture in professional contexts has other drivers. We report two different cases: The first case reports VR use in a social gathering during an online academic conference where participants from different countries did not know each other well and most experienced VR for the first time at this occasion. The second case is a high-tech company where employees meet in VR regularly for different kinds of internal meetings. Based on semi-structured interviews, our research gives insights into the role of avatars to create dynamics in virtual interaction and collaboration in professional meetings.

2   Case: Avatars in a Conference

In the first case, we created a social event in virtual reality at the Scandinavian Academy of Industrial Engineering and Management conference in November 2020 that gathered researchers from Nordic universities. The whole conference was conducted online via Zoom. At the end of the conference day, the two authors of this paper offered a virtual reality (VR) event. Of the 22 participants (including the authors), 17 agreed into an interview about their experiences afterwards, while two reflected on their experience in a group mail-exchange with each other and one of the authors, and one didn't reply on the invitation to an interview.

Most of the participants had not experienced VR before, only some had used it for gaming in the past, but not for professional meetings. Therefore, we offered an onboarding event prior to the conference to try the technology and create an own avatar on the platform. The aim was to create a feeling of security to participate in the real event. Furthermore, an experienced guide was participating in the VR-event to help participants in the virtual arenas and answer questions. Figure 1 shows a screenshot from the social event in one of the virtual arenas where the users gathered as avatars. We investigated how avatars in this VR setting would enable communication or create obstacles in a social event at a conference, which is usually aiming at get to know each other, allow an individual "branding" and establish a new professional connection for further collaboration.

In the preparation of the event, every participant could design an own avatar by choosing among a limited set of choices regarding clothes of different style and color, shoes, body length, body size, style and color of hairstyle, hats, googles and skin-color. It was possible to upload a photo of the user's face. This was used to generate the face of their avatar, but most participants did not do this. In the virtual arena, every avatar was labeled with the user's first name and the country of their university. Being represented by these avatars lead to advantages, but also to challenges when approaching and interacting with others in the virtual space.

Fig. 1. Informal talks in the social event in the virtual world

A participant mentioned that avatars are *"…interfaces between you and the other real person that makes it a little easier to break this ice…"* and to overcome shyness and get in contact with unknown people.

Another participant perceived avatars as difficult to find out who is behind an avatar: *"…you don't really see how old this person is; I cannot go through the room and look for the young PhD student who is similar to me"*. Even with avatars that look more professional like on a usual conference, it was difficult to find people with a similar experience level (as, e.g., PhD students that are mostly of young age). Additionally, *"it could be trickier to build a first time connection, so I was surprised how much harder it felt in the VR environment to talk to people I didn't know"*. The avatars furthermore do not allow to recognize the mood of a person: *"I cannot detect if this person looks kind of grumpy or annoyed"*. This *"…could be an easy way to approach that person, or this person is annoyed and just wants to be left alone"*.

3   Case: Avatars in Internal Professional Meetings

In the second case, we interviewed the high-tech company AdventureBox that have reached a point in their digitalization of internal collaboration where social Virtual Reality (VR) has become a "new normal" to them since three months back in time. The company has 20 employees distributed across the globe and is noted on the Swedish stock exchange.

The semi-structured interview was taking place as a group interview with four organizational members: the CEO, the initiator of social VR in the company and two other employees. Unlike in the first case, the interviewees did not express any obstacles with the visual appearance of avatars. The face of each avatar was based on a photo of the user, which made the avatar's face looks very similar to the user's dito. The interviewees argued that when participants intuitively link the look of the face with the body language of the avatar, it altogether makes up a valid representation of this person as a *"selfie in combination with body language, even a stronger representation that i.e. in Zoom"*. Figure 2 shows a group photo from a professional meeting in the virtual reality where the avatars wear the real faces of the AdventureBox employees.

Fig. 2. Virtual reality meeting at Adventure Box

The employees have managed to go beyond the look of avatars in order to focus on the collaborative process in the 3D virtual arena. They compared social VR with a video conference system, and actually thought that it can be easier to recognize a person being represented by an avatar than in a 2D-window in a video conference call: "It gives a feeling of closeness among the avatars, and among the users as a consequence of this". They suggest the concept of a "stand-up-meeting" in VR as a powerful tool for collaboration: "If you want to have a team-mission and you can't meet people abroad, this is possible in VR - you can give people a feeling of being under the same roof. In a geographically distributed organization, you can created a sense of belonging through "social VR", inclusion. Standup meetings are nicer in VR: it's easier to talk, it's a kind of intuitive".

4   Discussion and Conclusion

Avatars can play different roles in VR worlds. In a medical or rehabilitation context, the virtual body of an avatar can decrease cognitive load and improve motor and cognitive tasks of patients when they follow their avatar in the virtual world [5]. In other scenarios like gaming, users can create themselves a new identity, where they can try out being someone else, like a hero [6]. For scenarios in the social virtual reality it is not known enough about how self-presentation works and how this influences the users' interactivity [4]. Our research contributes to this call for research.

Reflecting on the two cases in this study, there are several dissimilarities in how the different users in the different contexts perceive the avatars in a professional setting; to be represented by an avatar and to interact with other users' avatars in a 3D virtual social or collaborative arena. First, there is an indication that trust and tension are a factors that can be essential elements when it comes to both the expectations on and a perception of the avatars. In the second case, social VR was used for internal collaboration where the participants conveyed that they now each other quite well professionally and they were able to collaborate through their avatars, while in the conference setting, participants did not know each other well. This puts high expectations on the avatars and their interaction – it is a tenser situation. Second, the visual appearance of the avatars, in combination with other "social marks", seems to be even more important in the situation of low trust and high tension, using the desire expressed by PhD students to be able to find other likeminded participants in the conference in case 1. Third, it plays a major role, which type of toolbox a VR platforms offers to construct avatars and how they appear in different kinds of HMDs, using the example that only the upper part of avatars body can be visible. Fourth, there is an aspect of time and change; the time it takes to implement and the "push" that is created – compared with the similar "push" the pandemic has had on the spread of video conferences.

References

1. Viglione, G.: How conferences will survive the coronavirus shock. Nature **582**, 166–167 (2020)
2. PwC. Seeing is believing. How virtual reality and augmented reality are transforming business and economy (2019). https://www.pwc.com/seeingisbelieving
3. Freeman, G., Zamanifard, S., Maloney, D., Adkins, A.: My body, my avatar: how people perceive their avatars in social virtual reality. In: Extended Abstracts of the 2020 CHI Conference on Human Factors in Computing Systems – Proceedings, pp. 1–8 (2020). https://doi.org/10.1145/3334480.3382923
4. Freeman, G., Maloney, D.: Body, avatar, and me: the presentation and perception of self in social virtual reality. In: Proceedings of the ACM on Human-Computer Interaction, pp. 1–27 (2021)
5. Gonzales-Franco, M., Cohn, B., Ofek, E., Burin, D.: The self-avatar follower effect in virtual reality. In: 2020 IEEE Conference on Virtual Reality and 3D User Interfaces (VR), pp. 18–25 (2020)
6. Kim, C., Lee, S.G., Kang, M.: I became an attractive person in the virtual world: users' identification with virtual communities and avatars. Comput. Hum. Behav. **28**, 1663–1669 (2012). https://doi.org/10.1016/j.chb.2012.04.004

Realistic Occlusion of Virtual Objects Using Three-Dimensional Hand Model

Vyacheslav Olshevsky(✉) ⓘ, Ivan Bondarets ⓘ, Oleksandr Trunov ⓘ,
and Artem Shcherbina ⓘ

Samsung R&D Institute Ukraine (SRK), 57 Lva Tolstogo Street, Kyiv 01032, Ukraine
{v.olshevskyi,i.bondarets,a.trunov,a.shcherbina}@samsung.com

Abstract. We develop a method for predicting virtual object occlusions during hand-object interaction in mixed reality. We reconstruct a 3D hand model from a monocular RGB camera frame and use it to predict occlusions. The quality of these occlusions, evaluated using dice coefficient, is at the same level as reported for other depth sensor and hand model based methods. Our model runs in real-time on off-the-shelf smartphone and gives a plausible experience of grabbing, rotating and translating virtual objects, which we confirmed through a dedicated user study. Volume penetration is the main reason for occlusion errors. However, the suitability of the object to the user scenario and its appealing look can compensate for the occlusion errors, and make a positive mixed reality experience.

Keywords: Mixed reality · Hand reconstruction · Occlusion

1 Introduction

User perception of virtual objects in mixed reality (MR) depends crucially on the ability of free-hand interaction with them [1,7,8]. Occlusion is an important visual cue for estimating the proximity of different objects, which comes naturally

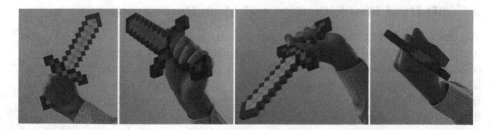

Fig. 1. Occlusion prediction using a reconstructed 3D hand model allows rotating virtual objects in mixed reality at any angle and move them around.

C. Stephanidis et al. (Eds.): HCII 2021, CCIS 1420, pp. 295–301, 2021.
https://doi.org/10.1007/978-3-030-78642-7_40

in the real world. In MR, however, the naturalness of hand-object interaction depends on the quality of the predicted occlusions, obfuscated by the lack of the hand depth information. We address occlusions via reconstruction of the three-dimensional (3D) hand model from a monocular camera image. The proposed method produces plausible occlusions and hand-object interaction at different angles as illustrated in Fig. 1.

Object occlusion is a long-standing problem. In case of static scenes the most popular approach consists in reconstruction of a 3D scene through SLAM algorithms. Object tracking is used to handle occlusions produced by non-deformable real objects. In highly dynamical environments such as hand-object interactions, scene reconstruction has insufficient precision, while tracking can not account for changing hand shape and view angle [3]. The techniques for estimating hand depth and handle occlusions either use depth sensors, stereo cameras, or monocular cameras. The latter techniques are most suitable for smartphone applications, but their usage has been limited because of a high computational cost.

In this work, we propose an occlusion prediction method, based on the hand model reconstruction, which runs in real-time on a smartphone. A 3D hand model is deduced from a single RGB camera frame, and the occlusion mask is computed from it. Feng et al. [3] have shown that occlusions, obtained in a similar way, have superior quality compared to the ones deduced by the Cost Volume Filtering [8], in terms of the reprojection error. Tang et al. [7] predicted occlusions directly, without hand model/depth reconstruction, and found them to be better than the occlusions based on the hand model [4], in terms of dice coefficient for predicted occlusion.

Our method reconstructs a full 3D model of the hand, hence it is more versatile than the direct occlusion prediction [7]. For instance, our method is easy to extend for casting realistic hand shadows. Unlike [3], we are able to reconstruct two hands in real-time on off-the-shelf smartphones. We have evaluated the proposed technique qualitatively using the occlusion dice coefficient. The occlusion quality of our method is on the same level with other present-day techniques. In addition, we have conducted a study which confirms the resulting MR experience is plausible to users.

2   Method

2.1   3D Hand Pose Estimation and Mesh Reconstruction

We employ a widely used 3D kinematic hand model which consists of 21 hand joints [5]. Our hand model reconstruction framework is based on a sequence of convolutional neural networks (CNNs). A Single Shot Detector [6] is used to localize user's hands on a frame from a monocular camera. A region of the camera frame containing the hand is then passed to the dedicated CNN which outputs 21 heatmaps of hand joints, parameters of the 3D kinematic hand model, and a semantic segmentation map. Additional small CNNs are used to verify the hand detection and find the left/right side of the hand. A template matching tracker [2] is used when the hand detector is unnecessary, to optimize the processing speed.

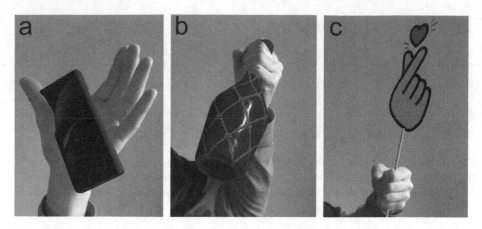

Fig. 2. Three objects that are used for this study in addition to Sword: Phone, Bottle, and Heart Sign.

Virtual hand mesh is recovered from the reconstructed 3D hand model following the approach of Zhang et al. [9]. Virtual objects are rendered as if they are occluded by the mesh and augmented into the real-world picture. The hand model reconstruction and 3D mesh generation for two hands performs at 30 frames per second on off-the-shelf smartphones such as Samsung Galaxy Note 10, used in this study.

2.2 Implementation

To evaluate our approach qualitatively and quantitatively we have developed an Android smartphone app which mimics simple hand-object interactions. A user can hold a virtual object, rotate it and move it anywhere in the camera field of view using a bare hand. Virtual object is augmented into the frame obtained from the smartphone's front camera and displayed on the screen. The virtual object appears when the user makes a grip hand pose, e.g., as shown in Figs. 1 and 2. The object is then rigidly bound to the specific joints of the kinematic hand model and can be rotated and translated with the hand. The object disappears when the user loosens the grip. This rather simple scenario allows, nevertheless, to study object occlusions during hand-object interaction at all possible distances and angles.

3 Evaluation

We have picked four virtual objects that are entertaining and convenient in the proposed scenario: Sword (Fig. 1), Phone, Bottle, and Heart Sign, shown in Fig. 2. We evaluated our method quantitatively using the occlusion dice coefficient metrics, and qualitatively via a user study. A Samsung Galaxy Note 10 smartphone was used in both experiments.

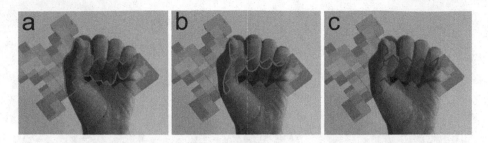

Fig. 3. An example of labelling used for dice coefficient estimation. The ground truth (a), the computed occlusion mask (b), the intersection of the above two regions (c). The 3D hand model is shown with a semi-transparent yellow color. (Color figure online)

3.1' Accuracy Evaluation

We evaluate the occlusions quantitatively in the following way. A semi-transparent virtual object and a 3D hand model are rendered on the screen during user interaction. The video from the screen is recorded, manually labeled, and then occlusion dice coefficients are computed for all labelled frames. The dice coefficient (F1 score) between the ground truth occlusion mask T and the generated occlusion mask M is computed over the intersection of the hand with the virtual object

$$D = \frac{2\,|T \cap M|}{|T \cup M|}. \tag{1}$$

The three regions are depicted in Fig. 3: the ground truth occlusion mask (where the real hand occludes the virtual object) T is green, the computed occlusion mask (where the 3D hand model occludes the object) M is red, and their intersection $T \cap M$ is blue.

We recorded 16 videos, in which four different users manipulated each of four virtual objects. Users were asked to rotate and translate the objects in different directions randomly, to ensure the occlusions happened at all possible angles. Users spent about 3 minutes of their time per object. One in 50 frames in each video was manually labelled to delineate the three zones: the ground truth occlusion, the predicted occlusion, and their intersection (Fig. 3). In total, we obtained about 100 labeled images per object (Table 1).

We compute the dice score according to Eq. 1 using the number of pixels in each labelled region, and average over all frames for the given object (Table 1). Bottle and Heart Sign exhibit $D \geq 0.85$, which compares to the best of results cited in [7] for depth sensor and hand model based occlusion models. Although we use a different set of objects, we can not directly compare the numbers, but our objects have similar grips and sizes to those used in [7].

The Sword and Phone objects give $D < 0.8$. These objects are larger than Bottle and Heart Sign, demanding a wider grip. Therefore, it is easier for the user to suddenly change the grip, or form a wrong grip, thus corrupt the occlusion. A similar problem was observed by Battisti et al. [1]. In their experiments, the hand penetrated into the virtual object due to undefined physical constraints of the object volume. Tang et al. [7] also came across this issue and dubbed it 'hand-object penetration problem'.

Table 1. Occlusion dice coefficients for different objects.

Object	No. of frames	Dice coefficient
Phone	105	0.797
Bottle	102	0.847
Heart Sign	93	0.890
Sword	98	0.755

3.2 User Study

For qualitative evaluation of our method, we conducted a user study. It involved 12 volunteers (7 females), aged $27 - 68$ (40 on average). Four subjects indicated they had no previous experience with augmented or virtual reality. Five participants had technical, while the rest – non-technical background. After a short introduction, a participant was given a smartphone where our Android app had been launched. The user was asked to freely interact with each of the four objects, in any order, for as long as he or she liked to. Normally 10 minutes was enough for users to experience each virtual object at all possible distances (obviously, limited by the span of user's hands and camera field of view) and various angles.

After that users answered the following questions using a 4-point Likert scale from -2 (very bad) to 2 (very good).

1. How realistic do the virtual objects fit in your hand?
2. How natural is the interaction with the virtual objects?

And rate the overall experience (appearance and interaction naturalness) with each object on a 5-point scale, from -2 (completely dislike) to 2 (like a lot).

More than one-half of all participants have positively rated both the occlusion quality (appearance of the virtual objects in hands) and the naturalness of interaction (rotation and translation) in the proposed mixed-reality scenario as shown in Fig. 4a. The correlation between assessed naturalness and appearance ranking is only 0.46, i.e., many users who liked the quality of predicted occlusions at the same time disapproved of the quality of interaction experience. Hence, both factors are important for the best mixed reality experience for the broad audience.

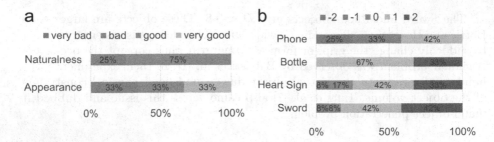

Fig. 4. Quiz results. a) Users rating of the overall mixed reality experience: the naturalness of hand-object interactions and the appearance of object occlusions. b) Relative comparison of the overall experience (both interaction and appearance) with different objects.

Three objects, Bottle, Heart Sign, and Sword made mostly positive impression (Fig. 4b). The Phone was disliked by most participants. It requires the widest grip, and is rigidly locked with the wrist, which makes occlusions look unnatural due to the penetration of fingers into the virtual volume. Interestingly though, that another virtual object, Sword, was liked by the 84% of the audience despite the analogous volume penetration problem (see Table 1). The informal feedback, collected from users after the study, suggests that the rigid binding to the palm is a severe limitation of the smartphone grip compared to the everyday experience. While most users mentioned that the Sword looked fun and was very natural to operate.

4   Conclusion and Discussion

We have proposed a real-time hand occlusion prediction method for augmented and mixed reality on smartphones, and evaluated it for simple object interactions: rotation and translation. The quality of occlusions, measured in terms of the dice coefficient is object-dependent, and is worse for the objects that require a wider grip due to penetration problem. However, the overall user impression from interacting with an object does not solely depend on the quality of occlusions. The suitability of the object to the scenario, its usefulness and appearance are highly important for the satisfactory MR experience.

Other authors have indicated that hand model based occlusion prediction is more precise and versatile than, e.g., depth sensor based methods. However, due to its computational complexity, it has never been studied on smartphones. Our contribution shows the feasibility of this approach, and opens new directions to make the smartphone MR experience more immersive, for instance, by realistic hand shadow prediction.

This study allowed to outline possible directions for future work on improvement of hand-object interaction in MR. First of all, it is a physics-based interaction between the hand model and the object, which will alleviate the penetration problem. The second important improvement is adaptation of the hand model optimization algorithm [3], which uses semantic segmentation to improve the 3D hand model. This will stabilize the hand model and improve occlusion quality.

References

1. Battisti, C., Messelodi, S., Poiesi, F.: Seamless bare-hand interaction in mixed reality. In: 2018 IEEE International Symposium on Mixed and Augmented Reality Adjunct (ISMAR-Adjunct), pp. 198–203 (2018). https://doi.org/10.1109/ISMAR-Adjunct.2018.00066
2. Chantara, W., Mun, J.H., Shin, D.W., Ho, Y.: Object tracking using adaptive template matching. IEIE Trans. Smart Process. Comput. **4**, 1–9 (2015)
3. Feng, Q., Shum, H.P.H., Morishima, S.: Resolving hand-object occlusion for mixed reality with joint deep learning and model optimization. Comput. Anim. Virtual Worlds **31**(4–5) (2020). https://doi.org/10.1002/cav.1956
4. Ge, L., et al.: 3D hand shape and pose estimation from a single RGB image. In: 2019 IEEE/CVF Conference on Computer Vision and Pattern Recognition (CVPR), pp. 10825–10834 (2019). https://doi.org/10.1109/CVPR.2019.01109
5. Lee, J., Kunii, T.L.: Model-based analysis of hand posture. IEEE Comput. Graph. Appl. **15**(5), 77–86 (1995). https://doi.org/10.1109/38.403831
6. Liu, W., et al.: SSD: single shot MultiBox detector. In: Leibe, B., Matas, J., Sebe, N., Welling, M. (eds.) ECCV 2016. LNCS, vol. 9905, pp. 21–37. Springer, Cham (2016). https://doi.org/10.1007/978-3-319-46448-0_2
7. Tang, X., Hu, X., Fu, C.W., Cohen-Or, D.: GrabAR: occlusion-aware grabbing virtual objects in AR. In: Proceedings of the 33rd Annual ACM Symposium on User Interface Software and Technology, UIST 2020, pp. 697–708. Association for Computing Machinery, New York (2020). https://doi.org/10.1145/3379337.3415835
8. Walton, D.R., Steed, A.: Accurate real-time occlusion for mixed reality. In: Proceedings of the 23rd ACM Symposium on Virtual Reality Software and Technology, VRST 2017. Association for Computing Machinery, New York (2017). https://doi.org/10.1145/3139131.3139153
9. Zhang, X., Li, Q., Zhang, W., Zheng, W.: End-to-end hand mesh recovery from a monocular RGB image. CoRR abs/1902.09305 (2019). http://arxiv.org/abs/1902.09305

Preliminary Findings from a Single Session of Virtual Reality Attentional Bias Modification Training in Healthy Women

Bruno Porras-Garcia[✉], Alana Singh, Helena Miquel, Marta Ferrer-Garcia, Sergio Lopez, Guillem Hopmans, Jesus Fleta, and José Gutiérrez-Maldonado

Department of Clinical Psychology and Psychobiology, University of Barcelona, Passeig de la Vall d'Hebron, 171, 08035 Barcelona, Spain
brporras@ub.edu

Abstract. A growing body of research has tried to modify automatic cognitive mechanisms, for instance body-related attentional bias (AB), in eating disorders (EDs). This study provides preliminary findings of an innovative body-related AB modification task using virtual reality (VR) and eye-tracking technologies. It aims to provide further information about other possible body-related variables that might influence the effectiveness of these interventions. Particularly, it assesses whether body image disturbances reported by healthy women are significant predictors of worse intervention outcomes. Twenty-six women participated in the study. Body dissatisfaction, body distortion levels and body-related AB were measured before and after a single session of the VR-AB modification task. All participants were embodied in a virtual avatar with their real measurements and underwent the task for 30 min. AB measures included the number of fixations and complete fixation time on weight-related areas of interest and were recorded using an eye-tracking device incorporated in the VR head-mounted display. Paired sample t-test analyses did not show any significant ($p > .05$) reduction in ED measures (including body-related AB and body image disturbances) after the intervention. Pearson correlation and linear regression analyses revealed that body distortion and body dissatisfaction significantly predicted a lower reduction of an AB levels toward weight-related body areas after the intervention. Our results suggest that body image disturbances may play a critical role in the effectiveness of AB modification training in a non-clinical sample. The combination of VR and eye-tracking technologies might open a wide range of possibilities for designing and developing new body-related interventions that aim to gradually retrain automatic body-related attentional processes in patients with EDs.

Keywords: Anorexia nervosa · Virtual reality body exposure · Full body illusion · Fear of gaining weight · Body image

1 Introduction

A phenomenon known as attentional bias (AB) describes the propensity to pay more attention to certain types of stimuli or information (e.g., disorder-relevant information)

© Springer Nature Switzerland AG 2021
C. Stephanidis et al. (Eds.): HCII 2021, CCIS 1420, pp. 302–309, 2021.
https://doi.org/10.1007/978-3-030-78642-7_41

than other sorts of information (Williamson et al. 2004). Previous studies have shown that in adult women with high body dissatisfaction and patients with eating disorders (EDs) this AB manifests as a tendency to focus more on self-reported unattractive body parts than other body parts (Jansen et al. 2005; Tuschen-Caffier et al. 2015; Bauer 2017).

Although there is a large body of research that assesses the presence of AB in EDs, very little has been done so far to apply the information obtained to improve the efficacy of available treatments. For example, mirror exposure is frequently used to intensify/enhance traditional cognitive behavioral therapy. However, its application is mainly aimed at the extinction of negative cognitive, emotional and behavioral responses to the self, rather than direct modification of attentional processes (Renwick et al. 2013).

AB modification training (ABMT) on the body has not yet been explored in patients with EDs, and only one study has been conducted with women who have high body dissatisfaction (Smeets and Jansen, & Roefs 2011). Dysfunctional body-related AB may be responsible for decreasing the effectiveness of body exposure-based treatments, as some patients may tend to avoid or look excessively at self-reported unattractive body areas, which interferes with the exposure-based task. Thus, new treatment techniques need to be developed by adding specific components designed to reduce body-related AB.

The main aim of this study is to develop an innovative body-related ABMT, using virtual reality (VR) and eye-tracking (ET) technologies. This study provides preliminary findings of a single session of ABMT among healthy women. Further information about other possible body-related variables that might influence the effectiveness of this intervention is provided by assessing whether body image disturbances reported by healthy women are significant predictors of intervention outcomes.

2 Method

2.1 Sample

This study was approved by the ethics committee of the University of Barcelona. The sample was composed of 26 undergraduate women ($M_{age} = 21.48$, $SD = 1.01$, $M_{BMI} = 21.66$, $SD = 2.36$) at the University of Barcelona, recruited through campus flyers and advertisements in social network groups. The exclusion criteria were a self-reported diagnosis of a current ED, a body mass index (BMI) of less than 17 (moderate thinness) or more than 30 (obesity; according to the World Health Organization [2004]), or a self-reported current severe mental disorder diagnosis (e.g., schizophrenia or bipolar disorder). Each participant was given an identification code to guarantee the confidentiality of the data.

2.2 Measures

Before starting the task (pre-evaluation) and at the end (post-evaluation), the following measures were assessed.

Body Image Disturbances Measures. Figural Drawing Scale for Body-Image Assessment (BIAS-BD; Gardner et al. 2009): this questionnaire allows the use of physical anthropometric dimensions of adult women and men by providing a series of human silhouettes. The questionnaire consists of two versions (A and B), each of which provides a different randomization of silhouettes to avoid an order effect bias. Participants were instructed to select one silhouette that they perceived as their current body size (perceived silhouette), and one that they wanted to have (desired body size). Afterwards, the participants' real silhouette was assessed according to their BMI. Body dissatisfaction (BIAS-O) was evaluated by calculating the discrepancy between perceived and desired body sizes. Body distortion (BIAS-X) was assessed by calculating the discrepancy between perceived and real body sizes. This questionnaire has good psychometric properties, with good test-retest reliability ($r = 0.86$) and good concurrent validity ($r = 0.76$) (Gardner et al. 2009).

AB Measures. In accordance with the Weight Scale body items of the Physical Appearance State and Trait Anxiety Scale questionnaire (PASTAS, Reed et al. 1991), the same areas of interest (AOIs) were individually drawn onto a 2D frontal view picture of the female avatar and were labeled as weight-related body parts (W-AOIs): i.e., thighs, buttocks, hips, stomach, legs and waist. The participant's visual fixation, defined as the visual act of sustaining one's gaze on a single location over a minimum duration (typically 100–200 ms) (Jacob and Karn 2003), was estimated by the following variables:

– *Number of fixations on W-AOIs (NF)*: number of available fixations on the specified area of interest group (i.e., weight-related AOIs).
– *Complete fixation time on W-AOIs (CFT)*: sum of the fixation duration at the specified area of interest group (i.e., weight-related AOIs) in milliseconds.

2.3 Instruments

Participants were exposed to an immersive virtual environment using a VR head-mounted display (HTC-PRO Eye) with a precise ET included (Tobii ET). In addition to the two controllers that HTC-PRO usually provides, three additional body trackers were used to achieve full body motion tracking. A young female avatar wearing a basic white t-shirt with blue jeans and black trainers was created. The avatar also wore a swim cap to avoid any influence of hairstyle. The virtual environment consisted of a room with a large mirror on the front wall. The mirror was large enough to reflect every limb of the body and was placed 1.5 m in front of the patients.

2.4 Procedure

The virtual avatar was generated by taking a frontal and lateral photo of the participant. To match the silhouette of the avatar to the actual silhouette of the participant, different parts of the pictures were adjusted. Simultaneously, the other researchers administered the pre-assessment questionnaires and answered the patient's questions. Next, the full body illusion (FBI) was induced over the virtual body (i.e., to perceive and regard a virtual body as their own real body) using two procedures: visuo-motor and visuo-tactile stimulation. Both procedures lasted three minutes (see Fig. 1).

Fig. 1. Pictures of the procedures to induce a full body illusion

Once the FBI was induced, the participants' gaze was tracked while they were asked to observe their virtual body in the mirror for 30 s, to assess body-related AB. During this process, and as a cover story, participants were told to stand still and avoid abrupt head movements while the virtual avatar position was being recalibrated.

The ABMT was based on an adaptation of the AB induction procedure proposed by Smeets and Jansen (2011). The training was developed through the visual selection of geometric figures (e.g., square, rectangle and circle) that fitted approximately with specific parts of the participant's body. Each of these figures had different colors. Participants were instructed to detect and identify the figures that appeared in different parts of the avatar's body (Fig. 2). In 45% of the trials, the geometric figures appeared on weight-related body parts, in another 45% of the trials the figures appeared on non-weight-related body parts. In the remaining trials (10%) the figures appeared on three neutral stimuli located next to the avatar (Fig. 2).

Fig. 2. Attentional bias modification training through virtual reality

2.5 Statistical Analyses

The analysis software Ogama (Open Gaze Mouse Analyzer) was used to transform the eye-tracking raw data into suitable quantitative data. The outcome of the intervention, including the AOIs data, was analyzed by the statistical software IBM SPSS Statistics v.25. Paired sample t-test analyses were run to assess differences before and after the ABMT in all measures. Furthermore, Pearson correlation analyses and simple regression analyses were run to assess whether higher body image disturbances prior to the task predicted a lower reduction of body-related AB levels after the intervention. To achieve this, additional data transformation was conducted by subtracting the difference between AB toward weight-related AOIs measures before and after the intervention (differences in CFT pre - CFT post, and NF pre-NF post).

3 Results

Paired sample t-test analyses did not show any significant ($p > .05$) reduction of ED measures (including body-related AB and body image disturbances) after the intervention (see Table 1).

Table 1. Pre- and post-intervention results

Measures	Pre-intervention M(SD)	Post-intervention M (SD)	Paired sample t-test	
			t	p
BIAS-O	8.40 (20.19)	11.00 (12.82)	−0.80	.430
BIAS-X	10.60 (16.41)	15.80 (9.97)	−1.589	.125
NF-W	22.60 (13.61)	22.00 (12.65)	0.816	.422
CFT-W	5336 (3806)	5190 (4994)	0.146	.885

Note: BIAS-X = body distortion, BIAS-O = body dissatisfaction, NF = Number of fixations, CFT = Complete fixation time on weight (W) areas of interest

However, Pearson correlation analyses showed statistically significant ($p < .05$) positive correlations between pre-intervention body-image disturbance measures and the difference between pre-and post-intervention in complete fixation time (Table 2).

Table 2. Pearson correlation analyses

	Difference CFT (pre-post)	Difference NF (pre-post)	BIAS-X pre	BIAS-O pre
Difference CFT (pre-post)				
Difference NF (pre-post)	0.696**			
BIAS-X pre	− 0.390*	− 0.289		
BIAS-O pre	− 0.369*	− 0.194	0.668**	

Note: BIAS-X = body distortion, BIAS-O = body dissatisfaction, CFT = complete fixation time, NF = number of fixations. *p value < .05, **p value < .01

Finally, linear regression analyses showed that having higher body distortion levels before the intervention marginally predicted a lower reduction of an AB toward weight-related body parts after the intervention (only at complete fixation time, $F(1,24) =$

4.125, p = 0.05). This accounted for 15% of the explained variability. Having higher body dissatisfaction levels before the intervention also marginally significantly predicted a lower reduction of an AB toward weight-related body parts after the intervention (only at complete fixation time, $F(1,24) = 4.564$, p = 0.07), which accounted for 13% of the explained variability (see Fig. 3).

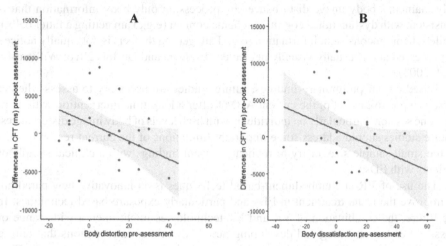

Fig. 3. Scatter plot assessing the linear relation between body distortion (a) and body dissatisfaction (b) values before the intervention, and the difference before and after the intervention in complete fixation time toward weight-related body parts.

4 Discussion

This study presented an innovative ABMT procedure using a combination of VR and ET technologies. Although research on the presence of AB in body image disturbances is extensive, very little has been done so far to apply the information obtained to improve the efficacy of available treatments.

The current preliminary findings indicated that there were no significant reductions in ED or AB measures after the ABMT. These findings are partially in line with those reported by Smeets et al. (2011), in which exposure to all body areas in a group of healthy women with body dissatisfaction did not lead to an increase in body satisfaction. However, the authors reported that when these women were trained to focus only on the three most attractive body parts, there was an increase in their body satisfaction levels (Smeets et al. 2011). Nonetheless, some methodological differences should be considered for both studies. First, the current study was conducted using a combination of VR and ET technologies, while the study Smeets and Jansen (Smeets et al. 2011) employed a computer-based task. In addition, our ABMT procedure was adapted to produce a balanced distribution of attention to body parts (i.e., weight and non-weight related body areas), instead of paying more attention to a specific group of body areas (e.g., attractive vs. unattractive) as in the other study.

Our results also suggest that body image disturbances may play a critical role in the effectiveness of AB modification training, even in a non-clinical sample. Higher body distortion and body dissatisfaction before the task significantly predicted a lower reduction of AB levels toward weight-related body areas, after the intervention. Previous research suggests a bidirectional relationship between body image disturbances and body-related AB (Rodgers and DuBois 2016). Dysfunctional body-related AB presumably maintains body image disturbances by processing only body information that is consistent with dysfunctional cognitive schema content (e.g., I am getting a fatter belly), while schema-inconsistent information (e.g., I am getting thinner) is not equally noticed or processed and is usually visually neglected (Rodgers and DuBois 2016; Williamson et al. 2004).

Based on our preliminary findings, future studies are necessary to assess whether there is a positive effect of the current ABMT after a long-time intervention with more than one session, particularly on individuals with high levels of body image disturbances. Future studies should address some important limitations of the current research, such as the small sample size, or try to replicate current findings with a clinical sample of patients with EDs.

The use of VR and embodiment-based techniques is an innovative new paradigm to improve the usual treatment in EDs and particularly exposure-based techniques. In the future, the combination of VR and ET technologies might open a wide range of possibilities for designing and developing new body-related interventions that aim to gradually retrain automatic body-related attentional processes in patients with EDs. These ABMTs may even be displayed in a wide range of emotionally salient situations for the patients (e.g., in a clothing shop, on the beach, in front of peers, etc.) or with a virtual body that gradually increases in weight.

Funding. This study was funded by the Spanish Ministry of Science and Innovation (Ministerio de Ciencia e Innovación, Spain/Project PID2019-108657RB-I00: Modification of attentional bias, with virtual reality, for improving anorexia nervosa treatment) and by AGAUR, Generalitat de Catalunya, 2017SGR1693.

References

Williamson, D.A., White, M.A., York-Crowe, E., Stewart, T.M.: Cognitive-behavioral theories of eating disorders. Behav. Modif. **28**, 711–738 (2004). https://doi.org/10.1177/0145445503259853

Jansen, A., Nederkoorn, C., Mulkens, S.: Selective visual attention for ugly and beautiful body parts in eating disorders. Behav. Res. Ther. **43**(2), 183–196 (2005). https://doi.org/10.1016/j.brat.2004.01.003

Tuschen-Caffier, B., Bender, C., Caffier, D., Klenner, K., Braks, K., Svaldi, J.: Selective visual attention during mirror exposure in anorexia and bulimia nervosa. PLoS ONE, **10**(12), e0145886 (2015). https://doi.org/10.1371/journal.pone.0145886

Bauer, A., et al.: Selective visual attention towards oneself and associated state body satisfaction: an eye-tracking study in adolescents with different types of eating disorders. J. Abnorm. Child Psychol. **45**(8), 1647–1661 (2017). https://doi.org/10.1007/s10802-017-0263-z

Smeets, E., Jansen, A., Roefs, A.: Bias for the (un)attractive self: On the role of attention in causing body (dis)satisfaction. Health Psychol. **30**, 360–367 (2011). https://doi.org/10.1037/a0022095

Gardner, R.M., Jappe, L.M., Gardner, L.: Development and validation of a new figural drawing scale for body-image assessment: the BIAS-BD. J. Clin. Psychol. **65**(1), 113–122 (2009)

Renwick, B., Campbell, I. C., Schmidt, U.: Review of attentional bias modification: a brain-directed treatment for eating disorders. Eur. Eating Disord. Rev. **21**(6), 464–474 (2013). https://doi.org/10.1002/erv.2248

Reed, D.L., Thompson, J.K., Brannick, M.T., Sacco, W.P.: Development and validation of the Physical Appearance State and Trait Anxiety Scale (PASTAS). J. Anxiety Disord. **5**, 323–332 (1991). https://doi.org/10.1016/08876185(91)90032-O

Jacob, R.J.K., Karn, K.S.: Eye tracking in human-computer interaction and usability research. ready to deliver the promises. In: Hyönä, J., Radach, R., Deubel, H. (eds). The Mind's Eye: Cognitive and Applied Aspects of Eye Movement Research, pp. 573–605. Elsevier Science, Amsterdam (2003) https://doi.org/10.1016/B978-044451020-4/50031-1

Rodgers, R.F., DuBois, R.H.: Cognitive biases to appearance-related stimuli in body dissatisfaction: a systematic review. Clin. Psychol. Rev. **46**, 1–11 (2016). https://doi.org/10.1016/j.cpr.2016.04.006

Portable Virtual Reality-Based Mirror Visual Feedback System for Home Rehabilitation

Beatriz Rey[1]([✉]) [ID], Alejandro Oliver[1], and Jose M. Monzo[2] [ID]

[1] Departamento de Ingeniería Gráfica, Universitat Politècnica de València, Camino Vera s/n, 46022 Valencia, Spain
bareyso@dig.upv.es, alolomol1@alumni.upv.es
[2] Instituto de Instrumentación Para Imagen Molecular (I3M), Centro Mixto CSIC—Universitat Politècnica de València, Camino Vera, s/n, 46022 Valencia, Spain
jmonfer@upvnet.upv.es

Abstract. Mirror visual feedback (MVF) is an ownership illusion that has been applied to manipulate the corporal schema in different kinds of patients. The affected limb is hidden behind a mirror, while the patient observes in the mirror the reflected image of the healthy limb, making him/her believe that it is the affected one. The goal of the present work is to develop a VR-based MVF application that can be used for home rehabilitation, complementing the sessions that take place in the hospital or therapist's office. In the developed application, the patient visualizes the environment from an egocentric perspective, seated in front of a table where a cube appears at specific moments. The exercise consists of grabbing the cube and moving it to another location. This movement is performed only with the healthy hand, although virtual movements can be observed in both hands. With VR, highly immersive experiences can be created and MVF parameters can be manipulated as needed, which is not possible with a real mirror. These factors, combined with the use of a stand-alone system, make the developed system highly suitable for MVF home rehabilitation.

Keywords: Virtual reality · Mirror visual feedback · Motor training

1 Introduction

Mirror visual feedback (MVF) [1] is an ownership illusion that has been applied to manipulate the corporal schema in different kinds of patients, such as patients with pain syndrome [2], stroke [3] or phantom limb pain [4]. The affected limb is hidden behind a mirror, while the patient observes in the mirror the reflected image of the healthy limb. That makes him/her believe that the reflected movements from the healthy limb are from the affected one.

Recent studies have proposed the use of Virtual Reality (VR), instead of the physical mirror, to provide the visual feedback needed in this illusion [5–8]. Two VR-related technologies are especially relevant for this application: head-mounted displays (HMDs) and motion capture or tracking systems [9]. HMDs generate stereoscopic images that

© Springer Nature Switzerland AG 2021
C. Stephanidis et al. (Eds.): HCII 2021, CCIS 1420, pp. 310–315, 2021.
https://doi.org/10.1007/978-3-030-78642-7_42

can be presented to the patients creating immersive experiences while isolating their vision from the real world. That way, the patient will only visualize the virtual hands that are included in the virtual environment. On the other hand, tracking devices are used to register the patients' real movements and assign them to those of an avatar in the virtual world. In VR-based MVF, the movements from the healthy arm are registered and this information is used as the basis to move the hands of the virtual model.

In recent years, many VR devices have arrived to the mass-market and enabled the use of this technology at home. That will make possible that procedures such as VR-based MVF, that has been traditionally applied in hospitals, rehabilitation centers and research facilities, can be applied in home-based rehabilitation.

The goal of the present work is to develop a VR-based MVF application for upper limbs that can be used for home rehabilitation, complementing the sessions that take place in the hospital or therapist's office.

2 Materials and Methods

2.1 Hardware

The application has been developed for Oculus Quest 2, a stand-alone VR system that allows its use at home without needing any additional hardware. It has a resolution of 1832 × 1920 pixels per eye, a refresh rate up to 90 Hz. It comes with two Oculus Touch controllers with several buttons. The position and orientation of the head mounted display and the controllers are tracked with an inside out optical system.

2.2 Software

The VR application has been developed using the real-time 3D engine Unity 3D, with the Oculus Integration tools to connect and interact with the Oculus Quest 2 headset and Oculus Touch Controllers.

2.3 VR Application

The virtual environment is a room, with a window and a door, and several pieces of furniture, including two tables, a sofa, shelves with books and a lamp. The environment can be visualized in Fig. 1. The patient visualizes the environment from an egocentric point of view, seated in front of a table.

The application has been programmed to let the participant perform a simple exercise with the virtual mirror hand (moving a cube from an initial to a final location) in a repetitive way, according to the configuration parameters included in an input file.

Input Parameters. The application reads the input parameters from an xml file. In this file, several configuration parameters that are needed for running the application are included: the healthy hand (left/right), the virtual hands that are shown in the virtual environment (left, right or both) and the different iterations of the task with the time between each pair of consecutive iterations. The parameters with their possible values are summarized in Table 1.

Fig. 1. Virtual environment used for the application.

Table 1. Configuration parameters that are included in the input xml file. The exercise iteration and time between iteration parameters are repeated as many times as iterations of the exercise are included in the training protocol

Parameter	Values
Healthy hand	Left/Right
Virtual hands	Left/Right/Both
Exercise Iteration (x n)	Integer number
Time between iterations (x n)	Time in seconds between an iteration and the next one

Exercise. The exercise consists of grabbing a cube that appears on the table and moving it to another place marked with a square on the table (the procedure can be observed in Fig. 2). Only the controller corresponding to the healthy hand that is indicated in the input file will be used.

To grab the cube, the participant should press and hold the grab button of the controller. In order to leave the cube, the button should be released.

Fig. 2. User grabbing a cube inside the virtual environment. Images corresponding to the left and right eye are shown.

Training Protocol. Several configurations and training protocols can be defined depending on the information included in the input file.

A possible configuration will be to show only the mirror hand in virtual reality. In this case, the patient will move the healthy hand in the real world, but in the virtual environment the exercise will be performed in a mirror way with the opposite hand.

Another possible configuration is to perform the exercise in the real world with the selected hand while, in the virtual environment, the movements can be observed in both hands. The active hand will reproduce its real-world movements, while the other hand will reproduce the mirror movements.

In both cases, a learning curve is expected, as the patient should learn to control the virtual hand with the movements of the opposite hand. Several repetitions of the exercise will be performed as detailed in the input file.

The cube will appear on the table in the moments corresponding to the different iterations and will disappear when it is correctly placed in its final location. If the participant leaves the cube before reaching the final location, the cube will return to the initial point. If the participant cannot successfully finish the task, the cube will disappear when the next iteration starts (and the next cube appears).

The session will finish when the different iterations have been performed.

Output Information. Information regarding the performance of each iteration will be saved in an output file at the end of the session. The included parameters for each iteration are detailed in Table 2.

Table 2. Information included in the output file for each iteration of the exercise.

Parameter	Description
Success (Yes / No)	It indicates if the iteration has been successfully finished
Maximum hand height (cm)	Maximum height of the hand during the trajectory
Reaching time (s)	Elapsed time to grab the cube (since the iteration start)
Holding time (s)	Time holding the cube
Task time (s)	Time until the cube disappears (since the iteration start)
Grabbing number	Number of times the cube is grabbed by the participant
Mean hand velocity (m/s)	Mean hand velocity during the iteration
Maximum hand velocity (m/s)	Maximum hand velocity during the iteration

3 Results and Conclusions

In the present work, a VR-based MVF prototype has been developed and it is in the process of being tested with volunteers. The main contribution of the current application is that it can be run in a stand-alone VR system, without requiring a computer or any additional hardware. Thus, it can be easily applied in the context of a home-based rehabilitation.

VR allows the creation of highly immersive experiences, required to generate embodiment [10]. This concept can be defined as a procedure that applies VR hardware and software to substitute the person body by a virtual one, usually with the goal of generating subjective illusions of body ownership and agency [11]. Body ownership is the illusory perception that a person can have that a virtual body of part of this virtual body belongs to him /her, and that it is the origin of their sensations [12]. Agency represents the fact that the person recognizes himself/herself as the cause of the actions and movements of their body [13]. Generating these illusions is a requisite for the success of any VR-based motor training procedure [14] and it is even more relevant for the success of the MVF procedure that we apply in the present work by means of VR.

Another contribution of VR in this field is based on the capability of this technology of generating experiences that will be impossible in the real world. In our case, VR allows a more precise manipulation of the MVF parameters, making possible interventions beyond a simple mirror representation, by controlling parameters such as the distance of the virtual limb or the delay of the feedback [6–8, 15].

All these factors make the developed system highly suitable for MVF home rehabilitation. Future works will focus on the validation of the system and in the definition of training protocols adapted for different kinds of patients.

Acknowledgement. This research was funded by Conselleria de Innovación, Universidades, Ciencia y Sociedad Digital, Comunitat Valenciana, Spain, grant number AICO/2019/029.

References

1. Ramachandran, V.S., Rogers-Ramachandran, D., Cobb, S.: Touching the phantom limb. Nature **377**(6549), 489–490 (1995)
2. Thieme, K., et al.: Pain inhibition in Fibromyalgia. J. Pain **12**(4), P73 (2011)
3. Hartman, K., Altschuler, E.: Mirror therapy for hemiparesis following stroke: a review. Curr. Phys. Med. Rehabil. Rep. **4**(4), 237–248 (2016)
4. Chan, B.L., Charrow, A.P., Howard, R., Pasquina, P.F., Heilman, K.M., Tsao, J.W.: Mirror therapy for phantom limb pain. New Engl. J. Med. **357**(21), 2206 (2007)
5. Osumi, M., et al.: Restoring movement representation and alleviating phantom limb pain through short-term neurorehabilitation with a virtual reality system. Eur. J. Pain **21**(1), 140–147 (2017)
6. Nierula, B., Martini, M., Matamala-Gomez, M., Slater, M., Sanchez-Vives, M.V.: Seeing an embodied virtual hand is analgesic contingent on colocation. J. Pain **18**(6), 645–655 (2017)
7. Martini, M.: Real, rubber or virtual: the vision of "one's own" body as a means for pain modulation. A narrative review. Consciousn. Cogn. **43**, 143–151 (2016)
8. Sato, K., et al.: Non-immersive virtual reality mirror visual feedback therapy and its application for the treatment of complex regional pain syndrome: an open-label pilot study. Pain Med. **11**(4), 622–629 (2010)
9. Perez-Marcos, D.: Virtual Reality experiences, embodiments, videogames and their dimensions in neurorehabilitation. J. Neuroeng. Rehabil. **15**(1), 1–8 (2018)
10. Longo, M.R., Schüür, F., Kammers, M.P., Tsakiris, M., Haggard, P.: What is embodiment? A psychometric approach. Cognition **107**(3), 978–998 (2008)
11. Kilteni, K., Normand, J.M., Sanchez-Vives, M.V., Slater, M.: Extending body space in immersive virtual reality: a very long arm illusion. PLoS ONE **7**(7), e40867 (2012)
12. Tsakiris, M.: My body in the brain: a neurocognitive model of body-ownership. Neuropsychology **48**(3), 703–712 (2010)
13. Spanlang, B., et al.: How to build an embodiment lab: achieving body representation illusions in virtual reality. Front. Robot. AI **1**, 9 (2014)
14. Gorisse, G., Christmann, O., Amato, E.A., Richir, S.: First-and third-person perspectives in immersive virtual environments: presence and performance analysis of embodied users. Front. Robot. AI **4**, 33 (2017)
15. Limanowski, J., Kirilina, E., Blankenburg, F.: Neuronal correlates of continuous manual tracking under varying visual movement feedback in a virtual reality environment. Neuroimage **146**, 81–89 (2017)

Virtual Reality for Industrial Heritage: The Thermal Power Plant of Aramon

Nancy Rodriguez[✉] (iD)

LIRMM – Univ Montpellier, CNRS, Montpellier, France
nancy.rodriguez@lirmm.fr

Abstract. The fast development of interactive technologies has impacted the field of Cultural Heritage by enriching museums, sites and exhibitions. As for Cultural Heritage, Industrial Heritage can also benefit from new technologies in order to create interactive experiences and advance the understanding and dissemination of industrial evolution. The thermal power plant of Aramon at the South of France has stopped its electricity production and will be dismantled. This site is rich in industrial heritage and cultural significance. A 3D model of the site as well as virtual tours would make possible, on the one hand, to create resources for educational purposes in order to introduce the public to energy production sites and, on the other hand, to keep the memory of the region's Industrial Heritage.

Keywords: Virtual reality · 3D models · Cultural heritage · Industrial heritage · Virtual heritage · Digital reconstruction

1 Introduction

Virtual reality allows, by the means of an immersive and interactive virtual environment, to explore environments that are inaccessible for various reasons such as distance, ethics, the need for non-destructive public access or safety of visitors. Virtual reality makes then possible to the general public to discover and visit distant, dangerous or unavailable sites.

For several years, Virtual Reality have become popular to cultural knowledge dissemination in the field of Cultural Heritage. According to the UNESCO definition, Cultural Heritage is "both a product and a process, which provides societies with a wealth of resources that are inherited from the past, created in the present and bestowed for the benefit of future generations" [1]. Using computer-based interactive technologies as Virtual Reality to Cultural Heritage is generally called Virtual Heritage [2]. As stated by Stone [3], technology allows "to record, preserve, or recreate artefacts, sites and actors of historic, artistic and cultural significance, and to deliver the results openly to a global audience in such a way as to provide formative educational experiences through electronic manipulations of time and space".

Industrial sites are important in terms of preservation of the trace of technological progress and landscape evolution. As stated by [4] there is less awareness about industrial heritage and its physical evidence is slowly disappearing.

C. Stephanidis et al. (Eds.): HCII 2021, CCIS 1420, pp. 316–321, 2021.
https://doi.org/10.1007/978-3-030-78642-7_43

Therefore, we think that like for its Cultural Heritage counterpart, Industrial Heritage can benefit from 3D models to preserve sites and machinery that will no longer exist, and exploit Virtual Reality for Industrial Heritage preservation, representation and dissemination [5].

The thermal power plant of Aramon at the South of France, a fuel oil power plant, was commissioned in 1977 to respond quickly to variations in electricity consumption in order to protect the network from power cuts. The power plant has stopped its electricity production in April 2016 and is being deconstructed. The site is being upgraded for the installation of renewable energies (photovoltaic). The complete dismantling of the site is planned for 2032. With the collaboration of EDF (Electricité de France, historical French energy operator) and the Campus des Métiers et des Qualifications (network bringing together the worlds of education, economy and research in the same territory) we started the 3D modeling of the power plant. Our aim is to create a virtual environment, with a view to helping courses of the Campus such as Systems Maintenance, Nuclear Environment and Industrial Control and Automatic Regulation for educational purposes, and also to preserve the memory of the region's industrial heritage.

The reminder of this paper is organized as follows. Section 2 presents related work. Section 3 discusses methodology and tools used to implement our virtual reality environment. Finally, section Conclusion summarizes the paper and describes our future work.

2   Related Work

As stated by [6], "virtual reality technology has become mature for facilitating the experience of and, as a consequence, the learning of culture and heritage". In the field of Industrial Heritage, [7] presents an interactive virtual tool allowing to explore an industrial power plant from the nineteenth century in Slovak city of Piešťany which was reconstructed from historical documents as archive technical documents, drawings and photographs. The machinery hall was reconstructed through 3D scanning from preserved and functional historic diesel engines form the Technical Museum in Vienna. This works shows how the immersion provided by Virtual Reality increase the effectiveness and attractiveness of learning activities about extinct significant Industrial Heritage in order to bring the history, culture and technology closer to the public.

[8] presents the restoration and reuse design of industrial heritage in virtual reality. The Abrase Wheel Factory located in Shengshou (China), has high artistic value and a potential to be transformed and reused. The original appearance of the former industrial buildings must be restored. In this project, virtual reality is integrated to facilitate simulations as well as allowing the augmentation of physical prototypes with interactive virtual content. [9] addresses an identified issue in heritage education i.e. the lack of context and personalization of conventional learning methods. Emerging technologies as augmented reality offer alternatives to customize, locate and contextualize learning. An application has been developed following their "Framework to Heritage Education" and validated by a study involving tourist and citizens in Cartagena de Indias (Colombia).

3 Development

There are several elements to consider when creating the virtual model of the plant: the capture and modelling of the environment, the software tools available and the possibilities of interaction.

3.1 Materials

On our first visit to the plant in February 2020, we took a guided tour of the facilities and took several photos. We also obtained several historical documents and aerial photographs from EDF (Fig. 1). Unfortunately, due to the Covid-19 crisis and lockdown measures in France we were unable to return to the physical site. We were therefore constrained to work with only these documents without the possibility of get more information or details to improve our model.

Fig. 1. Aerial view of the power plant of Aramon

3.2 3D Model

The 3D model of the plant was made in accordance with the available documents, by a group of students of the Master in Computer Science of the University of Montpellier (France) [10]. It was produced in Unity [11], a game engine allowing to create and manage interactive virtual environments. Unity offers several functionalities such as a physics engine, a mechanism to build animations and the possibility to easily integrate interaction devices.

At the first place, the layout plan of the site with the location of the various buildings was used to define the position in the 3D space of buildings models. Then the buildings have been modeling based on the available pictures. In addition to modelling via simple primitives and Unity ProBuilder [12], some standard industrial components models are from 3d models shared sites such as TurboSquid [13] and the Unity Asset Store. Some particular elements were created from scratch, like the chimney which has been built from a 3D cylinder object. Then, the Unity Pro Builder tool was used to work on its shape by selecting the angles and sides to be rounded or widened (Fig. 2).

Fig. 2. 3d model of the chimney

An interactive virtual screen has been placed in the main building to provide the visitor with information about the history of the plant (Fig. 3).

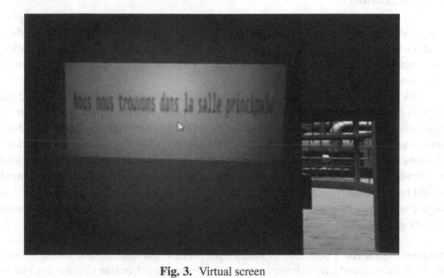

Fig. 3. Virtual screen

3.3 Interaction

A user-controllable character was integrated into the scene to allow environment exploration. Her movements are controlled using the keyboard, collisions are taken into account to provides a realistic exploration of the scene. The user can also change floor by using a virtual lift (Fig. 4).

Fig. 4. Virtual lift buttons

A video of the first version of the 3d model is available here: https://youtu.be/i7M CmDRb0Ow. At present, there is no a guided virtual visit implemented, the user can move around freely in the environment.

4 Conclusion

This paper presents a virtual reality application allowing the exploration of the 3D model of the thermal power plant of Aramon. To create this application, we collected documentation as aerial photographs and plans. These resources were used to reconstruct the industrial site.

This model is the base of our application which aims to allow immersion and peda-gogical experiences in the virtual plant. The real plant will disappear in ten or so years from now, therefore its 3d model would serve to bring energy production and industrial heritage closer to the public. Students will be able to relate the industrial machines and processes seen in class with the reconstructed plant. We are currently putting our efforts into developing a pedagogical scenario focused on particular machinery details (models would be obtained from photogrammetry) and in the definition of a virtual visit: views to give access to important information, how to arrange these views and the clues needed for navigation.

Acknowledgements. I would like to thank the staff of EDF and thermal plant, Nathalie Bruneau, Marilène Combes and Olivier Riviere, as well as Corine Negre from the Campus des Métiers et des Qualifications, and all the students who participate in the development of the application.

References

1. Heritage. UNESCO Culture for Development Indicators. https://en.unesco.org/creativity/sites/creativity/files/cdis/heritage_dimension.pdf. Accessed 21 Feb 2021
2. Jacobson, J., Holden, L. Virtual Heritage: Living in the Past. Techné: Research in Philosophy and Technology **10**(3) (2007)

3. Stone, R., Ojika, T.: Virtual heritage: what next? IEEE Multimedia **7**, 73–74 (2000)
4. Checa, D., Alaguero, M., Bustillo, A.: Industrial heritage seen through the lens of a virtual reality experience. In: DePaolis, L.T., Bourdot, P., Mongelli, A. (eds.) AVR 2017. LNCS, vol. 10324, pp. 116–130. Springer, Cham (2017). https://doi.org/10.1007/978-3-319-60922-5_9
5. Bekele, M.K., Champion, E.: A comparison of immersive realities and interaction methods: cultural learning in virtual heritage. Front. Robot. AI **6**(91) (2019)
6. Ch'ng, E., Cai, Y., Thwaites, H.: Guest editor's introduction. special issue on VR for culture and heritage: the experience of cultural heritage with virtual reality. Presence. **26**(3), iii–vi (2017)
7. Hain, V., Hajtmanek, R.: Industrial heritage education and user tracking in virtual reality. In: Cvetković, D. (ed.), Virtual Reality and Its Application in Education. IntechOpen (2019). https://www.intechopen.com/books/virtual-reality-and-its-application-in-education/industrial-heritage-education-and-user-tracking-in-virtual-reality
8. Jue, C., Chen, W.: Restoration and reuse design of industrial heritage based on virtual reality technology. IOP Conf. Ser.: Mat. Sci. Eng. **825**, 012–0215 (2020)
9. Mendoza, R., Baldiris, S., Fabregat, R.: Framework to heritage education using emerging technologies. Procedia Comput. Sci. **75**, 239–249 (2015)
10. Chetouan, A., Choukri, A., Di Marino, M., Hennani, S.: Visite virtuelle de la centrale thermique d'Aramon. Technical report, University of Montpellier (2020)
11. Unity. https://unity.com. Accessed 21 Mar 2021
12. Unity ProBuilder. https://unity3d.com/unity/features/worldbuilding/probuilder. Accessed 21 Mar 2021
13. TurboSquid. https://www.turbosquid.com. Accessed 21 Mar 2021

Development of an Operation Console in Virtual Reality for a Serious Game Designed as a Tool for User Training in Piloting an Unmanned Aerial Vehicle

André Salomão, Marcos Vinicius Golçalves, Milton Luiz Horn Vieira, and Nicolas Canale Romeiro[✉]

Universidade Federal de Santa Catarina, Florianópolis, Brazil

Abstract. In this article, we will demonstrate and go into details on how and why we designed an operation panel in virtual reality using gaming design, unmanned aerial vehicle, and virtual reality concepts as a part of a bigger scope serious game that aims to train new users into driving unmanned aerial vehicles to diverse situations replicated from real life. The creation of 3D assets for virtual reality environment requires the researcher to consider the application performance, being necessary to find ways to ensure we keep a steady performance while also sacrificing visual fidelity as minimum as required, our approach was to hide parts of the model not being seen in by the user and the creation of illusion with details in the asset's material.

Keywords: Virtual reality · Serious game · Unmanned aerial vehicle

1 Introduction

In this article, we will demonstrate and go into details on how and why we designed an operation panel in virtual reality using gaming design, unmanned aerial vehicle, and virtual reality concepts as a part of a bigger scope serious game that aims to train new users into driving unmanned aerial vehicles (UAV) to diverse situations replicated from real life.

Designing a serious game poses a series of challenges due to its nature of having to transfer knowledge to the player, to be considered serious, while also keeping it entertaining, to be considered a game [1], it creates a virtual environment that is dynamic and open to the development of activities that will teach a pre-determined subject in a specific context [2].

Games can be used as a tool to solve issues, and the designer should question itself if gaming can be the best solution and why [3]. To understand if gaming can be an effective tool in training users in the act of piloting an unmanned aerial vehicle, it is necessary to determine how its ecosystem works. In the context of this work, an unmanned aerial vehicle is defined as a generic aircraft with no human on board [4] that is part of a system also composed of a base station of control and antenna connection that works as a link between the vehicle and the base station [5].

This base station of control can be a box a size of a case or a notebook that can fit in a normal-sized bag, but it can also be a system structured in grounded stations with a size of a room away from where the unmanned aerial vehicle is flying, communicating with it through a satellite in an operation console used to send and receive information to and from the unmanned aerial vehicle. This operation console can be composed of tools such as a video camera for recognition, radars, weather, and chemical sensors [5].

The concept of virtual reality can be traced back as far as 1960 [6], but its definition can also be limited due to the technology of its time [7], LaValle [8] also defines it as "Inducing targeted behavior in an organism by using artificial sensory stimulation, while the organism has little or no awareness of the interference".

Regardless of which concept of virtual reality is used to define it, there are four characteristics presented in a virtual reality system: a virtual world, immersion, sensorial feedback, and interactivity [9]. The virtual world is the imaginary space manifested through media, aimed to create a virtual environment with objects and interactions with the user in a physical and immersive way. The immersion characteristic is the intent of virtual reality, to induce the user to feel like he is in a completely different context than the one he was in like he was present in the virtual world [8, 9]. For this immersion to occur, there must be sensorial feedback between the virtual world and the user, where the system should be able to track the user positional and orientation in real life and replicated it in the virtual world [7]. Interactivity is going to determine how the user is going to feel, live, and react to the virtual world presented to them.

Virtual reality is at its core, an organism composes of simulations and interactions able to track user's position and actions substituting or amplifying its feedback of one or more senses, with the user ending up feeling like they are immersed or even present in this imaginary created virtual world [9].

To design and create this virtual world, we decided to use a game engine, which is software used as a foundation for games but can also be modified for other types of uses [10] and implement game design concepts efficiently [11]. The game engine of choice was the "Unreal Engine 4", known to be able to develop applications that work in real-time, from traditional games to mobiles, virtual reality, and augmented reality [12]. Alongside a basic set of features included in virtual reality hardware, it was added support to the Leap Motion technology, responsible for tracking the player's fingers with high precision, low process power, and almost zero latency [13] to improve the player's input in the operational panel. The application's assets created in this article were also made using the free 3D modeling software Blender.

2   Fundamentals

In this chapter we will approach the two main fundamentals points of this article, the first one is related to the unmanned aerial vehicle, focusing on explaining how a generic system of it works and the second point will discuss virtual reality and what needs to be done from a technical point of view regarding the creation of 3D assets to its ecosystem.

2.1 UAV

An unmanned aerial vehicle is just one part of a system, which can change accordingly to its use, but we can define a generic UAV system that will have the following components: air vehicles, one or more ground control station (GCS), and/or mission planning and control stations (MPCS), payload, and data link and additionally can have launch and recovery subsystems, air-vehicle carriers, and other ground handling and maintenance equipment [14].

The GCS works as the operational center of the UAV system where all information like video, command, and telemetry data converges and are processed and displayed, working as a command post for the user that will be performing actions like mission planning, receiving mission assignments, reports from data and others relevant information to the unit. This generic GCS is shown in Fig. 1 but can also be noted that a GCS can also be something smaller in scale, like a case, containing little more than a remote control, a display, a way to process information and control the UAV [14].

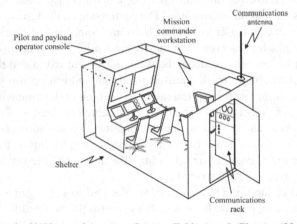

Fig. 1. UAV generic system. Source: Fahlstrom & Gleason (2012).

2.2 Virtual Reality

During tests conducted by Wolfartsberger, Zenisek, and Sievi [15], it is stated that VR productions keep a stable 100 frames per second and that models with high polygon count causing the frame rate to drop significantly. In the tests conducted by the authors, it was shown that a model with over 30 million polygons would cause the frame rate to drop to around 30 frames per second, which would most probably cause motion sickness. They then used software tools to reduce the complexity of the model and its polygon count to less than a million polygons, and with this version of the model, the frame rate would stabilize to an adequate level [15].

According to Tang & Ho [16], most CAD (Computer-aided Design) and CAID (Computer-aided Industrial Design) models are not suited directly to real-time rendering, due to the complexity of the models and textures. The authors suggest, to avoid having to use specific software to reduce model complexity, that the modeler uses specific modeling methods to make a VR-ready model. One of the suggestions is the use of shaders, a tool that calculates the normal of the faces creating the illusion of being a rounded face, instead of using subdivision. Another method the authors recommend is to use bevel modifiers with low segments, creating smoother edges and still maintaining low polygon count [16].

3   Development

For the development of a virtual environment of user training in piloting a UAV, it was necessary to look for visual references beyond the established ones in the fundamentals. Generic systems as a reference and technical guidance are necessary when creating a gaming asset, one to comprehend what we are trying to create and the other to understand the limitation of the technology we are working with.

So, our goal was to create two 3D assets, the first one will be named "high-poly model", which will be our starting point of development, and the second one will be called the "low-poly" model which will be our final goal for the asset that will be implemented inside virtual reality.

The GCS's panel of control was modeled after the model "Block 30/50" from the company named General Atomics Aeronautical, which produced this GCS that was used, at the time of the development of this research, by different departments in countries worldwide, including but not limited to the US (Department of Security and NASA), Italy, France [17]. Figure 2 represents the visual reference of this model.

Fig. 2. Block 30/50. Source: General Atomics Aeronautical (2019)

As this control panel is being created as an asset for a training application in virtual reality, it will be required to display information regarding the training exercise, while also enabling the user to control it, as necessary, so, the modeling process had to take these two considerations. To be able to easily display information the display panels in the control panel were modeled as a separated unit, but for the user, this difference is not noted, and the controls, that being the keyboard and the UAV Handler, were created also as a separated asset and inserted in the control panel, but they were designed to be used with the LEAP Motion technology, creating another layer of immersion for the user to control the UAV. The described process resulted in the "High-poly" models that are represented by Fig. 3.

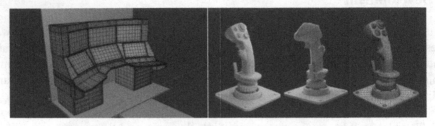

Fig. 3. Control panel (left) and handler (right) high poly versions.

As noted, both this control panel and UAV handler are going to be implemented in a virtual reality application, so the following step was to reduce the polygons count to reduce its impact on the application's performance as noted by [15, 16]. The result of this process can be seen in Fig. 4.

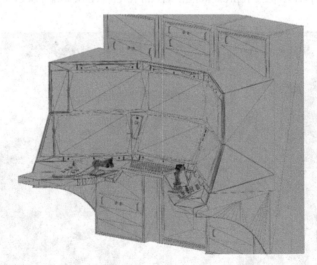

Fig. 4. Control panel low poly version.

All the assets were designed and modeled, except for the keyboard, to accomplish the fact that the user will be using it with LeapMotion technology or similars, using its hand as input to create an extra layer of immersion. The final version, in this case, the "low-poly" version, of these assets are implemented inside the virtual environment created using the Unreal Engine 4 gaming engine for the interaction of the user with it. Figure 5 also shows as closely as possible what we envision would be the user's point of view when interacting with it.

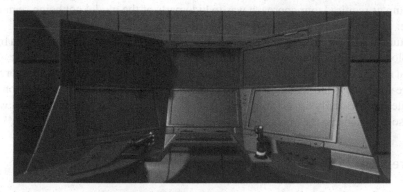

Fig. 5. Control panel final version.

The final asset inside Unreal Engine 4 virtual environment still retains some of the details we had in the High Poly Model, even though it is the Low Poly Model, to do so, we used a normal map based on the high poly model to create an illusion of detail without impacting the game's performance, we used normal maps applied to the main material, as seen in Fig. 6.

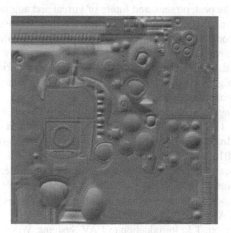

Fig. 6. Normal map.

4 Conclusion

The goal of this article was to demonstrate how and why we designed an operation panel in virtual reality for the piloting of an unmanned aerial vehicle. This research is a part of a bigger scope serious game project that will be used to train users into piloting these machines. The creation of 3D assets for virtual reality environment requires the researcher to take into account the application performance, being necessary to find ways to ensure we keep a steady performance while also sacrificing visual fidelity as minimum as required, our approach was to hide parts of the model not being seen in by the user and the creation of illusion with details in the asset's material.

Future works should take into consideration that this development was limited by the technology of its time, which means that future technology can help mitigate these issues and that researchers should, alongside the development of new technology, look for more creative solutions to the problems of developing 3D assets for virtual reality environment to create more visually appealing results that will help improve user immersion which will also help achieve the application's main goal.

References

1. Arnab, S., et al.: Mapping learning and game mechanics for serious games analysis. Br. J. Educ. Technol. **46**(2), 391–411 (2015)
2. Romero, M., Usart, M., Ott, M.: Can serious games contribute to developing and sustaining 21st century skills? Games Cult. **10**(2), 148–177 (2015)
3. Schell, J.: The Art of Game Design: A Book of Lenses, 2nd edn. CRC Press, Taylor & Francis Group, Boca Raton (2014)
4. Nex, F., Remondino, F.: UAV for 3D mapping applications: a review. Appl. Geomat. **6**(1), 1–15 (2014)
5. Fahlstrom, P.G., Gleason, T.J.: Introduction to UAV Systems. Wiley, Hoboken (2012)
6. Cipresso, P., et al.: The past, present, and future of virtual and augmented reality research: a network and cluster analysis of the literature. Front. Psychol. **9**(November), 1–20 (2018)
7. Jerald, J.: The VR Book: Human-Centered Design for Virtual Reality, 1st edn. Association for Computing Machinery and Morgan & Claypool Publishers, New York (2015)
8. LaValle, S.M.: Virtual Reality. Cambridge University Press, Cambridge (2017)
9. Sherman, W.R., Craig, A.B.: Understanding Virtual Reality: Interface, Application, and Design. Elsevier, Alpharetta (2003)
10. Gregory, J.: Game Engine Architecture. Taylor and Francis Group, LLC, Abingdon (2009)
11. Guana, V., Stroulia, E., Nguyen, V.: Building a game engine: a tale of modern model-driven engineering. In: Proceedings - 4th International Workshop on Games and Software Engineering, GAS 2015, pp. 15–21 (2015)
12. Unreal Engine: Unreal engine features (2018a). https://www.unrealengine.com/en-US/features. Accessed 26 Nov 2018
13. Leap Motion Developer: Leap motion documentation (2018). https://developer.leapmotion.com/documentation. Accessed 26 Nov 2018
14. Fahlstrom, P.G., Gleason, T.J.: Introduction to UAV Systems. Wiley, Hoboken (2012)
15. Wolfartsberger, J., Zenisek, J., Sievi, C.: Chances and limitations of a virtual reality-supported tool for decision making in industrial engineering. IFAC-PapersOnLine **51**(11), 637–642 (2018)
16. Ming Tang, Y., Ho, H.L.: 3D modeling and computer graphics in virtual reality. IN: Mixed Reality and Three-Dimensional Computer Graphics (2020)
17. General Atomics Aeronautical: Advanced Cockpit GCS (2019). http://www.ga-asi.com/advanced-cockpit-gcs. Accessed 17 July 2019

Health Data Management for Nursing Practice: An Intelligent, Holographic Mixed-Reality System

Syed Hammad Hussain Shah[1]([⊠]) [ID], Bjørnar Longva[1], Ibrahim A. Hameed[1] [ID], Mads Solberg[2], and Anniken Susanne T. Karlsen[1] [ID]

[1] Department of ICT and Natural Sciences, Faculty of Information Technology and Electrical Engineering, Norwegian University of Science and Technology, Aalesund, Norway
syed.h.h.shah@ntnu.no

[2] Department of Health Sciences in Aalesund, Faculty of Medicine and Health Science, Norwegian University of Science and Technology, Aalesund, Norway
https://www.ntnu.edu/employees/syed.h.h.shah

Abstract. The elderly population in need of long-term care is rising, adding to the workload of healthcare workers in nursing homes. Throughout a work day health workers often must perform the time consuming process of collecting various types of health data from the residents. A recent study has revealed that frontline nurses and caregivers spend over half of their time accessing and updating patient records instead of providing care. New technology could enhance these data-oriented operations, and free up time so that staff can care for patients in other ways. Intelligent human-computer interaction paradigms can enhance data retrieval, visualization, and communication processes efficiently in a way to improve the overall productivity during work. In this study, we present an intelligent holographic mixed reality (MR) system that leverages Microsoft Hololens for work practices of healthcare work in nursing homes. Supported by computer vision, this system provides automatic data retrieval, in addition to interactive data visualization and mid-air data entry mechanism. Using face recognition through the Hololens' visual sensors, the system recognizes individual patients, and automatically retrieves relevant health data and supports data entry.

Keywords: Mixed reality · Intelligent user interfaces · Eldercare · Nursing homes · Health Informatics

1 Introduction

Globally, 901 million people are above the age of 60 years. This number is expected to reach 1.4 billion by 2030. According to the Norwegian Institute of Public Health (NIPH), the population above 70 years accounts for 10% of the overall population in Norway, a number that will double by 2070 [1]. Due to the growing elderly

© Springer Nature Switzerland AG 2021
C. Stephanidis et al. (Eds.): HCII 2021, CCIS 1420, pp. 329–336, 2021.
https://doi.org/10.1007/978-3-030-78642-7_45

population, and the corresponding increase in demand for professional care, the workload on healthcare staff has gradually increased in nursing homes. In these institutions, health workers have to visit each resident multiple times throughout a day. During these visits, workers spend much time accessing and updating patient records, search, visualize and interpret patient information, to assess the overall health situation of each patient. These data are multidimensional, and include information about life history, medical issues, and critical parameters such as blood pressure, body temperature, sugar and oxygen level, medication, diet etc. Based on explorative interviews with health workers in a nursing home in Western Norway healthcare staff still use pen and paper for collecting data and then transforming these data for storage on a desktop computer. Recently, some nursing homes in the region have begun using mobile tablets to effectively collect, save and visualize health data. Although, the process of data collection and visualization has been digitized, these handheld 2D digital interfaces suffer from operational challenges. For instance, users must manually search patient records to visualize and interpret health data during follow-ups. Additionally, workers interact with multiple media, using both tablet and paper at the same time, when acquiring new or updating health data from patients. During this process, they also must operate different apparatuses, including devices for measuring body temperature, blood pressure, blood sugar and oxygen levels etc. A general complaint is that it is difficult to operate all these media in parallel. Furthermore, the COVID-19 pandemic has made it riskier to use hand-held devices and other materials near elderly residents, due to potential transmission issues. A recent survey based on interviews with 475 healthcare professionals in 7 countries found that nurses and caregivers spend more time dealing with tech problems and entering data than caring of patients [2]. The survey found that 56% of a front-line healthcare worker's time is spent accessing and updating patient records. 50% of the respondents reported that existing technology platforms waste time that could be spent helping patients and that there is a need to invest in better technology for future health crises [2]. To address these concerns, we propose that an enabling technology like holographic mixed reality (MR) can be a solution that can improve daily work practices among healthcare professionals. It does so by embedding interactive and intelligent digital interfaces in the care process, in ways that reduce time spent on accessing, visualizing, and updating patient-records. MR supports the coexistence of real world and virtual 3D objects (also called 'Holograms') in the same environment [3]. Users can interact with holograms that are projected from a transparent head-mounted display (HMD) while staying connected to the real world. This enables them to confidently move around in their situated environment, while having interactive graphical visuals superimposed on this environment. As such, this technology can be applied to a range of professional domains ranging from manufacturing, education, entertainment to healthcare [4]. Used correctly, mixed reality can support novel interactions with computational tools in a situated environment, and these interactions can be further leveraged by artificial intelligence (AI) and computer vision (CV), adding intelligence to these interfaces.

In this paper we propose an intelligent holographic MR system leveraged by AI and CV based on see-through HMD named Hololens 2. The system is built upon a new interaction paradigm, using a hands-free MR interface. Here, we adopt this system so that health workers can use it at elderly nursing homes to handle patient data in an efficient and safe way. Using this solution, health workers can search and visualize past patient data, and enter new data through interaction with the holographic 3D user interface. Furthermore, the system brings flexibility, since it enables users to keep the holographic interface at hand, while they move around in real world surroundings, interacting with people and objects. The purpose of the hands-free interface is to support health workers in quickly and easily switch between interactions with the holographic interface and the patient, all while keeping their peripheral vision clear. This setup would also reduce the risk of virus transmission because they do not have to continuously touch the device for inter-action, which can be sanitized at the end of visit. Microsoft is also providing an industrial edition of Hololens 2, which can be sanitized and is safe to use during in the context of the pandemic. Moreover, the process of patient search and data retrieval is automated in the system by using CV, so that it intelligently retrieves the patient data effortlessly. This retrieval is accomplished by recognizing the resi-dent's face, based on visual information received through the Hololens' RGB cam-era. After recognizing the patient, his/her profile is automatically searched in the database to retrieve the corresponding health data.

2 Related Work

In recent years, the use of MR have been tested in several applications. Although the usage of HMDs is in an early phase, compared to other portable devices such as tablets [5], there has been an increase in the number of HMD-based applications developed for training and daily work practices in various domains, including manufacturing, education, entertainment, and healthcare. In medical training, Matthew et al. [6] presented a study of a holographic MR application in Hololens for clinical and non-clinical practices in pathology. Researchers [6] based their application on the video-conference software 'Skype' [7] in Hololens. Wear-ing the Hololens, pathology assistants and trainees could receive instructions from a remote pathologist through audio and visual communication, supported by virtual annotations. The authors [6] concluded that Hololens introduces many novel opportunities that could enrich work practices in the field of pathology. In addition to clinical applications, the Hololens has potential for clinical and educational purposes in healthcare. In another study Bjelke Andersson et al. [8] developed a holographic MR application based on Hololens, for neurosurgi-cal training. When clinicians performed procedures in MR without experiencing the tactile, physical resistance of real bodies, they reported that the interac-tion felt unnatural due to lack of embodied sensation which could be improved by high quality graphics. Sean Hauze et al. [9] suggests, MR can be applied to the training of nursing students. They propose that if the Hololens can be successfully used for training nurses, it is possible that the system also could be adapted to daily work practices. Nurses play an essential role in the early detection of a patient's deteriorating health. Chia-Chi Teng et al. [10] developed an application to monitor multiple critical patients from a remote location using a mixed-reality interface with Hololens. Functionality in this application included live video and audio streaming, as well as visualization of vital signs collected from equipment in the patient's room. The nurses reported that the application was helpful and supportive. It is also known that augmented reality (AR) could support patients suffering from vision impairment. An AR-based assisting platform, known as "Bright", developed for visually impaired persons was presented by Bakshi et al. [11]. A voice-enabled application, Bright allowed users to communicate, it included an adjustable zoom overlay, text-to-speech, facial recognition and emergency contact to caregiver.

3 Proposed System

The system we have developed is based on the 'HoloLens 2' by Microsoft. Here, we use a client-server architecture as basis. The functions dedicated to the server include processing of information received from Hololens, handling data-related operations (such as data storage or retrieval and sending the useful response back to the client i.e. the Hololens). Hololens captures the image data through its RGB camera and sends it to the server for facial recognition, and provide visualization of data received from serverIt also gives opportunities for interaction with relevant information through a holographic 3D interface. Facial recognition is here used to match a human face from a digital image, or a video frame, against a database of faces for authentication. Figure 1 the proposed client-server architecture of the system.

We created a RESTful API for communication with the database to insert, update or delete data pertaining to the patient profile, and execution of different machine learning (ML) and CV algorithms, such as those for facial recognition. Data related to the patient profile includes a profile picture, relevant personal information, historical health data, medications profile, and past data of vital signs i.e., body temperature, blood pressure, heart rate and oxygen level, as measured at scheduled intervals by nurses.

Here, we have added intelligent functionality to the holographic MR interface through automatic face recognition, by using CV to retrieve relevant data about the recognized patient. We have also provided a holographic 3D button control in MR for taking a picture of patient's face using front facing photographic RGB camera in Hololens. Facial recognition is then applied on this image/video frame. Upon successful recognition of patient, the system automatically searches the patient profile and sends relevant data to the Hololens for visualization through holographic MR interface. A face detection and recognition API named as Dlib[1] is used for face recognition. Figure 2 shows the flow diagram of the process whereby patient data is intelligently retrieved. As the vital signs are measured at scheduled intervals, the system can visualize an overall trend of the health situation by

---

[1] http://dlib.net/.

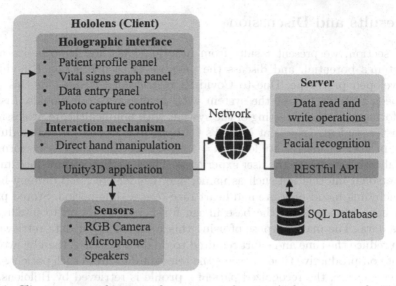

Fig. 1. Client-server architecture for automated patient's data entry and retrieval

mapping data in a graph to show an overall trend, aiding the worker to interpret
the health status of the patient over time. These graphs, which are created on the
server, use well-known libraries named 'Pandas' and 'Matplotlib'. They are sent
back to Hololens as images for visualization. Along with a search mechanism, we
also provided an MR interface in Hololens for data entry. The aim has been to
make it easy for health workers to keep the holographic interface pinned to the
device, so that it stays with them while they are mobile, while having the digital
interface ready at hand. This is made possible by embedding the spatial awareness system in Hololens. According to need, the health workers can also pin the
interface to a fixed real-world location.

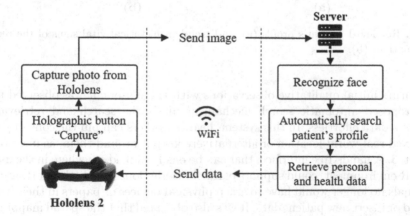

Fig. 2. Intelligent patient search

4   Results and Discussion

In this section, we present results from functional testing, hypothesize about the system's potential, and discuss the purpose of each functional module in the developed prototype. Due to Covid-19 restrictions, it has - at this point - not been possible to test the system with healthcare professionals. Instead, we performed functional testing of the system with non-healthcare professionals i.e., master students (n = 3) at NTNU's Campus in Aalesund, based on dummy patient profiles of master students (n = 4) to gauge the system's performance and qualitatively observe the user experience. These profiles include face images, basic personal information such as name, age, gender etc., and dummy health data, including blood pressure and heart rate over a time-period. Stored profile images have been used as the base image for face recognition to intelligently retrieve data. The main purpose of using this mechanism for data retrieval has been to reduce the time and effort required to do data searches, thereby avoiding waste of non-productive time to access the relevant data from each patient. After facial recognition, the recognized patient's profile is retrieved by Hololens, and relevant profile data is loaded into the main control panel (Patient profile panel) present in holographic MR interface as shown in Fig. 3a.

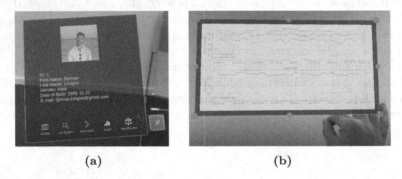

(a)   (b)

Fig. 3. Retrieved patient's profile (a), and trend in historical vital signs of the recognized patient (b)

During initial qualitative observations with these users, it was observed that the proposed automatic search mechanism made the search and retrieval of patient's data effortless. In this system, health workers can pin the control panel to a fixed real-world location or alternatively keep it around them, as mentioned in Sect. 3. A hands-free interface, that can be easily pinned anywhere in the user's 3D MR environment, could support parallel interactions with little effort, as professionals no longer would have to grasp physical devices or papers in their hands to read or insert new patient data. It was also observed that the spatial mapping of the holographic MR interface in 3D world, as mentioned above, offer users instant access to relevant data and easy navigation to 3D interface while doing parallel interactions with a fake patient. Furthermore, from the main control panel, user reported that it was easy to proceed to the graph panel (Vital signs graph panel), which offered a visualization of vital trends over time. Potentially, this can give health professionals an improved overview of the health situation and facilitate interpretations of health data. We have developed the panels in a way that they can be scaled, rotated, grabbed, and moved for making visualization more legible. Figure 3b shows the user interaction with graph panel, while moving and scaling it using direct hand manipulation. We have also provided an MR interface enabling the insertion of new data using holographic data-entry forms and a keyboard to provide mid-air text entry mechanisms in MR [12]. In this way, we hope to support health workers as they interact with patients, and enter or retrieve data through the hands-free digital interface. A hypothesis is that this hands-free interface could make it more convenient for healthcare workers to operate other instruments, such as those used for measuring vital signs.

5   Conclusion and Future Work

The present study has presented building blocks for a novel holographic mixed reality system based on Microsoft Hololens 2, and performed functional testing at initial level to qualitative observe the potential of proposed system for future use by healthcare workers during daily activities with elder patients in nursing homes. The functionalities presently embedded include intelligent patient search mechanisms, a holographic interface, a mid-air data entry mechanism in MR, and a set of interaction paradigms. There is no integration with actual health records in this early phase, due to data privacy concerns. Furthermore, COVID-19 restrictions implies that we have only performed system testing with students, and qualitatively observed their experiences at a university campus. Initial results, however, suggest that such a system can be useful for patient data management, as the digital interfaces support data entry and interpretation during multimodal interactions with patients. Hopefully, this new platform for data entry and retrieval, could free up time that is now used for data management, but which could better be used to care for patients in other ways.

In future work, the system will be developed for use in real-life situations with actual patient records. We also aim to make the interaction mechanisms more intelligent and responsive by adding additional features, such as a speech-based interface to the system. Moreover, analyzing past health records is a complex task. Therefore, we will apply data analytics on patient health data using machine learning techniques to summarize relevant and useful information. This would include important trends for interpreting the patient's health status. Furthermore, we aim to enable health workers to customize the interface so that users can easily select what sort of information they want to visualize.

Acknowledgement. This work was supported by the Norwegian University of Science and Technology (NTNU).

References

1. Organization, W. H. Ageing And Health. https://www.who.int news-room/fact-sheets/detail/ageing-and-health%20%5C#:~:text=Today% 5C%2C%5C%20125% 5C%20million%5C%20people%5C%20are%20%5C% 20aged%5C%2080%5C%20 years%5C%20or%5C%20older
2. SOTI: Critical Technology for Critical Care: The State of Mobility in Health- care 2020/21 Report. https://www.soti.net/industries/healthcare/mobilityreport/
3. Microsoft: Mixed Reality. https://docs.microsoft.com/en-us/windows/mixed-reality/discover/mixed-reality
4. Lindlbauer, D., Feit, A.M., Hilliges, O.: Context-aware online adaptation of mixed reality interfaces. In: Proceedings of the 32nd Annual ACM Symposium on User Interface Software and Technology, pp. 147–160 (2019)
5. Daling, L., Abdelrazeq, A., Sauerborn, C., Hees, F.: A comparative study of aug-mented reality assistant tools in assembly. In: Ahram, T., Falcão, C. (eds.) AHFE 2019. AISC, vol. 972, pp. 755–767. Springer, Cham (2020). https://doi.org/10. 1007/978-3-030-19135-1_74. ISBN: 978-3-030-19135-1
6. Hanna, M.G., Ahmed, I., Nine, J., Prajapati, S., Pantanowitz, L.: Augmented reality technology using Microsoft HoloLens in anatomic pathology. Arch. Pathol. Laborat. Medi. **142**, 638–644 (2018). ISSN: 0003–9985
7. Technologies, S. Skype: Communication Tool. https://www.skype.com
8. Andersson, H.B., BØrresen, T., Prasolova-FØrland, E., McCallum, S., Estrada, J.G.: Developing an AR application for neurosurgical training: lessons learned for medical specialist education. In: 2020 IEEE Conference on Virtual Reality and 3D User Interfaces Abstracts and Workshops (VRW), pp. 407–412 (2020). https://doi. org/10.1109/VRW50115.2020.00087
9. Hauze, S., Hoyt, H., Marshall, J., Frazee, J., Greiner, P.: An evaluation of nurs-ing student motivation to learn through holographic mixed reality simulation. In: 2018 IEEE International Conference on Teaching, Assessment, and Learning for Engineering (TALE), pp. 1058–1063 (2018). https://doi.org/10.1109/TALE.2018. 8615347
10. Teng, C.-C., et al.: Mixed reality patients monitoring application for critical care nurses. In: Proceedings of the Third International Conference on Medical and Health Informatics 2019, Xiamen, China, pp. 49–53. Association for Comput-ing Machinery (2019). ISBN: 9781450371995. 3340037.3340050. https://doi.org/ 10.1145/3340037.3340050
11. Bakshi, A.M., Simson, J., de Castro, C., Yu, C.C., Dias, A.: Bright: an augmented reality assistive platform for visual impairment. In: 2019 IEEE Games, Entertain-ment, Media Conference (GEM), pp. 1–4 (2019). GEM.2019.8811556. https://doi. org/10.1109/GEM.2019.8811556
12. Gupta, A., Samad, M., Kin, K., Kristensson, P.O., Benko, H.: Investigating remote tactile feedback for mid-air text-entry in virtual reality. In: 2020 IEEE International Symposium on Mixed and Augmented Reality (ISMAR), pp. 350–360 (2020)

VAMR Basketball on Head-Mounted and Hand-Held Devices with Hand-Gesture-Based Interactions

Eric Cesar E. Vidal Jr.(✉) ⬤ and Ma. Mercedes T. Rodrigo ⬤

Ateneo de Manila University, Katipunan Avenue, 1108 Quezon City, Philippines

Abstract. Virtual, Augmented, and Mixed Reality (VAMR)-based sports sim-ulators may help facilitate learning and training for students confined within closed/cramped spaces (e.g., during a pandemic), and allow disabled or disadvan-taged players to participate in the said sports alongside non-disabled peers. This work explores the development of a VAMR basketball simulator that uses hand gestures to accurately mimic the real-world performance of basketball moves such as throwing and shooting. Furthermore, the simulator is developed simultaneously for both head-mounted (VR/AR headsets) and hand-held (smartphone/tablet) form factors, facilitating deployment of the same simulator over multiple hardware con-figurations. This eliminates the need to force students to use one platform for online learning, and would also allow for future real-time networked multi-user support across different form-factor devices. This model also paves the way for future user studies comparing the efficacy of head-mounted and hand-held modes for simulating basketball and other sports in VAMR.

Keywords: CAVE and multi-participant environments · Education and training · Gaming · Human factors · Mobile systems · Presence in VAMR

1 Introduction

Traditional sports games, such as basketball, have been a popular subject of computer-based simulations for entertainment, teaching and training. Computer-generated virtual environments provide users the opportunity to participate in such sports while in remote places [1, 2]. Such virtual environments are realized using Virtual, Augmented, and/or Mixed Reality technologies, collectively referred to as VAMR.

The increased reliance on distance-based learning due to the COVID-19 pandemic means that the task of keeping students motivated and engaged in learning activities has become more challenging than ever. Hergüner et al.'s study found that positive attitudes towards online learning amongst students of sports sciences directly contribute to an improvement in said students' readiness to learn online [3]. An online learning environment that is not easily accessible to students for reasons relating to instructional delivery, usability, or cost/availability, will likely impair students' learning attitudes, or worse, prevent participation in the learning activity altogether. Therefore, creating a

C. Stephanidis et al. (Eds.): HCII 2021, CCIS 1420, pp. 337–344, 2021.
https://doi.org/10.1007/978-3-030-78642-7_46

sports learning environment that is easily accessible to a wide range of students is an important key towards successful online learning of sports.

This ease-of-access problem initially appears to be adequately addressed via the adoption of VAMR-based sports simulations in the curriculum. In contrast to more traditional methods such as lecturing and passive multimedia, VAMR deals with the problem of instructional delivery by putting users in direct exposure to sports scenarios, with an emphasis on learning-by-doing, e.g., players would physically learn how to shoot a free throw, pass the ball to a teammate, and execute offensive or defensive plays step-by-step. In addition, the novelty effect of using a VAMR-based learning tool for the first time may significantly increase student motivation [4]. However, studies of VAMR applications reveal that the novelty effect may wear out over prolonged use, and any underlying usability issues, such as repetitiveness of bodily motion, discomfort from equipping/holding the device, user weariness, and frustration, become increasingly distracting over time [5].

Alongside these usability issues, cost and availability issues are also important factors for students. VAMR devices can be very expensive, with high-end devices such as Microsoft HoloLens selling for thousands of dollars and is outside of the typical student's budget. More recently, Augmented Reality on mobile phones and tablets are increasingly used as cheaper alternatives to full-fledged Virtual Reality headsets. However, this market fragmentation causes further availability issues for educators: an educator may not be able to mandate the use of the exact same hardware platform for a given class, which would force additional costs on students who already own some other VAMR-capable device. Standardization efforts of VAMR application programming interfaces, such as OpenXR [6], would allow applications to be written once for multiple platforms, solving this fragmentation problem. However, OpenXR is currently not available on all platforms (notably on iOS and Android handheld devices), and even then, developers still need to contend with per-platform variations, such as widely divergent field-of-view (FOV) display angles and sensor configurations across device models. Furthermore, mobile phones typically do not ship with OpenXR-ready input controllers, forcing developers to implement non-OpenXR alternatives, such as hand gesture tracking via the phone's front-facing camera [7].

This paper specifies and addresses these usability, cost, and availability issues, by documenting the design of a proof-of-concept, cross-platform VAMR basketball simulator. Basketball was chosen due to the popularity of the sport in the authors' home country, Philippines, as well as the fact that basketball's basic moves of ball passing and ball shooting are intuitively translated into hand gestures (whether tracked via controller input or front-facing camera) across all VAMR-capable devices, making the said sport a practicable starting point towards a later, more comprehensive study of VAMR use in overall sports teaching.

Parallel to the objective of teaching sports, another potential use of VAMR-based sport simulation is to enable the sport to be played by people who otherwise could not participate in a real-world sporting event due to disabilities. A VAMR-based simulation can theoretically allow multiple levels of computer assistance. In the case of basketball, this includes easier movement around the playing court, easier execution of passing/shooting actions, full/partial guidance of shots, and player height adjustment.

Such assistive features potentially increase the accessibility of a VAMR sports simulator even further for a wider variety of users and are thus considered in this paper.

2 Simulator Design

The design of our work-in-progress basketball simulator fundamentally follows an iterative process, as the on-going research explores new ideas and variations on existing ideas in terms of user control and interface. The simulator is currently designed as a freeform basketball court "sandbox", with a player able to freely interact with the ball and court with working physics, e.g., the user can aim and throw the ball anywhere on the court, including both goal baskets.

The features of our simulator were mostly inspired by the following previous work: an academic free-throw simulator [8] implemented using an XVR CAVE (a projected whole-room VR system) and motion tracking provided by Polhemus/DTrack magnetic trackers attached to the player's hand; and, a commercial simulator [9] that was designed specifically for the HTC VIVE headset and controllers. The academic simulator focused primarily on free-throw simulation and was thus limited to visualizing the free throw shot's direction and speed. On the other hand, the commercial simulator is more sandbox-like, allowing the player to shoot from any position in a half-court.

2.1 Hardware and Software Requirements

Our simulator is written in Unity version 2019.4, a commercial game engine that supports several extension frameworks to enable VR and AR rendering, but currently does not support OpenXR natively. For the simulator, it was decided to use the SteamVR extension framework to enable the use of a third-party hand gesture recognition plugin, HTC's VIVE Hand Tracking SDK. Unity's built-in XR subsystem is used for Microsoft HoloLens, which includes support for finger-pointing and tapping gestures.

Meanwhile, mobile platforms are supported using Unity's AR Foundation extension framework. Hand gesture support is not available by default; instead, the authors' own AMDG framework [7] is used. The AMDG framework offers users a handheld VAMR interaction style where the user's primary hand executes actions, while the other hand holds the device up near the eyes (see Fig. 1, right), providing a VAMR experience without the need for a headset. AMDG supports open-hand, closed-hand, and finger-pointing gestures. The AMDG hand detection engine has been updated to support people occlusion detection (available on iOS A12 devices and later) and LiDAR-based depth mapping (available on iPad Pro 2020 and iPhone 12 Pro).

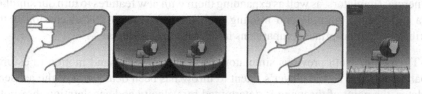

Fig. 1. Head-mounted (left) versus hand-held (right) configurations.

Table 1 summarizes the specific hardware and software configurations used to make our simulator available on four different types of devices: HTC VIVE, Microsoft HoloLens 1, iPhone 11 and iPad Pro 2020. These platforms were consciously chosen to cover a wide range of VAMR hardware archetypes while minimizing hardware acquisition costs and development time: the VIVE is a wide-FOV VR headset that is tethered to a computer, the HoloLens is a see-through AR headset with limited FOV but does not require a connected computer, and the iPhone and iPad are mobile handheld devices coming in small and large form factors, respectively. Other platforms, such as the Oculus Quest 2, HoloLens 2 and Android-based handheld devices, may be supported in later versions of the simulator as the hardware becomes available to the authors.

Table 1. Hardware and software configurations supported by the basketball simulator.

	HTC VIVE	Microsoft HoloLens 1	iPhone 11	iPad Pro 2020
Form factor	Tethered VR headset	Untethered AR headset	Mobile phone	Mobile tablet
Hand gesture support	Full support (via VIVE Hand Tracking SDK)	Finger-pointing and tapping only	Full support (via AMDG)	Full support (via AMDG)
Hand gesture capture hardware	VIVE front-facing camera	HoloLens depth camera	Front-facing camera with people occlusion detection	LiDAR scanner
Additional software libraries	SteamVR 1.16.10 VIVE Hand Tracking SDK 0.9.4	n/a	AR Foundation 2.1.16 AMDG OpenCV for Unity 2.4.3	AR Foundation 2.1.16 AMDG OpenCV for Unity 2.4.3

As a special case, since the HoloLens 1 hardware can only detect finger-pointing gestures, for this application, all open-hand gestures can also be done via finger-pointing (i.e., all subsequent references to open-hand and finger-pointing are equivalent).

2.2 Features Implemented

Our simulator borrows main features from the two previously described academic and commercial simulators, as well as expanding them with new features to turn our simulator into a full-fledged learning and training tool. Each feature in this discussion is thus described with appropriate comparisons to the previous systems.

Ball-Throwing. Both previous simulators track the player's hand motion to estimate the ball's motion after the player's intent to throw has been detected. For the academic simulator, the point of throwing is determined by velocity and acceleration thresholds;

once these thresholds were exceeded, the position, velocity, and acceleration at that point in time are sampled and used as the ball's initial parameters, and then simulated further using a Matlab ode45 solver. The commercial simulator, on the other hand, uses the VIVE controller's grip button to determine whether the ball has been released, and collects real-time position measurements of the VIVE controller to calculate velocity; the actual computation is unfortunately not documented due to the simulator's commercial nature. However, since the VIVE was the flagship hardware of the SteamVR platform, it is suspected that the computation is similar to that of the SteamVR plugin's throw computation [10]. SteamVR uses two possible estimation strategies for computing the release velocity of a thrown object when using the VIVE controller: a simple estimation that uses the previous three frames of hand positions to calculate the velocity on release, and an advanced estimation that buffers up to 10 frames of previous hand positions, finds the frame with the peak speed, and calculates the velocity with the help of the previous and next frame surrounding the peak frame.

For our simulator, since hand gestures are used instead of controllers, it was initially decided that the closed-hand gesture would be used to initialize ball-throwing, and the open-hand gesture would be used to signal the point of release, with the in-between motion of the hand used for estimating ball velocity (see Fig. 2). However, there is a noticeable delay in the detection of the open-hand gesture, possibly causing unexpected throwing behavior. Also, the HoloLens equivalent gesture (bringing a finger down then up to throw) may seem unintuitive for users. Thus, an alternate mode that uses velocity thresholds, similar to that of the academic simulator, is available as an option. The option is presented so that future usability testing may determine which method (close-move or close-move-open) would be ideal for actual use. The velocity (i.e., speed and direction) of the throw is then calculated using the last 3 frames, as with SteamVR.

Fig. 2. Shooting. From left to right: closed hand, forward movement, open hand (optional).

Player Teleport/Turning. The previous commercial simulator allows for easier movement around the court via the standard SteamVR "teleport" command. Teleportation can be used by disabled or less-athletic people to move around the virtual court without having to physically move in the real world. A teleport command is executed by pressing a physical controller's touch pad, which then shows a visual indication of the destination location of the player, and releasing the touchpad teleports the player to the said location. In addition, pressing the left or right edges of the touch pad allows players to rotate their viewpoint counterclockwise or clockwise, respectively. All viewpoint changes resulting from teleport or turning are instantaneous, with no in-between motion; this is recommended by the creators of SteamVR to prevent motion sickness.

This feature is likewise implemented in our simulator but is activated using hand gestures instead; the user points at a location on the floor and taps that location to teleport. However, if the teleport is instantaneous as with SteamVR, this gives a possibly unfair playing advantage to teleporting users over physically-moving users.

To reintroduce balance, it was decided to add a delay in the form of a circular progress bar (see Fig. 3). The progress bar fills up over time, and completion time is proportional to the travel distance; releasing the tap before completion shall cancel the teleport action. The teleport is also cancelled by moving the hand left or right, which causes a viewpoint rotation action to occur instead.

Fig. 3. Teleporting. From left to right: point, tap (with progress bar), release to teleport.

Presence Indicators. A persistent problem in VAMR is the diminished ability of users to establish the presence of other virtual objects, due to the limited field-of-view (FOV) of the hardware. This problem is especially severe on Microsoft HoloLens with an FOV of only 30° (horizontal). For example, sudden turning and movement can make the player lose their bearings and consequently lose track of the positions of the ball or goal. The previous commercial simulator avoided this problem by truncating the court into a half-court (so only one goal basket is available), and a new ball is automatically thrown at the user after every shot to ensure that the user always sees the ball. This simplification unfortunately rules out full-court simulation with multiple players.

To address this problem, our simulator uses icons at the edges of the visible screen (see Fig. 4) to act as presence indicators pointing to the off-screen positions of objects. When the player does not possess the ball, a ball icon indicates the off-screen position of the ball. If the ball is currently possessed by the player, a presence indicator of the player's (correct) goal appears instead.

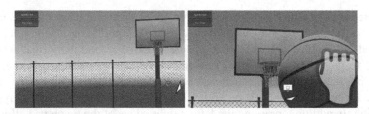

Fig. 4. Presence indicators. Left: missing ball. Right: correct goal location.

Shooting Assistance. To assist people with disabilities, our simulator offers multiple levels of shooting assistance. While this is partly supported by the commercial simulator, which offers two slider bars for controlling shot power and angle auto-correction, the configurable parameters for our simulator are altered to specifically provide disability assistance or training as opposed to just simplifying the simulation for casual use.

The first parameter is an automatic power adjustment variable, which, when set to 0, makes it so that initial speed of the ball is automatically calculated from the player's distance from the goal. When set to 1, the full speed is taken from the magnitude of the player's own hand movement. A value between 0 and 1 has the effect of amplifying weaker shots and attenuating stronger shots. Players can start at 0 to effectively allow a simple "close-open" gesture to launch the ball (perfect for beginners or disabled players), then gradually increase the value to 1 as they get better at estimating shot power.

The second parameter is an angle adjustment variable, which works similarly to angle auto-correction. However, instead of correcting the angle to always make the goal (which is not very useful for progressive training), a slider value of 0 uses the player's forward gaze as the ball's direction, 1 uses the direction of the player's hand movement vector, and in-between values interpolate between these two vectors. This way, players who are still developing their shooting aim can intuitively use their gaze instead to guide the shot (and still learn the proper angles for taking shots, which may be enough for the needs of younger users in physical education programs).

A third parameter, not present in the previous simulator, is player height adjustment. Controlling the player's height can be useful to allow shorter or disabled players experience ball shooting in the same way as standing or taller players. Conversely, taller players can also use this setting as a handicap for training.

3 Simulator Prototype Issues and Evaluation

As mentioned in the previous section, the simulator's design was iterated upon, and features were added or improved as needed. Early versions of the simulator did not incorporate teleportation and used only "close-open" gestures (with no interim hand movement) for shooting. Teleportation was initially added as an option that can only be triggered using external controllers (or the touchscreen on iOS devices) but is later simplified to be performed as a hand gesture by using context sensitivity: pointing towards the ground allows teleportation, while pointing upwards allows throwing. This simplifies interaction immensely and eliminates the need for separate controllers.

The current design of the simulator is geared towards implementing multi-user support, which inspired the implementation of teleportation progress bars. Future multi-user support would add gestures for throwing the ball towards teammates and stealing the ball from opponents. The system will also have to allow for event-based scripting to handle refereeing (e.g., moving into the space of another player should cause a foul event, which in turn can auto-arrange players into a free-throw configuration). Event-based scripting can also enable directed learning activities, such as training for consecutive free throws, 3-point shots, or ball-passing exercises. This can further be expanded to visualization and execution of playing tactics, similar to [11].

An evaluation of the system would involve observed user trials, with users testing the system on each supported device and evaluating their usability based on metrics such as SUS [12]. While these tests are currently not possible due to global pandemic lockdowns, it will be useful in the future to gauge the system's effectiveness as a learning and training tool, and to perform cross-evaluation of different device configurations, both head-mounted and hand-held.

4   Conclusion

This study developed a VAMR basketball simulator intended for distance-based learning and training, with features to assist disabled or disadvantaged players. The simulator primarily uses hand-gesture-based interaction to eliminate the need for additional input devices. The simulator is designed for both head-mounted and hand-held platforms to maximize its potential userbase, allow for future cross-platform networking, and permit forthcoming usability comparisons of head-mounted and hand-held form factors for effective VAMR-based sports training.

References

1. Soltani, P., Morice, A.H.P.: Augmented reality tools for sports education and training. Comput. Educ. **155**, 103923 (2020)
2. Pato, A.S., Remilllard, J.D.: eSport: Towards a Hermeneutic of Virtual Sport. (eSport: hacia una hermenéutica del deporte virtual). Cultura, Ciencia y Deporte (2018)
3. Hergüner, G., Yaman, Ç., Sari, S.Ç., Yaman, M.S., Dönmez, A.: The effect of online learning attitudes of sports sciences students on their learning readiness to learn online in the era of the new coronavirus pandemic (Covid-19). Turkish Online J. Educ. Technol. **68** (2021)
4. Huang, W.: Investigating the novelty effect in virtual reality on STEM learning. Ph.D. dissertation, Arizona State University (2020)
5. Rodrigo, M.M.T., Vidal, E.C.J.E., Caluya, N.R., Agapito, J., Diy, W.D.: Usability study of an augmented reality game for philippine history. Presented at the 24th international conference on computers in education, Mumbai, India (2016)
6. Khronos Group Inc.: The OpenXR Specification: What is OpenXR? https://www.khronos.org/registry/OpenXR/specs/1.0/html/xrspec.html#_what_is_openxr. Accessed 19 Mar 2021
7. Vidal, E.C.E., Rodrigo, M.M.T.: Hand gesture recognition for smartphone-based augmented reality applications. In: Chen, J.Y.C., Fragomeni, G. (eds.) HCII 2020. LNCS, vol. 12190, pp. 346–366. Springer, Cham (2020). https://doi.org/10.1007/978-3-030-49695-1_23
8. Covaci, A., Postelnicu, C.-C., Panfir, A.N., Talaba, D.: A virtual reality simulator for basket-ball free-throw skills development. In: Camarinha, L.M., Shahamatnia, E., Nunes, G. (eds.) DoCEIS 2012. IAICT, vol. 372, pp. 105–112. Springer, Heidelberg (2012). https://doi.org/10.1007/978-3-642-28255-3_12
9. Boninblue Design Laboratory: VR SHOOT AROUND - Realistic basketball simulator, https://store.steampowered.com/app/671740/. Accessed 11 Nov 2020
10. Valve Software: SteamVR Unity plugin. https://github.com/ValveSoftware/steamvr_unity_plugin. Accessed 22 Mar 2021
11. Tactic Training. IEEE Trans. Vis. Comput. Graph. PP, (2020). https://doi.org/10.1109/TVCG.2020.3046326
12. Sauro, J.: A practical guide to the system usability scale: Background, benchmarks & best practices. Measuring Usability LLC (2011)

Virtual Control Interface: A System for Exploring AR and IoT Multimodal Interactions Within a Simulated Virtual Environment

Zezhen Xu$^{(\boxtimes)}$ ⓘ, Powen Yao$^{(\boxtimes)}$ ⓘ, and Vangelis Lympouridis$^{(\boxtimes)}$ ⓘ

USC Viterbi School of Engineering, Los Angeles, CA 90089, USA
{zezhenxu,powenyao,el_829}@usc.edu

Abstract. This paper discusses the development of Virtual Control Interface (VCI), a Virtual Reality (VR) system for simulating and exploring multimodal context-sensitive interactions between Augmented Reality (AR) glasses and Internet of Things (IoT) devices.

Current trends in controlling IoT devices focus on using existing control interfaces such as smartphones. Parallel technological trends indicate that AR glasses are likely to become the next consumer terminal. Therefore, there is a need to explore a new paradigm for IoT control interfaces that leverages the benefits of AR.

Towards developing future-proof AR-IoT interfaces, we observed the HCI community's challenges in using existing hardware to explore the full potential and the limitations of future AR-IoT interfaces. That became the foundation for developing VCI.

This paper provides an overview of the advantages and shortcomings of developing such interfaces on smartphones, state-of-the-art AR/Mixed Reality (MR) glasses, and our proposed VR simulated AR environment. This overview outlines how our proposed system could be a superior choice for researchers to investigate, challenge assumptions, prototype, develop, and experimentally test AR-IoT interactions and interfaces with currently available technologies.

Furthermore, we present the three pillars we followed to guide the design and development of VCI to make it resemble an actual AR-IoT framework as much as possible while abstracting parts that have little to no effect on AR-IoT HCI research. These pillars are: design transferable architecture, use viable multimodal interactions and explore user interfaces in real-life scenarios.

These three principles informed the VCI's system architecture built upon three main subsystems: handling multi-modal user input, IoT device emulation and connectivity, and managing the AR user interface (UI).

Finally, we provide a heuristic evaluation and future work for VCI.

Keywords: Smart home · Internet of Things · Augmented reality · Virtual reality · AR-IoT · Multimodal interaction · Virtual Control Interface

© Springer Nature Switzerland AG 2021
C. Stephanidis et al. (Eds.): HCII 2021, CCIS 1420, pp. 345–352, 2021.
https://doi.org/10.1007/978-3-030-78642-7_47

1   Introduction

Current trends in controlling the Internet of Things (IoT) smart devices are focused on using existing control devices such as smartphones. Control interfaces on smartphones are spatially separated from the devices they operate, making them less intuitive as the users need to remember the association from device names to physical devices. Using these interfaces becomes exponentially more challenging the more devices a smart home has.

Parallel trends indicate that Augmented Reality (AR) glasses are likely to become the next consumer terminal. Therefore there is a need to explore a new paradigm for IoT control interfaces that leverages the benefits they bring. Towards developing future-proof AR-IoT interfaces, we face the challenge that both AR and IoT are still years away from mass adoption and rely on hardware advancements. It is challenging to explore the potential and the limitations of a future-proof AR-IoT interface using existing off-the-shelf hardware.

We propose a speculative design and engineering framework to explore these systems and interfaces while testing assumptions of using AR and IoT devices experimentally. We build our solution under a Virtual Reality (VR) framework that enables a first-person experience on how AR could integrate into a future smart home. It focuses on rapid prototyping upon various human-computer interaction layers built on a systems architecture that allows multimodal interfacing with emulated smart devices within a game engine.

The proposed Virtual Control Interface (VCI) system is a VR framework for simulating and exploring multimodal context-sensitive interactions between AR and IoT devices. We incorporate hand tracking, voice recognition, and eye tracking together as input to explore various augmented control interfaces and scenarios in a future smart home.

2   Overview of Developing for AR-IoT

Existing demos have already showcased possibilities for controlling IoT devices through AR-IoT interfaces on smartphones [1,6,7] and in state-of-the-art AR/MR glasses [4].

There is also increasing interest from researchers and developers to explore the possibilities of AR applications using head-mounted devices within the context of interfacing with IoT. Therefore, there is an unmet need to find ways to accelerate these explorations and better understand what users might need in the future to research and develop these applications. A robust framework that could offer the tools to prototype and closely resemble a future AR-IoT system and explore its full potential is crucial to obtain meaningful results from user testing.

Within the current development of the extended reality (XR) continuum, AR and VR have many similarities and differences; regardless, they both belong to the next computing platform, often referred to as the era of spatial computing.

A helpful way to join both mediums' strengths is to emulate AR in VR environments as what we have seen, for example, in the Cave-AR system proposed by Marco Cavallo et al. [5].

We will now briefly explore the advantages and shortcomings of developing and exploring AR-IoT interactions on smartphones, state-of-the-art AR/MR glasses, and in a simulated VR environment. This exploration illustrates how our proposed method of emulating AR-IoT interactions in VR could result in a better experience, reduce costs, remove unnecessary hardware limitations, and provide a scalable architecture for HCI researchers.

2.1   Developing AR-IoT on Smartphones

Smartphones are the most used AR devices today, with two of the largest AR platforms - iOS [2] and Android. The vast number of existing devices, users, and developers behind the smartphone industry provides researchers with a broader audience for testing and established AR development frameworks such as ARKit, ARCore, and AR Foundation.

Nonetheless, the AR experience on smartphones is somewhat limited compared to that of future AR glasses due to its form factor. Smartphones' 2D screens do not display depth information and have a small field of view (FOV), resulting in non-immersive AR experiences. Furthermore, smartphones are not wearables, so users need to hold smartphones with their hands. Using smartphones this way builds fatigue, and users loses the ability to perform two-hand gestures or fully engage with their surroundings. As a result, AR applications on smartphones usually use touch screens as the primary interaction modality. The hardware limitations of smartphones cause a degraded user experience incomparable to what future AR glasses could offer. Although accessible, AR-IoT paradigms developed on smartphones are limited and not directly transferable to future AR glasses.

2.2   Developing AR-IoT on the State-of-the-Art AR/MR Glasses

It is becoming more common for researchers to conduct AR-IoT research on existing AR/MR glasses. Current AR glasses' form factor will be similar to future commercialized AR glasses, so AR-IoT interactions developed on current state-of-the-art AR/MR glasses are potentially directly transferable to future AR glasses. Researchers can also leverage existing AR/MR backend services and frontend frameworks. Simultaneous Localisation and Mapping (SLAM), object recognition and tracking, spatial anchors, hand tracking, voice recognition and cloud services are valuable tools and services that can help with the AR-IoT interaction research and development process.

On the other hand, exploring AR-IoT interactions on the current state-of-the-art AR/MR glasses suffers from the high cost and hardware limitations of AR/MR glasses and IoT devices. Researchers need to purchase AR/MR glasses, physical IoT devices, and physically equip spaces when exploring current and future real-life scenarios. The current state-of-the-art AR/MR glasses have limited hardware capabilities such as a narrow field of view (FOV), low resolution projecting screens, restricted computational power, color and shadow rendering issues and limited sensor integrations to support future interaction modalities. In addition, current IoT devices are not designed for AR controlled use cases. They lack critical hardware components for localization and standards for communicating with AR glasses. Furthermore, researchers cannot experiment with future IoT devices not yet produced by manufacturers.

Apart from cost and hardware limitations, developing AR-IoT solutions on current hardware would also cost much time. Most of the current AR glasses are developer editions, which means their experimental software and hardware features are prone to change. On the IoTs' side, researchers need to spend time connecting, tracking, and controlling physical IoT devices supporting multiple standards, which can deviate a lot of the effort and time put into the AR-IoT interaction design research.

2.3   Developing AR-IoT on VR Simulated AR Environments

Developing AR-IoT interactions and experiences in a simulated VR environment combines the advantages of developing on smartphones and state-of-the-art AR/MR glasses. VR headsets have established and commercialized platforms, like smartphones, and their form factor roughly resembles that of AR/MR glasses. Testing in VR provides a sense of presence as if the testing users and researchers are in the scene they want to explore. We can effectively simulate close to real-life AR experiences in VR and leverage VR headsets' mature ecosystem.

This approach can reduce the cost of exploring and experimenting with AR-IoT interactions in different scenarios. Within a VR simulation, researchers can set up multiple scenes such as smart home, an office or a warehouse with various simulated IoT devices in a relatively short amount of time and at minimum cost.

In addition, this approach lifts hardware limitations researchers face when using AR/MR glasses. VR headsets have much better screens with higher refresh rate and resolution and larger FOVs than state-of-the-art AR/MR glasses. Unlike in the real world, in a VR simulation, we can emulate unlimited amounts of IoT devices, the positioning system necessary to locate IoT devices, and a unified data transmission layer to send and receive data to control IoT devices.

A simulated VR solution is scalable and can provide a lot of flexibility and freedom to researchers. Researchers can add new input modalities into existing scenes when new sensors are commercialized. They can extend the scenes with IoT products that might exist in the future to explore and develop future-facing AR-IoT interactions.

With this approach, every part required to build an AR-IoT experience, including the emulated AR glasses and their operating system, IoT devices, environments and scenarios, are developed in game engines. Researchers can make rapid iterations by designing, scripting, building, and experiencing their speculative designs and interaction scenarios in a single pipeline.

3   Core Principles

As we have seen, developing AR-IoT solutions in a VR simulated AR environment has many advantages. The experience produced can be relatively close to that of the actual future where AR glasses are adopted.

Using a VR simulated environment, our goal is to rapidly prototype and explore multimodal AR-IoT interactions in current and future real-life scenarios.

To achieve that, we need to make this framework resemble an actual AR-IoT infrastructure as close as possible while abstracting parts that have little to no effect on AR-IoT HCI research.

We identified three pillars to guide us to develop such a system.

1. Build VCI's architecture with inspirations initially taken from existing smart home frameworks that could translate to future AR-IoT architectures.
2. Support viable existing multi-modal interactions or those that can most likely exist in future AR glasses.
3. Enable explorations of AR-IoT user interfaces and interactions within current real-life or future scenarios.

4   System Architecture

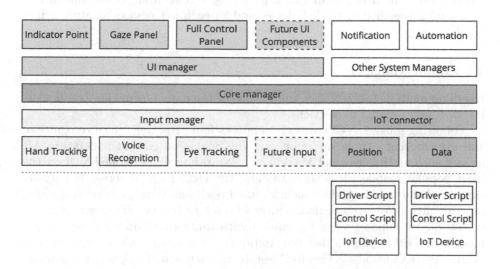

Fig. 1. Overview of VCI's High-Level System Architecture

We designed the system architecture shown in Fig. 1 for VCI with the three pillars. The "core manager" drives three main parts of VCI: "IoT connector", "Input manager", and "UI manager" to work together.

4.1   IoT Connector

In a real-life scenario that involves an AR-IoT setting, the AR glasses are physi-cally separated from the IoT devices they will be controlling. AR glasses need to track IoT devices' position in space and transmit data to them using a standard protocol. Following pillar 1 and 3, VCI's architecture provides the capability to emulate the separation between emulated AR glasses and IoT devices. It also needs a protocol for researchers to set up emulated IoT devices in new scenes when exploring everyday scenarios and interactions.

The dotted line in Fig. 1 reflects a clear separation between the AR glasses and the emulated IoT devices in VCI. Each emulated IoT devices include a driver script that conforms to a unified standard protocol defined by VCI. VCI's IoT connector is constantly looking for IoT devices in the scene, tracking their position, and registering their driver scripts as the manifest file. Researchers can add new types of emulated IoT devices by describing their characteristics and controllable actions in their driver script. Each device also includes a control script that emulates embedded software that would come with physical IoT devices to control their actions.

At the implementation level, the core manager issues actions through user intentions gathered from the UI manager and other system components to the IoT connector. The IoT connector will send the actions to corresponding IoT devices' driver scripts by looking up device information gathered when regis-tering them. The driver scripts then parse the actions from VCI's standard to instructions specified by the IoT device and let each IoT devices' control scripts handle it.

4.2   Input Manager

Handling multiple forms of user input is one of the requirements for experiment-ing with multi-modal interactions.

Following pillar 2, VCI currently supports hand tracking, voice recognition, and eye-tracking - three key input methods viable on current and future AR glasses such as Hololens and Magic Leap. We primarily developed VCI on the most popular mobile VR headset to date, the Oculus Quest series. It natively supports hand tracking, which includes hand positioning and gesture recognition functionalities. We further enhance its hand tracking functionalities with MRTK-Quest [8]. We support voice recognition with unity's built-in voice recognition module and other plugins that use Android's voice recognition feature, such as "Game Voice Control" [3]. Oculus Quest, on the hardware level, does not support native eye-tracking. Within VR, we can speculate with average accuracy where a user is looking at within the virtual environment by projecting a ray cast from the center of the field of view. To make this more apparent to the user, we are placing a small dot at the center of the screen. The users can look around and place the dot on the devices they want to control to simulate gazing at them.

4.3   UI Manager

UI manager provides a software interface for HCI researchers to develop and manage AR UI components for controlling devices with ease. The UI manager takes in parsed user input, sends and receives IoT devices' data seamlessly through the core manager's help and its underlying Input manager and IoT connector. Following pillar 3, we built and experimented with three UI components in VCI under a smart home setting.

Fig. 2. Indicator point   **Fig. 3.** Gaze panel   **Fig. 4.** Full control panel

Indicator Point and Quick Actions. VCI indicates the exact position of smart devices to the user with indicator points attached to each device. These are grey-boarded white dots, as shown in Fig. 2. All indicator points contain an icon at the center. The icon classifies the device's type to inform the user which device they picked when they want to control it. In every simulated environment, users can discover smart home devices by looking around and finding the indicator points associated with them.

VCI offers a set of quick actions to users to control primary settings on smart devices rapidly. The users do not even need to look at the devices to perform such interactions. By pointing their hand to where the device is and dragging the indicator point horizontally or vertically, the user can control an attribute along that axis - examples include adjusting the temperature of an AC unit, the brightness of a light, or the height of the blinds on a window.

Gaze Panel with Context-Aware Voice Commands. VCI knows which device a user wants to control from gaze input. When the system is confident that the user wants to use a device, a gaze panel appears beside the indicator point corresponding to the device, as shown in Fig. 3. Gaze panel provides information about the IoT devices and voice command suggestions to the user.

Because VCI knows where the user is looking, VCI supports context-aware voice commands. It shortens the voice commands by removing the need for the users to explicitly say the name of the device and allowing vague commands that could have multiple meanings on different types of devices. For example, a user can look at a smart light and say "turn off". Only that light will be turned off.

Full Control Panel. Quick actions and voice commands alone cannot handle all possible interactions with smart home IoT devices in an everyday scenario. To solve this problem, VCI provides a full control panel, as shown in Fig. 4. It is where all other secondary or advanced functions can reside. The user can access the full control panel by dragging an indicator point towards them. These full control panels are customizable per device.

Within the VCI system's architecture and development framework, researchers can add more UI components to the system and experience their interactions in VR within a few hours, thanks to the underlying mechanics that handle user inputs and IoT device simulation and connectivity.

5   Evaluation and Future Work

VCI is a system that lets researchers experiment with AR-IoT multimodal interactions in real-life current or future simulated environments with low cost and a rapid development process. We built the framework, emulated a smart home environment and simulated different everyday scenarios, UI components, and interactions demonstrated in the paper with a team of 9 students within a semester. We have received overwhelmingly positive feedback from users after using VCI, but moving forward, we are seeking more testing with experts from the HCI and IoT communities.

We plan to extend the system to a few more prototyping environments, including a smart office and a smart warehouse, and explore more multimodal interactions within those environments.

References

1. http://smartarhome.com/
2. Augmented reality. https://www.apple.com/augmented-reality/
3. Game voice control [offline speech recognition]: Audio: Unity asset store. https://assetstore.unity.com/packages/tools/audio/game-voice-control-offline-speech-recognition-178047description
4. Avidigitaly: Xr-os: Ar & iot app - control lights and smart home iot devices like a jedi! July 2019. https://www.youtube.com/watch?v=PyhvXZcC4cA
5. Cavallo, M., Forbes, A.G.: Cave-AR: a VR authoring system to interactively design, simulate, and debug multi-user AR experiences. In: 2019 IEEE Conference on Virtual Reality and 3D User Interfaces (VR), pp. 872–873 (2019). https://doi.org/10.1109/VR.2019.8798148
6. Jo, D., Kim, G.J.: In-situ AR manuals for IoT appliances. In: 2016 IEEE International Conference on Consumer Electronics (ICCE), pp. 409–410 (2016). https://doi.org/10.1109/ICCE.2016.7430669
7. Lee, J., Lee, K., Nam, B., Wu, Y.: Iot platform-based IAR: a prototype for plant o m applications. In: 2016 IEEE International Symposium on Mixed and Augmented Reality (ISMAR-Adjunct), pp. 149–150 (2016). https://doi.org/10.1109/ISMAR-Adjunct.2016.0063
8. Provencher: provencher/mrtk-quest. https://github.com/provencher/MRTK-Quest

Virtual Equipment System:
Expansion to Address Alternate Contexts

Powen Yao[✉] [iD], Vangelis Lympouridis[iD], and Michael Zyda

USC Viterbi School of Engineering, Los Angeles, CA 90089, USA
{powenyao,el_829,zyda}@usc.edu

Abstract. Virtual Equipment System (VES) is a body-centric 3D User
Interface design framework built to advance the development of interfaces
that capitalize on user's proprioception in immersive environments. In
a previous poster paper submitted to HCII last year, we focused on the
application of this framework in developing a series of virtually embodied
interfaces for adjusting auditory and visual user settings. We outfitted
the user with Virtual Equipment that correspond to the user's sensory
organs. For example, by interacting with Virtual Headphones and performing gestures, the user can adjust the audio volume of the system.
Similarly, the user can interact with Virtual Goggles to adjust brightness
settings.

Since then, we have expanded the development of the VES and its
functionalities. In particular, to support additional contexts in the form
of a set of Virtual Equipment known as Equipment Set or simply as Set.

A user can simultaneously be "wearing" several Equipment Sets, each
designed for a specific context. That is to say, multiple Equipment Sets
affect the user at the same time, though the user can only interact with a
Set at a time. With simple actions, however, the user can switch between
different Sets and access the functionalities of the Set within the context
of its use. So far, we have built three demos to showcase VES in different
contexts: Auditory and Visual user settings, privacy settings using VES
in combination with the Voodoo Doll technique, and telematic sensory
settings through the use of Alternate Avatars.

Keywords: Virtual Equipment System · 3D user interface · Virtual
reality

1 Introduction

Many Virtual Reality (VR) games have brought the concept of personal equipment for users; The user may find a watch on the wrist, a helmet on the head,
or a gun in the hip holster. These equipment are an imitation of real-life equipment and function similarly to their real-world equivalents, both cosmetically
and functionally. For example, a gun holstered away at the side can be picked
up and used to shoot projectiles. Regardless of whether the gun fires a 9mm

© Springer Nature Switzerland AG 2021
C. Stephanidis et al. (Eds.): HCII 2021, CCIS 1420, pp. 353–360, 2021.
https://doi.org/10.1007/978-3-030-78642-7_48

bullet, a fireball, or a orb of darkness, the interaction with the equipment is very similar to what we see in real life.

It is important to note that physical laws in virtual reality do not need to be the same as the ones in our actual reality. In the game Half-Life: Alyx [4], the user can access ammo by grabbing over the shoulder and the user immediately finds the ammo appropriate for the weapon at hand. In the game Raw Data [3], the user can reload pistols simply by moving pistols to where the holsters are. In an extreme example, in the VR Game Fantastic Contraption [1], the user can pull out different building components such as sticks and wheels from the ear, top of the head, and so on. These components are far bigger than what a person can reasonably equip. There are also infinite copies stored in the same location. They are equipment only in the sense that they are objects that follow the user's body at a specific location.

These games showed that user interfaces and user interactions in virtual reality do not have to follow the laws of our reality. We refer to this quality as hyper-physical interface properties and define it as the properties of a user interface with a virtual manifestation that follows physical laws and phenomena that are not necessarily found in our physical world.

2   Virtual Equipment System

Our previous work with Virtual Equipment System (VES) [5] explored hyper-physicality and hyper-physical interfaces as applied to a Virtual Equipment System. Our initial proposal [6] called for the use of Virtual Headphones and Virtual Goggles that serve as shortcuts for users to adjust their sensory settings. Our more recent work also applied it to user privacy by combining VES with the Voodoo DOll technique [2] as well as applying VES to user's avatar variations.

In these contexts, the user would access the equipment placed at the eye slot for very different reasons. In the context of the sensory settings, it is to interact with Virtual Goggles to adjust the brightness of the experience as well as other visual-related settings. In the context of user privacy, it is to interact with the user's privacy representation of eyes to control eye-tracking, eye color, pupil reflection, and other privacy settings. In the context of Avatar & Representation, it would be a shortcut for grabbing an Arcane Eye which the user can place in the world to later see through.

Given there are many different interactions that can be associated with a given context for the same body part, the equipment would either have to be multi-purposed or there needs to be multiple equipment at the same body part. As multi-purpose equipment could be diluted in its efficiency, we look to hyper-physical interactions to address the issues of having multiple equipment at the same body part. The user needs to be able to quickly switch the Set he is wearing in order to access the right Virtual Equipment for his intended interaction (Fig. 1).

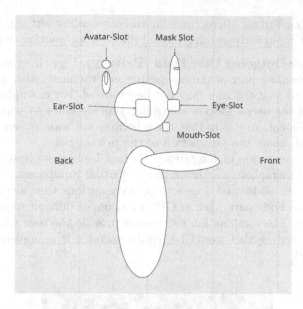

Fig. 1. For the latest configuration of the standard VES context, the user is equipped with the Avatar Tool in the Avatar-Slot and Privacy Mask Tool in the Mask-Slot.

3   Potential Contexts for VES

There are many different contexts that one may want to use Virtual Equipment System for. We propose that the users have multiple Virtual Equipment Sets worn at the same time. Each Set is collection of Virtual Equipment and typically intended and geared toward a specific context. Some possible contexts are: Sensory, Privacy, Management, Cosmetic, Avatar, Dev, and App/Game Specific.

Of the many contexts, we believe the first three should be universal and supported on an Operating System (OS) level. By supporting them at the OS-level, it would allow users a familiar and universal interface to fall back on regardless of the VR world they are in.

In any given context, there may be multiple Sets associated with that context. For example, the user may have many different Game-Specific Sets for a fantasy game, such as a Warrior Set, a Thief Set, and a Wizard Set.

3.1   Different Sets and Their Contexts

Sensory Set for Incoming Sensory Data. In any VR application, the user benefits from being able to quickly adjust sensory settings. This is one of the candidate for universal implementation as without sensory inputs to the user, there would be no VR. Users would use the Virtual Equipment located near their sensory organs to adjust and access its corresponding settings.

While not strictly incoming sensory data, interaction settings are also included here as they tend to be grouped together in traditional menus. This may include interacting with a Virtual Microphone for audio recording settings, Virtual Controller to adjust input settings, and Virtual Shoe for locomotion settings.

Privacy Set for Outgoing User Data (Privacy). Users in virtual reality are increasingly becoming part of the computing environment, with data collected (with permission) that the user may not be aware of. For example, the activity and location of the user's motion controller provide clues to what the user is doing at the moment. Any data that the user may not want others to receive or utilize would fall under the jurisdiction of the privacy Set.

In our implementation of the privacy Virtual Equipment System, we utilize the voodoo doll metaphor in addition to the Virtual Equipment System to provide the user with additional access to privacy options that are not normally associated with a body part, such as GPS location, or difficult to get to, such as the user's heart. The combination techniques provide the user with a powerful and intuitive interface that would be highly useful if it is implemented at the OS-level (Fig. 2).

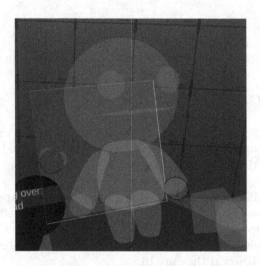

Fig. 2. VES combined with Voodoo Doll Metaphor for the privacy context The user's left controller has grabbed the Heart organ, allowing the user to enable/disable tracking for pulse rate

Management Set for VES Management. This Set utilizes a special instance of the VES where the user can manage settings related to Virtual Equipment Systems. Broadly, the user would be able to manage which Virtual Equipment Sets to use, swap out the equipment equipped within a Virtual Equipment Set, and fine tune the position of the equipment slots.

Given that VES involves whole body interaction, it is ideal for VES to also be adjusted in the same manner. The user should be able to move Equipment slots using the same motion controller in the same way that he would access an equipment stored in that slot. Using a traditional 2D menu would increase the time needed to customize the interaction to the user's end result.

This is the third candidate for being a universal VES Set as its role becomes increasingly crucial once the user is dealing with more than one Equipment Set.

Cosmetic Set for Outgoing User Data (Cosmetic). In an multi-user environment, the user may want to look a certain way to the other users. In many games featuring equipment, the user typically has equipment that looks a certain way and provides gameplay bonuses to the user. Some games also have the option of wearing cosmetic or vanity equipment that override the appearance of the functional equipment the user has equipped. Similarly, in VR, the user may have a Set for this context. The user would appear to others as wearing whichever equipment they have on in this Set. The user would also be able to interact with these equipment to access its related cosmetic settings. For example, the user may interact with the eye-patch worn at the eye-slot to change to a different eye equipment such as a monocle.

Fig. 3. In the Alternate Avatar Context, the user is placing an Alternate Avatar that the user can later see, hear, or speak through. The user can also possess the Alternate Avatar to become that avatar

Avatar Set for Using Alternate Avatars. In this Set, the user has access to Equipment that allow the user to place Alternate Avatars and its lesser versions in the world as shown in 3, which affects how the player can manifest in the virtual world. The user can also see, hear, or speak through placed Alternate Avatars, allowing the user to be present in multiple locations at a moment's notice. For example, the user may place an Arcane Eye from the Eye Slot that he can use to see through even after leaving the area.

The avatar equipment also serves as a metaphor for possession. The user may place equipment associated with different body parts on other characters to experience the world through their perspective. For example, the user may place the eye equipment at another user to request the VR equivalent of remote desktop to see what that user sees.

Dev Set for Development or Debug. In this Set, the user is provided equipment that is expected to aid with the development process. For example, the user may interact with the equipment at the eye slot to see the world as wireframe constructions, shaded, or in terms of UV Charts. Alternatively, with the Dev Set and context, the user may see code or data associated with each objects in the world and can then modify them. This functionality is likely to be app-specific. While any VR experience should have a Dev Set, it would not be universal as it is not intended for everyday users.

App/Game-Specific Set. Last but not least, are Sets that are specific to the application or the game the user is playing. For example, a user may be playing a fantasy VR games with swords and shields or the user may be using a VR drawing application and interact with the equipment in the eye slot to see different lighting conditions or different layers.

4 Changing Sets for Different Contexts

We have provided many different contexts in which a specific Set may be useful. As the context may change rapidly based on the user's intention, there needs to be a way to quickly change the current Virtual Equipment Set based on the context the user is in. In the basic example, Sets and contexts are synonymous.

Set Switch Tool. The Set Switch Tool is an Virtual Equipment that is used to switch the current Set to the one associated specifically with the Set Switch Tool. In the case of the Privacy Set, it's the privacy mask where the mask serves as a metaphor for user's privacy. In the case of Avatar Set, it's the Avatar Tool that's shaped like a doll.

For the current implementation, the two Set Switch Tools have been deliberately placed in a location that is harder to reach in order to avoid accidental interactions. The Set Switch tool can belong in many different Sets, but it always has a specific Set (context) that it is associated with. Interacting with the Set Switch Tool is meant to switch the current Set to that associated Set.

The Set Switch Tool provides three potential methods to switching Sets. The first is through the hover state, the second is through the activate action, the third is through the drop action at the Universal Set Switch Tool.

Set Switch Tool - Hover Interaction. As the user hovers a motion controller over the Set Switch Tool, the active Set switches to the Set associated with the tool. As soon as the user stops hovering a motion controller over the tool, the Set reverts back to what it was previously.

This means that the user can simultaneously use the other controller to interact with the equipment in the new Set. Thus, the user with the Sensory Set equipped can move one hand over to the Avatar Tool in a hover state while the other hand grab the Arcane Eye instead of the Virtual Goggles in the eye slot. This is shown in Fig. 4.

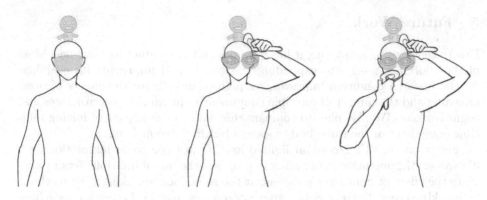

Fig. 4. Left to Right: 1) User is equipped with Virtual Goggles and the Avatar Tool which functions as a Set Switch Tool. 2) The User moves and hovers one controller over the Avatar Tool to trigger the Set switch. The Equipment Set is now switched to the Avatar Set with Arcane Eyes. 3) The user grabs Arcane Eyes from Avatar Set

Set Switch Tool - Activate Action. The user can grab the Set Switch Tool and push the trigger button to activate the Set Switch Tool. The activation will toggle the current mode on or off, depending on its existing state. Once toggled on, the user would be equipped with the associated Set until the it is changed again.

This is best used when the user would need to switch the current Set for a while. It also has the benefit of allowing interaction with just one hand.

Set Switch Tool - Drop Action. The user may also grab the Set Switch Tool and drop it in the Universal Set Switch Tool. Similar to dropping a Virtual Equipment in the Alt Node, dropping it in the Universal Set Switch Tool serves as a way to trigger a Set switch.

Universal Set Switch Tool. The user may not always have access to the Set Switch Tool for a given Set that he wants to switch to. As the number of contexts and sets a user has equipped grow, it will become increasingly difficult to place a Set Switch Tool in each Set to switch to the other contexts/Sets. This is where the Universal Set Switch Tool come in.

The Universal Set Switch Tool is similar to a regular Set Switch Tool but its associated Set is the VES Management Set. Its Equipment Gesture can be associated with iterating through the Sets that the user have equipped so the user can perform left and right gestures to cycle through the Sets. Alternatively, each direction can correspond to a particular Set so the user could use Up gesture to switch to Sensory Set, Left gesture to Privacy Set, and so on.

This Universal Set Switch Tool would be placed at an easily accessible location, but not frequently accessed to avoid accidental interaction. A possible location would be the chest. It is easy for the user to access, but does not carry as much association with specific senses such as the eyes or the ears.

The Universal Context Switch Tool can also be combined with the Voodoo Doll technique to provide the user with a way to customize Sets without the need for whole-body interaction.

5   Future Work

Due to the ongoing pandemic, it has been difficult to conduct user studies. Most of the effort has gone into expanding the system and improving its usability. As the research condition improves, we plan to investigate the effects of overcrowding and the impact of multiple equipment in proximity on error rates and cognitive load. We also plan to compare this data to the impact of having multiple equipment in the same body location but in different Sets.

Furthermore, VES has so far limited itself to just controller interaction with 3D space. Although this paper already proposes the use of multiple Sets to alleviate the effect of multiple equipment at the same location along with methods to quickly access different Sets, other approaches may be better for switching Sets. For example, a multi-modal approach using speech recognition may be a better approach that should be provided to the users when available.

6   Conclusion

Virtual Equipment System offers the user the ability to quickly access different equipment, each representing different options and interactions. Furthermore, we can apply the Virtual Equipment System to different contexts to re-use the same system more broadly. As the contexts increase, we utilize the concept of Equipment Sets that are equipped simultaneously with one Set active at a time to better address the need of having multiple equipment in the same body location. This concept also includes new equipment to aid users in managing the increasingly growing amount of contexts and Equipment Sets that they may encounter.

References

1. Northway Games, R.G.C.: Fantastic contraption. [Digital] (2016)
2. Pierce, J.S., Stearns, B.C., Pausch, R.: Voodoo dolls. In: Proceedings of the 1999 symposium on Interactive 3D graphics - SI3D '99. ACM Press (1999). https://doi.org/10.1145/300523.300540
3. Survios: Raw data. [Digital] (2017)
4. Valve: Half-life: Alyx. [Digital] (2020)
5. Yao, P., Lympouridis, V., Zhu, T., Zyda, M.: Interfacing with sensory options using a virtual equipment system. Symposium on Spatial User Interaction. ACM, October 2020. https://doi.org/10.1145/3385959.3421723
6. Yao, P., Zhu, T., Zyda, M.: Designing Virtual Equipment Systems for VR. In: Stephanidis, C., Antona, M. (eds.) HCII 2020. CCIS, vol. 1225, pp. 137–144. Springer, Cham (2020). https://doi.org/10.1007/978-3-030-50729-9_19

Mixed Reality Application and Interaction of Chinese Traditional Furniture in the Digital Scene Construction from Chinese Ancient Paintings

Dehua Yu(✉)

Beijing Institute of Technology, Beijing 100081, China

Abstract. The study focused on display and interaction of Chinese traditional furniture including shape, structure and its ancient usage scenarios. The aim of the interaction mixed with real and virtual scene is to direct the participants to experience the ancient living scene of Chinese traditional furniture, learn the background of Chinese unique shape and structure of Chinese traditional furniture. The study is the attempt of design application of MR technology, sensor technology to Chinese cultural heritage study and protection. A digital scene of the painting "Celebrating 60th Birthday in Bamboo Garden" drawn by Ji lv and Wenying Lv who are palace painters in middle Ming Dynasty would be constructed with real and virtual Chinese ancient furniture and living things. With the help of MR technology, the participants would join in the digital scene of ancient living scene, directed by virtual waiters to experience the fix and unfix process of Chinese traditional furniture, set up literati communication scene of antique appreciation, poetry and painting, and so on. Six Chinese traditional high and low dual-purpose tables with different shapes and structures would be chosen to be saved in six boxes, which can be randomly selected by the participants to experience the fix and unfix process.

Keywords: Mixed reality · Chinese traditional furniture · Interaction

1 Introduction

Chinese traditional furniture plays an important role in Chinese traditional culture. There are four excellent factors of Chinese traditional furniture: elegant shape, strong structure, coordinated proportion and rational material. The paper would explore the possible interactive exhibition with AR/MR technology, motion capture and sensor technology to attract more people to experience the artful and ingenious structures and usage of Chinese traditional furniture.

A digital scene of the painting "Celebrating 60th Birthday in Bamboo Garden" drawn by Ji lv and Wenying Lv who are palace painters in Ming Dynasty would be constructed with real and virtual Chinese ancient furniture and living things [1].

© Springer Nature Switzerland AG 2021
C. Stephanidis et al. (Eds.): HCII 2021, CCIS 1420, pp. 361–366, 2021.
https://doi.org/10.1007/978-3-030-78642-7_49

2   Achieved Interactive Exhibition Effect

2.1   Visitors Interact with Virtual Character with Sensor Technology

Previous exhibition study puts a real folding chair besides the virtual folding chairs, and there are some directions to let the participants sit on the real folding chair. The action of sitting would trigger the pressure sensor installed on the seat of the folding chair, which would trigger the animation of virtual characters in the painting to interact with the participants with eyes, talks or motion (see Fig. 1).

Fig. 1. Visitors interact with virtual character with pressure sensor technology.

2.2   Control of Virtual Waiter in the Painting with Motion Capture Technology

Previous exhibition study has already achieved the motion match between research people and virtual characters by means of motion capture sensor technology [2]. The research people who wears motion capture sensor hardware has matched the virtual waiter in the painting, and the virtual waiter would follow the full-body action and movement of the research people. In the restored digital scene of the painting "Celebrating 60th Birthday in Bamboo Garden", the virtual waiter would interact with visitors, and direct the participants to experience the fix and unfix process of Chinese traditional high and low dual-purpose tables (see Fig. 2).

Fig. 2. The virtual waiter would interact with visitors freely followed by research people.

3   Mixed Reality Application and Interaction

3.1   Mix with Real and Virtual Furniture in Mixed Reality Environment

The study would build waiters serving scene around the table, and through the MR Glasses visitors can immerse in the rockworks, busy waiters and tables around them. Some waiters are preparing fruits and desserts, some waiters are boiling tea, and some are delivering the tea to their masters. The busy and lively atmosphere would infected the visitors who wear MR Glasses, and it seems that the visitors are also personally in the environment, feeling comfortable and rich literary life in Bamboo Garden in middle Ming Dynasty (see Fig. 3).

Fig. 3. Mix and interaction of real and virtual furniture with MR Glasses.

A table by the rockery is solid wood table with lacquer, on which there are guqin, fruit plate and food box. In the mixed reality scene, the waiters are busy with tea, fruit and dessert. The table is common in ordinary life to support general articles for daily use in middle Ming Dynasty. There would be more similar tables with dual-purpose tables shown in the mixed reality scene.

The study would build the officials watching the cranes dancing in the garden. Three officials with official costume are sitting in the folding chair, enjoying the cranes which indicate longevity. Similar folding chairs would be shown in virtual and real way. Virtual officials can sit on the virtual folding chair, inviting the participants to sit on the real folding chairs, and enjoy the same atmosphere of dancing cranes.

3.2 The Experience of Fix and Unfix Process of Chinese Traditional High and Low Dual-Purpose Tables

Chinese traditional high and low dual-purpose Tables [3] are common outdoor furniture in Ming and Qing Dynasty, especially in garden, suburb and hunting area (see Fig. 4). It is also appropriate in the garden of the painting "Celebrating 60th Birthday in Bamboo Garden".

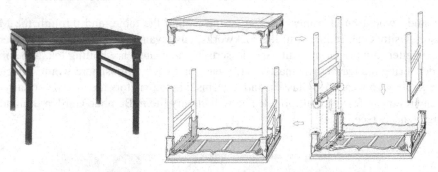

Fig. 4. The mortise and tenon structure of Chinese traditional high and low dual-purpose tables collected by the Imperial Palace.

Six different Chinese traditional high and low dual-purpose tables would be chosen ahead (see Fig. 5). The study would set up six virtual boxes on the floor of the garden, in which six different Chinese traditional high and low dual-purpose tables would be saved. The virtual waiter would direct the participants to open the box, take out the folding table on the rock, and unfix their legs to change the short tables to high tables. Finally, the high table would be put besides the rockworks, supporting the tea tray, food container or just a flower vase. They can also put the writing brush, Xuan paper and inkstone on the table, if they want to set the scene of calligraphy and drawing. Six boxes have six different and unique shapes and structures, showing vivid Chinese cultural gene. While the real six Chinese traditional high and low dual-purpose tables would be displayed one side to give a reference.

The process of fix and unfix would be mixed with real and virtual furniture and living things. All the participants' actions would be captured by sensors which triggered the

Fig. 5. The experience of fix and unfix process of Chinese traditional high and low dual-purpose tables with MR technology.

interaction of the virtual waiter. During the process, the participants would enjoy the interaction with virtual ancient literati in the finished real and virtual scene.

4 Conclusion

The study focused on the digitization display and interaction of Chinese traditional furniture and its culture it contains. With the help of motion capture, sensor, MR technology, people would have chance to immerse in the mixed reality display environment, interacting with real and virtual furniture, which direct people to experience Chinese traditional culture and living condition. Mixed reality technology is a good way to mix real furniture with virtual furniture, which give the participants the unique mixed atmosphere to enjoy.

Acknowledgments. This paper is supported financially by MOE (Ministry of Education in China) Project of Humanities and Social Sciences Research Youth Fund (Project No.19YJC760144).

References

1. Zhao, B.: Drawing Collection of the Palace Museum, vol. 8, p. 26. Palace Museum Press, Beijing (2011)

2. Yu, D.: Motion capture and virtual reality application in the interactive exhibition of chinese traditional furniture. In: Karwowski, W., Ahram, T., Etinger, D., Tanković, N., Taiar, R. (eds.) IHSED 2020. AISC, vol. 1269, pp. 209–214. Springer, Cham (2021). https://doi.org/10.1007/978-3-030-58282-1_34
3. Dehua, Y., Jiang, K.: Mortise and Tenon structure of chinese traditional high and low dual-purpose table. Packag. Eng. **41**(25), 162–169 (2020)

VR-DesignSpace: A Creativity Support Environment Integrating Virtual Reality Technology into Collaborative Data-Informed Evaluation of Design Alternatives

Maryam Zarei(✉) and Steve DiPaola

Simon Fraser University, Burnaby, Canada
{mzarei,sdipaola}@sfu.ca

Abstract. In the Architectural, Engineering, and Construction (AEC) projects, the project team continuously evaluates and reflects on alternative design solutions during the design process. However, there are limited computational tools to support the real-time collaborative analysis of design alternatives and practical data-driven decision-making. This paper investigates the potential integration of Virtual Reality (VR) technology into the design process to augment real-time collaborative evaluation and reflection on design solutions in a data-informed architectural design context. We argue that: (a) the collaborative assessment of design ideas requires to occur in an immersive 3D environment since architectural design space and interactions are inherently three-dimensional; (b) reducing the cognitive load of shifting between various tools and multiple interfaces during the examination of alternatives augments decision-making accuracy and efficiency; (c) the collaboration experience can benefit from the advantages of VR over physical reality in addition to simulation of preferable in-person collaborations and interactions. To address these high-level considerations, we propose a technical approach for designing and implementing an interactive Creativity Support Virtual Environment called VR-DesignSpace, inspired by VirtualCoLab, an immersive scientific collaboration system used in the mathematics domain. VR-DesignSpace system facilitates real-time interactions between designers, clients, and stakeholders involved in an AEC project to promote evaluation and decision-making tasks. It also augments the interactions between the design team and the design solutions space. For future work, we develop a prototype VR-DesignSpace system using Tivoli Cloud VR and assess the system's functionality in an architectural design setting through a formative expert review.

Keywords: Virtual Reality · Human-Computer Interaction · User Experience Design · Real-Time Interaction · Comparative Design Analytics

© Springer Nature Switzerland AG 2021
C. Stephanidis et al. (Eds.): HCII 2021, CCIS 1420, pp. 367–374, 2021.
https://doi.org/10.1007/978-3-030-78642-7_50

1   Introduction

Digital collaboration has become increasingly prevalent due to the pandemic, particularly in the AEC domain, where the projects heavily rely on teamwork. Demand for innovative technologies and approaches to support asynchronous collaborative architectural design exploration and decision-making has been strong constantly [2]. Now, *real-time* virtual collaboration is also in demand.

This study presents an approach to the design and development of shared virtual environments for supporting collaborative design exploration and reflection tasks during the architectural design process. Our proposed system, VR-DesignSpace, is an interactive creativity support Virtual Environment (VE) that aims to enhance the collaborative design evaluation experience by combining the features of current design tools used frequently in the design and incorporating new techniques and interactions.

2   Background

2.1   Design Data Analytics

Data-driven decision-making is gaining popularity in architectural design. Designers value consideration of design performance in the generation and selection of design options to balance building form and performance metrics concerns [5,11]. Continuous evaluation and reflection on architectural design ideas is an essential task in AEC projects. This evaluation starts from the early design stages when the architectural designers explore, compose, and compare multiple alternative solutions based on their forms and performance data. It continues to the final stages as designers, clients, and stakeholders of the project collaboratively decide on the most potential proposed solutions for further development and finalization. For evaluation of design space, multiple computational systems are proposed. However, there is a need for a more robust and seamless interaction between design form exploration and performance analysis. [1,2,5,11]. Notably, current tools fall short in the cohesive simultaneous presentation of all design data to facilitate comprehensive analysis and decision-making in multidisciplinary teams. This bottleneck emphasizes the importance of designing and implementing innovative systems that combine existing resources' strengths while also addressing their limitations.

2.2   Collaborative Virtual Environments

Development of a Collaborative Virtual Environment (CVE) for supporting creative activities such as design exploration and decision-making necessitates a comprehensive design and implementation guideline. This task is particularly complex since, in the design of such environments, the requirements might be uncertain and tied to the dynamic and evolving needs of users. In this regard, it is worthwhile to examine possibilities for supporting these ill-defined design activities through a variety of existing tools and techniques. When various tools and approaches combine according to users' needs, they may lead to new applications that solve the problem more efficiently [7]. Existing research on related subjects, such as virtual collaboration, virtual learning environments, or immersive 3D geo-visualization platforms [6,7,10], can be used to direct the design and development of new CVEs that foster creative practices in architectural design.

3   Methodology

We use Design Study Methodology in this research. Design studies are a subset of the broader field of problem-driven research, in which the aim is to collaborate with users to solve their real-world problems [5,11]. This paper reports designing and developing an in-progress project addressing a real-world Human-Computer Interaction (HCI) problem in the AEC industry. As the first phase, based on a literature review, we identified challenges of current computational design systems and the demand for supporting the real-time collaborative data-informed evaluation of design alternatives. We contribute to the high-level considerations for designing a system solution addressing the above domain problem. Besides, inspired by the VirtualCoLab, an immersive scientific collaboration tool [3], we propose a solution concept (Fig. 1) for addressing the identified gap. We studied the detailed technical aspects of implementing such systems by using emerging technologies such as Tivoli Cloud VR [8].

In the next phase, we build a prototype of the VR-DesignSpace system with the required features for interactions with a design project. We evaluate this version in an architectural design context to assess the system's functionality

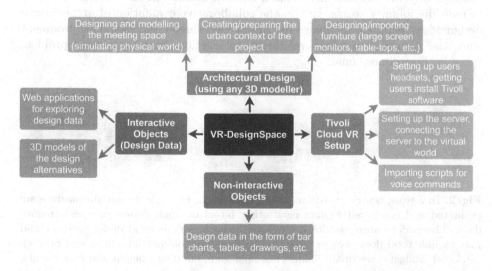

Fig. 1. A conceptual diagram showing different components of VR-DesignSpace and a high-level summery of implementation considerations

through qualitative research and test its utility, likability, and usefulness [6] during design review meetings. We also validate the proposed high-level considerations to provide feedback and new guidelines for future improvements.

4 High-Level System Considerations

As mentioned, the current computational tools have limitations in supporting the *real-time* collaborative evaluation of design alternatives and practical decision-making. We propose three high-level system considerations derived from the literature review [6] to address current tools' limitations.

4.1 Task Environment and Problem Space Consistency

A data-driven architectural design project may consist of various data, including 3D form compositions (Fig. 2), geometries, performance metrics visualizations (Fig. 3), images, technical drawings, sketches, plain textual and numeric data, and so on. Architects apply different methods to visualize and present these complex design data to communicate their ideas [1, 2, 4, 5, 11]. Non-technical audiences usually find these representations and visualizations difficult to comprehend quickly. On the other hand, an essential phase of the design is receiving feedback from the clients and stakeholders who may not have a professional background in AEC areas [2, 6]. Therefore, it is crucial to present design data easily understandable by all the project's team members. Designers present three-dimensional design data through two-dimensional non-immersive illustrations, which adds an unnecessary level of task layer to understanding design data and consequently, hinders the effective and efficient evaluation of design alternatives in multidisciplinary teams. Hence, the collaborative evaluation of architectural design ideas requires an immersive interactive three-dimensional environment since the nature of architectural design interactions and the overall problem space is three-dimensional.

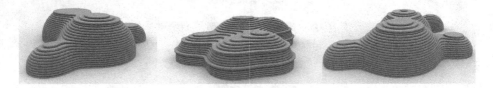

Fig. 2. In a team-centric real-time design evaluation, multiple design alternatives are evaluated and compared against each other based on their forms and performance data. The performance metrics are unique in each architectural design project and may include total floor area per function (residential, commercial, office, and others), total cost/budget, view quality index, net solar gain, building's height and floor counts, and so on.

4.2   Cognitive Load Consideration

Designers use multiple computational tools throughout the design process based on the task at hand and the level of required design resolution. Current interactive systems require the user to switch between several windows or tools to complete design exploration tasks. In some cases, they need large screens to display multiple interfaces simultaneously, which might not be a sustainable, accessible approach [5, 11]. The cognitive load of shifting between multiple interfaces during the design exploration impacts the accuracy and efficiency of design alternative solutions analysis by distracting user's concentration. Users must be enabled to quickly access entire design space data and concentrate their attention on particular data based on their needs.

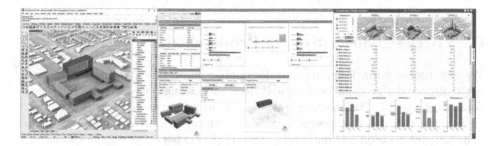

Fig. 3. Design form and performance data presented in visual analytics dashboards [11]. These interfaces help the project's team to make data-informed decisions more reliably and faster.

4.3   User's Virtual Experience Augmentation

Non-immersive spaces mainly do not support natural interactions comparable to how users experience and communicate in the real world. Interactions based on keyboards and mouse for input and a monitor for output, for instance, have very different properties than interactions in the real world [9]. The human experience in virtual environments can be augmented by replicating the good features of in-person collaboration experiences and interactions and benefiting from the potentials of virtual human-space and human-design interaction techniques (multi-user interactions).

5   Inspiration from VirtualCoLab

DiPaola et al. [3] designed and developed VirtualCoLab (Fig. 4) to understand better how mathematicians and other professionals can cooperate and interact with one another using 3D virtual environments, particularly when they are not in the same physical location. VirtualCoLab creates a shared experience that provides distant participants with a sense of telepresence using 3D environments with rich media features (e.g. browsers, movies, and chat), avatar embodiment, and spatial user interfaces [3].

Fig. 4. VirtualCoLab: The avatar in a virtual colab can communicate with web-based displays and collaborate with peers in a physical colab [3].

6   VR-DesignSpace System Proposal

We experiment with designing and developing innovative systems for enhancing real-time design collaboration and decision-making based on the high-level considerations. VR-DesignSpace (Fig. 5) is a virtual interactive environment for supporting simultaneous design form and performance presentation, real-time collaborative decision-making, and human digital experience augmentation.

System: VR-DesignSpace setup uses free, open-source software called Tivoli Cloud VR [8]. Using Tivoli, we build a scalable virtual environment (meeting space) where the design team can join using their computers and VR headsets to communicate and interact with each other from anywhere on the planet. Similar to VirtualCoLab, this immersive environment provides rich media including 3D design models, browsers, videos, and spatial user interfaces displaying performance data visualizations to help design exploration [3]. An architect designs and creates meeting space components based on architectural standards, existing meeting rooms, and innovative user interactions that may not be easily possible in a physical world.

Human-Environment Interactions: VR-DesignSpace supports rich interactions between the users and VE's elements. The user can interact with displays and interactive table-top interfaces, which visualize the alternatives' performance data in bar charts, parallel coordinates plots (PCP), and tables [5,11]. Web-based computational design tools such as DesignSense [1] and D-ART [2] can be connected to these displays. These design analytics applications support the exploration of design space and collaborative evaluation of design alternatives by displaying design form and performance side by side [1,2,5]. Users have control over the number of these digital displays placed in the space for showcasing different aspects of the project. Free from the real-world limitations of resources and space, these displays are re-sizable and can be placed or suspended in any location in the virtual room. Users can *clone* them per their needs or juxtapose multiple interfaces for their comparison tasks. The virtual environment allows teleportation to the virtual *urban context* of the project. For instance, if the design team needs to inspect the project's site location to analyze existing buildings in the context and evaluate their impact on the design, they can easily *fly* there and visit the context from different perspectives. In the real world, this activity is challenging, time-taking and inefficient.

Human-Design Interactions: In VR-DesignSpace, the design team can verbally interact with design models or performance data visualizations. Using voice commands, they adjust the scales, materials (colours), positions, proportions, and orientations of 3D models in the environment to analyze them better or make on-demand changes. Each team member can clone and interact with the design data (multi-user interactions with both forms and performance metrics), independently evaluate design alternatives, or present their ideas to the team.

Human-Human Interactions: The ability to display human movements and gestures during conversations is the key distinction between VR-DesignSpace and the video-conferencing systems used by design teams for collaboration. Each participant has an *avatar* that represents her presence in the VE. By making digital communications more natural, virtual body language and AI-powered facial expressions change the way people interact and experience the VE.

Fig. 5. A conceptual prototype of VR-DesignSpace system [3]

7   Conclusion and Future Work

We experimented with existing tools to understand how they can bind together to provide a new method of addressing design exploration and reflection challenges. We introduced the idea of VR-DesignSpace as a real-time collaboration system built in a virtual environment for architectural designers, which allows presenting 3D design data in a more immersive way. Moreover, it enhances design exploration through human-environment, human-design, and human-human interactions. VR-DesignSpace brings together multiple computational design tools and creates an immersive experience for design teams working on data-oriented design decision-making tasks. In the subsequent phases, we will build the prototype and test it to gain knowledge on such systems' design and development.

References

1. Abuzuraiq, A.M., Erhan, H.: The many faces of similarity - a visual analytics approach for design space simplification. In: Proceedings of the 25th CAADRIA Conference, vol. 1, pp. 485–494 (2020)
2. Alsalman, O., Erhan, H., Haas, A., Abuzuraiq, A.M., Zarei, M.: Design analytics and data-driven collaboration in evaluating alternatives. In: Proceedings of the 26th CAADRIA Conference, p. 10 (2021, in press)
3. DiPaola, S., Tolmie, J., Dugaro, S.: VirtualCoLab - immersive scientific collaboration. https://dipaola.org/lab/research/virtualcolab/. Accessed 20 Mar 2021
4. Erhan, H., Abuzuraiq, A.M., Zarei, M., Alsalman, O., Woodbury, R., Dill, J.: What do design data say about your model? - a case study on reliability and validity. In: Proceedings of the 25th CAADRIA Conference. vol. 1, pp. 557–567 (2020)
5. Erhan, H., Zarei, M., Abuzuraiq, A.M., Haas, A., Alsalman, O., Woodbury, R.: FlowUI: Combining directly-interactive design modelling with design analytics. In: Proceedings of the 25th CAADRIA Conference, vol. 1, pp. 475–484 (2020)
6. Fernando, T., Wu, K.C., Bassanino, M.: Designing a novel virtual collaborative environment to support collaboration in design review meetings. J. Inf. Technol. Construct. **18**, 372–396 (2013)
7. Impedovo, D., Pirlo, G., Stasolla, E.: Integrated virtual environments for collaborative real-time activities: the Co.S.M.O.S. prototype. Je-LKS : J. e-Learn. Knowl. Soc. **7**(2), 59–68 (2011). https://doi.org/10.20368/1971-8829/521
8. Meeks, C., Deprez, M.: Tivoli Cloud VR. https://tivolicloud.com/. Accessed 20 Mar 2021
9. Men, L., Bryan-Kinns, N., Bryce, L.: Designing spaces to support collaborative creativity in shared virtual environments. Peer J. Comput. Sci. **5**(e229), 39 (2019). https://doi.org/10.7717/peerj-cs.229
10. Sasinka, C., et al.: Collaborative immersive virtual environments for education in geography. Int. J. Geo-Inf. **8**(3) (2019).https://doi.org/10.3390/ijgi8010003
11. Zarei, M., Erhan, H., Abuzuraiq, A.M., Alsalman, O., Haas, A.: Design and development of interactive systems for integration of comparative visual analytics in design workflow. In: Proceedings of the 26th CAADRIA Conference, p. 10 (2021, in press)

A Customized VR Rendering
with Neural-Network Generated Frames
for Reducing VR Dizziness

Zhexin Zhang[1(✉)], Jun-Li Lu[1,2(✉)], and Yoichi Ochiai[1,2(✉)]

[1] Research and Development Center for Digital Nature, University of Tsukuba,
Tsukuba, Japan
jacobzhang@digitalnature.slis.tsukuba.ac.jp,
{jllu,wizard}@slis.tsukuba.ac.jp
[2] Faculty of Library, Information and Media Science, University of Tsukuba,
Tsukuba, Japan

Abstract. This research is to develop a NN system that generates
smooth frames for VR experiences, in order to reduce the hardware
requirement for VR therapy. VR is introduced as a therapy to many
symptoms, such as Acrophobia, for a long, but not yet broadly used. One
of the main reason is that a high and stable frame rate is a must for a comfortable VR experience. Low fresh rate in VR could cause some adverse
reactions, such as disorientation or nausea. These adverse reactions are
known as "VR dizziness". We plan to develop a NN system to compress
the frame data and automatically generate consecutive frames with extra
information in real-time computation. Provided with the extra information, the goal of compressing NN is to conclude and abandon textures
that are dispensable. Thereafter, it would compress left and right frames
in VR into a data frame with all necessary information. Subsequently,
we send it to clients, the client put the data frame into rebuilding GAN
system and get three pairs of frames. After applying some CV methods
such as filtering and alias, these frames are shown on users' HMD. Furthermore, the compressed data can be transported easily, which allows
medical facilities to build a VR computing center for multiple clients,
making VR more broadly available for medical usages.

Keywords: Computer vision · Virtual Reality · Neural Network ·
Generative adversarial network

1 Introduction

VR is introduced as a therapy to many symptoms, such as Acrophobia, for long,
but not yet broadly used. One of the main reason is that a high and stable frame
rate is a must for a comfortable VR experience. Recent research has shown that
VR experience need at least 90 Frames Per Second (FPS) to be comfortable
[5]. Otherwise, it could cause some adverse reactions, such as disorientation or
nausea [6]. These adverse reactions are known as "VR dizziness" [8].

© Springer Nature Switzerland AG 2021
C. Stephanidis et al. (Eds.): HCII 2021, CCIS 1420, pp. 375–380, 2021.
https://doi.org/10.1007/978-3-030-78642-7_51

The main reason of frame dropping can be: slow rendering, transmitting delay, etc. Thus it requires high-performance graphical devices which makes VR a high-cost therapy. However, even with that a graphical device system, there can also be some cases where the frame dropping happens. For example, a quick head turn would force all objects in the view to be re-rendered and raise the burden of rendering abruptly.

We plan to develop a NN system to compress the frame data and automatically generate consecutive frames with extra information [9] in real-time computation. Provided with extra information, the goal of compressing NN is to conclude and abandon textures that are dispensable. Thereafter, it would compress left and right frames in VR into a data frame with all necessary information. Subsequently, we send it to clients, the client put the data frame into rebuilding GAN system and get three pairs of frames. After applying some CV methods such as filtering and alias, these frames are shown on users' HMD. Furthermore, the compressed data can be transported easily, which allows medical facilities to build a VR computing center for multiple clients, making VR more broadly available for medical usages [10].

2   Related Works

Many VR treatment has already been developed in recent years, Wagner et al. [1] analyzed a typical instance of crossing a road in VR. They took avoiding motion sickness as a vital factor in experiment design. Recently, a lot of research that use VR as a treatment [2–4] has been done. Plenty of them are aiming on cognitive illness [10]. Which makes it important to keep visual cognition experience stable and fluent in VR.

3   Methodologies

3.1   High FPS Screens

In non-VR gaming experience, higher FPS display is a classical way of reducing dizziness and burden of brain. Usually, gaming with a higher FPS display means more smooth experience. At present, common VR experience are in the fresh-rate 90 Hz. Multiple research has shown that any FPS lower than 90-Hz may cause severe VR-dizziness. We plan to use a 144-Hz Screen. Recently, various small 144-Hz screens have been released the market. Most are used as smartphone screen.

3.2   Frame Interpolation

With Higher FPS, the burden of graphical device will rise as well, which is a problem we will face. Our solution is to generate the interpolation frames by GAN system. We plan to insert 2 frames at every interval, and turn a 48-Hz VR experience into 144-Hz.

3.3   How GAN Works in Limited Time

As Fig. 2 shows, the time the GAN system is given cannot be longer than the render time of one frame. In our method, the GAN does not generate a full frame, but only a smaller area called "Patch". by replacing the pixel map in the patch area, we suppose that it can deceive user's eyes and make the VR experience more fluent on low-performance graphical devices. The exact position of the patch is also decided by NN system.

4   Performance Enhancement by GAN

VR experience become unsmooth when intervals between frames changes in sudden. Which is usually caused by a abrupt rise of rendering workload. For example, a quick head turn changes the viewpoint and every visible objects need to be re-rendered [1]. Rendering workload can vary to several times larger than normal under some certain conditions. However, a NN takes designated time to handle a frame, so we are supposed to be able to avoid frame skipping issues.

4.1   Optimizing Visual Experiences in VR

It is trivial that a frame generated by a GAN can never be more accurate than a rendered frame. However, accuracy is not the most important thing in VR experience. For instance, human eyes prefer moving objects with motion blur. Also, an accurate VR experience usually means more polygons to render. And therefore means more rendering burden for VR engine.

Some research has shown that the fluency of a VR experience is considerably influenced by the Peripheral vision [11].

5   Compressing and Reconstructing Frames

Our NN system can also be used to lower a burden of information transfer where the VR headset is connected to rendering device in a indirect way using a compress-reconstruct method.

In a compress-reconstruct process, on rendered frame and extra information are compressed into a data frame, which are then transferred. After that, the texture NN can reconstruct the data frame into 3 frames by patching. This can lower the burden of transferring data. In our NN system, given the extra information, such as the motion of a user, we extract necessary graphic textures by a NN and thus generate patches by a GAN. NNs are trained by VR usage data of users.

6 Deep Learning Method

We plan to train the NN system with a HNN feature map method.

6.1 HNN Feature Map Method

The Frame firstly go through a Hourglass NN, to figure out the area that needed patching. The feature map is attached to the frame as a channel. After that it goes through a RNN structure where the feature map are treated just like the other channels.

6.2 Training Loss

In our training process we use a full-144 Hz frame sequence as the data set. We take every 3 frames as a batch, the first frame, along with the motion vector, is given as the input for GAN. The second and third are considered Ground Truth(GT). With eye tracking method we suppose the GAN will generate a fake frame that matches the following 2 conditions by patching: the fake frame should be close to GT in low frequency, and the fake frame should avoid spatial aliasing around visual focus.

7 Experimental Setting

We plan to use Vive Pro Eye[1], a VR headset with embedded eye tracker.

7.1 Signal Capturing and Handling

In experiment we plan to use a video capture card to transmit visual signals. After that the signals are used as input of NN systems. The Frames are actually stretched by optical lens in the VR headset before be seen. But here we handle these signals as they are showed on plains. We assume that the NN system can figure it out as a feature. The more we apply CV methods to it, the less difference will the loss make on NN in the backward process.

---

[1] https://www.vive.com/jp/product/vive-pro-eye/overview/.

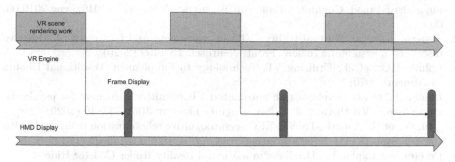

Fig. 1. Working timeline and dataflow of VR application. Comparing with the traditional method.

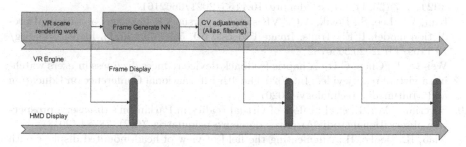

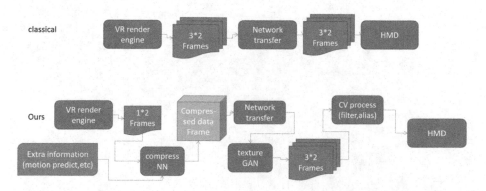

Fig. 2. In our VR rendering, we propose a system with neural networks that generate revised frames from a VR engine.

References

1. Wagner, S., et al.: Difficulty factors for VR cognitive rehabilitation training - crossing a virtual road. Comput. Graph. (2019). https://doi.org/10.1016/j.cag.2019.06.009
2. Segawa, T., et al.: Virtual reality (VR) in assessment and treatment of addictive disorders: a systematic review. Front. Neurosci. **13** 1409 (2020)
3. Lohne, P.O., et al.: Utilizing VR Technology to Supplement Traditional Phobia Treatment (2020)
4. Lambe, S., et al.: Developing an automated VR cognitive treatment for psychosis: gameChange VR therapy. J. Behav. Cognit. Therapy **30**(1), 33–40 (2020)
5. Tan, W., et al.: A method of VR-EEG scene cognitive rehabilitation training. Health Inf. Sci. Syst. **9**(1), 1–9 (2020). https://doi.org/10.1007/s13755-020-00132-6
6. Pereira, A.: Explaining Dizziness in a Virtual Reality Roller Coaster Ride
7. Khan, A., Zhijiang, Z., Yu, Y., Khan, M., Yan, K., Aziz, K.: GAN-Holo: generative adversarial networks-based generated holography using deep learning. Complexity **2021**, 1–7 (2021). https://doi.org/10.1155/2021/6662161
8. Kim, W., Lee, S., Bovik, A.C.: VR sickness versus VR presence: a statistical prediction model. IEEE Trans. Image Process. **30**, 559–571 (2021). https://doi.org/10.1109/TIP.2020.3036782
9. Wei-Te, T., Chen, C-H.: A haptic feedback device reduces dizziness in users watching a virtual reality video. In: 2020 The 4th International Conference on Education and Multimedia Technology (2020)
10. Severiano, M.I.R., et al.: Effect of virtual reality in Parkinson's disease: a prospective observational study. Arquivos de neuro-psiquiatria **76**(2), 78–84 (2018)
11. Xiao, R., Benko, H.: Augmenting the field-of-view of head-mounted displays with sparse peripheral displays. In: Proceedings of the 2016 CHI Conference on Human Factors in Computing Systems (CHI 2016). Association for Computing Machinery, New York, NY, USA, pp. 1221–1232 (2016). https://doi.org/10.1145/2858036.2858212

Security and Privacy Issues in HCI

Scaling the Phish: Advancing the NIST Phish Scale

Fern Barrientos, Jody Jacobs(✉), and Shaneé Dawkins ⓘ

National Institute of Standards and Technology, Gaithersburg, MD 20899, USA
{fernando.barrientos,jody.jacobs,shanee.dawkins}@nist.gov

Abstract. Organizations use phishing training exercises to help employees defend against the phishing threats that get through automatic email filters, reducing potential compromise of information security and privacy for both the individual and their organization. These exercises use fake and realistic phishing emails to test employees' ability to detect the phish, resulting in click rates which the organization can then use to address and inform their cybersecurity training programs. However, click rates alone are unable to provide a holistic picture of why employees do or do not fall for phish emails. To this end, the National Institute of Standards and Technology (NIST) created the Phish Scale methodology for determining how difficult a phishing email is to detect [1]. Recent research on the Phish Scale has focused on improving the robustness of the method. This paper presents initial results of the ongoing developments of the Phish Scale, including work towards the repeatability and validity of the Phish Scale using operational phishing training exercise data. Also highlighted are the ongoing efforts to minimize the ambiguities and subjectivity of the Phish Scale, as well as the design of a study aimed at gauging the usability of the scale via testing with phishing exercise training implementers.

Keywords: Usable cybersecurity · Cybersecurity awareness training · Phishing · NIST Phish Scale

1 Introduction

Over half of all emails sent and received are spam; and an ever-growing number of those messages contain malicious threats [2]. Moreover, 10% of spam messages manage to get through email filters, and phishing emails account for approximately one-third of those emails [3]. Phishing emails are malicious threats designed to deceive and extract sensitive information from the email's recipient [4]. The phishing cyber threat exploits vulnerabilities in organizations of all types and sizes, including industry, academia, and government [5–8]. A major problem with phishing is that it targets what is possibly the most vulnerable element within any security system, the human user. While spam filters are capable of filtering phishing emails based on their sender, format, and verbiage, there are still phishes which get through this net, and it is these emails which can wreak havoc on an otherwise secured system. By clicking links and volunteering personally

C. Stephanidis et al. (Eds.): HCII 2021, CCIS 1420, pp. 383–390, 2021.
https://doi.org/10.1007/978-3-030-78642-7_52

identifiable information, those who have been successfully phished can end up costing themselves and their organizations a significant amount of money in recovery efforts and time lost.

To help combat the phishing threat, organizations strive to improve phishing awareness via embedded phishing training exercises. These exercises provide organizations data – click decisions in an operational environment – from realistic, safe, and controlled training experiences. However, these click decision data that show when an email user did or did not click on a link or attachment in a phish do not tell the whole story. The National Institute of Standards and Technology (NIST) Phish Scale (NPS) was conceived to provide context to these data – click rates – and to better understand why people do or do not fall for a phish [4]. The NPS is a method for determining how difficult or easy a phishing email is to detect [1] by considering both the characteristics of the email itself and the user context of the email's recipient. Ongoing research on the use of the NPS is intended to improve its robustness, validity, and ease of use. The goal of the research presented in this paper was to assess the repeatability and validity of the NPS when applied to phishing emails used during embedded phishing awareness training exercises.

2   Applying the Phish Scale

The Phish Scale was created to provide a metric for training implementers to gain a better understanding of the variability in click rates resulting from their phishing training exercises. The output of the NPS – a difficulty rating – can be used to provide context to these click rates. Steves, et al. previously described the NPS, its development, and its components in elaborate detail [1, 9]; a high level summary is presented below.

The NPS method is comprised of two major components. The first component is a measure of the observable characteristics, or cues, of the email itself (e.g., spelling, grammar). The more cues in a phish, the easier it is to detect. The second component, the premise alignment, measures how well an email aligns with the context of one's work. The higher the premise alignment, the more difficult the phish is to detect. For example, a phish that requests payment of an invoice is more difficult to detect (high premise alignment) to an individual in the accounts payable division. While the same invoice phish might be more easily to detect to a system architect whose job duties do not include payment of invoices. The NPS includes two separate approaches to determining the premise alignment – a *Formulaic Approach* and *Blended Perspective* [9]; the former approach is the focus of the analysis in this paper. When analyzed collectively, these two NPS components produce a difficulty rating for a target audience's susceptibility to a particular phishing email (Table 1). Phishing emails with a High premise alignment and Few cues are usually harder for individuals to detect. Conversely, emails with Low premise alignment and Many cues are easier to detect by individuals.

3   Research Methodology

One of the goals of this research presented in this paper is to gauge the repeatability of applying the NPS to phishing emails. To this end, the NPS was evaluated to measure the

Table 1. Determining detection difficulty

Number of cues	Premise alignment	Detection difficulty
Few (more difficult)	High	Very difficult
	Medium	Very difficult
	Low	Moderately difficult
Some	High	Very difficult
	Medium	Moderately difficult
	Low	Moderately to Least difficult
Many (less difficult)	High	Moderately difficult
	Medium	Moderately difficult
	Low	Least difficult

agreement between independent ratings of phishing exercise emails. This effort began with the process of reevaluating the phishing emails from a previously published paper on the NPS [9]. First, a team of NIST researchers (n = 3) who were not among the original authors of the NPS independently applied the NPS to the ten phishing emails originally published by Steves, et al. [9]. The team then met to assess and compare the individual scores for both cues and premise alignment. Points of divergence in cue counts or premise alignment element scores were discussed and ultimately resolved by averaging the scores of the team members. Finally, the team's consolidated scores and difficulty rating were evaluated against the previously published findings.

Another goal of this research is to validate the metric by applying the NPS to a broader set of phishing data. The first step toward this goal is presented in this paper; the NPS was applied to three additional phishing emails used in embedded phishing awareness training exercises throughout 2020 (see Appendix). The aforementioned steps were repeated in this effort – independent ratings by research team members followed by discussion and resolution of scoring conflicts. The results of these two research efforts are presented in Sect. 4.

4   Results

This section covers the results of our analysis of applying the NPS to the ten original phishing emails as well as the three additional phishing emails. As mentioned in the previous section, these 13 emails (ten original, three new) were independently rated by members of the research team and consolidated into final scores for the cue count and premise alignment. Each email was ultimately given an overall detection difficulty rating (referred to throughout the remainder of this section as the "new" scores and ratings).

For the original ten emails, the new scores and ratings were compared to the prior published work (see Sect. 3). This comparison is detailed in Table 2, where cue and premise alignment categories are specified for each phishing email, followed by the associated numerical score in parentheses. In addition to these data, the click rates (showing the percentage of email users who clicked in the email) for the phishing exercise associated with each phish are presented in Table 2.

When comparing cues, there is clear variance in the actual scores between the new and original analysis for the individual phishing emails. However, when abstracting up to their corresponding cue categories, agreement between the new categorical data and the original categorical data was met in 90% of these phishing emails. In regard to the premise alignment, the more subjective component of the NPS, an even greater variance is seen in the actual scores given by both new and original ratings. The effects of this numerical variance can be seen in the agreement between new categories and the original categories where ratings only matched up in 40% of the phishing emails. Lastly, in large part due to the variance in the results of applying the premise alignment component, the detection difficulty ratings were agreed upon in 50% of the ten original phishing emails when comparing the original data to the new data. Given the five possible ratings on the scale of detection difficulty, it is important to note that while 50% of the new ratings did not match the original ratings, the differences were only by a factor of one (e.g., "very" to "moderately" rather than "very" to "least"). Additionally, when comparing the original detection difficulty ratings and click rates to the new ratings and corresponding click rates, the new ratings exhibit a similar pattern to the original ratings in how they line up with the click rates.

Table 2. Comparison of NIST Phish scale ratings for original phish emails

Phish email	Cues (new)	Cues (original)	Premise alignment (new)	Premise alignment (original)	Difficulty (new)	Difficulty (original)	Click rates
E1	Few (6)	Few (7)	Low (10)	High (30)	Moderate	Very	49.3%
E2	Some (10)	Some (14)	Medium (13)	High (24)	Moderately	Very	43.8%
E3	Few (7)	Few (8)	Medium (16)	High (24)	Very	Very	20.5%
E4	Some (9)	Few (6)	Medium (14)	High (18)	Moderately	Very	19.4%
E5	Some (9)	Some (11)	Low (9)	Medium (14)	Moderately to least	Moderately	11.6%
E6	Some (13)	Some (13)	Low (0)	Low (10)	Moderately to least	Moderately to least	11.0%
E7	Many (18)	Many (18)	Medium (13)	Medium (16)	Moderately	Moderately	9.1%
E8	Some (9)	Some (12)	Medium (12)	Medium (12)	Moderately	Moderately	8.7%
E9	Some (14)	Some (11)	Low (−1)	Low (2)	Moderately to least	Moderately to least	4.8%
E10	Some (10)	Some (12)	Medium (13)	Low (4)	Moderately	Moderately to least	3.2%

Table 3 features the averaged calculations for the three independent raters of the current study. The click rates for emails E11 and E12 align well with their respective detection difficulty ratings, according to the pattern exhibited in the application of the NPS to the previous ten emails. However, the click rates for email E13 do not fully align with the established detection difficulty rating scale. The trend of the NPS has been for emails with a click rate as low as 2.8% to have a "least" or "moderately to least" difficulty rating.

Table 3. NIST Phish Scale ratings for new phish emails

Phish emails	Cues	Premise alignment	Detection difficulty	Click rates
E11	Some (12)	Low (4)	Moderately to least	12.7%
E12	Many (18)	Low (9)	Least	5.4%
E13	Many (16)	Medium (13)	Moderately	2.8%

The NPS has the ability to contextualize click rates with its detection difficulty ratings. However, there are some unexpected factors which may inflate click rates which could lead to the disagreement between click rates and detection difficulty ratings (as exhibited by E13). For example, when a phishing email appeared to come directly from an authority figure in upper management, it elicited serious concerns and a deeper sense of action by the email recipient than was measurable by the NPS, ultimately leading to an increased click rate and the aforementioned disagreement. These factors are intended to be addressed in future iterations of NPS development.

5 Discussion and Future Work

This paper presents an initial look into the ongoing validation effort of the NPS. The results discussed in the previous section show the margin of error in the NPS difficulty rating determination; there can be a slight variance in independent scores of a phishing email, yet that variance is not reflected in the resulting detection difficulty rating. This provides insight into the development of future iterations of the NPS; however, additional validation testing is needed, including testing with larger and more diverse datasets. To this end, the NPS is currently being tested with a variety of large datasets (both public and nonpublic) from universities, private companies, and other government agencies. The findings from applying the NPS to a variety of datasets will be used to improve future iterations of the NPS. These efforts are aimed at ensuring the NPS's accuracy and validity.

NIST is conducting a research study to determine the usability and applicability of the NPS. The study invited both federal and non-federal organizations with robust phishing programs to apply the NPS in their organizations, aligning with their existing embedded phishing awareness training programs. Following their use of the NPS, training implementers were asked to provide detailed feedback and recommendations about their use of the NPS. This valuable real-world information resulting from the study will determine the effectiveness of the NPS in unique organizational environments, how usable the NPS is, and how organizations use the NPS to contextualize phishing exercise click rates.

As mentioned throughout this paper, NPS research is ongoing. Current efforts to improve repeatability, to evaluate validity, and to assess the usability of the NPS are expected to lead to a more streamlined version of the NPS that would be beneficial to organizations to provide clarity, functionality, and adaptability of the metric. Future iterations of the NPS will incorporate various modifications grounded in findings from the research. Revisions currently being considered for adoption and inclusion are: 1) for the observable cues component, reducing subjectivity, increasing identification accuracy, and minimizing redundancy across the scale, 2) refining the cue counting method by incorporating a weighting metric to address cue saliency, and 3) restructuring the premise alignment's five elements to be more efficient, reducing the total number of elements and adopting proven methodologies for determination of premise alignment element scores. Additionally, insights gleaned from the aforementioned usability study, including the identification of successful practices and strategies, and lessons learned will be used to refine future iterations of the NPS.

6 Conclusion

The NPS helps organizations and phishing awareness training implementors in two primary ways. Firstly, by contextualizing message click and reporting rates for a target audience, and secondly by providing a way to characterize actual phishing threats so training implementors can reduce the organization's security risk. Organizations should tailor their cybersecurity and privacy awareness training program to their unique environment while still meeting their organizations' mission and risk tolerance. Likewise, the NPS goes beyond the face value of an email by accounting for the environment, roles, and responsibilities of people within an organization. Tailoring training to the types of threats their organization faces helps them maintain a resilient security and privacy posture. Additionally, when click rates and quantitative and qualitative metrics from the NPS are viewed holistically, they can signal to an organization that training approaches and objectives, delivery methods, training frequency or content necessitate alterations to be effective in combating the ever-changing phishing threat landscape.

Disclaimer. Certain commercial entities, equipment, or materials may be identified in this document in order to describe an experimental procedure or concept adequately. Such identification is not intended to imply recommendation or endorsement by the National Institute of Standards and Technology, nor is it intended to imply that the entities, materials, or equipment are necessarily the best available for the purpose.

Appendix

Note: Logos have been blinded from the phishing email images below (Figs. 1, 2 and 3).

Fig. 1. E11: E-card phish

Fig. 2. E12: Document review phish

COMPANY CONFIDENTIAL Upcoming public announcement

GC   o **General Counsel's Office <noreply@account-maintenance.com>**   Tuesday, May 19, 2020 at 9:32 AM
     To: o Doe, Jane (Fed)

Open Message

Click Here for more info and help

NOTICE: If you have concerns about the validity of this message contact the sender directly
or your account representative.

Secured by   Copyright ©   All right reserved.

Fig. 3. E13: Public Announcement phish

References

1. Steves, M.P., Greene, K.K., Theofanos, M.F.: A phish scale: rating human phishing message detection difficulty. In: Proceedings 2019 Workshop on Usable Security. Workshop on Usable Security, San Diego, CA. (2019). https://doi.org/10.14722/usec.2019.23028
2. Ezpeleta, E., Velez de Mendizabal, I., Hidalgo, J. M.G., Zurutuza, U.: Novel email spam detection method using sentiment analysis and personality recognition. Logic J. IGPL, **28**(1), 83–94 (2020). https://doi.org/10.1093/jigpal/jzz073
3. Cyren: Email Security Gap Analysis: Aggregated Results. (2017). https://pages.cyren.com/rs/944-PGO-076/images/Cyren_Report_GapAnalysisAgg_201711.pdf. Accessed Jan 2021
4. Greene, K.K., Steves, M., Theofanos, M., Kostick, J.: User context: an explanatory variable in phishing susceptibility. In: Proceedings of 2018 Workshop Usable Security (USEC) at the Network and Distributed Systems Security (NDSS) Symposium (2018)
5. Aaron, G., Rasmussen, R.: Global phishing survey 2016: Trends and domain name use. Anti-Phishing Working Group. June 2017. https://docs.apwg.org/reports/APWG_Global_Phishing_Report_2015-2016.pdf. Accessed Aug 2017
6. Hong, J.: The state of phishing attacks. Commun. ACM **55**(1), 74–81 (2012)
7. SonicWall: 2019 SonicWall Cyber Threat Report (2019). https://www.sonicwall.com/resources/white-papers/2019-sonicwall-cyber-threat-report. Accessed Aug 2020
8. Symantec: Internet Security Threat Report. vol. 24 (2019). https://www.symantec.com/security-center/threat-report. Accessed Aug 2020
9. Steves, M., Greene, K., Theofanos, M.: Categorizing human phishing difficulty: a Phish scale. J. Cybersec. **6**(1), tyaa009 (2020). https://doi.org/10.1093/cybsec/tyaa009

Privacy Concerns in Chatbot Interactions: When to Trust and When to Worry

Rahime Belen Saglam[1], Jason R.C. Nurse[1(✉)], and Duncan Hodges[2]

[1] University of Kent, Canterbury, UK
{R.Belen-Saglam-724,J.R.C.Nurse}@kent.ac.uk
[2] Cranfield University, Defence Academy of the UK, Shrivenham, UK
d.hodges@cranfield.ac.uk

Abstract. Through advances in their conversational abilities, chatbots have started to request and process an increasing variety of sensitive personal information. The accurate disclosure of sensitive information is essential where it is used to provide advice and support to users in the healthcare and finance sectors. In this study, we explore users' concerns regarding factors associated with the use of sensitive data by chatbot providers. We surveyed a representative sample of 491 British citizens. Our results show that the user concerns focus on deleting personal information and concerns about their data's inappropriate use. We also identified that individuals were concerned about losing control over their data after a conversation with conversational agents. We found no effect from a user's gender or education but did find an effect from the user's age, with those over 45 being more concerned than those under 45. We also considered the factors that engender trust in a chatbot. Our respondents' primary focus was on the chatbot's technical elements, with factors such as the response quality being identified as the most critical factor. We again found no effect from the user's gender or education level; however, when we considered some social factors (e.g. avatars or perceived 'friendliness'), we found those under 45 years old rated these as more important than those over 45. The paper concludes with a discussion of these results within the context of designing inclusive, digital systems that support a wide range of users.

Keywords: Artificial intelligence · Chatbots · Conversational agents · Data privacy · Trust · Personal information · Human factors

1 Introduction

Chatbots are software programs that can simulate a conversation in natural language, and are a promising technology for customer services in various contexts (e.g., finance, health care and tourism). Providing personalised experiences enables the provision of more effective user services. Personalisation is the ability

© Springer Nature Switzerland AG 2021
C. Stephanidis et al. (Eds.): HCII 2021, CCIS 1420, pp. 391–399, 2021.
https://doi.org/10.1007/978-3-030-78642-7_53

to dynamically adapt functionality to an individual to better suit user needs [1]. In a chatbot context, it is accomplished through the effective processing of a user's responses, and the identification and adaptation to information in disclosed during the conversation. Despite the advantages of chatbots, this process can often led to a tension between the requirements for service quality and the need for user privacy. These are both important topics within the context of human-computer interaction [10].

Information disclosure to chatbots and factors that have an impact on it have been widely studied in the literature and the privacy concerns are often identified as a barrier to individual's disclosing information [3,5,8,9]. However, the main issues that lead to privacy concerns in chatbot interactions and the design practices that challenge data privacy principles, are often overlooked. Hence, in this study, we provide the perspective of British citizens privacy concerns surrounding the design practices of AI-based chatbots.

We conducted an empirical study with 491 participants where four main challenges or ambiguities in agent design have been evaluated. These are, third-party access to personal information, inappropriate use of information once shared with chatbots, loss of control over personal data, and finally, ambiguities regarding the deletion of personal data. In addition, we investigated the factors that help to build trust in user/human-chatbot interaction. We investigated five factors for this purpose; the gender of the chatbot, use of a chatbot avatar, the quality of responses received from the chatbot, the friendliness of the chatbot, and the grammatical correctness of the language used by the agent. Our findings contribute to the literature by providing insights from a UK perspective on the main privacy concerns particular to chatbot design. These results can help to design user-centered solutions prioritising and respecting the privacy concerns of users.

2   Literature Review

Folstad et al. [2] categorised the factors perceived to affect trust in chatbots for customer service into two high-level groups; factors concerning the chatbots and factors concerning the service environment. Quality in interpretation of the user requests and advice in response to request were given as factors in the first category. They were followed by human-likeliness, self presentation (which describes the chatbot's communication of what it can do and its limitations) and professional appearance. Professional appearance in this context was defined as being thoughtfully developed and the chatbot providing grammatically correct responses. The authors reported three factors concerning the service environment; brand of the service provider, security and privacy aspects of the service, and the perceived risk associated with using the chatbot. The ability for the chatbot to correctly interpret the user requests and the advice in the response were the most frequently reported factors identified by the participants. Ischen et al. [4] investigated to what extent privacy concerns in chatbot interactions have an impact on users' attitudes and their adherence to the recommendations provided by the chatbot. In addition, findings revealed that information disclosure is indeed influenced by privacy concerns.

Even though the privacy concerns or perceived risk are a well-known factors that have impact on trust to chatbots, to the best of our knowledge, there is no study that investigates the issues behind perceived risk in user-chatbot interactions. However, some design practices in AI-based chatbots introduce several challenges to design privacy aware solutions. In their study, Saglam and Nurse identified open issues in agent design from a data privacy perspective where GDPR (General Data Protection Regulation) has been used as privacy regulation [7]. The lack of algorithmic transparency, the difficulties in managing consent, and the difficulties in exercising the right to be forgotten, are some of the open issues raised.

In this current study, bearing in mind the nature of chatbot technology and the challenges they provide for assuring data privacy, we prepared a survey where participants were asked to evaluate their concerns regarding deleting their personal information, third-party sharing, and losing control over their personal data. Our results contribute to formulate privacy concerns in chatbot design taking into account the design practices of this technology.

3   Method

We implemented a survey on the SurveyMonkey platform and asked participants to provide their opinions on two issues; potential risks that result in concerns in chatbot interaction and the factors that lead them to trust a chatbot. Before those questions, we posed questions to collect informed consent from the participants. Demographic characteristics of the participants (age group, gender, and educational level) were also collected. The chatbot-centered questions used a 7-point Likert scale and asked the following questions:

- To what extent do you agree or disagree with the following statements?
  - After using a chatbot, I would feel that others know about me more than I am comfortable with.
  - After using a chatbot, I would worry that any personal information that I shared with it could be inappropriately used
  - After using a chatbot, I believe that I would have control over who can get access to any personal information that I shared with it
  - After using a chatbot, I would worry about how to delete any personal information that I shared with it
- How important are each of the following factors in determining whether you trust a chatbot or not?
  - The gender of the chatbot
  - Whether the chatbot has an avatar (picture or visual depiction)
  - The quality of responses received from the chatbot
  - The friendliness of the chatbot
  - The grammatical correctness of the language used.

3.1   Participants

This study's ultimate goal is to explore the perspective of British citizens on the privacy concerns of chatbot interactions. Therefore, we recruited participants using Prolific[1], which allowed us to reach a representative sample of UK citizens based on gender, age and ethnicity. We included six attention checking questions and excluded the participants who failed in more than one attention question.

Within the 491 valid participants 49.7% self-identified as male, and 10.4% being aged between 18 and 24, 19.2% between 25 and 34, 15.9% between 25 and 44, 18.9% between 45 and 54 and 35.6% being 55 and over. When considering the highest-level of the participant's education 15.5% achieved a GCSE-level of education[2], 28.1% achieved an A-level or equivalent[3], 34.4% achieved an undergraduate degree, 18.7% a postgraduate degree and 3.3% a doctorate.

3.2   Analysis

The analysis conducted for this study was a mixture of descriptive and quantitative statistics. Proportional-odds logistic regression models [6] were built to model the effects of age, gender and education. Ordinal regression, such as the proportional-odds logistic regression used in this study, is a common approach to modelling problems where the dependent variable (in this case, the Likert response) is ordinal. The model coefficients provide an insight into the effects of these variables on how participants rate their concerns or levels of trust.

4   Results

4.1   When to Worry?

We asked our participants to evaluate three main concerns: privacy concerns around others knowing more than they are comfortable with after chatbot interaction; worries around inappropriate use, and how to delete personal information. We also asked their beliefs on whether they would have control over who can access their personal information. The results from this are shown in Fig. 1.

Our findings reveal that UK citizens are most frequently concerned about how to delete personal information. Followed by concerns about whether the data would be inappropriately used.

When we perform a logistic regression analysis to examine the influence of user factors (age group, gender, education) on these concerns, we found no interaction from the gender or education variables. However, the proportional odds logistic regression model results revealed a significant age effect in the top three concerns. This effect is shown in Fig. 2. The logistic-regression models show statistical significance (at a 5% significance level) for both the 45 to 55 age group and the over 55 age group.

---

[1]   https://www.prolific.co/.
[2]   Typically taken at 15 years of age.
[3]   A subject-based qualification between typically forming the period from leaving compulsory education to pre-university education.

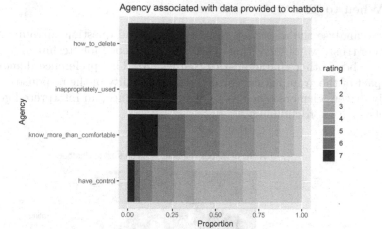

Fig. 1. The responses from the data privacy concerns.

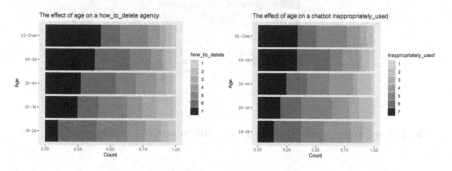

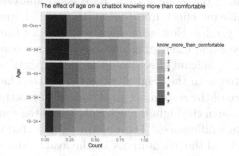

Fig. 2. The effect of age on the data privacy concerns.

4.2   When to Trust?

When we analyse the responses given to our second question surrounding what engenders trust, we observe that there is a preference for 'technical' quality in chatbots above other characteristics (see Fig. 3). This preference demonstrates the impact of the grammatical correctness and quality of the response over more 'socially-driven' elements such as an avatar's presence, an interpreted gender or concepts such as 'friendliness'.

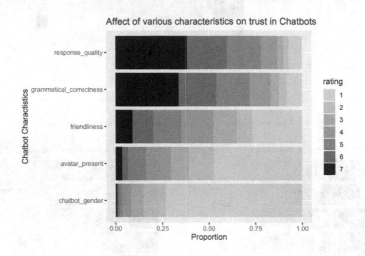

Fig. 3. The responses when considering the characteristics which engender trust.

When we performed the same logistic regression analysis on this data, we again found no significant effect from either the participants' education level or the self-described gender. However, when we consider the participant's age, we again begin to see some interesting effects. When we consider the response quality, we can see no significant effect from the participants' age. There was also no age effect associated with the gender presented by the chatbot. The effect of age on the importance of the response's grammatical correctness was significant, although small for those in the highest age bracket, and the remaining age-groups exhibited no significant differences. The remaining two characteristics, whether an avatar was present and the 'friendliness' of the avatar, did have an effect from the age of the participant. These characteristics are shown in Fig. 4 with those under 45 considering these characteristics more important when engendering trust with a chatbot.

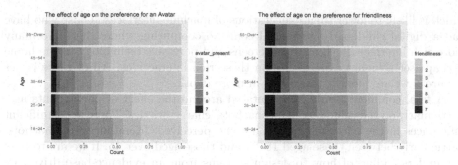

Fig. 4. The effect of age on the chatbot characteristics that engender trust.

5   Discussion and Conclusion

This study aimed to investigate users' privacy concerns and to understand features that are important to build trust in services mediated by chatbots.

The first emerging issue is the feeling of the loss of agency over data provided to a chatbot, with significant concerns over the ability to delete data and concerns around how the data would be used. The chatbot effectively decouples the individual disclosing the data from the final users of the data. This decoupling reduces the user's saliency of the value gained to the user from each disclosure; this has been shown to reduce the desire to disclose data [5]. Hence, we should reduce this gap where possible and ensure users perceive they maintain agency over their data. The significant effect from the age of the respondent is an important observation. Suppose we are looking to build inclusive, digital systems that responsibly support citizens and user-bases. In that case, designers should be aware that these age groups may have more significant concerns in their use of chatbots. A system that explicitly addresses these concerns early in the interaction is likely to enable better disclosures and outcomes for all users.

The second emerging issue was the chatbot characteristics that engender trust in a chatbot. The factors which had the most significant effect were the response quality and the grammatical correctness of the responses. These factors represent the most salient cue to a user about the 'competence' of the designer, builder and operator of the chatbot. It is perhaps not surprising that this engenders trust in the chatbot—and it is noteworthy that this was consistent across all users independent of age, gender and education.

However, there was an age effect associated with the effect of two of the chatbot's characteristics. We identified that those under 45 were significantly more likely to use an avatar and the chatbot's 'friendliness' when deciding whether to trust a chatbot. This separation between those over 45 and those under 45 appears several times in this dataset. We hypothesise that this relates to the Xennials, who had an analogue childhood but a digital adulthood. These individuals will have had the introduction to technology with a very un-human interface, which is likely to lower their expectations of machine interfaces. Those who have had a digital childhood and indeed come to computing where there are many more rich interfaces such as touchscreens and pervasive technology in the home perhaps set a higher expectation on these rich interactions. All of these issues are areas we are looking to explore in more depth.

A final comment would be orientated around the effect of participants age, particularly on the value placed on chatbots' characteristics. There are significant differences in the effect of avatars and the perceived 'friendliness' of chatbots, particularly between those aged 18–24 and those aged over 45. If we are to base our understanding of how to design systems from an evidence-base driven by this younger cohort, we risk creating systems that are not effective for all ages.

Acknowledgements. This work is funded by the UK EPSRC 'A Platform for Responsive Conversational Agents to Enhance Engagement and Disclosure (PRoCEED)' project (EP/S027211/1 and EP/S027297/1).

References

1. Fan, H., Poole, M.S.: What is personalization? perspectives on the design and implementation of personalization in information systems. J. Organ. Comput. Electron. Comm. **16**(3–4), 179–202 (2006)
2. Følstad, A., Nordheim, C.B., Bjørkli, C.A.: What makes users trust a chatbot for customer service? an exploratory interview study. In: Bodrunova, S.S. (ed.) INSCI 2018. LNCS, vol. 11193, pp. 194–208. Springer, Cham (2018). https://doi.org/10.1007/978-3-030-01437-7_16
3. Ghosh, C., Eastin, M.S.: Understanding users' relationship with voice assistants and how it affects privacy concerns and information disclosure behavior. In: Moallem, A. (ed.) HCII 2020. LNCS, vol. 12210, pp. 381–392. Springer, Cham (2020). https://doi.org/10.1007/978-3-030-50309-3_25
4. Ischen, C., Araujo, T., Voorveld, H., van Noort, G., Smit, E.: Privacy concerns in chatbot interactions. In: Følstad, A., et al. (eds.) CONVERSATIONS 2019. LNCS, vol. 11970, pp. 34–48. Springer, Cham (2020). https://doi.org/10.1007/978-3-030-39540-7_3
5. Lee, H., Park, H., Kim, J.: Why do people share their context information on social network services? a qualitative study and an experimental study on users' behavior of balancing perceived benefit and risk. Int. J. Hum.-Comput. Studi. **71**(9), 862–877 (2013)
6. McCullagh, P.: Regression models for ordinal data. J. R. Stat. Soc. Ser. B (Meth.) **42**(2), 109–142 (1980). http://www.jstor.org/stable/2984952
7. Sağlam, R.B., Nurse, J.R.C.: Is your chatbot GDPR compliant? open issues in agent design. In: Proceedings of the 2nd Conference on Conversational User Interfaces, pp. 1–3 (2020)
8. Suganuma, Y., Narita, J., Nishigaki, M., Ohki, T.: Understanding the impact of service trials on privacy disclosure. In: Stephanidis, C., Antona, M. (eds.) HCII 2020. CCIS, vol. 1226, pp. 605–612. Springer, Cham (2020). https://doi.org/10.1007/978-3-030-50732-9_78

9. Treiblmaier, H., Chong, S.: Trust and perceived risk of personal information as antecedents of online information disclosure: results from three countries. In: Global Diffusion and Adoption of Technologies for Knowledge and Information Sharing, pp. 341–361. IGI Global (2013)

10. Williams, M., Nurse, J.R.C., Creese, S.: Smartwatch games: encouraging privacy-protective behaviour in a longitudinal study. Comput. Hum. Behav. **99**, 38–54 (2019)

Sharing Secrets with Agents: Improving Sensitive Disclosures Using Chatbots

Oliver Buckley[1]([✉]), Jason R. C. Nurse[2], Natalie Wyer[1], Helen Dawes[3], Duncan Hodges[4], Sally Earl[1], and Rahime Belen Saglam[2]

[1] University of East Anglia, Norwich, UK
o.buckley@uea.ac.uk
[2] University of Kent, Canterbury, UK
[3] Oxford Brookes University, Oxford, UK
[4] Defence Academy of the UK, Cranfield University, Shrivenham, UK

Abstract. There is an increasing shift towards the use of conversational agents, or chatbots, thanks to their inclusion in consumer hardware (e.g. Alexa, Siri and Google Assistant) and the growing number of essential services moving online. A chatbot allows an organisation to deal with a large volume of user queries with minimal overheads, which in turn allows human operators to deal with more complex issues. In this paper we present our work on maximising responsible, sensitive disclosures to chatbots. The paper focuses on two key studies, the first of which surveyed participants to establish the relative sensitivity of a range of disclosures. From this, we found that participants were equally comfortable making financial disclosures to a chatbot as to a human. The second study looked to support the dynamic personalisation of the chatbot in order to improve the disclosures. This was achieved by exploiting behavioural biometrics (keystroke and mouse dynamics) to identify demographic information about anonymous users. The research highlighted that a fusion approach, combining both keyboard and mouse dynamics, was the most reliable predictor of these biographic characteristics.

Keywords: Chatbot · Conversational agent · Disclosure · Biometrics · Keystroke dynamics · Mouse dynamics · Information inference

1 Introduction

Conversational agents, also known as chatbots, are applications that interact with users in increasingly empathetic and humanistic ways. These technologies have seen a significant rise in popularity and prevalence, in part thanks to assistants such as Siri and Alexa being embedded in consumer hardware. While these assistants will typically focus on everyday tasks and enquiries there is a growing shift to their use in contexts where users are required to disclose sensitive information, for example, in healthcare.

The ubiquity and uptake of chatbots has continued to grow, despite a number of key questions remaining unanswered. These include areas such as how

C. Stephanidis et al. (Eds.): HCII 2021, CCIS 1420, pp. 400–407, 2021.
https://doi.org/10.1007/978-3-030-78642-7_54

a chatbot's characteristics may be used to maximise the depth and accuracy of disclosures that are linked to sensitive information. This is particularly pertinent when considering applications where honest and frank disclosures are prerequisites for an improved service outcome. Additionally, there are a number of privacy and security concerns associated with chatbots, which need to be appropriately managed to enable a better service provision [11].

The Platform for Responsive Conversational Agents to Enhance Engagement and Disclosure (PRoCEED) project aims to address these issues, and provide a framework for delivering agents that are both effective and efficient in their interactions. In this paper we provide a summary of the research to date, along with key findings in relation to agent design and report on two key studies. The remainder of the paper is structured as follows: Sect. 2 provides an overview of related material, Sect. 3 outlines the methodology used in the studies, Sect. 4 reports on the initial results and findings and finally, Sect. 5 discusses our conclusions and future work.

2   Related Work

As our societal dependence on technology increases, then so does the need for organisations to develop communications that are capable of managing the increasing volume of users. Currently, chatbots are largely seen as a tool for first line customer support, offering a balance between limited organisation resources and providing the users with efficient and direct answers. For example, Juniper Research [9] estimates that annual cost savings derived from the adoption of chatbots could reach $7.3 billion globally by 2023.

The increasing trend towards the use of chatbots, by both government and industry, highlights the need for a greater appreciation of how individuals interact with them and the factors that determine the efficiency of this engagement. This is crucial if they are to increase service effectiveness and efficiency, given the reluctance, historically, to engage with agents [3]. However, a significant portion of research in this domain focuses on creating increasingly human-like agents [7], and developing methods that maximise an individual user's engagement [12]. While these represent important aims, they highlight a lack of research focused on understanding which aspects of an agent encourage user engagement and which of these aspects support deeper and more accurate disclosures.

There are a range of factors that influence how willing individuals are to engage and disclose the correct information to agents, which can relate to the agent itself (e.g. humanity, avatar), the medium (e.g. text, voice) or the individual (e.g. age, need). The literature provides indications about the features that are likely to affect engagement, with the perceived 'humanity' of the agent being vital. Epley et al. [6] suggest that adapting the characteristics of agents makes anthropomorphism more likely. This anthropomorphisation and its nature is something that is determined by the attributes of the perceiver. Specifically, individuals who are more motivated to engage in social interaction (e.g., the chronically lonely) or those who are more motivated to establish control over their environments (e.g., those wishing to show expertise in their domain) have been shown to be more prone to anthropomorphise agents [5].

Existing research on the use of chatbots for the disclosure of sensitive information has often been limited by the technology. Elmasri and Maeder [4] developed a chatbot to engage with 18–25-year olds to understand alcohol consumption. While the work found that individuals did disclose small amounts of information, and were generally positive about the agent they were largely frustrated by the technical solution. Similarly, in the education sector Bhakta et al. [2] present research that used simple chatbots to cover a range of sensitive topics such as sexual health, drug use and plagiarism. This work found that the use of a chatbot resulted in more words than a standard non-interactive survey, which was considered to be a greater engagement. While more words may constitute increased engagement, the elicitation of more sensitive information requires a more nuanced approach.

The research in this project is informed by broader research into conversational agents and user interactions. Hill et al. [7] concluded that humans communicate differently when they know they are directly interacting with a machine. Their experiments revealed that participants sent twice as many messages to chatbots as they did to humans. There is research (e.g. Jenkins et al. [8]) that suggests that users expect conversational agents to behave and communicate in a very human-like way, whereas other studies (Bailenson et al. [1]) highlight an increase in the depth of disclosures when engaging with a more machine-like agent.

In this project we focus on understanding the depth of disclosure and how the characteristics of both the agent and the user can impact this level of information sharing. The studies in this paper highlight the methods used to quantify the sensitivity of particular disclosures as well as our approach to automatically understand the characteristics of the user.

3   Methodology

The project to date consists of two studies designed to better understand the core characteristics of an agent when considering disclosure, and to inform agent design. Firstly, we discuss a 491-individuals study that aimed to investigate the types of information that people with different characteristics are comfortable sharing with a chatbot vs. a human. The second study presents a 240-person experiment to infer demographic information from mouse and keyboard usage.

3.1   Understanding Information Disclosure

The perceived sensitivity of personal information is central to the privacy concerns and information disclosure behavior of individuals. Such perceptions motivate how people disclose and share information with others. In this part of the study, we investigated the perspective of citizens in the United Kingdom about three main issues related to chatbot-mediated information disclosure. Firstly, we identified the factors that lead to certain data items being considered sensitive by the participants. Secondly, we asked them to evaluate the perceived sensitivity of different data items and finally, we analysed how demographic characteristics of the participants (such as age, gender, education), anonymity, context (health vs finance) and interaction means (chatbot-mediated vs human-mediated) influence the perception of sensitivity on an individual level.

In order to understand reasons or factors that lead participants to consider certain personal data as more sensitive, we asked individuals to give their reasons in open-ended questions and conducted a thematic content analysis to identify emerging themes in their responses. Whilst to assess the sensitivity ratings covered in the second part of the study, we used hierarchical cluster analysis and grouped data items based on their perceived sensitivity. Finally, to model the effect of demographic characteristics, anonymity, context and interaction means, we built proportional-odds logistic regression models. Using those models, we explored the effects of these factors on comfort levels of people while disclosing sensitive information.

3.2   Inferring Demographic Information Using Keystroke and Mouse Dynamics

As identified previously it is clear that encouraging successful disclosures from individuals requires a tailored experience that acknowledges the individual differences between users. Logically, if a chatbot is to provide a tailored experience to a user it must have a way of assessing a set of characteristics about the user in order to select the most appropriate experience. In this study we look to model the ability to infer user characteristics, in this case demographic information such as age and gender, from how the user is interacting with the chatbot.

This study used a custom web-application that facilitated the collection of large volumes of mouse and keystroke dynamic data, in both controlled and uncontrolled scenarios. Participants were required to complete five distinct tasks: three gathering data associated with the use of a mouse and two gathering data from keyboard kepresses.

To gather data about the use of a mouse, participants were shown single cross hairs, and were required to click the centre of the target. Once they clicked within 100 px of the centre of the target they were presented with a new target, with participants asked to click five targets in total. This used a similar approach to that devised by Van Balen et al. [13]. Additionally, more natural mouse data was gathered during the initial phases of the study, when asking users to provide demographic data. In order to collect keystroke data, participants were required to copy a short passage of text from Bram Stoker's Dracula and then to write a brief description of the plot of the last movie that they watched. This approach is designed to both provide data collection which is comparable against all participants and then free collection (e.g. writing creatively rather than copying), to better mimic reality. The study collected data from 239 participants, and used a combination of features resulting in a total of 241 features in total.

4   Initial Results

4.1   Understanding Information Disclosures

The thematic analysis of the responses given for the factors that lead participants to consider a data item to be sensitive identified several common factors. Our findings confirmed the importance of the risk of harm, trust of the interaction means, public availability of data, context of the data, and the re-identification risk in disclosure behavior. Additionally, we found other factors had an impact upon the comfort level of individuals while disclosing information. These factors included concerns about the reactions from others, concerns regarding personal safety or mental health, and the consequences of disclosure on loved ones.

Assessment of the sensitivity ratings of different data items and clustering results demonstrate that from a UK perspective, passwords are the most sensitive data type where 92% of participants gave it the highest rating. Bank account credentials, credit card number are other items appearing in the same high sensitivity category. The next category, sensitive data items, included formally identifiable information such as national ID number and passport number. Accordingly, the least sensitive items were hair colour, gender and height which are unhelpful to identify individuals and are typically observable.

Focusing specifically on chatbots, the proportional-odds logistic regression models that were built in the third part of the study demonstrated that there is a preference for disclosure to humans (over chatbots) especially in a health context. Participants were more comfortable disclosing their health information such as medical diagnosis, chronic diseases and mental health issues directly to a human. This impact was less visible in the finance domain where only the credit score and income level data items showed a significant effect. Therefore, finance may well be a potential context where chatbots can be utilised.

4.2   Inferring Demographic Information Using Keystroke and Mouse Dynamics

As discussed previously the ability to dynamically adapt the chatbot to the user provides the opportunity to present the chatbot that is most likely to elicit deep and accurate disclosures. This section explores the results from the study looking to automatically identify biographic characteristics of the user and hence support the personalisation of the chatbot.

Using a variety of machine learning approaches we explored the ability to predict the characteristics of the users from their interactions with the computer via the keyboard and mouse, the data was randomly split with 95% for training and 5% for testing, utilising random undersampling to account for class imbalance, this process was performed 100 times for each experiment. The research also explored the effect of accurate feature engineering by reducing the number of features used by the classifiers, this used the ANOVA F-values between the label and the features to identify the most discriminatory features. The set of features associated with the mouse dataset was smaller and hence we only present the results for the full dataset. Initial results are shown in Table 1, which shows the performance for a variety of classification techniques. We would anticipate these scores could be improved by more rigorous feature engineering and tuning of the model parameters but the performance is included as an indication of the classification accuracy.

Table 1. Accuracy scores for each biometric (keystroke, mouse dynamics and a combined measure of the two) and its ability to predict soft biometric features.

	N. features	Keystrokes				Mouse				Combination			
		Gender	Handedness	Age	Electronic Hours	Gender	Handedness	Age	Electronic Hours	Gender	Handedness	Age	Electronic Hours
Random Forest (100)	all	0.57	0.61	0.20	0.06	0.60	0.55	0.23	0.11	0.64	0.58	0.25	0.09
	150	0.58	0.53	0.21	0.12	-	-	-	-	0.66	0.58	0.26	0.13
	100	0.60	0.56	0.20	0.17	-	-	-	-	0.68	0.64	0.27	0.17
Decision Trees (3, 5)	all	0.50	0.58	0.16	0.15	0.58	0.57	0.23	0.10	0.52	0.63	0.20	0.21
	150	0.51	0.58	0.17	0.18	-	-	-	-	0.54	0.67	0.21	0.16
	100	0.52	0.58	0.18	0.19	-	-	-	-	0.58	0.68	0.23	0.20
Decision Trees (10, 3)	all	0.57	0.69	0.15	0.10	0.57	0.52	0.22	0.16	0.54	0.81	0.22	0.05
	150	0.51	0.74	0.16	0.10	-	-	-	-	0.56	0.74	0.21	0.07
	100	0.50	0.66	0.18	0.09	-	-	-	-	0.54	0.81	0.22	0.05
SVM	all	0.44	0.32	0.14	0.02	0.50	0.38	0.14	0	0.44	0.30	0.14	0.01
	150	0.52	0.29	0.15	0.02	-	-	-	-	0.51	0.31	0.15	0.02
	100	0.55	0.29	0.15	0.03	-	-	-	-	0.60	0.31	0.17	0.03
Gaussian Naive Bayes	all	0.50	0.26	0.18	0.10	0.54	0.64	0.26	0.13	0.46	0.32	0.20	0.10
	150	0.50	0.33	0.18	0.08	-	-	-	-	0.53	0.42	0.24	0.15
	100	0.54	0.43	0.24	0.11	-	-	-	-	0.53	0.54	0.28	0.22
KNN	all	0.50	0.6	0.11	0.11	0.58	0.41	0.18	0.14	0.52	0.58	0.14	0.16
	150	0.54	0.54	0.12	0.08	-	-	-	-	0.58	0.56	0.18	0.18
	100	0.52	0.55	0.20	0.13	-	-	-	-	0.59	0.08	0.20	0.12

The results of our study clearly showed that using a combination of both keystroke and mouse features led to a more accurate prediction of a soft biometric characteristic, regardless of the biometric being predicted, the classifier being used, or the number of features the machine learning model was trained on. This was the case even when the biometric was not predicted with a large degree of accuracy (age and the number of hours spent on electronic devices).

In addition to this, our study found that the Mouse Dynamic features were more discriminatory than the Keystroke Dynamic features. This is seen in both the accuracy scores when comparing mouse and keyboard data. It is also seen in the combined data set, after the feature engineering stage the data set contains a disproportionate number of features from the mouse dataset.

As can be seen from Table 1 the best results were achieved using a combination of mouse and keyboard dynamics, indicating that it is possible to infer some of user characteristics from their interaction but at a relatively low accuracy.

5   Conclusions and Future Work

In this paper we present initial results for two studies, which aim to understand sensitive information disclosures and identifying soft biometrics using a fusion of keystroke and mouse dynamics. The first study determined participants perceptions with regards to the sensitivity of information across various domains. The key finding was that finance represented the area where participants would be most comfortable disclosing sensitive data to a chatbot.

We also identified from the literature that a dynamic chatbot which identified characteristics of the user and then provided a tailored service is likely to produce deeper and more accurate disclosures. Hence a second study considered the ability to automatically identify demographic information about a user based solely on their interactions with a chatbot (e.g. how they used the mouse and keyboard). The goal being that these assessments could drive the personalisation of the chatbot. Whilst we demonstrate it is possible to infer these user characteristics the accuracy is generally low. This indicates that for chatbots it may not be appropriate to infer these characteristics with a degree of confidence suitable for tailoring the experience.

The two studies in this paper will provide some of the early results from a larger project focusing on the provision of tailored chatbots to improve the sensitive disclosures made by users of these systems. The project is currently undertaking a Wizard-of-Oz (e.g. as seen in Kerly and Bull [10]) style experiment, which aims to understand how the perceived humanity of a chatbot impacts the depth of sensitive disclosures.

These experimental studies will be further contextualised with a number of case studies, exploring the application of chatbots in sensitive domains and providing mechanisms to ensure that the resulting digital services are inclusive and consider the needs of all of those using these services.

Acknowledgements. The research presented in this paper forms part of the *A Platform for Responsive Conversational Agents to Enhance Engagement and Disclosure (PRoCEED)* project funded by the Engineering and Physical Sciences Research Council, UK (EP/S027424/1, EP/S027211/1, EP/S027297/1, EP/S027467/1).

References

1. Bailenson, J.N., Yee, N., Merget, D., Schroeder, R.: The effect of behavioral realism and form realism of real-time avatar faces on verbal disclosure, nonverbal disclosure, emotion recognition, and copresence in dyadic interaction. Presence: Teleoperators Virtual Environ. **15**(4), 359–372 (2006). https://doi.org/10.1162/pres.15.4.359
2. Bhakta, R., Savin-Baden, M., Tombs, G.: Sharing secrets with robots? In: EdMedia+ Innovate Learning, pp. 2295–2301. Association for the Advancement of Computing in Education (AACE) (2014)
3. Drift: The 2018 state of chatbots report (2018). https://www.drift.com/wp-content/uploads/2018/01/2018-state-of-chatbots-report.pdf

4. Elmasri, D., Maeder, A.: A conversational agent for an online mental health intervention. In: Ascoli, G.A., Hawrylycz, M., Ali, H., Khazanchi, D., Shi, Y. (eds.) BIH 2016. LNCS (LNAI), vol. 9919, pp. 243–251. Springer, Cham (2016). https://doi.org/10.1007/978-3-319-47103-7_24
5. Epley, N., Waytz, A., Akalis, S., Cacioppo, J.T.: When we need a human: motivational determinants of anthropomorphism. Soc. Cogn. **26**(2), 143–155 (2008). https://doi.org/10.1521/soco.2008.26.2.143
6. Epley, N., Waytz, A., Cacioppo, J.T.: On seeing human: a three-factor theory of anthropomorphism. Psychol. Rev. **114**(4), 864 (2007)
7. Hill, J., Randolph Ford, W., Farreras, I.G.: Real conversations with artificial intelligence: a comparison between human-human online conversations and human-chatbot conversations. Comput. Hum. Behav. **49**, 245–250 (2015). https://doi.org/10.1016/j.chb.2015.02.026
8. Jenkins, M.-C., Churchill, R., Cox, S., Smith, D.: Analysis of user interaction with service oriented chatbot systems. In: Jacko, J.A. (ed.) HCI 2007. LNCS, vol. 4552, pp. 76–83. Springer, Heidelberg (2007). https://doi.org/10.1007/978-3-540-73110-8_9
9. Juniper Research: Bank Cost Savings via Chatbots to Reach $7.3 Billion by 2023, as Automated Customer Experience Evolves (2019). https://www.juniperresearch.com/press/press-releases/bank-cost-savings-via-chatbots-reach-7-3bn-2023
10. Kerly, A., Bull, S.: The potential for chatbots in negotiated learner modelling: a Wizard-of-Oz study. In: Ikeda, M., Ashley, K.D., Chan, T.-W. (eds.) ITS 2006. LNCS, vol. 4053, pp. 443–452. Springer, Heidelberg (2006). https://doi.org/10.1007/11774303_44
11. Sağlam, R.B., Nurse, J.R.C.: Is your chatbot GDPR compliant? Open issues in agent design. In: Proceedings of the 2nd Conference on Conversational User Interfaces. CUI 2020. Association for Computing Machinery, New York (2020). https://doi.org/10.1145/3405755.3406131
12. Sundar, S.S., Bellur, S., Oh, J., Jia, H., Kim, H.S.: Theoretical importance of contingency in human-computer interaction: effects of message interactivity on user engagement. Commun. Res. **43**(5), 595–625 (2016). https://doi.org/10.1177/0093650214534962
13. Van Balen, N., Ball, C., Wang, H.: Analysis of targeted mouse movements for gender classification. EAI Endorsed Trans. Secur. Saf. **4**(11) (2017)

Investigating What You Share: Privacy Perceptions of Behavioural Biometrics

Sally Earl[(✉)] [ID], James Campbell [ID], and Oliver Buckley [ID]

School of Computing Science, University of East Anglia, Norwich NR4 7TJ, UK
{s.earl,j.campbell1,o.buckley}@uea.ac.uk
http://www.uea.ac.uk

Abstract. This study examines people's perceptions of biometrics, in the context of the inherent privacy concerns surrounding behavioural biometrics as an alternative to conventional password systems. We present the knowledge and opinions of behavioural biometrics collected in this study. The main theme which is present throughout the research is that users have privacy concerns around behavioural biometrics, but that these concerns do not necessarily translate into privacy-conscious actions.

Keywords: Behavioural biometrics · Privacy · Perceptions

1 Introduction

Biometrics are becoming increasingly common as an alternative to conventional password and passcode systems, whether this be the use of a fingerprint to unlock a laptop or their face to open a mobile phone.

One of the reasons for the shift towards biometrics is the underlying issues associated with creating good passwords. It has long been stated that it is difficult for users to create passwords which are both memorable and secure [8], and many of the measures which websites and companies use to try to increase security can make things worse, for example [1,12]. Additionally, users tend to be reluctant to use security measures which are an inconvenience [6]. Biometrics have the advantage of removing any cognitive load from the user - as they do not need to remember any information or have a specific item on their person.

Behavioural biometrics create a unique profile of a person through looking at how they act [17]. The key difference between physical and behavioural biometrics is that physical biometrics have a static measurement, whereas behavioural biometrics are dynamic.

While the public are likely to be familiar with physical biometrics due to their ubiquity in day-to-day life, behavioural biometrics are less likely to be at the forefront of their consciousness. Previous studies (such as in Furnell and Evangelatos [7] and Buckley and Nurse [4]) have looked at perceptions of biometrics both physical and behavioural, but none have focused on exclusively behavioural biometrics.

C. Stephanidis et al. (Eds.): HCII 2021, CCIS 1420, pp. 408–415, 2021.
https://doi.org/10.1007/978-3-030-78642-7_55

One large difference between physical and behavioural biometrics is that behavioural biometrics can frequently be gathered without the user's knowledge, unlike physical biometrics which usually require an action of the user. As a result of this, behavioural biometrics have the potential to be more privacy-infringing than physical biometrics.

In recent years, online privacy has become at the forefront of public consciousness, with the UK ICO [10] noting an increase of 70% of contacts from the general public surrounding issues of data privacy since the implementation of the Data Protection Act 2018. As a result, any technological development which has the potential to interfere with privacy may cause a lack of trust from users.

In this study we aimed to not only gather more information about people's knowledge and trust of behavioural biometrics, but also how this might link to their perceptions of privacy.

2   Literature Review

Many different behavioural biometrics have been studied, with 28 having been identified by Yampolskiy and Govindaraju [17]. Of these biometrics, the most commonly studied are Gait (the way a person walks), Keystroke Dynamics (the way a person types), Mouse Dynamics (the way a person uses their mouse), Signature (the dynamic movement when a person signs their name), and Voice (the way a person speaks).

Several studies have been completed regarding perceptions of biometrics. In 2007 Furnell and Evangelatos [7] found 45% of participants felt passwords were inadequate for large-scale systems, and most had positive opinions towards biometrics. The study found that the behavioural biometrics studied were ranked as being less reliable than the physical biometrics, with keystroke dynamics in particular being ranked as not at all reliable. Keystroke dynamics were also the biometric the participants were least aware of. This trend can also be seen in a study by Krupp et al. [13], which looked at attitudes to biometrics within Germany, and found that whilst voice biometrics and facial recognition were known, they were not well-accepted. This trend is again seen in a study by Buckley and Nurse [4], with the behavioural biometrics being ranked as least secure (again, with the caveat that these biometrics were also those which were less familiar to the participants).

Studies throughout the last decade have found that people have seen biometrics as a secure authentication method [2,5,13]. Despite these positive opinions of biometrics; however, studies still show people prefer using passwords to other methods including biometrics and other password alternatives (such as graphical passwords) [19].

Some previous studies have discussed the potential privacy issues and other ethical concerns of biometrics. Norval and Prasopoulou [15] found that there was a wide variety of attitudes towards biometrics, with some seeing biometrics as intrusive, whilst others saw them as more neutral. A similar dichotomy has been found in other studies, with some users preferring passwords due to their lack of privacy concerns, despite security issues, and others preferring biometrics due to their heightened security, regardless of risk [18]. Zimmerman and Gerber [19] found that signature elicited the most privacy concerns of the authentication methods used. The authors also found that privacy concerns and preferred authentication method did not directly relate to one another, with fingerprint being the second most-liked authentication method, but also having high security concerns. None of these studies considered how a participant's existing opinions on privacy might factor into their feelings on biometrics generally.

When discussing biometrics, it is also important to note that the knowledge (or lack thereof) that a participant has may effect their understanding of the potential benefits and issues. Mwapasa et al. [14] highlights the knowledge-gap between potential users of biometric systems and those who implement and write policies concerning them, particularly in countries with high illiteracy levels. As a result of this, it is important to note that users do not necessarily have all the information available to make informed choices.

Based on the literature above, this research looks to understand user's perceptions of biometrics and contrast this with their knowledge on the subject. Furthermore, we look to incorporate online social media presence data to understand if the perceptions of biometrics, match their own online privacy settings.

3   Method

In order to facilitate data collection, we designed a survey for this study, comprised of a mixture of closed and open-ended questions. Prior to study launch, we obtained ethical approval from our University.

Participant recruitment took place primarily through the Prolific platform, which allowed us to obtain a diverse pool of respondents. This recruitment was supplemented with more ad-hoc recruitment from the general public, primarily through social media, and snowball sampling [9].

Our survey began with collecting a range of demographic data from participants including gender, age, and highest level of education. Additionally, we collected data on what social networks participants used, and whether their accounts were public or private.

We then asked a number of questions which focused on participant's opinions on privacy; to allow us to use this as a baseline for their opinions on behavioural biometrics.

The study then followed closely that of Buckley and Nurse [4], asking participants to define what they felt was meant by the term 'behavioural biometrics'. We then presented them with a list of behavioural biometrics (Gait, Keystroke Dynamics, Mouse Dynamics, Voice, and Signature/Handwriting) to see which they had previously heard of. We chose these specific behavioural biometrics as they were the biometrics identified in [17] which were most likely to be usable in a variety of situations. Similarly to the previous study, we then asked participants to rank the domains of Airport, Banking, Home, Mobile Devices, and Online Shopping in terms of need for security, then rank which behavioural biometrics (if any) they would trust to secure each domain. This was to ascertain how secure they felt each biometric was (as if they trusted a biometric in the domain they felt was the most needing security, they likely trusted the biometric). Our study concluded with asking participants whether they felt behavioural biometrics infringed on their privacy, and asking them to recall how many days we planned to retain their data.

The data analysis consisted of a variety of quantitative and qualitative techniques. For the closed questions we used statistical methods for analysis, including looking for correlation using the Pearson Chi-Squared test. For the open-ended questions, we first used Thematic Analysis [3], which allowed us to manually explore all the data to find patterns and themes.

4   Results

Our survey received a total of 238 responses. Of these, 104 were female and 134 were male. A significant minority of our participants (40%) were aged 19–25, with 72% of our participants being aged 30 or below. As a result of this, it is important to note there is a bias towards younger people within our data, all of whom will have grown up with access to the internet and technology.

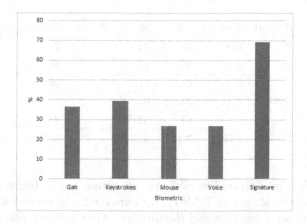

Fig. 1. Percentage of participants who had heard of each biometric

Before participants were asked their opinions on behavioural biometrics, we first asked them what they thought was meant by the term, and conducted thematic analysis on the responses. The most commonly occurring theme was that the participants did not know, with 20% responding such. Other common themes included the idea of monitoring a user's actions on a computer or online, with many participants explicitly mentioning monitoring social media behaviour. Other themes in the data included monitoring of a person's actions or patterns,

and the use of identification or determination of personal features and characteristics. A not insubstantial number of participants guessed or knew behavioural
biometrics had something to do with monitoring an action or behaviour of some
sort.

After participants had given their definition, they were then given an accurate
definition of behavioural biometrics. When asked if they had ever heard of any
of the behavioural biometrics considered in our study, only signature had been
heard of by a majority of our participants (69%) (Fig. 1). This is likely to be
in part due to a misunderstanding conflating signing for something and the
biometric, as considered in [4].

Our results are similar to those found in [4], with the exception of voice,
which only 26% of our participants had heard of. This seems unlikely, as voice
recognition has been used by banks for several years, including all of the UK's
Big 4 banks (Barclays, HSBC, Lloyds Group, and NatWest Group). Additionally
this result is significantly below that of Buckley and Nurse [4], who found over
60% of their participants had heard of voice biometrics. It is unclear what factor
has caused this discrepancy.

Table 1. Breakdown of rankings of security in each domain, with the lower the value
indicating the higher need for security.

	Airport	Banking	Home	Mobile devices	Online shopping
1	80	104	40	12	2
2	52	103	39	18	26
3	36	27	64	61	50
4	33	4	34	95	72
5	37	0	61	52	88
Average	2.5588	1.7101	3.1555	3.6597	3.9160

We also asked participants to rank specific situations in terms of their need
for security (results shown in Table 1). As expected, the areas ranked as most
needing security were banking and the airport. After this, we asked our participants which biometrics they would trust in each domain, to give us an idea of
which biometrics they trust the most. Voice biometrics was most consistently
ranked the most trusted biometric.

The feasibility of each individual biometric to provide security in each situation seems to have been taken into account somewhat. This can be seen when
looking at the ranking for gait analysis, which despite coming last in 3 of the
domains, it came second in the other two (home and the airport). This makes
sense that for online shopping and mobile devices, gait would be unlikely to be
a feasible authentication method.

When asked about whether behavioural biometrics infringed on their privacy,
just over 50% of our participants reported being unsure (Fig. 2). Of the remainder, more felt behavioural biometrics were privacy infringing than felt they were

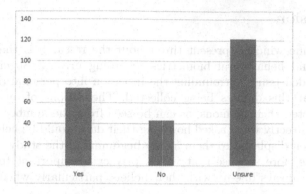

Fig. 2. Participants' response to the question "Do you think behavioural biometrics infringe on your privacy"

not. This is unsurprising, given the majority of the participants reported being concerned or very concerned about their privacy online.

Our participants' lack of certainty in the potential implications of behavioural biometrics is highlighted by 25 of our participants responding they felt behavioural biometrics gathered lots of personal data, whilst 25 other participants responded that they did not. These are in direct opposition to each other, showing either a lack of understanding by our participants, or alternatively a real disagreement about whether behavioural biometric data actually constitutes further personal data.

It is important to note here that the EU agrees with the latter of these 2 positions, with GDPR counting behavioural biometrics as 'special category data,' meaning it must be processed within specific settings. One of these is 'explicit consent'. The guidance from the ICO states that explicit consent in terms of biometric authentication must include the ability to opt-out [11]. This shows that the EU's opinions on the privacy and consent concerns surrounding behavioural biometrics are similar to many members of the public.

When asked if they thought behavioural biometrics infringed on privacy, our participants highlighted their desire to have knowledge of the information being gathered, and the ability to consent to it (with this idea being present 28 times). This again helps indicate that the GDPR requirements for explicit consent reflect the opinions of the public. Whilst this view has been explicitly expressed by our participants, their actions did not necessarily reflect it. 72.27% of the participants incorrectly selected a specific number of days which were specified in the Terms and Conditions at the beginning of the survey. This is not an uncommon finding, with previous studies showing that 79.7% of their participants agreed to the terms and conditions without reading them [16]. This highlights an ethical dilemma, that whilst users wish to be notified of behavioural biometric collection, ensuring they receive this information is difficult. This means that users may lose trust in sites they use if they later discover behavioural biometric collection.

5   Conclusion

The main theme which is present throughout the research is that users have concerns around behavioural biometrics regarding privacy. Specifically, these concerns included issues surrounding the intrusion into personal data, and the knowledge that this data is being collected. The actions of our users; however, contradicted their opinions, as can be seen from the number of users that responded incorrectly when asked how long their data would be held for, despite this having been displayed to them at the beginning of the study.

We can therefore surmise that whilst privacy is important to users, their actions do not always line-up with their beliefs, particularly when convenience is involved.

Future work should focus on improving the privacy implications of collecting behavioural biometric data, without compromising on the usability of a system. Further discussion is needed to understand perceptions of biometrics, and how their reputation and use as a form of security can be improved.

References

1. Adams, A., Sasse, M.A.: Users are not the enemy. Commun. ACM **42**(12), 40–46 (1999)
2. Bhagavatula, R., Ur, B., Iacovino, K., Kywe, S.M., Cranor, L.F., Savvides, M.: Biometric authentication on iPhone and android: usability, perceptions, and influences on adoption (2015)
3. Braun, V., Clarke, V.: Thematic analysis (2012)
4. Buckley, O., Nurse, J.R.: The language of biometrics: analysing public perceptions. J. Inf. Secur. Appl. **47**, 112–119 (2019)
5. Cornacchia, M., Papa, F., Sapio, B.: User acceptance of voice biometrics in managing the physical access to a secure area of an international airport. Technol. Anal. Strateg. Manag. **32**, 1–15 (2020)
6. Fagan, M., Khan, M.M.H.: Why do they do what they do?: a study of what motivates users to (not) follow computer security advice. In: Twelfth Symposium on Usable Privacy and Security ({SOUPS} 2016), pp. 59–75 (2016)
7. Furnell, S., Evangelatos, K.: Public awareness and perceptions of biometrics. Comput. Fraud Secur. **2007**(1), 8–13 (2007)
8. Gehringer, E.F.: Choosing passwords: security and human factors. In: IEEE 2002 International Symposium on Technology and Society (ISTAS 2002). Social Implications of Information and Communication Technology. Proceedings (Cat. No. 02CH37293), pp. 369–373. IEEE (2002)
9. Goodman, L.A.: Snowball sampling. Ann. Math. Statist. **32**(1), 148–170 (1961). https://doi.org/10.1214/aoms/1177705148
10. Information Commissioner's Office: Information commissioner's annual report and financial statements 2019–20. Technical Report. Information Commissioner's Office (2020)
11. Information Commissioner's Office (2020). https://ico.org.uk/for-organisations/guide-to-data-protection/guide-to-the-general-data-protection-regulation-gdpr/special-category-data/what-are-the-conditions-for-processing/#conditions1

12. Inglesant, P.G., Sasse, M.A.: The true cost of unusable password policies: password use in the wild. In: Proceedings of the SIGCHI Conference on Human Factors in Computing Systems, pp. 383–392 (2010)
13. Krupp, A., Rathgeb, C., Busch, C.: Social acceptance of biometric technologies in germany: a survey. In: 2013 International Conference of the BIOSIG Special Interest Group (BIOSIG), pp. 1–5. IEEE (2013)
14. Mwapasa, M., et al.: "Are we getting the biometric bioethics right?"-the use of biometrics within the healthcare system in Malawi. Glob. Bioeth. **31**(1), 67–80 (2020)
15. Norval, A., Prasopoulou, E.: Seeing like a citizen: exploring public views of biometrics. Polit. Stud. **67**(2), 367–387 (2019)
16. Steinfeld, N.: "I agree to the terms and conditions": (how) do users read privacy policies online? An eye-tracking experiment. Comput. Hum. Behav. **55**, 992–1000 (2016)
17. Yampolskiy, R.V., Govindaraju, V.: Taxonomy of behavioural biometrics. In: Behavioral Biometrics for Human Identification: Intelligent Applications, pp. 1–43. IGI Global (2010)
18. Zimmermann, V., Gerber, N.: "If it wasn't secure, they would not use it in the movies" – security perceptions and user acceptance of authentication technologies. In: Tryfonas, T. (ed.) HAS 2017. LNCS, vol. 10292, pp. 265–283. Springer, Cham (2017). https://doi.org/10.1007/978-3-319-58460-7_18
19. Zimmermann, V., Gerber, N.: The password is dead, long live the password-a laboratory study on user perceptions of authentication schemes. Int. J. Hum. Comput. Stud. **133**, 26–44 (2020)

Unnecessary Input Heuristics and PayJoin Transactions

Simin Ghesmati[1,3]([✉]), Andreas Kern[2,3], Aljosha Judmayer[2,3],
Nicholas Stifter[2,3], and Edgar Weippl[2,3]

[1] Vienna University of Technology, Vienna, Austria
[2] University of Vienna, Vienna, Austria
[3] SBA Research, Vienna, Austria
{sghesmati,akern,ajudmayer,nstifter,eweippl}@sba-research.org

Abstract. Over the years, several privacy attacks targeted at UTXO-based cryptocurrencies such as Bitcoin have been proposed. This has led to an arms race between increasingly sophisticated analysis approaches and a continuous stream of proposals that seek to counter such attacks against users' privacy. Recently, PayJoin was presented as a new technique for mitigating one of the most prominent heuristics, namely *common input ownership*. This heuristic assumes that the inputs of a transaction, and thus the associated addresses, belong to the same entity. However, a problem with PayJoin is that implementations can accidentally reveal such transactions if the corresponding inputs from involved parties are not chosen carefully. Specifically, if a transaction is formed in a way such that it contains seemingly unnecessary inputs, it can be identified through so-called *unnecessary input heuristic (UIH)*. What is not yet clear is the impact of naive coin selection algorithms within PayJoin implementations that may flag such transactions as PayJoin. This paper investigates the resemblance of PayJoin transactions to ordinary payment transactions by examining the significance of the unnecessary input heuristic in transactions with more than one input and exactly two outputs which is the common template of recent PayJoin transactions.

Keywords: PayJoin · Bitcoin · Privacy · Blockchain · Mixing · Unnecessary input heuristic · Optimal change heuristic

1 Introduction

Blockchain-based cryptocurrencies such as Bitcoin have gained significant interest by a wider audience in recent years. Hereby, the topic of transaction privacy has received considerable attention as research clearly highlights that storing every transaction in the network within a publicly accessible ledger can have a serious effect on user privacy. Previous studies [1,2] report some of the possible attacks that can reveal the identities of different entities and effectively find their relationships within UTXO(unspent transaction output)-based blockchains such

© Springer Nature Switzerland AG 2021
C. Stephanidis et al. (Eds.): HCII 2021, CCIS 1420, pp. 416–424, 2021.
https://doi.org/10.1007/978-3-030-78642-7_56

as Bitcoin. Several techniques have been proposed to remedy these privacy issues. In Bitcoin, the amount (also referred to as coins) associated with an address can be transferred to another address through a transaction. Transactions consist of input and output addresses. Each input address should be signed by its private key to unlock transferring the coins from that address. It is assumed that all the inputs in a transaction are controlled by the same user. This leads to a so-called *common input ownership heuristic* [1] which helps to cluster all the addresses that belong to the same user. To prevent effectiveness of this heuristic, CoinJoin was proposed by G. Maxwell in 2013 in which the users jointly create a transaction with their inputs and their desired outputs and then each of the users separately signs her input. Users have to send the same amount of coins to the desired outputs to prevent any linkage between the inputs and the outputs, which in turn leads to the distinguishability of these equal-sized output transactions in the blockchain. In recent years, the PayJoin [3–5] protocol, which follows the basic idea of CoinJoin, has been proposed to enhance the privacy of Bitcoin transactions, whereby the intended recipient of a transaction adds some of her *own* unspent transaction outputs to the inputs of the sender's transaction to break the so-called *common input ownership heuristic* [1]. The technique has been proposed as a Bitcoin Improvement Protocol BIP78 [6]; however, a naive implementation of the protocol, specifically in regard to the coin selection by participants, has the potential to flag such transactions as a PayJoin.

This paper evaluates the significance of *unnecessary input heuristic* on PayJoin transactions and discusses possible solutions to better blend in these transactions. In particular, the contributions of this paper are as follows:

– We compare the different definitions of unnecessary input heuristic (UIH).
– We provide an empirical analysis of the different UIH approaches.
– We extend upon existing discussions and describe possible countermeasures for PayJoin technique.

The remaining part of the paper is structured as follows: We first provide definitions and background information on PayJoin transactions in Sect. 2. Section 3 examines the definition of unnecessary input heuristic, reports extracted transaction statistics from Bitcoin, analyzes them via this heuristic. We then discuss research challenges specific to the PayJoin protocol in Sect. 4.

2   PayJoin Transactions

The concept of PayJoin was first proposed in a blog-post by BlockStream, called Improving Privacy Using Pay-to-EndPoint (P2EP) [3]; shortly after, BustaPay [4] was proposed in the Linux Foundation, Gibson provided more details under the name of PayJoin [5]. PayJoin solves the distinguishability of equal-size CoinJoin transactions by adding at least one UTXO of the recipient to the UTXO inputs of the transaction (Fig. 1), which provides plausible deniability. Simplified, it can be considered as performing a CoinJoin while paying someone else. The protocol effectively breaks one of the most prominent heuristics that can be employed to de-anonymize Bitcoin users, namely common input ownership. By breaking this heuristic, the utilization of the PayJoin protocol by some users can also provide privacy to other users. Further, the protocol also intends to hide the true payment amount, as the total output of the transaction will be the sum of the payment amount and the recipient's input amounts.

To run the protocol [6], the recipient (Bob) sends his address and the amount to the sender (Alice), using BIP21 URI. The sender creates and signs a transaction (original transaction) in which she sends the specified amount to the recipient's address. She also provides her change address to receive the remainder, and then sends the transaction to the recipient. The recipient checks the transaction and creates a new transaction (PayJoin proposal) by appending his inputs to the transaction created by the sender. The recipient then alters the output amount by adding his input amounts. He signs his inputs and sends this PayJoin proposal to the sender. The sender checks and signs the PayJoin transaction and broadcasts it to the network. The recipient is also able to broadcast the original transaction if there was any problem in creating the PayJoin transaction. At the time of writing, the protocol has been implemented by Joinmarket wallet, Samourai wallet (Stowaway), Wasabi wallet, Blue wallet and BTCPay. Users can create their own stores in BTCPay to receive PayJoin transactions (e.g., for selling their services). The senders (or buyers) can pay to the recipients through the aforementioned wallets that support PayJoin transactions. Currently, PayJoin transactions are formed as multiple inputs and exactly two outputs, which we consider as interesting transactions in this paper.

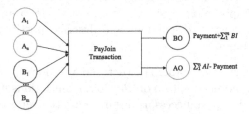

Fig. 1. A sample PayJoin transaction

3   Optimal Change/Unnecessary Input Heuristic

Whenever the sum of the inputs is larger than the payment amount, a so-called change address is created in Bitcoin to return the remainder of the coins to the sender [1]. Over the years, several heuristics have been implemented to aid address attribution. In this section, we want to look at one of the heuristics, which can be directly used to identify PayJoin transactions, amongst all transactions with more than one input and exactly two outputs.

UIH1 (Optimal change address): The *optimal change* heuristic was introduced to detect the change address of a transaction. It has been implemented by blockchain analysis tools such as blocksci [2] to cluster addresses. This heuristic flags the smallest output as a change address if it is smaller than the smallest input [2].

UIH2 (Unnecessary Input): This heuristic flags transactions as abnormal, if the largest output could be paid without the smallest input.

In practice, there exist several nuanced variants of UIH1 and UIH2, which we discuss in the following.

BlockSci UIH1 [2]: *"If there exists an output that is smaller than any of the inputs it is likely the change."*[1]

BlockStream UIH1[2]: *"This heuristic gives an indication that one output is more likely to be a change because some inputs would have been unnecessary if it was the payment."*

Gibson UIH1 [5]: *"One output is smaller than any input. This heuristically implies that output is not a payment, and must therefore be a change output."*

BlockSci UIH2 [2]: *"If a change output was larger than the smallest input, then the coin selection algorithm would not need to add the input in the first place."*[3]

BlockStream UIH2: *"If the sum of the inputs minus minimum input covers the larger output and transaction fee, the transaction has seemingly unnecessary inputs that are not typically added by consumer wallet software with a less sophisticated coin selection algorithm."*

Gibson UIH2 [5]: *"One input is larger than any output. This heuristically implies that this is not a normal wallet-created payment."*

Gibson, A. [5] and BlockStream definitions need double-checking for UIH1 and UIH2; however, UIH2 by [5] does not cover the situation when the subset sum of the inputs is enough for paying the larger output. There is also a degree of uncertainty over the definition of UIH2, as different coin selection algorithms or input consolidation can violate this heuristic [7], however, creating those kinds of transactions by PayJoin protocol has the potential to make these kinds of transactions suspicious. Avoiding UIH1 and UIH2 is an open question amongst PayJoin developers, and what is not yet clear is the anonymity set that can be achieved by avoiding these heuristics. The discussion among the developers refers to the statistics that were provided on gist and then published in [5]. The statistics provide the number of transactions with more than one input and exactly two outputs for 885 blocks in one week of the December 2018. To clarify how these transactions appear in practice, we refer to these real PayJoin

---

[1] We consider the BlockSci definition in a simpler form, ignoring the transaction fee for data categorization.

[2] https://github.com/Blockstream/esplora/blob/cbed66ecee9f468802cf1f073c204718b eac30d7/client/src/lib/privacy-analysis.js\#L47-L70.

[3] A comprehensive definition can be considered as $(sum(in) - min(in) >= sum(out) - min(out) + TX.fee)$.

Algorithm 1. BlockSci UIH1 and UIH2 according to BlockSci !UIH1

if $min(out) < min(in)$ then
  Transaction is UIH1
else
  Transaction is UIH2
end if

Algorithm 2. BlockStream UIH1 and UIH2

if $(Sum(in) - min(in) >= max(out) + TX.fee)$ then
  Transaction is UIH2
else if $(Sum(in) - min(in) >= min(out) + TX.fee)$ then
  Transaction is UIH1
end if

Algorithm 3. Gibson UIH1 and UIH2

if $min(out) < min(in)$ then
  Transaction is UIH1
end if
if $max(in) > max(out)$ then
  Transaction is UIH2
end if

---

transactions that can be categorized by UIH1[4] and UIH2[5]. As can be seen, one performed such as normal payment transactions (UIH1) and the other has unnecessary input (UIH2)[6]. PayJoin technique is recently implemented and there is not enough ground truth, however, in our manual inspection to find BTCPay PayJoin transactions and in the transactions that we created using BTCPay, we found that BTCPay does not prevent UIH2 and some of the transactions are formed such that they can be flagged as UIH2.

3.1 Transactions Statistics via the Unnecessary Input Heuristic

We Parsed Bitcoin blockchain and extracted all the interesting transactions over a week in September from 2009 to 2020, and then apply different definitions to shed light on the significance of avoiding UIH1 and UIH2 in PayJoin transactions as well as to compare the statistics obtained by different definitions. We Parsed Bitcoin blockchain and extracted all the transactions with more than one input and exactly two outputs for 885 blocks in one week of the September from 2009 to 2020, the statistics of which are indicated in Fig. 2. Due to practical constraints, this paper cannot provide comprehensive data for all the transactions which are performed in the Bitcoin blockchain.

---

[4] https://blockstream.info/tx/8cb0af96f1a2693683621758acbf3b7a7ad69a69672c61e1 44941d666f72da2a.

[5] https://blockstream.info/tx/58d68b22ab96b87a11c1fbd3090fee23f96f71a4115f96210 ba776d0ae7d8d55.

[6] In the second transaction, different nSequence fields also reveal that the inputs were added by different wallets, however, wallet fingerprinting is beyond the scope of this paper.

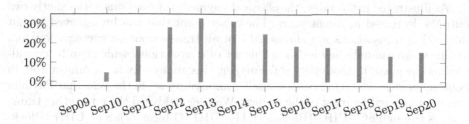

Fig. 2. Percentage of interesting transactions from total transactions

Table 1. UIH1 and UIH2 transactions

885 Blocks Start from	SC–UIH1‡ G–UIH1°	ST–UIH1×	SC–UIH2	ST–UIH2	G–UIH2	SC–UIH1% G–UIH1%	ST–UIH1%	SC–UIH2%	ST–UIH2%	G–UIH2%
3-Dec-18	145264	145003	122828	122684	83513	54.20%	54.09%	45.80%	45.76%	31.20%
9-Sep-09	1	1	0	0	0	100.00%	100.00%	0.00%	0.00%	0.00%
9-Sep-10	56	56	33	33	16	62.90%	62.92%	37.10%	37.08%	18.00%
9-Sep-11	5258	5282	2323	2288	466	69.40%	69.67%	30.60%	30.18%	6.10%
9-Sep-12	21107	20982	32164	32137	21551	39.60%	39.39%	60.40%	60.33%	40.50%
9-Sep-13	44308	44277	27448	27258	15539	61.70%	61.70%	38.30%	37.99%	21.70%
9-Sep-14	64926	65432	55308	54653	36083	54.00%	54.42%	46.00%	45.46%	30.00%
9-Sep-15	100210	100699	106913	105518	84373	48.40%	48.62%	51.60%	50.94%	40.70%
9-Sep-16	133802	133345	82436	82359	57103	61.90%	61.67%	38.10%	38.09%	26.40%
9-Sep-17	124684	123971	90398	90197	60583	58.00%	57.64%	42.00%	41.94%	28.20%
9-Sep-18	140864	140474	112492	112428	74070	55.60%	55.45%	44.40%	44.38%	29.20%
9-Sep-19	144879	144143	88588	88544	69510	62.10%	61.74%	37.90%	37.93%	29.80%
9-Sep-20	171532	170790	93180	93120	75295	64.80%	64.52%	35.20%	35.18%	28.40%
Average						58.04%	57.98%	41.96%	41.77%	27.18%

‡ SC stands for BlockSci. × ST stands for BlockStream. ° G stands for Gibson.

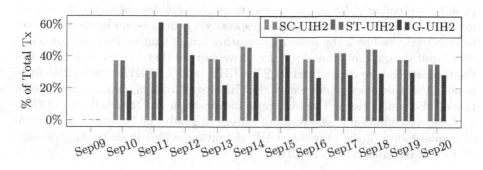

Fig. 3. Percentage of UIH2 transactions

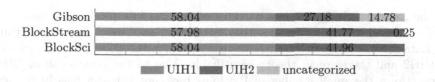

Fig. 4. % of transaction categories by BlockSci, BlockStream, and Gibson definitions

As illustrated in the table, the classical payment transactions with exactly two outputs decreased in recent years. The other point that can be achieved is that interesting transactions are almost 20% of all transactions on average. PayJoin at this stage can only be hidden in this set of transactions, which can be considered as the possible anonymity set. Further, this anonymity set is almost 15% in September 2020 which indicates a smaller anonymity set in the year that PayJoin was implemented by most of the wallets. We then analyzed the interesting transactions through SC−UIH1 (BlockSci), G−UIH1 (Gibson [5]), ST−UIH1 (BlockStream), SC−UIH2 (BlockSci !UIH1), ST−UIH2 (BlockStream), and G−UIH2 (Gibson [5]). We also extracted the data for 885 blocks in December 2018 to compare our results with the statistics in [5].

We applied algorithms 1, 2, and 3 to categorize transactions by different definitions of UIH1 and UIH2. The results of our research are reported in Table 1 which shows a breakdown of transactions by the different UIH1 and UIH2 categories. As can be seen in the selected blocks during September 2020, 64.8% of transactions are categorized as SC−UIH1 transactions, in which the change address is identifiable while 35.2% are SC−UIH2 which contain unnecessary input. Due to the small number of transactions in the selected data during September 2009, we exclude this year in the following statistical reports. The results obtained from the preliminary analysis show that on average nearly 58.04% of transactions are categorized as SC−UIH1 compared to around 41.96% as SC−UIH2. An interesting aspect we observe is the high ratio of SC−UIH2 and ST−UIH2 transactions, which shows almost 40% of transactions did not follow normal coin selection algorithms and were created with unnecessary input. Figure 3 illustrates the chart of UIH2 transactions by different algorithms. The peak in September 2012 for the transactions that are categorized as SC−UIH2 and ST−UIH2 (60.40% and 60.33%, respectively) could be an interesting point to investigate and seek the reason for creating lots of transactions with unnecessary input during that time. From Fig. 4 we can see that 57.98% and 41.77% of the transactions are categorized by ST−UIH1 and ST−UIH2, while 0.25% fit in none of the categories, which shows that Blockstream algorithm can not categorize all the transactions. The high ratio of uncategorized transactions (14.78%) by Gibsons' definition is as a result of considering only the largest input, instead of a subset sum of the inputs in UIH2 definition, which leads to flagging only 27.18% of the transactions as UIH2.

4   Discussion

At the time of writing, implementations of the PayJoin protocol remain relatively new and we conjecture that they are not yet used much in practice; thus, the data-set will likely not include many PayJoin transactions that are created as UIH2 and therefore in theory identifiable. Due to the large ratio of UIH2 transactions, the small number of PayJoins have not led to a bias in the last evaluation period (Sep 20), where they could have occurred. This might change if the reason for the high ratio of UIH2 transactions can be identified. A manual investigation of some of the UIH2 transactions revealed that there are transactions which can be categorized as internal address reuse, i.e., spending the UTXOs of the same address. This circumstance can separate these transactions from others, indicating that they are not PayJoin transactions. Further analysis is required to investigate the high number of UIH2 transactions. One of the possible countermeasures to avoid UIH2 in PayJoin transactions would be adding the input by the recipient such that it overtakes the change address of the sender (AO in Fig. 1); in this manner, the minimum output would be less than the minimum input which results in creating the transaction as an ordinary one.

On the one hand, the PayJoin protocol has the potential to cause privacy problems for both the sender and the recipient. If the adversary assumes common input ownership heuristic for all the inputs, she links the inputs to the previous transactions of the other participant. The sender may encounter a serious problem if she is not knowledgeable about PayJoin technique and the way it is created. In the current implementation of the wallets, the actions that should be done to send the coins as PayJoin is similar to sending the coins as an ordinary payment. Thus, the novice user is involved in a mixing technique, while she might not know the consequence of linking her inputs to the recipient inputs. In the worst case, if the recipient's input is related to the Darknet or criminal activities, the user may get into trouble. If the community seeks a technique that can increase the user's privacy by making the common input ownership heuristic less effective, they should also consider the privacy of the user who gets involved in these transactions. Any side effects as a result of lacking the knowledge by the user should be avoided. On the other hand, PayJoin transactions may render cluster analysis more difficult than before, as it creates false positives in the analysis leading to more super clusters.

In its current state, PayJoin is only described for transactions with more than one input and two outputs. This leads to an anonymity set of 15.4% compared to the total number of transactions according to our extracted data for September 2020 (Fig. 2). Moreover, it appears that classical payment transactions have been decreasing over the past years. Therefore, PayJoin should also be extended to transactions with more than two outputs to increase the anonymity set. As one of the main contributions of PayJoin is breaking the common input ownership heuristic, it can also poison the heuristic for a larger set of transactions.

Acknowledgment. This work is supported by COMET SBA-K1 and the Austrian Research Promotion Agency (FFG) via project number 874019.

References

1. Meiklejohn, S., et al.: A fistful of bitcoins: characterizing payments among men with no names. In: Proceedings of the 2013 Conference on Internet Measurement Conference, pp. 127–140. Association for Computing Machinery, New York (2013)

2. Kalodner, H., et al.: BlockSci: design and applications of a blockchain analysis platform. In: 29th USENIX Security Symposium (USENIX Security 20), pp. 2721–2738. USENIX, (2020). Change Address Heuristics. https://citp.github.io/BlockSci/reference/heuristics/change.html. Accessed 20 Sep 2020
3. Improving privacy using Pay-to-End Point (P2EP). https://blockstream.com/2018/08/08/en-improving-privacy-using-pay-to-endpoint/. Accessed 20 Sep 2020
4. Bustapay BIP: a practical sender/receiver coinjoin protocol. https://lists.linuxfoundation.org/pipermail/bitcoin-dev/2018-August/016340.html. Accessed 20 Sep 2020
5. PayJoin. https://joinmarket.me/blog/blog/payjoin/. Accessed 23 Aug 2020
6. BIP78: A simple payjoin proposal. https://github.com/bitcoin/bips/blob/master/bip-0078.mediawiki. Accessed 20 Sep 2020
7. BitCoin Privacy. https://en.bitcoin.it/wiki/Privacy. Accessed 20 Sep 2020

Smooth Transition of University Members to Multifactor Authentication

Yukio Ishihara$^{(\boxtimes)}$ and Ryuichiro Matsuzaki

Shimane University, 1060 Nishikawatsu-cho, Matsue-shi, Shimane 690-8504, Japan
{iyukio,rmatsu}@ipc.shimane-u.ac.jp

Abstract. In recent years, multifactor authentication becomes the mainstream to prevent illegitimate access especially caused by compromised passwords. In this study, we design and build an application system for Shimane University members to make transition to multifactor authentication. For smooth transition, we set requirements including that the transition should be triggered by each of the members at any time. After four months of operation, it is shown that the system works successfully.

Keywords: Multifactor authentication · Conditional access · Azure Active Directory

1 Introduction

In recent years, phishing emails remain relentless and are expected to continue [1]. Phishing for IDs and passwords reportedly seems not to be of interest to phishing frauds due to increasing use of multifactor authentication (hereinafter called MFA), however it still be one of major threats to companies, educational institutions etc. MFA provides a protective platform for users based on not only their passwords but also their own devices. In contrast, SFA or single factor authentication provides simple protection only by passwords. Thus, it is strongly recommended that MFA is introduced without delay to prevent any illegitimate access, which could be due to compromised passwords.

In Shimane University, we use Microsoft Azure Active Directory [2] to manage the members' accounts, and we make available to the members Microsoft 365 cloud-based services including Outlook on the web (emails), Office for the web (documents, spreadsheets), Teams (video conferences), OneDrive (personal storage) etc. Expectedly the amount of data stored on the cloud is growing, however the data are protected only by SFA. Thus, there is an urgent need for MFA, and it is also required to make as smooth transition to MFA as possible.

In 2020, Ibaraki University in Japan introduced MFA to all the members in a short period of time [3]. They exploited Microsoft Forms [4] to guide staff members and students individually towards MFA. This approach allowed each member to apply for MFA and set up their own device at any time they prefer.

We take a similar approach to those of Ibaraki University. Besides MFA, an additional protection style is introduced that any access from outside Shimane University is blocked (hereinafter call Blocked), and also the members are allowed to choose either MFA or Blocked depending on their work styles.

C. Stephanidis et al. (Eds.): HCII 2021, CCIS 1420, pp. 425–430, 2021.
https://doi.org/10.1007/978-3-030-78642-7_57

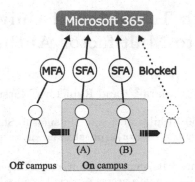

Fig. 1. Protection styles.

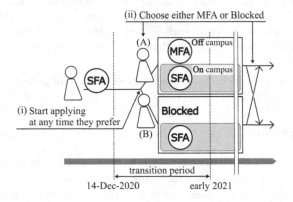

Fig. 2. Requirements for our system

2   Requirements for Our Application System

In Shimane University, all the data stored on Microsoft 365 cloud are protected only by SFA, therefore, we plan to use Microsoft Azure MFA [5], where sign-in attempts to Microsoft 365 must be approved by users' own devices all times. However, we decide to bypass the approval process when accessing it on-campus in order to balance usability and protection as shown in Fig. 1.

Now considering how all the university members can be guided smoothly to MFA/Blocked, we figure out two requirements: (i) The simultaneous transition towards MFA/Blocked would be likely to cause chaos to the members even though announcement is made in advance because there would be sudden interruption to continuous use of the services for a certain period of time, especially emailing. This worrisome scenario should be avoided as mentioned in [3]. Therefore, the transition should be triggered by individuals, and it should complete in as short time as possible. (ii) The majority of the university members work on/off-campus while the other work only on-campus. The former will require MFA when accessing Microsoft 365 off-campus as shown in Fig. 1 (A). The latter

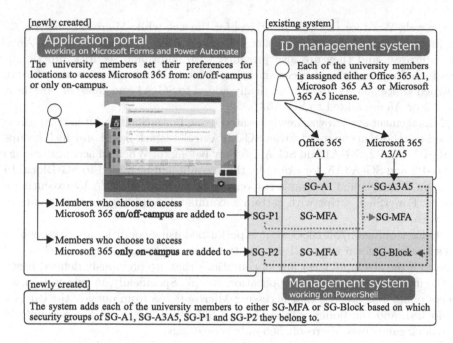

Fig. 3. Overview of our application system.

cannot access it off-campus, or their access will be Blocked as shown in Fig. 1 (B). The work style varies depending on their job title. Thus, our application system should enable the members to choose one of these two on demand. Figure 2 summarizes the requirements (i) and (ii) for our application system.

3   Overview of Our Application System

We developed our application system comprised of Application portal, Management system and ID management system as shown in Fig. 3. We also created five independent groups of SG-P1, SG-P2, SG-A1, SG-A3A5, SG-MFA and SG-Block, specifically known as Security Group in Azure Active Directory, to control the application flow as shown in Fig. 2.

Application portal was newly created using Microsoft Forms and Microsoft Power Automate. The university members sign in to the portal and submit their preferences: want to access Microsoft 365 on/off-campus or only on-campus. After the submissions, their accounts are automatically added by Power Automate to either group: SG-P1 (access on/off-campus) or SG-P2 (access only on-campus).

ID management system is an existing system that handles entry, modification, and removal of members' accounts. Upon the entry, each account is assigned one of Microsoft licenses: Office 365 A1, Microsoft 365 A3 or Microsoft 365 A5. Office 365 A1 is provided by Microsoft for free with Office apps such as Outlook on the web, Word for the web and Excel for the web while Microsoft 365 A3/A5 are provided with desktop versions of Office apps, known as Microsoft 365 Apps for enterprise, and they are also provided with additional security functionalities including conditional access mentioned later. Members' accounts who are assigned Office 365 A1 are automatically added to SG-A1 and those of Microsoft 365 A3 or A5 are added to SG-A3A5.

Management system was newly created using PowerShell and it is responsible to add members' accounts to either SG-MFA or SG-Block based on which groups of SG-P1, SG-P2, SG-A1 and SG-A3A5 they belong to. When an account belongs to SG-P2 and SG-A3A5, for example, the account will be added to SG-Block. In addition, Management system is responsible to turn on/off MFA by executing a specific PowerShell script with certain accounts when adding these accounts to SG-MFA.

As for turning on/off Blocked, it is performed using conditional access, which is a security platform where all sign-in attempts to Microsoft 365 are checked and allowed if the attempts meet any of conditions that are previously defined based on the user's location, device, application etc. [6]. Specifically, in this system, an access policy was created that accessing Microsoft 365 from outside the campus is blocked, and the policy was applied to SG-Block. Thus, all the accounts in SG-Block can access Microsoft 365 only on-campus.

The system performs the above task at about 10-min intervals. Note that any accounts in SG-A1 cannot be in SG-Block, or any members who are assigned Office 365 A1 must use MFA because Office 365 A1 does not include the conditional access functionality. Most of the university members are assigned Microsoft 365 A3 or A5 license while visiting professors, part-time lecturers etc. are assigned Office 365 A1 license.

With regard to the requirement (i): the transition to MFA/Blocked should be triggered by individuals and it should also complete in as short time as possible, described in Sect. 2, the university members are able to sign in to Application portal at any time they prefer, then choose one of the two options: access Microsoft 365 on/off-campus or access it only on-campus. Within 10 min, Management system will complete the settings for MFA or Blocked, respectively. After that, those who have chosen the former are required to register their own mobile devices, which are used to approve their sign-in attempts and to deny any illegitimate access. Thus, (i) is satisfied.

With regard to the requirement (ii): our application system should enable the members to choose either MFA or Blocked on demand, the members are able to sign in again to Application system and choose the other option. Thus, (ii) is also satisfied.

4   Transition to MFA/Blocked

On December 14, 2020, we announced to the university members about transition to MFA/Blocked along with its instructions, which was made available on the web pages. We also set a time limit until the end of March 2021 for the

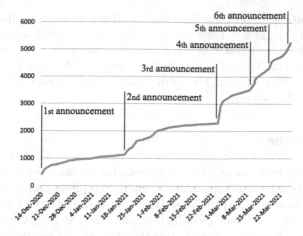

Fig. 4. Number of the members who were in either MFA or Blocked protection style on each day between December 14, 2020 and March 26, 2021.

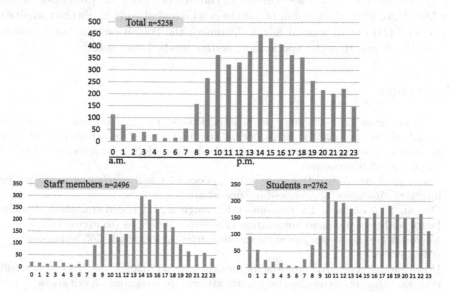

Fig. 5. Times when the members applied for MFA or Blocked.

transition. Figure 4 shows the number of members who were in either MFA or Blocked protection style on each day. There was gradual and steady increase after December 14, 2020, and it was over 5,000 members on March 26, of which 172 members were in Blocked. Figure 5 shows a histogram of what time the members applied or made transition to MFA/Blocked. More members made the transition during the daytime while a small number of members did during the night. This is because working hours of some members are at night especially in the university hospital, and also there is a distinctive tendency that students made the transition until late hour.

Our application system handled the members' transitions during the day and night, and we did not have any troubles after the first announcement on December 14, 2020. As a result, it was shown that the application system meeting the two requirements (i) and (ii) worked successfully although it was still going for the rest of 3,000 members. The future work includes a survey to quantify the effectiveness of the system.

5   Conclusions

In this study, we built an application system for Shimane University members to make transition to a secure platform where two protection styles were made available: sign-in attempts to Microsoft 365 from outside the campus must be approved using the members' own devices, and these attempts are just blocked. To make the transition as smooth as possible, the system was designed to satisfy two requirements: (i) the transition should be triggered by individuals, and (ii) the system should enable the members to choose one of the two protection styles. On March 26, 2021, the number of members who had already made the transition was over 5,000 out of around 8,500. Although the transition was not complete yet, it was shown that the application system worked successfully.

References

1. Cybercriminals kick-off 2021 with sweepstakes, credit card, delivery scams. Trend Micro Inc. (2021). https://www.trendmicro.com/vinfo/be/security/news/cybercrime-and-digital-threats/cybercriminals-kick-off-2021-with-sweepstakes-credit-card-delivery-scams
2. Microsoft Azure Active Directory. https://docs.microsoft.com/en-us/azure/active-directory/fundamentals/active-directory-whatis
3. Ohtaki, Y., Nishihara, T., Yamamoto, K., Noguchi, H.: Rapid transition to multi-factor authentication and automation of routine operations (to appear)
4. Microsoft Forms. https://www.microsoft.com/en-us/microsoft-365/online-surveys-polls-quizzes
5. How it works: Azure AD multi-factor authentication (2020). https://docs.microsoft.com/en-us/azure/active-directory/authentication/concept-mfa-howitworks
6. What is conditional access? https://docs.microsoft.com/en-us/azure/active-directory/conditional-access/overview

Security Rules Identification and Validation: The Role of Explainable Clustering and Information Visualisation

Luca Mazzola[1]([✉])(iD), Florian Stalder[1](iD), Andreas Waldis[1](iD),
Patrick Siegfried[1](iD), Christian Renold[1], David Reber[2], and Philipp Meier[2]

[1] School of Information Technology, HSLU - Lucerne University of Applied Sciences
and Arts, Suurstoffi 1, 6343 Rotkreuz, Switzerland
{luca.mazzola,florian.stalder,andreas.waldis,patrick.siegfried,
christian.renold}@hslu.ch
[2] SECUDE International AG, Werftestrasse 4a, 6005 Luzern, Switzerland
{david.reber,philipp.meier}@secude.com

Abstract. In the context of data access and export control from enterprise information systems, one of the issue is the generation of the rules. Currently, this time consuming and difficult task is highly based on experience. Expert security analysts merge their experience of Enterprise Resource Planning (ERP) systems with the random exploration of the logs generated by the system to try to envision the most relevant attack paths. This project allowed to explore different approaches for creating support for human experts in security rule identification and validation, while preserving interpretability of the results and inspectability of the approach used. This resulted in a tool that complements the security engine by supporting experts in defining uncommon patterns as security-related events to be monitored and vetted by the event classification engine. The result is a promising instrument allowing the human inspection of candidate security-related relevant events/patterns. Main focus being the definition of security rules to be enforced by the specific security engine at run-time. An initial evaluation round shows a positive trend into the users' perception, even tough a miss of contextual information still hinders its usage by more business-oriented profiles.

Keywords: ERP · Rule-based security system · Data access and export control · Security classification · Interpretable decision support system · eXplainable AI · Anomaly detection · Model inspectability · Results interpretability

1 Introduction

In the context of data access and export control from Enterprise Information Systems (EIS), one of the issue is the generation of the rules. Currently, this time consuming and difficult task is highly based on experience. In fact, identification and formalisation of rules for security system is a challenging tasks,

© Springer Nature Switzerland AG 2021
C. Stephanidis et al. (Eds.): HCII 2021, CCIS 1420, pp. 431–438, 2021.
https://doi.org/10.1007/978-3-030-78642-7_58

requiring deep understanding of the functioning of the system to be monitored, to their specific data flows and deep expertise with the security engine at hand, to correctly design rules that enforce the identified risky patterns. To make even more complex this exercise there is need to understand the peculiarities and customisation that each big company requires in its main Enterprise Resource Planning (ERP), as one of the most important aspects of the logs is the tables and resources accessed but also the specific function used for the data elaboration.

Expert security analysts merge their experience of ERP systems with the random exploration of the logs generated by the system to try to envision the most relevant attack paths [16]. This has clearly shortcomings, starting from the difficulty and expensiveness of hiring those experts (usually external consultants), to the lack of guarantee to have covered most of all the relevant security conditions, passing through the impossibility to anyone else in the company to vet and validate the security rules developed. Adding to that, in particular for complex and distributed environment such as for multinational large companies, the granularity of this approach is too coarse to guarantee the smoothness of access together with a safe enough data protection level [10]. The main problem of this type of reactive system is the creation of the inference engine that will analyse in real-time the information requested, compare it with the user profile and its previous operativity and classify its risk level [5]. The most common approach is a rule-based system, where business and security experts jointly try to identify and formalise the relevant conditions for instructing the system know how to act [18]. On top of it, this is a complex, time-consuming and resource-limited activity, as only already identified behaviours or attack patterns will be considered and mapped [11]. This document reports an approach developed for using easily explainable unsupervised clustering and information visualisation, towards a support system for rule-based security classification.

Stemming from expertise in data science, we are testing feasible ways to apply a data-driven approach to the activity of supporting the experts in identifying patterns and most relevant data dimensions for data protection in business-relevant information system [13]. To achieve this role of Decision Support System (DSS) within this project requires that the results produced by the data-driven approach can be communicated and interpreted by domain and security experts, not guaranteed to be acquainted with general data sciences approaches. This means that no black- and grey-box approach is well suited, particularly Deep Learning methods [3,14]. The choice of not providing fully automatically generated rules is based on a twofold consideration: on the one side, it is very important to not disrupt the operativity of the company by blocking too many fully legitimate data access. On the other side, the presence of the "human in the loop" guarantees the validation and a higher tolerance against false patterns emerging from data analysis [6]. Additionally, visualisation is a well-known tool for awareness elicitation, such as in the case of personal habits and attitudes [7], for social and political discourse [17], for complex activities by multiple humans within software development projects [8] or for anomaly detection in maritime traffic [12].

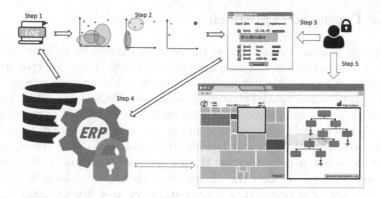

Fig. 1. The approach developed, from ERP access logs export to rules generation, trough unsupervised clustering and visual inspection of outliers. The final ruleset exploration is also supported for validation purposes.

2   Requirements Elicitation

The first step has been to identify the necessary functional and non-functional properties that such a DSS for security rule identification should offer. As the rules are specific for the company business and organisation, we selected and involved a multinational partner working in the production of large consume alimentary goods as the test-bed for this project. Experts from its side helped in the discussion and identification of the main needs for such a system. We built on the top of an already existing real-time analysis for data export of SAP-stored information that is able to contextually decide its statistical probability of data exploitation [1] using, among others, a specialised classification about including personal and/or financial relevant information. The export actions will be logged, classified and, as consequence, the corresponding actions might be notified, blocked or the exported data get encrypted. This will prevent unauthorised or unexpected profiles to access, even by mistake, business or regulatory sensitive knowledge about the company and its operations. However this translates cascade into an action on the specific transaction. Due to the fact that the decision has a deep effects on the functioning of the ERP/EIS, is taken only based upon human validation of the rule engine configuration. Thius, on top of the *effectiveness* on the rule suggestions generation, the most important requirements identified were *simplicity*, *interpretability*, and *scalability*, to support the "human-in-the-loop". The first and second points are highly interrelated, as both deal with the amount of information and the abstraction used for presenting it. Scalability affects instead the possibility to use the approach in near real-time and to test multiple configuration. These points will be part of further exploration, as not necessary for a first demonstrator.

3   The Proposed Approach

The proposed approach is to support the security experts by an integrated process, as represented in Fig. 1. The generated logs (Step 1) are exported from the ERP system and (Step 2) clustered in an unsupervised manner, using a noise resistant density-based spatial clustering called DBSCAN [4,15]. This approach, coupled with a semi-automatic identification of the DBSCAN parameters (the radius ϵ and the *minPts*), is adopted under the assumption that risky export operations are represent by event logs in infrequent part of the space, meaning that they lie in low-density regions. By its iterative application till a specified termination condition is met, the algorithm is then able to identify (last part of Step 2) a set of episodes that represent prototypes. By additionally ranking these outliers based on their score and computing the importance of each data dimension, the interface can present (Step 3) a simplified interface where a security professional can generate a security rule, by generalisation. Allowing the expert to select which dimensions and values are relevant for the security rule, a twofold objective is achieved: the human experience is embedded in the resulting ruleset and the rules is a fuzzy extension of the prototype point, by removing irrelevant data aspects (including noise). The generated rule can then be exported back to the security component into the ERP system (Step 4), for run-time labelling and protection. Additionally, the experts and other internal human resources in the company interested in understanding the typology of security logs and the corresponding ruleset can be explored (Step 5). This will improve the comprehensibility of the process and can also support the validation of the security model, in case of need.

3.1   Clustering and Anomaly Detection

The interpretation of outliers requires an anomaly metric. This metric describes the degree of anomaly for a given point. The degree of anomaly represents the divergence of a given point from the cluster characteristics. Some measurements used to define our parameters are the followings:

$$D = \begin{cases} \frac{contDist + catDist}{2} & \text{average} \\ \frac{\#contDist}{(\#contDist + \#catDist)}(\#contDist + \#catDist) & \text{weighed\_average} \end{cases} \tag{1}$$

$$R = rank(\frac{D}{\max D}) \tag{2}$$

$$knn = (1 - D)^2 * (R <= K) \tag{3}$$

$$peaks = (\mu_{knn} > \mu_{\mu_{knn}}) * (\mu_{knn} == \max((R <= K) * \mu_{knn})) \tag{4}$$

$$mdpp = \max D_{peaks} \tag{5}$$

where:

contDist euclidean distance between each datapoint.
  catDist distances between categorical features.
    rank ranks each point according to the calculated distances.
    μ_{knn} mean of *knn*.
    $\mu_{\mu_{knn}}$ average of μ_{knn}.

Unsupervised Outlier Detection. In our approach we use iterative clustering: At the first iteration a clustering algorithm calculates a membership of a cluster for each point. Outliers are grouped together in a separate cluster. For every further iteration, the outliers from the previous step are used as input for the next execution of the clustering algorithm. The level of irregularity is defined by

$$\text{Level of irregularity} = \begin{cases} 0 & \text{point is never classified as outlier} \\ n & \text{point is classified as outlier after } n^{\text{th}} \text{ iteration} \end{cases}$$

Thereby, we can assign a level of irregularity to every point. The Local Outlier Factor (LOF) - as in [2] - is a density based algorithm. It calculates a factor indicating the degree of anomaly or novelty. All the points below a certain threshold are classified as anomalies. This is sued to verify the results of iterative clustering. In addition, it allows to compare the outliers of one level based on the factors of the LOF algorithm. Iterative clustering was applied with three iteration steps. This algorithm returns factors based on pre-computed distances. Experiments were performed using datasets of different sizes (2500, 5000, 10000 points) to determine the optimal initialisation parameters ($<K$-neighbours, radius $r>$).

K-Neighbour: K is heuristically estimated by the formula:

$$K_{pred} = \left\lceil \sqrt{\frac{N}{\max D}} \right\rceil \tag{6}$$

where

  K estimated number of neighbours
  N number of data points
  D distance between two points

By running multiple experiments varying only the value assumed by the K parameter, we measured the effects in term of number of outliers, percentage of summed outlier factors, and the mean LOF of a given point. This shows that our heuristic estimated for K_{pred} is close enough to an optimal value, as inferred by the application of the elbow method [9].

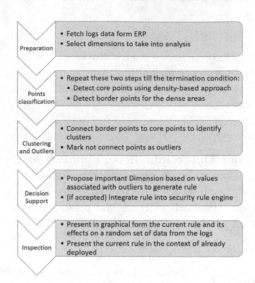

Fig. 2. The implemented pipeline highlights the main logical steps of our architecture. Each task is then implemented as a specialised module in the web service-based platform that is adopted for the project.

Radius r: In the second experiment, K is fixed and radius r is variable. The results of one execution are compared against multiple runs of the iterative clustering approach. Thereby, K is estimated as mentioned in Eq. 6 and r is estimated by:

$$r_{pred} = \mu_{\text{max-dist}} + 2 * \sigma_{\text{max-dist}} \tag{7}$$

where:

$\mu_{\text{max-dist}}$ Mean of the values from *mdpp*. See Eq. 5 for details.

$\sigma_{\text{max-dist}}$ Standard deviation of the values from *mdpp*.

This experiment was executed adopting 40 different values of r: 20 between $\frac{2*r_{pred}}{3}$ and r_{pred} and the remaining 20 from r_{pred} to 1, both using an independent logarithm scale. Using number of outliers, percentage of the summed outlier factors, and mean factor of an outlier we showed that our initial heuristic choice was sensible and produced acceptable results. In this way, we demonstrate that a general heuristic-based initialisation of the algorithm is feasible.

The implemented architecture is based on Restful web services, that provide partial results, as from the pipeline presented in Fig. 2. Minimalist user interfaces as web applications allow the security experts to interact with the results generated, such as to inspect the proposed outliers as security-related risk prototype, considering also the rank of the different dimensions with respect of a particular case. Also the visualisation for the rules tree and the treemap for logs coverage is implemented using an AJAX-based framework. This guarantee portability and Independence from a specific ERP/EIS, requiring only a server to run and a browser to interact with the human operator.

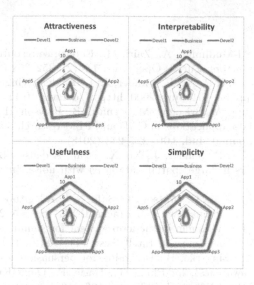

Fig. 3. Initial evaluation of 5 different approaches for communicating the clusters and the outliers found by our algorithm: users with different profiles participated in this first validation round. The blue line represents security related developers, while the grey one collects software developers and ERP system integrators. The third one, in the orange colour, collects users related more closely to the business side, such as profile specialised in controlling, in business development and in marketing.

4 Conclusions

An initial evaluation round showed a positive trend into the users' perception, despite the fact that a lack of contextual information still hinders its usage by more business-oriented profiles. Figure 3 present a comparisons on the four identified dimensions of attractiveness, interpretability, usefulness and simplicity. Next steps will be to collect qualitative feedback and thus improve the solution. Concurrently, the implementation partner is working to bring into production this demonstrator within their commercial solution for data access and export protection software.

Acknowledgement. The research leading to this work was partially financed by *Innosuisse* - Swiss federal agency for Innovation, through a competitive call. The project 29926.1 IP-ICT is called *IAC: Intelligent Automatic Configuration* (https://www.aramis.admin.ch/Grunddaten/?ProjectID=42722). The authors would like to thanks all the people involved on the implementation-side at SECUDE International AG (https://secude.com/) for all the constructive and fruitful discussions and insight into the functioning of a security engine and the characterisation of security event types. **Final Note:** the work briefly described here is under review for an U.S. Patent, with application number 17/174,837.

References

1. Al-Mashari, M., Al-Mudimigh, A., Zairi, M.: Enterprise resource planning: a taxonomy of critical factors. Eur. J. Oper. Res. **146**(2), 352–364 (2003)
2. Breunig, M., Kriegel, H.P., Ng, R., Sander, J.: LOF: identifying density-based local outliers. vol. 29, pp. 93–104, June 2000. https://doi.org/10.1145/342009.335388
3. Dekhtiar, J., Durupt, A., Bricogne, M., Eynard, B., Rowson, H., Kiritsis, D.: Deep learning for big data applications in CAD and PLM-research review, opportunities and case study. Comput. Ind. **100**, 227–243 (2018)
4. Ester, M., Kriegel, H.P., Sander, J., Xu, X., et al.: A density-based algorithm for discovering clusters in large spatial databases with noise. In: KDD, vol. 96, pp. 226–231 (1996)
5. Kamarudin, M.H., Maple, C., Watson, T., Safa, N.S.: A logitboost-based algorithm for detecting known and unknown web attacks. IEEE Access **5**, 26190–26200 (2017)
6. Kim, B., Pardo, B.: A human-in-the-loop system for sound event detection and annotation. ACM Trans. Interact. Intell. Syst. (TiiS) **8**(2), 1–23 (2018)
7. Kim, T., Hong, H., Magerko, B.: Designing for persuasion: toward ambient eco-visualization for awareness. In: Ploug, T., Hasle, P., Oinas-Kukkonen, H. (eds.) PERSUASIVE 2010. LNCS, vol. 6137, pp. 106–116. Springer, Heidelberg (2010). https://doi.org/10.1007/978-3-642-13226-1_12
8. Lanza, M., Hattori, L., Guzzi, A.: Supporting collaboration awareness with real-time visualization of development activity. In: 2010 14th European Conference on Software Maintenance and Reengineering, pp. 202–211. IEEE (2010)
9. McInnes, L., Healy, J.: Accelerated hierarchical density based clustering. In: 2017 IEEE International Conference on Data Mining Workshops (ICDMW), pp. 33–42. IEEE (2017)
10. Monk, E., Wagner, B.: Concepts in Enterprise Resource Planning. Cengage Learning, Boston (2012)
11. Ning, P., Jajodia, S.: Intrusion detection techniques. The Internet Encyclopedia (2004)
12. Riveiro, M., Falkman, G., Ziemke, T.: Improving maritime anomaly detection and situation awareness through interactive visualization. In: 2008 11th International Conference on Information Fusion, pp. 1–8. IEEE (2008)
13. Sanders, N.R.: Big Data Driven Supply Chain Management: A Framework for Implementing Analytics and Turning Information into Intelligence. Pearson Education, London (2014)
14. Schreyer, M., Sattarov, T., Reimer, B., Borth, D.: Adversarial learning of deepfakes in accounting. arXiv preprint arXiv:1910.03810 (2019)
15. Schubert, E., Sander, J., Ester, M., Kriegel, H.P., Xu, X.: DBSCAN revisited, revisited: why and how you should (still) use DBSCAN. ACM Trans. Database Syst. (TODS) **42**(3), 1–21 (2017)
16. She, W., Thuraisingham, B.: Security for enterprise resource planning systems. Inf. Syst. Secur. **16**(3), 152–163 (2007)
17. Valkanova, N., Jorda, S., Tomitsch, M., Vande Moere, A.: Reveal-it! the impact of a social visualization projection on public awareness and discourse. In: Proceedings of the SIGCHI Conference on Human Factors in Computing Systems, pp. 3461–3470 (2013)
18. Wiegenstein, A., Schumacher, M., Jia, X.: Apparatus and method for detecting, prioritizing and fixing security defects and compliance violations in SAP® ABAP code, US Patent 8,402,547, 19 Mar 2013

An IOT Security Awareness and System Hardening Advisory Platform for Smart Home Devices

Aimee Shepherd$^{(\boxtimes)}$ and Edward Apeh$^{(\boxtimes)}$

Faculty of Science and Technology, Bournemouth University, Poole, UK
{s5001169,eapeh}@bournemouth.ac.uk

Abstract. This poster will demonstrate the work currently being undertaken to develop the proposed platform for IoT Security and System Hardening Advisory. It will highlight the current state of art for IOT security awareness and system hardening advisory. It will also present the investigation into the use of end-user approaches such as crowdsourcing and gamification to facilitate the sharing of security related information on SMART home devices within a community of end-users, retailers and manufacturers. Also, it will present the design of the experiments to evaluate the proposed platform's performance in engaging its users and its provisioning of a continuous feedback loop of identification and recommended resolution of SMART home devices security issues.

Keywords: Internet of Things · SMART home devices · End user engagement

1 Introduction

The recent proliferation and dependence on SMART home devices has resulted in a corresponding increase in evolving threats and attacks on the IOT devices that makeup the SMART home. There is therefore a clear need for providing continuous up to date threat information and hardening recommendations for smart devices from off the shelf to end of life.

Figure 1 highlights a direct correlation with the rise of installed bases to the rise of different attack vectors with, for instance, a 40% surge in global ransomware, 19% increase in intrusion attempts, and 30% rise in IoT malware [2].

This extended poster abstract will present the work currently being undertaken to develop an IOT security awareness and system hardening advisory platform for smart home devices. It highlights the current state of art for IOT security awareness and system hardening advisory. It presents the investigation into the use of end-user approaches such as crowdsourcing and gamification to facilitate the sharing of security related information on SMART home devices within a community of end-users, retailers and manufacturers. Finally, the poster presents the design of the experiment to evaluate the proposed platform's performance in engaging its users and its provisioning of a continuous feedback loop of identification and recommended resolution of SMART home devices security issues.

© Springer Nature Switzerland AG 2021
C. Stephanidis et al. (Eds.): HCII 2021, CCIS 1420, pp. 439–446, 2021.
https://doi.org/10.1007/978-3-030-78642-7_59

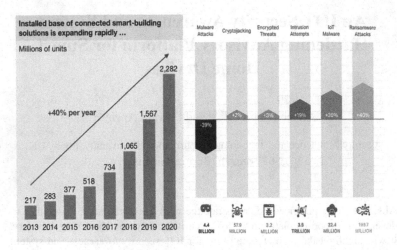

Fig. 1. A side-by-side illustration of the rapid expansion of smart building solutions over 7 years alongside the increase in the attacks on smart home IOT devices [1].

2 Background Information

Smart home systems include a wide range of mobile and/or web solutions for monitoring, controlling and automating functions in the home.

The connected IOT devices that make up smart home systems (i.e. Internet-connected "thing" ranging from power grids to smart doorbells) is set to be 41.6 billion by 2025. This increase in IOT devices has been matched by an increase in the number and sophistication of IOT device attacks over time as shown in Fig. 2 [2].

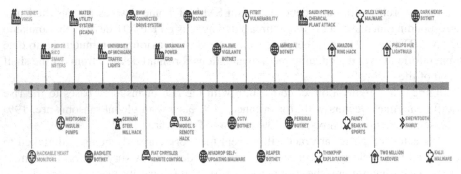

Fig. 2. A timeline of attacks and exploitations on IoT.

Most attacks on smart home systems tend to take advantage of the out-of-the box default settings on smart home systems. Furthermore, threat actors have also exploited the non-technical awareness of end-users. As more consumers adopt IoT solutions in the home, their role in the overall security and privacy of IoT increases. Consumers are also required therefore, to take a more active role in purchasing and in their home security and privacy.

In addition, competition and pressure to bring products to market results in shortcuts taken during the manufacturing and design processes. A recent report by GOV UK has highlighted that one of the key factors influencing the level of cyber security, or lack thereof, in consumer IoT devices is a lack of consumer awareness of what to look for in a device to ensure it is secure. Furthermore, the report highlighted how without a unified standard to mark a device's security level, consumers have no clear way of determining whether the device they have purchased will protect their data [3]. Whilst there is a limited number of materials available for end users, such as the NCSC's one pager on how to purchase secure IoT devices, they do not provide a place where consumers can understand their devices security level and the reasoning behind it [5].

Along with a general lack of awareness of the threat posed to IOT devices, there is a lack of physical hardening is a key impact on the rise of IoT attacks [4]. These have all combined to increase the attacks and severity on the IOT devices that make up the smart home system. The proposed solution aims to provide a system to improve the lack of hardening and awareness for not only consumers but also manufacturers and retailers.

A survey conducted by the IT security firm Trend Micro has revealed that 86% of IT and security decision makers around the world believe their organisations need to enhance their awareness of IoT Threats [2].

This statistic demonstrates clearly the need for a solution for all users of IoT devices, inside the organisations and outside.

The eight most common vulnerabilities in IoT devices named by OWASP include insecure network services, lack of secure update mechanisms and the lack of physical hardening. Hackers actively exploit weaknesses in IoT security not to attack the devices themselves, but as a point for all kinds of malicious behavior. Such as, DoS attacks, malware distribution, spamming/phishing, click fraud, credit card theft [3].

The proposed solution will allow for the eight most common vulnerabilities to become more publicly aware by end users of smart home devices and also advise them on how they can harden their devices, to further protect them from potential threat actors.

3 Current Solutions and Their Shortcomings

Existing approaches to address the lack of awareness and advisory of the evolving threats posed by smart home devices tend to range from bug bounty programmes to patch management. These solutions are however limited in their coverage and often miss out on vital input and involvement of non-technical end-users. Furthermore, existing approaches tend to be more reactive than proactive in the detection and resolution of security issues of SMART home devices.

InfraGard a partnership between the FBI and the private sector provides a platform for association of persons who represent businesses, academic institutions, state and local law enforcement agencies, and other participants dedicated to sharing information and intelligence to prevent hostile acts against the United States. However, it has very little provision for the engagement and sharing vulnerabilities or issues with the general public. Furthermore, the catch-all nature of the InfraGard platforms makes it challenging to identify SMART home devices threats.

The NCSC have created a platform, working with small to medium sized enterprises, charities, legal and accountancy sectors, as an e-learning training package. The aim is to ensure that staff are staying safe online, it covers areas on why cyber security is important and how attacks happen. Again, a short coming of this is that it is not available publicly and therefore proves there is a gap in the market for the proposed solution which is discussed in the next section.

These existing solutions whilst providing information about cyber threats have very little end user engagement – especially in terms of reporting and feedback provision of IOT device vulnerabilities and threats. The end user is the key actor in how IoT's will shape the future and without their continuous feedback throughout the life of an IoT device, limited improvements will be made [5].

4 Proposed Solution

To address these shortcomings, an IOT security awareness and system hardening advisory platform for smart home devices is proposed. The proposed platform will incorporate crowdsourced security information from SMART home devices end-user with processed information on SMART home devices vulnerability obtained from CVE and/or NVD. The aim is to curate, analyse and present security issues of SMART home devices along with the relevant recommendations for addressing them to manufacturers, retailers and end-users.

Gamification is the use of video game elements in non-gaming systems to improve user experience and user engagement [7].

In persuasive technology, video games and game aspects have been studied as potential means to shape user behaviour in directions intended by the system designer or to instill embedded values. The proposed solution aims to in still gamification embedded in the solution as well rewarding users for completing tasks as such, to ensure that the system hardening advisory aspect of this solution is understood and taken on board by end users.

This will allow manufacturers to really reach into each demographic of end user and understand the use and functionality of their devices more ensuring that the market of IoT can become richer and smarter over time.

Crowdsourcing will also be a main aspect of the end user interaction feature of this system. Crowdsourcing is a problem-solving model based on the combination of human and machine computation, it is the act of outsourcing work to an undefined, networked labour using and open call for participation [8].

The proposed solution will use crowdsourcing in the form of community forums to allow end users, manufacturers and retailers of such devices to communicate open and freely on all topics concerning The Internet of Things and Smart Devices. Table 1 shows the use cases of the proposed solution.

Nelson's heuristics will be used throughout the project to analyse how the users will interact with this system and requirements will be based on these scenarios. Nelson's heuristics will be a continual part of the agile evaluation process throughout the entirety of the project lifetime.

Key features of the proposed system will be a feed (determined by CVE entries), either listed by brand or device of the current status of the home device. For example, Amazon's Alexa will be shown in a user engaging way with pictures and underneath

Table 1. Use cases of the proposed solution

	Use case
Manufacturers and retailers	Manufacturers will use this system to navigate through the IoT devices that they are interested in and through the feed from the CVE they will discover whether any devices of interest currently have any known vulnerabilities The system will provide details on how they can advise users to harden their system Further, they can interact with end users through community forums to engage regarding feedback or any concerns
End users	End users will use the system to understand how their smart home devices work and how they can further protect themselves in the home environment whilst using their smart devices to the best of their ability They will interact with manufacturers and retailers through forums and crowdsourcing to engage regarding feedback, concerns or any issues

there will be shown its current vulnerability status using a traffic light system. Moreover, the use of gamification will ensure that users find the system 'fun' to use and increases the amount of time they spend learning about their smart home devices.

Crowdsourcing will be used to gather feedback and knowledge from end users to further improve future and existing devices.

Further, community forums will be highly encouraged by engaging topic titles to ensure that users feel comfortable using these. These crowdsourcing forums will encourage users to give feedback on the devices they own or are looking to own on any issues or simple recommendations to improve the useability to the manufacturer/retailer.

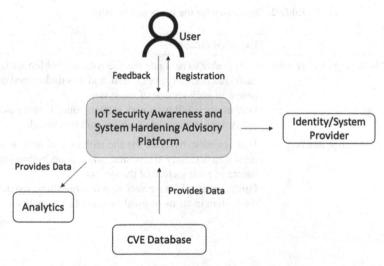

Fig. 3. A context diagram of the proposed solution.

Figure 3 highlights a brief context diagram of the proposed solution. "User" in figure will be defined as all end users, manufacturers and retailers that will use the system.

The key benefits to the proposed solution include:

1. Improved feedback loop – with the use of crowdsourcing and open community forums, end users of smart home devices will have the open space to engage with other users, manufacturers and retailers freely. This aspect is something that hasn't been seen in terms of IoT devices and therefore it will greatly increase the feedback loop of this market.
2. End user engagement – the use of these crowdsourcing community forums will allow for the end user engagement to increase and also the knowledge of our end users of smart home devices and therefore the whole experience of owning a smart home device increase. End users are more likely to recommend products and services once they understand them more.
3. End user interaction – due to the increase in knowledge about their device, be it security, functionalities or usability, the interaction with smart home devices with inevitably increase. This could mean the purchasing of more devices for their home and greatly increase sales and understanding of IoT devices, consequently increasing the reputation of smart home devices as this sector grows.

4.1 Testing and Evaluation

The system will undergo testing and evaluation with different demographics to ensure that all perspective users of the system will be able to navigate this with ease.

Below in Table 2 you can find a test specification which will be used to conduct the testing once the system has been produced. The caveat to this may be that particular details of the may be adjusted or changed to suit the end results.

Table 2. Test cases for the proposed solution

Test case	Expected outcome
User in 18–24 range to navigate the site	User is able to navigate the site with no problems where each area is clearly signposted, and it is understood the nature of each section of the system Further, they will have very minimal questions regarding the system in terms of useability and functionality
User in 25–40 range to navigate the site	User is able to navigate the site with no problems where each area is clearly signposted, and it is understood the nature of each section of the system Further, they will have very minimal questions regarding the system in terms of useability and functionality

(continued)

Table 2. (*continued*)

Test case	Expected outcome
User in over 40 range to navigate the site	User is able to navigate the site with no problems where each area is clearly signposted, and it is understood the nature of each section of the system Further, they will have very minimal questions regarding the system in terms of useability and functionality
Corporate manufacturer or retailer to navigate the site	User is able to navigate the site with no problems where each area is clearly signposted, and it is understood the nature of each section of the system Further, they will have very minimal questions regarding the system in terms of useability and functionality
End user to create a new thread in the community forums	End user is able to navigate freely to the community page where they will easily find the button of how to create a new thread and they are able to conduct themselves through the process of creating the thread with ease
End user to post in an existing thread	End user is able to navigate freely to thread in question and is able to post a comment or reply to this thread with ease and minimal questions
Manufacturer/retailer to create and reply on a thread	User is able to navigate freely to thread in question and find the reply section and easily reply to the thread as expected with minimal questions
Manufacturer/retailer to push notify an end user of security hardening recommendation	User is able to navigate to the dashboard where they can push notifications either to a specified thread or new thread, or they can push to all users of the system regarding system hardening advise
Manufacturer/retailer to navigate the vulnerabilities to find a particular known vulnerability	User is able to navigate to the vulnerabilities tab and find the vulnerability in question or view the top 5 vulnerabilities

After testing has been completed, a review of this will be undertaken to investigate whether the expected outcomes meet the actual outcomes. Moreover, any changes that may be needed will be noted and the system adapted accordingly.

5 Summary and Conclusion

In conclusion, it is apparent that the existing solutions in the area of IoT security awareness and system hardening advisory are not adequate for regular home end users of such devices. Therefore, the proposed solution aims to cover these shortcomings and provide a system which is open sourced and benefits the manufacturers, retailers and end users of these devices. Such, it will ensure that the system is user friendly and tailored to all possible users to further increase engagement.

6 Future Work

Future work of this system will be in the area of gaining a high user engagement with the plan to make the system completely open sourced and free to use.

The main focus will be ensuring the system is easy to navigate for all users and increase the feedback that manufacturers and retailers gain for the smart devices that are already in the market. Further, the use of gamification will be developed to ensure that all learning methods for different personalities are covered for a higher engagement and retention of information.

References

1. Memoori: How many connected devices are there now in smart buildings? (2021). https://mem oori.com/buildings-make-majority-connected-devices-much-building-now-connected/
2. Prnewswire.com: New SonicWall research finds aggressive growth in ransomware, rise in IoT attacks (2020). https://www.prnewswire.com/news-releases/new-sonicwall-research-finds-aggressive-growth-in-ransomware-rise-in-iot-attacks-301162392.html
3. UK, G.: The Cyber Aware Perception Gap,1st edn. GOV.UK, UK (2016). https://assets.publis hing.service.gov.uk/government/uploads/system/uploads/attachment_data/file/684609/BT_ CYBER_AWARE_V11_280218.pdf. [ebook]
4. Rentz, P.: OWASP releases latest top 10 IoT vulnerabilities. TechWell (2019). https://www.tec hwell.com/techwell-insights/2019/01/owasp-releases-latest-top-10-iot-vulnerabilities
5. Sarah, L.: NCSC's new cyber security training for staff now available (2020). https://www. ncsc.gov.uk/blog-post/ncsc-cyber-security-training-for-staff-now-available
6. Federal Bureau of Investigation: InfraGard | Federal Bureau of Investigation (2019). https:// www.fbi.gov/about/partnerships/infragard
7. Webster, M.: Definition of GAMIFICATION (2021). https://www.merriam-webster.com/dic tionary/gamification
8. Webster, M.: Definition of CROWDSOURCING (2021). https://www.merriam-webster.com/ dictionary/crowdsourcing

A Smartphone User Verification Method Based on Finger-Writing of a Simple Symbol

Atsushi Takahashi, Yohei Masegi, and Isao Nakanishi(✉)

Tottori University, Tottori 680-8552, Japan
nakanishi@tottori-u.ac.jp

Abstract. Writer verification based on finger-writing of a simple symbol on a touch screen is proposed herein. The users write a simple and well-known symbol, for example, a circle, triangle, or square. In addition, the users write the symbol using their finger instead of a pen on a tablet. This allows more convenience with the use of the proposed method. However, it was observed that the original approach and obtained verification performance were not reliable. In this work, we create a new database using thirty participants. By examining individual features extracted from the database, the risk of misjudgment is found. In order to solve this problem, a coordinate transformation method is introduced. Moreover, normalization is examined for fusing individual features by comparing three normalization methods. The proposed method with appropriate coordinate transformation and normalization achieves an equal error rate of 10.6% even when all participants write only a simple circle.

Keywords: Writer verification · Simple symbol · Finger writing · Coordinate transformation · Normalization

1 Introduction

With the progress of recent technologies, cellular phones have been replaced by smartphones. We can interact with anyone using smartphones, anytime, anywhere. Smartphones have become indispensable in our daily lives. On the other hand, the risk of leakage of personal information is increasing.

For person authentication, passwords, PIN codes, or patterns [1–3] have been used in smartphones. However, these require users to remember them. Therefore, there is a risk of forgetting them or mistaking them when entering them into an authentication system. These are inconvenience for users. Also, there is a risk of their being known by others. This makes it possible to spoof an authentication system.

Biometrics authentication has attracted attention since users never forget biometric data and never mistake to present them to an authentication system. As such modalities of biometrics, face-images, iris-images, and fingerprints are generally used and categorized as static biometrics, of which information can be

ⓒ Springer Nature Switzerland AG 2021
C. Stephanidis et al. (Eds.): HCII 2021, CCIS 1420, pp. 447–454, 2021.
https://doi.org/10.1007/978-3-030-78642-7_60

extracted stable, and it results in higher authentication performance. However, these modalities always appear on the body surface. Therefore, it is easy to steal their data (images) by others using a digital camera and to perform a spoofing attack using a counterfeit produced by the stolen data.

On the other hand, there are dynamic biometrics such as signatures, voiceprints, and gaits (walking motions). In particular, we focus on the signature, which verifies users by the writing of users' signatures [4–6] and has been used for authentication in personal digital assistant (PDA) systems [7–11], which equips a stylus pen and a tablet display. However, using the dedicated pen when signing is inconvenient for users. In recent years, it becomes general to write (touch) directly by a finger on a touchscreen instead of using the stylus pen [12–23]. However, to write a signature with a finger on a small touchscreen of a smartphone is very inconvenient for users. In addition, writing a signature requires users to spend a long time and it is also inconvenient for users. As a result, the signature is no longer used as an authentication method in smartphones.

Writer verification is to verify whether genuine users or not by the act of writing [24]. We have proposed a novel user (writer) verification method, where users write a symbol that is simple, well-known, and never forgotten and mistaken, for example, a circle, a cross, a triangle, or a square [25]. To write a simple symbol makes usability the highest. On the other hand, the descriptive content of the proposed method is well known to everyone and simple, so that to adopt some verification method based on pattern matching makes it very easy to imitate what users write. The security level may become low. However, if verification using extracted "habits" as individual features from written data and/or writing process is applied to the proposed method, a certain level of security is guaranteed. In other words, individual features independent of descriptive contents should be extracted in the proposed method. However, this original approach and obtained verification performance were not reliable since there were only 19 participants and extraction of individual features and fusion of these features were not fully discussed.

2 User Verification Based on Finger-Writing of a Simple Symbol

In this study, we assume user verification, where an applicant who wants to use a smartphone specifies one of the enrolled users. He/she writes a simple symbol, writing data are verified and judged whether he/she is genuine compared with the template relevant to the specified user. The verification is achieved based on Euclidian distance matching. The obtained distance is compared with a threshold that is determined in advance of verification; then, if the distance is smaller than the threshold, the applicant is regarded as a genuine user. If the distance is larger than the threshold, the applicant is regarded as ingenuine/imposter user. The threshold is empirically determined.

2.1   Finger-Writing Database

First, we constructed a new database using 30 participants to obtain more reliable results for performance evaluation. Simple symbols were a circle, triangle, and square. The smartphone used in this work was Arrows NX F-04G produced by Fujitsu Limited, Japan. Its specifications are summarized in Table 1. As the developing environment, Android Studio was used.

Table 1. Specifications of the used smartphone.

OS	Android 5.0
CPU	MSM8994 2.0 GHz
RAM	3 GB
ROM	32 GB
Display	5.2-in. IPS (1440 × 2560)
Size	146 × 70 × 8.8 mm
Weight	155 g

Fig. 1. A style for finger-writing.

All participants were sitting a chair and wrote a symbol freely: some participants held a smartphone in their dominant hand and wrote a symbol with a thumb of the same hand, and some participants held the smartphone in their nondominant hand and wrote a symbol with an index finger of their dominant hand. A style for finger-writing a simple symbol is presented in Fig. 1. All participants wrote each symbol twenty times. As a result, there are 1800 data (30 participants × 3 symbols × 20 times) in a database.

2.2   Individual Features

We selected 40 individual features which are considered being independent of descriptive contents as follows, **SP**: coordinate values at the starting point, **EP**: coordinate values at the ending point, **MinX**: the minimum value in x coordinate, **MinY**: the minimum value in y coordinate, **MaxX**: the maximum value in x coordinate, **MaxY**: the maximum value in y coordinate, **MinP**: coordinate values (x and y) in the minimum pressure, **MaxP**: coordinate values in the maximum pressure, **MinT**: coordinate values in the minimum touching-area, **MaxT**: coordinate values in the maximum touching-area, **MinS**: coordinate values in the minimum speed, **MaxS**: coordinate values in the maximum speed, **MinA**: coordinate values in the minimum acceleration, **MaxA**: coordinate values in the maximum acceleration. **DX**: distance between the maximum and the minimum x, **DY**: distance between the maximum and the minimum y, **MC**: the means of coordinate values, **DSE**: distance between the starting and the end points, **WA**: writing area, **WT**: writing time, **MP**: the mean of pressure, **Pmin**: the minimum of pressure, **Pmax**: the maximum of pressure, **MT**: the mean of touching-area, **Tmin**: the minimum of touching-area, **Tmax**: the maximum of touching-area, **MS**: the mean of speed, **Smin**: the minimum of speed, **Smax**: the maximum of speed, **MA**: the mean of acceleration, **Amin**: the minimum of acceleration, **Amax**: the maximum of acceleration, **PS**: pressure at the starting point, **TS**: touching-area at the starting point, **SS**: speed at the starting point, **AS**: acceleration at the starting point, **PE**: pressure at the end point, **TE**: touching-area at the end point, **SE**: speed at the end point, and **AE**: acceleration at the end point. When using the coordinate values x and y, each individual feature has two dimensions (elements).

2.3   Coordinate Transformation and Normalization

Through the analysis of the features obtained from the database, we found a risk of mis-verification. For example, as illustrated in Fig. 2 (a), an extreme example could be assumed, where two symbols written by different participants A and B coincidentally have the maximum finger-pressure at the same point. In this case, these two participants cannot be discriminated using only the maximum finger-pressure point.

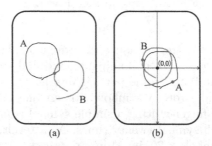

(a)   (b)

Fig. 2. Two circle symbols written by two participants.

This mis-verification is caused by different writing areas. Thus, by adjusting the different areas, as illustrated in Fig. 2 (b), this problem could be addressed. This adjustment is achieved by extracting the centroids of the two symbols and then matching their coordinates. This process is called coordinate transformation 1 (CT1) hereafter. In addition to such an origin relocation, it is possible to transform the cartesian coordinates to polar equivalents. In the polar coordinates, each sampled point is expressed by a vector, that is, length and angle, and not the x and y coordinate values. This is called coordinate transformation 2 (CT2).

We had confirmed which coordinate transformation including not using transformation was suitable for each feature in advance. As a result, the CT2 was found to be effective for most of the features. However, the most suitable representation of coordinate values depended on the features. Therefore, suitable coordinate representation for each feature should be selected in verification.

In order to achieve higher verification performance, it is better to use individual features in combination than to use them alone. However, when fusing individual features, the normalization of their values is needed since their range of fluctuation is different from each other. Without the normalization, the influence of features with a small fluctuation range on verification could be ignored by that of features with a large fluctuation range. Thus, we had examined well-known three normalization methods, the min-max method, the MAD method, and the Z-score method [26] in advance and confirmed that the min-max and Z-score methods were superior to the MAD method.

2.4   Verification Performance When Fusing Features

Finally, we evaluated the verification performance when fusing the obtained features. However, there are 40 features, so that the number of their combinations results in a large set. Thus, we investigated in the following 10 cases, **All**: all features (number of features was 40), **Off**: off-line features (11), **On**: on-line features (29), **Start**: features of coordinate data, pressure, touching-area, speed, acceleration at the starting point during the writing, **End**: features of coordinate data, pressure, touching-area, speed, acceleration at the endpoint during the writing, **Area**: the mean, minimum, and maximum values and the minimum and maximum coordinate data for touching-area features, **Pres.**: the mean, minimum, and maximum values and the minimum and maximum coordinate data for pressure features, **Speed**: the mean, minimum, and maximum values and the minimum and maximum coordinate data for speed features, **Accel.**: the mean, minimum, and maximum values and the minimum and maximum coordinate data for acceleration features, and **Good**: features that achieved good performance, i.e., those whose EERs are less than the mean value of EERs for all features; therefore, the number of features depends on the symbols and normalization methods[1].

---

[1] For instance, 25 features, SP(CT2), EP(CT2), MinX(CT1), MinY(CT0), MaxX (CT0), MaxY(CT2), MinS(CT2), MinP(CT2), MaxP(CT2), MinT(CT2), MaxT (CT2), MinA(CT2), DX, DY, MC, WA, WT, Pmax, MT, Tmax, MS, MA, PE, SE, and AE when using the min-max method and writing ○, where CT0 indicates the case using the original coordinate.

The number of data for making a template was 10; therefore, 10 data from 20 data of each participant were used for making a template and the remained 10 data were used in verification. Assuming the spoofing, other participants' 29×10 data were used as forged symbols for each participant.

A false rejection rate (FRR) corresponds to the ratio of the number of symbols that are written by genuine participants but mistakenly decided as being not genuine to the number of symbols that are written by genuine participants. A false acceptance rate (FAR) is the ratio of the number of symbols that are written by other participants but mistakenly decided as being genuine to the number of symbols that are written by other participants. Error rate curves, namely the FAR and the FRR, were plotted by changing the threshold, which is a security level. In general, these FAR and FRR curves have a trade-off characteristic, and when these curves have a crossing point, it corresponds to the equal error rate (EER). The verification performance was evaluated using the EER, and smaller EER implies better performance.

The number of cross-validations was set as 10. In each cross-validation, 10 data for generating a template from 20 data are changed, and EERs obtained from the 10 cross-validations were averaged.

The results for the three symbols are shown in Table 2. The cases where the EERs were the smallest in three normalization method are colored in red. The columns with EER difference from the smallest one of over than 1% are colored in blue and the columns with EER difference of less than 1% are not colored. The best verification performance of EER = 10.6% was obtained when fusing "Good" features using the min-max method with the circle symbol.

Table 2. EERs (%) when fusing features in three symbols.

(a) Circle

Features	Min-max	Z-score
ALL	11.0	11.9
Off	14.2	13.9
On	13.0	12.7
Start	20.0	18.1
End	15.7	14.2
Pres.	18.0	17.9
Area	17.2	17.7
Speed	16.7	16.3
Accel.	18.5	18.4
Good	10.6	11.0

(b) Triangle

Features	Min-max	Z-score
ALL	14.9	16.8
Off	17.5	16.3
On	16.7	18.1
Start	22.1	18.5
End	19.0	16.1
Pres.	18.9	18.2
Area	18.8	19.0
Speed	23.6	22.6
Accel.	26.1	25.2
Good	12.3	12.4

(c) Square

Features	Min-max	Z-score
ALL	12.8	14.7
Off	16.7	17.3
On	15.0	16.0
Start	20.0	17.6
End	16.4	14.4
Pres.	15.4	15.7
Area	17.2	17.9
Speed	21.5	22.2
Accel.	25.1	25.1
Good	11.4	11.5

3 Conclusions

To develop the writer verification system based on the finger-writing of a simple symbol on a touchscreen, we created a finger-writing database using 30 participants and examined the effectiveness of coordinate transformation for extracting individual features and normalization for fusing the features. As a result, the best performance of EER = 10.6% was obtained using suitable coordinate transformation and normalization, even when all the 30 participants only wrote a simple circle symbol on a touchscreen. This shows the feasibility of the proposed method.

In this work, we used a simple verification method of Euclidian distance matching. For further works, we are planning to introduce a learning-based verification method such as support vector machines. Furthermore, the information of finger-orientation on a touchscreen which was used in Ref. [14] may be applicable as an individual feature in the proposed method. We are now trying to extract such a finger-orientation feature from a smartphone. Another challenge is to further increase the number of participants for improving the reliability of the results obtained in this paper.

References

1. Schlöglhofer, R., Sametinger, J.: Secure and usable authentication on mobile devices. In: Proceedings of the 10th International Conference on Advances in Mobile Computing & Multimedia (2012)
2. Rogowski, M., Saeed, K., Rybnik, M., Tabedzki, M., Adamski, M.: User authentication for mobile devices. In: Saeed, K., Chaki, R., Cortesi, A., Wierzchoń, S. (eds.) CISIM 2013. LNCS, vol. 8104, pp. 47–58. Springer, Heidelberg (2013). https://doi.org/10.1007/978-3-642-40925-7_5
3. Shafique, U., et al.: Modern authentication techniques in smart phones: security and usability perspective. Int. J. Adv. Comput. Sci. Appl. 8(1), 331–340 (2017)
4. Jain, A.K., Griess, F.D., Connell, S.D.: On-line signature verification. Pattern Recogn. 35(12), 2963–2972 (2002)
5. Dimauro, G., Impedovo, S., Lucchese, M.G., Modugno, R., Pirlo, G.: Recent advancements in automatic signature verification. In: Proceedings of the 9th International Workshop on Frontiers in Handwriting Recognition, pp. 179–184 (2004)
6. Fierrez, J., Ortega-Garcia, J.: On-line signature verification. In: Jain, A.K., Flynn, P., Ross, A.A. (eds.) Handbook of Biometrics. Springer, New York (2007). https://doi.org/10.1007/978-0-387-71041-9_10
7. Sayeed, S., Samraj, A., Besar, R., Hossen, J.: Online hand signature verification: a review. J. Appl. Sci. 10(15), 1632–1643 (2010)
8. El-Henawy, I.M., Rashad, M.Z., Nomir, O., Ahmed, K.: Online signature verification: state of the art. Int. J. Comput. Technol. 4(2), 664–678 (2013)
9. Diaz, M., Ferrer, M.A., Impedovo, D., Malik, M.I., Pirlo, G., Plamondon, R.: A perspective analysis of handwritten signature technology. ACM Comput. Surv. 51(6), 1–39 (2019)
10. Ricci, R., et al.: The "SECUREPHONE" a mobile phone with biometric authentication and e-signature support for dealing secure transactions on the fly. In: Proceedings of the International Conference on Security and Cryptography, pp. 9–16 (2006)

11. Martinez-Diaz, M., Fierrez, J., Krish, R.P., Galbally, J.: Mobile signature verification: feature robustness and performance comparison. IET Biometrics **3**(4), 267–277 (2014)
12. Sae-Bae, N., Ahmed, K., Isbister, K., Memon, N.: Biometric-rich gestures: a novel approach to authentication on multi-touch devices. In: Proceedings of the 30th ACM Conference on Human Factors in Computing Systems, pp. 977–986 (2012)
13. Luca, A.D., Hang, A., Brudy, F., Lindner, C., Hussmann, H.: Touch me once and I know it's you! Implicit authentication based on touch screen patterns. In: Proceedings of 2012 Conference on Human Factors in Computing Systems, pp. 987–996 (2012)
14. Frank, M., Biedert, R., Ma, E., Martinovic, I., Song, D.: Touchalytics: on the applicability of touchscreen input as a behavioral biometric for continuous authentication. IEEE Trans. Inf. Forensics Secur. **8**(1), 136–148 (2013)
15. Sae-Bae, N., Memon, N.: Online signature verification on mobile devices. IEEE Trans. Inf. Forensics Secur. **9**(6), 933–947 (2014)
16. Martinez-Diaz, M., Fierrez, J., Galbally, J.: Graphical password-based user authentication with free-form doodles. IEEE Trans. Hum. Mach. Syst. **46**(4), 607–614 (2016)
17. Antal, M., Zsolt, L.: Biometric authentication based on touchscreen swipe patterns. In: Proceedings of 9th International Conference Interdisciplinarity in Engineering, pp. 8–9 (2015)
18. Patel, V.M., Chellappa, R., Chandra, D., Barbello, B.: Continuous user authentication on mobile devices: recent progress and remaining challenges. IEEE Sig. Process. Mag. **33**(4), 49–61 (2016)
19. Kumar, R., Phoha, V.V., Serwadda, A.: Continuous authentication of smartphone users by fusing typing, swiping, and phone movement patterns. In: Proceedings of 8th IEEE International Conference on Biometrics: Theory, Applications, and Systems (2016)
20. Nguyen, T., Sae-Bae, N., Memon, N.: DRAW-A-PIN: authentication using finger-drawn PIN on touch devices. Comput. Secur. **66**, 115–128 (2017)
21. Al-Showarah, S.: The effectiveness of dynamic features of finger based gestures on smartphones' touchscreens for user identification. Int. J. Interact. Mobile Technol. **11**(1), 133–142 (2017)
22. Ku, Y., Park, L.H., Shin, S., Kwon, T.: Draw it as shown: behavioral pattern lock for mobile user authentication. IEEE Access **7**, 69363–69378 (2019)
23. Tolosana, R., Vera-Rodriguez, R., Fierrez, J., Ortega-Garcia, J.: BioTouchPass2: touchscreen password biometrics using time-aligned recurrent neural networks. IEEE Trans. Inf. Forensics Secur. **15**, 2616–2628 (2020)
24. Sreeraj, M., Idicula, S.M.: A survey on writer identification schemes. Int. J. Comput. Appl. **26**(2), 23–33 (2011)
25. Takahashi, A., Nakanishi, I.: Authentication based on finger-writing of a simple symbol on a smartphone. In: Proceedings of International Symposium on Intelligent Signal Processing and Communication Systems, pp. 411–414, November 2018
26. Ross, A.A., Nandakumar, K., Jain, A.K.: Handbook of Multibiometrics. Springer, Boston (2006). https://doi.org/10.1007/0-387-33123-9

Analysis of Multi-attribute User Authentication to Against Man-in-the-Room Attack in Virtual Reality

Jiawei Wang and BoYu Gao[✉]

College of Cyber Security, Jinan University, Guangzhou, China
bygao@jnu.edu.cn

Abstract. With the popularity of Virtual Reality (VR), most of VR applications focus on content creation and experience design, while the security and privacy of VR applications has been ignored. For example, the Man-in-the-room (MITR) attack is well known for tapping user interactions in VR, including the user's behaviors, real-time conversations, screenshots and computer audio, etc. Therefore, to provide secure and usable user authentication become one of crucial problems for VR applications. In this work, we propose a multi-attribute user authentication method to against MITR attack in VR. Specifically, any combinations of these selected attributes and values can be password for the certain user. The presented objects that conform to the password from the random object group are provided by our designed principles for identity authentication. The user then can select any presented attributes and values for authentication. Through this process, the attacker could not easy to guess the password even via a MITR attack. We designed a pilot study and evaluated the effectiveness and security of the proposed authentication method. By imitating the behavior of the MITR attacker, the authentication schemes under different settings are used to test the influence of different variables in the proposed security scheme. The experimental result shows that the proposed scheme can effectively resist invisible attack. This work-in-progress can give preliminary suggestions to against MITR for securing VR applications.

Keywords: User authentication · Man-in-the-room attack · Virtual Reality

1 Introduction

With the popularity of Virtual Reality (VR), numerous applications emerged to enable new experiences for traditional fields (i.e., games, shopping, etc.). However, most of VR application designers ignored one of crucial problems in designing VR applications, the security and privacy [3]. Especially, the traditional user authentication methods are no longer secure to meet the requirements of VR applications. For example, attackers can join the user's virtual reality while remaining invisible, which is called Man-in-the-room (MITR) attack. MITR attackers can tap user interactions in VR, including the user's behaviors, screenshots, chatting conversations and computer audio, etc. Therefore, for a user authentication scheme that inputs a fixed password, once the attacker successfully executes MITR attack during user authentication, the user's password will be stolen.

© Springer Nature Switzerland AG 2021
C. Stephanidis et al. (Eds.): HCII 2021, CCIS 1420, pp. 455–461, 2021.
https://doi.org/10.1007/978-3-030-78642-7_61

Fig. 1. (a) user can define the password using attribute-based authentication with this gaze interaction. (b) failed login. (c) successful login.

The core idea of the traditional identity authentication anti-shoulder surfing attack scheme is to incorporate an indirect secret transformation method, which can separate the visible password input process from the password itself [8, 9]. Similarly, we adopt this methodology to secure user authentication in VR.

In this work, we propose a novel multi-attribute user authentication by using virtual objects along with multiple attributes in VR (Fig. 1). Users can select the preferred object's attributes and the corresponding values of attributes as the password. The users were asked to unlock by selecting any displayed combinations of selected attributes. The core idea of our method is that the user authenticates through a randomly generated object with multiple attributes instead of entering a fixed password, so that the authentication process is separated from the password itself to improve the security of the scheme, including resistance to MITR attacks. In addition, we simulate MITR attacks to evaluate the security of the proposed method, and provide preliminary suggest for user authentication in VR.

2 Related Work

From the prior works, we classified VR user authentication scheme into three categories.

(1) Knowledge-based authentication, users can input the registered numeric ID or virtual patterns [1, 5–7], it is easy to use, but also easy to be observed and leak the input information.
(2) Biometric-based authentication, users can rely on the fingerprint, iris [10] or human visual information to lock or unlock the VR applications [4], however, these schemes are efficient and safe while required specific additional hardware support.
(3) Behavioral biometric, the interaction behavior can be modeled and used as a unique biometric authentication method (i.e., gait [11], body motion [2, 14], electroencephalography [12], etc.), but these new schemes are still in the development stage and the number of test experimenters is small, besides, most of them also require additional hardware.

From our observations, all three categories user authentication can be easily recorded when facing up with the Man-in-the-room attack [3]. For biometric-based authentication and behavioral biometric, even if the user authentication information is stolen by the MITR attacker, because the user's biometrics cannot be forged, the attacker is unable to impersonate the user to log in. However, these solutions need to collect the user's biological characteristics, and cannot be compatible with applications without designated hardware. Therefore, majority VR applications adopt the knowledge-based authentication, and some existing works showed the feasible solutions for VR applications.

Most of knowledge-based VR user authentication schemes transfer traditional mobile-side schemes directly to the VR environment, and the user is authenticated by entering a fixed password (i.e. [5–7]). In this case, if the attacker records the user's password input screenshots, attacker can successfully steal the user's password. It is not secure enough using such traditional authentication in VR. Such limitations motivate us to further explore this research question, how to secure the inputting while keeping usability for authentication.

3   Multi-attribute User Authentication Method

The overview of our proposed multi-attribute user authentication is illustrated in Fig. 2. The method proposed in this article is divided into two modules, one is user setup module that the user sets a password, and the other is user authentication module that the user performs authentication based on the password. The detailed description of these two modules is as follow.

User Setup Module

Step 1. The user sets password attributes. The user selects a set of attribute types T_p from all the provided N attribute types T as password attributes.

Step 2. The user sets values of password attributes. For each attribute $t(t \in T_p)$, the user selects a set of attribute values V_T as the password and gets the password attribute value $V_p = \{V_p[t] | t \in T_p\}$. As shown in Fig. 2 (Top), the grayed-out attributes and attribute values represent that they are selected by the user, and the user password is

$$\{t : V_p[t] | t \in T_p\} = \{Type2 : V_p[2], \ldots, Typex : V_p[x], \ldots\}$$
$$= \{Type2 : \{V[2][1], V[2][i_2]\}, \ldots, Typex : \{V[x][2], V[x][i_x], V[x][m_x]\}, \ldots\}$$

User Authentication Module

Step 1. The system generates verification objects. The system generates K random verification objects on the authentication interface according to the following rules.

- Every verification object has N attribute types and each attribute has and only has one attribute value which is randomly generated.

- The K verification objects generated every time satisfy the rule as far as possible that the attribute values corresponding to at least two attribute types of any two objects are different.
- There are at least K_{min} verification objects match to the user's password.

Step 2. The user selects the verification object for authentication. The user observes each object that appears on the authentication interface and judges whether it matches to the user's password. As shown in Fig. 2 (Bottom), if verification object y satisfies $\forall x \in \{1, 2, \ldots, N\}, (x \notin T_p \vee V[x][j_{yx}] \in V_p[x])$, then it is called y *match to the user's password*. The user can only pass the authentication by selecting all objects that meet the password setting, and selecting more or less will fail to log in.

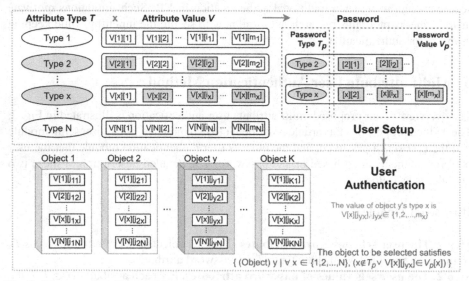

Fig. 2. The overview of the multi-attribute-based user authentication, consisting of two parts, the one is user password setting (Top), the other one is user authentication (Bottom). The password includes the object type and its corresponding attribute (i.e., password: {numbers: {1,2}, animal: {dog}}), the users can select the objects and its corresponding attributes as the password. After setting up the password, the possible candidates are displayed for selection.

Our authentication method is extensible. Objects in the physical world have unlimited types of attributes, and their corresponding attribute values may also be unlimited (i.e., the serial number of an object can be any string). Thus, in theory, the number of attribute types N and the number of attribute type attribute values $\{m_i | i = \{1, 2, \ldots, N\}\}$ in the method can approach infinity. Users can choose their own specific password attributes from great quantity of attributes types and their corresponding attribute values, that are easier for the user to remember or cannot be easily distinguished by others. For instance, musicians can choose the tone, and color-blind person can exclude color as one of their password attributes. Furthermore, the method can be used in conjunction with other identity authentication schemes. The method itself has no requirements for hardware devices, and is suitable for all types of VR devices and environments. It can be used as a backup solution for hardware-required authentication scheme (i.e., biometric-based authentication [4, 10] or behavioral biometric [2, 11, 12]) when devices are missing or fail.

Compared with the traditional two-dimensional space, VR environment has immersion, imagination, and immersion (3Is) [13]. These features improve the availability of our method. Immersion and immersion further increase the scalability of the method. For example, the geographic information and the interactive reaction can be used as the attribute type of the verification object. In addition, immersion and imagination make the method more vivid and more convenient for users to remember and choose.

4 Preliminary Results

To evaluate the effectiveness and security of such an authentication method, we design an initial test to quantify the security of the Man-in-the-room attack for multi-attribute-based user authentication in VR. We implemented the MITR attack strategy, and evaluated the security of the method under different variable settings, and based on the results, we gave suggestions for the implementation of the method.

In the experiment, we assume that the MITR attacker has seen three successful authentication of the legitimate user and the attacker can make attempts three times to impersonate user to log in. That is, the attacker pretends to be the legitimate user and performs three authentications, and as long as one passes the attack, this attack is considered successful.

We set up the number of mimic attacks under every variable setting as 100, and the experiment results are shown in Fig. 3. Based on the experimental results, we found that when the number of objects and its attributes were small, the percentage of successful attacks was not consistent among the displayed objects. However, with the increasing number of attributes, the consistency of changes with the same number of objects and attributes were presented. In addition, the level of security for this multi-attribute based user authentication increased with the increasing of displayed items. In particular, we easily found the peak from the experimental results. For example, when k was 3 and 6, the percentage of successful attacks increased, as expected, when k was 9, 12, and 15, the security was enhanced as the displayed items increased.

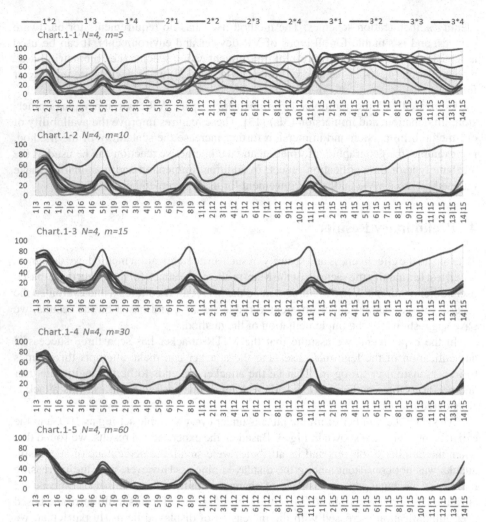

Fig. 3. The percentage of successful attacks under different number of objects and attributes, the horizontal axis represents the displayed items for selection, while vertical axis represents the percentage of successful attacks. The different pairs of N*m are illustrated in each condition. (a) N = 4, m = 5. (b) N = 4, m = 10. (c) N = 4, m = 15. (d) N = 4, m = 30. (e) N = 4, m = 60.

5 Conclusion and Future Work

In this work-in-progress paper, we proposed a multi-attribute-based user authentication method to against the man-in-the-room attack, and the results gave preliminary findings about the design of multi-attributes authentication in VR. In particular, we evaluated the security of the program, and the experimental results show that through appropriate variable settings, the program can effectively resist the MITR attack. In future, we will continue this method with a full-scale user study to evaluate the security and usability of the proposed method.

Acknowledgement. This work was supported by the National Natural Science Foundation of Guangdong (No. 2021A1515012629) and China (No. 61902147, 61932011), and by the Guangzhou (No. 202102021131) and Guangdong (No. 2019B1515120010) Basic and Applied Basic Research Foundation.

References

1. George, C., et al.: Investigating the third dimension for authentication in immersive virtual reality and in the real world. In: 2019 IEEE Conference on Virtual Reality and 3D User Interfaces (VR). IEEE (2019)
2. Pfeuffer, K., et al.: Behavioural biometrics in VR: identifying people from body motion and relations in virtual reality. In: Proceedings of the 2019 CHI Conference on Human Factors in Computing Systems (2019)
3. Casey, P., Baggili, I., Yarramreddy, A.: Immersive virtual reality attacks and the human joystick. IEEE Trans. Dependable Secure Comput. (2019)
4. Luo, S., et al.: OcuLock: exploring human visual system for authentication in virtual reality head-mounted display. In: 2020 Network and Distributed System Security Symposium (NDSS) (2020)
5. Yu, Z., Liang, H., Fleming, C., Man, K.L.: An exploration of usable authentication mechanisms for virtual reality systems. In: 2016 IEEE Asia Pacific Conference on Circuits and Systems (APCCAS), Jeju, Korea (South), pp. 458–460 (2016). https://doi.org/10.1109/APCCAS.2016.7804002
6. George, C., et al.: Seamless and secure VR: adapting and evaluating established authentication systems for virtual reality. In: NDSS (2017)
7. Mathis, F., et al.: RubikAuth: fast and secure authentication in virtual reality. In: Extended Abstracts of the 2020 CHI Conference on Human Factors in Computing Systems (2020)
8. Roth, V., Richter, K., Freidinger, R.: A PIN-entry method resilient against shoulder surfing. In: Proceedings of the 11th ACM Conference on Computer and Communications Security (2004)
9. Sun, H.-M., Chen, S.-T., Yeh, J.-H., Cheng, C.-Y.: A shoulder surfing resistant graphical authentication system. IEEE Trans. Dependable Secure Comput. **15**(2), 180–193 (2018)
10. Boutros, F., Damer, N., Raja, K., Ramachandra, R., Kirchbuchner, F., Kuijper, A.: On benchmarking iris recognition within a head-mounted display for AR/VR applications. In: 2020 IEEE International Joint Conference on Biometrics (IJCB), Houston, TX, USA, pp. 1–10 (2020). https://doi.org/10.1109/IJCB48548.2020.9304919
11. Shen, Y., et al.: GaitLock: protect virtual and augmented reality headsets using gait. IEEE Trans. Dependable Secure Comput. **16**(3), 484–497 (2019)
12. Li, S., et al.: Brain signal authentication for human-computer interaction in virtual reality. In: 2019 IEEE International Conference on Computational Science and Engineering (CSE) and IEEE International Conference on Embedded and Ubiquitous Computing (EUC). IEEE (2019)
13. Burdea, G.C., Coiffet, P.: Virtual Reality Technology. Wiley, Hoboken (2003)
14. Lu, Y., Gao, B., Long, J., Weng, J.: Hand motion with eyes-free interaction for authentication in virtual reality. In: 2020 IEEE Conference on Virtual Reality and 3D User Interfaces Abstracts and Workshops, pp. 715–716 (2020)

AI and Machine Learning in HCI

Attacks and Anomaly Detection in IoT Network Using Machine Learning

Amani Alzahrani[1,2,3](✉), Tahani Baabdullah[1,2,4](✉), and Danda B. Rawat[1,2](✉)

[1] Data Science and Cybersecurity Center (DSC2), Washington, DC, USA
{Amani.alzahrani,Tahani.baabdullah}@bison.howard.edu,
danda.rawat@howard.edu
[2] Howard University, Washington, DC 20059, USA
[3] Shaqra University, Riyadh, Kingdom of Saudi Arabia
[4] Princess Nourah Bint Abdul Rahman University, Riyadh, Kingdom of Saudi Arabia

Abstract. Internet of Things (IoT) has been recently one of the fastest-growing technologies around the world. Despite the rise of IoT devices, IoT has greatly changed the mode of communication. As of any system, IoT technology might be subjected to various anomalies and security issues such as authentication, authorization, data protection, network security, and access control. Usually, these security issues can arise through data transmission from/to IoT devices. This is what constitutes anomalies in IoT. Usually, with the technology evolving, these anomalies are increasing day in day out. Thus, there is a high need for intrusion detection systems (IDSs) to tackle IoT attacks and prevent exploiting vulnerabilities. This forces researchers and developers of IoT to start contemplating on how they should be using different technologies to help detect these anomalies and have them addressed. One such technology is machine learning (ML). In this paper, we compared the performance of different ML techniques in detecting IoT network attacks accurately. The models were trained with different size of data to show how each model performs while the data size increased to help generalize the model. The machine learning (ML) algorithms that have been used in the paper are: Logistic Regression (LR), Gaussian Naive Bayes (Gaussian NB), Multi-layer Perceptron Artificial Neural Network (ANN), Random Forest (RF), and Gradient Boosting classifier (GBC). We found out that RF and GBC models showed the best performance compared with other models with 99% accuracy.

Keywords: Internet of Things · IoT · Intrusion detection · IDS · Anomaly detection · Machine learning

1 Introduction

1.1 Internet of Things (IoT)

The concept of Internet of Things (IoT) is that it extends the internet to connect both internetworking devices and non-IP components, such as television, light, fan, refrigerator, camera and air-conditioner. IoT device is everywhere around us in home and

© Springer Nature Switzerland AG 2021
C. Stephanidis et al. (Eds.): HCII 2021, CCIS 1420, pp. 465–472, 2021.
https://doi.org/10.1007/978-3-030-78642-7_62

businesses, like manufacturing organizations, vehicular networks, industries, grid companies, health organization and more. The main purpose of IoT is to deliver a higher level of services to society and businesses. Thus, nodes of the network are formed of all things in the worldwide attached with embedded electronics and information technology to work like important components and to generate precious information depending on desired requirements of that network. Due to the increment of IoT usage, there will be over 20.5 billion IoT devices connected by 2020, also there will be more than three trillion US dollars spent on IoT hardware. IoT is one of the main components of building blocks of smart home and cities [1]. As known about IoT network, it is connections of large numbers of sensors and heterogenous devices, thus recognizing one thing can cause security challenges or issues, such as privacy issues, governance of the system, access control, and overall architecture. The main significant aspects of IoT network are considered security and privacy. IoT network desires to reach these three security requirements: confidentiality, integrity, and availability in order to achieve security aspects. IoT environment is considered a de-centralized network as fog network, and it is definitely different from being a centralized network as cloud network. Therefore, implementing detection techniques/methods becomes an essential processing to increase security of IoT networks through detection abnormal behavior or patterns of the IoT networks. Hence, the level of security of IoT systems can be robust because of applying detection techniques of abnormal behaviors or patterns of the IoT networks, such as comparison header analyzer intrusion detection system (IDS), vector space representation using a Multilayer Perceptron (MLP), machine learning, or deep learning [1]. The growing of IoT devices has increased the numbers of cyber-attacks, network threats, security and privacy issues as side effects of this IoT network. Inappropriately, these security issues and concerns have not solved yet and need more attention to prevent and detect them in early stage. Thus, IoT security is an interesting research topic to realize potential threats and vulnerabilities to find solutions and countermeasures to provide a large number of reliable services [2–4].

1.2 Anomaly Detection in IoT

Due to the limitations of IoTs computational capabilities and storage capacities, there are many security and privacy issues and vulnerabilities of IoT devices, for example authentication, authorization, data protection, network security, and access control. As known, complexity and multidisciplinary arrangements are the features of IoT systems. It is a big challenge to preserve the security requirement of the IoT system due to their vulnerabilities and the wide-scale attack surface. Thus, the security solutions should comprise holistic considerations to obtain the desired security requirements of the IoT system. Subsequently, the probability of physically accessing of IoT devices by intruders is very high in IoT networks because of the unattended environment that IoT devices typically work in. Intruders can get private information through eavesdropping of the communication channel as long as IoT devices are usually connected over wireless networks. Limitation of computations and power resources are considered the main reasons behind the incapability of IoT devices to support complex security structures. Hence, it is very complicated and challenging task to secure IoT systems due to the weakness of its capabilities. IoT systems have the features of being accessible and available for anyone, anywhere and anytime that impact on attack vectors or surfaces to be easily accessible by attackers. Therefore, the probabilities of IoT systems threating are definitely increased. As known, threats are the actions by attackers to exploit security vulnerabilities in a system and execute negative impacts on it. Hence, there are many threats and attacks that affect negatively on IoT systems, for example passive attacks such as eavesdropping, and active threats such as spoofing, Sybil, man-in-the-middle (MITM), malicious packets and denial of service (DoS) attacks [5].

2   Related Works

Many research papers have presented methods of using machine learning (ML) and deep learning (DL) models in order to improve and support the security of the IoT systems via using robust intrusion detection systems (IDS). In these survey papers [7, 8], data mining and machine learning methods were used to ensure cybersecurity through supporting IDS. Hence, it focused on the security via utilizing data mining and machine learning models, also it explained the misuse and anomaly detections in cyber field [5, 7, 8]. A Decision Tree (DT) as a basis classifier with another ML classifiers were used in security applications, for example intrusion detection, as mentioned in [9, 10]. This study analyzed the traffic of fog-based networks to detect the source of the malicious packets, and to detect Distributed Denied of Services (DDoS) attacks in order to secure IoT devices [11]. Support Vector Machine (SVM) are used in intrusion detection systems in many security applications due to its efficiency of the memory storage [12, 13]. Naïve Bayes (NB) classification is used to detect network traffic to either normal or abnormal packet through its ability to apply all features independently to filtering network traffic. Thus, it is used for anomaly detection [14, 15]. K-nearest neighbors (KNN) algorithm is also used for network intrusion detection and anomaly detection [16, 17]. This paper [18] presented a model to detect R2L (Remote-to-Local) and U2R (User-to-Root) attacks of the IoT environment, and this model provided a high accuracy of detection these kinds of attacks. Therefore, the model used two-tier classification, NB and KNN classifiers, to decrease the dimensionality of the features and to improve effectiveness by applying two layers of feature reduction [18]. In this paper [19], network intrusion detection and anomaly detection were applied by using Random Forests (RF) algorithm. All of these algorithms RF, SVM, KNN and ANN were used for DDoS detection in IoT systems as mention in [20]. Therefore, their method focused on avoiding extra computational overhead and enhancing the system applicability to real-time classification through using limited feature sets. As a result, RF was the best classifier, and it gave the highest classification results compared to the other classifiers. The experiment in this paper [21] was applied on the network traffic data from 17 IoT devices belonged to nine categories of IoT devices. This study adopted to train a multi-class classifier using RF algorithms through utilizing the features of the network traffic and recognizing the IoT device categories from the white list. As a result, the paper approved that ML algorithms and particularly RF have the capability to identify and recognize IoT devices that are unauthorized to belong to that network [21]. As known, the basic task of Principal Component Analysis (PCA) is to realize a real-time intrusion detection in IoT systems based on feature selection. As mentioned in [22], the model applied the PCA for feature reduction, and it also used SoftMax regression and KNN algorithms for classifications. The conclusion was that the combination of using PCA, SoftMax regression and KNN classifiers produced an effective system used in real time in IoT environments due to its effectiveness of time and computing capabilities [22].

3 System Methods

3.1 Dataset Description

The dataset used in this project was collected by monitoring and collecting the network logs using Ultrasonic Sensor with Arduino and NodeMCU [23]. Data preprocessing including cleaning, feature extraction and selection was already implemented on the dataset. These steps converted the data into feature vectors. We use Feature Scaling to bring all values to same magnitudes. In the dataset, there are 477,426 samples and 14 features without any missing data. The dataset contains six balance classes represented the attack types as shown in the table below.

3.2 Data Analysis

To train the models, we splatted the dataset into three parts: training set, validation set, and test set. The test set represents 20% of the total dataset with 95486 records, and the remained data, 381940 records, are for training and validation the models which represent 80%. K fold cross-validation technique has been used to avoid any overfitting.

Table 1. Description of dataset classes

Class	Category	Total num.	Description
0	Normal/Original	79035	Data that is correct and is accurate
1	Wrong Setup	82285	Data that as a result of the wrong system setup
2	Distributed Denial of service (DDoS)	79020	Attack where too many ambiguous packets flood a server, making services unavailable to service users
3	Data Type Probing	79002	It is a malicious device that writes different data types instead of intended data types
4	Scan Attack	79052	Process of scanning a computer system with the aim of getting information. It is usually done using a hardware component
5	Man-in-the-Middle (MITM)	79032	In this type of hack, hacker intercepts communication and alters the communication between two devices without their knowledge

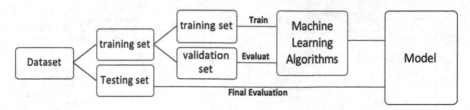

Fig. 1. System model flow diagram

We feed the models with different size of data. We trained each model by adding 20% samples of dataset each time until we covered the whole data. Then, the performance was measured using Cross entropy loss and accuracy. Figure 1 illustrates our model architecture (Table 1).

Since our dataset is labeled, several supervised learning algorithms were used which are Logistic Regression (LR), Gaussian Naive Bayes (GaussianNB), Multi-layer Perceptron artificial Neural Network (ANN), Random Forest (RF) and Gradient Boosting classifier (GBC). Four-fold cross-validation was applied on the dataset using each of these models. We feed the models with different numbers of samples and capture the performance using Cross entropy loss in each subset. Then, find the best model performance based on the test accuracy for the whole dataset.

4   Experiment Results and Evaluation

By training the dataset using four-fold cross validation and different machine learning models, Fig. 2 and 3 shows the model performance using Cross entropy loss and the accuracy results for each subset from the training and validation dataset.

From the figures above, it can be inferred that RF, GBC, and ANN have performed best both in training and validation sets. The three models record accuracy of around 100% accurate on training samples and 99% on the validation samples. It is obvious that RF and GBC had the same accuracy with all different size of data. However, ANN accuracy of 20% samples of the data is 97% and from 40% of data and up, it reached the accuracy of %99. Regarding cross-entropy loss, RF has the lowest loss with 0.00003 training set and 0.000006 in the validation set, then GBC with 0.0004 loss in both the training and validation set. Whereas ANN records 0.05 loss in both the training and validation set.

LR and NB performance were lower in the case of both training and validation samples with 87%, 89% accuracy, and 0.27 loss, 0.26 loss, respectively for training and validation sets. The table below summarizes all models' performance results.

After completing the training phase, the models were tested by applying them on a new dataset which was never shown to these models before to get the final performance evaluation. The accuracy results were almost the same as the validation accuracy results, as shown in Table 2.

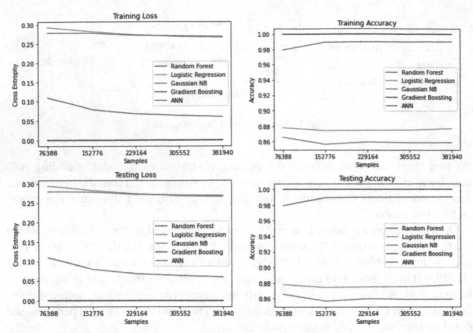

Fig. 2. Training and testing loss for different algorithms

Fig. 3. Training and testing accuracy for different algorithms

Table 2. Training performance results of models.

Class	Training Acc	Validation Acc	Training loss	Validation loss
RF	**100%**	**99%**	**0.00003**	**0.00006**
LR	87%	87%	0.26	0.26
NB	85%	85%	0.27	0.27
GBC	100%	99%	0.0004	0.0004
ANN	99%	99%	0.05	0.05

After completing the training phase, the models were tested by applying them on a new dataset which was never shown to these models before to get the final performance evaluation. The accuracy results were almost the same as the validation accuracy results, as shown in Table 3.

Table 3. Testing performance results of models.

Model	Test set Acc
NB	99%
GBC	99%
ANN	98%
RF	87%
LR	85%

5 Conclusion

IoT systems are more complex nowadays than ever before. This complexity is because of increased data and requirements of the systems, with various fields being in need of IoT to achieve their automation. With the gradual growth of embedded devices, the number of devices connected worldwide can be greater than the entire planet population. Thus, there will be gradual growth of anomalies and security issues. In this paper, we used different machine learning algorithms to detect the intrusion attacks in IoT systems. We tested the models with different size of datasets and observed their performance by measuring cross entropy loss and accuracy for each model. We found out that RF and GBC models showed the best performance, with %99 accuracy, to detect attacks in IoT systems compared with the other algorithms used in this paper.

References

1. Nandy, T., et al.: Review on security of internet of things authentication mechanism. IEEE Access. **7**, 1–36 (2019)
2. Nia, A.M., Jha, N.K.: A comprehensive study of security of internet-of-things. IEEE Trans. Emerg. Top. Comput. **5**(4), 586–602 (2017)
3. Babiceanu, R.F., Seker, R.: Big data and virtualization for manufacturing cyber-physical systems: a survey of the current status and future outlook. Comput. Ind. **81**, 128–137 (2016)
4. El-Hajj, M., Fadlallah, A., Chamoun, M., Serhrouchni, A.: A survey of internet of things (IoT) authentication schemes. Sensors **19**(5), 1141 (2019)
5. Al-Garadi, M.A., Mohamed, A., Al-Ali, A.K., Du, X., Ali, I., Guizani, M.: A survey of machine and deep learning methods for internet of things (IoT) security. IEEE Commun. Surv. Tutor. **22**(3), 1646–1685 (2020)
6. Xiao, L., Wan, X., Lu, X., Zhang, Y., Wu, D.: IoT Security Techniques Based on Machine Learning, arXiv preprint arXiv:1801.06275 (2018)
7. Buczak, A.L., Guven, E.: A survey of data mining and machine learning methods for cyber security intrusion detection. IEEE Commun. Surv. Tutor. **18**(2), 1153–1176 (2016)
8. Mishra, P., Varadharajan, V., Tupakula, U., Pilli, E.S.: A detailed investigation and analysis of using machine learning techniques for intrusion detection. IEEE Commun. Surv. Tutor. **21**(1), 686–728 (2018)
9. Goeschel, K.: Reducing false positives in intrusion detection systems using data-mining techniques utilizing support vector machines, decision trees, and naive Bayes for off-line analysis. In: SoutheastCon, pp. 1–6. IEEE (2016)

10. Kim, G., Lee, S., Kim, S.: A novel hybrid intrusion detection method integrating anomaly detection with misuse detection. Expert Syst. Appl. **41**(4), 1690–1700 (2014)
11. Alharbi, S., Rodriguez, P., Maharaja, R., Iyer, P., Subaschandrabose, N., Ye, Z.: Secure the internet of things with challenge response authentication in fog computing. In: 2017 IEEE 36th International Performance Computing and Communications Conference (IPCCC), pp. 1–2. IEEE (2017)
12. Liu, Y., Pi, D.: A novel kernel SVM algorithm with game theory for network intrusion detection. KSII Trans. Internet Inf. Syst. **11**(8) (2017)
13. Buczak, A.L., Guven, E.: A survey of data mining and machine learning methods for cyber security intrusion detection. IEEE Commun. Surv. Tutor. **18**(2), 1153–1176 (2015)
14. Agrawal, S., Agrawal, J.: Survey on anomaly detection using data mining techniques. Procedia Comput. Sci. **60**, 708–713 (2015)
15. Swarnkar, M., Hubballi, N.: OCPAD: one class Naive Bayes classifier for payload based anomaly detection. Expert Syst. Appl. **64**, 330–339 (2016)
16. Li, L., Zhang, H., Peng, H., Yang, Y.: Nearest neighbors based density peaks approach to intrusion detection. Chaos Solitons Fractals **110**, 33–40 (2018)
17. Syarif, A.R., Gata, W.: Intrusion detection system using hybrid binary PSO and K-nearest neighborhood algorithm. In: 2017 11th International Conference on Information & Communication Technology and System (ICTS), pp. 181–186. IEEE (2017)
18. Pajouh, H.H., Javidan, R., Khayami, R., Ali, D., Choo, K.-K.R.: A two-layer dimension reduction and two-tier classification model for anomaly-based intrusion detection in IoT backbone networks. IEEE Trans. Emerg. Top. Comput. **7**(2), 314–323 (2016)
19. Chang, Y., Li, W., Yang, Z.: Network intrusion detection based on random forest and support vector machine. In: 2017 IEEE International Conference on Computational Science and Engineering (CSE) and Embedded and Ubiquitous Computing (EUC), vol. 1, pp. 635–638. IEEE (2017)
20. Doshi, R., Apthorpe, N., Feamster, N.: Machine Learning DDoS Detection for Consumer Internet of Things Devices, arXiv preprint arXiv:1804.04159 (2018)
21. Meidan, Y., et al.: Detection of Unauthorized IoT Devices Using Machine Learning Techniques, arXiv preprint arXiv:1709.04647 (2017)
22. Zhao, S., Li, W., Zia, T., Zomaya, A.Y.: A dimension reduction model and classifier for anomaly-based intrusion detection in internet of things. In: Dependable, Autonomic and Secure Computing, 15th International Conference on Pervasive Intelligence & Computing, 3rd International Conference on Big Data Intelligence and Computing and Cyber Science and Technology Congress (DASC/PiCom/DataCom/CyberSciTech), pp. 836–843. IEEE (2017)
23. Kaggle. https://www.kaggle.com/speedwall10/iot-device-network-logs. Accessed 21 Nov 2019

A Machine Learning Approach
to Football Match Result Prediction

Luca Carloni, Andrea De Angelis, Giuseppe Sansonetti[✉],
and Alessandro Micarelli

Department of Engineering, Roma Tre University,
Via della Vasca Navale 79, 00146 Rome, Italy
{ailab,gsansone}@dia.uniroma3.it

Abstract. This paper describes the design and implementation of predictive models for sports betting. Specifically, we focused on exploiting Machine Learning (ML) techniques to predict football match results. To this aim, we realized an architecture that operates in two phases. First, it extracts data from the Web through scraping techniques. Then, it gives the collected data in input to different ML algorithms. Experimental tests showed encouraging performance in terms of the Return on Investment (ROI) metric.

Keywords: Machine learning · Artificial neural networks · Sport bets

1 Introduction

Recent technological advances in Machine Learning (ML) [29] (e.g., Deep Learning [14,22]) play a central role in our lives. ML designs the services of our cities [8], recommends which places [21] may be of interest to us (e.g., cultural heritage resources [23] or restaurants [3]) and how to reach them [9]. It suggests to us which news articles [6] or research papers [13] to read, which music artists and songs to listen to [19], which movies to watch [2], which products to buy [4], and even people to hang out with [11]. It is, therefore, natural that we turn to ML even when it comes to betting our money on sports events.

In this paper, we illustrate a forecasting system aimed to profit in the sports betting market using ML techniques. More specifically, we adopted Logistic Regression, K-Nearest Neighbors, Support Vector Machine, Naïve Bayes, and Random Forest, as well as a four-layer Artificial Neural Network (ANN). Those ML techniques were compared with each other using the prediction accuracy as an evaluation metric. The comparative analysis we carried out led us to choose the ANN as the learning technique since it allowed us to achieve better results. Subsequently, through simulation and prediction trials, we assessed the system performance. Finally, the system was also tested in predicting results related to matches still to be played. The performance in terms of Return on Investment (ROI) has been encouraging, which motivates us to pursue our research activities in this area.

© Springer Nature Switzerland AG 2021
C. Stephanidis et al. (Eds.): HCII 2021, CCIS 1420, pp. 473–480, 2021.
https://doi.org/10.1007/978-3-030-78642-7_63

2   Related Work

Among the first approaches advanced in the research literature to predict the result of sports events is the one illustrated in [26], in which the author proposes the use of least squares to make predictions on football and basketball matches. Since then, there have been numerous contributions on the same topic. For instance, in [10] the authors argue that regression models allow for more accurate results than those provided by domain experts. Furthermore, human experts are unable to process the publicly available data efficiently. Loeffelholz *et al.* [16] put forward the use of neural network models on a dataset of 620 games. One of the reasons why neural networks are so widely used in this domain lies in their flexibility in defining the class to be identified. For instance, in [1] the authors use two classes (home goals and away goals), while in [18] the class expresses the probability of winning. In [7], the authors describe a model, named *pi-football*, that takes advantage of a Bayesian Network to predict the outcome of football matches belonging to the English Premier League (EPL). This model takes into account both objective and subjective information, also weighing the available data through degrees of uncertainty. However, apart from a few authoritative exceptions, the results obtained in the first decade of the 2000s are generally not particularly encouraging. In [12], Haghighat *et al.* suggest that this is due to the limited size of the datasets. They, therefore, propose to consider player-level statistics as well and to adopt more advanced ML models. The advent of Deep Learning (DL) has provided a new boost to the entire domain. For example, in [17] the author illustrates an experimental evaluation conducted on different DL models on US National Basketball Association (NBA) matches. Interestingly, the author shows that significant results in terms of profit could be attained only by integrating statistics data with features extracted by experts from video recordings. The authors of [15] describe a convolutional neural network-based approach for the prediction of the outcome of basketball games, where the convolutional layer allows the system to exploit player-level data. They also suggest that correlating the prediction of the results with the predictions made by bookmakers is not helpful for the accuracy of the final results. In [20], the authors illustrate a system based on a Multi-Layer Perceptron (MLP) for predicting the outcome of football matches and show that it outperforms approaches based on traditional ML algorithms like Support Vector Machine (SVM) and Random Forest. Tiwari *et al.* [28] propose a model for predicting the result of football matches that makes use of Recurrent Neural Networks (RNNs) and Long Short-Term Memory (LSTM). To increase the model performance, the authors consider any events during the match and their consequences on the final result. In [5], the authors study the potential provided by ANNs by thoroughly analyzing ANN-based approaches for predicting the outcome of sports events and identifying what they believe are the challenges still to be solved. Consequently, they propose a prediction system based on the CRISP-DM model [24]. In [27], the authors propose to use different ML techniques to predict the outcome of football matches based on features related to not only the game but also the players.

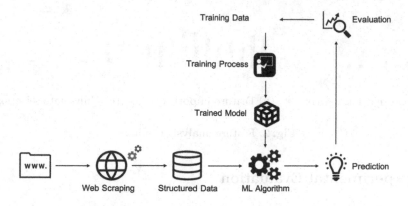

Fig. 1. The overall system architecture.

3 System Architecture

The overall architecture of the proposed system is shown in Fig. 1. The system works in two phases. In the first phase, the extraction of the betting odds is performed using a web scraping technique. These odds are related to the top betting markets such as *1X2*, *over-under 2.5*, and *goal-no goal*. Specifically, with the 1X2 market, we mean the type of bet that can be made to predict the outcome of a match, with the over-under 2.5 market we mean the market that takes into account the sum of the number of goals scored within a single match, with the goal-no-goal market we mean whether or not the match ended with at least one goal. In the second phase, the collected data is taken as input, and predictions are made through ML techniques. The web scraping operation was carried out from June to December 2020, through which we collected the following data:

- Number of countries: 12;
- Number of matches: 49,319;
- Number of seasons: for the highest leagues all the seasons starting from 2008–2009 until 2019–2020, for lower leagues from 2010–2011 until 2018–2019;
- Number of original features: 47;
- Missing cells: 349,215.

This data was subjected to a data cleaning operation, which reduced the number of matches to 36,461. Before applying the Machine Learning techniques, it was essential to carry out a relevance analysis of the features available. The objective of this analysis is to identify the most relevant features and discard the least relevant ones, which could harm the forecasting model and, consequently, reduce its accuracy. Among the techniques used there are Univariate Selection, Feature Importance, and Correlation Matrix. The example graphs shown in Fig. 2 are related to the over-under 2.5 market. These analyzes allowed us to reduce the total number of features to 31, thereby improving performance in terms of accuracy as well as computational efficiency.

(a) Correlation matrix　　　(b) Feature importance　　　(c) Univariate selection

Fig. 2. Feature analysis results.

4   Experimental Evaluation

Once the data extraction, cleaning, and analysis procedures were completed, ML techniques were applied to the data just learned. This process occurred in two phases. Initially, we employed different ML techniques to understand which of them was the most efficient for that specific market. Once the best technique for that market had been identified, it was then reused for incoming matches. The different ML models were:

- Logistic Regression;
- K-Nearest Neighbors;
- Support Vector Machine;
- Naïve Bayes;
- Random Forest;
- Four-layer Artificial Neural Network.

Subsequently, through the use of simulation and prediction techniques, we wanted to evaluate the effectiveness and efficiency of the system. Figure 3 shows the results in terms of accuracy for the over-under 2.5 market by applying the different ML techniques. It can be noted that ANN outperformed the other methods. The comparative analysis, therefore, led us to choose the ANN as the learning technique, since - as we have seen - it is more efficient than the other classification methods tested. Based on the previous results, we used the ANN as a model for the testing phase. The data was divided according to the classic 80-20 method: 80% of the data was used to train the network, while the remaining 20% was used as a test-set. We performed two experimental sessions. In the first session, we used the Return on Investment (ROI) as a metric to evaluate the probability of gaining a profit from an investment. ROI is defined as the ratio between the gain/loss realized by an investment and its initial cost. More specifically, we evaluated the system by monitoring the ROI trend as the threshold varied, which was set on the output of the neural network. It varied from the value of 0.9 up to 0.1: if the match was higher than the considered threshold, then it was considered for that market, else it was not taken into consideration. Figure 4 shows some example graphs. On the x-axis, there is the number of matches that are higher than the aforementioned threshold, on the y-axis, the ROI value. As can be expected, the number of matches increases as

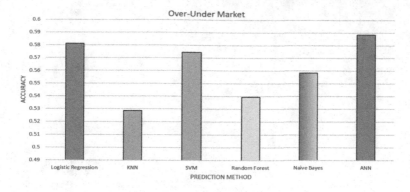

Fig. 3. Comparative analysis results.

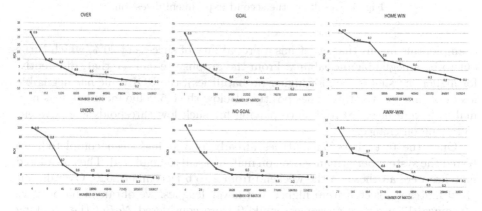

Fig. 4. Results of the first experimental session.

the threshold value decreases, but this does not mean having a higher profit since the probability of winning is reduced. This session was repeated for each market that was scrapped. From the graphs it is possible to notice that there is a positive ROI value for high thresholds, generally starting from 0.6, 0.7. This is since for lower values we are in the area of complete randomness.

In the second experimental session, we wanted to compare the proposed approach with a baseline system that, differently, always plays the lowest odd for the given market. Taking once again the over-under 2.5 market as an example, this means that if we want to play the over for a game, the baseline system places credits on the over only if the betting odd is lower than that of the under, while our system places credits on the over only if the match is higher than the set threshold value. The obtained results are shown in Fig. 5. We can note how the baseline system has a negative ROI, which happens for every market. This information confirms that the baseline system approach does not lead to profits. We can also observe that, for low threshold values, our system does not lead to gains, but this is predictable. Taking a threshold value equal to 0.2 as an

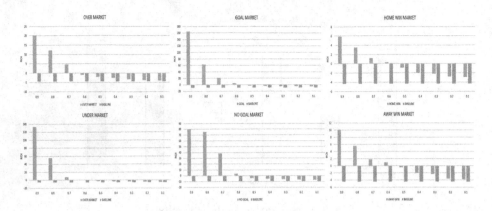

Fig. 5. Results of the second experimental session.

example, this means that event has a probability of success of 20%, which turns out to be a negligible probability. From the graphs, we can see that, differently, for higher thresholds (i.e., for higher probabilities), the ROI value has negligible losses or, most of the time, goes positive. Below the 0.5 value included, it is normal to have a negative ROI since playing for such low thresholds is equivalent to relying on chance.

Once the test phase on matches already played had been completed, we tested the system performance even on matches still to be played. The considered matches were all those on the weekend from 4 to 6 December 2020. Overall, out of 89 matches selected from higher and lower leagues, we obtained 65 positive outcomes, 13 negative outcomes, while 9 were considered *NoBet* (i.e., looking at the different probabilities it was deemed not convenient to place credits on that match), or credits were placed but the game was not played for different reasons. Even after this test, the ROI was calculated: placing 10 credits on each game, we reached a gain of 999.7 credits out of 790 played, with a net gain of 209.7 and an overall ROI of 26.54%, that is, an encouraging final result.

5   Conclusions and Future Work

In conclusion, we first developed a web scraping system, which retains the opening and closing betting odds of football matches belonging to different national leagues. Then, we employed different prediction techniques with diverse classification algorithms. Finally, we carried out experimental trials aimed to show the efficiency and effectiveness of the proposed system, also testing it on matches still to be played with good final results.

Among the possible future developments, there is undoubtedly the possibility of taking any temporal variation of odds for each archived match. This was not done as the scrapped betting sites did not report those variations for archived matches. Furthermore, for matches still to be played, it is possible to retain any change in odds up to the last available at the scraping time. We can also think of replacing the ANNs with Recurrent Neural Networks, which are very efficient in managing instances belonging to different time intervals. Finally, we can integrate the data extracted from online betting sites with user-generated content on social media. For example, in [25], the authors use tweet posts to increase the accuracy of a US National Football League (NFL) match outcome forecasting system.

References

1. Arabzad, S.M., Tayebi Araghi, M., Sadi-Nezhad, S., Ghofrani, N.: Football match results prediction using artificial neural networks; the case of Iran pro league. J. Appl. Res. Ind. Eng. **1**(3), 159–179 (2014)
2. Biancalana, C., Gasparetti, F., Micarelli, A., Miola, A., Sansonetti, G.: Context-aware movie recommendation based on signal processing and machine learning. In: Proceedings of the 2nd Challenge on Context-Aware Movie Recommendation, CAMRa 2011, pp. 5–10. ACM, New York (2011)
3. Biancalana, C., Gasparetti, F., Micarelli, A., Sansonetti, G.: An approach to social recommendation for context-aware mobile services. ACM Trans. Intell. Syst. Technol. **4**(1), 10:1–10:31 (2013)
4. Bologna, C., De Rosa, A.C., De Vivo, A., Gaeta, M., Sansonetti, G., Viserta, V.: Personality-based recommendation in e-commerce. In: CEUR Workshop Proceedings, Aachen, Germany, vol. 997. CEUR-WS.org (2013)
5. Bunker, R.P., Thabtah, F.: A machine learning framework for sport result prediction. Appl. Comput. Inform. **15**(1), 27–33 (2019)
6. Caldarelli, S., Feltoni Gurini, D., Micarelli, A., Sansonetti, G.: A signal-based approach to news recommendation. In: CEUR Workshop Proceedings, Aachen, Germany, vol. 1618. CEUR-WS.org (2016)
7. Constantinou, A.C., Fenton, N., Neil, M.: pi-football: a Bayesian network model for forecasting association football match outcomes. Knowl.-Based Syst. **36**, 322–339 (2012)
8. D'Aniello, G., Gaeta, M., Orciuoli, F., Sansonetti, G., Sorgente, F.: Knowledge-based smart city service system. Electronics **9**(6), 1–22 (2020)
9. Fogli, A., Sansonetti, G.: Exploiting semantics for context-aware itinerary recommendation. Pers. Ubiquit. Comput. **23**(2), 215–231 (2019). https://doi.org/10.1007/s00779-018-01189-7
10. Forrest, D., Simmons, R.: Forecasting sport: the behaviour and performance of football tipsters. Int. J. Forecast. **16**(3), 317–331 (2000)
11. Gasparetti, F., Sansonetti, G., Micarelli, A.: Community detection in social recommender systems: a survey. Appl. Intell. (2020)
12. Haghighat, M., Rastegari, H., Nourafza, N.: A review of data mining techniques for result prediction in sports. Adv. Comput. Sci. Int. J. **2**, 7–12 (2013)
13. Hassan, H.A.M., Sansonetti, G., Gasparetti, F., Micarelli, A.: Semantic-based tag recommendation in scientific bookmarking systems. In: Proceedings of the 12th ACM Conference on Recommender Systems, pp. 465–469. ACM, New York (2018)
14. Hassan, H.A.M., Sansonetti, G., Gasparetti, F., Micarelli, A., Beel, J.: Bert, elmo, USE and infersent sentence encoders: the panacea for research-paper recommendation? In: Tkalcic, M., Pera, S. (eds.) Proceedings of ACM RecSys 2019 Late-Breaking Results, vol. 2431, pp. 6–10. CEUR-WS.org (2019)

15. Hubácek, O., Sourek, G., Zelezný, F.: Exploiting sports-betting market using machine learning. Int. J. Forecast. **35**(2), 783–796 (2019)
16. Loeffelholz, B., Bednar, E., Bauer, K.W.: Predicting NBA games using neural networks. J. Quant. Anal. Sports **5**(1), 1–17 (2009)
17. Maymin, P.Z.: Wage against the machine: a generalized deep-learning market test of dataset value. Int. J. Forecast. **35**(2), 776–782 (2019)
18. McCabe, A., Trevathan, J.: Artificial intelligence in sports prediction. In: Proceedings of the Fifth International Conference on Information Technology: New Generations, ITNG 2008, USA, pp. 1194–1197. IEEE Computer Society (2008)
19. Onori, M., Micarelli, A., Sansonetti, G.: A comparative analysis of personality-based music recommender systems. In: CEUR Workshop Proceedings, Aachen, Germany, vol. 1680, pp. 55–59. CEUR-WS.org (2016)
20. Rudrapal, D., Boro, S., Srivastava, J., Singh, S.: A deep learning approach to predict football match result. In: Behera, H.S., Nayak, J., Naik, B., Pelusi, D. (eds.) Computational Intelligence in Data Mining. AISC, vol. 990, pp. 93–99. Springer, Singapore (2020). https://doi.org/10.1007/978-981-13-8676-3_9
21. Sansonetti, G.: Point of interest recommendation based on social and linked open data. Pers. Ubiquit. Comput. **23**(2), 199–214 (2019). https://doi.org/10.1007/s00779-019-01218-z
22. Sansonetti, G., Gasparetti, F., D'Aniello, G., Micarelli, A.: Unreliable users detection in social media: deep learning techniques for automatic detection. IEEE Access **8**, 213154–213167 (2020)
23. Sansonetti, G., Gasparetti, F., Micarelli, A., Cena, F., Gena, C.: Enhancing cultural recommendations through social and linked open data. User Model. User-Adap. Inter. **29**(1), 121–159 (2019). https://doi.org/10.1007/s11257-019-09225-8
24. Shearer, C.: The CRISP-DM model: the new blueprint for data mining. J. Data Warehous. **5**(4), 13–22 (2000)
25. Sinha, S., Dyer, C., Gimpel, K., Smith, N.A.: Predicting the NFL using Twitter. In: Proceedings of the 2nd Workshop on Machine Learning and Data Mining for Sports Analytics co-located with ECML PKDD 2013, pp. 28–38 (2013)
26. Stefani, R.T.: Football and basketball predictions using least squares. IEEE Trans. Syst. Man Cybern. **7**(2), 117–21 (1977)
27. Stübinger, J., Mangold, B., Knoll, J.: Machine learning in football betting: prediction of match results based on player characteristics. Appl. Sci. **10**(1), 46 (2020)
28. Tiwari, E., Sardar, P., Jain, S.: Football match result prediction using neural networks and deep learning. In: Proceedings of ICRITO 2020, pp. 229–231 (2020)
29. Vaccaro, L., Sansonetti, G., Micarelli, A.: An empirical review of automated machine learning. Computers **10**(1), 11 (2021)

User-Centric Explainability in Fintech Applications

Sahil Deo[1,2] and Neha Sontakke[2(✉)]

[1] Hertie School of Governance, Berlin, Germany
[2] CPC Analytics, Berlin, Germany
mail@cpc-analytics.com
http://www.cpc-analytics.com/

Abstract. Fintech applications such as robo-financial advisors (RAs) are complex algorithmic decision making systems, which gained prominence with their claim to democratize finance. Lack of transparency and explanations for these automated decisions leads to a trust deficit for users, limiting the potential of these applications. Our research aims to analyse the effectiveness of user-centric explanations in conveying the decision-making logic of complex algorithmic systems. Our user study tests techniques from explainable AI, varying in complexity and transparency. The quantitative aspects of our study determine the efficacy and usability of explanations and the qualitative aspects measure the effect of explanations on users and system usability. Our study finds trust and confidence of users in the system is positively correlated with comprehension and transparency provided by the presence of an explanation. There is a notable reduction in comprehension and trust between transparent white and opaque black box explanations of algorithms. This study is designed to aid policymakers and regulators in order to understand user needs which are crucial to designing better policies around algorithmic explainability for RAs.

Keywords: Explainable AI · User research · Financial technology · HCI · Usability · Artificial Intelligence

1 Introduction

The financial services sector is one of the torchbearers for applications driven by Artificial Intelligence (AI). One such service is wealth management provided by RA applications, automated web-based data-driven investment advisory algorithms. Used to estimate the best plans for trading, investment, portfolio rebalancing, or tax saving, for each individual as per their preferences. RA recommendation process begins when a user fills a questionnaire and is classified in risk classes (from low to high risk). The output is often a set of fund allocations based on parameters such as fund risk and size. However, unlike human advisors, RAs provide no reasons for their decisions, and this shortcoming reduces the trust

© Springer Nature Switzerland AG 2021
C. Stephanidis et al. (Eds.): HCII 2021, CCIS 1420, pp. 481–488, 2021.
https://doi.org/10.1007/978-3-030-78642-7_64

that users repose in their advice. RAs could bring about a large positive impact for consumers, if guided in the right direction by stakeholders and allowed to serve consumers in a fair, equitable way [1]. Our objective is to bridge this trust deficit. Explainable AI (XAI) can generate human-understandable explanations of algorithmic processes. The goal of XAI is to ask and address "how" and "why" questions related to algorithms [2]. These explanations play a crucial role in fostering user trust and technology acceptance [3]. Our approach tests the effect of user-centric explanations using techniques from explainable AI, to bridge this trust deficit, by conducting a user study with 105 human subjects on a custom-built RA. In addition to assessing the user interpretation of the explanations we measure their effect on the usability of the whole application. This extended summary provides a glimpse of the essential aspects of the experiment design and its key results.

1.1   User Requirements

A review of relevant literature reveals user expectations from explanations. Apart from answering "how"s and "why"s of algorithm logic, explanations need to provide a heuristic understanding of complex systems through narratives and mental models. Explanations should cover cause and effect relationships between features and outcomes, abductive inference (reverse engineer logic), counterfactual reasoning (effects of changing input variables), comparative reasoning (experimenting as a "neighbour"/social proof) and contrastive reasoning (Why A not B?). Our strategy addresses user requirements through descriptive visual, tabular and textual explanations. Explanation efficacy is examined through a survey. Ideally, each explanation should provide users with background knowledge to understand explanations, useful justifications (causes, desires, and logic), pragmatic goals (intention of explanation), and functional capabilities (limitations and coverage) [2–4].

1.2   Research Questions and Objectives of the Study

RQ1: How is user trust and system perception influenced by explanations?
RQ2: How do explanations affect the usability of the RA complex algorithmic system as a whole?
RQ3: How do explanations and consequently user opinions vary based on the complexity of algorithm and nature of explanations? (white vs. black box explanations)
RQ4: How does user perception of explanations system usability change in context of demographic group membership. For example, users from different age groups, risk categories, backgrounds, prior RA or investment knowledge, etc.
RQ5: How could the information gathered on user comprehension, opinions, and usability of explanations contribute towards the broader picture of generic guidelines for innovative inclusion? In order to aid developers and designers of ADS to help regulators better frame policies in the future.

2 Experiment Design

The experiment follows a hybrid approach of application and human grounded evaluation of explanations. An custom-built RA equipped with an explanation strategy is provided to participants of the user study. After each explanation, over 50 survey questions are used to determine comprehension, interpretation and usability of explanations.

2.1 Robo Advisory System and Explanations

A replica fintech RA application is given for experimentation to user study participants. This application is built to recommend mutual funds to user study participants. Two decisions made by a RA application directly concerning users are: risk profiling and asset allocation. Understanding the rationale behind these decisions is crucial and thus the focus of our explanation strategy. Two different machine learning models form the heart of the system. The first model creates a user profile after gathering user preferences, capturing useful information regarding investor objectives and limitations. But its primary purpose is to assign a risk category to each user. The second creates a mutual fund profile by classifying mutual funds into the same divisions of risk, based on a large amount of historical data gathered through 30 variable factors associated with each fund. A third algorithm links mutual funds to users based on profile matching through a set of different parameters (risk, objective, duration and amount of investment).

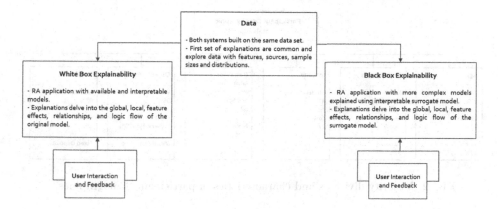

Fig. 1. Approaches to system explainability.

2.2 Black-Box and White-Box Explanations

Explanations of both algorithms in the system are generated using two different approaches (Refer Fig. 1). First, white box explanations are generated under conditions of complete relatively transparent availability of algorithms. Here, user risk is calculated using a decision tree algorithm (98% accuracy) which is inherently explainable. The mutual fund risk is calculated using a more complex support vector machine (95% accuracy). The difference in the complexity of the white box algorithms provides an additional point of view to evaluate user understanding. In the black-box system, both algorithms are made complex support vector machines (probabilistic kernels, 93% and 95% accuracy) and their explanations are generated through simplified inherently explainable algorithms acting as **surrogate models** (both above 80% cross validation accuracy) [5]. Both systems use the same training and testing data. One of the systems shown to users can be viewed here: https://white-box-explanations.herokuapp.com/.

2.3 User Sampling

Our sampling strategy is purposive and theoretical. Through user iterations we gather key concepts and areas of division that could lead to relevant and impactful results. Target audience for RA application is any person above the age of 18 interested or currently investing in funds, bonds, stocks, etc. The RA systems and survey are web-based, distributed to users through a link. Initially, using quota sampling, users are chosen based on a wide range of traits such as: differing age groups, dependents, incomes etc. This sample population also consists of amateur and professional investors. The initial sample recruited co-workers and acquaintances that fit a criterion for sampling iteration. The next iteration is snowball sampling, where previous participants pass the link to unknown and uncurated set of individuals.

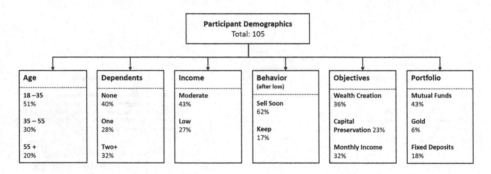

Fig. 2. Majority divisions and characteristics of participant demographics.

2.4 Participant Demographics

The survey had participants from mixed nationalities (India, Germany, and United States). From 105 participants, 54 interacted with the black box system and 51 with white box (Refer Fig. 2). Over a duration of four months, each participant received ample time for testing and analysis of explanations. Most participants were young, with few dependents, mostly stable incomes and a self-reported interest in wealth-based investments. Based on user preferences 52% are recommended moderate-high or high (in cases of high income and high stability) risk funds by the algorithm. White-box and black-box users show less than 10% deviation in each individual demographic.

3   Results

Explanation evaluation is done through a hybrid survey; qualitative questions understand user thoughts and opinions after each explanation while the quantitative aspects measure explanation comprehension.

3.1   User Comprehension

User comprehension is tested using the quantitative survey with close ended questions that require participants to analyse every explanation. Beginning with **localized explanations**, each user is asked to provide personal information and select investment preferences via a RA questionnaire. Then, user risk algorithm assigns a risk category to each users based on these preferences. The weight and impact (positive or negative) of each preference towards a risk decision is given through LIME local explanations. Here, 66% of the white and 64% of black box participants accurately answer questions on personalized local user risk.

Next, participants are shown **model specifications** for both user and mutual fund risk algorithms. Model specifications convey technical details such as performance metrics, function, sampling strategies etc. 63.8% of the white box participants answer questions relevant to user risk correctly, while 73% were correct for mutual fund specifications. For black box, 51% were correct about user risk and 53% about mutual fund risk.

Global feature importance explanations are calculated through average marginal contribution of a feature value over all possible permutations. This explanation conveys a generalised-holistic view of the importance of each feature towards a prediction class. In each systems, global importance of user and mutual fund risk is presented to participants. White box users answered relevant questions with 80% accuracy, while black box users with 53%. This percentage is the average of two algorithms.

A **decision tree** constructed on training and predicted outcome data represents hierarchical rules followed by the algorithm in a human- understandable format. Decision boundaries used to partition one class from another are expressed as if-then rules/conditions. 77% of white and 83% of black box participants followed the logic correctly. Although highly comprehensive, these depict highly simplified limited logic in a linear tree-like hierarchy.

The SHAP **feature effect and behaviour** explanations are the most technical and complex explanations. These explanations allow in-depth, feature-wise, and class-wise global comparative view of feature behaviour learnt by the model. White box comprehension was 67% for the user risk algorithm and 57% for the mutual fund risk algorithm. However, for black box, 34% were accurate for user risk questions and 26% for the mutual risk questions (Fig. 3).

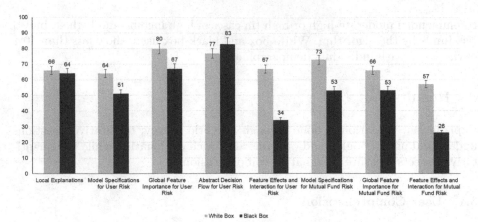

Fig. 3. User comprehension and accuracy for white and black box explanations. Data is normalized to percentage values. For both systems, the 95% confidence interval lies between ±5 points.

The trend of reduced black-box accuracy and comprehension can be seen across all explanations. An increase in explanation complexity results in a proportional and drastic decrease in black box user comprehension. However, this decrease is due to the surrogate model approximation used to generate black box explanations. The approximation used by a surrogate model in the black box algorithm causes details to be captured with a lower degree of precision. Therefore, lower comprehension is not due to an error in understanding the graph, it is due low explanation clarity due to approximation.

3.2 Usability of Explanations

User comprehension determines the interpretability of explanations. User opinions and trust convey the effectiveness of explanations. Both these factors are taken into consideration while determining usability. A large number of users from both systems found all explanations useful. However, white box users prefer global feature explanations while black box users prefer model specifications, the least preferred explanations according to white box users. On their own, model details provide an overview of the model performance but do not divulge a lot of information regarding the decision logic. They can only provide a preliminary idea of the model, its intent, functions, and performance. However, users can detect the lack of clarity and precision in explanations caused by black box approximation. In such cases, they prefer the clarity offered by model specifications. Therefore, in cases where a clear explanation is not possible, external data or features familiar to users should be shown, (such as the data sources in model specifications) to increase comprehension and trust in the system (Fig. 4).

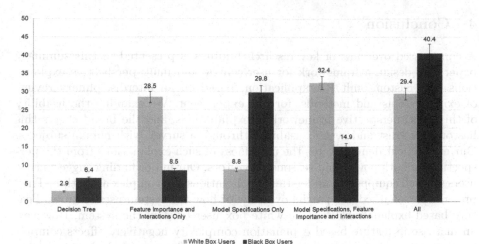

Fig. 4. Depicts explanation preference. A majority of users like all explanations. However, model specifications have a 21% increase in preference for black box explanations. While feature importance and interactions show a 18% reduction in popularity.

3.3 User Trust

The qualitative survey gathers the system users' opinions and thoughts on the explanations and the system. The primary goal of these questions is to understand participant psyche. This includes behavioural aspects (such as challenging areas, points of frustration, fatigue, etc.), general thoughts on specific explanation difficulties or usability, and measuring the effect of explanations on user trust. In this summary paper, only findings related to user trust are presented.

Trust **in explanations** is measured by trust in the data used to train algorithms along with the ability of explanations to convey decision making logic behind system recommendations. Trust **in the system** is measured using direct qualitative questions posed to participants in the survey. Data sources and variables for fund risk were well-known amongst 65% of seasoned RA users, and were trusted highly trusted (66% of white and 55% of black box users). Next, 70% of white box and 49% of black box participants though that knowing the extent of variables used through the feature based explanations in the system, has increased their trust in the system.

Participants were asked to rate their understanding of the system, before and after explanations. For white box, an initial average rating of 5.8/10 increased by 2 points on average. For black box, the average increase is less than 1 point. This indicates that explanations play a crucial role in helping users understand the system. Moreover, 61% of white box and 55% of the black box users reported increased **trust in the system** due to provided explanations. Therefore, user trust in the system is positively correlated with the presence of explanations. However, increase of clarity and precision, leads to good quality explanations which can further increase user trust.

4   Conclusion

A compressed overview of key research findings is presented in this summary paper. We design a framework for user-centric and multi-perspective explanations of a custom-built RA application, based on an interdisciplinary review of existing tools and methods, for our experiment. We examine the usability of this multi-perspective framework of explanations, and the broad effects this has on user trust and system usability through a survey with human subjects. Our experiment demonstrates the usefulness of such explanations from the perspectives of both novice and seasoned investors. Our major finding suggests that users are well equipped to understand explanations of a complex algorithm. They prefer a personalised but partial overview of how the system uses features. Feature based explanations increase white box user trust in the system. However, an increase in feature based explanation complexity negatively affects comprehension and usability in the black box approximation approach. In which case model specifications are the preferred explanations.

Overall, explanations are found to be positively correlated with user trust and consequently increase usability of the system. Therefore, explanations of algorithmic decision logic would benefit users as well as the developers of complex decision making systems.

References

1. Laboure, M., Braunstein, J.: Democratising finance: the digital wealth management revolution (2017). https://voxeu.org/article/digital-wealth-management-revolution
2. Hoffman, R.R., et al.: Metrics for Explainable AI: Challenges and Prospects (2018)
3. Shin, D.: The effects of explainability and causality on perception, trust, and acceptance: implications for explainable AI. Int. J. Hum.-Comput. Stud. (2020). https://doi.org/10.1016/j.ijhcs.2020.102551
4. Alexander, V., et al.: Why trust an algorithm? Performance, cognition, and neurophysiology. Comput. Hum. Behav. (2018). https://doi.org/10.1016/j.chb.2018.07.026
5. Arrieta, A.B., et al.: Explainable artificial intelligence (XAI): concepts, taxonomies, opportunities and challenges toward responsible AI. Inf. Fusion (2020). https://doi.org/10.1016/j.inffus.2019.12.012

Effective Movie Recommendation Using User Frequency Based Collaborative Filtering Algorithm

Litao Fan, Zhao Huang, and Chao Qi[✉]

School of Computer Science, Shaanxi Normal University, Xi'an 710119,
People's Republic of China
qichao@snnu.edu.cn

Abstract. Although a variety of collaborative recommendation methods have become available, they are still facing the challenges of increasing their accuracy and validity. This study uses the inverse user frequency to improve the impact of user frequency on item cosine similarity. It is novel collaborative filtering based on the cosine similarity. The improved cosine similarity is used to calculate the similarity between items. Finally, the corresponding target user recommendation results are generated. The experiments show that our proposed technique significantly outperforms the others collaborative filtering techniques, which is helpful to improve the recommendation performance.

Keywords: Collaborative filtering · Cosine similarity · User frequency

1 Introduction

The recommendation systems [1] provide users with personalized products or services. They are becoming more and more important and successful in e-commerce [2], and have been widely used in other applications, such as YouTube, and social networks. Generally, the recommendation systems will construct the personal information of the product and establish user's personal information according to user's previously recorded behaviors. Thereafter, the prediction of user item rates has not been evaluated. Based on the prediction, the system will make recommendations. Various recommendation generation techniques have been proposed and widely used in commercial environments. Among them, the collaborative filtering (CF) method is the most successful recommendation technique. However, the current recommendation system still faces major challenges. For example, a large score prediction error can lead to low recommendation accuracy and cold start problems [3]. The collaborative filtering algorithm [4] is an important part of the recommendation system, and it focuses on the calculation of similarity with items or users. The common similarity calculation method is the cosine similarity [5]. In order to improve the accuracy of recommendation and reduce the score prediction error of unrated items, this paper reports a cosine similarity calculation method based on user frequency, which solves the influence of user frequency on item similarity. By doing so, it can obtain more accurate calculation results of similarity and improve the performance of recommendations [6].

C. Stephanidis et al. (Eds.): HCII 2021, CCIS 1420, pp. 489–494, 2021.
https://doi.org/10.1007/978-3-030-78642-7_65

2 Literature Review

A large number of studies in the areas of recommendation algorithm have been conducted in order to provide better performance for target users. The precision of similarity calculation between items or users is the key of recommendation algorithm. Traditional similarity methods such as, Cosine similarity [7] and Pearson similarity [8] are usually used to calculate the similarity between users. However, it can be argued that although these studies can improve the accuracy of score prediction to a certain extent, they lack of vital considerations of high dependence on the number of common scores in calculating the similarity of the recommendation algorithm. This may result in the inaccurate recommendations. The similarity calculation can be improved by addressing other factors, such as the influence of user's emotional factors on preference [9]. Dhawan et al. [10] have used project-based collaborative filtering to generate suggestions and used different project similarity measures. Evidence from literature indicates that when cosine similarity is used to calculate similarity, the accuracy of the recommendation algorithm can be improved by addressing the factors of user preferences.

3 Research Method

3.1 Basic Algorithm

The basic idea of ItemCF is to recommend items that are similar to the items they have liked before.

ItemCF algorithm generally includes two steps:

Step1: Calculate the similarity between items.
Step2: Generate a final recommendation list for the target user based on the user's historical behavior and the similarity information between different items.

The formula for similarity between items is shown as follows:

$$w_{ij} = \frac{|N(i) \cap N(j)|}{\sqrt{|N(i)||N(j)|}} \tag{1}$$

The ItemCF algorithm will encounter the problem of 0 similarity when calculating the similarity between different items. At this time, a user-item look-up table can be established, that is, a list of items that he has acted for each user. After obtaining the similarity information between different items, the following formula can be used to calculate the interest of current user u in a specific item j:

$$p_{uj} = \sum_{i \in N(u) \cap S(j,K)} w_{ji} r_{ui} \tag{2}$$

Where, $N(u)$ is the set of items for which the user has acted, $S(j,K)$ is the set of K neighbors of item j, w_{ji} represents the similarity between two items j and i, and r_{ui} represents user u's pair of items. The degree of interest of i (under the implicit data set, if the target user u has ever acted on the item i, then $r_{ui} = 1$, otherwise $r_{ui} = 0$). The meaning of this formula is: if an item is more similar to an item that the user previously liked, then it is more likely to be recommended and rank higher in the recommended list.

3.2 The Impact of User Frequency on Item Similarity

For the item similarity calculation formula, the reason why two items are similar is that many users have interacted with them, and each user has contributed to the similarity of different items.

For example, there is a user who works as a movie reviewer. Users watched more than a dozen movies every day and watched thousands of movies in total during his work. This means that the user's behavior has contributed to the similarity of more than a thousand movies, but it is clear that the user is not watching movies out of their own interest. In fact, not all of these movies are similar. In other words, when calculating item similarity, we should reduce the contribution of frequency users to item similarity calculation. Therefore, we should take user frequency into consideration when calculating the similarity:

$$w_{ij} = \frac{\sum_{u \in N(i) \cap N(j)} \frac{1}{\log(|N(u)| + \alpha)}}{\sqrt{|N(i)||N(j)|}} \tag{3}$$

This paper proposes the ItemCF algorithm of this similarity calculation formula. The algorithm believes that low frequency users should contribute more to the similarity between different items than frequency users.

4   Results and Discussion

4.1   Baselines Description

To confirm the validity of our results, we compare them with the results obtained by the two recommendation methods.

- **ItemCF:** ItemCF is based on the assumption that a user's favorite movies are related to the movies they have known and liked.
- **ItemCF-IUF:** ItemCF-IUF is based on the following assumption: the contribution of frequency users to item similarity should be less than that of low frequency users, so an IUF (Inverse User Frequence) parameter is added to modify the calculation formula of item similarity.

4.2   Effectiveness Evaluation

The performance of our method is evaluated and compared with ItemCF and ItemCF-IUF on the MovieLens 100k dataset. This dataset contains 100,000 ratings (scoring scores from 1–5) from 943 users in 1682 movies, and each user has rated at least 20 movies. Moreover, we divided the data set into two parts, including 80% training part and 20% testing part. The training part is used to estimate the model, and the test part is used for the evaluation. In order to analyze the accuracy of our method, the study adopted the general information retrieval evaluation measures, such as Recall, Precision and F1-Score. The Precision (4), Recall (5) and F1-Score (6) metrics are defined as follows:

$$precision = \frac{TP}{TP + FP} \tag{4}$$

$$recall = \frac{TP}{TP + FN} \tag{5}$$

$$F1 - score = \frac{2 * precision * recall}{precision + recall} \tag{6}$$

Where, TP is the number of recommendations in the top-N list considered right by the testing set; FP is the number of recommendations in the top-N list considered wrong by TS; FN is the number of recommendations considered right by testing set but not in the top-N list.

4.3 Experimental Results on Recommendations

The results of the precision, recall, and F1-score are shown in Figs. 1, 2, and 3 f respectively.

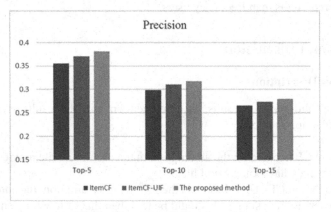

Fig. 1. The comparisons of precision

The x-axis of each graph represents the number of recommended movies, and the y-axis represents the values of Precision, Recall, and F1-score. The results show that the recommendation method considering user frequency has better performance. Compared with the evaluation-based methods, the proposed method that uses user similarity shows better results. This indicates that having the consideration of user frequency level can make a better understanding of the user preferences.

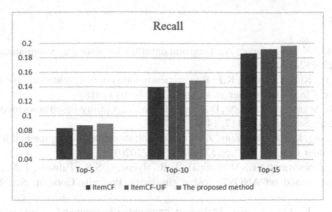

Fig. 2. The comparisons of recall

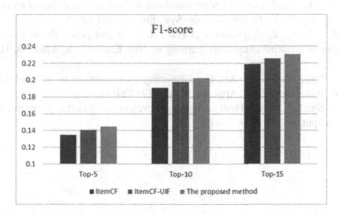

Fig. 3. The comparisons of F1-score

5 Conclusion

In this study, we proposed an Item-CF recommendation method based on user frequency, which addresses the influence of user frequency to item similarity. Users with high user frequency should contribute less to the item similarity than users with low user frequency. Our proposed recommendation method is evaluated based on the Movielens 100k dataset. Experiment results demonstrate that our proposed method is significantly outperforms the other baselines in Top-N recommendation on the evaluation metrics of precision, recall and F1-score.

Acknowledgement. This study was supported by research grants funded by the "National Natural Science Foundation of China" (Grant No. 61771297).

References

1. Milovančević, N.S., Gračanac, A.: Time and ontology for resource recommendation system. Phys. A **525**, 752–760 (2019)
2. Hwangbo, H., Kim, Y.S., Cha, K.J.: Recommendation system development for fashion retail e-commerce. Electron. Commer. Res. Appl. **28**, 94–101 (2018)
3. Zihayat, M., Ayanso, A., Zhao, X., Davoudi, H., An, A.: A utility-based news recommendation system. Decis. Support Syst. **117**, 14–27 (2019)
4. Feng, C., Liang, J., Song, P., Wang, Z.: A fusion collaborative filtering method for sparse data in recommender systems. Inf. Sci. **521**, 365–379 (2020)
5. Sejal, D., Ganeshsingh, T., Venugopal, K.R., Iyengar, S.S., Patnaik, L.M.: Image recommendation based on ANOVA cosine similarity. Procedia Comput. Sci. **89**, 562–567 (2016)
6. Gao, L., Dai, K., Gao, L., Jin, T.: Expert knowledge recommendation systems based on conceptual similarity and space mapping. Expert Syst. Appl. **136**, 242–251 (2019)
7. Wei, J., Meng, F., Arunkumar, N.: A personalized authoritative user-based recommendation for social tagging. Future Gener. Comput. Syst. **86**, 355–361 (2018)
8. Wang, S.-L., Wu, C.-Y.: Application of context-aware and personalized recommendation to implement an adaptive ubiquitous learning system. Expert Syst. Appl. **38**, 10831–10838 (2011)
9. Deng, S., Wang, D., Li, X., Xu, G.: Exploring user emotion in microblogs for music recommendation. Expert Syst. Appl. **42**, 9284–9293 (2015)
10. Dhawan, S., Singh, K.: Jyoti: High rating recent preferences based recommendation system. Procedia Comput. Sci. **70**, 259–264 (2015)

API Design for Multidimensional Integration Library

Erika Hernández-Rubio[1], Miriam Pescador-Rojas[2], Ramses Fuentes Pérez[2], Diego D. Flores-Nogueira[2], and Amilcar Meneses Viveros[3]([⌂])

[1] Instituto Politécnico Nacional, ESCOM, SEPI-ESCOM, Mexico City, Mexico
ehernandezru@ipn.mx
[2] Instituto Politécnico Nacional, Mexico City, Mexico
[3] Departamento de Computación, Cinvestav-IPN, Mexico City, Mexico
ameneses@cs.cinvestav.mx

Abstract. API is the medium in which programmers interact with frameworks and libraries. This allows programmers to develop code with other programming layers and middleware layers. The API is the set of names of functions, classes, methods, and data types needed to interact with the different layers in a compute platform through frameworks and libraries. Also, heterogeneous systems are standard in current computing platforms. The learning curve for developing or running parallel programs can be steep. An API is suitable in order to reduce the learning curve for use parallel heterogenenous computing libraries. The API hides the particular characteristics of the execution of a task in different computing units. An API is presented for a heterogeneous parallel multidimensional integration library based on Gaussian quadratures in this work. The control to select the best execution unit depends on an artificial intelligence module that decides to depend on the problem's size to be solved.

Keywords: API design · Multidimensional integration · Heterogeneous computing

1 Introduction

Current systems are developed using frameworks and libraries provided by third parties. To use these frameworks efficiently requires a good API design [10]. The design of the API guarantees the adoption of frameworks and libraries by programming users [1,2,4]. In software engineering, software's quality is achieved using various methodologies, and API design has caught the attention of designers in recent years. It have been made proposals to ensure the API's quality, mainly in the object-oriented paradigm or in Web environments [5,7,12]. In mathematical libraries, where only functions and constants are defined, functions definition are common in structured programming paradigm and would be included as class methods in object oriented programming paradigm. Also, with advances in processor technology, it is common to have heterogeneous computing

© Springer Nature Switzerland AG 2021
C. Stephanidis et al. (Eds.): HCII 2021, CCIS 1420, pp. 495–499, 2021.
https://doi.org/10.1007/978-3-030-78642-7_66

platforms, that is, with different technologies for execution units, for example; combining CPUs and GPUs or CPUs and FPGAs [3,13]. To provide functions libraries to take advantage of these technologies, decision mechanisms must be incorporated to decide which execution unit can solve a problem with the best performance. The advantage of the API is that it hides implementation details. For libraries with heterogeneous parallel programming, the API hides the implementation details regardless of whether the program uses a multicore processor or GPU. An API is presented for a heterogeneous parallel multidimensional integration library based on Gaussian quadratures in this work. Using Machine Learning techniques, it is possible to improve performance without the user intervening in the decision to select the process unit where the functions are to be executed.

2   API's Design Guide

API is the medium in which programmers interact with frameworks and libraries. API allows programmers to develop code with other programming layers and, middleware layers. The API is the set of names of functions, classes, methods and, data types that are needed to interact with the different layers in a compute platform through frameworks and libraries [1,4,10]. Also, heterogeneous systems are standar in current computing platforms. The learning curve for developing or running parallel programs can be steep. API must have some characteristics: as useful, easy to use and easy to learn, leads to readable code, hard to misuse, easy to extend and complete [1,2]. Also, a minimal API could be easy to learn, and the API does not incorporate implementation elements [1].

3   Heterogeneous Parallel Architectures

Current computing platforms have various execution units, which can execute different instructions sets than those used by a traditional CPU [3,13]. These types of systems are called heterogeneous. Examples of these systems include combinations of CPUs with GPUs or CPUs with FPGA devices. Examples of these systems include combinations of CPUs with GPUs or CPUs with FPGA devices. In particular, the combinations of CPU with GPU are heterogeneous parallel architectures, and the programs that run on these systems are heterogeneous parallel programs [6].

Parallel heterogeneous systems have various combinations. The most common ones are simpler with a multicore processor with one GPU card, a multicore processor with several GPU cards, and systems with two multicore processors with several GPU cards. Regardless of the configuration of CPUs and GPUs, heterogeneous parallel programs must take care of memory accesses, because the use of the GPU has an overhead due to the fact that data must be transferred between the main memory of the computer to the memory of the GPU card.

4   Multidimensional Integration

Multidimensional integration is a tool for several problems in the economy, physics, and chemistry, among others [8,9]. Unfortunately, in most cases, the integral does not have an analytical solution, so we choose to have numerical solutions that approximate the value of the integral that we want to obtain. The numerical methods to approximate the solution are well known as the Riemann sums, the Gaussian quadrature methods, the Stieltjes methods, or simulation by Monte Carlo methods [9,11,14].

Quadrature integration methods make an approximation to the integral 1. To do this, the nodes x_i and the weights w_i must be calculated. The user chooses the number of nodes and weights.

$$\int_a^b f(x)dx = \sum_{i=1}^{\infty} w_i f(x_i) \tag{1}$$

To extend the integral in d dimensions, tensor products are used to distribute weights and abcisssas to the hypervolume Ω, such that we obtain the following equation.

$$\int_\Omega W(X)f(X)dX \tag{2}$$

Where X is a d-dimensional vector, and W is a weight tensor that covers d-dimensions. A detailed explanation of this method can be seen in [9].

5   The API

The multidimensional integral library has a set of functions to solve integral numerically from 3 to 6 dimensions using gaussian quadrature method [9]. These functions are parallelized in OpenMP to run on multicore processors and CUDA to run on GPU cards.

The Gaussian quadrature integration algorithm must calculate the abscissa and weights. Arrays are used to store these values according to the number of evaluation points desired. Integration functions can have a shorter execution time sequential or in parallel on a CPU or GPU, depending on the number of evaluation points, the dimensionality, and the function to be evaluated. The use of the library must be transparent for users, such that it is not necessary for the user to know execution attributes such as the number of threads or number of thread blocks.

The user give the pointer of a function to be integrated, limits of integration, and the number of points, as parameters to library functions. Table 1 shows the name of the main library functions and the task they solve. The name of these functions init with letters "GL" correspond to Gaussian Library. All of these functions have seven arguments and return a double value. The first argument is the pointer, for the integral return value. The second argument is the pointer to the function. Thus functions have a double value as an argument and return

Table 1. Multidimensional integration library API

Name	Description
GL_Integral	The main function. This function hides the execution unit
GL_CUDA	This parallel function solves the integration on the GPU card
GL_OMP	This parallel function solves the integration on the multicore processor
GL_SEC	This sequential function solves the integration on a processor core

a double value. The third argument is corresponds to the dimension. The fourth argument is the number of points. The next two arguments corresponds to the limits of integration. Finally, these functions return the total execution time.

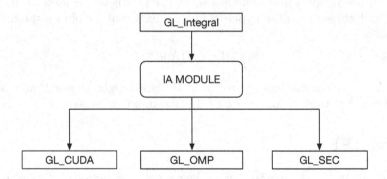

Fig. 1. API hierarchy diagram

Figure 1 shows the hierarchy diagram API. In this way, the user should only use the GL_Integral function for integration in multiple dimensions. Only if user needs to use a specific type of execution they can use GL_CUDA, GL_OMP or GL_SEC.

6   Conclusions

The programmer is the end-user of a library or framework. API design allows the use of frameworks and libraries to be transparent to the user. In heterogeneous environments, the API reduces the learning curve.

In this work, an API for multidimensional integrations running in parallel heterogeneous systems is presented. The API is minimum with only one function it is possible execute in sequential or parallel mode (in OMP or CUDA) depending on the size of the problem, represented by dimension and number of points. It is possible to hide the heterogeneous platform with this function. In case of user needs to execute the function in special mode it is possible to call the specific functions. All functions have the same parameters: pointer to the functions to be integrated, limits of integrations, and a number of points.

Acknowledgment. The authors thank the facilities and financial support given by the Instituto Politécnico Nacional (SIP project 20201079), as well as the Section of Research and Graduate Studies (SEPI) of ESCOM-IPN and Cinvestav-IPN, provided to accomplish this publication.

References

1. Blanchette, J.: The little manual of API design. Trolltech, Nokia (2008)
2. Bloch, J.: How to design a good API and why it matters. In: Companion to the 21st ACM SIGPLAN Symposium on Object-Oriented Programming Systems, Languages, and Applications, pp. 506–507 (2006)
3. Brodtkorb, A.R., Dyken, C., Hagen, T.R., Hjelmervik, J.M., Storaasli, O.O.: State-of-the-art in heterogeneous computing. Sci. Program. **18**(1), 1–33 (2010)
4. Henning, M.: API design matters. Commun. ACM **52**(5), 46–56 (2009)
5. Masse, M.: REST API Design Rulebook: Designing Consistent RESTful Web Service Interfaces. O'Reilly Media, Inc., Newton (2011)
6. Mittal, S., Vetter, J.S.: A survey of CPU-GPU heterogeneous computing techniques. ACM Comput. Surv. (CSUR) **47**(4), 1–35 (2015)
7. Mulloy, B.: Web API design (2013)
8. Nechuiviter, O., Iarmosh, O., Kovalchuk, K.: Numerical calculation of multidimensional integrals depended on input information about the function in mathematical modelling of technical and economic processes. In: IOP Conference Series: Materials Science and Engineering, vol. 1031, p. 012059. IOP Publishing (2021)
9. Quintero-Monsebaiz, R., Meneses-Viveros, A., Carranza, F., Cortés-Castillo, C.G., González-Zamudio, A., Vela, A.: Multidimensional adaptative and deterministic integration in cuda and openmp. J. Supercomput. (2021, accepted paper)
10. Reddy, M.: API Design for C++. Elsevier, Amsterdam (2011)
11. Todorov, V., Apostolov, S., Dimov, I., Fidanova, S., Poryazov, S., Dimitrov, Y.: An optimal monte carlo algorithm for a class of multidimensional integrals. rN **4**(2c1c2), 2c1c2 (2020)
12. Tulach, J.: Practical API Design: Confessions of a Java Framework Architect. Apress, New York (2008)
13. Zahran, M.: Heterogeneous computing: here to stay. Commun. ACM **60**(3), 42–45 (2017)
14. Zaremba, S.: Some applications of multidimensional integration by parts. Ann. Polon. Math. **1**, 85–96 (1968)

The Impact of Ethical Issues on Public Understanding of Artificial Intelligence

Yerin Kim[1] and Jang Hyun Kim[2(⊠)]

[1] Department of Applied Artificial Intelligence, Sungkyunkwan University, Seoul 03063, Korea
yerinee95@skku.edu
[2] Department of Interaction Science/Department of Human-AI Interaction,
Sungkyunkwan University, Seoul 03063, Korea
alohakim@skku.edu

Abstract. The suspension of the chatbot service "Luda" has raised numerous questions for South Korean society on ethical issues in dealing with artificial intelligence (AI). While the primary reason for suspension was the chatbot's hate speech against the LGBT community, the chatbot itself was also a target for sexual harassment from manipulative users. Moreover, the service provider "Scatter Lab" had to go through an investigation for possible violations of the Personal Information Protection Act.

The aim of this research is to systematically examine the public's expectations and concerns over AI and to retrieve implications from the perspective of human – AI interaction. Using big data analysis incorporated with natural language processing, the research analyzed news and comments related to Luda and found that the main concern of the public on data was regarding its collection process and content. Based on a qualitative analysis of the literature, the main source of such concerns was enhanced AI literacy which was also induced by the complex ethical issues related to Luda.

Keywords: Artificial intelligence · AI ethics · AI literacy

1 Introduction

The suspension of the chatbot service "Luda" has raised numerous questions for South Korean society on the ethical issues in dealing with artificial intelligence (AI). While the primary reason for the suspension was the chatbot's hate speech against the LGBT community, the chatbot itself was also a target for sexual harassment from manipulative users [1]. Moreover, the service provider "Scatter Lab" had to go through an investigation for possible violations of the Personal Information Protection Act in the process of collecting data [2]. Eventually, even after the service was suspended, the chatbot triggered a highly confrontational gender debate and criticism against Scatter Lab.

It should be noted that such controversies over AI related ethical issues are not new. In 2016, a chatbot called "Tay", developed by Microsoft, was shut down after the chatbot posted racist tweets [3]. In 2019, a "human review" of voice data collected

© Springer Nature Switzerland AG 2021
C. Stephanidis et al. (Eds.): HCII 2021, CCIS 1420, pp. 500–507, 2021.
https://doi.org/10.1007/978-3-030-78642-7_67

for improving AI speakers brought about a serious backlash against major companies like Google and Apple [4]. It is clear that these repeated ethical issues and their media coverage are making a cumulative impact on public understanding of AI. Since public opinion can be a "powerful force" in technology development [5], it is important to understand what exact concerns the public have whenever such ethical issues arise and how people perceive them.

The aim of this research is to systematically examine the public's expectations and concerns over AI from the Luda incident and to retrieve implications from the perspective of human - AI interaction. Using an interdisciplinary approach, the paper will investigate the impact that Luda has had on people's perception of AI and implications for the AI industry in general. In order to do so, a big data analysis using news articles on Luda and related comments was conducted. Combined with this quantitative analysis, a qualitative analysis covering news comments and related literature was conducted.

2 Methods

To examine the public's understanding of the Luda incident, news articles and related comments were collected from Naver which is the biggest search engine in Korea. The data collection period was from December 23rd 2020, which was the date Luda was released, to February 18th, 2021. Based on the search word "이루다 (Luda)" and "인공지능 (Artificial Intelligence)," 1,135 news articles and 27,875 comments were collected.

After preprocessing, a semantic network of the collected text data was drawn out. Furthermore, some of the keywords with higher centrality and clusters of words with statistically significant linkage in terms of co-occurrence were identified. Using centrality indices, a researcher can measure the relative importance of a word and the clusters of words can reveal certain themes that exists in the given text [6]. For centrality Bonacich Power Centrality of each word was measured and for word clustering Girvan-Newman grouping method was utilized. A natural language processing tool *Optimind*[1] was used for visualizing semantic network analysis, calculating centrality, and clustering words. Considering the different characteristics of each data set, news and comment data were analyzed separately.

3 Results

3.1 News Data

Table 1 shows the top 15 words with the highest Bonacich Power Centrality from the news data. From words such as "Data," "User," "Consent," "Collection," it is shown that the news articles mainly focused on the possible violation of personal information protection from the data collection process. To provide more details, Scatter Lab utilized Kakaotalk conversations of people to train Luda and the data was collected from their other application called the "Science of Relationship." The Science of Relationship was a paid service in which people provided their Kakaotalk data to receive an analysis report

---

[1] Optimind (Version 3.0).

on based on a specific conversation. The main debate was about whether Scatter Lab has explicitly asked for consent to the users of Science of Relationship that their data could be used for purposes other than the analysis report [7].

Table 1. Top 15 words with the highest Bonacich Power Centrality.

	Words from news articles				Words from comments		
	Words in Korean	Words in English	Bonacich Power Centrality		Words in Korean	Words in English	Bonacich Power Centrality
1	데이터	Data	556.84	9	관리	Manage	279.42
2	활용	Utilize	470.344	10	삭제	Delete	279.42
3	학습	Learning (Training)	391.91	11	사용	Use	249.233
4	수집	Collection	390.636	12	동의	Consent	238.852
5	이용	Utilization	387.242	13	중심	Center	225.846
6	이용자	User	365.231	14	때문	Because	196.955
7	출시	Launch	334.663	15	서비스	Service	193.233
8	기반	Foundation	288.198				

Figure 1 shows the group network which is the network of the word cluster extracted from the original semantic network. The result was manually translated from Korean to English. It shows the similar focus on the personal information leakage and the ongoing investigation. It can be inferred that the word "science" is from the Science of Relationship.

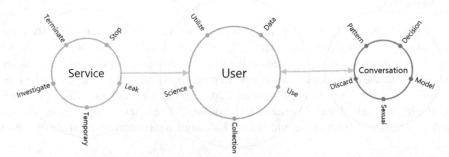

Fig. 1. Group Network from news data and the representative words from each cluster

3.2 Comments Data

Table 2 shows the top 15 words with the highest Bonacich Power Centrality from the comments data. While the comments paid more attention to the sexual harassment and hate speech than the news, one can see that the data was still the main issue in the comments as well.

Table 2. Top 15 words with the highest Bonacich Power Centrality from comments

	Words from news articles				Words from comments		
	Words in Korean	Words in English	Bonacich Power Centrality		Words in Korean	Words in English	Bonacich Power Centrality
1	사람	People	63.4183	9	대화	Conversation	15.0432
2	문제	Problem	26.4798	10	혐오	Hate	13.7887
3	데이터	Data	23.3591	11	어떻게	How	12.8472
4	생각	Think	22.808	12	윤리	Ethics	12.0432
5	성희롱	Sexual harassment	21.7091	13	범죄	Crime	11.8351
6	인권	Human right	18.7777	14	이해	Understand	11.1682
7	처벌	Punishment	18.3583	15	동성애	Homosexuality	9.92727
8	학습	Learning (Training)	17.8435				

Figure 2 shows the group network extracted from the comments data. The group network clearly shows the perception that the problem is the data and the data collected without any consent should entirely be discarded. Another topic in the group network is about granting human rights to the AI. However, the Korean word "운운", which was translated as "mention", has certain negative connotations in Korean context. Therefore, it can be seen how overall public perception is that it is absurd to give human rights to an AI.

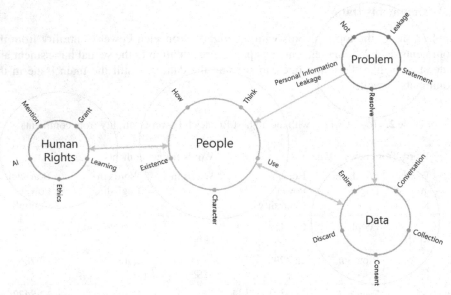

Fig. 2. Group Network from comments data and the representative words from each cluster

4 Discussion

From the analysis, it is evidently shown that the Luda incident has triggered a major concern on "data" from the public's point of view. The results implied that the concerns on the data had two aspects. One was about the legitimacy and transparency of the data collection process. The public sentiment towards the data collection for Luda was highly negative saying that the Kakaotalk conversation was collected without consent and hence needs to all be discarded. The second aspect was about the quality and the morality of the data itself which has largely been determined by the people in society. The logical framework that connected "people" with "problem" from the group network of comments data manifested the public's understanding that the problem is the people who generated such discriminatory data. The following comments illustrate this viewpoint.

- "Isn't it the people's fault from the beginning? Luda just said what she learnt from what people said."
- "AIs don't create any knowledge. They just acquire the data that people have created and hence can only acquire data full of prejudice."

One of the main reasons why people focused on the data can be explained by AI literacy, especially on machine learning. According to Long and Magerko, a "critical engagement with data and machine learning" is one of the key aspects of AI literacy [8]. To achieve that, one must recognize the human role in AI and know that the computers learn from data. Furthermore, it is important to understand that initial training data can affect the result of the algorithm. Through an extensive literature review, Long and Magerko highlighted that people should be able to "investigate who created the dataset, how the data was collected and what the limitations of the dataset were [8]." The complex ethical issues regarding Luda have encouraged the public to engage in all these three aspects and hence has elevated the public's AI literacy.

5 Conclusion

In conclusion, it is shown that the main concern of the public regarding the chatbot Luda incident was its data. People showed a negative attitude towards the data collection process of Luda and the discriminatory tendency of the data itself. The reason behind this focus on data was the enhanced AI literacy that the incident brought about. From the complex ethical issues raised by Luda, people were encouraged to actively engage in investigating the creation and collection process of the data. Moreover, Luda also provided an opportunity for the public to understand the limitations of the dataset and the resulting consequences. As a result, in order to prevent such backlash from the public in the future, the focus should not be about simply filtering words and trying to make the chatbot sound better on the superficial level. Instead, what's necessary is to engage deeper with the public discourse on AI and to contemplate how to acquire a better data set. The most basic way of doing that will be the transparent and legitimate collection of data and, ultimately, it will lead to the AI industry's responsibility to contribute to a healthier society as stated in the Asilomar AI Principles [9].

Appendix

The Original Semantic Network of News Articles

The Original Semantic Network of News Comments

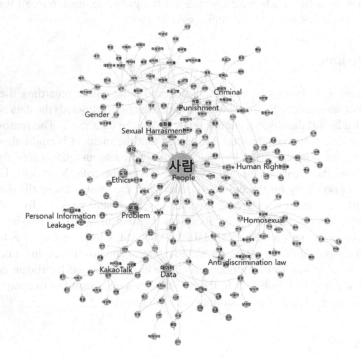

References

1. McCurry, J.: South Korean AI chatbot pulled from Facebook after hate speech towards minorities, 14 January 2021. https://www.theguardian.com/world/2021/jan/14/time-to-properly-socialise-hate-speech-ai-chatbot-pulled-from-facebook. Accessed 26 Mar 2021
2. Kim, E.: (News focus) CHATBOT Luda CONTROVERSY leave questions over AI ethics, data collection, 13 January 2021. https://en.yna.co.kr/view/AEN20210113004100320. Accessed 26 Mar 2021
3. Wolf, M.J., Miller, K.W., Grodzinsky, F.S.: Why we should have seen that coming: comments on microsoft's tay "experiment", and wider implications. ORBIT J. **1**(2), 1–12 (2017)
4. Sawers, P.: Apple and GOOGLE halt human Voice-data reviews over privacy backlash, but transparency is the real issue, 2 August 2019. https://venturebeat.com/2019/08/02/apple-and-google-halt-human-voice-data-reviews-over-privacy-backlash-but-transparency-is-the-real-issue/. Accessed 26 Mar 2021
5. Dafoe, A.: AI governance: a research agenda. Governance of AI Program, Future of Humanity Institute, University of Oxford, Oxford, UK (2018)
6. Kim, L., Kim, N.: Connecting opinion, belief and value: semantic network analysis of a UK public survey on embryonic stem cell research. J. Sci. Commun. **14**(1), A01 (2015)
7. Lokesh. Lee LUDA: A CHATBOT developed by SCATTERLAB gone wrong, social Media Rampage, 17 Feb 2021. http://www.forumgrad.com/lee-luda-a-chatbot-developed-by-scatterlab-gone-wrong-social-media-rampage/. Accessed 26 Mar 2021

8. Long, D., Magerko, B.: What is AI literacy? Competencies and design considerations. In: Proceedings of the 2020 CHI Conference on Human Factors in Computing Systems, pp. 1–16, April 2020
9. AI principles, 11 April 2018. https://futureoflife.org/ai-principles/. Accessed 26 Mar 2021

Multi-input Deep Convolutional Neural Network Based on Transfer Learning for Assisted Diagnosis of Alzheimer's Disease

Wenyuan Ling, Zhiwei Qin, Zhao Liu$^{(\boxtimes)}$, and Ping Zhu

Shanghai Jiao Tong University, Shanghai 200240, People's Republic of China
{Lingwenyuan,qinzhiwei,hotlz,pzhu}@sjtu.edu.cn

Abstract. Alzheimer's Disease is the most common form of dementia which initially impairs the memory and finally progresses to death. There is no effective treatment for this irreversible disease. The latest innovations in multimodal neuroimaging data and artificial intelligence technology made it possible to detect this disease in the early stage, which has become a major research area in neuroscience. We proposed a deep learning algorithm using pre-train Restnet50 that takes both gray matter and white matter into account which would have a potential improvement to the existing CAD methods of AD diagnosis is utilized for the classification of brain images among Cognitively Normal (CN), Early Mild Cognitive Impairment (EMCL), Late Mild Cognitive Impairment (LMCI), Alzheimer's Disease (AD), ensuring very precise and accurate diagnosis.

Keywords: Alzheimer's disease · MRI classification · Deep learning · Transfer learning · Gray matter · White matter

1 Introduction

Alzheimer's disease (AD) is a progressive neurodegenerative brain disease with memory and cognitive deterioration. It has been acknowledged to affect patients' quality of life physically and psychologically. According to a report by the Alzheimer's Association, AD has already acknowledged as the fifth-leading cause of death and its worldwide prevalence is projected to reach 60 million by 2050 [1]. There is no effective treatment of AD on the ground due to its unfathomed etiology and pathogenesis. Thus, a robust method of accurately diagnosing AD is desirable.

Previous studies have reported that the development of Alzheimer's disease is accompanied by damage to nerve cells in brain regions involved in memory and a reduction in the volume of grey matter and the hippocampus [2]. This intermediate transition between Normal and AD is acknowledged as Mild Cognitive Impairment (MCI) [3], playing an important role in early diagnosis due to its high conversion rate to AD.

Neuroimaging techniques have been employed in numerous studies [4–20] to detect pathological variations associated with AD and to predict the MCI-to-AD conversion. Common practices of dementia diagnosis are the use of MRI, PET, Computed Tomography (CT), single-photon emission computed tomography (SPECT) [5], and diffusion

© Springer Nature Switzerland AG 2021
C. Stephanidis et al. (Eds.): HCII 2021, CCIS 1420, pp. 508–514, 2021.
https://doi.org/10.1007/978-3-030-78642-7_68

tensor imaging (DTI) [6]. Magnetic Resonance Imaging (MRI) has been the most extensively employed imaging modality for its wide availability and good diagnostic accuracy with moderate cost.

Many Computer-Aided Diagnosis (CAD) systems are developed using machine learning techniques to detect the structural, functional changes in the brain and classify MRI based on their features.

2 Related Works

Machine learning methods for AD classification are mainly composed of conventional machine learning methods with precomputed medical descriptors and deep learning methods. The former methods usually extract representative features and support vector machine (SVM), random forest (RF) voxel-based morphometry (VBM) methods were widely used for MRI analysis. Risacher et al. [7] used values from segmented regions of interest (ROI) and calculated the hippocampal volumes grey matter (GM) density as input image features. Song et al. [8] extracted 93 ROIs from the MRI and PET scans and combined the multimodal features through a multi- kernel SVM in order to improve AD classification accuracy.

Deep learning algorithms, with automatic prominent feature extraction and end-to-end training, have shown broad prospects in CAD. Bijen Khagip et al. [9] employed pre-trained Alexnet CNN as a generic feature extractor of 2D images and classifying a number of patients as an AD, MCI, or NC yielding a classification accuracy of 77.62%. Blessy C Simon et al. [10] using a transfer learning approach, modified and trained three networks, namely AlexNet, ResNet-18, and GoogleNet to classify 3000 images with high accuracy. At the same time, previous work have proven that multi-modal data can provide more information to train the network. Liu et al. [11] trained a deep neural network contained auto-encoders to combine multimodal features which were extracted from 83 ROIs of PET and MRI scans.

In the processing flow of MRI, we take Luxit Kapoor's [12] method as a reference. It was initially employed in the process of detecting brain tumors in MRI images. The general steps detecting the brain regions in MRI are Pre-processing, Filtering, Segmentation, and Post-processing.

Although some methods have achieved good results in AD classification, there are still shortcomings worthy of our attention. Firstly, previous researches on the assisted diagnosis of AD mainly focus on the structural alterations in gray matter (GM). With further etiological researches on AD, a relation between white matter (WM) and AD development has been proved. Therefore, a deep learning algorithm that takes both GM and WM into account would have a potential improvement to the existing CAD methods of AD diagnosis. Secondly, EMCI and LMCI classification is a particularly difficult problem. There are a limited number of studies to investigate the effectiveness of focusing on localized MRI areas to differentiate and classify EMCI and LMCI groups of which distinction would allow early intervention.

In our work, we propose a multi-input deep convolutional neural network (CNN) with transfer learning for MRI image classification. The aim of this work is to develop a computer-based diagnosis system that provides additional support for the medical staff to support their diagnosis evidence. The proposed network will divide the image into one of the four categories: Alzheimer's Disease (AD), Early Mild Cognitive Impairment (EMCI), Late Mild Cognitive Impairment (MCI), and Normal Controls (NC), accurately predicting patients' conditions through MRI.

3 Methodology

Figure 1 illustrates the proposed framework in three phases: (1) image pre-processing stage where the entire brain MRI images are segmented into different parts, (2) feature extraction and combination stage where informative features needed for classification are extracted from the images and fused into a matrix; and (3) classification stage, where fused features are fed to classical machine learning classifier to produce the final prediction.

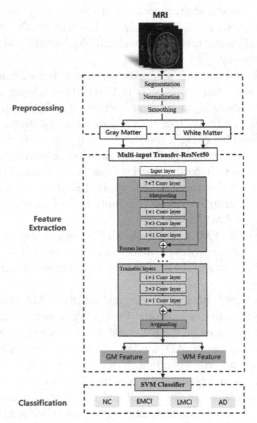

Fig. 1. Flowchart of MRI images classification process.

3.1 Data Collection

Ninety subjects from the ADNI (http://adni.loni.usc.edu/) database were selected randomly in our study, respecting roughly a 1:1:1:1 ratio (NC: EMCI: LMCI: AD). We have taken factors such as gender, education, age, and demographic characteristics into account to ensure the balance of the four types of data. The brain MRI images are collected from the ADNI datastore in DICOM format. ADNI is a multisite study that aims to improve clinical trials for the prevention and treatment of Alzheimer's Disease. A huge collection of data including MRI, fMRI, PET of various other modalities are available for all the classes of dementia (Table 1).

Table 1. Distribution of Data Set collected from ADNI.

NC	EMCI	LMCI	AD
23	22	21	24

3.2 Preprocessing

The main intention of preprocessing methods is to remove error removed and to enhance the brain MR Image. Pre-processing can be subdivided into 4 periods: brain extraction, skull removal from MR images, image enhancement, and data amplification. The first three steps can be done using SPM in MATLAB. With the help of standard ADNI pipeline, brain MR Image enhancement. Correction of gradient warping and B1 nonuniformity are done as post-acquisition. Finally, The raw MRI images are preprocessed and segmented into three parts: grey matter (GM), white matter (WM), and cerebrospinal fluid (CSF). Skull stripping is performed to remove non-brain tissues.

In addition, we used 2D sagittal MRI slices as network input for data enhancement. About 200 sagittal slices can be segmented by MRI, from which 20–30 slices are selected to form the data set (Figs. 2 and 3).

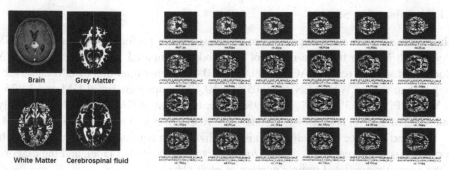

Fig. 2. Pre-processed brain images

Fig. 3. Expanded data set from MRI slices

3.3 Feature Selection and Classification

By comparing the performance of GoogleNet, VGG, and Resnet on the dataset, we finally chose the pre-trained Resnet50 to extract the image features. The traditional convolutional network or fully connected network will have the problems of information loss and loss when information is transmitted, and it will lead to gradient disappearance or gradient explosion so that the deep network cannot be trained. ResNet solves this problem to a certain extent, by directly transferring the input information to the output and protecting the integrity of the information, the whole network only needs to learn the part of the difference between the input and the output, thus simplifying the learning goal and the difficulty. ResNet50 has two basic blocks, named Conv Block and Identity Block, where the input and output dimensions of the Conv Block are different, so they cannot be concatenated, its role is to change the network dimension; the input and output dimensions of the Identity Block are the same, that can be connected in series to deepen the network.

We build resnet-gray model and resnet_white model to capture features of GM and WM simultaneously for training. The feature extraction model is based on a pre-trained Resnet50 with transfer learning and expanded to a double-channel architecture to adapt for multiple types of inputs. The features extracted from images of both GM and WM are combined to provide more comprehensive information for classification. Ultimately, the SVM classifier outputs the predicted categories of the MRI images.

In the experiment, gray matter and white matter were input separately for feature extraction and classification. Then we use multi-input features from gray matter and white matter to classify the same dataset and compare the results. The classification and efficiency of single feature and multi-input feature are compared from Accuracy (ACC), Sensitivity (SEN), Specificity (SPE), and Area under the receiver operating characteristic curve (AUC). In this work, the same set of options are set for all the networks so that the comparison can be performed specifically for the different network architectures with the same set of parameters and the same set of data. The mini-batch size is set as 50 and all the networks are trained up to 15 epochs.

4 Results

4.1 A Subsection Sample

The result shows a clear improvement of classification performance when using GM along with WM as multiple inputs of the model, compared with using GM or WM alone. GM + WM reaches ACC of 99.05%, 10.4% higher than that of GM and 11.2% higher than that of WM; SEN of 99.05%, a 10.42% improvement of GM and 11.25% of WM; SPE of 99.3%, 9.3%, and 3.9% higher than that of GM and WM respectively; and AUC of 99.9%, increases 2.1% and 1.6% respectively compared to GM and WM.

The performance of the algorithm is visualized by a confusion matrix, in which the vertical axis is the real label, the horizontal axis is the predicted label, and the diagonal is the correctly predicted sample number of each class.

Table 2 shows the comparison between this paper and other published results. In our paper, we have done the classification of 4 classes whereas most of the paper focused on 3 class problems. Still, our classification results of the 4 classes are comparable or better than the published results (Fig. 4).

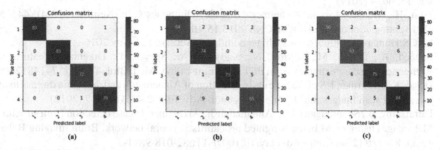

Fig. 4. (a) Confusion matrix of GM + WM training (b) Confusion matrix of GM training (c) Confusion matrix of WM training

Table 2. Comparing the proposed model with different models.

Feature types	ACC (%)	SEN (%)	SPE (%)
GM + WM	97.047	95.048	96.689
GM	88.621	88.620	96.190
WM	87.803	87.802	95.896
Madusanka [13]	86.633	84.212	86.242
Choi [14]	92.300	93.300	91.100
Hosseini-Asl E [15]	89.117	88.300	89.115

5   Conclusion

In this study, the deep learning method is utilized for the classification of different classes of Alzheimer's disease under the method of transfer learning. Based on the comparison and evaluation of related work done to classify Alzheimer's disease, the proposed method could substantially improve the accuracy of the diagnosis of AD by making full use of the features extracted from both gray matter and white matter. We demonstrate with our contribution that the proposed model outperforms the previous methods in all four classification tasks. The ability to diagnose and classify AD and MCI at an early stage enables clinicians to make more informed decisions at later stages for clinical intervention and treatment planning. The application of the computer-aided diagnosis system of AD will be highly possible in the future, which can greatly reduce the risk of AD and improve the quality of the elderly's life.

References

1. Alzheimer's Association: 2017 Alzheimer's disease facts and figures. Alzheimer's Dementia, vol. 13, no. 4 (2017)
2. Jahn, H.: Memory loss in Alzheimer's disease. Dialogues Clin. Neurosci. **15**(4), 445–54 (2013).https://doi.org/10.31887/DCNS.2013.15.4/hjahn
3. LNCS Homepage. http://www.springer.com/lncs. Accessed 21 Nov 2016
4. Sayeed, A., Petrou, M., Spyrou, N., Kadyrov, A., Spinks, T.: Diagnostic features of Alzheimer's disease extracted from PET sinograms. Phys. Med. Biol. **47**(1), 137–148 (2002)
5. Desai, K.D., Parmar, P.S.: Effective early detection of Alzheimer's and dementia disease using brain MRI scan images. Int. J. Emerg. Technol. Adv. Eng. **2**(4), 414–417 (2012)
6. Duraisamy, B., Shanmugam, J.V., Annamalai, J.: Alzheimer disease detection from structural MR images using FCM based weighted probabilistic neural network. Brain Imaging Behav. **13**(1), 87–110 (2018). https://doi.org/10.1007/s11682-018-9831-2
7. Risacher, S.L., Saykin, A.J., Wes, J.D., Shen, L., Firpi, H.A., McDonald, B.C.: Baseline MRI predictors of conversion from MCI to probable AD in the ADNI cohort. Curr. Alzheimer Res. **6**(4), 347–361 (2009)
8. Zhang, F., et al.: Semantic association for neuroimaging classification of PET images. J. Nuclear Med. **55**(Suppl. 1), 2029–2029 (2014)
9. Khagi, B., Lee, C.G., Kwon, G.: Alzheimer's disease classification from brain MRI based on transfer learning from CNN. In: 2018 11th Biomedical Engineering International Conference (BMEiCON), Chiang Mai, Thailand, pp. 1–4 (2018). https://doi.org/10.1109/BMEiCON.2018.8609974
10. Simon, B.C., Baskar, D., Jayanthi, V.S.: Alzheimer's disease classification using deep convolutional neural network. In: 2019 9th International Conference on Advances in Computing and Communication (ICACC), Kochi, India, pp. 204–208 (2019). https://doi.org/10.1109/ICACC48162.2019.8986170
11. Liu, S., et al.: Multimodal neuroimaging feature learning for multiclass diagnosis of Alzheimer's disease. IEEE Trans. Biomed. Eng. **62**(4), 1132–1140 (2015)
12. Kapoor, L., Thakur, S.: A survey on brain tumor detection using image processing techniques. In: 7th International Conference on Cloud Computing, Data Science & Engineering (2017)
13. Madusanka, N., Choi, H.K., So, J.H., et al.: Alzheimer's disease classification based on multi-feature fusion. Curr. Med. Imaging Rev. **15**(2), 161–169 (2018)
14. Choi, B.K., et al.: Convolutional neural network-based MR image analysis for Alzheimer's disease classification. Curr. Med Imaging Rev. **16**(1), 27–35 (2020). https://doi.org/10.2174/1573405615666191021123854. PMID: 31989891
15. Hosseini-Asl, E., Keynton, R., El-Baz, A.: Alzheimer's disease diagnostics by adaptation of 3D convolutional network. In: 2016 IEEE International Conference on Image Processing (ICIP), pp. 126–130. IEEE (2016)
16. Goceri, E., Songul, C.: Biomedical information technology: image based computer aided diagnosis systems. In: International Conference on Advanced Technologies, Antalaya, Turkey (2018)
17. Gocer, E.: Diagnosis of Alzheimer's disease with sobolev gradient based optimization and 3D convolutional neural network. J. Numer. Methods Biomed. Eng. **35**(7), e3225 (2019)
18. Goceri, E.: Fully automated classification of brain tumors using capsules for Alzheimer's disease diagnosis. IET Image Process (2019)
19. Goceri, E., Songül, C.: Computer-based segmentation, change detection and quantification for lesions in multiple sclerosis 2017. In: International Conference on Computer Science and Engineering (UBMK) Antalya, Antalya, Turkey, 5–7 October 2017, pp. 177–182 (2017)
20. Kim, J.P., et al.: Machine learning based hierarchical classification of frontotemporal dementia and Alzheimer's disease. Neuroimage Clin. **23**, 101811 (2019)

Rheumatism Information Extraction from Electronic Medical Records Using Deep Learning Approach

Ning Liu[1], NanNan Gai[2(✉)], and Zhao Huang[1]

[1] School of Computer Science, ShaanXi Normal University, Xi'an 710119, People's Republic of China
{ningliu,zhaohuang}@snnu.edu.cn
[2] Xi'an No. Five Hospital, Xi'an 710119, People's Republic of China

Abstract. With the increasing adoption of Electronic Medical Records (EMRs) system, how to extract and use the medical data resources stored in the EMR is starting to attract the attention of researchers. Recently, Natural language processing (NLP) has been used as a common method to process text information in the EMR, which can also be used for Text categorization, Sentiment analysis, Word segmentation, Part-of-speech tagging, etc. Named Entity Recognition (NER) is the primary task of NLP, which can effectively identify valuable information in the text. For these reasons, this work aims to explore the NER model in the field of Rheumatism and the influence of text annotation methods on the performance of NER model. The results show that having compared with four different deep learning models, our proposed approach has achieved the higher level of accuracy. In addition, we found that the reduction of annotation types can improve the performance of the NER model applied to Rheumatism.

Keywords: Named entity recognition · Deep learning · Electronic medical records · Rheumatism

1 Introduction

Patients with Rheumatic Diseases (RD) have various symptoms. Some symptoms are quite similar with other diseases, such as mouth sores, skin conditions, which may lead to misdiagnosis. Therefore, there is a need to establish a rheumatism knowledge base to assist physicians to obtain more precise information about RD, so as to reduce the rate of misdiagnosis and the burden of physicians.

In recent years, the adoption of the EMR is gradually increasing, replacing the traditional paper records in a large number of health care organizations and hospitals. Physicians enter a variety of patient medical information into the EMR during the treatment process, such as the patients' physical examination, symptom description, the diagnosis results and treatment approaches [1]. Therefore, these abundant medical data resources stored in the EMR can be used for the construction of rheumatism knowledge base,

© Springer Nature Switzerland AG 2021
C. Stephanidis et al. (Eds.): HCII 2021, CCIS 1420, pp. 515–522, 2021.
https://doi.org/10.1007/978-3-030-78642-7_69

which can provide deeper insight into patient treatment. However, most of the data are unstructured, and it is difficult to extract effective information directly from these data.

To overcome this challenge, researchers find that NLP can be used to analyze unstructured text information and extract useful information [2]. NLP has many tasks, such as feature extraction, sequential labeling tasks [3], among which NER is considered a primary clinical NLP task [4]. A variety of NER methods has been used in practices, such as rule-based methods, statistics-based methods, and machine learning methods [5]. Recently, since the power of deep learning has been recognized in aspect of learning ability, it has attracted the attention of researchers, which is widely applied in the field of clinical NER and shows its great performance [6].

The main purpose of this study is to explore which combination of deep learning model and CRF model is more suitable for identifying rheumatic-related entities from EMR, so as to help establish a rheumatic knowledge base. The study uses the popular Long Short-Term Memory (LSTM), Gated Recurrent Unit (GRU) and their variants are combined with the CRF model. The Root Mean Square Prop (RMSprop) algorithm was used to optimize the performance of these models. By comparing the performance of these hybrid models, the results show that a NER model is suitable for rheumatism. Besides, we compared the effects of two different annotation methods on NER model training, and found that the change in the number of text annotation categories would have an impact on the performance of NER model.

2 Methods

2.1 LSTM and GRU

The LSTM model is a special Recurrent Neural Networks (RNN) model. RNN is a network for modeling sequence data, which can store text information and effectively reduce local dependencies. However, the model has the weakness of vanishing gradients. In order to improve this weakness, Hochreiter and Schmidhuber [7] proposed LSTM model. The LSTM model can effectively deal with the long-distance dependence problem by continuously updating the memory cell through the input gate and forget gate.

Later, the GRU model was proposed, and its structure was simpler than LSTM [8]. The input gate and forget gate of GRU model are combined into update gate, and the tasks of passing information and forgetting information can be handled by a unit. Therefore, the model needs fewer parameters and shorter time to train.

2.2 BiLSTM and BiGRU

Because the data transmission in the LSTM and GRU models is unidirectional, only the information from the past can be obtained. However, in order to label the characters in the sentence correctly, it is necessary to obtain the contextual information. The Bidirectional Long Short-Term Memory (BiLSTM) and Bidirectional Gated Recurrent Unit (BiGRU) are proposed to capture contextual information from both directions (i.e., forward and backward) [9, 10].

2.3 Deep Learning Model and CRF

CRF has the powerful inference ability and can make full use of contextual information, such as words and sentences as features to support the model to obtain abundant information. If the CRF model and the deep learning model are combined into a hybrid model, this hybrid model will check the contextual consistency while predicting the label, thereby improving the accuracy of the model annotation results.

2.4 RMSprop

RMSprop is an optimization algorithm proposed by Hinton. It is an extension of the stochastic gradient descent algorithm, which can solve the problem of vanishing learning rates. The formula used in the RMSprop algorithm is as follows [11].

$$v_t = \rho v_{t-1} + (1-\rho)g_t^2 \tag{1}$$

$$\omega_{t+1} = \omega_t + \Delta\omega_t = \omega_t - \frac{\lambda}{\sqrt{v_t + \epsilon}}g_t \tag{2}$$

where v_t is the exponential average of squares of gradients. g_t is the gradient at time t. λ is the initial learning rate.

3 Experiment

3.1 Dataset

The dataset used in our experiment is collected from Xi'an No. Five Hospital, which contains 143 rheumatism patients. The dataset is randomly divided into 70% training set (including 100 patients) and 30% testing set (including 43 patients).

3.2 Text Filtering

The dataset contains relevant medical records of patients, but some contents are not useful in this study. Therefore, there is a need to filter data manually, mainly including the following two aspects:

Delete Wrong Data. When there are too many patients, it will make physicians suffer from cognitive overload, which may cause them to input wrong sentences into EMR. For example, "双侧4字征阳性"is incorrectly entered as "双侧4字征阳性性". These wrong sentences will affect the accuracy of NER, so we need to delete these wrong sentences in advance.

Delete Irrelevant Data. EMR contains some basic information of the patient, such as name, phone number. This information has nothing to do with the diagnosis of rheumatism. Hence, these privacy-related data need to be manually removed, leaving primary data about the RD.

3.3 Data Annotation

With the professional guidance of rheumatologists, the data of EMR are partitioned into four types: clinical symptoms, physical examinations, diagnosis results, and disease treatments. To refine the data in the rheumatology knowledge base, as shown in Table 1, we divide these four types into eight categories of clinical named entity.

Table 1. The definition and corresponding examples of eight entities

Entity	Definition	Example
DescriptionSign	The feeling of clinical symptoms	关节肿胀 (Joint Swelling)
PositionSign	The location of clinical symptoms	膝盖 (Knees)
DegreeSign	The degree of clinical symptoms	轻度关节肿胀 (Mild Joint Swelling)
ItemTest	The name of the general examinations	血沉 (Erythrocyte Sedimentation Rate (ESR))
ResultTest	The result of general examinations	N% 80.5%
TypeDisease	The name of the disease	类风湿关节炎 (Rheumatoid Arthritis)
DegreeDisease	The severity of the disease	轻度类风湿关节炎 (Mild Rheumatoid Arthritis)
DrugsDisease	The information of drugs given by the physician, including the method of taking drugs, adverse reactions, etc.	一日三次 (Three Times A Day)

Table 2. An example of the annotated sequence

Sentence	Annotated results
患者自诉于3月前无明显诱因出现颈椎、双肩关节疼痛，活动受限。 (The patient said that three months ago, he had pain in the cervical spine and shoulder joints without reason, and felt restrained when moving these parts.)	患(O)者(O)自(O)诉(O)于(O)3(O)月(O)前(O)无(O)明(O)显(O)诱(O)因(O)出(O)现(O)颈(B-PositionSign)椎(E-PositionSign)、(O)双(B-PositionSign)肩(I-PositionSign)关(I-PositionSign)节(E-PositionSign)疼(B-DescriptionSign)痛(E-DescriptionSign)，(O)活(B-DescriptionSign)动(I-DescriptionSign)受(I-DescriptionSign)限(E-DescriptionSign)。(O)

We label each Chinese character in the dataset using BIOES (i.e., Begin, Inside, Outside, End, and Single) labeling method. An example of the annotated sequence is shown in Table 2. There are three stages for text annotation process. In the first stage, we randomly select some samples for labeling to determine the annotation rules. Then, all data are manually labeled based on the established annotation rules. The last stage is to check the annotated results and modify the errors.

3.4 Comparison of NER Methods

Performance Metrics. In this experiment, the loss function and accuracy are used as the performance metrics of these NER models.

Loss function can be used to calculate the inconsistency between the predicted value and the true value. The smaller the loss rate, the better the annotation performance of the model.

Accuracy is the ratio of the number of samples correctly classified by the classification model (including positive and negative samples) and the total number of samples. In this experiment, it refers to the proportion of correct text annotation.

Results and Discussions. We use Python to implement NER models for rheumatism, and combines the RMSprop algorithm to optimize these model's performance. Table 3 summarizes the comparison results of the implemented RMS-LSTM-CRF, RMS-GRU-CRF, RMS-BiLSTM-CRF, and RMS-BiGRU-CRF on the testing set. From the left side of Table 3, we can draw the following conclusions.

The performance of RMS-GRU-CRF model is better than the RMS-LSTM-CRF model, and the RMS-BiGRU-CRF model outperforms the RMS-BiLSTM-CRF model. The experimental result proves that whether the structure of the model is unidirectional or bidirectional, the GRU model always performs better than LSTM in rheumatism NER.

The latter two bidirectional models can achieve higher accuracy and lower loss rate. For the clinical data of rheumatism patients, the same characters in different sentences represent different entity. For example, the entity types of " 关节(joints)" in the " 右肩关节压痛(right shoulder joint is tendered)" and " 类风湿关节炎(rheumatoid arthritis)" are PositionSign and TypeDisease respectively. In order to correctly label the " 关节(joints)" in different sentences, the NER model needs to have the ability to understand the semantics of sentences. As a result, the accuracy of the latter two models with better ability to obtain contextual information is higher.

Table 3. The comparison results on the testing set

Methods	BIOES		BIO	
	Loss (%)	Accuracy (%)	Loss (%)	Accuracy (%)
RMS-LSTM-CRF	47.04	87.06	37.59	90.67
RMS-GRU-CRF	39.14	89.78	37.53	91.48
RMS-BiLSTM-CRF	33.62	92.05	24.69	93.15
RMS-BiGRU-CRF	33.45	93.12	22.06	94.77

3.5 Comparison of Labeling Patterns

In addition to BIOES, there is a common labeling patterns BIO (Begin, Inside, and Outside). In principle, compared with BIOES, BIO only needs to label three types of word. For instance, a single character is no longer labeled as S, but is regarded as the beginning of a word and labeled as B. In other words, using BIO annotation method may make it easier for the model to predict the entity types of the character.

The second experiment is to verify whether the change of annotation types will affect the performance of the NER model. We label the dataset using the BIO labeling patterns and train all models again. In order to further demonstrate the effect of two different annotation methods, we choose best-performing RMS-BiGRU-CRF model to label text. Table 4 shows the comparison between the model labeling and manual labeling after training with different labeling patterns.

It can be found from Table 3 that the loss rate of all models decreases and the accuracy increases after using the BIO annotation method. Especially for the first two models, the accuracy increases significantly. Table 4 shows that the RMS-BiGRU-CRF model trained using the BIO predicts fewer wrong annotations, and the error rate is reduced from 20% to 6%. These experimental results confirm that in this work, the fewer annotation types in the dataset, the better the performance of the trained NER model.

Table 4. The comparison of model labeling with manual labeling

Text	True (BIOES)	Predict (BIOES)	True (BIO)	Predict (BIO)
双	B-PositionSign	B-PositionSign	B-PositionSign	B-PositionSign
上	I-PositionSign	I-PositionSign	I-PositionSign	I-PositionSign
肢	I-PositionSign	I-PositionSign	I-PositionSign	I-PositionSign
肌	I-PositionSign	I-PositionSign	I-PositionSign	I-PositionSign
肉	E-PositionSign	E-PositionSign	I-PositionSign	I-CheckResult
无	S-DegreeSign	S-DegreeSign	B-DegreeSign	B-DegreeSign
压	B-DescriptionSign	B-Description-Sign	B-DescriptionSign	B-DescriptionSign
痛	E-DescriptionSign	E-DescriptionSign	I-DescriptionSign	I-DescriptionSign
…	…	…	…	…
双	B-PositionSign	B-PositionSign	B-PositionSign	B-PositionSign
膝	E-PositionSign	E-PositionSign	I-PositionSign	I-PositionSign
活	B-DescriptionSign	B-Description-Sign	B-DescriptionSign	B-DescriptionSign
动	I-DescriptionSign	E-DescriptionSign	I-DescriptionSign	I-DescriptionSign
正	I-DescriptionSign	I-CheckResult	I-DescriptionSign	I-DescriptionSign
常	E-DescriptionSign	E-CheckResult	I-DescriptionSign	I-DescriptionSign
。	O	O	O	O

4 Conclusion

In this study, we compared four different NER models and two different labeling patterns based on rheumatism data stored in EMR. We found that the RMS-BiGRU-CRF model trained using the BIO annotation method is more suitable for rheumatism NER. The experimental results indicate that the performance of the NER model can be enhanced with the growth of the ability to obtain contextual information. In addition, for rheumatism NER, the performance of the NER model would be increased if the annotation types of the labeling patterns were reduced.

The purpose of this study to explore a suitable method for identifying disease symptoms, diagnosis results and other information of rheumatism patients' medical record. This is the preparation for the construction of knowledge base. And our future tasks are using the implemented hybrid model to extract the information from EMR, and determining the correct correspondence between diseases and symptoms. Finally, we will construct a rheumatism knowledge base to assist physicians in diagnosing RD, so as to improve the level of medical services.

Acknowledgments. This work was supported by the National Natural Science Foundation of China (Grant No. 61771297).

References

1. Bhatia, P., Busra Celikkaya, E., Khalilia, M.: End-to-end joint entity extraction and negation detection for clinical text. In: Shaban-Nejad, A., Michalowski, M. (eds.) W3PHAI 2019. SCI, vol. 843, pp. 139–148. Springer, Cham (2020). https://doi.org/10.1007/978-3-030-24409-5_13
2. Sung, S.-F., Chen, K., Wu, D.P., Hung, L.-C., Su, Y.-H., Hu, Y.-H.: Applying natural language processing techniques to develop a task-specific EMR interface for timely stroke thrombolysis: a feasibility study. Int. J. Med. Inform. **112**, 149–157 (2018)
3. Zhou, M., Duan, N., Liu, S., Shum, H.-Y.: Progress in neural NLP: modeling, learning, and reasoning. Eng. (Beijing) **6**, 275–290 (2020)
4. Lee, W., Kim, K., Lee, E.Y., Choi, J.: Conditional random fields for clinical named entity recognition: a comparative study using Korean clinical texts. Comput. Biol. Med. **101**, 7–14 (2018)
5. Yin, M., Mou, C., Xiong, K., Ren, J.: Chinese clinical named entity recognition with radical-level feature and self-attention mechanism. J. Biomed. Inform. **98**, 103289 (2019)
6. Zhao, S., Cai, Z., Chen, H., Wang, Y., Liu, F., Liu, A.: Adversarial training based lattice LSTM for Chinese clinical named entity recognition. J. Biomed. Inform. **99**, 103290 (2019)
7. Hochreiter, S., Schmidhuber, J.: Long short-term memory. Neural Comput. **9**, 1735–1780 (1997)
8. Morchid, M.: Parsimonious memory unit for recurrent neural networks with application to natural language processing. Neurocomputing **314**, 48–64 (2018)
9. Liu, G., Guo, J.: Bidirectional LSTM with attention mechanism and convolutional layer for text classification. Neurocomputing **337**, 325–338 (2019)

10. Zhu, Q., Zhang, F., Liu, S., Wu, Y., Wang, L.: A hybrid VMD–BiGRU model for rubber futures time series forecasting. Appl. Soft Comput. **84**, 105739 (2019)
11. Huk, M.: Stochastic optimization of contextual neural networks with RMSprop. In: Nguyen, N.T., Jearanaitanakij, K., Selamat, A., Trawiński, B., Chittayasothorn, S. (eds.) ACIIDS 2020. LNCS (LNAI), vol. 12034, pp. 343–352. Springer, Cham (2020). https://doi.org/10.1007/978-3-030-42058-1_29

AI Facilitator Allows Participants to Conduct a Friendly Discussion and Contribute to Feasible Proposals

Tatsuya Oyama, Chihiro Sasaki, Chika Oshima(✉), and Koichi Nakayama

Saga University, Saga 840-8502, Japan
karin27@sa3.so-net.ne.jp, knakayama@is.saga-u.ac.jp

Abstract. This paper added an AI facilitator function to a discussion board system (DBS) for the purpose of guiding a discussion in an appropriate direction. Each participant who uses the DBS on their individual screen can express their own opinions by moving words to boxes made for each item to be discussed. The improved DBS (ver. 2.1) presented comments to those participants who had not spoken or operated any words on the screen for a designated period of time. When all participants in the discussion placed the same word in the same box, the word color changed to green. Here, four participants held an online discussion with their cameras off using DBS ver. 2.1. The results of a questionnaire showed that the prompts from DBS encouraged the participants to talk and add the words to the boxes. The sight of the green-colored text gave participants a feeling of pleasure, knowing that the other participants agreed with their opinion. Contrary to the experimenter's hypothesis, there were no disagreements, because all participants recognized an idea as "excellent." However, the idea came to be a realistic and immediately feasible proposal, because the participants discussed it by asking each other whether they had placed the same word in the same box, although the underlying assumption of DBS is that the participants will not disclose to each other the words they put into the boxes.

Keywords: DBS · Decision making · Online discussion

1 Introduction

Peer pressure [1] can occur easily in discussions. A person serving as a facilitator may guide such discussions, to ensure they run smoothly and in an appropriate direction. The functions of a facilitator can be roughly divided as follows [2]:

Function 1: Provide objectives and deliverables and design an optimal process for discussion.
Function 2: Prevent emotional conflict among discussion participants and avoid the "pitfalls of groupthink."
Function 3: Inspire discussion by asking questions or by using a guiding framework.

© Springer Nature Switzerland AG 2021
C. Stephanidis et al. (Eds.): HCII 2021, CCIS 1420, pp. 523–530, 2021.
https://doi.org/10.1007/978-3-030-78642-7_70

Function 4: Increase participants' faith in the results of the discussion and build consensus.

The Discussion Board System (DBS) [3, 4] was developed to help realize the facilitator's functions. To achieve Function 1, DBS ver. 1.0 displayed boxes, which were made for each item to be discussed. To address Function 2, a screen is provided so that none of the participants can see each other. DBS extracts words from the participants' utterances, and each participant may express their own opinions by moving the words into boxes as they see fit. Most discussion support systems allow participants to share their opinions, often through keywords of conversations that are represented in a two-dimensional space [5], or by voicing opinions in online discussions [6], and ideas that might be buried are displayed in text chat [7]. After the discussion, the DBS can also reveal the words in the boxes (each participant's opinions), although without disclosing when and who put each word into the box. Therefore, this box area can be considered a "semi-personal space" [3].

The results of an experiment using DBS ver. 1.0 suggested that the boxes allow participants to decide on the final conclusion of the items to be discussed within a set time. Moreover, there were differences between the words in the boxes on each participant's screen and the words they considered to be "the conclusion of this discussion." This result suggested that semi-personal space was effective for reducing peer pressure [3]. By contrast, participants did not always speak using the words in the boxes to reveal their individual opinions. This was necessary for achieving Function 3.

With the above in mind, an artificial intelligence (AI) facilitator was implemented in DBS ver. 2.0 [4]. This newer version automatically displays comments that encourage participants to voice their opinions. When all participants put the same word in the same box, the display color for the word changes to green. The results of an experiment using DBS ver. 2.0 suggested that the comments were a trigger to speak and/or move the words on the screen. In contrast, after the word turned green, one of the participants deleted the word from the box on his screen. Hence, the DBS was necessary for reconfirming with each participant whether or not they agreed with the word changing to green. The results indicated that the contents of the comments offered by the AI should be improved to encourage participants to share their opinions more.

This paper proposes DBS ver. 2.1, which improves the AI comments and adds a function to reconfirm participants' views on the agreed words. These improvements can realize Function 4. The overall usability of the system is also improved with this version.

2   Discussion Board System ver. 2.1

2.1   Basic Design

Figure 1 indicates a display of DBS ver. 2.1. As in DBS ver. 1.0 and 2.0 [3, 4], the boxes made for each item to be discussed are displayed in a category area (Function 1). The participants can know the progress of the discussion by the accumulation status of the words in the boxes.

Participants cannot see each other's category areas (Function 2), therefore each is free to express their own opinions by moving the words into boxes as they see fit.

The comment area presents the comments as text information; this is a revision from DBS ver. 2.0 (Function 3). Moreover, an animation AI character speaks these comments using Web Speech API with some behaviors. The comments, in particular, encourage those participants who have not spoken or moved any words on the screen for a certain period of time to join in the discussion. At the beginning of the discussion, DBS 2.1 shows the comments, which indicate the items to be discussed in the AI character's voice.

If all participants in the discussion add the same word to the same box, the word's color changes to green (Function 4). The participants can then know that the other participants agreed with the word. DBS 2.1 adds a dialog box for each participant to reconfirm whether or not they agree with the word's placement in the box.

The parking area allows a participant to add any word they are considering adding to the box. Those words that someone puts into the box are also displayed in the parking area.

A timer in the upper left corner of the screen shows the time remaining for the discussion.

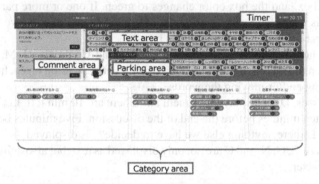

Fig. 1. Display of discussion board system ver. 2.1 (Color figure online)

2.2 Extracting and Displaying Words

When the discussion starts, DBS extracts the words from participants' utterances and displays them in the text area. All participants see the same words in the text area of each screen. The utterances are recognized and translated into text data using Speech Recognition, a Web speech API. The text data are parsed using kuromoji.js, a Japanese morphological analysis engine, or a named entity extraction API. Then, DBS extracts words from the text data. These words include nouns and groups of nouns connected by adnominal particles. For example, "no," in Japanese, is an adnominal particle that connects two nouns, as in "*kyozai no kenkyu* (study of teaching materials)," "*ane no kuruma* (my sister's car)." The extracted words are sent to and registered on a server. DBS inquires of the server at a certain interval. If a new word is found, DBS acquires and displays the word on each participant's screen. A text create function also allows the participants to add words themselves.

2.3 Display Comments

DBS 2.1 can display nine comments (A–I) during the discussion. At the beginning of the discussion, before transitioning to the screen shown in Fig. 1, DBS shows the theme of the discussion, the number of items to be decided, and the limited time (Comment A).

Figure 2 shows an algorithm indicating Comments B–D. These comments are displayed on the screens of all participants at regular intervals.

When all participants add the same word to the same box, the word's color changes to green. Then, Comment E, "All participants added [*applicable word*] to [*applicable box*]. Do you agree/disagree with this word?" is shown in a dialog box. When all participants agree with the word, a check mark appears to its left. If one or more participants disagrees with this word, DBS delivers Comment F, "Would you like to give your opinion concerning this word?" above the applicable box.

When all participants press the confirm button of a box including some words, Comment G, "Is [*applicable box*] decided?" appears in a dialog box. When all participants agree with this box, DBS displays Comment H, "This box has been decided" above the applicable box, and the box color changes to green. If one or more participants disagrees with this word, DBS displays Comment I, "Would you like to give your opinion concerning this box?" above the applicable box.

Figures 3 and 4 show the algorithms for indicating Comments J–M. These comments appear on the screen of the applicable participant depending on each participant's situation, talking and/or moving the words.

As time passes, DBS displays Comment N, "There are 10 min left. Let's summarize our opinions" ten minutes before the end of the discussion. Five minutes before the end, Comment O, "Is there anything else we have to decide?" is displayed.

Comments A, E, G, N, and O are not only displayed as text, but also delivered audibly by the AI character.

3 Experiment

3.1 Aim

This section examines the usefulness of the facilitator function implemented in DBS ver. 2.1.

3.2 Method

Four third-year university students (Participants E–H) participated in an experiment. One was female, the other three were male. They were paid a small reward to compensate for their time. All participants connected to DBS ver. 2.1 from their own personal computers at home. They could hold voice conversations using Microsoft Teams, but could not see each other's faces. DBS was always displayed on their computer screen. The screen and audio of each participant was recorded using DemoCreator software.

The subject for the discussion was "planning a memorable and moving program for a kindergarten graduation," a fictional scenario. The conditions were as follows: the preparation period was 3 weeks from today, the budget was 20,000 yen, the audience was 20 children aged 5 to 6 (10 girls and boys each), the time of the program is 15–30 min, the location is on the premises of the kindergarten, and the performers are the four discussion participants. The items to be decided during the discussion were: the program theme, the time of the performance, things to have ready, role divisions, and precautions. In addition, secret information that differed among participants was supplied. For example, one piece of information was "The teachers' program is a magic show."

After the discussion, the participants answered a questionnaire.

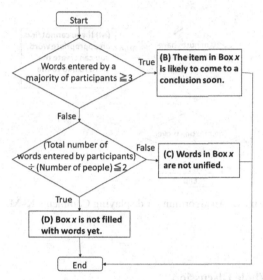

Fig. 2. An algorithm for displaying Comments B–D.

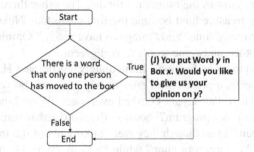

Fig. 3. An algorithm for displaying Comment J.

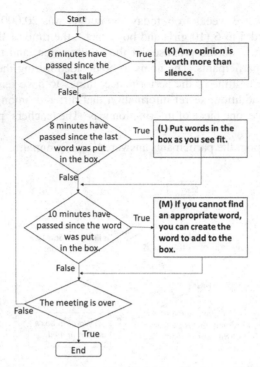

Fig. 4. An algorithm for displaying Comments K–M.

4 Results

4.1 Flow of the Whole Discussion

When the experiment began, the discussion did not start easily. After 16 min, Participant F proposed a treasure hunt as the program's theme. The other three verbally expressed their agreement. The treasure hunt became the first candidate. Next, they moved on to the topics of "performance time" and "things to have ready." Opinions for these topics were proposed smoothly, and some words turned green.

Next, they moved to "role division." Immediately, Participant H proposed "a person who goes to buy sweets, a person who goes to buy a picture book, and a person who makes a voucher." Then, Participant G asked everyone, "What kind of words did you put in the box for 'what is a program?' because the word *Takarasagashi* (treasure hunt) had not tuned to green," even though they were talking about the treasure hunt. Participant F answered "like a treasure hunt," while Participants E, G, and H had answered "takarasagashi."

When they decided on the role divisions, Participant G added his own name using the character input function. Then, Participant F was asked to make new words by other participants, even though this function was available to all participants.

Finally, their discussion moved to the item "precautions." All items that needed to be discussed were addressed before the time limit was reached.

4.2 Moving Words into Boxes

Participants F, G, and H placed the same 13 words in the boxes. Participant E placed the same words in the box for 13 out of 14 words. The participants moved the same words at almost the same time.

4.3 Questionnaire Results

Due to space limitations, answers to only a few of all questions are shown. When the comments were displayed, the participants' thoughts were as follows:

- It was a good chance to break the ice.
- I thought that we should summarize the discussion.
- I thought that I have to say something.
- I thought that I have to move the words to the boxes.
- When I tried to express my opinion or listen to the opinions of others, the AI character spoke, and I lost my concentration.

When Comment E, "Do you agree/disagree with this word?" was displayed, the participants thoughts were as follows:

- I lost my concentration.
- I think that this comment was not necessary, because the word had already been judged once as an agreement.
- After displaying the comment, I pressed the "agree" button without thinking too much because I decided to agree with the word.

The results of questionnaire made clear that each participant agreed with the conclusions of the discussion. Some participants answered that the reason why everyone agreed with the overall conclusion was that a "treasure hunt" was an excellent idea. One of the participants evaluated that the idea as very realistic, in terms of time, money, and personnel. Furthermore, the participants were able to discuss the idea until it was ready for action.

5 Discussion

An original specification of DBS was that each participant would be able to move the words according to their own opinions on their own screen, which could not be seen by other participants (a semi-personal space). However, in this experiment, there were many cases in which a participant asked the others about their actions, such as, "What did you put in the box of [applicable box]?" and "Would you create an additional word, [applicable word]?".

There are several possible reasons for these unexpected uses of DBS. First, there may have been a lack of instruction before the experiment. Second, the idea of presenting a treasure hunt was so appealing that no participant had any doubts about it, and all agreed.

Therefore, they discussed the details of the idea with confirming their agreement with one another, so they could make a feasible proposal immediately.

The comments from DBS were opportunities for the participants to speak and move the words into boxes. In contrast, some AI voice comments interfered with the participants' utterances and thinking.

6 Conclusion

Our Discussion Board System aims to allow discussion participants to express their opinions and to reach a conclusion smoothly from various opinions. This paper proposed DBS ver. 2.1, which implements functions to automatically display comments that encourage participants to speak during discussions. Further, the color of any word that all participants add to the same box changes, in order to inform them that they have all agreed with the word.

In the experiment, unlike our expectation, there were no instances of conflict or peer pressure. Many words changed to green because the participants agreed with so many items. It was suggested that the function of changing the word to green encourages the conclusion of the discussion in favor of more realistic proposals.

In the future, DBS aims to serve as an AI facilitator that can make comments by focusing not only on the moved words, but also on spoken words.

References

1. Asch, S.E.: Opinions and social pressure. Sci. Am. **193**, 31–35 (1955). https://www.jstor.org/stable/24943779
2. Mori, T.: Facilitator Training Course. Diamond Inc., Tokyo (2007).(in Japanese)
3. Sasaki, C., Oshima, C., Kajihara, S., Nakayama, K.: Reaching a final consensus in a discussion: the impact of real-time intention expression related to categories. In: 13th International Conference on Human System Interaction, pp. 106–111. IEEE Press, New York (2020). https://doi.org/10.1109/HSI49210.2020.9142630
4. Oyama, T., Sasaki, C., Oshima, C., Kajihara, S., Nakayama, K.: Analysis of the impact of the discussion support system on discussions. In: SSI2020. The Society of Instrument and Control Engineers, Japan (2020). (in Japanese)
5. Nishimoto, K., Sumi, Y., Kadobayashi, R., Mase, K., Nakatsu, R.: Group thinking support with multiple agents. Syst. Comput. Jpn. **29**, 21–31 (1998). https://doi.org/10.1002/(SICI)1520-684X(199812)29:14%3C21::AID-SCJ3%3E3.0.CO;2-S
6. Ito, T., Imi, Y., Ito, T., Hideshima, E.: COLLAGREE: a facilitator-mediated large-scale consensus support system. In: Collective Intelligence, pp. 10–12, Colabria (2014)
7. Theeramunkong, T., Skulimowski, A.M.J., Yuizono, T., Kunifuji, S. (eds.): KICSS 2015. AISC, vol. 685. Springer, Cham (2018). https://doi.org/10.1007/978-3-319-70019-9

Dynamic Course of Action Analysis with Uncertainty of Information in Wargaming Environment

Adrienne Raglin(✉) ⓘ, John Richardson, Mark Mittrick, and Somiya Metu ⓘ

US CCDC DEVCOM Army Research Laboratory, 2800 Powder Mill Rd, Adelphi, MD 20783, USA

{adrienne.raglin2.civ,john.t.richardson7.civ, mark.r.mittrick.civ,somiya.metu.civ}@mail.mil

Abstract. Human information interaction (HII) focuses on the ability to capture, communicate, and understand the problems, tasks, ideas, and concepts which can be applied to ultimately generate courses of action (CoA) and make decisions. The complexities in each part of HII make it a challenging area to research. One of these challenges is the inherent variability that comes with human decision makers. Another challenge is the nuances of the interactions needed to solve the problem or complete a task. Additionally, there is also the challenge of the imperfect nature of information. These challenges, like the elements of HII, are intertwined, which adds to the complexity of the problem. Previous research in the information element and its imperfect nature has led to work in creating an uncertainty of information (UoI) paradigm, which is represented as a numerical value. A strength of the UoI concept is the descriptors which are used to express the causal reasoning behind the uncertainty. These descriptors are taken from Gershon's terminology and act as taxonomies to enable an easier way of understanding and communicating uncertainty, particularly for decision making. As this research is expanded, the utilization of human computer interaction (HCI) as a technique that allows for the investigation of UoI and the elements of HII dynamically is extremely important. The HCI technique utilized for this work is the wargaming simulation environment. Through wargaming, we can investigate and understand how CoA and their corresponding decisions (when there is UoI) are made so that the mission objectives are optimally achieved.

Keywords: Uncertainty of Information · Decision Making · Simulation · Course of action · Reinforcement learning · Wargaming · Human Information Interaction · Human Computer Interaction

1 Introduction

Human Information Interaction is an area of study that focusses on people's interaction with information. Concepts from this discipline can be applied in CoA analysis and decision making. Although the intricacies of HII are not completely understood, continued

C. Stephanidis et al. (Eds.): HCII 2021, CCIS 1420, pp. 531–539, 2021.
https://doi.org/10.1007/978-3-030-78642-7_71

research particularly for the military is critical. Current military operations necessitate seamless integration of human and automated capabilities especially in generation of CoAs and their analysis for informed decision making. One of the subfields of HII is Human Computer Interaction that focusses on design, evaluation, and implementation of interactive computing systems for utilization by humans. This paper describes an HCI technique which utilizes a war gaming engine for the analysis of CoA with Uncertainty of Information. First, we describe Uncertainty of Information and how it can be potentially used for informed and up-to-date decision making. We then talk about our approach of using reinforcement learning for course of action analysis utilizing scenarios in StarCraft II Engine. We present our results from the simulations and conclude with future work.

2   Uncertainty of Information

There is an increased dependence on a variety of data coming from multiple sources needed to make decisions particularly for those related to command and control (C2). This increase will continue as teams of humans and agents within a multi-domain bat-tlespace must work in partnership utilizing the data at hand and adapt as this data changes. Unfortunately, the data from these various sources does not come with guaranteed per-fection and certainty, adding to the complexities and challenges for decision making. This has led to our research in Uncertainty of Information (UoI). The main objective of the UoI concept is to incorporate terminology into the computation to aid decision making and to analyze the consequential impact of uncertainty on decision making. Thereby, integrating a level of reasoning into intelligent systems supporting decision making tasks.

In the current implementation of the UoI algorithms (Raglin et al. 2020), we have chosen four data sources categories. These categories are *visualization*, *information*, *networks*, and *devices*. We also have selected seven taxonomies based on the ideas from Gershon's taxonomy (Gershon 1998) work on the imperfect information as variable descriptor to represent uncertainties associated with the source categories. The seven taxonomies are:

- *Inconsistent*: Uncertainty due to a source that varies or do not stay the same.
- *Corrupt*: Uncertainty due to a source containing errors.
- *Questionable*: Uncertainty due to a source that lacks information or its questionable.
- *Disjoint*: Uncertainty due to a source that lacks cohesion or organization.
- *Incomplete*: Uncertainty due to a source that is unfinished or not complete.
- *Imprecise*: Uncertainty due to a source that lacks exactness or detail.
- *Complicated*: Uncertainty due to a source that is convoluted or confusing.

The expression for the UoI can be expressed simply as:

$$UoI = \sum_{i=1, n=1}^{m,n} T_i * S_n, \tag{1}$$

where T represents the taxonomies, S represents the source categories. At each decision point the UoI values can be used to help determine which CoAs to take. Ideally the action associated with the lowest possible UoI value would lead to the best decision. While that is ideal, sometimes it is not always possible to take the action or make the decision with the lowest uncertainty. This has been the motivation behind this aspect of the research.

3 Reinforcement Learning

In this paper we address two questions:

(1) Can we train an agent to complete a path finding task where its CoA is influenced by UoI?
(2) How does the level of influence impact the CoA?

  To investigate these questions we used StarCraft II (SC2) as our wargaming simulator. We developed a path finding scenario in SC2 and used reinforcement learning (RL) to train the path finding agent. Reinforcement learning is a technique where the agent learns from its experience to solve the problem. For our RL agent we used the agent developed by (Waytowich et al. 2019), which is an Asynchronous Advantage Actor-Critic (A3C) (Mnih et al. 2016) agent built to work with SC2 via PySC2 (Vinyals et al. 2017), and our own reward function. The experiments were run on a Lambda Deep Learning Machine using 10 workers. The reward function is an integer rating that defines how well the agent performed in the scenario. The RL agent learns by taking actions to optimize the reward.

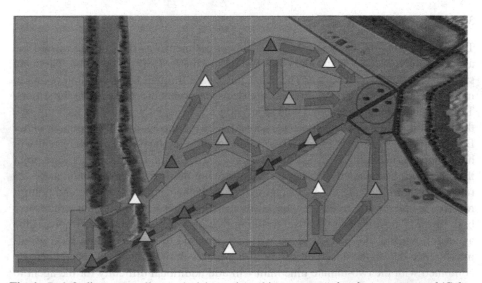

Fig. 1. Path finding map: yellow = decision point, white = suggested, red = not suggested (Color figure online)

3.1 StarCraft II Scenario

The scenario assumes that pathways are known, but there is uncertainty associated with determining the agent's CoA to navigate the paths. As a result, the UoI value is used to suggest the most desirable path. In this initial exploration the impact of UoI in the SC2 environment required us to consider a 'snapshot' scenario where the technical details of determining the UoI suggestion were abstracted away. To design our path finding scenario we considered UoI at its most superficial level. At this level the UoI algorithm reduces to a 'yes' or 'no' suggestion for a decision point. Consequently, in the path finding task each intersection is a decision point and will be binary. There will be two paths leading away from the decision point, one representing the 'yes' decision and the other representing 'no'. In the scenario we consider UoI to signify confidence in the data suggesting the 'yes' path is desirable, and lack of confidence in suggesting the 'no' path is desirable. In the scenario, it is not elaborated upon, but desirability could be due to any operational environment (OE) attributes, from weather effects to hostile opposition. The agent is free to take any path to solve the task, but our goal is to train it to use the UoI suggestion. To conduct our experiment it was first necessary to construct the path finding scenario in SC2. As a baseline for the scenario, an existing map based on our work with a tactical military scenario (Richardson and Mittrick 2020) was used. The majority of the map was made impassable except for a series of interconnected paths leading from the start point to the end point (See Fig. 1). At the start point there is a single unit controlled by the agent. The agent has two minutes to travel from the start point to the end point via any pathway. Backtracking was allowed in this experiment.

3.2 Reward Function

The reward function that was created for this experiment was designed to reward the agent for moving towards the end point and taking the UoI suggested paths. There are six decision points on the map. The agent must pass through three decision points to make it to the end point. As a result, the decision points are placed into three tiers. Tier 1 includes the first decision point, Decision 1. The agent will always pass through this decision point. Tier 2 includes the second decision the agent will encounter, either Decision 2 or Decision 5. Finally, Tier 3 will include the final decision the agent will have to make, including Decision 3, Decision 4, or Decision 6. At each decision point the agent will be awarded $+25$ reward for following the UoI suggested path, and -25 reward for not following the UoI suggested path. If the agent reaches the end point it receives a $+50$ reward. If the agent backtracks and explores each decision it will receive both rewards, positive and negative, resulting in a net zero reward. Furthermore, if the agent follows the 'no' path its speed will be decreased to simulate some form of OE interference due to the uncertain nature of the path's desirability. This speed decrease combined with the two-minute time limit will add additional difficulty for the agent to reach the end point when traversing the 'no' path. The speed decrease does not make it impossible to reach the end point within the time limit, but does limit exploration. Furthermore, the pathways are divided into segments (See Fig. 2 that give reward for moving towards the end point. The cumulative rewards (See Table 1) are evenly divided among the pathway segments.

Fig. 2. Path segmenting

Table 1. Reward function

Event	Reward
Decision point: suggested path	+25
Decision point: not suggested path	−25
Path: Tier 1 -> Tier 2	+10
Path: Tier 2 -> Tier 3	+20
Path: Tier 3 -> End point	+30
Reaching endpoint	+50

To evaluate our research questions a series of RL experiments using our scenario and a series of modifications were conducted. First, to determine if the agent would learn to reach the end point using the UoI suggested path, we used the original scenario during training. Next, three more experiments were conducted with the successive removal of the reward associated with each decision tier to explore the impact of fewer UoI suggestions. In a final experiment, Decision 1 was set to suggest 'no' for each path, with a reward of −25 when taking either path.

4 Results and Analysis

For each scenario variant the optimal reward is deterministic (See Table 2). The relevant training curves, referenced in Table 2 indicate the agents' success in optimizing the path finding task.

For Scenario A the smoothed curve shows that the agent was able to learn to reach the optimal reward. The training curve reveals there was an extended period of stagnant exploration before the agent explored alternative paths and found the optimal route. The agent learned to collect the reward for making three suggested decisions.

In Scenario B the agent was once again able to learn to reach the optimal reward. In several episodes the workers are actually exceeding the optimal score. Investigation of this anomaly revealed that the agent that the agent discovered a loophole in the path segmenting that allowed it to earn an additional +20 in rewards. As a result the smoothed

Table 2. Optimal reward

Scenario	Optimal reward
A: All decision points active (Fig. 3)	185
B: Tier 1 decision point rewards removed (Fig. 4)	160
C: Tier 1, 2 decision point rewards removed (Fig. 5)	135
D: Tier 1, 2, 3 decision point rewards removed (Fig. 6)	110
E: Tier 1 decision point rewards no suggested path (Fig. 7)	135

curve was trending above the optimal score in the time steps observed. This exploit was possible in the remaining scenarios but does not appear to have had an impact on their learning.

Next, the agent in Scenario C did not achieve the optimal score. Instead, the smooth curve suggests the agent selected the direct straight line path from the start point to the end point. The negative reward collected for choosing the 'no' path at the single decision point on that path did not cause the agent to find alternative paths to the end point in the time-steps observed.

Furthermore, the agent in Scenario D does optimize its score. The optimal score is again achieved by taking the direct path from the start point to the end point, although in this scenario there is no negative reward for choosing the 'no' path as in Scenario C.

Finally, Scenario E does not optimize its reward. In fact, the smooth curve indicates that the agent never learned to achieve a reward above −5. This is an interesting result, as it suggests that the initial big negative reward made it impossible for the agents to overcome.

Returning to the questions we posited earlier in the paper, the results show that under the experimental conditions it is possible to use RL techniques to train an agent to

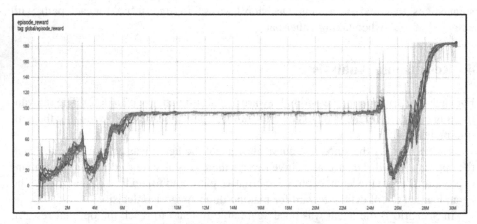

Fig. 3. Training curve - all decision points active

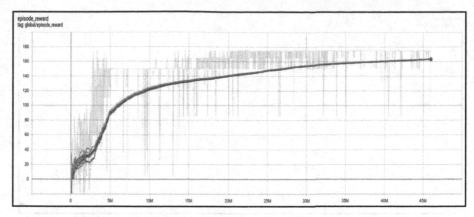

Fig. 4. Training curve: Tier 1 decision point rewards removed

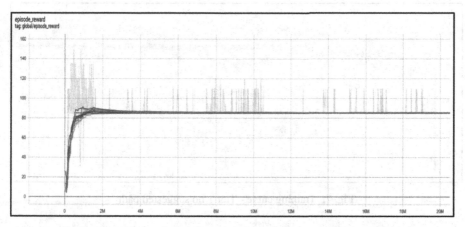

Fig. 5. Training curve: Tier 1, 2 decision point rewards removed

complete a path finding task using a CoA influenced by UoI. Initial results also indicate that the level of influence does impact the agent's ability to optimize the task. Scenario C revealed that a UoI suggestion near the end of the task was ignored in favor of completing the task. To further test this observation we could reproduce these experiments with the removal of the Tier rewards conducted in reverse order. This would provide further insight into whether it is the number of influenced decision points or their position within the task flow that has the greatest impact. Scenario E provides some evidence that position may have a large impact, as modifying the reward structure of the initial decision point caused the agent to fail.

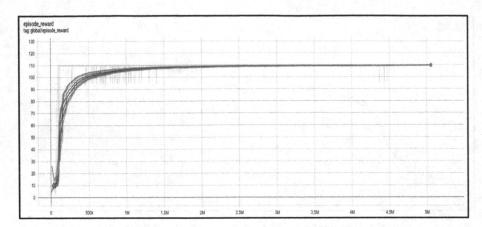

Fig. 6. Training curve: Tier 1, 2, 3 decision point rewards removed

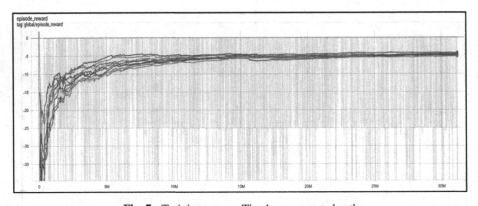

Fig. 7. Training curve - Tier 1 no suggested path

5 Conclusion and Future Work

In conclusion, although the 'snapshot' scenarios used in this initial work are basic examples they have allowed us to explore a testbed for further investigation. In the future, we plan to replace the UoI abstraction we used for decision points with a dynamic representation that will allow for stochastic pathways. In addition, increasing the density of decision points to reflect context within the operational environment will enable more complex course of actions.

References

Gershon, N.: Visualization of an imperfect world. IEEE Comput. Graph. Appl. **18**(4), 43–45 (1998)

Mnih, V., Badia, A.P., Mirza, M., Graves, A., Lillicrap, T.P., Harley, T., Kavukcuoglu, K.: Asynchronous Methods for Deep Reinforcement Learning (2016). arXiv:1602.01783

Raglin, A., Metu, S., Lott, D.: Challenges of simulating uncertainty of information. In: Stephanidis, C., Antona, M., Ntoa, S. (eds.) HCII 2020. CCIS, vol. 1293, pp. 255–261. Springer, Cham (2020). https://doi.org/10.1007/978-3-030-60700-5_33

Richardson, J., Mittrick, M.: Game Simulation for Agent-based Command and Control Experimentation. MORS Symposium – Poster (2020)

Vinyals, O., et al.: StarCraft II: A New Challenge for Reinforcement Learning (2017). arXiv:1708.04782v1

Waytowich, N., Barton, S.L., Lawhern, V., Warnell, G.A.: Narration-based Reward Shaping Approach using Grounded Natural Language Commands (2019). arXiv:1911.00497

Feature Fused Human Activity Recognition Network (FFHAR-Net)

Anmol Singhal[(✉)], Mihir Goyal[(✉)], Jainendra Shukla[(✉)],
and Raghava Mutharaju[(✉)]

Indraprastha Institute of Information Technology (IIIT-Delhi), Delhi, India
{anmol17332,mihir17166,jainendra,raghava.mutharaju}@iiitd.ac.in

Abstract. With the advances in smart home technology and Internet of Things (IoT), there has been keen research interest in human activity recognition to allow service systems to understand human intentions. Recognizing human objectives by these systems without user intervention, results in better service, which is crucial to improve the user experience. Existing research approaches have focused primarily on probabilistic methods like Bayesian networks (for instance, the CRAFFT algorithm). Though quite versatile, these probabilistic models may be unable to successfully capture the possibly complex relationships between the input variables. To the best of our knowledge, a statistical study of features in a human activity recognition task, their relationships, etc., has not yet been attempted. To this end, we study the domain of human activity recognition to improve the state-of-the-art and present a novel neural network architecture for the task. It employs early fusion on different types of minimalistic features such as time and location to make extremely accurate predictions with a maximum micro F1-score of 0.98 on the Aruba CASAS dataset. We also accompany the model with a comprehensive study of the features. Using feature selection techniques like Leave-One-Out, we rank the features according to the information they add to deep learning models and make further inferences using the ranking obtained. Our empirical results show that the feature *Previous Activity Performed* is the most useful of all, surprisingly even more than time (the basis of activity scheduling in most societies). We use three Activities of Daily Living (ADL) datasets in different settings to empirically demonstrate the utility of our architecture. We share our findings along with the models and the source code.

Keywords: Human activity recognition · Activities of Daily Living · Deep learning

1 Introduction

The growing need for automation tools and technologies across several domains such as healthcare, smart homes, and service robotics has led to extensive

---

A. Singhal and M. Goyal—Contributed equally to this work.

© Springer Nature Switzerland AG 2021
C. Stephanidis et al. (Eds.): HCII 2021, CCIS 1420, pp. 540–547, 2021.
https://doi.org/10.1007/978-3-030-78642-7_72

research in building systems that recognize and process human intentions. The goal is to develop robust, scalable tools that perform efficiently, even in adverse circumstances and can work according to the user's requirements. Such a system that identifies and prioritizes users' needs without any explicit instructions or command is crucial to enhancing the overall experience.

Human activity recognition is an important area of research for building efficient, intelligent home systems. It identifies the day-to-day actions a user performs in real-time based on specific environmental factors and sensor values. Recognizing human actions is a challenging task as we need to determine all the significant environmental factors that may influence an action. Moreover, since each user follows a different schedule, it becomes even more difficult for a system to recognize human activity in situations where multiple people live together. Therefore, we require complex models to distinguish underlying patterns in the user schedule. We also need to analyze how significantly various features like time, location, and user's previous action affect the current activity.

Over the years, there have been several efforts to develop accurate and robust models using probabilistic approaches and machine learning. Human activity recognition is modeled as a multi-class classification task, where the classes refer to the set of user actions performed in the environment. Probabilistic approaches like CRAAFT [13] and SPEED [1] algorithms and probabilistic graphical models (PGMs) have been proposed for this task. With increased access to sensor data, many machine learning algorithms like the Naive Bayes classifier and Support Vector Machines (SVMs) have also been used to model user behavior. Although these models are effective solutions, as the amount of smart home user data increased explosively, the need for more powerful deep learning-based systems has emerged [22] Probabilistic models make many assumptions about the data distribution including correlation between features which may not necessarily be true when dealing with complex real-world data. Following are our contributions.

- We propose Feature-Fused Human Activity Recognition Net (FFHAR-Net), which uses a neural network architecture and employs fusion on different minimalistic features, including time, location, previous activity etc. We demonstrate our architecture's utility empirically using three Activities of Daily Living (ADL) datasets in different settings.
- We perform a comprehensive study of the features used in FFHAR-Net using feature selection techniques like Leave-One-Out and rank the features according to the information they add in determining the user action.

2 Related Work

We discuss some of the existing literature related to our proposed approach. This falls into the two broad categories of human activity recognition and fusion.

2.1 Human Activity Recognition

Human Activity Recognition (HAR) is an important task to consider when dealing with smart-home technology. Over the years, researchers have used several approaches to model the problem effectively and achieve accurate results. Some of the earliest methods used for HAR include sequence matching algorithms, and the usage of rulesets [7,9]. More sophisticated data-based techniques involving Markov, Bayesian and machine learning methods have emerged in recent years. Variations of the Markov model [15,19,20], including graph-based methods like Probabilistic Graphical Models (PGMs) and other Markov-based permutations like Hierarchical Hidden Markov Models (HHMMs), are popular approaches to HAR. They look at the problem at a higher level before transitioning to a more granular classification. As the access to good quality data has increased, several machine learning methods, including techniques like regression [12], deep learning-based neural networks (NNs) [18,22] and reinforcement learning (Q learning) [2], have been proposed. Hybrid models that span Bayesian and machine learning methods [3,4,17] have also emerged.

Using contextual features from the environment efficiently is a crucial aspect of predicting human behavior. In this regard, several approaches have used an extensive set of features to perform the task [13,21]. Some algorithms have performed transformations to the features extracted from sensor values to model complex relationships [10]. On the other hand, we use a simplistic set of features, making our model results easier to interpret without negatively affecting the performance. It also makes it possible to perform a comprehensive feature analysis that has not been attempted before to the best of our knowledge.

2.2 Fusion

In the case of multimodal input data collected through various sensors, an ensemble-based technique called fusion has proven to be a powerful method. Fusion aims to mix relevant information from individual sensors and use a combined feature vector to solve a given problem. Several works done in domains, including healthcare, agricultural and art technologies, have used fusion [8,11,14,16] and have shown improved performance. Due to the effectiveness of fusion as an ensemble method, we also use early-fusion for FFHAR-Net.

3   Approach

Let M be the number of activities that the user performs. The ith activity description a_i is of the form [Day, Time, Hour, Minute, Location, Prev Activity] with a corresponding annotation label y_i where each element of a_i represents the value of their namesake and y_i represents the activity the user performed. Our prediction task comprises of using an activity's description to predict its annotation label.

3.1   Datasets

One of the key applications of the human activity recognition problem is related to the activities of daily living, a person's daily self-care activities. These activities are common across most cultures worldwide and provide ample opportunities to model deep learning networks. We use three datasets from the CASAS

Project[1] called Aruba [5], Milan [6] and Tulum [5]. These datasets detail the environment of three smart homes with varying conditions monitored over different time periods. The Aruba dataset features a smart home of a woman whose children and grandchildren visit regularly. The data was collected for about seven months. The Milan dataset is about a smart home of a woman with a pet whose children visit regularly. The data was collected for about four months. Lastly, the Tulum dataset monitored a smart home with two married residents for about seven months.

3.2 Data Preprocessing

Each of the datasets has been annotated with activity labels by CASAS. For each entry in a dataset, there are four parameters associated with it with an optional 5th parameter. The first four parameters describe date, time, sensor name and the sensor's value, respectively, while the optional 5th parameter is the annotated label if an activity was detected. Given the nature of our problem, we only keep the entries that contain the annotated label. Each dataset contains a mapping of the sensor to its location in the smart home. We use this mapping to obtain user location for each entry. We describe the feature set in Table 1.

Table 1. Description of the feature set for each entry

Feature name	Description
Day	The day of the entry
Time	Total time (in minutes) passed from the start of the day
Hour	The hour of the day at which the entry was made
Minute	The minute of the hour at which the entry was made
Location	The user location for the entry
Previous activity	The previous activity of the user

3.3 FFHAR-Net

FFHAR-Net is a four-layer neural network architecture that allows the prediction of human activities. Each feature acquired from the data is categorical in nature. To this end, we encode each feature into its one-hot vector representation for the model input. A feed-forward layer follows each of these vectors that extracts high-level representations of the features. FFHAR-Net employs the use of early fusion to combine the information from each feature representation effectively. Each representation is concatenated into a single vector before processing further in the form of feed-forward layers and appropriate activations. The model output is a one-hot vector representation of the class prediction. We depict the preprocessing and architecture for FFHAR-Net in Fig. 1.

---

[1] http://casas.wsu.edu/.

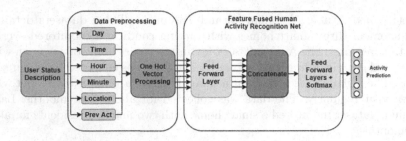

Fig. 1. FFHAR-Net architecture

4   Evaluation

4.1   Baselines

We compare FFHAR-Net against state-of-the-art deep learning baselines in the domain of human activity recognition. We use works based on BPNN [22] and DBN-ANN [4]. These models, unlike FFHAR-Net, use several features, including the values of sensors in smart homes. To make a fair comparison, we use their proposed architectures on our feature set.

4.2   Experimental Setup

We tune FFHAR-Net's hyper-parameters using Grid Search. We summarize here the range of hyperparameters tuned on – size of feed-forward layers $\in \{8, 16, 32, 64\}$, dropout $\delta \in \{0.0, 0.1, 0.25, 0.5\}$, learning rate $e \in \{0.1, 0.01, 0.001, 0.0001\}$ and optimiser $\in \{$Adam, RMSProp$\}$. We implement all the models with Keras and Google Colaboratory using ReLU as our hidden layer activation function and Softmax as our final activation function. We choose the highest performing model based on the training phase on our validation set.

5   Results and Analysis

5.1   Results

The micro F1 scores of the baselines and FFHAR-Net on all the three datasets is given in Table 2. FFHAR-Net outperforms the baselines on all the datasets by a significant margin. This can be attributed to the use of the early-fusion technique. It enhances FFHAR-Net's ability to learn a better representation of features which significantly improves its understanding of the complex relationships that may exist in the data.

Table 2. Micro F1 score obtained on all three datasets

Dataset	BPNN	DBN-ANN	FFHAR-Net
Aruba	0.932	0.965	**0.978**
Milan	0.611	0.730	**0.912**
Tulum	0.741	0.740	**0.770**

5.2 Feature Study

We use both statistical and empirical experiments to analyze the usefulness of the features and their relative importance. For the former, we employ the use of Joint Mutual Information (JMI), which quantifies the dependence of the target value on individual features. For the latter, we use the Leave-One-Out (LOO) method to train models using subsets of features to rank them with respect to the performance they contribute. We present the rankings of features on all the three datasets based on JMI and LOO in Table 3.

Table 3. Ranking for each feature for all three datasets based on JMI and LOO (in the ascending order of ranks)

Feature rank	Aruba	Milan	Tulum
Joint Mutual Information (JMI)	Previous activity	Location	Location
	Location	Previous activity	Previous activity
	Hour	Minute	Hour
	Minute	Hour	Minute
	Time	Time	Time
	Day	Day	Day
Leave-One-Out (LOO)	Previous activity	Previous activity	Previous activity
	Location	Location	Location
	Minute	Hour	Hour
	Hour	Time	Time
	Time	Minute	Day
	Day	Day	Minute

It is apparent from the study that *Location* and *Previous Activity* are the best performing features and *Day* performs the worst. While the latter result seems reasonable, the former is quite surprising. Time has been considered the basis of human schedules. To have *Time* not be ranked the best is quite interesting. While this may be true for just the chosen datasets, further research may validate this more concretely for a generalized setting.

6 Conclusion

Human Activity Recognition proves to be an exciting field of study with a great scope of research. It has applications in a variety of fields like smart homes, healthcare and robotics. Taking advantage of the massive good quality datasets available, we present a strong neural network architecture that employs early fusion and outperforms other state-of-the-art deep learning approaches in the domain. We further perform a study of the feature set used using the statistical and empirical methods of Joint Mutual Information and Leave-One-Out. The research shows 'Previous Activity' to be the most informative of the features, outperforming 'Time', the basis of human schedules. On the other hand, 'Day' performs the worst. We believe this opens an avenue for research to solidify this belief for other domains related to Activities of Daily Living.

Acknowledgement. Raghava Mutharaju and Jainendra Shukla are partly supported by the Infosys Center for AI (CAI) and Jainendra Shukla is also partly supported by the Center for Design and New Media at IIIT-Delhi.

References

1. Alam, M.R., Reaz, M.B.I., Mohd Ali, M.A.: Speed: an inhabitant activity prediction algorithm for smart homes. IEEE Trans. Syst. Man Cybern. - Part A: Syst. Hum. **42**(4), 985–990 (2012). https://doi.org/10.1109/TSMCA.2011.2173568
2. Ali, F.M., Lee, S.W., Bien, Z., Mokhtari, M.: Combined fuzzy state q-learning algorithm to predict context aware user activity under uncertainty in assistive environment. In: 2008 Ninth ACIS International Conference on Software Engineering, Artificial Intelligence, Networking, and Parallel/Distributed Computing, pp. 57–62 (2008). https://doi.org/10.1109/SNPD.2008.13
3. Chen, C., Das, B., Cook, D.: Energy prediction based on resident's activity (2010)
4. Choi, S., Kim, E., Oh, S.: Human behavior prediction for smart homes using deep learning. In: 2013 IEEE RO-MAN, pp. 173–179 (2013)
5. Cook, D.: Learning setting-generalized activity models for smart spaces. IEEE Intell. Syst. **27**, 32–38 (2012)
6. Cook, D., Schmitter-Edgecombe, M.: Assessing the quality of activities in a smart environment. Methods Inf. Med. **48**(5), 480–5 (2009)
7. Das, S.K., Cook, D.J., Battacharya, A., Heierman, E.O., Lin, T.-Y.: The role of prediction algorithms in the MavHome smart home architecture. IEEE Wirel. Commun. **9**(6), 77–84 (2002). https://doi.org/10.1109/MWC.2002.1160085
8. Goel, P., Goyal, M., Shah, R.: Arten-net: an emotion classification system for art (student consortium). In: 2020 IEEE Sixth International Conference on Multimedia Big Data (BigMM), pp. 302–306 (2020)
9. Jakkula, V., Cook, D.: Mining sensor data in smart environment for temporal activity prediction (2007)
10. Jouini, R., Lemlouma, T., Maalaoui, K., Saidane, L.A.: Employing grey model forecasting GM(1,1) to historical medical sensor data towards system preventive in smart home e-health for elderly person. In: 2016 International Wireless Communications and Mobile Computing Conference (IWCMC), pp. 1086–1091 (2016). https://doi.org/10.1109/IWCMC.2016.7577210

11. Liu, K., Li, Y., Xu, N., Natarajan, P.: Learn to combine modalities in multimodal deep learning. ArXiv abs/1805.11730 (2018)
12. Minor, B., Cook, D.J.: Regression tree classification for activity prediction in smart homes. In: Proceedings of the 2014 ACM International Joint Conference on Pervasive and Ubiquitous Computing: Adjunct Publication, UbiComp 2014 Adjunct, p. 441–450. Association for Computing Machinery, New York (2014). https://doi.org/10.1145/2638728.2641669
13. Nazerfard, E., Cook, D.J.: CRAFFT: an activity prediction model based on Bayesian networks. J. Ambient Intell. Humaniz. Comput. 6(2), 193–205 (2014). https://doi.org/10.1007/s12652-014-0219-x
14. Petscharnig, S., Schöffmann, K., Benois-Pineau, J., Chaabouni, S., Keckstein, J.: Early and late fusion of temporal information for classification of surgical actions in laparoscopic gynecology. In: 2018 IEEE 31st International Symposium on Computer-Based Medical Systems (CBMS), pp. 369–374 (2018). https://doi.org/10.1109/CBMS.2018.00071
15. Rao, S.P., Cook, D.J.: Identifying tasks and predicting actions in smart homes using unlabeled data. In: Proceedings of the Machine Learning Workshop on the Continuum from Labeled to Unlabeled Data (2003)
16. Seeland, M., Rzanny, M., Alaqraa, N., Wäldchen, J., Mäder, P.: Plant species classification using flower images–a comparative study of local feature representations. PLOS ONE 12, e0170629 (2017). https://doi.org/10.1371/journal.pone.0170629
17. Shuai, Z., Oh, S., Yang, M.H.: Traffic modeling and prediction using camera sensor networks. In: Proceedings of the Fourth ACM/IEEE International Conference on Distributed Smart Cameras, ICDSC 2010, pp. 49–56. Association for Computing Machinery, New York (2010). https://doi.org/10.1145/1865987.1865996
18. Vintan, L., Gellert, A., Petzold, J., Ungerer, T.: Person movement prediction using neural networks (2004)
19. Kang, W., Shin, D., Shin, D.: Detecting and predicting of abnormal behavior using hierarchical Markov model in smart home network. In: 2010 IEEE 17Th International Conference on Industrial Engineering and Engineering Management, pp. 410–414 (2010). https://doi.org/10.1109/ICIEEM.2010.5646583
20. Wu, E., Zhang, P., Lu, T., Gu, H., Gu, N.: Behavior prediction using an improved hidden Markov model to support people with disabilities in smart homes. In: 2016 IEEE 20th International Conference on Computer Supported Cooperative Work in Design (CSCWD), pp. 560–565 (2016). https://doi.org/10.1109/CSCWD.2016.7566051
21. Wu, Z., Liu, A., Zhou, P., Su, Y.F.: A Bayesian network based method for activity prediction in a smart home system. In: 2016 IEEE International Conference on Systems, Man, and Cybernetics (SMC), pp. 001496–001501 (2016). https://doi.org/10.1109/SMC.2016.7844449
22. Xu, G., Liu, M., Li, F., Zhang, F., Shen, W.: User behavior prediction model for smart home using parallelized neural network algorithm. In: 2016 IEEE 20th International Conference on Computer Supported Cooperative Work in Design (CSCWD), pp. 221–226 (2016). https://doi.org/10.1109/CSCWD.2016.7565992

Choreography Composed by Deep Learning

Ryosuke Suzuki[✉] and Yoichi Ochiai

University of Tsukuba, Tsukuba, Japan
ryosuke.suzuki@digitalnature.slis.tsukuba.ac.jp,
wizard@slis.tsukuba.ac.jp

Abstract. Choreography is a type of art in which movement is designed. Because it involves many complex movements, a lot of time is spent creating the choreography. In this study, we constructed a dataset of dance movements with more than 700,000 frames using dance videos of the "Odotte-mita" genre. Our dataset could have been very useful for recent research in motion generation, as there has been a lack of dance datasets. Furthermore, we verified the choreography of the dance generated by the deep learning method (acRNN) by physically repeating the dance steps. To the best of our knowledge, this is the first time such a verification has been attempted. It became clear that the choreography generated by machine learning had unique movements and rhythms for dancers. In addition, dancing machine-learning-generated choreography provided an opportunity to make new discoveries. In addition, the fact that the model was a stick figure made the choreography vague, and, although it was difficult to remember, it created varied dance steps.

Keywords: Choreography · Dance · Deep learning

1   Introduction

Choreography is an art form in which movement is designed, and because of its many complex movements, can be time consuming to create. In particular, it takes a great deal of time and effort to create new and innovative choreography, something we have never danced or seen before. Therefore, synthesizing dances and generating new choreographies is very useful for choreographers as it provides easy inspiration. In addition, it can benefit other fields, such as the generation of character movements for animation and games and for human behavior research.

In this study, we constructed a motion dataset by scraping dance videos of the "Odotte-mita" genre from the web and estimating their skeletons. To do so, we used the algorithms OpenPose [4], a skeleton detection algorithm for monocular cameras using deep learning, and 3d pose baseline vmd [9], which transforms the 2D pose data obtained from it into a 3D image. In addition, we trained a network called acRNN, which has been successfully used to synthesize

© Springer Nature Switzerland AG 2021
C. Stephanidis et al. (Eds.): HCII 2021, CCIS 1420, pp. 548–555, 2021.
https://doi.org/10.1007/978-3-030-78642-7_73

dance movements [19], with the dataset we built and generated choreography. Moreover, by physically dancing the generated choreography, we verified the effect of generating dance with deep learning on choreography.

The main contribution of this study is the construction of a dataset of dances with complex movements, totaling approximately 700,000 frames, and the usability of dances generated by deep learning using the dataset.

2 Related Work

The study of human motion has been investigated using a variety of approaches. In this section, we first introduce the literature on the prediction, synthesis, and generation of human motion and explain the significance of conducting this study.

2.1 Motion Prediction

The "prediction" of motion is traditionally done by statespace models, and traditional approaches include bilinear spatio-temporal basis models [1], hidden Markov models [3], Gaussian process latent variable models [18], linear dynamic models [14], and restricted Boltzmann machines [16]. Recently, there has also been research using deep learning methods, such as RNN and GAN. Among them, a model called HP GAN [2] and a model called the adversarial geometry aware encoder decoder model [7] have also been developed. However, since these studies are only "predictions" of motion, there is no variation in the output motion, and there are limitations in generating a variety of movements.

2.2 Motion Synthesis

In motion "synthesis," some methods separate body parts and synthesize them, while others divide the motion into short sequences and synthesize them. For example, Lee et al. provided a source of motion to enable a robot or animated character to perform improvised dances to music. They aimed to inspire choreographers by suggesting reasonable dance moves from the music and having the user synthesize the motions separately for the head, torso, left arm, right arm, and lower body [8]. There is also a technique that divides and composes the image by the torso, neck, left leg, shoulder, and arm. Bin Umino et al. reduced dance movements into elemental movements by dividing them along a short time axis, and generated new choreography by arranging and combining the divided movements along the time axis again [17]. This kind of choreography is called "analytical synthetic choreography," and the Motion Archive contains 247 elemental movements of ballet and 58 elemental movements of modern dance. The "synthesis" of such movements is to generate unprecedented and novel movements and choreographies by combining movements that have been divided in some way. However, in this method, the generation of movements has to be done by the user, and the system cannot perform the generation completely independently.

2.3 Motion Generation

For motion generation, database-driven frameworks such as motion graphs have been proposed based on the use of simulation-based techniques and large-scale human motion capture data, and, more recently, deep learning methods such as RNN and GAN have been used. There are two types of methods that use deep learning: those that use GANs and those that use RNNs. In terms of RNN-based methods, Zhou et al. developed a model called auto-conditioned Recurrent Neural Network (acRNN) and presented a robust framework that can synthesize complex motions such as dance and martial arts without querying a database [19]. This model is an RNN that uses a special type of memory called long short-term memory (LSTM). While all previous studies have focused on the synthesis of relatively simple human movements over very short periods of time, this model has demonstrated the ability to generate over 18,000 frames. Although we have not yet proven infinite stability, we have shown state-of-the-art qualitative results in motion generation. However, in these studies, they are viewed as physical movements and not studied from the perspective of choreography in dance. In addition, there is a limit to the number and type of dance motion datasets, which limits the generation of dances.

3 Method

3.1 Dataset Construction

First, we need a motion dataset for the dance, so we start by building it. We will use "youtube dl" [15] to scrape videos tagged with "Odotte-mita" from Nico Nico Douga. "Odotte-mita" are videos of ordinary people dancing to their favorite music. We collected more than 2,000 videos. The collected dance videos were narrowed down to those taken at fixed points, and the skeletal coordinates of the dancers were estimated using OpenPose [4]. Next, blank frames that could not be estimated by OpenPose were removed and divided into different folders. This was done to convert to 3D; the previous frame of the frame to be estimated is used as a reference, so any blank frame will cause an error. From 2D skeletal coordinate data, 3D skeletal coordinates can be estimated using "3d pose baseline vmd" [9] and "3dpose gan vmd" [10]. In addition, if we estimate the depth of the video using "FCRN Depth Prediction vmd" [11] and estimate it with "VMD 3d pose baseline multi" [12] using the above output, we can output a vmd file. Finally, because acRNNs are trained in bvh files, the generated vmd files are converted to bvh files using "mio 0.1" [5] and "MMDBVHToSLBVH master" [6]. The MMDBVHToSLBVH master is used to handle unnecessary coordinate information. For example, the hair of Hatsune Miku's model is also included in the bvh file when using only mio 0.1, so it is necessary to remove it. In this way, dance motion data were constructed from "Odotte-mita" videos. The dataset we built spanned over 700,000 frames.

3.2   Learning and Generation

The network used for training was an acRNN [19]. An acRNN is an RNN that uses a special type of memory called long short-term memory (LSTM). In this study, we trained on the dataset prepared in Sect. 3.1, with 200,000 iterations and a sequence length of 180. In addition, the original code was trained and generated with 57 joints, but because the dataset we created used the COCO model, we rewrote the code so that it could train and generate with 18 joints. The learning process took approximately two days, and the generation took only a few tens of seconds. The generation was performed with a weight of 120,000 and an FPS of 60 (Fig. 1).

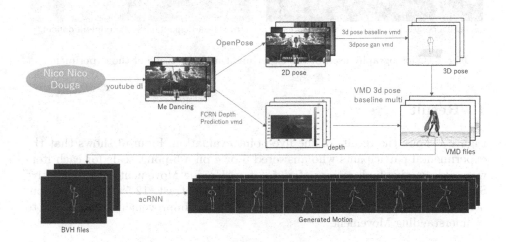

Fig. 1. Overview of our method

3.3   Experiment with Actual Dancing

To verify the impact of the choreography generated in Sect. 3.2, we conducted an experiment in which the participants actually danced. We asked as an experimental task for the participants to memorize the generated choreography for 20 min while watching it on their smartphones and then answer a questionnaire using a Google form. The choreography to be learned by the experimental participants was shown by a stick figure model dancing using a BVH player [13], and uploaded to YouTube for sharing.

In the questionnaire used in the experiment, the participants were asked to rate the choreography on a five-point scale for two items: "The movement was unique" and "The rhythm was unique." In addition, we asked the participants to rate the usefulness of the three items of "creative support," "skill improvement," and "movement understanding/learning" on a five-point scale and to provide reasons for their responses in free text. Eight experimental participants (four males and four females) were collected from the dancers. One was a member of the laboratory of this study. The age of the experimental participants ranged from 19 to 25 years (mean 21.25 ± 2.435), and their dancing experience ranged from 4 to 21 years (mean 13.87 ± 5.027) (Fig. 2).

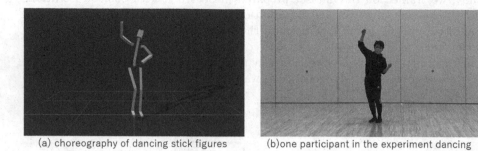

(a) choreography of dancing stick figures   (b)one participant in the experiment dancing

Fig. 2. Choreography used in the experiment and the scene of the experiment

4   Result

Figure 3 shows the results of the five-point evaluation. Figure 3 shows that the experimental participants who answered 5 or 4 on a 5-point scale for each item were able to give high ratings of 87.5% for "Unique Movement" and "Creative Support" and 62.5% for "Unique Rhythm". In contrast, 12.5% of the respondents did not give a very high rating to "Technical Improvement" and 37.5% to "Understanding Movement".

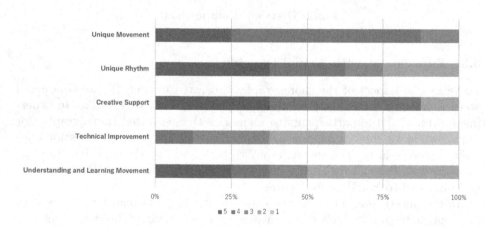

Fig. 3. Results of 5-point evaluation

4.1 Usefulness for Creative Support

As for creative support, there were many comments such as "feasible choreography that I would never have come up with on my own" and "this is not a dance that I have danced or seen before". There were also comments that predicted that the choreography generated by machine learning gave the dancers new insights, such as "I felt it was useful enough to discover a new sense of tempo and rhythm." In contrast, the experimental participants who gave a low score of 2 commented that it was difficult to understand the front and back of the body and that there were some movements that were impossible for humans. It is possible that it is difficult to remember the choreography due to the fact that a stick figure model is dancing in the video.

4.2 Usefulness for Technical Improvement

As for technical improvements, there were opinions such as "it does not affect the technical aspect" and "the footsteps are ambiguous." The choreography generated in this case does not seem to have a significant effect on the technical aspect. However, we also received positive comments such as, "It may be an opportunity to learn new movements," and "It is useful as material in the sense that it refines movements that we do not usually think about."

4.3 Usefulness for Understanding and Learning Movement

Regarding the understanding of the movements, there were comments such as "the movements are unclear," "the movements are difficult to learn," and "I cannot see the movements in detail". This may have been due to the fact that the movement model was a stick figure, and the structure of the movement was difficult to understand. However, opinions such as "For intermediate and higher objects with some basic training, we think it is useful for practicing and training to learn choreography and movement" suggest that it can be useful for experienced persons.

5 Discussion

The results in Sect. 4 show that the choreography generated by machine learning in this study has unique movements and rhythms for dancers. This suggests that the system in this study may be useful for supporting creative work. In addition, dancing machine-learning-generated choreography provided us with an opportunity to make new discoveries. However, it is thought that further innovations are needed in terms of technical improvement, understanding of movements, and learning. Since it was difficult to remember the choreography because the model was a stick figure, we would like to conduct the experiment again by having a fleshy model dance. However, in the free description at the end of the presentation, "the same video can be received in various ways by different dancers, and I felt that it could be used in the initial stage of choreography. I couldn't receive detailed information such as the fingers, but to some extent the dancer's imagination could make up for it, so I felt it had potential as a support rather than a complete choreography. I felt that it had more potential as a support than a complete choreography." This may be due to the fact that the model was a stick figure and the choreography looked ambiguous, which created diversity in the movements when learning. Another comment was, "I thought that if someone who had never danced before did it, they would have more variety in their movements than someone who had experience."

6   Conclusion

In this study, we constructed a dataset of dance motions spanning more than 700,000 frames using dance videos of the "Odotte-mita" genre. The dataset could also be very useful for recent research on movement generation, as dance datasets have been lacking.

Furthermore, we verified the choreography of the dance generated by deep learning (acRNN) by performing the dance. To the best of our knowledge, this is the first attempt at such a verification. It became clear that the choreography generated by machine learning had unique movements and rhythms for dancers. In addition, dancing machine-learning-generated choreography provided an opportunity to make new discoveries. In addition, the fact that the model was a stick figure made the choreography vague, and although it was difficult to remember, it created diversity in the movements.

References

1. Akhter, I., Simon, T., Khan, S., Matthews, I., Sheikh, Y.: Bilinear spatiotemporal basis models. ACM Trans. Graph. **31**, 1–12 (2012)
2. Barsoum, E., Kender, J., Liu, Z.: HP-GAN: probabilistic 3D human motion prediction via GAN. arXiv preprint arXiv:1711.09561 (2017)
3. Brand, M., Hertzmann, A.: Style machines. In: ACM International Conference on Computer Graphics and Interactive Techniques (SIGGRAPH) (2000)
4. Cao, Z., Simon, T., Wei, S., Sheikh, Y.: Realtime multi person 2D pose estimation using part affinity fields. In: CVPR (2017)
5. esetomo: mio (2009). https://github.com/esetomo/mio
6. esetomo: Mmdbvhtoslbvh (2012). https://github.com/esetomo/MMDBVHToSLBVH
7. Gui, L.-Y., Wang, Y.-X., Liang, X., Moura, J.M.F.: Adversarial geometry-aware human motion prediction. In: Ferrari, V., Hebert, M., Sminchisescu, C., Weiss, Y. (eds.) ECCV 2018. LNCS, vol. 11208, pp. 823–842. Springer, Cham (2018). https://doi.org/10.1007/978-3-030-01225-0_48
8. Lee, M., Lee, K., Lee, M., Park, J.: Dance motion generation by recombination of body parts from motion source. Intell. Serv. Robot. **11**(2), 139–148 (2017). https://doi.org/10.1007/s11370-017-0241-x
9. miu200521358: 3d-pose-baseline-vmd (2018). https://github.com/miu200521358/3d-pose-baseline-vmd

10. miu200521358: 3dpose_gan_vmd (2018). https://github.com/miu200521358/3dpos e_gan_vmd
11. miu200521358: Fcrn-depthprediction-vmd (2018). https://github.com/miu200521 358/FCRN-DepthPrediction-vmd
12. miu200521358: Vmd-3d-pose-baseline-multi (2018). https://github.com/miu20052 1358/VMD-3d-pose-baseline-multi
13. olympe: Bvh player (2014). http://lo-th.github.io/olympe/BVH_player.html
14. Pavlovic, V., Rehg, J., MacCormick, J.: Learning switching linear models of human motion. In: Advances in Neural Information Processing Systems (NIPS) (2001)
15. rg3: youtube-dl (2018). https://github.com/rg3/youtube-dl
16. Taylor, G., Sigal, L., Fleet, D., Hinton, G.: Dynamical binary latent variable models for 3D human pose tracking. In: IEEE Conference on Computer Vision and Pattern Recognition (CVPR) (2010)
17. Umino, M., Soga, A., Hirayama, M.: Blended choreography of ballet and contemporary dance by using 3DCG motion data (2007)
18. Urtasun, R., Fleet, D., Geiger, A., Popovic, J., Darrell, T., Lawrence, N.: Topologically constrained latent variable models (2008)
19. Zhou, L., Li, Z., Xiao, S., He, C., Huang, Z., Li, H.: Auto conditioned recurrent networks for extended complex human motion synthesis. In: ICLR (2018)

Identifying Individual Cats by Their Chewing Sounds Using Deep Learning

Yu Suzuki[1]([⊠]) and Akane Osawa[2]

[1] School of Project Design, Miyagi University, 1-1 Gakuen,
Kurokawa-gun, Taiwa-cho, Miyagi 981-3298, Japan
suzu@myu.ac.jp
[2] Hitachi Solutions East Japan, Miyagi, Japan

Abstract. Social interest in animal welfare inclined toward reducing animal stress and in environmental enrichment oriented toward reproducing the natural living environments of animals is growing. To achieve these, observing and understanding the behavior of individual animals, in an environment with multiple animals, in detail is necessary. This research aims to achieve the individual identification of an animal without causing them unnecessary stress. In this research, we evaluated the sound of chewing as an individual discriminator for cats, one of the most familiar animals. The proposed system can analyze cat behavior without causing stress because it identifies a cat without attaching a tag. As an example of the application of the individual discriminator, we developed a food container that can identify individual cats.

Keywords: Animal computer interaction · Animal identification

1 Introduction

Keeping multiple animals in the same space is common; for example, in some homes, multiple animals such as dogs and cats live in the same room and in zoos, many cages have multiple animals. Social interest in animal welfare, which seeks to prevent stress to animals, and in environmental enrichment, which seeks to recreate the original living environment of animals is growing. In homes and zoos, where multiple animals are kept, providing appropriate care for each animal is necessary.

The most common method of identifying individual animals is to attach a physical tag, such as a collar or ear tag to the animal. However, this method causes stress to the animal. In this research, we aim to identify individual animals while avoiding this consequence.

2 Method for the Individual Identification of Animals

2.1 Individual Identification with Tags

Pet products that can monitor the behavior of animals and manage the health of animals are available; for example, a collar-type wearable device [4] can record

© Springer Nature Switzerland AG 2021
C. Stephanidis et al. (Eds.): HCII 2021, CCIS 1420, pp. 556–560, 2021.
https://doi.org/10.1007/978-3-030-78642-7_74

an animal's activities such as running, walking, eating, and sleeping. A toilet system can also be used to automatically record animal urination data for health management. These products enable owners to know the behavior of their pets while they are away from home and are useful for health management. However, when using these products with multiple pets, the owner has to attach a special tag to each pet for individual identification.

2.2   Individual Identification with Biological Features

Recently, biometrics has been attracting attention as a method of individual identification. Biometrics involves technology that uses physical or behavioral characteristics to identify individuals. Unlike conventional identification technologies, biometrics does not involve a tag-based identification method, but a method that uses differences among individuals. Two types of features are used in biometrics: physical and behavioral features. For physical features, the nose pattern of a cat [2] and the face of a chimpanzee [3] have been used.

Behavioral features have been used for biometric authentication of humans, such as human interface for the touch operation of smartphones [1], but they have not been fully applied to animals. If identifying individuals based on their behavioral characteristics is possible, it would be possible to do so for animals as well.

3   Method for Individual Identification Using the Behavioral Features of Animals

3.1   Target Animal and Goals

In this research, we use behavioral information to identify individual cats. By using behavioral information for identification, cats can maintain a normal life in a normal environment. We aim to achieve optimal environmental enrichment and animal welfare without causing stress to cats.

3.2   Use of Chewing Sounds

In this research, we try to identify individual cats using their food chewing sounds. There are two main reasons for using the chewing sounds to identify individual cats. First, the sounds generated while eating food are diverse, involving chewing, breathing, meowing and purring, and are likely to include individual differences. Second, cats tend to eat food in multiple portions. Therefore, individual identification is effective even when cats are left alone at home.

4   Individual Identification Using Chewing Sounds

In this study, we developed an individual discriminator using machine learning to identify individual cats by their chewing sounds. Of the several types of machine learning methods, we used a learning method called supervised learning in this research and created the supervised data using the labeled chewing sounds of individuals. The machine learning used in this discriminator is based on Deep Learning, in which artificial intelligence extracts features from training data. Python was used for the development of the discriminator. The process flow of the individual discriminator is as follows:

1. Collect training data by recording chewing sounds several times.
2. Extract the features of the collected chewing sounds by using mel-frequency cepstral coefficients (MFCCs).
3. Create an individual discriminator trained using the feature data.

4.1 Collection of Chewing Sounds

To create training data, we recorded the chewing sound of each animal several times. As shown in Fig. 1, the chewing sounds were recorded for two cats owned by the author. All data were labeled after removing noise other than the chewing sounds and silent intervals occurring before chewing. As a result, we collected 815 s of chewing sounds from Cat A and 1260 s from Cat B. To standardize the conditions, both cats were fed the same type of dry food for recording.

(a) Cat A   (b) Cat B

Fig. 1. Two cats eating dry food.

4.2 Feature Extraction from Chewing Sounds

In this research, MFCC was used as a feature. To obtain MFCCs, low-frequency parts are extracted finely, and high-frequency parts are extracted coarsely according to the characteristics of human hearing. MFCC-extraction is a method used for extracting features of human voice, but it can also be used for classifying music and instrumental sounds, so we decided to utilize this feature in this research.

Fig. 2. A food container for cats with a built-in discriminator.

4.3   Creation of an Individual Discriminator

First, we attempted to create a learning model using machine learning. To create a model using machine learning, we referred to the scilkit-learn algorithm cheat-sheet and tried four types of algorithmic classifiers: SVC (Support Vector Classifier), KNN (K-Nearest Neighbors), Randomforest, and GradientBoosting as EnsembleClassifiers. As a result, the correct answer rate was approximately 60%–70%. By adjusting the parameters of each classifier, the accuracy was slightly improved, but the learning time became longer.

Next, we attempted to create a model using deep learning to improve the accuracy and shorten the learning time. TensorFlow, which is also used for Google's voice search, was used as a backend to create the model using the Keras library. When the created models were evaluated by cross-validation, devising models with an accuracy of more than 90% was possible. By storing the models and weights with good learning results, we were able to perform discrimination with only the time required to load the good models and weights. As the results were satisfactory, we used the model created by deep learning as an individual discriminator.

5   Food Container with a Built-In Discriminator

As an application of the developed discriminator, we made a food container for cats with a built-in discriminator. Figure 2 shows the food container and a cat in the middle of a meal. The food container has three functions: cat identification, measurement of food intake, and notification. The food container identifies the cat and measures the amount of food the cat has eaten. When the cat eats a meal, the container sends a message to the owner which contains the identified cat name and amount of the meal eaten by the cat.

The food container is equipped with a load cell, amp module, and Arduino Uno. The owner can receive the notification from Slack and the LINE app. Therefore, obtaining data on the diet of each individual cat is possible.

As a result of using this food container on two cats, we confirmed that it can correctly identify each cat and send notifications. However, noises such as a human voice cause some false identification.

6 Conclusions

In this research, we identified individual cats using the differences in their chewing sounds. We were able to identify individual cats without stressing them because there was no need to attach tags to the cats themselves. By creating a food container capable of individual identification and weight measurement, we have shown that cats can maintain their normal lives, and their owners can manage their health and watch over them.

As a future project, we will develop an individual identification method utilizing various behavioral characteristics. In this research, we focused on cats, but we would like to make similar efforts with other animals to realize animal welfare.

References

1. Bo, C., Zhang, L., Li, X.Y., Huang, Q., Wang, Y.: Silentsense: silent user identification via touch and movement behavioral biometrics. In: Proceedings of the 19th Annual International Conference on Mobile Computing & Networking, pp. 187–190 (2013)
2. Chen, Y.-C., Hidayati, S.C., Cheng, W.-H., Hu, M.-C., Hua, K.-L.: Locality constrained sparse representation for cat recognition. In: Tian, Q., Sebe, N., Qi, G.-J., Huet, B., Hong, R., Liu, X. (eds.) MMM 2016. LNCS, vol. 9517, pp. 140–151. Springer, Cham (2016). https://doi.org/10.1007/978-3-319-27674-8_13
3. Schofield, D., et al.: Chimpanzee face recognition from videos in the wild using deep learning. Sci. Adv. 5(9), eaaw0736 (2019)
4. Yonezawa, K., Miyaki, T., Rekimoto, J.: Cat@log: sensing device attachable to pet cats for supporting human-pet interaction. In: Proceedings of the International Conference on Advances in Computer Entertainment Technology, pp. 149–156 (2009)

Smartphone-Based Recognition Aid of Upward Staircases with People for the Visually Impaired

Hotaka Takizawa[1]([✉]), Genki Sekita[1], Makoto Kobayashi[2], Akihisa Ohya[1], and Mayumi Aoyagi[3]

[1] University of Tsukuba, Tsukuba 305-8573, Japan
takizawa@cs.tsukuba.ac.jp
[2] Tsukuba University of Technology, 305-8520 Tsukuba, Japan
[3] Aichi University of Education, 448-8542 Kariya, Japan

Abstract. Many visually impaired individuals often use upward staircases to move to other floors, but it is difficult for them to find distant upward staircases. Several assistive systems have been proposed in the past, and the recent trends are smartphone-based systems. This paper described a CNN-based recognition method of upward staircases. The recognition method was a key technology for our smartphone-based assistive system. In the method, GoogLeNet models were used as CNNs. Two types of image data augmentation were used beforehand. One was the data augmentation based on the Affine transformation, and the other was the data augmentation based on the Cutout technique, where square- and human-type masks were arranged in the grid positions of images. These masks were able to emulate situations where upward staircases were partially occluded by persons. These data augmentation produced four image datasets and therefore four GoogLeNet models, which were applied to the 560 images of actual 28 environments. There were upward staircases in the 14 environments, and not in the other 14 environments. The recognition accuracy was evaluated by F-measures. When the square-type masks were used, the maximum F-measure was 0.95.

Keywords: Visually impaired individuals · Upward staircases · CNN

1 Introduction

World Health Organization reported that the number of visually impaired individuals was at least 2.2 billion worldwide [1]. They often face to difficulties in their daily life. Recognition of staircases is one of such difficult tasks. When they want to move to other floors, they often use staircases, but they cannot find distant staircases by use of white canes.

There were many obstacle detection systems for visually impaired users. These systems can detect staircases as dangerous objects, but cannot help such users know whether there are staircases [2]. Several assistive systems can notify

© Springer Nature Switzerland AG 2021
C. Stephanidis et al. (Eds.): HCII 2021, CCIS 1420, pp. 561–566, 2021.
https://doi.org/10.1007/978-3-030-78642-7_75

the users about upward staircases by use of laser pointers [3] and RGB-D sensors [4–6]. They were the prototype systems, and therefore it was difficult for many users to obtain.

We proposed several smartphone-based system to assist visually impaired users to find target objects such as escalators [7] and restroom pictograms [8]. The users panned the cameras of their smartphones to promising directions, and took the images of environments. If the objects were found in the images, the smartphones output voice guidance to the users.

In this paper, upward staircases are recognized as target objects by a CNN-based method. GoogLeNet [9] models are used as CNNs. Two types of image data augmentation are used beforehand. One is the data augmentation based on the Affine transformation, and the other is the data augmentation based on the Cutout technique [10]. The recognition method was applied to the images of upward staircases with and without persons.

1.1   Affine-Based Data Augmentation

Each image is reduced to three sizes. Regions of interest (ROI) are set at the centers of the images, and are translated to eight directions. At each position, the ROI is rotated in six directions. These processes generate $189\ (= 3 \times 9 \times 7)$ images from one image.

1.2   Cutout-Based Data Augmentation

In general, there are often one or more persons on upward staircases, and their numbers and positions are various. It is difficult to collect the training images of all the patterns. In this paper, we use the Cutout technique where training images are partially masked by square-type regions. The positions of the masks are randomly changed in every epochs of the training phase of CNN.

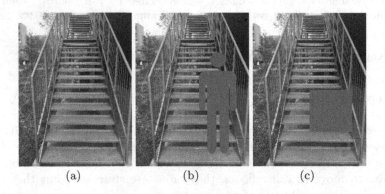

(a)   (b)   (c)

Fig. 1. (a) Image of upward staircases. (b) Image masked by a human-type mask. (c) Image masked by a square-type mask.

In this paper, we propose an improved Cutout-based technique that uses human-type masks as well as square-type masks. These masks are set at the 10×10 grid positions of training images, which are input into CNN at all once in the training phase. The pixel values of the masks are set to be the mean values of the images. Figure 1 shows the example image of upward staircases and the images masked by human- and square-type masks.

The human-type masks can emulate situations where steps are partially occluded by persons. In addition, by setting the masks at the grid positions, occlusion patterns can be expressed comprehensively.

2   Experiments

2.1   Image Datasets for Training

310 and 310 images of environments with and without upward staircases, respectively, were taken by use of iPhone6. There were no persons in these environments. From the 620 images, four image datasets were generated as follows:

1. Dataset 1: the 620 images.
2. Dataset 2: $117,180 \ (= 310 \times 2 \times 189)$ images generated by applying the Affine-based data augmentation.
3. Dataset 3: $62,000 \ (= 310 \times 2 \times 100)$ images generated by applying the Cutout-based data augmentation with *square*-type masks.
4. Dataset 4: $62,000$ images generated by applying the Cutout-based data augmentation with *human*-type masks.

2.2   Image Datasets for Testing

14 and 14 environments with and without upward staircases were selected, respectively. 560 images were taken by use of the same smartphone, and four image datasets were produced as follows:

1. Dataset A: 140 images of upward staircases without any persons.
2. Dataset B: 140 images of upward staircases with one person.
3. Dataset C: 140 images of upward staircases with two persons.
4. Dataset D: 140 images of other objects such as sidewalks and buildings.

2.3   Results

Four GoogLeNet models were trained by use of the four image datasets, respectively. These GoogLeNet models were tested by use of the following three image dataset combinations:

1. Dataset A and D
2. Dataset B and D
3. Dataset C and D

Table 1. Recognition accuracy of upward staircases.

	DS combination	F measure
DS1	A and D	0.77
	B and D	0.54
	C and D	0.51
DS2	A and D	0.87
	B and D	0.86
	C and D	0.78
DS3	A and D	0.95
	B and D	0.92
	C and D	0.92
DS4	A and D	0.82
	B and D	0.82
	C and D	0.82

The images in the dataset combinations were input to the GoogLeNet models, which output the probabilities of the images being upward staircases. The recognition accuracy was evaluated by F-measures.

Table 1 lists the F-measures. DS1, 2, 3 and 4 represent Dataset 1, 2, 3, and 4, respectively, and "A and D", "B and D", and "C and D" represent the dataset combinations. For example, 0.77 was obtained by applying the GoogLeNet model trained by DS1 to the dataset combination A and D.

DS1	20%	0%	25%
DS2	38%	68%	100%
DS3	96%	100%	100%
DS4	0%	100%	97%

Fig. 2. Images of upward staircases without and with persons.

DS1	0%	49%
DS2	0%	2%
DS3	0%	100%
DS4	0%	69%

Fig. 3. Images of other objects.

Figure 2 shows the images of upward staircases with their probabilities. In the first image, there were no persons, whereas in the second and third images, there were one and two persons, respectively. The rows of DS1, 2, 3, and 4 represent the probabilities obtained by the GoogLeNet models trained by DS1, 2, 3, and 4, respectively. The model failed to recognize all the images when trained by DS1, but succeeded when trained by DS3. The model with DS4 failed the first image and succeeded the second and third images. Square-type masks were effective, but human-type masks should be improved.

Figure 3 shows the images of other objects. The first image was recognized correctly, but the second image was failed when DS3 and 4 were used. It was possible that floor terraces were mistakenly recognized as steps.

3 Conclusion

This paper proposed a CNN-based recognition method of upward staircases. GoogLeNet models were used as CNNs. Two types of image data augmentation were used. The recognition method was applied to the 560 images of the actual 28 environments, and the recognition accuracy was evaluated by F-measures. The maximum F-measure was 0.95. One of our future works is to improve the shapes of masks in Cutout.

Acknowledgment. This work was supported in part by the JSPS KAKENHI Grant Number 19H04500.

References

1. WHO: World health organization, media centre, visual impairment and blindness, fact sheet n° 282 (2017). http://www.who.int/mediacentre/factsheets/fs282/en/. Accessed 15 Jan 2018

2. Kaur, P., Kaur, S.: Proposed hybrid color histogram based obstacle detection technique. In: Proceedings of the Third International Symposium on Computer Vision and the Internet, VisionNet 20116, pp. 88–97. Association for Computing Machinery, New York (2016)
3. Yasumuro, Y., Murakami, M., Imura, M., Kuroda, T., Manabe, Y., Chihara, K.: E-cane with situation presumption for the visually impaired. In: Carbonell, N., Stephanidis, C. (eds.) UI4ALL 2002. LNCS, vol. 2615, pp. 409–421. Springer, Heidelberg (2003). https://doi.org/10.1007/3-540-36572-9_32
4. Filipe, V., Fernandes, F., Fernandes, H., Sousa, A., Paredes, H., Barroso, J.: Blind navigation support system based on Microsoft Kinect. In: Proceedings of the 4th International Conference on Software Development for Enhancing Accessibility and Fighting Info-exclusion (DSAI 2012), Douro Region, Portugal, pp. 94–101 (2012)
5. Wang, S., Pan, H., Zhang, C., Tian, Y.: RGB-D image-based detection of stairs, pedestrian crosswalks and traffic signs. J. Vis. Commun. Image Represent. **25**(2), 263–272 (2014)
6. Takizawa, H., Yamaguchi, S., Aoyagi, M., Ezaki, N., Mizuno, S.: Kinect cane: an assistive system for the visually impaired based on the concept of object recognition aid. Pers. Ubiquit. Comput. **19**(5), 955–965 (2015). https://doi.org/10.1007/s00779-015-0841-4
7. Nakamura, D., Takizawa, H., Aoyagi, M., Ezaki, N., Mizuno, S.: Smartphone-based escalator recognition for the visually impaired. Sensors **17**(5), 1057 (2017)
8. Iwamoto, T., Takizawa, H., Aoyagi, M.: A preliminary study on recognition of restroom signs by use of SVM and CNN (in Japanese). IEICE Technical reports (WIT), No. 180, pp. 11–14. IEICE (2018)
9. Szegedy, C., et al.: Going deeper with convolutions. In: 2015 IEEE Conference on Computer Vision and Pattern Recognition (CVPR), pp. 1–9 (2015)
10. Devries, T., Taylor, G.W.: Improved regularization of convolutional neural networks with cutout. CoRR, Vol. abs/1708.04552 (2017)

Towards Commonsense Reasoning in AAL Environments

Athanasios Tsitsipas[✉][ID] and Lutz Schubert[ID]

Institute of Information Resource Management, University of Ulm, Ulm, Germany
{athanasios.tsitsipas,lutz.schubert}@uni-ulm.de

Abstract. Ambient Assisted Living (AAL) is an application of Smart Environments, dealing with elderlies and their caregivers' assistance in their daily life within their enhanced apartments. An AAL environment needs constant observation of the inhabitant's activities to inform caregivers of critical situations respectively to react to them, such as the patient leaving the flat with the stove still on. Setting up an AAL environment is costly and complicated, as all sensors are tailored to the specific situation. Various industrial systems or research activities exist to monitor the environment and apply a rule-based inference to detect the multiple conditions as far as possible. There are, however, a range of standard day-to-day sensors, such as light switches, window sensors etc., which do not directly monitor patient conditions but allow for inference about a situation, e.g. whether a person has left the flat. We call this "lifted" contextual information. Also, there is much uncertainty in such environments, such as sensor malfunctions, power loss, or connectivity issues. Hence, a situation awareness system should freely combine and switch between combinations of sensors for identifying and verifying the current situation, respectively, inferences drawn from it. For example, confirm that the person has left the flat by checking for a webcam movement. This resembles our ability to use commonsense when we look at possible sensor readings on a dashboard. We make plain inferences based on a hypothesis on the given evidence. Such a system needs to make logical connections between different data and contribute to a derived information. We propose developing a logic-based system using the sensor events as evidence for a commonsense reasoning task.

Keywords: Commonsense reasoning · Knowledge representation · Probabilistic theory · Event Calculus

1 Introduction

Reasoning about an environment in the context of smart homes gained significant attention in the last two decades. Researchers have been developing concepts and tools to employ miscellaneous artificial intelligence (AI) techniques for ambient assisted living (AAL) environments [13]. Such systems target the well-being of the inhabitants [18], via health monitoring [8], energy-efficient appliance operation [11] and personalised service adaptation [12]. AI applications in AAL

© Springer Nature Switzerland AG 2021
C. Stephanidis et al. (Eds.): HCII 2021, CCIS 1420, pp. 567–572, 2021.
https://doi.org/10.1007/978-3-030-78642-7_76

environments perceive the inhabitant via the surrounding sensors and automatically adapt or make decisions. This component eventually exhibits reasoning capabilities and systematic decision support; see [14] for a recent survey. An essential aspect of those systems is detecting and recognising human activities or situations (such as left the apartment) and detecting emergencies (such as falls). It is of high relevance for the ageing population, where an AAL system [9] would notify or act promptly in scenarios of significance. However, such ecosystems' complexity requires high maintenance costs and complex relations to achieve semantic interoperability to recognise activities in focus. There can be many situations worth identifying using sensors in a single room, ranging from "is someone present" to "is the water boiling". Considering an entire home, we may end up with hundreds of such situations, and an office building could have thousands. This leads to increasing numbers of sensors to cover all the above situations, driving the economic and maintenance costs to higher levels.

This paper focuses on the reusability and repurposing of existing day-to-day sensors in the environment (e.g., light switches, contact sensors). As such, they do not directly offer the property in need (e.g., situation or activity) but allow their incorporation in an inference task, as "lifted" contextual information. One with a naive knowledge of physics may exercise a hypothesis evaluation about the situation using sensor results as evidence. We offer a solution to encode this Commonsense Knowledge (CK) in rules with the different combinations of sensors while forming a model for recognising the situation in need. The rules mentioned above contain a form of uncertainty in their definition. More specifically, we employ a Markov Logic Network (MLN) for developing a probabilistic model to support the uncertain varieties of different compositions of sensors, expressed as commonsense logic rules, for identifying the situation in need. The inference task also contains a set of meta-rules, which encode the interaction between the sensor events and their interpretation effects. The paper gives a quick overview of the approach and a discussion over state of the art in reasoning in AAL environments. We conclude with a short outlook and future steps.

2   Proposed Approach

This section will briefly describe our approach to representing the situation recognition from "lifted" contextual information (i.e., sensor information) using CK and its uncertainty aspects. In our case, we use the term "CK" to metaphorically argue behind the transfer of knowledge one has behind a naive understanding of physics of how sensors work. For general definitions of CK, see [6]. For example, one knows that a light bulb in operation, in simple words, emits light and gets hotter over time; this accounts for commonsense. As such, using environmental properties (of light intensity and ambient temperature), we may reason behind the followings situations via explanations of the sensor readings (accounts as knowledge): *(i)* a light switch is flipped on, *(ii)* someone is present in the room, *(iii)* but could also possibly mean that there is a fire in the room; and many others. Specifically, for the situation in *(iii)*, the readings of a light sensor and a temperature sensor may not be enough. An additional sensor (e.g., an air quality sensor) will increase the explanation's accuracy ("there is fire"). One may observe a factor of uncertainty regarding the reasoning behind some sensor readings, as much as a process of Commonsense Reasoning (CR) does.

We automate this form of CR, using symbolic representations of sensor data in logic-based rules over continuous time. MLN is a robust framework that combines both logical and probabilistic reasoning [16]. It allows us to declare a stochastic model at a high level using first-order logic. Besides, we use the well-defined temporal formalism of Event Calculus (EC), a many-sorted predicate calculus, to reason about events and their effects [10]. A hybrid approach of the two was presented by Skarlatidis et al. [19], developing a dialect of EC to model the inertia laws for recognising complex events in an annotated video surveillance dataset. Their work inspired us to select the technologies for dealing with uncertain knowledge and extract situations of interest from continuous sensor data.

The construction of a first-order knowledge base is expressive, powerful and uses unambiguous semantics for its syntactic rules. Constructing an MLN Knowledge Base (KB) is a set of tuples $\langle w, F \rangle$, where w is the confidence value to the rule formula F. Each first-order *formula* contains different atoms connected with logical operators. Each *atom* is a predicate symbol applied to a tuple of *terms*, representing an object in the domain. A *term* can be a constant (e.g., a sensor type - ContactSensor, MotionSensor), a variable (which ranges over a domain - a range of constants) or a function (applied over terms also).

Using the domain-independent predicates from the EC dialect (MLN-EC) in [19], we create CK formulas that reflect different sensors' compositions to recognise a situation of interest. EC's main components are the *event* and the *fluent* (a property whose value changes over time). In our system, the *events* are "lifted" contextual information from the sensor data. They are low-level symbolic representations of sensor data, matching primitive shape-based patterns - we name them *shapeoids*. The *fluents* are the monitored situations whose value persists over time. The meta-rules of EC encode the so-called *inertia laws* [17], which dictate that something continuous to hold unless it is indicated otherwise (e.g., terminated by an event). The variables and functions start with a lowercase letter. The predicates and constants with an uppercase letter.

The offline statistical relation framework of MLN, combined with the meta-rules of Event Calculus, offers a formal, but at the same time, a powerful probabilistic logic-based method for complex event recognition [19]. Open-source implementations of MLN exists, such as Alchemy[1], Tuffy[2], LoMRF[3]. For our purpose, we use LoMRF as its implementation is in Scala, matching the language of any modern data processing framework (e.g., Apache BEAM[4]), to realise a

---

[1] http://alchemy.cs.washington.edu/.
[2] http://i.stanford.edu/hazy/tuffy/.
[3] https://lomrf.readthedocs.io/.
[4] https://beam.apache.org/.

holistic architecture for online inferences from streaming data. Also, LoMRF has the most recent development cycle than any of the other tools.

Finally, we envisage an architecture for our approach and turn it into a holistic system and a complete pipeline that spawns over the following steps/components:

- Modelling CK and representing a different set of sensor compositions as alternatives for monitored situations.
- Extract low-level symbolic representations of streaming sensor data, matching primitive shape-based patterns - named shapeoids.
- Initiate dynamic inference processes (i.e., inference in MLN) on incoming streaming shapeoid events while posing queries for the recognition.

3   Related Work

Several different approaches have been pursued over the years to encode CK [6] and perform CR [7]. In AAL, the notion of CR is applied when there is a creation of a symbolic knowledge base and perform reasoning upon these symbols. In a recent survey [4], the authors contacted a study for augmenting the situation of AAL and the kinds of solutions applied in such environments. The pervasiveness of sensor devices in smart environments enables systems to "read" and understand the environmental behaviour from sensor data [3, 20, 21]. The task of reasoning in AAL, bases mostly on the probes of information installed in the environments (i.e., sensors) and the context they are applied for (e.g., the inhabitant, daily activities etc.). A fundamental step in a reasoning task, is the initial representation of the entities and their connections (if any). Many use the concept of ontologies [5] as a shared conceptual model of the world, to facilitate the core knowledge representation. The authors in [15] distinguish between lightweight ontologies, storing only the formal hierarchies and relationships, and heavyweight ontologies, adding inference rules for semantic interpretations. Nonetheless, we concur that some situations do not exist implicitly in the data or are challenging to collect and annotate.

The inference process for reasoning with ontologies is monotonic; a new observation will not change already inferred knowledge. For instance, in [1], the authors use a hybrid system incorporating an ontological representation of data and a non-monotonic inference process using answer set logic for sensor data [2] targeting AAL environments. However, their approach does not handle rule uncertainty, although they model their semantics in a model that supports fallible logic. Besides, their approach does not support a formal grounded theory at the meta-level, dictating logic and supporting the CR mode [7]. We opt for integrating fundamental domains from formal grounded theories, probabilistic theory and modern dynamic data processing solutions to automate the CR in smart environments.

4   Conclusion and Future Steps

This paper introduced an approach to use "lifted" contextual information from sensor data and introduce sensor data interpretation via CR rules. A naive knowledge of physics coupled with background domain knowledge of a smart environment opts for detecting occurrences of certain situations. As such, declaring these logical "inference" sentences results in a human-readable form of reasoning that incorporates commonsense logic.

Due to the uncertain nature of making a hypothesis about given observations, we use MLN to soften the constraints against the possible world where the logical sentences are satisfied. The inertia rules must remain as hard constraints. The choice of a bounded environment, such as AAL, narrows down the available knowledge for encoding it with our method. The approach does not foresee an infinite amount of encoded inference rules, as inference in MLN may become intractable if we make too many open-world assumptions in the CK rules. The complexity of the system relies on the definition of the CK rules. However, our approach's novelty is the redundancy in detecting the desired situation via alternatives from ones' CK with the available nearby sensors, considering that we normally use direct means for sensing (e.g., use a contact sensor to detect if the door is open).

As future steps, we want to demonstrate in a dynamic scenario of how the sensor data patterns (shapeoids) relate to semantic interpretations (CK rules). Moreover, an evaluation with a real dataset is foreseen to examine the scalability of the approach.

Acknowledgements. This work was partially funded by the Federal Ministry of Education and Research (BMBF) of Germany under Grant No. 01IS18072.

References

1. Alirezaie, M., et al.: An ontology-based context-aware system for smart homes: E-care@ home. Sensors **17**(7), 1586 (2017)
2. Baral, C.: Knowledge Representation, Reasoning and Declarative Problem Solving. Cambridge University Press, Cambridge (2003)
3. Barnaghi, P., Ganz, F., Henson, C., Sheth, A.: Computing perception from sensor data. In: 2012 IEEE Sensors, pp. 1–4. IEEE (2012)
4. Calvaresi, D., Cesarini, D., Sernani, P., Marinoni, M., Dragoni, A.F., Sturm, A.: Exploring the ambient assisted living domain: a systematic review. J. Ambient Intell. Human. Comput., 1–19 (2016). https://doi.org/10.1007/s12652-016-0374-3
5. Compton, M., et al.: The SSN ontology of the W3C semantic sensor network incubator group. J. Web Semant. **17**, 25–32 (2012)
6. Davis, E.: Logical formalizations of commonsense reasoning: a survey. J. Artif. Intell. Res. **59**, 651–723 (2017)
7. Davis, E., Marcus, G.: Commonsense reasoning and commonsense knowledge in artificial intelligence. Commun. ACM **58**(9), 92–103 (2015)
8. Falcionelli, N., et al.: Indexing the event calculus: towards practical human-readable personal health systems. Artif. Intell. Med. **96**, 154–166 (2019)

9. Köckemann, U., et al.: Open-source data collection and data sets for activity recognition in smart homes. Sensors **20**(3), 879 (2020)
10. Kowalski, R., Sergot, M.: A logic-based calculus of events. In: Schmidt, J.W., Thanos, C. (eds.) Foundations of Knowledge Base Management. Topics in Information Systems, pp. 23–55. Springer, Heidelberg (1989). https://doi.org/10.1007/978-3-642-83397-7_2
11. Lu, C.H., Wu, C.L., Weng, M.Y., Chen, W.C., Fu, L.C.: Context-aware energy saving system with multiple comfort-constrained optimization in M2M-based home environment. IEEE Trans. Autom. Sci. Eng. **14**(3), 1400–1414 (2015)
12. Marsa-Maestre, I., Lopez-Carmona, M.A., Velasco, J.R., Navarro, A.: Mobile agents for service personalization in smart environments. J. Netw. **3**(5), 30–41 (2008)
13. Mekuria, D.N., Sernani, P., Falcionelli, N., Dragoni, A.F.: Reasoning in multi-agent based smart homes: a systematic literature review. In: Leone, A., Caroppo, A., Rescio, G., Diraco, G., Siciliano, P. (eds.) ForItAAL 2018. LNEE, vol. 544, pp. 161–179. Springer, Cham (2019). https://doi.org/10.1007/978-3-030-05921-7_13
14. Mekuria, D.N., Sernani, P., Falcionelli, N., Dragoni, A.F.: Smart home reasoning systems: a systematic literature review. J. Ambient Intell. Human. Comput. **12**(4), 4485–4502 (2019). https://doi.org/10.1007/s12652-019-01572-z
15. Poli, R., Obrst, L.: The interplay between ontology as categorial analysis and ontology as technology. In: Poli, R., Healy, M., Kameas, A. (eds.) Theory and Applications of Ontology: Computer Applications, pp. 1–26. Springer, Dordrecht (2010). https://doi.org/10.1007/978-90-481-8847-5_1
16. Richardson, M., Domingos, P.: Markov logic networks. Mach. Learn. **62**(1–2), 107–136 (2006). https://doi.org/10.1007/s10994-006-5833-1
17. Shanahan, M., et al.: Solving the Frame Problem: A Mathematical Investigation of the Common Sense Law of Inertia. MIT Press, Cambridge (1997)
18. Si, H., Kawahara, Y., Morikawa, H., Aoyama, T.: A stochastic approach for creating context-aware services based on context histories in smart home. Cogn. Sci. Res. Paper-Univ. Sussex CSRP **577**, 37 (2005)
19. Skarlatidis, A., Paliouras, G., Artikis, A., Vouros, G.A.: Probabilistic event calculus for event recognition. ACM Trans. Comput. Logic (TOCL) **16**(2), 1–37 (2015)
20. Teixeira, T., Dublon, G., Savvides, A.: A survey of human-sensing: methods for detecting presence, count, location, track, and identity. ACM Comput. Surv. **5**(1), 59–69 (2010)
21. Ur, B., McManus, E., Pak Yong Ho, M., Littman, M.L.: Practical trigger-action programming in the smart home. In: Proceedings of the SIGCHI Conference on Human Factors in Computing Systems, pp. 803–812 (2014)

Preventing Discrepancies Between Indicated Algorithmic Certainty and Actual Performance: An Experimental Solution

Johanna M. Werz[1]([⊠]), Konstantin Zähl[2], Esther Borowski[3], and Ingrid Isenhardt[3]

[1] IMA, RWTH Aachen University, Dennewartstr. 27, 52068 Aachen, Germany
johanna.werz@ima.rwth-aachen.de
[2] Institut für Unternehmenskybernetik E.V., Aachen, Germany
[3] IMA, RWTH Aachen University, Aachen, Germany

Abstract. Demands for transparency in algorithms and their processes increase as the usage of algorithmic support in human decision-making raises. At the same time, algorithm aversion – abandoning algorithmic advice after seeing an algorithm err – persist [1]. The current paper proposes a way to investigate the effect of transparency, i.e., disclosing an algorithm's certainty about its future performance, on the usage of algorithms even when they err. A respective experimental setting requires varying algorithmic certainty while keeping the algorithm's error rate constant. However, experiencing discrepancy between the certainty information and the actual performance could distort participants' behavior. The paper, therefore, proposes a solution to the question: How can a study design prevent a discrepancy between indicated success rate and observable performance?

This poster describes an experimental weight estimation task that allows to measure advice deviation from the recommendation. It introduces a way to choose probability values so that the amount of observed algorithmic errors that occur is equally likely for two different probability conditions. With this design, researchers are able to manipulate the success probability disclosed by an algorithm while providing a sequence of algorithmic advice with a constant number or errors. This provides a way to prevent discrepancy between the indicated certainty and the actual performance in comparable experimental conditions.

The poster describes the process as well as the resulting test material. It furthermore discusses the benefits as well as limitations of the proposed study design.

Keywords: Algorithm aversion · Transparency · Augmented decision-making · Algorithmic performance · Human computer interaction

1 Introduction

Nowadays, algorithmic advice influences multiple aspect of our modern world: Be it dating, navigation, music choice or shopping [2]. In a professional context, too, people increasingly rely on algorithms to structure huge amounts of data and prepare decisions.

C. Stephanidis et al. (Eds.): HCII 2021, CCIS 1420, pp. 573–580, 2021.
https://doi.org/10.1007/978-3-030-78642-7_77

As algorithms are outperforming humans in many domains, e.g. [3], human decision making can profit from algorithmic advice.

Despite people appear to be confident in algorithms and are increasingly using their advice [2], the effect called algorithm aversion persists: When observing an algorithm err, people stop using it even if it deteriorates their decisions [1, 4]. One way to overcome this effect could be to adjust users' expectation in algorithmic capabilities, i.e. by telling them that the algorithm entails some uncertainty [5]. However, an experimental set-up that combines both a certainty measure (e.g., average success rate) with an actual erring algorithm is not trivial. Such an experimental setting needs to vary algorithmic certainty while keeping the algorithm's error rate constant to allow for comparison between certainty conditions. However, users should not experience any discrepancy between the certainty information given and the actual performance as this might introduce feelings of confusion. The paper, therefore, addresses the following question: How can the predicted accuracy of an algorithm be altered while keeping its performance stable? That is, how can probability calculations prevent users from experiencing discrepancy between indicated success rate and observable performance?

2 Theoretical Background

Previous studies have investigated advice utilization in participants by employing a Judge-Advisor System (JAS), e.g. [6, 7]. In a JAS paradigm participants have to formulate an initial judgement for a given task, get advice, and then give their final judgement [8]. This design provides the opportunity to measure the weight of advice (WOA), which is the ratio of the final judgment in relation to the initial judgment [9]. In many studies that investigate algorithm aversion, wizard-of-Oz-designs are used to vary the available information of an algorithmic advisor and measuring its effect on WOA. Experimental conditions, e.g., vary available information about others using the algorithm [10], available explanations [11], or about the type of task [2].When humans interact with algorithms, several studies show that they expect them to be perfect [12, 13]. When experiencing a violation of this expectation, e.g. when seeing an algorithm err, users deter it – algorithm aversion occurs [4]. Disclosing uncertainty of algorithms along with its advice could be a means to regulate expectation about algorithmic results in advance and to overcome algorithm aversion [5].

However, information about the algorithm's certainty can be framed in several ways. Depending on the nature of the task, uncertainty on the one hand is a success/error rate (for tasks with distinct correct or false outcomes). It can be disclosed positively (e.g. as 90% confident) or negatively (e.g. 10% unsure). On the other hand, uncertainty can be a precision measure that refers to the degree of variance, with which algorithm results are scattered around a true target value (e.g. confidence interval).

The uncertainty value, i.e. a clear success or error probability, has already been investigated in algorithm research when participants – without any error experience – had to decide whether a human or a machine should perform a task, e.g. [14, 15]. This might be because "The result is 90% likely to be correct" is easy to understand. What is more, such a statement is also likely to occur in real algorithmic advice settings. Many current supervised machine learning algorithms for classification tasks are evaluated by so-called train-test split [16, 17]. The data is split into two parts: one to train the algorithm and one to test its predictive performance. This leads to claims about algorithmic performance such as "The algorithm predicts the results correctly in 87% of the cases". That is, an algorithmic success rate is both easy to understand and close to reality.

However, a hypothetical 90% success rate does not guarantee the occurrence of one error in ten trials. Rather, the sequence of algorithmic decisions during the experiment is a result of a random experiment that has a specific probability of actual occurrence. The uncertainty information determines this probability and, thereby, influences how plausible the algorithm's behavior appears to the participant. Experiencing discrepancy between proposed algorithmic certainty and actual error occurrence could lead to surprised or disappointed users and a biased variable of interest, the weight of advice.

At the same time, the experimental settings such as those used to investigate algorithm aversion are characterized by a certain variable being kept constant whereas independent variable(s) of interest are varied to allow for comparison [2, 4, 6, 7, 12–15]. To be able to investigate the effect of algorithmic certainty on the usage of sometimes erring algorithms, as proposed in the current study, a constant number of algorithmic errors across different algorithmic certainty levels is required. However, they have to occur equally likely to allow for comparison and to uphold a plausible setting for participants. An experimental design solution based on probability calculations is required and will be presented in the following.

3 Suggested Method

3.1 Fundamental Idea and Assumptions

To allow for varying algorithmic certainty levels while presenting realistic outcomes to the users, we propose an experimental set-up with a mathematical process to determine certainty levels and a sequence of realistic outcome values. The following decisions must be made initially:

- The amount of trials n
- The amount of errors m
- The probability of such a sequence of errors p_{seq}
- Whether the algorithmic advice is binary (true/false) or continuous (e.g., weight estimates)

The calculation of certainty levels bases on the assumption that each prediction made by one algorithm has a constant probability p_{true} of being right and $p_{false} = 1 - p_{true}$ of being false. Based on that observing m errors in a sequence of n trials can be interpreted as the result of a Bernoulli experiment of two possible outcomes with fixed probabilities:

$$P(m \text{ errors}, p_{true}) = \binom{n}{m} p_{false}^m \, p_{true}^{n-m} \tag{1}$$

We are looking for two different values $p_{true,low}$ and $p_{true,high}$ for one lower and one higher algorithmic certainty level condition. The probability values can be chosen in a

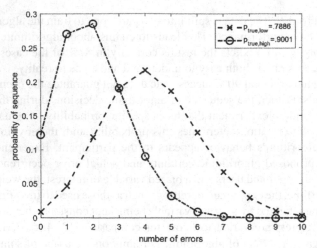

Fig. 1. Two Binomial distributions for $p_{true,low} = 0.7886$ and $p_{true,high} = 0.9001$ ($n = 20$) intersecting at $m = 3$.

way that they produce two Binomial distributions that intersect at m errors (see Fig. 1). Observing a sequence of m errors would therefore be equally likely for both conditions.

The following Sect. 3.1 describes how to determine those certainty levels that satisfy given parameters of n, m and p_{seq}. Afterwards, Sect. 3.2 presents a method of how to adapt the results from Sect. 3.1 for tasks involving continuous estimates.

3.2 Determining Low and High Certainty Values

For a given number of errors m in a sequence of length n there is an infinite amount of possible sequence probabilities p_{seq}. The following procedure leads to possible value sequences:

1. Chose a sequence length n and a number of errors m. Then chose a preferred sequence probability p_{seq}. Given these parameters, the Eq. (1) becomes:

$$(1 - p_{true})^m \, p_{true}^{n-m} = C$$

which is a polynomial of degree $\max(m, n - m)$ and with constant $C = \dfrac{p_{seq}}{\binom{n}{m}}$.

2. Solve the polynomial for p_{true} and dismiss solutions other than $0 < p_{true} < 1$.
3. Chose the lowest solution value as $p_{true,low}$ and the highest as $p_{true,high}$. If there are less than two solutions, or the two probabilities are too close, repeat with a smaller sequence probability p_{seq} or different m and n.

   For the present experiment, we chose the length of $n = 20$ trials with $m = 3$ errors. The sequence probability is set to 19% and the corresponding probability values are determined as $p_{true,low} = 0.7886$ and $p_{true, high} = 0.9001$.

3.3 Transfer to Continuous Estimation Tasks

Apart from tasks with binary true-false results, there are also tasks involving a continuum of possible answers, with varying deviations from the correct answer. Examples are estimation tasks of, i.e., lengths or weights. Assuming an unbiased estimator with a Gaussian distribution, estimates are scattered around the true value with a range described by the standard deviation. For such continuous estimation tasks, errors can be defined as estimates that deviate from the true value by a set margin (e.g., $\pm 20\%$).

That means that, for a given success probability p_{true} of the algorithm, estimates of a wizard-of-Oz algorithm should be sampled from a normal distribution $N(\mu, \sigma^2)$, with mean μ equal to the true target. The standard deviation σ is scaled in a way that a sample is within the defined margin with a probability of p_{true}. Using a z-table for the standard normal distribution, σ can be calculated from $z(p_{\text{true}}/2)$. The following equation must hold

$$\frac{z(p_{\text{true}}/2)}{\sigma_{STD}} = \frac{0.2 * \mu}{\sigma}$$

with $\sigma_{STD} = 1$ and $0.2 * \mu$ the maximum acceptable distance to the true value. Solving for σ gives

$$\sigma = \frac{0.2 * \mu}{z(p_{\text{true}}/2)}.$$

For each trial, a sample is drawn from a normal distribution defined by the above-mentioned μ and σ. For the current experiment, twenty alleged algorithmic estimates have to be calculated for each participant as everybody gets to estimate $n = 20$ trials. Only sequences with errors occurring at the sixth, tenth and 14th trial are presented to participants, to keep the number and positional effect of errors constant across conditions. These algorithmic estimates are used as weight estimates in a wizard-of-Oz experimental setting described in the following.

4 Proposed Experimental Design

To exemplify the above-described principals in an experiment that investigates the effect of disclosed certainty measures on algorithm aversion, the following experimental online study was designed. In a wizard-of-Oz design set up online, participants read about the cover story according to which they are participating in a study that evaluates the performance of a weight estimating algorithm. They read that they will see pictures of fruits and vegetables and have to estimate the weight of the displayed foods. Estimates deviating more than 20% of the real weight will be considered errors.

Without their knowledge, participants take part in one of three conditions: high certainty, low certainty or control group. Each group receives the same text describing algorithm and task. The two certainty groups additionally read the sentence "The algorithm errs in 78.9%/90.1% of cases", for the low and high certainty condition, respectively. These error rates are the results of the above-described procedure.

Participants run through 20 trials. Each trial follows the JAS paradigm. Participants first have to indicate an initial guess on a slider, before they see an algorithmic estimate (see Fig. 2). In the two certainty conditions, this algorithmic advice mentions the condition-dependent success rate of the algorithm again.

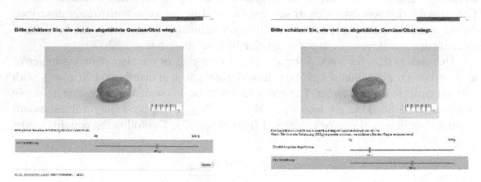

Fig. 2. After an initial guess (left), participant are presented with an algorithmic estimation (right). They read about the algorithms uncertainty rate (except in the control condition) and can adjust their estimation.

In a next step, participants can adjust their estimation and then receive the result of the estimation. The true value is displayed together with the algorithmic result and the participant's final estimation. Estimates are labelled as correct (green letters) or false (red letters), and visualized along a scale (see Fig. 3). After the 6th, 10th and 14th, participants learn that the algorithm gave wrong advice. The values of both correct and false algorithmic advice is generated using the above-described method.

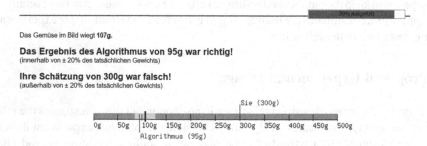

Fig. 3. Feedback page about true weight and estimates: first row indicates the true weight, followed by the algorithmic results and the participant's final as well as initial (small letters below) estimate.

After 20 trials, the participants are asked to retell the displayed success rate as a control question and indicate their individual estimate of the algorithm's performance. Before a debriefing about the Wizard-of-Oz design and the true background of the study, participants answer several questionnaires containing questions about trust in the estimation algorithm and one about their perceived control of technology, followed by some demographic questions.

To compare the effect of certainty condition on advice taking after errors, trials before and after error are of interest. Therefore, the weight on advice (WOA), the relation of final estimation to initial estimation, is calculated for each trial. An ANOVA then tests the interaction of WOA before and after algorithmic errors with certainty condition for significance. The described method makes this comparison across conditions possible thanks to the fact that in all conditions errors are equally likely to occur and do occur equally often – thereby preventing discrepancies between proposed algorithmic certainty and its actual performance.

5 Discussion

The described method offers the opportunity to investigate algorithm aversion with plausible levels for different conditions of high and low algorithmic certainty. With this set up, researchers can experimentally compare the effect of different certainty conditions in combination with the weight on advice in trials following an error in comparison to those without error experience.

One limitation is that the number of mistakes, of total trials as well as the certainty values must be selected beforehand and – having set up the experiment – cannot be changed easily. Furthermore, certainty levels are fixed within conditions and on (two) predefined values. Solving the discrepancy between indicated algorithmic certainty and actual performance therefore comes at the cost of flexibility. What is more, participants could still perceive the errors together with the uncertainty level – despite its equal mathematical probability – as being unrealistic. To this end, at the very end the study entails a question of how the certainty is perceived. Another drawback is a high effort of 20 trials for participants. This can lead to a reduced engagement. An incentive for the best estimates could try to uphold motivation.

Eventually and despite several limitation, the proposed method provides the opportunity to compare different algorithmic performance certainties with the reaction following actual errors. The mathematical process enables a plausible experimental setting in which proposed certainty values corresponds to actual performance. This setup can be used to investigate algorithm aversion but also be adapted to other re-search questions entailing similar variables.

References

1. Burton, J.W., Stein, M.-K., Jensen, T.B.: A systematic review of algorithm aversion in augmented decision making. J. Behav. Decis. Mak. **33**, 220–239 (2020). https://doi.org/10.1002/bdm.2155
2. Logg, J.M., Minson, J.A., Moore, D.A.: Algorithm appreciation: People prefer algorithmic to human judgment. Organ. Behav. Hum. Decis. Process. **151**, 90–103 (2019). https://doi.org/10.1016/j.obhdp.2018.12.005
3. Grove, W.M., Zald, D.H., Lebow, B.S., Snitz, B.E., Nelson, C.: Clinical versus mechanical prediction: a meta-analysis. Psychol. Assess. **12**, 19–30 (2000). https://doi.org/10.1037/1040-3590.12.1.19

4. Dietvorst, B.J., Simmons, J.P., Massey, C.: Algorithm aversion: people erroneously avoid algorithms after seeing them err. J. Exp. Psychol. Gen. **144**, 114–126 (2014). https://doi.org/10.1037/xge0000033
5. Werz, J.M., Borowski, E., Isenhardt, I.: When imprecision improves advice: disclosing algorithmic error probability to increase advice taking from algorithms. In: Stephanidis, C., Antona, M. (eds.) HCII 2020. CCIS, vol. 1224, pp. 504–511. Springer, Cham (2020). https://doi.org/10.1007/978-3-030-50726-8_66
6. Önkal, D., Goodwin, P., Thomson, M., Gönül, S., Pollock, A.: The relative influence of advice from human experts and statistical methods on forecast adjustments. J. Behav. Decis. Mak. **22**, 390–409 (2009). https://doi.org/10.1002/bdm.637
7. Prahl, A., Swol, L.V.: Understanding algorithm aversion: when is advice from automation discounted? J. Forecast. **36**, 691–702 (2017). https://doi.org/10.1002/for.2464
8. Sniezek, J.A., Henry, R.A.: Accuracy and confidence in group judgment. Organ. Behav. Hum. Decis. Process. **43**, 1–28 (1989). https://doi.org/10.1016/0749-5978(89)90055-1
9. Bonaccio, S., Dalal, R.S.: Advice taking and decision-making: an integrative literature review, and implications for the organizational sciences. Organ. Behav. Hum. Decis. Process. **101**, 127–151 (2006). https://doi.org/10.1016/j.obhdp.2006.07.001
10. Alexander, V., Blinder, C., Zak, P.J.: Why trust an algorithm? performance, cognition, and neurophysiology. Comput. Hum. Behav. **89**, 279–288 (2018). https://doi.org/10.1016/j.chb.2018.07.026
11. Yeomans, M., Shah, A., Mullainathan, S., Kleinberg, J.: Making sense of recommendations. J. Behav. Decis. Mak. **32**, 403–414 (2019). https://doi.org/10.1002/bdm.2118
12. Dzindolet, M.T., Pierce, L.G., Beck, H.P., Dawe, L.A.: The perceived utility of human and automated aids in a visual detection task. Hum Factors. **44**, 79–94 (2002). https://doi.org/10.1518/0018720024494856
13. Madhavan, P., Wiegmann, D.A.: Similarities and differences between human–human and human–automation trust: an integrative review. Theor. Issues Ergon. Sci. **8**, 277–301 (2007). https://doi.org/10.1080/14639220500337708
14. Castelo, N., Bos, M.W., Lehmann, D.R.: Task-dependent algorithm a version. J. Mark. Res. **56**, 809–825 (2019). https://doi.org/10.1177/0022243719851788
15. Longoni, C., Bonezzi, A., Morewedge, C.K.: Resistance to medical artificial intelligence. J Consum Res. **46**, 629–650 (2019). https://doi.org/10.1093/jcr/ucz013
16. Hastie, T., Tibshirani, R., Friedman, J.: The Elements of Statistical Learning: Data Mining, Inference, and Prediction, Second Edition. Springer Science & Business Media (2009)
17. Goodfellow, I., Bengio, Y., Courville, A.: Deep Learning. MIT Press, Cambridge (2016)

Artificial Intelligence in Pilot Training and Education – Towards a Machine Learning Aided Instructor Assistant for Flight Simulators

Shuiqiao Yang[1]([✉]) [iD], Kun Yu[1] [iD], Thorsten Lammers[2] [iD], and Fang Chen[1] [iD]

[1] Data Science Institute, University of Technology Sydney,
Ultimo, NSW 2007, Australia
shuiqiao.yang@uts.edu.au
[2] Centre for Advanced Manufacturing, University of Technology Sydney,
Ultimo, NSW 2007, Australia

Abstract. The aviation industry was set to see unprecedented growth over the next two decades. Key occupations predicted to be in shortage included not only pilots, but also flight instructors. Undoubtedly, Covid-19 is currently having a huge impact on the industry. Nevertheless, the current environment further strengthens the need for pilots to maintain their training. Consequently, there is pressure to deliver high-quality training outcomes for an increasing number of pilots and trainees with limited resources available. Current simulator-based training schemes are limited by placing a significant reliance on the personal experience of flight instructors to assess pilot performance. Finding ways to increase the quality and efficiency of simulator-based training is therefore of high importance. With recent advances in artificial intelligence, it is possible to use machine learning techniques to extract latent patterns from massive datasets, to analyze pilot trainees' activities, and to provide feedback on their performance by processing hundreds of different parameters available on flight simulators. An ML-aided pilot training and education framework is needed that exploits the power of the ML techniques for more objective performance evaluation. In this paper, we describe a conceptual framework for such a system and outline steps toward the development of a full digital instructor system with the potential to overcome current limitations and enabling comprehensive and meaningful feedback that is tailored to the individual need of the trainee.

Keywords: Aviation industry · Conceptual framework · Flight maneuver

1 Introduction

As a special form of education, pilot training is a critical component for the aviation industry and closely relates to flight safety and flight task execution. Well-trained, highly proficient and professional pilots are extremely important

C. Stephanidis et al. (Eds.): HCII 2021, CCIS 1420, pp. 581–587, 2021.
https://doi.org/10.1007/978-3-030-78642-7_78

for the safety of humans and airplanes [12]. The training process establishes a primary interface between pilots and the potential environment that they will face during real flight operations. Currently, most of the pilot training processes are conducted in a full flight simulator which stimulates actual flight environments and makes the pilot training affordable and safe. For instance, a full flight simulator can simulate accurate force feedback for the pilot's flight controls through the simulator system [5]. Equipped with various systems to simulate all the different flight status parameters (e.g. acceleration, altitude, velocity etc.), the flight simulator can generate a large amount of flight and pilot activity data during the training process [10]. With an ability to process large scale datasets and automatically extract hidden features that are difficult to be identified by human beings, machine learning (ML) techniques have developed rapidly in recent years and have been applied in many real-world applications such as computer vision, speech recognition, natural language processing, robotics and medical diagnosis [8]. Overall, ML is capable of processing complex datasets, provide quantitative feedback, extract hidden features, and automatically make decisions.

In this paper, we propose a conceptual framework that utilizes supervised ML techniques to extract the latent patterns from the multi-modal data generated by the flight simulator, to build models to characterize the flight tasks, and to recognize the pilot trainees' operational behaviors during the training processes. This framework first trains a supervised ML model to learn the standard pilot operations for the training task using the data generated by experts or teachers. Then, the trained model will be used to provide feedback to pilot trainees during the training process. Overall, the goal of this paper is to propose a framework that utilizes ML algorithms to examine trainee performance in a simulated environment and provide qualitative performance information to aid instructor assessment and enable more effective feedback to trainees in real time.

The remainder of this paper is organized as follows. We first provide the technical background of current pilot training schemes. Then, we review related academic works of ML-related applications in the aviation industry. Afterwards we describe the proposed conceptual ML-aided pilot training framework before concluding with a short summary.

2   Technical Background

Flight simulation has been adopted as an integral element in the development of the aviation industry and has contributed significantly to flight safety over the last few decades [2]. It has become an essential means for both civil airlines and military organizations to safely train pilots at an affordable cost. Currently, with the ongoing development of hardware and software technologies, flight simulators are becoming more sophisticated to provide training for a wide range of tasks [3]. Figure 1 shows a flight simulator for a modern civil airline, in which the cabin includes a full replica of the actual flight deck [1]. It includes different subsystems, such as pilot controls, visual, sound and motion, to provide high fidelity cues to the pilots. Additionally, there is a data acquisition system which

Fig. 1. Illustration of a civil full flight simulator [1].

captures pilot control inputs and simulator state information at a sampling rate (typically 50–60 Hz) to record hundreds of inputs and simulator states. This data can be used for pilot trainee performance analysis [3].

The instructor station is located at the rear of the cabin, enabling the instructor to observe the operational behaviors of the pilot trainee. In a typical flight training process, the pilot trainee will be accompanied by an instructor for learning and performance evaluation. The flight instructor usually sits behind the trainee to observe the trainee's actions [1]. The flight instructor can introduce simulations of faults, monitor the flight situation, and observe the pilot trainee's control actions [7]. When the training processes are finished, the flight instructor will prepare a debrief report for the trainee in a limited time frame. The report includes the judgement of instructor for the various control actions of the pilot [7]. However, a few challenges have been identified for this instructor-based performance assessment [1,7]:

- High possibility for an instructor to miss relevant actions of the trainee pilot due to the limited visibility and possible sight obstruction of flight instructor and high instructor workload in boost moments.
- Trainee evaluation is heavily based on the individual experience of instructors. Therefore, the feedback from the instructors is highly subjective and lacks evidence.
- Limited real-time identification and feedback of incorrect pilot activities or risky behaviors during the training process. Very limited retrospective analysis is available to identify the missed performance aspects for pilot trainees.

Modern flight simulators incorporate hundreds of different parameters capturing every aspect of the flight status, such as altitude, velocity, pedal inputs, etc. [3,4]. The pilot training process leads to a huge amount of data being generated. Identification of the latent operational patterns for pilot trainees can help understand their operational deficiencies quantitatively and objectively, which marks a great difference from the traditional instructor-based subjective feedback. By combining pilot training related data from a flight simulator and advanced ML techniques, it seems promising to develop an intelligent digital instructor system that can provide real-time, objective and quantitative assessments, as well as a detailed diagnosis of the practice processes to the pilot trainees.

3 Related Work

Although the application of machine learning (ML) in the context of flight simulation is a very young field of research, some key contributions have been made. For example, Giddings et al. [6] have studied the problem of defining the relationships between the pre-aptitude, proficiency tests, and success in pilot training. They have collected data with labels from the Air Force Personnel Center and applied different supervised ML models such as random forest, K-nearest neighbors and neural networks to predict the success patterns for pilots based on their historical testing records. Wilson et al. [14] have studied the problem of gaze classification to evaluate the performance for aviators to analyze if the pilot trainee would scan too rapidly, omit, or fixate – which are common errors when scanning the horizon, and cross-checking instruments. Traditionally, the examination for the gaze of pilot trainees relies on a manual check from flight instructors. They have proposed to use ML to replace the flight instructors for this task. They transform the gaze or scan patterns into heatmaps and adopt deep convolutional neural networks to classify the heatmaps into different level of qualities to help the flight instructors for quick reviewing. Memarzadeh et al. [11] have proposed to detect the outliers in flight data using convolutional variational auto-encoders. They argue that the current state-of-the-art ML models show great ability in processing high-dimensional time series data (like the sequential, time-stamped data generated by a flight simulator). Shmelova et al. [13] have proposed to use ML and text analysis to train the air traffic controllers to decrease human factor-related accident rates. Li et al. [9] have explored the factors in flight simulators that could improve the human-machine interaction efficiency. They have adopted meta-cognitive strategy to help pilots to coordinate cognitive resources and gradually form flight experience based on their characteristics. While these presented works provide insightful analyses of singular aspects within the pilot training process, our proposed conceptual framework focusses on a more comprehensive analysis based on a variety of aspects such as various control inputs to the simulator for the pilot trainees and also aims at facilitating the judgement for flight instructors due to the various challenges mentioned in Sect. 2.

4 Conceptual Model

In order to exploit the potentials of using ML for pilot training, we propose to utilize supervised ML algorithms to learn the latent reverse mapping functions between the flight status and the corresponding operational inputs in a maneuver. A flight simulator records two types of data: one type for capturing the simulated aircraft states and the other for capturing the operator's control

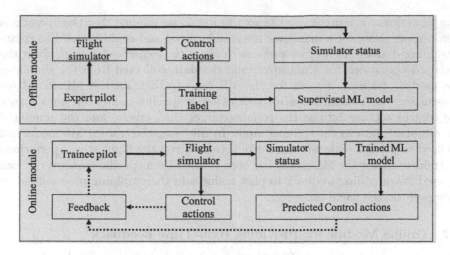

Fig. 2. Conceptual framework for ML-aided pilot training and education (the solid arrow lines denote the data flows and the dotted arrow lines denote the feedbacks).

actions. The control actions performed by the trainee lead to the corresponding changes of the flight states such as attitude, altitude and airspeed. It is nontrivial to explicitly define the mapping functions given the large amount of control inputs and state variables, but supervised ML algorithms could easily capture the relations between them by using the status signals as training data and the control signals as the corresponding label information. It is intuitive the actions of pilots with different proficiency levels would result in different simulated aircraft states and the associated control actions when conducting the same maneuver.

To create such training and labelling data pairs, we assume that the expert pilots can perform standard control operations and their generated data from the flight simulators can accurately reflect the mapping relations between flight status and control actions. Hence, it is possible for us to train the supervised ML algorithms using the training datasets collected from experts. After the supervised ML model has been trained, those datasets can be used to predict the expert-level control signals given the current flight status performed by pilot trainees, thus differences and feedbacks could be provided to the trainees in real time. The proposed framework utilizes supervised ML techniques as a novel tool to assist pilot training. As shown in Fig. 2, it involves two core modules: an offline module to use the expert pilots' behavior data to train supervised ML models; and an online module to provide the trainee pilot with feedback.

4.1 Offline Module for Standard Pilot Operation Learning

The offline module contains supervised ML models that are trained with labelled data to learn the standard operations for different maneuvers. The purpose of the offline module is to train the supervised ML model to learn the expert-level control actions for a maneuver. As seen in Fig. 2, we assume that the operations from expert pilots for a maneuver are standardized and could be used to create a training dataset. Hence, we propose to allow the expert pilot to perform the standard operations for a maneuver and the data collected from the simulator are used as training dataset for the ML model. To train the ML model for recognizing the standard control actions on a specific maneuver, we can use the control actions data as the training target (i.e., labels) and the simulated aircraft state data as the training input. In this way, the trained ML model can be used to predict expert-level control actions given the flight status performed by trainees. After the ML model has been trained for a specific maneuver, it can be used for providing feedback to pilot trainees in their training processes when they perform the same maneuver.

4.2   Online Module for Providing Real-Time Feedback

The online module shown in Fig. 2 is designed for providing comprehensive real-time feedback to pilot trainees. In the traditional pilot training process, the instructors have limited time to prepare the debrief report to the trainees and the feedback from the instructors can also be subjective. Using the online module, the real-time data collected from the simulator will be separated into two parts: the flight status data and the control action data. The trained ML models can learn the relations between the flight status and control actions. When given the state data of the simulator operated by a pilot trainee, the differences between the expert-level control actions and the current pilot trainee's control actions can be computed. Thus, detailed feedback can be provided to the trainee in real time. Based on the new ML-aided pilot training framework, the pilot trainees are expected to gain a better understanding of their control behaviors as the control difference between the trainee and the expert can be provided as feedback in real-time. Also, for each control input to the simulator, the pilot trainee can view the difference be-tween themselves and the expert. Therefore, the ML models can provide more comprehensive and detailed feedback to pilot trainee. At the same time, the flight instructor may also have access to more evidence supporting them for preparing the debrief report.

5   Conclusion

Pilot training has always been an essential element of the aviation industry. Well-trained pilots are essential for increasing the safety of various flight activities. In this paper, we review the current pilot training practices that are based on the feedback from flight instructors and explain the drawbacks of the current instructor-based evaluation system. Based on the rapid progress in the development of ML techniques, we propose a framework that exploits the power of ML methods for better pilot training. In the framework, the standard operational patterns for different maneuvers are learned by the supervised ML models. After that, the pilot trainee can be provided with real-time feedback in a more comprehensive way, utilizing the prediction capabilities of trained ML models. We believe that our proposed framework provides a starting point for a development initiative and can also be generalized to other professional training and education contexts such as medical surgery training, operation of precision instruments, etc. In the future, we will exploit the proposed conceptual framework into the real flight simulators and develop a reliable digital assistant in pilot training.

References

1. Allerton, D.: The impact of flight simulation in aerospace. Aeronaut. J. **114**(1162), 747–756 (2010)
2. Baarspul, M.: A review of flight simulation techniques. Prog. Aerosp. Sci. **27**(1), 1–120 (1990)
3. Boril, J., Jirgl, M., Jalovecky, R.: Using aviation simulation technologies for pilot modelling and flight training assessment. Adv. Mil. Technol. **12**(1) (2017)
4. Boril, J., Jirgl, M., Jalovecky, R.: Use of flight simulators in analyzing pilot behavior. In: Iliadis, L., Maglogiannis, I. (eds.) AIAI 2016. IAICT, vol. 475, pp. 255–263. Springer, Cham (2016). https://doi.org/10.1007/978-3-319-44944-9_22
5. Feng, T., Zhao, C.Q.: Design and research of electric control load system of flight simulator. DEStech Trans. Eng. Technol. Res. (ICEEA) (2016)
6. Giddings, A.C.: Predicting pilot success using machine learning (2020)
7. Hays, R.T., Jacobs, J.W., Prince, C., Salas, E.: Flight simulator training effectiveness: a meta-analysis. Mil. Psychol. **4**(2), 63–74 (1992)
8. LeCun, Y., Bengio, Y., Hinton, G.: Deep learning. Nature **521**(7553), 436–444 (2015)
9. Li, Q., et al.: Human-machine interaction efficiency factors in flight simulator training towards Chinese pilots. In: Cassenti, D.N., Scataglini, S., Rajulu, S.L., Wright, J.L. (eds.) AHFE 2020. AISC, vol. 1206, pp. 26–32. Springer, Cham (2021). https://doi.org/10.1007/978-3-030-51064-0_4
10. Mangortey, E., et al.: Application of machine learning techniques to parameter selection for flight risk identification. In: AIAA Scitech 2020 Forum, p. 1850 (2020)
11. Memarzadeh, M., Matthews, B., Avrekh, I.: Unsupervised anomaly detection in flight data using convolutional variational auto-encoder. Aerospace **7**(8), 115 (2020)
12. Orlady, L.M.: Airline pilot training today and tomorrow. In: Crew Resource Management, pp. 469–491. Elsevier (2010)
13. Shmelova, T., Sikirda, Y., Rizun, N., Lazorenko, V., Kharchenko, V.: Machine learning and text analysis in an artificial intelligent system for the training of air traffic controllers. In: Research Anthology on Reliability and Safety in Aviation Systems, Spacecraft, and Air Transport, pp. 237–286. IGI Global (2021)
14. Wilson, J., Scielzo, S., Nair, S., Larson, E.C.: Automatic gaze classification for aviators: using multi-task convolutional networks as a proxy for flight instructor observation. Int. J. Aviat. Aeronaut. Aerosp. **7**(3), 7 (2020)

End-To-End Deep Learning for pNN50 Estimation Using a Spatiotemporal Representation

Sayyedjavad Ziaratnia[1]([✉]), Peeraya Sripian[1], Tipporn Laohakangvalvit[1], Kazuo Ohzeki[2], and Midori Sugaya[1]

[1] College of Engineering, Shibaura Institute of Technology, 3-7-5, Toyosu, Koto-ku, Tokyo 135-8548, Japan
{am20008,peeraya,tipporn,doly}@shibaura-it.ac.jp
[2] Faculty of Engineering, Tokyo International Institute of Technology, 1-7-3, Nishi-Shinjuku, Shinjuku-ku, Tokyo 160-0023, Japan

Abstract. Various industries widely use emotion estimation to evaluate their consumer satisfaction towards their products. Generally, emotion can be estimated based on observable expressions such as facial expression, or unobservable expressions such as biological signals. Although used by many research, the Facial Expression Recognition has a lack of precision for expressions that are very similar to each other or a situation where the shown expression differs from the real subject's emotion. On the other hand, biological signal indexes such as pNN50 can act as a supportive mechanism to improve emotion estimation from observable expressions such as facial expression recognition method. pNN50 is a reliable index to estimate stress-relax, and it originates from unconscious emotions that cannot be manipulated. In this work, we propose a method for pNN50 estimation from facial video using a Deep Learning model. Transfer learning technique and a pre-trained Image recognition Convolutional Neural Network (CNN) model are employed to estimate pNN50 based on a spatiotemporal map created from a series of frames in a facial video. The model which trained on low, middle, and high pNN50 values, shows an accuracy of about 80%. Therefore, it indicates the potential of our proposed method, and we can expand it to categorize the more detailed level of pNN50 values.

Keywords: pNN50 Estimation · rPPG · Convolutional Neural Network · Deep Learning

1 Introduction

Remote emotion estimation can play an important role and be of much benefit during this time of the covid-19 pandemic, where many governments are asking their citizens to stay at home as a preventive measure. For example, it can be used as a feedback system in an online meeting or an online classroom. Also, it can be applied to improve human interaction with various intelligent systems such as robotics [1, 2] and automobiles [1, 3].

© Springer Nature Switzerland AG 2021
C. Stephanidis et al. (Eds.): HCII 2021, CCIS 1420, pp. 588–593, 2021.
https://doi.org/10.1007/978-3-030-78642-7_79

Emotion is difficult to measure because they are sometimes fleeting, concealed, and contradictory [4]. Nowadays, there are two conventional approaches for emotion estimation: (1) emotion estimation based on observable expressions such as facial expression [5, 6], and (2) emotion estimation based on unobservable expressions using biological signals [7]. However, both approaches have few limitations that prevent them from going beyond the research level and being applicable in people's daily lives. The Facial Expression Recognition method can be integrated into various environments due to their remote-based approach for emotion categorizing. However, in some scenarios when expressions are very similar to each other, or the shown expression differs by the real subject's emotion, facial expression recognition may not produce a stable accuracy. In the second approach, emotion can be estimated using biological signals such as heart rate variability (HRV), brain wave, etc. However, to measure those biological signals, it is necessary to attach sensors to human directly. This limits the operation domain to an experimental environment.

This study mainly focuses on pNN50, an obtainable index from HRV, as it can be used to estimate emotion more precisely than observable approaches [8]. pNN50 is a reliable index to estimate stress-relax [9] and originates from unconscious emotions that can estimate human's actual emotion. In this work, we propose a remote method for pNN50 estimation from facial video using a spatiotemporal map with a Convolutional Neural Network (CNN) model. Our proposed method could be used to act as a supportive mechanism to improve current observable emotion estimation methods such as facial expression recognition.

2 Background

In this section, we briefly overview the concepts used in this study.

2.1 Remote Photoplethysmography (rPPG)

Remote photoplethysmography (rPPG) allows contactless measurement of human cardiac activity by analyzing pulse-induced slight color changes on the human skin surface from a video camera. This technology leads to numerous applications for video health monitoring and also allows non-contact assessment of other physiological indexes [10].

2.2 pNN50

pNN50 refers to successive peak intervals (RR_i) of HRV in a time frame that differing by more than 50 ms ($NN50$) divided by total number of peak intervals (N) in that time frame [9].

$$NN50 = \sum_{i=1}^{N} (|RR_{i+1} - RR_i| > 50 \text{ ms}) \qquad (1)$$

$$pNN50 = \frac{NN50}{N} \qquad (2)$$

3 Proposed Method and Implementation

The purpose of this study is to realize remote pNN50 estimation from facial video with a CNN model. The contribution of this method is carried out in threefold:

1. First, a series of frames are used to detect the face inside them and apply skin segmentation to get only the skin pixels, and then the face is divided into a number of blocks for further processing.
2. Second, based on the created blocks, the average of each color channel inside of each block is calculated to create a spatiotemporal map that represents the changes in skin color over time.
3. Third, using a transfer learning technique and a pre-trained image recognition CNN model (VGG-16), the pNN50 estimation model based on a spatiotemporal map was implemented.

3.1 Facial Video Dataset

UBFC-RPPG dataset [11] is used to verify and prove the principles of our proposed method. This dataset is specifically designed for remote photoplethysmography (rPPG) measurement tasks. It contains 42 videos from 42 different subjects which each video is about 1–2 min long. The videos were recorded by a Logitech C920HD Pro camera with a resolution of 640x480 in an uncompressed 8-bit RGB format.

3.2 Data Pre-processing

The employed method for data pre-processing is based on RhythmNet [12]. First, face detection and skin segmentation have been applied for T frames to get the ROI of the face and removing the background pixels. Then, the facial area is divided into n ROI blocks; next, each RGB channel (Red, Green, Blue) signal is extracted to create a spatiotemporal map based on the mean color channel for each block. Figure 1 shows the data pre-processing flow.

3.3 Feature Extraction

For feature extraction we used VGG-16 which is a convolutional neural network model proposed by K. Simonyan and A. Zisserman [13] and has been trained on ImageNet [16] which is an open-source repository of images, consisting of 1000 classes and over 1.5 million images.

3.4 Model Training

Since our approach is to apply transfer learning into VGG-16, we trained the model from block five, and prior blocks have been frozen for feature extraction. Finally, the model structure after block five has been changed based on our proposed method for pNN50 estimation.

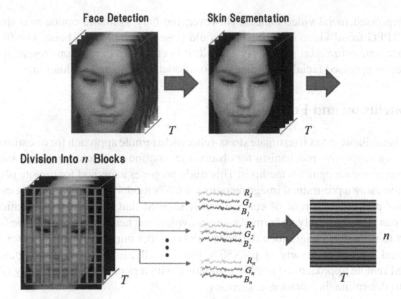

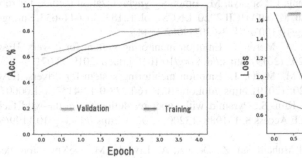

Fig. 1. Data pre-processing

4 Result (Proof of Concepts)

To prove the concept of remote pNN50 estimation and our proposed method, the model has trained on three categories, low, middle, and high pNN50 values. The obtained result shows an accuracy of 80%, which indicates the potential of our proposed method for remote pNN50 estimation. Figures 2 and 3 illustrate the accuracy and loss of the model.

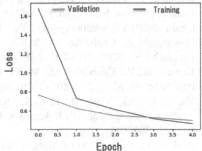

Fig. 2. Training and validation accuracy   **Fig. 3.** Training and validation loss

5 Discussion

One of the limitations of this study was the lack of the facial video samples. To our knowledge, there is no investigation about the effect of number of frames and compressed video on the accuracy of remote pNN50 estimation. Therefore, we preferred to use a non-compressed facial video dataset. However, the only available option was the the UBFC-RPPG facial video dataset which could pose the problem of being insufficient for an accurate estimation model. As a result, it is crucial to expand our research, and use other compressed facial video datasets for model training and evaluation.

6 Conclusion and Future Work

pNN50 is a reliable index to estimate stress-relax and a remote approach for its estimation can act as a supportive mechanism for observable emotion estimation methods such as facial expression recognition methods. This study proposes a method for remote pNN50 estimation using a pre-trained Image recognition CNN model based on a spatiotemporal map. Our preliminary proof of concept result showed that the remote estimation of pNN50 can be successfully performed using convolutional neural networks. In the future we plan to use other facial video databases and conduct our experiment to extend the model and estimate a variety of pNN50 values. Finally, our goal is to compare the proposed remote approach for pNN50 estimation with a photoplethysmography (PPG) sensor to determine the obtainable accuracy.

Acknowledgements. This work was partially supported by JSPS KAKENHI Grant Number JP19K20302.

References

1. Spezialetti, M., Placidi, G., Rossi, S.: Emotion recognition for human-robot interaction: recent advances and future perspectives. Front. Rob. A I, 7 (2020). https://doi.org/10.3389/frobt.2020.532279
2. Kajihara, Y., Sripian, P., Feng, C., Sugaya, M.: Emotion synchronization method for robot facial expression. In: Kurosu, M. (ed.) HCII 2020. LNCS, vol. 12182, pp. 644–653. Springer, Cham (2020). https://doi.org/10.1007/978-3-030-49062-1_44
3. Kowalczuk, Z., Czubenko, M., Merta, T.: Emotion monitoring system for drivers. IFAC-PapersOnLine **52**(8), 200–205 (2019). https://doi.org/10.1016/j.ifacol.2019.08.071
4. Kowalczuk, Z., Czubenko, M., Merta, T.: Emotion monitoring system for drivers. IFAC-PapersOnLine **52**(8), 200–205 (2019). https://doi.org/10.1016/b978-0-12-415781-1.00007-8
5. Vo, T., Lee, G., Yang, H., Kim, S.: Pyramid with super resolution for in-the-wild facial expression recognition. IEEE Access **8**, 131988–132001 (2020). https://doi.org/10.1109/access.2020.3010018
6. Burkert, P., Trier, F., Afzal Muhammad, Z., Dengel, A., Liwicki, M.: DeXpression: deep convolutional neural network for expression recognition (2015)
7. Sugaya, M., Watanabe, I., Yoshida, R., Chen, F.: Human emotional state analysis during driving simulation experiment using bio-emotion estimation method. In: 2018 IEEE 42nd Annual Computer Software and Applications Conference (COMPSAC) (2018). https://doi.org/10.1109/compsac.2018.10301
8. Ikeda, Y., Sugaya, M.: Estimate emotion method to use biological, symbolic information preliminary experiment. In: Schmorrow, D.D.D., Fidopiastis, C.M.M. (eds.) AC 2016. LNCS (LNAI), vol. 9743, pp. 332–340. Springer, Cham (2016). https://doi.org/10.1007/978-3-319-39955-3_31

9. Kim, H.G., Cheon, E.J., Bai, D.S., Lee, Y.H., Koo, B.H.: Stress and heart rate variability: a meta-analysis and review of the literature. Psychiatry Invest. **15**(3), 235–245 (2018). https://doi.org/10.30773/pi.2017.08.17
10. Wang, W.: Robust and automatic remote photoplethysmography. Technische Universiteit Eindhoven (2017)
11. Bobbia, S., Macwan, R., Benezeth, Y., Mansouri, A., Dubois, J.: Unsupervised skin tissue segmentation for remote photoplethysmography. Pattern Recogn. Lett. **124**, 82–90 (2017). https://doi.org/10.1016/j.patrec.2017.10.017
12. Niu, X., Shan, S., Han, H., Chen, X.: RhythmNet: end-to-end heart rate estimation from face via spatial-temporal representation. IEEE Trans. Image Process. **29**, 2409–2423 (2020). https://doi.org/10.1109/tip.2019.2947204
13. Simonyan, K., Zisserman, A.: Very deep convolutional networks for large-scale image recognition. CoRR, abs/1409.1556 (2014)

Author Index

Printed in the United States
by Baker & Taylor Publisher Services